Lecture Notes in Computer Science 14585

Founding Editors

Gerhard Goos
Juris Hartmanis

The series Lecture Notes in Computer Science (LNCS), including its subseries Lecture Notes in Artificial Intelligence (LNAI) and Lecture Notes in Bioinformatics (LNBI), has established itself as a medium for the publication of new developments in computer science and information technology research, teaching, and education.

LNCS enjoys close cooperation with the computer science R & D community, the series counts many renowned academics among its volume editors and paper authors, and collaborates with prestigious societies. Its mission is to serve this international community by providing an invaluable service, mainly focused on the publication of conference and workshop proceedings and postproceedings. LNCS commenced publication in 1973.

Christina Pöpper · Lejla Batina

Editors

Applied Cryptography and Network Security

22nd International Conference, ACNS 2024
Abu Dhabi, United Arab Emirates, March 5–8, 2024
Proceedings, Part III

 Springer

Editors
Christina Pöpper ⏺
New York University Abu Dhabi
Abu Dhabi, United Arab Emirates

Lejla Batina ⏺
Radboud University Nijmegen
Nijmegen, The Netherlands

ISSN 0302-9743   ISSN 1611-3349 (electronic)
Lecture Notes in Computer Science
ISBN 978-3-031-54775-1   ISBN 978-3-031-54776-8 (eBook)
https://doi.org/10.1007/978-3-031-54776-8

This Springer imprint is published by the registered company Springer Nature Switzerland AG
The registered company address is: Gewerbestrasse 11, 6330 Cham, Switzerland

Paper in this product is recyclable.

Preface

ACNS 2024, the 22nd International Conference on Applied Cryptography and Network Security, was held in Abu Dhabi, United Arab Emirates, on March 5–8, 2024. The conference covered all technical aspects of applied cryptography, network and computer security and privacy, representing both academic research work as well as developments in industrial and technical frontiers.

The conference had two submission deadlines, in July and October 2023. We received a total of 238 submissions over the two cycles (230 unique submissions incl. eight major revisions from the first submission cycle that were resubmitted as revisions in the second submission cycle). From all submissions, the Program Committee (PC) selected 54 papers for publication in the proceedings of the conference, some after minor or major revisions. This led to an acceptance rate of 23.5%.

The two program chairs were supported by a PC consisting of 76 leading experts in all aspects of applied cryptography and security whose expertise and work were crucial for the paper selection process. Each submission received around 4 reviews from the committee. Strong conflict of interest rules ensured that papers were not handled by PC members with a close personal or professional relationship with the authors. The program chairs were not allowed to submit papers and did not handle any submissions they were in conflict with. There were an additional 55 external reviewers, whose expertise the PC relied upon in the selection of papers. The review process was conducted as a double-blind peer review. The authors of 10 submissions rejected from the July deadline, but considered promising, were encouraged to resubmit to the October deadline after major revisions of their paper. From these 10 papers invited for a major revision, 8 papers got resubmitted to the second cycle, 5 of which were finally accepted.

Alongside the presentations of the accepted papers, the program of ACNS 2024 featured three invited talks given by Elisa Bertino, Nadia Heninger, and Gene Tsudik. The three volumes of the conference proceedings contain the revised versions of the 54 papers that were selected, together with the abstracts of the invited talks.

Following a long tradition, ACNS gives a best student paper award to encourage promising students to publish their best results at the conference. The award recipients share a monetary prize of 2,000 EUR generously sponsored by Springer.

Many people contributed to the success of ACNS 2024. We would like to thank the authors for submitting their research results to the conference. We are very grateful to the PC members and external reviewers for contributing their knowledge and expertise and for the tremendous amount of work and time involved in reviewing papers, contributing to the discussions, and shepherding the revisions. We are greatly indebted to Mihalis Maniatakos and Ozgur Sinanoglu, the ACNS'24 General Chairs, for their efforts and overall guidance as well as all the members of the organization committee. We thank the steering committee, Moti Yung and Jianying Zhou, for their direction and valuable advice throughout the preparation of the conference. We also thank the team at Springer for handling the publication of these conference proceedings, as well as Shujaat Mirza for working on the preparation of the proceedings volumes.

March 2024   Lejla Batina
                                                                 Christina Pöpper

Organization

General Co-chairs

Michail Maniatakos   New York University Abu Dhabi, UAE
Ozgur Sinanoglu   New York University Abu Dhabi, UAE

Program Committee Co-chairs

Christina Pöpper   New York University Abu Dhabi, UAE
Lejla Batina   Radboud University, The Netherlands

Steering Committee

Jianying Zhou   SUTD, Singapore
Moti Yung   Google, USA

Local Arrangements Chair

Borja García de Soto   New York University Abu Dhabi, UAE

Publicity Chair

Elias Athanasopoulos   University of Cyprus, Cyprus

Web Chair

Christoforos Vasilatos   New York University Abu Dhabi, UAE

Poster Chair

Charalambos Konstantinou   KAUST, KSA

Registration Chair

Rafael Song   New York University Abu Dhabi, UAE

Workshop Chair

Martin Andreoni   Technology Innovation Institute, UAE

Publication Chair

Shujaat Mirza   New York University, USA

Student Travel Grants Chair

Lilas Alrahis   New York University Abu Dhabi, UAE

Program Committee

Adwait Nadkarni	William & Mary, USA
Alexander Koch	CNRS and IRIF, Université Paris Cité, France
Alexandra Dmitrienko	University of Wuerzburg, Germany
Amr Youssef	Concordia University, Canada
An Braeken	Vrije Universiteit Brussel, Belgium
Anna Lisa Ferrara	University of Molise, Italy
Archita Agarwal	MongoDB, USA
Atefeh Mohseni Ejiyeh	UCSB, USA
Benjamin Dowling	University of Sheffield, UK
Chao Sun	Osaka University, Japan
Chiara Marcolla	Technology Innovation Institute, UAE
Chitchanok Chuengsatiansup	The University of Melbourne, Australia
Christine Utz	CISPA Helmholtz Center for Information Security, Germany
Christoph Egger	Université Paris Cité and CNRS and IRIF, France
Claudio Soriente	NEC Laboratories Europe, Spain
Colin Boyd	NTNU-Norwegian University of Science and Technology, Norway
Daniel Dinu	Intel
Daniel Gardham	University of Surrey, UK

Daniel Slamanig	Universität der Bundeswehr München, Germany
Dave Singelee	KU Leuven, Belgium
Devashish Gosain	MPI-INF, Germany
Diego F. Aranha	Aarhus University, Denmark
Dimitrios Vasilopoulos	IMDEA Software Institute, Spain
Dominique Schröder	Friedrich-Alexander Universität Erlangen-Nürnberg, Germany
Eleftheria Makri	Leiden University, The Netherlands
Elena Dubrova	Royal Institute of Technology, Sweden
Elena Kirshanova	Technology Innovation Institute, UAE
Elif Bilge Kavun	University of Passau, Germany
Fatemeh Ganji	Worcester Polytechnic Institute, USA
Florian Hahn	University of Twente, The Netherlands
Francisco Rodríguez-Henríquez	Technology Innovation Institute, UAE
Ghassan Karame	Ruhr University Bochum, Germany
Gustavo Banegas	Qualcomm, France
Hyungsub Kim	Purdue University, USA
Jean Paul Degabriele	Technology Innovation Institute, UAE
Jianying Zhou	Singapore University of Technology and Design, Singapore
João S. Resende	University of Porto, Portugal
Karim Eldefrawy	SRI International, USA
Katerina Mitrokotsa	University of St. Gallen, Switzerland
Katharina Krombholz	CISPA Helmholtz Center for Information Security, Germany
Kazuo Sakiyama	UEC, Tokyo, Japan
Kehuan Zhang	The Chinese University of Hong Kong, China
Khurram Bhatti	Information Technology University (ITU), Pakistan
Lukasz Chmielewski	Masaryk University, Czech Republic
Mainack Mondal	Indian Institute of Technology, Kharagpur, India
Marc Manzano	SandboxAQ, USA
Matthias J. Kannwischer	QSMC, Taiwan
Melissa Azouaoui	NXP Semiconductors, Germany
Monika Trimoska	Eindhoven University of Technology, The Netherlands
Monowar Hasan	Washington State University, USA
Mridula Singh	CISPA Helmholtz Center for Information Security, Germany
Murtuza Jadliwala	University of Texas at San Antonio, USA
Nabil Alkeilani Alkadri	CISPA Helmholtz Center for Information Security, Germany

Nils Ole Tippenhauer   CISPA Helmholtz Center for Information
                              Security, Germany
Olga Gadyatskaya   Leiden University, The Netherlands
Paulo Barreto   University of Washington – Tacoma, USA
Pino Caballero-Gil   University of La Laguna, Spain
Pooya Farshim   IOG & Durham University, UK
Sathvik Prasad   North Carolina State University, USA
Sebastian Köhler   University of Oxford, UK
Shahram Rasoolzadeh   Radboud University, The Netherlands
Sherman S. M. Chow   The Chinese University of Hong Kong, China
Silvia Mella   Radboud University, The Netherlands
Sinem Sav   Bilkent University, Turkey
Sofía Celi   Brave Software, Portugal
Sudipta Chattopadhyay   Singapore University of Technology and Design,
                              Singapore
Sushmita Ruj   University of New South Wales, Australia
Tako Boris Fouotsa   EPFL, Switzerland
Tibor Jager   University of Wuppertal, Germany
Tien Tuan Anh Dinh   Deakin University, Australia
Tran Quang Duc   Hanoi University of Science and Technology,
                              Vietnam
Valeria Nikolaenko   A16Z Crypto Research, USA
Vera Rimmer   KU Leuven, Belgium
Willy Susilo   University of Wollongong, Australia
Xiapu Luo   The Hong Kong Polytechnic University, China
Zheng Yang   Southwest University, China

Additional Reviewers

Afonso Vilalonga   Gregor Seiler
Alexander Karenin   Jean-Philippe Bossuat
Anshu Yadav   Jelle Vos
Astrid Ottenhues   Jenit Tomy
Beatrice Biasioli   Jérôme Govinden
Behzad Abdolmaleki   Jiafan Wang
Benjamin Terner   Jodie Knapp
Callum London   Joel Frisk Gärtner
Enrique Argones Rúa   Jorge Chávez-Saab
Erkan Tairi   Karl Southern
Fabio Campos   Laltu Sardar
Gareth T. Davies   Laurane Marco
Gora Adj   Li Duan

Lorenz Panny
Marcus Brinkmann
Nada El Kassem
Nan Cheng
Nusa Zidaric
Octavio Pérez Kempner
Okan Seker
Patrick Harasser
Paul Huynh
Paul Gerhart
Pradeep Mishra
Quan Yuan
Raghav Bhaskar
Ritam Bhaumik
Robert Merget

Sacha Servan-Schreiber
Sebastian Faller
Sebastian Ramacher
Semyon Novoselov
Shahram Rasoolzadeh
Sylvain Chatel
Tianyu Li
Valerio Cini
Victor Miller
Viktoria Ronge
Vir Pathak
Vojtech Suchanek
Vukašin Karadžić
Yangguang Tian

Abstracts of Keynote Talks

Applying Machine Learning to Securing Cellular Networks

Elisa Bertino

Purdue University, Indiana, USA

Abstract. Cellular network security is more critical than ever, given the increased complexity of these networks and the numbers of applications that depend on them, including telehealth, remote education, ubiquitous robotics and autonomous vehicles, smart cities, and Industry 4.0. In order to devise more effective defenses, a recent trend is to leverage machine learning (ML) techniques, which have become applicable because of today's advanced capabilities for collecting data as well as high-performance computing systems for training ML models. Recent large language models (LLMs) are also opening new interesting directions for security applications. In this talk, I will first present a comprehensive threat analysis in the context of 5G cellular networks to give a concrete example of the magnitude of the problem of cellular network security. Then, I will present two specific applications of ML techniques for the security of cellular networks. The first application focuses on the use of natural language processing techniques to the problem of detecting inconsistencies in the "natural specifications" of cellular network protocols. The second application addresses the design of an anomaly detection system able to detect the presence of malicious base stations and determine the type of attack. Then I'll conclude with a discussion on research directions.

Real-World Cryptanalysis

Nadia Heninger

University of California, San Diego, USA

Abstract. Cryptography has traditionally been considered to be one of the strong points of computer security. However, a number of the public-key cryptographic algorithms that we use are fragile in the face of implementation mistakes or misunderstandings. In this talk, I will survey "weapons of math destruction" that have been surprisingly effective in finding broken cryptographic implementations in the wild, and some adventures in active and passive network measurement of cryptographic protocols.

CAPTCHAs: What Are They Good For?

Gene Tsudik

University of California, Irvine, USA

Abstract. Since about 2003, CAPTCHAs have been widely used as a barrier against bots, while simultaneously annoying great multitudes of users worldwide. As their use grew, techniques to defeat or bypass CAPTCHAs kept improving, while CAPTCHAs themselves evolved in terms of sophistication and diversity, becoming increasingly difficult to solve for both bots and humans. Given this long-standing and still-ongoing arms race, it is important to investigate usability, solving performance, and user perceptions of modern CAPTCHAs. This talk will discuss two such efforts:

In the first part, we explore CAPTCHAs in the wild by evaluating users' solving performance and perceptions of unmodified currently-deployed CAPTCHAs. We obtain this data through manual inspection of popular websites and user studies in which 1,400 participants collectively solved 14,000 CAPTCHAs. Results show significant differences between the most popular types of CAPTCHAs: surprisingly, solving time and user perception are not always correlated. We performed a comparative study to investigate the effect of experimental context – specifically the difference between solving CAPTCHAs directly versus solving them as part of a more natural task, such as account creation. Whilst there were several potential confounding factors, our results show that experimental context could have an impact on this task, and must be taken into account in future CAPTCHA studies. Finally, we investigate CAPTCHA-induced user task abandonment by analyzing participants who start and do not complete the task.

In the second part of this work, we conduct a large-scale (over 3,600 distinct users) 13-month real-world user study and post-study survey. The study, performed at a large public university, was based on a live account creation and password recovery service with currently prevalent captcha type: reCAPTCHAv2. Results show that, with more attempts, users improve in solving checkbox challenges. For website developers and user study designers, results indicate that the website context directly influences (with statistically significant differences) solving time between password recovery and account creation. We consider the impact of participants' major and education level, showing that certain majors exhibit better performance, while, in general, education level has a direct impact on solving time. Unsurprisingly, we discover that participants find image challenges to be annoying, while checkbox challenges are perceived as easy. We also show that, rated via System Usability Scale (SUS), image tasks are viewed as "OK", while checkbox tasks are viewed as "good". We explore the cost and security of reCAPTCHAv2 and conclude that it has an immense cost and no security. Overall, we believe that this study's results prompt a natural conclusion: reCAPTCHAv2 and similar reCAPTCHA technology should be deprecated.

Contents – Part III

Blockchain

Mirrored Commitment: Fixing "Randomized Partial Checking"
and Applications 3
    Paweł Lorek, Moti Yung, and Filip Zagórski

Bitcoin Clique: Channel-Free Off-Chain Payments Using Two-Shot
Adaptor Signatures 28
    Siavash Riahi and Orfeas Stefanos Thyfronitis Litos

Programmable Payment Channels 51
    Ranjit Kumaresan, Duc V. Le, Mohsen Minaei,
    Srinivasan Raghuraman, Yibin Yang, and Mahdi Zamani

Fair Private Set Intersection Using Smart Contracts 74
    Sepideh Avizheh and Reihaneh Safavi-Naini

Powers-of-Tau to the People: Decentralizing Setup Ceremonies 105
    Valeria Nikolaenko, Sam Ragsdale, Joseph Bonneau, and Dan Boneh

Smart Infrastructures, Systems and Software

Self-sovereign Identity for Electric Vehicle Charging 137
    Adrian Kailus, Dustin Kern, and Christoph Krauß

"Hello? Is There Anybody in There?" Leakage Assessment of Differential
Privacy Mechanisms in Smart Metering Infrastructure 163
    Soumyadyuti Ghosh, Manaar Alam, Soumyajit Dey,
    and Debdeep Mukhopadhyay

Security Analysis of BigBlueButton and eduMEET 190
    Nico Heitmann, Hendrik Siewert, Sven Moog, and Juraj Somorovsky

An In-Depth Analysis of the Code-Reuse Gadgets Introduced by Software
Obfuscation 217
    Naiqian Zhang, Zheyun Feng, and Dongpeng Xu

ProvIoT : Detecting Stealthy Attacks in IoT through Federated Edge-Cloud
Security   241
  Kunal Mukherjee, Joshua Wiedemeier, Qi Wang, Junpei Kamimura,
  John Junghwan Rhee, James Wei, Zhichun Li, Xiao Yu, Lu-An Tang,
  Jiaping Gui, and Kangkook Jee

Attacks

A Practical Key-Recovery Attack on LWE-Based Key-Encapsulation
Mechanism Schemes Using Rowhammer   271
  Puja Mondal, Suparna Kundu, Sarani Bhattacharya,
  Angshuman Karmakar, and Ingrid Verbauwhede

A Side-Channel Attack on a Higher-Order Masked CRYSTALS-Kyber
Implementation   301
  Ruize Wang, Martin Brisfors, and Elena Dubrova

Time Is Money, Friend! Timing Side-Channel Attack Against Garbled
Circuit Constructions   325
  Mohammad Hashemi, Domenic Forte, and Fatemeh Ganji

Related-Tweak and Related-Key Differential Attacks on HALFLOOP-48   355
  Yunxue Lin and Ling Sun

Users and Usability

How Users Investigate Phishing Emails that Lack Traditional Phishing Cues . . .   381
  Daniel Köhler, Wenzel Pünter, and Christoph Meinel

Usable Authentication in Virtual Reality: Exploring the Usability of PINs
and Gestures   412
  H. T. M. A. Riyadh, Divyanshu Bhardwaj, Adrian Dabrowski,
  and Katharina Krombholz

Living a Lie: Security Analysis of Facial Liveness Detection Systems
in Mobile Apps   432
  Xianbo Wang, Kaixuan Luo, and Wing Cheong Lau

Author Index   461

Blockchain

Mirrored Commitment: Fixing "Randomized Partial Checking" and Applications

Paweł Lorek[1,5], Moti Yung[2,3], and Filip Zagórski[1,4(✉)]

[1] Wroclaw University, Wrocław, Poland
filip.zagorski@gmail.com
[2] Columbia University, New York, USA
[3] Google, New York, USA
[4] Votifica, Wrocław, Poland
[5] Tooploox, Wrocław, Poland

Abstract. Randomized Partial Checking (RPC) [16] was proposed by Jakobsson, Juels, and Rivest and attracted attention as an efficient method of verifying the correctness of the mixing process in numerous applied scenarios. In fact, RPC is a building block for many electronic voting schemes, including Prêt à Voter [6], Civitas [9], Scantegrity II [5] as well as voting-systems used in real-world elections (*e.g.,* in Australia [4]). Mixing is also used in anonymous transfers of cryptocurrencies. It turned out, however, that a series of works [17,18] showed subtle issues with analyses behind RPC. First, that the actual security level of the RPC protocol is way off the claimed [16] bounds. The probability of successful manipulation of k votes is $(\frac{3}{4})^k$ instead of the claimed $\frac{1}{2^k}$ (this difference, in turn, negatively affects actual implementations of the notion within existing election systems. This is so since concrete implemented procedures of a given length were directly based on this parameter). Further, privacy guarantees [11] that a constant number of mix-servers is enough turned out [17] to also not be correct. We can conclude from the above that these analyses of the processes of mixing are not trivial.

In this paper, we review the relevant attacks, and we present Mirrored-RPC (mRPC) – a fix to RPC based on "mirrored commitment" which makes it optimally secure; namely, having a probability of successful manipulation of k votes $\frac{1}{2^k}$.

Then, we present an analysis of the privacy level of both RPC and mRPC. We show that for n messages, the number of mix-servers (rounds) needed to be ε-close to the uniform distribution in total variation distance is lower bounded by:

$$r(n, \varepsilon) \geq \log_2 \binom{n}{2}/\varepsilon.$$

This proof of privacy, in turn, gives insights into the anonymity of various cryptocurrencies (*e.g.,* Zerocash [23]) using anonymizing pools. If a random fraction q of n existing coins is mixed (in each block), then to achieve full anonymity, the number of blocks one needs to run the protocol for, is:

$$rb(n, q, \varepsilon) \geq -\frac{\log n + \log(n-1) - \log(2\varepsilon)}{\log(1 - q^2)}.$$

© The Author(s), under exclusive license to Springer Nature Switzerland AG 2024
C. Pöpper and L. Batina (Eds.): ACNS 2024, LNCS 14585, pp. 3–27, 2024.
https://doi.org/10.1007/978-3-031-54776-8_1

1   Introduction

Mix nets, introduced by Chaum [7], constitute an important technique used in many privacy-preserving technologies. For instance, mix nets are a crucial part of many voting systems providing assurance that encrypted ballots posted by voters are correctly decrypted (and tallied). A list of schemes that use mix nets includes systems deployed in publicly binding elections: Estonia, Norway, Switzerland, Australia, USA [4,5,10,13,27]. But applications of mix nets are much wider: anonymous messaging [22], anonymous routing [8], and oblivious RAM [24]. To find a more elaborate list of applications and techniques for verifiable mix nets the reader is encouraged to read [15].

This paper focuses on a central prominent technique by Juels, Jakobsson, and Rivest called Randomized Partial Checking (RPC) [16]. The original Chaumian mix net was designed in the "honest but curious" model, to guarantee senders' privacy provided that at least one mix server is honest. But, a single malicious mix server could replace any number of ciphertexts. In order to decrease the possibility of this happening, RPC was proposed. In RPC, the more ciphertexts are replaced by a server the higher the probability of detecting malfeasance is. The main difference between RPC and other proof-of-shuffle techniques (like [12,26]) is that RPC is much more efficient than other techniques, but provides just a *strong evidence* of correct operations instead of a *proof* of correct operations (but luckily, this confidence is sufficient for many applications). Due to its efficiency, the RPC approach is used in end-to-end voter verifiable systems like Prêt à Voter [6], Scantegrity II [5], and coercion-resistant Civitas [9]. The above have been implemented and applied in real elections. Then, as interest in implementing the technique grew, a series of works [17,18] scrutinized it, and showed that the actual security level of the RPC protocol is way off the initial claim: the probability of successful manipulation of k votes is $(\frac{3}{4})^k$ instead of $\frac{1}{2^k}$ as claimed in [16]. These attacks [17] affected the implementations of Scantegrity and Civitas systems. The level of privacy was affected as well [17]. More on attacks on RPC see Sect. 2.3.

Related Work: Recently [14], a new RPC-type protocol was proposed, where optimal verifiability tolerance $(\frac{1}{2})^k$ is achieved. The protocol assumes that there is a special auditor that becomes the last mix server. After the auditor/mix server publishes decrypted messages it reveals its private keys. While such an approach works in theory, the new protocol role can raise trust-related issues, *e.g.*, now one needs to assume that the special auditor and the second to last mix server do not cooperate (and this configuration solves one weakness by introducing another!). Aside from the proposed attacks, the authors of [18] proposed changes to the protocol that can fix certain attacks, but then they noted that other attacks (which they, in fact, proposed) are "equally harmful." Then, given their finding, they conclude: "This seems to be an inherent problem for RPC mix nets, without an obvious fix."

Our Contributions: We present Mirrored Randomized Partial Checking (mRPC), a protocol that has exactly the same participants, roles, and trust assumptions as the original RPC. The only difference is that a (mirrored) commitment (a commitment to a different value) is published during the protocol execution and one additional value is opened and checked during the audit phase (per message, per server). These changes, in turn, allow us to achieve optimal verifiability tolerance $(\frac{1}{2})^k$ - compared to $(\frac{3}{4})^k$ in the original RPC. The difference between $1/2^k$ and $(3/4)^k$ is highly significant when considering practical parameters (see Fig. 1). We also show how many mix servers $r(n, \varepsilon)$ are required to mix n messages so that the distribution on permutations (mapping senders to decrypted messages) is ε-close to the uniform distribution on all n-element permutations (in total variation distance). Our proof works for both versions of RPC: Scheme One (Independent Random Selections) and Scheme Two (Pairwise Dependent Selections)[1]. Analysis (Lemma 6) of Scheme One is applicable to (un)linkability in blockchains, while analysis (Lemma 7) of Scheme Two (RPC) is related to anonymity guarantees of election protocols.

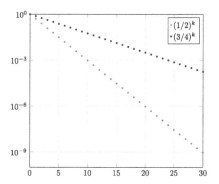

Fig. 1. mRPC guarantees better security level than original RPC. The probability of undetected manipulation of k messages is $(1/2)^k$ for mRPC and $(3/4)^k$ for RPC. x-axis corresponds to k-the number of modified entries; y-axis is the probability of undetectable manipulation.

1.1 Notation

We denote by $[n] = \{1, \ldots, n\}$. Security analysis uses standard assumptions about primitives used by Chaumian RPC mix nets: (1) public key encryption scheme ($\mathcal{E} = \langle \mathsf{KeyGen}, \mathsf{Enc}, \mathsf{Dec} \rangle$) used for Chaumian RPC to be IND-CCA2-secure [3], (2) commitment scheme is perfectly hiding and computationally binding (*e.g.*, Pedersen scheme [21]), (3) the encryption scheme allows for proof of correct decryption.

2 Chaumian Randomized Partial Checking (RPC) Mix Net

We try to closely follow [18] when describing the protocol. A decryption mix net [7] consists of a public, append-only *bulletin board*, mix servers $M_1, \ldots, M_r$, message senders $S_1, \ldots, S_n$ (sometimes we will call them voters) and *auditors*.

---

[1] As most authors we refer to Pairwise Dependent Selection scheme as to original RPC.

2.1 Protocol Description

The goal of the protocol: mix servers jointly decrypt messages sent by senders (voters), while auditors verify if the decryption process was performed correctly. The following steps are performed.

Setup Phase. Every mix server M_j generates two public/private key pairs $(pk_{2j-1}, sk_{2j-1}), (pk_{2j}, sk_{2j})$ and publishes its public keys pk_{2j-1}, pk_{2j} on the bulletin board.

Submit Phase. Every sender S_i chooses her input plaintext m_i (sometimes we refer to m_i as to a ballot/vote) and submits to the bulletin board B a ciphertext generated in the following process. She first encrypts m_i using pk_{2r} obtaining $c_{2r}^i = \mathsf{Enc}(pk_{2r}, m_i)$. Then, she repeats the following process for $j = 2r - 1, 2r - 2, \ldots, 0$:

$$c_j^i = \mathsf{Enc}(pk_j, c_{j+1}^i),$$

and submits c_0^i to the bulletin board B.

Mixing Phase. The sequence $C_0 = \langle c_0^1, \ldots, c_0^n \rangle$ of ciphertexts submitted by senders to B is the input to the mixing phase. We denote by $C_0[i] = c_0^i$ and similarly for other sequences.

   C_0 is fetched by the first server M_1 which outputs C_2 (each M_j performs two mixing steps $C_{2j-2} \rightsquigarrow C_{2j-1}$ and then $C_{2j-1} \rightsquigarrow C_{2j}$) that is an input to M_2, and so on.

   The output produced by M_r (the last mix server): C_{2r} should contain a permuted list of unencrypted input messages $m_1, \ldots, m_n$.

   The steps performed by each $M_j, j < r$ are following:

1. **Duplicate Elimination.** M_j removes duplicate entries from its input C_{2j-2}, leaving only a single copy of each entry. Moreover, all messages that correspond to decryption failures $\bot$ are removed. Denote by C'_{2j-2} the resulting sequence, and by $l \le n$ the number of messages of C'_{2j-2}.
2. **First Mixing.** M_j chooses uniformly at random a permutation π_{2j-1} of $[l]$ and posts on B the sequence C_{2j-1}, where $C_{2j-1}[i] = \mathsf{Dec}(sk_{2j-1}, C'_{2j-2}[\pi_{2j-1}])$.
3. **Second Mixing.** M_j performs the same steps as during the first mixing: selects uniformly at random a permutation π_{2j} of $[l]$. Then it posts on B the sequence C_{2j} where $C_{2j}[i] = \mathsf{Dec}(sk_{2j}, C'_{2j-1}[\pi_{2j}])$.
4. **Posting Commitments.** M_j posts two sequences of commitments on B:
   (a) commitments to the values $\pi_{2j-1}^{-1}(1), \ldots, \pi_{2j-1}^{-1}(l)$,
   (b) commitments to the values $\pi_{2j}(1), \ldots, \pi_{2j}(l)$.

For the clarity of presentation we assume no duplicate elimination took place, *i.e.*, $l = n$.

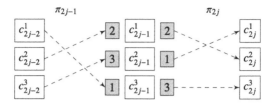

Fig. 2. Original RPC: commitments to $\pi_{2j-1}^{-1}(i)$ and to $\pi_{2j}(i)$ are in shaded squares. Dashed edges/arrows remain secret.

2.2   RPC Audit

During the audit phase, each mix server M_j opens half of the commitments. A set $I_j \subset \{1, \ldots, n\}$ is computed by *e.g.*, xor-ing random bit strings provided by the auditors.

AL If $i \in I_j$ then the mix server M_j is supposed to:
   1 open the left link for i, *i.e.*, M_j is supposed to open its i-th commitment from its first sequence of commitments, which should be a commitment on the value $\pi_{2j-1}^{-1}(i)$.
   2 post a (non-interavtive zero-knowledge) proof demonstrating that indeed $C_{2j-1}[i]$ is obtained from decrypting $C'_{2j-2}[\pi_{2j-1}^{-1}(i)]$ using sk_{2j-1}.
AR If $i \notin I_j$ then the mix server M_j is supposed to:
   1 open the right link: the commitment to the value $\pi_{2j}(i)$.
   2 post a (non-interactive zero-knowledge) proof that $C_{2j}[\pi_{2j}(i)]$ is obtained from decrypting $C_{2j-1}[i]$ using sk_{2j}.

Set I_j defines a corresponding challenge string (also called audit string) $B_j = b_{j,1} b_{j,2} \ldots b_{j,n}$ for $b_{j,i} \in \{0, 1\}$, where $b_{j,i} = 0$ if and only if $i \in I_j$.

Example 1 (RPC audit). Let us assume that the jth server committed to the values presented in the Fig. 2 and during the audit, an audit string $B_j = 010$ was selected ($I_j = \{1, 3\}$). Commitments to $\pi_{2j-1}^{-1}(1)$, $\pi_{2j-1}^{-1}(3)$ and to $\pi_{2j}(2)$ are opened. Corresponding proofs of correct decryptions are shown (along solid arrows) *e.g.*, that c_{2j-1}^2 correctly decrypts to c_{2j}^1 under the public key pk_{2j}. It is visualized on Fig. 3.

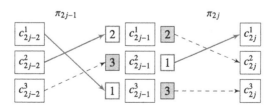

Fig. 3. RPC audit example for server M_j and audit string $B_j = 010$. Dashed edges and corresponding commitments remain hidden.

2.3 Attacks on RPC

In this section we describe and analyse attacks on RPC. The first attack was presented in [18] and later described in [17].

Attacks by the Last Mix Sever. To ilustrate the attack by the last mix-server, let us consider the following example with $n = l = 3$ votes. Let $m_1 = m_2 = A$ (2 votes for candidate A) while $m_3 = B$ (1 vote for B). Say, the honest permutation is $\pi_{2r} = (2, 1, 3)$ (Fig. 2), however, M_r is cheating and it publishes commitments to $\pi'_{2r} = (1, 1, 3)$ (which is not a permutation) (Fig. 4).

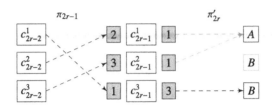

Fig. 4. Example: attack by the last mix server. A vote for B is copied while a vote for A is removed.

The audit string is of the form $B_r = b_{r,1}b_{r,2}b_{r,3}$. The value of $b_{r,3}$ is irrelevant for this attack, we are thus left with four choices for $b_{r,1}b_{r,2}$. All four situations are depicted in Fig. 5. If $b_{r,1} = b_{r,2} = 1$ then M_r is asked to open $\pi'_{2r}(1)$ and $\pi'_{2r}(2)$ and the cheating is detected. In all other cases, the cheating is not detected (since there are two entries pointing to the same element). In other words, one can detect a single message manipulation with probability $1/4$.

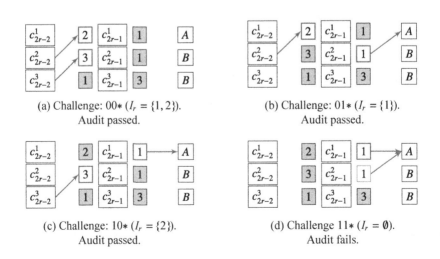

(a) Challenge: $00*$ ($I_r = \{1, 2\}$). Audit passed.

(b) Challenge: $01*$ ($I_r = \{1\}$). Audit passed.

(c) Challenge: $10*$ ($I_r = \{2\}$). Audit passed.

(d) Challenge $11*$ ($I_r = \emptyset$). Audit fails.

Fig. 5. RPC detects a single message manipulation just with probability $\frac{1}{4}$.

Attacks by Any Mix Server. Here, we present an attack that was proposed in [17]. This attack can be performed by any server. Let $l = n = 3$ and consider the server M_j with honest inverse permutation $\pi_{2j-1}^{-1} = (2, 3, 1)$ (Fig. 2), however the server publishes commitments to $\pi_{2j-1}'^{-1} = (1, 3, 1)$ (Fig. 6).

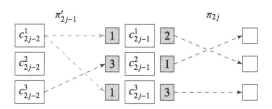

Fig. 6. Example: attack on any layer by server M_j. The result of the attack can be: a vote for B is copied while a vote for A is removed.

If the audit string $b_{j,1}b_{j,2}b_{j,3}$ is such that $b_{j,1} = b_{j,3} = 0$, then the server is asked to open $\pi_{2j-1}'^{-1}(1)$ and $\pi_{2j-1}'^{-1}(3)$ and the manipulation is detected. Note that in any other case for values of $b_{j,1}$, $b_{j,3}$, it is not detected. All four situations for values of $b_{j,1}$, $b_{j,3}$ are depicted in Fig. 7.

Summarizing, such a manipulation is detected with probability $1/4$ (and thus it is undetected with probability $3/4$) in case of one manipulation. In general, when k messages are manipulated, the probability of not detecting it is $(3/4)^k$ (for details see Theorem 1 in [18]).

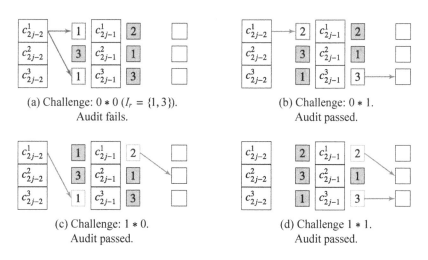

(a) Challenge: $0 * 0$ ($I_r = \{1, 3\}$).
Audit fails.

(b) Challenge: $0 * 1$.
Audit passed.

(c) Challenge: $1 * 0$.
Audit passed.

(d) Challenge $1 * 1$.
Audit passed.

Fig. 7. RPC detects a single message manipulation just with probability $\frac{1}{4}$.

3   Mirrored Randomized Partial Checking (mRPC)

In this section, we present a fix to RPC which we call Mirrored-RPC (mRPC) protocol and prove that it guarantees optimal level of manipulation detection *i.e.,* manipulation of k messages is detected with probability $1 - (1/2)^k$.

In RPC protocol, each mix server publishes two lists of commitments to the "middle column" (ciphertexts that are the result of the first mixing phase, see Fig. 2), more precisely server M_j for each entry i publishes:

- commitments to $\pi_{2j-1}^{-1}(i)$ (where data comes from), and
- commitments to $\pi_{2j}(i)$ (where data goes to).

In mRPC commitments are published on the "outer columns" – see Fig. 8. This change allows for detecting manipulations with higher probability than the original RPC.

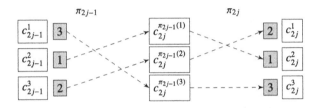

Fig. 8. mRPC: For each entry of a left column, a commitment to "where to" is published and a commitment to "where from" for entries of a right column is published (In the original RPC these commitments are only published for the entries that are the result of **first mixing.**).

3.1   Protocol Description

Setup phase The setup is exactly the same as in the original RPC (Sect. 2.1).

Submit phase This phase is exactly the same as in the original RPC (Sect. 2.1).

Mixing phase The mixing phase stays almost the same as the *Mixing phase* of the original RPC (see Sect. 2.1) the only difference is in the part: *Posting commitments*.

1. **Duplicate elimination** the same as in original RPC.
2. **First mixing** – the same as in original RPC.
3. **Second mixing** – the same as in original RPC.
4. **Posting commitments** M_j posts **two** sequences of commitments on B:
    (a) commitments to the values $\pi_{2j-1}(1), \ldots, \pi_{2j-1}(l)$,
    (b) commitments to the values $\pi_{2j}^{-1}(1), \ldots, \pi_{2j}^{-1}(l)$.

Note that RPC in **Posting commitments** phase in step 4a posts: $\pi_{2j-1}^{-1}(1), \ldots,$ $\pi_{2j-1}^{-1}(l)$ and in step 4b posts: $\pi_{2j}(1), \ldots, \pi_{2j}(l)$. Similarly as in RPC, for clarity of presentation, we assume no duplicate elimination took place in mRPC, *i.e.,* $l = n$.

3.2   mRPC Audit

During the audit phase, each mix server M_j opens half of the commitments. A set $I_j \subset \{1,\ldots,n\}$ is computed by *e.g.*, xor-ing random bit strings provided by the auditors. Set I_j defines a corresponding challenge string (also called audit string) $B_j = b_{j,1}b_{j,2}\ldots b_{j,n}$ for $b_{j,i} \in \{0,1\}$, where $b_{j,x} = 0$ if and only if $x \in I_j$.

AL If $x \in I_j$ *i.e.*, $b_{j,x} = 0$, then the mix server M_j is supposed to:
   1 (bidirectional checking):
     (a) publish value y;
     (b) then open $z = \pi_{2j-1}(y)$ and check if $z = x$;
   2 post a non-interactive zero-knowledge proof demonstrating that indeed $C_{2j-1}[x]$ is obtained from decrypting $C'_{2j-2}[y]$ using sk_{2j-1}.

AR If $x \notin I_j$ *i.e.*, $b_{j,x} = 1$, then the mix server M_j is supposed to:
   1 (bidirectional checking):
     (a) publish value y;
     (b) open the commitment to $z = \pi_{2j}^{-1}(y)$ and check if $z = x$.
   2 post a non-interactive zero-knowledge proof that $C_{2j}[y]$ is obtained from decrypting $C_{2j-1}[x]$ using sk_{2j}.

Example 2 (mRPC Audit). Let us assume that the jth server committed to the values presented in Fig. 8. The audit is presented in Fig. 9. During the audit phase, an audit string $b = 010 = b_1b_2b_3$ (defining the corresponding $I_j = \{1,3\}$). The jth server needs to publish:

AL for $x \in \{1,3\}$:
   1. for $x = 1$, $y_1 = 2$, $z = \pi_{2j-1}(y_1) = 1 = x$, a non-interactive ZKP that $C_{2j-1}[1]$ is obtained from decrypting $C_{2j-2}[2]$;
   2. for $x = 3$, $y_3 = 1$, $z = \pi_{2j-1}(y_3) = 3 = x$, a non-interactive ZKP that $C_{2j-1}[3]$ is obtained from decrypting $C_{2j-2}[1]$;
AR for $x \in I_j^c = \{2\}$:
   1. for $x = 2$, $y_2 = 1$, $z = \pi_{2j}^{-1}(y_2) = 2 = x$, a non-interactive ZKP that $C_{2j}[1]$ is obtained from decrypting $C_{2j-1}[2]$.

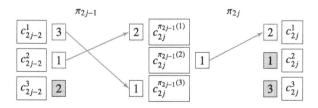

Fig. 9. mRPC audit example for server M_j with $B_j = 010$. Dashed edges and corresponding commitments remain hidden.

3.3   Attack Examples on mRPC

Attack by the Last Mix Server. Let us reconsider the attack described in Sect. 2.3. The dishonest "permutation" together with all commitments is depicted in Fig. 10.

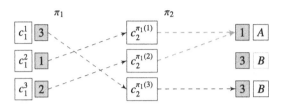

Fig. 10. Attack by the last mix server in mRPC.

For $b_{r,1} = b_{r,2} = 1$, the cheating is detected (Fig. 11 (d)). However, this is not the only situation when the manipulation is detected.

– Assume that the server commits to $\pi_{2r}'^{-1} = (1, *, 3)$. Consider $b_{r,1} = 0, b_{r,2} = 1$. In RPC server M_r is asked to open $\pi_{2r}'(2) = y = 1$, in mRPC the server is additionally asked to open $\pi_{2j}'^{-1}(y) = \pi_{2j}'^{-1}(1)$, which is 1 and the cheating is detected – Fig. 11(b).
– Assume that the server commits to $\pi_{2r}'^{-1} = (2, *, 3)$. Consider $b_{r,1} = 1, b_{r,2} = 0$. Then M_r is asked to open $\pi_{2r}'(1) = y = 1$ and additionally $\pi_{2r}'^{-1}(1) = 2$. This case is presented in Fig. 15(c).

In any case (for manipulated permutations), the manipulation will caught for 2 audit strings $b_{r,1}b_{r,2}$ out of 4, thus with probability 1/2. All options are depicted in Fig. 11.

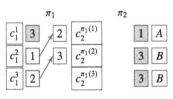

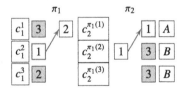

(a) Challenge string: 00*.
Audit passed.

(b) Challenge string: 01*. For $x = 2$ value $y = 1$ is published but opened commitment $z = 1 \neq x$. Audit failed.

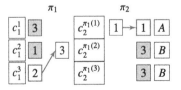

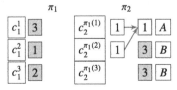

(c) Challenge: 10*.
Audit passed.

(d) Challenge 11*. For $x = 2$, $y = 1$ is published but opened commitment is for $z = 1 \neq x$. Audit failed.

Fig. 11. A view of a bulletin board after the audit step of mRPC.

Attacks by Any Mix Server. Let us continue the setup Sect. 2.3. The attack, in the presence of additional commitments is presented in Fig. 12.

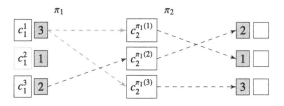

Fig. 12. Attack on any layer in mRPC.

Again, once $b_{j,1} = b_{j,3} = 0$, the manipulation is detected. Consider cases:

- Assume that server commits to $\pi'_{2j-1} = (3, *, 2)$. Consider $b_{j,1} = 0, b_{j,3} = 1$. In RPC server M_j is asked to open $\pi'^{-1}_{2j-1}(1) = y = 1$, in mRPC server is additionally asked to open $\pi'_{2j-1}(1)$ which is 3 and the manipulation is detected.
- Assume now that the commitment is $\pi'_{2j-1} = (1, *, 2)$. Then in case $b_{j,1} = 1, b_{j,3} = 0$ the server must open $\pi'^{-1}_{2j-1}(3)$ which commits to 1.

In any case (for manipulated permutations), the manipulation will be detected in two out of four possibilities for $b_{j,1}$ and $b_{j,3}$, i.e., with probability $1/2$. All the situations (for $\pi'_{2j-1} = (3, 1, 2)$) are presented in Fig. 13, other cases are "symmetric" (see Fig. 15).

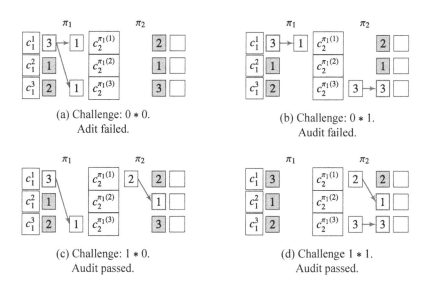

(a) Challenge: $0 * 0$.
Adit failed.

(b) Challenge: $0 * 1$.
Audit failed.

(c) Challenge: $1 * 0$.
Audit passed.

(d) Challenge $1 * 1$.
Audit passed.

Fig. 13. mRPC ggdetects a single message manipulation with probability $\frac{1}{2}$. For the same settings, RPC succeeds in detecting only with probability $\frac{1}{4}$.

The same attack as in Sect. 2.3 (Attacks by the last mix server) is presented, except in the first row of the last column, commitment is to row 2 from the middle column. The attack is then detected for different challenge strings but still with 50% probability (Fig. 14).

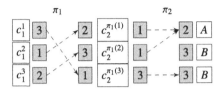

Fig. 14. Attack by the last mix server in mRPC.

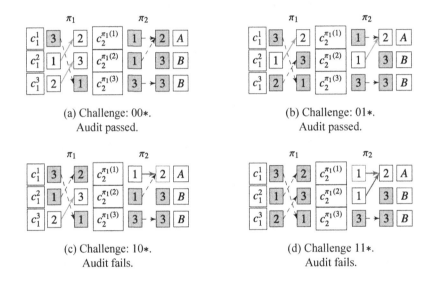

(a) Challenge: 00∗.
Audit passed.

(b) Challenge: 01∗.
Audit passed.

(c) Challenge: 10∗.
Audit fails.

(d) Challenge 11∗.
Audit fails.

Fig. 15. The same attack as in Sect. 3.4 is presented but with attacker committing to different values.

3.4   Security of mRPC

Lemma 1. *For mRPC, the probability of undetectable modification of k entries by any mix server M_j, during one mixing step is upper bounded by $\frac{1}{2^k}$.*

Proof. We will show the proof for an odd $(2j - 1)$ mixing step, the reasoning for an even $(2j)$ mixing step is similar. The input to the mix server M_j is a list of ciphertexts $C_{2j-1} = \langle c_{2j-1}^1, \ldots, c_{2j-1}^n \rangle$ published by the server M_{j-1} (or the users/voters for $j = 1$).

During the *Mixing phase*, M_j posts:

- the result of the *First mixing*, ciphertexts: $C_{2j} = \langle c_{2j}^1, \ldots, c_{2j}^n \rangle$,
- commitments $t_1, \ldots, t_n$.

If M_j is honest then for some $\pi_{2j-1} \in S_n$ and $y = \pi_{2j-1}(x)$ for all $x \in [n]$ the following equations hold:

$$t_x = \mathsf{Comm}(y), \tag{1}$$

$$c_{2j}^y = \mathsf{Dec}_{sk_{2j-1}}(c_{2j-1}^x). \tag{2}$$

During the audit step if $b_{j,y} = 0$ ($y \in I_j$) the following steps are performed:

AL.1 (bidirectional checking):
  1. M_j publishes z,
  2. M_j opens commitment $t_z = \mathsf{Comm}(y')$ to y',
  3. auditor checks if $y = y'$.
AL.2 (proof of correct decryption):
  1. M_j publishes the proof that Eq. 2 holds for y and z,
  2. auditor verifies the proof.

If M_j is dishonest and decides to manipulate k entries from positions in a set $A \subset \{1, \ldots, n\}$ ($|A| = k$) it means that M_j will not be able to pass *AL.2* part of the audit for $x \in A$.

M_j may try to post commitments to different positions but since the commitment check **AL.1** is bidirectional, a single entry from C_{2j-1} can be mapped only to a single entry in C_{2j}. And since C_{2j} lacks entries corresponding to ciphertexts from positions in A it will be detected in the **AL.2** part of the check whenever for such an entry a challenge bit 0 will be chosen.

Since there are k positions with that property, the probability of not detecting that k entries were dropped (replaced) is equal to $1/2^k$.

The main theorem is a direct conclusion from Lemma 1.

Theorem 1 (mRPC security). *For mRPC, the probability of undetectable modification of k entries by any mix server is upper bounded by $\frac{1}{2^k}$.*

4   Privacy Guarantees of RPC and mRPC

4.1   Constant Number of Mix-Servers

In [11] it was shown that for a scenario when votes are cast only on one of the two candidates, the constant number of mix servers is enough.

Here we show that for arbitrary messages (*e.g.*, for Australian-type ballots), a constant number of mix-servers is not enough.

Example 3 (Bulletin board leaks information). RPC auditing process may reveal a lot of information about voters' preferences. Figure 16 presents an extreme example. There are two candidates A, B and 8 voters $v_1, \ldots, v_8$. With only $r = 2$ mixing servers, a lot of information may be available to an adversary, even when he just observes publicly accessible information.

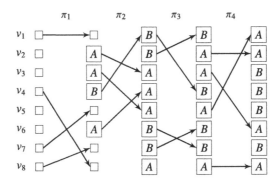

Fig. 16. RPC for small number of mix servers may reveal a lot of information. Just by observing bulletin board, an adversary may say that voters $\{v_1, v_4, v_7, v_8\}$ cast votes $\{A, B, B, B\}$ while voters $\{v_2, v_3, v_5, v_6\}$ cast votes: $\{A, A, A, B\}$.

The situation becomes much worse if an adversary knows exactly how some voters voted. For the example at Fig. 16, knowlede that v_4 voted for A reveals that v_1, v_7, v_8 voted for B.

Example 4 (Anonymity for arbitrary messages.). For a general case, when there are more types of messages (*e.g.,* ballots in Australia), senders' privacy is still at risk. In the most general case, every message is unique. The insight behind privacy definition is achieved in the following way: for an adversary, every permutation should be possible with almost the same probability – *i.e.,* distribution on permutations generated by the RPC process should be close to the uniform distribution.

By π we denote a permutation obtained by applying permutations $\pi_1, \ldots, \pi_4$, and revealing parts of them during the audit phase (see Fig. 17). It is easy to see that $P[\pi = (*, *, 5, *, *, 7, *, *)] = 0 = P[\pi = (*, *, 7, *, *, 5, *, *)]$ (it is impossible that message 5 was sent by v_3 at the same time when message 7 was sent by v_6, and vice versa). There are a lot of other permutations that are impossible to achieve.

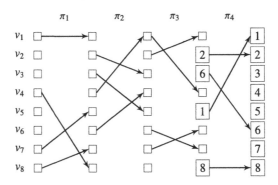

Fig. 17. RPC for a small number of mix servers may reveal a lot of information. The probability that senders v_2, v_3 sent messages $5, 7$ respectively is equal 0. One can exclude a lot of other combinations. A similar analysis can be applied to linkability of many crypto-currencies, *e.g.,* Zerocash [23].

Definition 1. *For mix-server entries x_i, x_j, we denote by $M_{at}(x_i, x_j) = t$ if M_t was the first mix-server for which entries were both audited during the same step. By audited by server M_k we mean that both x_i and x_j were assigned the same audit bits.*

Note that if entires x_i, x_j were audited in M_t then the entries were *mixed* – someone observing only revealed links does not know their relative ordering.

Lemma 2. *For any entries x_i, x_j the probability that they will be mixed for the first time in the k-th mix-server is equal to $\frac{1}{2^k}$, i.e., $P\left(M_{at}(x_i, x_j) = k\right) = \frac{1}{2^k}$.*

Lemma 3. *Let r be the number of mix-servers, and n be the number of processed entries. If $\binom{n}{2} \geq 2^r$ then with high probability there exists a pair of entries $i, j \in \{1, \ldots, n\}$ such that $M_{at}(x_i, x_j) > r$.*

The proof of Lemma 3 follows from a birthday paradox argument.

By $\text{RPC}_{r,n}$ we mean a random permutation obtained by processing n messages through an RPC cascade of r mix-servers having the knowledge on so far opened links. By $\mathcal{L}(\text{RPC}_{k,n})$ we denote the distribution of the scheme at step $k \leq r$ and by $\mathcal{U}(\mathcal{S}_n)$ we denote the uniform distribution, both on $\mathcal{S}_n$ – a set of permutations of n elements. We will use a *total variation distance* between two distributions μ, ν on a common finite state space $\mathbb{E}$ as

$$\text{TVD}[\mu, \nu] = \frac{1}{2} \sum_{e \in \mathbb{E}} |\mu(e) - \nu(e)|.$$

The conclusion of Lemma 4 is that a constant number of mix-servers is not enough to privately process arbitrary messages.

Lemma 4. *Let r be the number of mix-servers, and n be the number of processed entries. If $\binom{n}{2} \geq 2^r$ and in the last server m left links are open, then*

$$\text{TVD}\left[\mathcal{U}(\mathcal{S}_n), \mathcal{L}(\text{RPC}_{r,\sqrt{2^r}})\right] > 1 - \frac{2\,m(n-m)}{n(n-1)} \overset{(*)}{\geq} \frac{1}{2} - \frac{1}{2(n-1)},$$

where equality in $(*)$ is achieved for $m = n/2$ (say n is even).

The proof of Lemma 4 is in Appendix A.1, the bound is depicted in Fig. 18.

4.2 Mixing Time

In this section, we show the required number of mix-servers to achieve high level of privacy. The main result concerning the privacy of RPC and mRPC is the following.

Lemma 5. *Let n be the number of processed entries by a r-server RPC mix or mRPC. If*

$$r = r(n, \varepsilon) \geq \log_2\left[\binom{n}{2}\middle/\varepsilon\right]$$

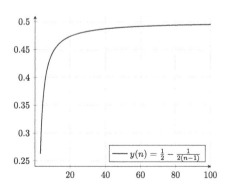

Fig. 18. Lower bound on $\text{TVD}\left[\mathcal{U}(\mathcal{S}_n), \mathcal{L}(\text{RPC}_{r,n})\right] \geq \frac{1}{2} - \frac{1}{2(n-1)}$.

then

$$\text{TVD}\left[\mathcal{U}(S_n), \mathcal{L}(RPC_{r,n})\right] \leq \varepsilon.$$

We start – Lemma 6 – with the RPC/mRPC Scheme One, i.e., the case when each server is asked to open left/right connections independently. Moreover, we assume that each entry is opened with some predefined probability $p \in (0, 1)$. Note that it is equivalent to actually considering $2r$ servers, each performing a single permutation – we consider however r servers, each performing two permutations, to be consistent with lemmas related to Scheme Two.

Afterwards, in Lemma 7 we show the result for Scheme Two. Lemma 5 is a direct consequence of the latter (substitute $p = 1/2$).

Lemma 6. *Let n be the number of processed entries by a r-server RPC or mRPC mix Scheme One. Each server is asked to open any connection independently with probability $p \in (0, 1)$. If*

$$r = r(n, \varepsilon) \geq \frac{1}{2} \log_{\frac{1}{1-(1-p)^2}} \left[\binom{n}{2}/\varepsilon\right]$$

then

$$\text{TVD}\left[\mathcal{U}(S_n), \mathcal{L}(RPC_{r,n})\right] \leq \varepsilon.$$

The proof of Lemma 6 is in Appendix A.2, it is based on strong stationary times (SST, introduced in [1,2]), a tool from a Markov chain theory.

Remark. It is worth mentioning that SST T from Lemma 6 (see its proof) resembles SST constructed in [19] for riffle shuffle scheme. Note that the RPC and the riffle shuffle are quite different – in RPC full permutation is applied in each step and each connection is revealed with probability p, whereas in riffle shuffle only the specific type of permutation in each step is performed and p corresponds to revealing some bits used to perform it. Note also that it takes $\frac{1}{2} \log_{\frac{1}{1-(1-p)^2}} \left[\binom{n}{2}/\varepsilon\right]$ for RPC to mix, whereas it takes $\log_{\frac{2}{1-(1-p)^2}} \left[\binom{n}{2}/\varepsilon\right]$ for riffle shuffle to mix.

Let us consider the following example.

Example 5. Consider $n = 6$ an assume that $B_1 = 001010, B_2 = 010011$, i.e., in first steps outgoing connections from nodes $1, 2, 4$ and 6 are revealed and in the second step the outgoing connections from nodes $1, 3$, and 4. With this knowledge, the adversary knows that with equal probability one of the permutations is possible:

$$(4, 1, 6, 3, 2, 5), (4, 1, 2, 3, 6, 5), (4, 6, 1, 3, 2, 5), (4, 2, 1, 3, 6, 5),$$
$$(4, 6, 2, 3, 1, 5), (4, 2, 6, 3, 1, 5), (4, 1, 6, 5, 2, 3), (4, 1, 2, 5, 6, 3),$$
$$(4, 6, 1, 5, 2, 3), (4, 2, 1, 5, 6, 3), (4, 6, 2, 5, 1, 3), (4, 2, 6, 5, 1, 3).$$

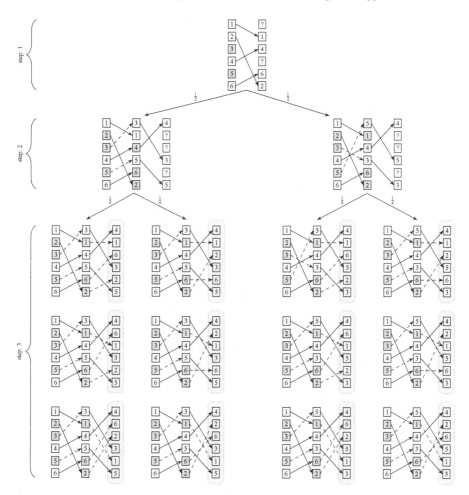

Fig. 19. 3 steps of execution of RPC for $n = 6$. All options for unrevealed nodes shown. Revealed connections depicted as solid lines (corresponding nodes are red), unrevealed ones as dashed lines (corresponding nodes are gray). After these three steps Y_3 has the uniform distribution on 12 permutations emphasized by gray regions. (Color figure online)

All possible situations are depicted in Fig. 19. In Fig. 20, one realization of this example is depicted – then all the pairs are mixed, thus the resulting permutation is random. (Note that for $n = 6$ such a situation happens on average after processing by $\frac{1}{2} \log_{\frac{4}{3}} \binom{6}{2} =$ 4.7 servers).

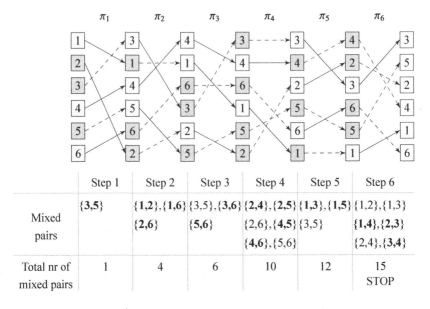

	Step 1	Step 2	Step 3	Step 4	Step 5	Step 6
Mixed pairs	{3,5}	{1,2},{1,6} {2,6}	{3,5},{3,6} {5,6}	{2,4},{2,5} {2,6},{4,5} {4,6},{5,6}	{1,3},{1,5} {3,5}	{1,2},{1,3} {1,4},{2,3} {2,4},{3,4}
Total nr of mixed pairs	1	4	6	10	12	15 STOP

Fig. 20. Sample execution of mixing of $n = 6$ elements. Newly mixed pairs are in **bold**. In this example after 6 steps an adversay has no knowledge on the final permutation (all $\binom{6}{2} = 15$ pairs are mixed). After three steps his knowledge is depicted in Fig. 19.

In the following Lemma 7 we show the result for Scheme Two.

Lemma 7. *Let n be the number of processed entries by a r-server RPC or mRPC mix Scheme Two. Each server is asked to open any left link independently with probability $p \in (0, 1)$, then the right links corresponding to non-opened left ones, are open.*

$$r = r(n, \varepsilon) \geq \log_{\frac{1}{2p(1-p)}} \left[\binom{n}{2}/\varepsilon\right]$$

then

$$\text{TVD}\left[\mathcal{U}(\mathcal{S}_n), \mathcal{L}(RPC_{r,n})\right] \leq \varepsilon.$$

The proof of Lemma 7 is in Appendix A.3. Note that for p close to 0 or 1 there will be many pairs mixed in step $2k - 1$ or $2k$. The worst situation i.e., the smallest number of mixed pairs (on average) will be for $p = 1/2$. For cases $n \in \{100, 10\,000, 1\,000\,000\}$ the average number of steps, as a function of p is depicted in Fig. 21.

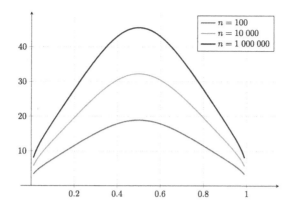

Fig. 21. Average number of RPC servers needed to mix $n \in \{100, 10\,000, 1\,000\,000\}$ entries (for $\varepsilon = \frac{1}{100}$). In the worst case $p = 1/2$ we need 19 servers on average.

5   Application: CryptoCurrency Unlinkability

In most popular cryptocurrencies, payments are performed between pseudonyms. Since transactions are published on a public ledger, payment transactions remain traceable. There were a couple of approaches that introduce untraceability to blockchain cryptocurrencies: Zerocoin [20], Zerocash [23] (used in ZCash), CryptoNote [25] (used in Monero).

In this section, we want to show a link between Lemma 6 and the anonymity guarantees of various cryptocurrencies. We assume that the anonymization protocol is similar to the one that is used in Zerocash. If one wants to measure the anonymity level of a given system in total variation distance then it corresponds to the mixing time of RPC Scheme One which is expressed in Lemma 6. Instead of applying the following equation:

$$r(n, p, \varepsilon) \geq \frac{1}{2} \log_{\frac{1}{1-(1-p)^2}} \left[\binom{n}{2} / \varepsilon \right] = -\frac{\log n + \log(n-1) - \log(2\varepsilon)}{2 \log(1 - (1-p)^2)}$$

it seems simpler is simpler think about the function of $q = 1 - p$ – here q corresponds to the fraction of entries being in a mix. Then let $rb(n, q, \varepsilon) = r(n, p, \varepsilon)$:

$$rb(n, q, \varepsilon) \geq \frac{1}{2} \log_{\frac{1}{1-q^2}} \left[\binom{n}{2} / \varepsilon \right] = -\frac{\log n + \log(n-1) - \log(2\varepsilon)}{2 \log(1 - q^2)}$$

One needs to approximate n, e.g., by applying the simplifications (1) and (2) below; then $nq = n(1 - p)$ would be the average number of transactions (or from/to addresses) in a single block. The number $rb(n, q, \varepsilon)$ denotes the required number of mix-servers so the resulting permutation is ε close in total variation distance to the uniform distribution on n elements. Since each server performs two independent permutations, the required number of steps is equal to $2rb(n, q, \varepsilon)$ (Fig. 22).

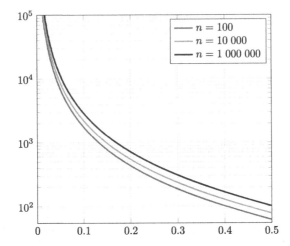

Fig. 22. Number of rounds (for cryptocurrencies the number of blocks) $2rb(n, q, \varepsilon)$ needed to be processed for a system with n entries to be close to the uniform distribution, as a function of q, ε. The x-axis of the plot is q – the probability of selecting an element to the mix $\varepsilon = 1/100$.

To give insights, we make a series of further simplifications:

(1) each transaction is of a nominal value (*e.g.*, 1 BTC/1 ETH/...),
(2) each pseudonym (public key) is linked with a single nominal value,
(3) each coin is selected to be used in a payment transaction independently, uniformly at random with probability $1 - p$ (in the Lemma 6 p corresponds to the opened links).

Then, assuming that all transactions are "shielded", with the data of 5/1/2022 (source: https://bitinfocharts.com) the results are following:

– for Ethereum $1.63 \cdot 10^{13}$ blocks (For $n = 120\ 606\ 657$, $p = \frac{186}{n}$, $\varepsilon = \frac{1}{10}$) would be needed ($2.56 \cdot 10^9$ days),
– for Bitcoin $6.03 \cdot 10^9$ blocks ($3.54 \cdot 10^7$ days).

6 Conclusions

We presented Mirrored Randomized Partial Checking (mRPC), the protocol that eliminates attacks on Randomized Partial Checking. Proposed mRPC makes minimal changes to the original protocol but allows for upper bounding probability of successful attack by an adversary to $(\frac{1}{2})^k$ - compared to $(\frac{3}{4})^k$ in the original RPC. The presented approach can be applied to fix Civitas and Scantegrity II voting systems.

We also provided an analysis of privacy guarantees offered by RPC. Our analysis gives also insights into the level of anonymity of cryptocurrencies. We conclude that due to the need for many steps (high value of $rb(n, q, \varepsilon)$ for small values of q) and the need for speedy transactions (that enforce low values of q), de-anonymization will be open to some attacks due to insufficient mixing.

A   Proofs

A.1   Proof of Lemma 4

Proof. Recall that I_j is a subset of $[n]$ for which left link is reveleaed (challenge bit is set to 0). Let us denote $S_{j,0} = I_j$ and $S_{j,1} = [n] \setminus I_j$, i.e., those messages for which right link is revealed (challenge bit 1). In terms of an audit string $B_j = b_{j,1}b_{j,2}\ldots b_{j,n}$, we may rewrite $S_{j,b} = \{i : b_{j,i} = b\}$.

If two elements x, y are not mixed in the M_j mix, it means that $x \in S_{j,b}$ and $y \in S_{j,1-b}$ for $b \in \{0, 1\}$.

Let us compare distance between the uniform distribution $\mathcal{U}(S_n)$ on n-element permutations to the distribution $\mathcal{L}(\mathsf{RPC}_{r,n})$ when $n \geq \sqrt{2^r}$.

From Lemma 3 there exists two mix entries x, y that are not yet mixed after r steps, with high probability. It means that $x \in S_{1,b_1}, S_{2,b_2}, \ldots, S_{r,b_r}$ and $y \in S_{1,1-b_1}, S_{2,1-b_2}, \ldots, S_{r,1-b_r}$ for $b_1, \ldots, b_c \in \{0, 1\}$.

Let $\mathcal{S}_n^0$ be the set of all permutations for which $x \in S_{r,b}$ and $y \in S_{r,1-b}$ for $b = 0, 1$. From the assumptions we have that $|S_{r,0}| = m$. From Lemma 3, with high probability, only permutations from $\mathcal{S}_n^0$ have nonzero probabilities in distribution $\mathcal{L}(\mathsf{RPC}_{r,\sqrt{2^r}})$. In other words, we can write that the probability of σ under $\mathcal{L}(\mathsf{RPC}_{r,\sqrt{2^r}})$ is $f(\sigma)$ such that

$$
f(\sigma) \quad
\begin{cases}
> 0 & \text{if } \sigma \in \mathcal{S}_n^0, \\
= 0 & \text{otherwise},
\end{cases}
$$

for some distribution f on $\mathcal{S}^0$ (Fig. 23).

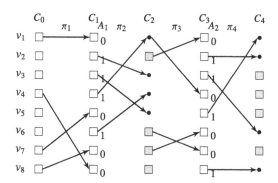

Fig. 23. Representation of sets $S_{1,0}, S_{1,1}$ for M_1 and sets $S_{2,0}, S_{2,1}$ for M_2. Audit/challenge bits A_1, A_2 for M_1, M_2 are presented next to columns C_1, C_3. Sets $S_{j,0}$ are denoted by ■ and sets $S_{j,1}$ are denoted by •.

Now, let us compute the distance between uniform distribution and the distribution $\mathcal{L}(\mathsf{RPC}_{r,n})$ for a set of permutations $\mathcal{S}_n^0$ such that m left links were opened, i.e., $|I_r| = |S_{r,0}| = m$.

$$\mathrm{TVD}\left[\mathcal{U}(S_n), \mathcal{L}(\mathrm{RPC}_{r,n}) \,\middle|\, |S_{r,0}| = m\right] =$$

$$= \frac{1}{2}\left(\sum_{\substack{\sigma \in S_n^0 \\ |S_{r,0}|=m}} \left|f(\sigma) - \frac{1}{n!}\right| + \sum_{\substack{\sigma \notin S_n^0 \\ |S_{r,0}|=m}} \frac{1}{n!}\right) \geq \frac{1}{2}\left(\sum_{\substack{\sigma \in S_n^0 \\ |S_{r,0}|=m}} \left(f(\sigma) - \frac{1}{n!}\right) + \sum_{\substack{\sigma \notin S_n^0 \\ |S_{r,0}|=m}} \frac{1}{n!}\right)$$

$$= \frac{1}{2} + \frac{1}{2}\left(\sum_{\substack{\sigma \notin S_n^0 \\ |S_{r,0}|=m}} \frac{1}{n!} - \sum_{\substack{\sigma \in S_n^0 \\ |S_{r,0}|=m}} \frac{1}{n!}\right) \qquad = \frac{1}{2} + \frac{1}{2n!}\left(n! - 2|\{\sigma \in S_n^0 : |S_{r,0}| = m\}|\right)$$

$$= 1 - \frac{|\{\sigma \in S_n^0 : |S_{r,0}| = m\}}{n!}$$

Noting that

$$|\{\sigma \in S_n^0 : |S_{r,0}| = m\}| = 2m(n-m)(n-2)!$$

we have

$$\mathrm{TVD}\left[\mathcal{U}(S_n), \mathcal{L}(\mathrm{RPC}_{r,n}) \,\middle|\, |S_{r,0}| = m\right] \geq 1 - \frac{2\,m(n-m)}{n(n-1)}.$$

The worst-case is exactly half left links are open (say n is even), i.e., $m = n/2$, then

$$\mathrm{TVD}\left[\mathcal{U}(S_n), \mathcal{L}(\mathrm{RPC}_{r,n}) \,\middle|\, |S_{r,0}| = m\right] \geq \mathrm{TVD}\left[\mathcal{U}(S_n), \mathcal{L}(\mathrm{RPC}_{r,n}) \,\middle|\, |S_{r,0}| = n/2\right]$$
$$\geq 1 - \frac{2\frac{n}{2}\frac{n}{2}}{n(n-1)} = \frac{1}{2} - \frac{1}{2(n-1)}.$$

A.2   Proof of Lemma 6

Proof. We will use some tools from Markov chain theory. We will consider two chains $\{X_t\}_{t\geq 0}, \{Y_t\}_{t\geq 0}$ on S_n. We set $X_0 = Y_0$ to be the identity permutation (note that $\mathrm{RPC}_{0,n}$ is the identity permutation).

Recall that server j performs permutations π_{2j-1} and π_{2j}, in total $2r$ permutations are performed.

Concerning X_{t+1}: it is X_t to which we apply a uniformly random permutation $\pi_t = (\pi_t(1), \ldots, \pi_t(n))$ (note that then $X_t \sim \mathcal{U}(S_n)$ for any $t \geq 1$).

Note that in Scheme One each server performs independently identical (in distribuion) steps. That is why we will look at the distribution after each application of π_t.

Concerning Y_t, this is X_t with the following extra knowledge. Let $B_t = b_{t,1}, \ldots, b_{t,n}$ be the n random bits chosen independently from the distribution $P(b_{t,i} = 0) = p = 1 - P(b_{t,i} = 1)$.

Now assume that the entries $S_{j,0} = \{j : b_{t,j} = 0\}$ from the permutation π_t are opened. Y_t has distribution of X_t provided we have a knowledge of $B_1, \ldots, B_t$. This corresponds to $\mathrm{RPC}_{t,n}$. Since $\{Y_t\}_{t\geq 0}$ is ergodic and aperiodic, the uniform distribution is the stationary distribution. By $\mathcal{L}(Y_t)$ we denote the distribution of Y_t.

We will use the strong stationary times (SST) approach (introduced in [1,2]). We say that T is an SST for $\{Y_k\}$ if for any permutation σ we have $P(Y_t = \sigma | T = t) = 1/n!$. For such SST we have $\mathrm{TVD}\left[\mathcal{L}(Y_k), \mathcal{U}(S_n)\right] \leq P(T > t)$ (see, e.g., Theorem 6 in [1]).

Let us define

$$T_{ij} = \min\{t : b_{t,i} = b_{t,j} = 1\},$$

i.e., this is the first time that both elements i and j were not opened. At this time the relative ordering of i and j is random (since π_k is uniformly random). Note that the probability that this will not happen in one step is $1 - (1 - p)^2$ (at least one entry was opened), thus $P(T_{ij} > t) = (1 - (1 - p)^2)^t$.

Now, let T be the first time when all the pairs of elements were not opened in at least one step. It means that all $\binom{n}{2}$ pairs are in random relative order – and that means that the permutation itself is random (since π_t's are uniformly random). In other words, T is an SST for $\{Y_t\}$. We may compute

$$\text{TVD}\,[\mathcal{L}(Y_k), \mathcal{U}(S_n)] \leq \qquad P(T > t) \qquad = P\left(\bigcup_{1 \leq i < j \leq n} \{T_{ij} > t\}\right)$$

$$\leq \sum_{1 \leq i < j \leq n} P(T_{ij} > t) = \sum_{1 \leq i < j \leq n} \left(1 - (1 - p)^2\right)^t = \binom{n}{2}\left(1 - (1 - p)^2\right)^t.$$

Taking $t = \log_{\frac{1}{1-(1-p)^2}} \left[\binom{n}{2}/\varepsilon\right]$, we have $\text{TVD}\,[\mathcal{L}(Y_k), \mathcal{U}(S_n)] \leq \varepsilon$. In total there are $t = 2r$ permutations, thus the proof is completed.

A.3 Proof of Lemma 7

Proof. The proof is similar to the proof of Lemma 6. The t-th server applies two permutations π_{2t-1} and π_{2t}, then each left link is opened independently with probability p, i.e., $B_{2t-1} = b_{2t-1,1}, \ldots, b_{2t-1,n}$ with i.i.d. $P(b_{2t-1,j} = 0) = p = P(b_{2t-1,j} = 1), j = 1, \ldots, n$. However the audit string B_{2t} is uniquely determined:

$$B_{2t} = (b_{2t,1}, \ldots, b_{2t,n}) = (1 - b_{2t-1,1}, \ldots, 1 - b_{2t-1,n}).$$

The situation is depicted in Fig. 24. Again, let

$$T_{ij} = \min\{t : b_{t,i} = b_{t,j} = 1\},$$

i.e., this is the first moment that elements i and j were not opened in the same permutation. Consider steps $2t - 1$ and $2t$: the elements i and j will be both opened in the same step if i) they are both revealed in step $2t - 1$; ii) they are both not opened in step $2t - 1$ (since then they surely will be in next step). Thus, the pair will not be mixed in steps $2t - 1$ and $2t$ with probability $2p(1 - p)$. We have

$$P(T_{ij} > 2t) = (2p(1 - p))^t.$$

Again, since all permutations π_t's are random, the first moment T when all the pairs are mixed is an SST, and we have (consider t even)

$$\text{TVD}\,[\mathcal{L}(Y_t), \mathcal{U}(S_n)]$$

$$\leq P(T > t) = P\left(\bigcup_{1 \leq i < j \leq n} \{T_{ij} > t\}\right)$$

$$\leq \sum_{1 \leq i < j \leq n} P(T_{ij} > 2t/2) = \sum_{1 \leq i < j \leq n} (2p(1 - p))^{\frac{t}{2}}$$

$$= \binom{n}{2}(2p(1 - p))^{\frac{t}{2}}.$$

Taking the last step, *i.e.*, $t = 2r$ we have that $r = \log_{\frac{1}{2p(1-p)}} \left\lceil \binom{n}{2}/\varepsilon \right\rceil$ what completes the proof.

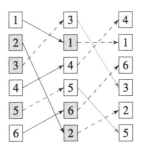

Fig. 24. Situation similar to Fig. 20: π_1 and π_2 and $B_1 = 001010$ are the same as there, but now B_2 is determined by B_1, namely $b_i^2 = 1 - b_i^1$ – opened connections depicted in red.

References

1. Aldous, D., Diaconis, P.: Shuffling cards and stopping times. Am. Math. Mon. **93**(5), 333–348 (1986)
2. Aldous, D., Diaconis, P.: Strong uniform times and finite random walks. Adv. Appl. Math. **8**(1), 69–97 (1987)
3. Bellare, M., Desai, A., Pointcheval, D., Rogaway, P.: Relations among notions of security for public-key encryption schemes. In: Krawczyk, H. (ed.) CRYPTO 1998. LNCS, vol. 1462, pp. 26–45. Springer, Heidelberg (1998). https://doi.org/10.1007/BFb0055718
4. Burton, C., Culnane, C., Heather, J.: Thea Peacock, Peter YA Ryan, Steve A Schneider, Vanessa Teague, Roland Wen, Zhe Xia, and Sriramkrishnan Srinivasan. Using prêt à voter in victoria state elections. EVT/WOTE, 2 (2012)
5. Carback, R.T., et al.: The scantegrity voting system and its use in the takoma park elections. In: Real-World Electronic Voting, pp. 253–292. Auerbach Publications (2016)
6. Chaum, D., Ryan, P.Y.A., Schneider, S.: A practical voter-verifiable election scheme. In: di Vimercati, S.C., Syverson, P., Gollmann, D. (eds.) ESORICS 2005. LNCS, vol. 3679, pp. 118–139. Springer, Heidelberg (2005). https://doi.org/10.1007/11555827_8
7. Chaum, D.L.: Untraceable electronic mail, return addresses, and digital pseudonyms. Commun. ACM **24**(2), 84–90 (1981)
8. Chen, C., Asoni, D.E., Barrera, D., Danezis, G., Perrig, A.: Hornet: high-speed onion routing at the network layer. In: Proceedings of the 22nd ACM SIGSAC Conference on Computer and Communications Security, pp. 1441–1454 (2015)
9. Clarkson, M.R., Chong, S., Myers, A.C.: Civitas: toward a secure voting system. In: 2008 IEEE Symposium on Security and Privacy (S&P 2008), pp. 354–368. IEEE (2008)
10. Gjøsteen, K.: The Norwegian internet voting protocol. In: Kiayias, A., Lipmaa, H. (eds.) Vote-ID 2011. LNCS, vol. 7187, pp. 1–18. Springer, Heidelberg (2012). https://doi.org/10.1007/978-3-642-32747-6_1
11. Gomułkiewicz, M., Klonowski, M., Kutyłowski, M.: Rapid mixing and security of Chaum's visual electronic voting. In: Snekkenes, E., Gollmann, D. (eds.) ESORICS 2003. LNCS, vol. 2808, pp. 132–145. Springer, Heidelberg (2003). https://doi.org/10.1007/978-3-540-39650-5_8

12. Groth, J., Ishai, Y.: Sub-linear zero-knowledge argument for correctness of a shuffle. In: Smart, N. (ed.) EUROCRYPT 2008. LNCS, vol. 4965, pp. 379–396. Springer, Heidelberg (2008). https://doi.org/10.1007/978-3-540-78967-3_22
13. Haenni, R., Koenig, R.E., Locher, P., Dubuis, E.: Chvote system specification (2017)
14. Haines, T., Müller, J.: Optimal randomized partial checking for decryption mix nets. In: Baek, J., Ruj, S. (eds.) ACISP 2021. LNCS, vol. 13083, pp. 277–292. Springer, Cham (2021). https://doi.org/10.1007/978-3-030-90567-5_14
15. Haines, T., Müller, J.: Sok: techniques for verifiable mix nets. In: 2020 IEEE 33rd Computer Security Foundations Symposium (CSF), pp. 49–64 (2020)
16. Jakobsson, M., Juels, A., Rivest, R.L.: Making mix nets robust for electronic voting by randomized partial checking. In: USENIX Security Symposium, San Francisco, USA, pp. 339–353 (2002)
17. Khazaei, S., Wikström, D.: Randomized partial checking revisited. In: Dawson, E. (ed.) CT-RSA 2013. LNCS, vol. 7779, pp. 115–128. Springer, Heidelberg (2013). https://doi.org/10.1007/978-3-642-36095-4_8
18. Küsters, R., Truderung, T., Vogt, A.: Formal analysis of Chaumian mix nets with randomized partial checking. In: 2014 IEEE Symposium on Security and Privacy, pp. 343–358. IEEE (2014)
19. Lorek, P., Kulis, M., Zagórski, F.: Leakage-resilient riffle shuffle. In: Blömer, J., Kotsireas, I.S., Kutsia, T., Simos, D.E. (eds.) MACIS 2017. LNCS, vol. 10693, pp. 395–408. Springer, Cham (2017). https://doi.org/10.1007/978-3-319-72453-9_32
20. Miers, I., Garman, C., Green, M., Rubinm, A.D.: Zerocoin: anonymous distributed e-cash from bitcoin. In: 2013 IEEE Symposium on Security and Privacy, pp. 397–411. IEEE (2013)
21. Pedersen, T.P.: Non-interactive and information-theoretic secure verifiable secret sharing. In: Feigenbaum, J. (ed.) CRYPTO 1991. LNCS, vol. 576, pp. 129–140. Springer, Heidelberg (1992). https://doi.org/10.1007/3-540-46766-1_9
22. Piotrowska, A.M., Hayes, J., Elahi, T., Meiser, S., Danezis, G.: The loopix anonymity system. In: 26th {USENIX} Security Symposium ({USENIX} Security 17), pp. 1199–1216 (2017)
23. Sasson, E.B., et al.: Zerocash: decentralized anonymous payments from bitcoin. In: 2014 IEEE Symposium on Security and Privacy, pp. 459–474. IEEE (2014)
24. Toledo, R.R., Danezis, G., Echizen, I.: Mix-ORAM: using delegated shuffles. In: Proceedings of the 2017 on Workshop on Privacy in the Electronic Society, pp. 51–61 (2017)
25. van Saberhagen, N.: Cryptonote v 1.0 (2012). https://cryptonote.org/whitepaperv1.pdf (2021)
26. Wikström, D.: A commitment-consistent proof of a shuffle. In: Boyd, C., González Nieto, J. (eds.) ACISP 2009. LNCS, vol. 5594, pp. 407–421. Springer, Heidelberg (2009). https://doi.org/10.1007/978-3-642-02620-1_28
27. Douglas Wikström. Verificatum (2018). https://www.verificatum.org/

Bitcoin Clique: Channel-Free Off-Chain Payments Using Two-Shot Adaptor Signatures

Siavash Riahi[1] and Orfeas Stefanos Thyfronitis Litos[2(⊠)]

[1] TU Darmstadt, Darmstadt, Germany
[2] Imperial College London, London, UK
o.thyfronitis-litos@imperial.ac.uk

Abstract. Blockchains suffer from scalability limitations, both in terms of latency and throughput. Various approaches to alleviate this have been proposed, most prominent of which are payment and state channels, sidechains, commit-chains, rollups, and sharding. This work puts forth a novel commit-chain protocol, Bitcoin Clique. It is the first trustless commit-chain that is compatible with all major blockchains, including (an upcoming version of) Bitcoin.

Clique enables a pool of users to pay each other off-chain, i.e., without interacting with the blockchain, thus sidestepping its bottlenecks. A user can directly send its coins to any other user in the Clique: In contrast to payment channels, its funds are not tied to a specific counterparty, avoiding the need for multi-hop payments. An untrusted operator facilitates payments by verifiably recording them.

Furthermore, a novel technique of independent interest is used at the core of Bitcoin Clique. It builds on Adaptor Signatures and allows the extraction of the witness only after *two* signatures are published on the blockchain.

1 Introduction

Blockchain technologies have gained increasing popularity in the past decade as they provide a robust, secure, and decentralized infrastructure that allows parties to make monetary transactions, as well as execute applications. The main ingredient used in virtually all blockchains are consensus protocols, which guarantee that all honest parties have received and agree on the latest state of the system. Unfortunately, because of their distributed nature, public blockchains do not scale well in terms of throughput and latency [1]. For example, Bitcoin needs at least 1h to finalize a new transaction [2] and can process around 7 transactions per second, in contrast to centralized, trusted payment processors that achieve instant finality and can process tens of thousands of transactions per second.

To tackle this issue, *off-chain* protocols were introduced. An off-chain protocol allows parties to make transactions without involving the blockchain and only come on-chain in case of disputes, vastly increasing throughput. The first

C. Pöpper and L. Batina (Eds.): ACNS 2024, LNCS 14585, pp. 28–50, 2024.
https://doi.org/10.1007/978-3-031-54776-8_2

type of widely deployed off-chain protocols is *payment channels* [3–7]. Two parties open a channel with a single on-chain transaction, locking their funds into a "joint account". They can then pay each other many times entirely off-chain, via a fast two-party protocol. An honest party can always unilaterally retrieve its rightful funds on-chain, thus it does not need to trust its counterparty.

Nevertheless, locking coins for exclusive use with a single counterparty is a severe limitation. *Payment Channel Networks* (PCNs) [6,7] mitigate this by enabling *atomic multi-hop payments*. A routing algorithm specifies a path of channels between the payer and the payee, then each intermediary receives funds in one channel and atomically sends the same amount (minus a fee) to the other.

In order for a channel to serve as an intermediate hop, it needs to have enough balance on one of the two sides of the channel. Unfortunately, intermediary channels are often used excessively in one direction, leading to *channel imbalance*. *Payment Channel Hubs* (PCHs) [8–10] were introduced to mitigate this. A PCH is a PCN node that offers liquidity and reliability in exchange for higher fees.

To deliver on these guarantees, the PCH must have the capacity to handle a scenario in which all parties simultaneously pay all their coins to the same party. This needs a large amount of locked funds: Consider a PCH with n clients, each of which owns c coins in its channel with the hub. The latter must have $(n-1)c$ coins in its channel with each client P in order to support everyone else each giving c coins to P, for a grand total of $n(n-1)c$ coins locked by the hub. Due to these scalability issues, practical hubs restrict the allowed payments and charge the users high fees to compensate for the opportunity cost of their locked funds.

To tackle this limitation of PCHs, an alternative off-chain approach that foregoes channels completely was introduced: *plasma* or *commit-chain* protocols [11]. Here a separate log of transactions between participating users is maintained by an *untrusted* operator that periodically commits the latest system state on-chain efficiently. Due to this need for on-chain commitments, contrary to PCNs, commit-chains do not achieve *instant finality*. Still, they greatly reduce the required operator *collateral* while maintaining high throughput and low fees. In most such protocols the operator either needs no collateral at all or has to lock nc coins, a linear improvement compared to PCHs. A popular subcategory of commit-chains are *rollups* [12,13]. They store all transaction data on-chain, but carry out the associated computation off-chain.

To date, all commit-chain protocols need the Turing-complete capabilities of, e.g., Ethereum [14] to validate exit requests and disputes. In this work we present *Bitcoin Clique*, the first commit-chain protocol suitable for blockchains with a limited scripting language such as Bitcoin [2]. Clique enables its users to pay each other off-chain without having to lock coins with a specific counterparty, therefore completely avoiding the issues that PCNs face. A payment only needs the active participation of the payer, the payee and an untrusted *operator*. To achieve this we leverage `OP_CHECKTEMPLATEVERIFY` (`OP_CTV`) [15], an opcode that is a prime candidate for inclusion in the next Bitcoin soft fork, as well as a novel technique of independent interest which builds on Adaptor Signatures [16]. At a high level, the latter enables the atomic exchange of a signature for a secret that satisfies a specific relation. This is useful for a range of applications [17–20].

Extending this primitive, we create a method to disclose the secret upon the publication of *two* adapted signatures instead of just one.

As we formally prove, Bitcoin Clique achieves security and scalability, needing only three off-chain messages per payment and a single on-chain transaction of minimal size at fixed intervals. Building on top of Bitcoin brings commit-chains to blockchains with constrained scripting capabilities, providing Bitcoin users more versatility of off-chain solutions and expanding the use cases of the cryptocurrency. Furthermore, it informs designers of future blockchains that pursue minimal on-chain scripting capabilities without compromising on the achievable off-chain functionality.

Similarly to other commit-chains and optimistic rollups [13], our solution only finalizes payments upon an on-chain commitment. We find this to be an acceptable tradeoff in exchange for drastically higher throughput than on-chain payments, as well as more flexibility and less collateral than payment channels.

1.1 Our Contributions

We provide *Bitcoin Clique*, the first commit-chain that is compatible with Bitcoin and other UTXO-based blockchains, enabling trustless off-chain payments between commit-chain users with superior throughput and lower fees than on-chain transactions, while avoiding the shortcomings of payment channels. We use of two special tools to design our protocol: Firstly, we employ the to-be-added OP_CTV opcode, which enables securely updating the state of Clique with the active participation of just a single party, the *operator*. Secondly, we leverage our novel technique at the heart of our construction, which extends Adaptor Signatures and underpins a punishing mechanism against users that try to maliciously obtain twice their rightful coins upon exiting. Relevant security properties are defined and formally proven.

1.2 Related Work

Off-Chain Channels. There has been extensive work on off-chain channels. The first line of works focused on off-chain payments over blockchains with a limited scripting language such as Bitcoin [4–6,21–24]. In [25] the Lightning Network (LN) [6] is formally proven secure in the UC framework [26]. State channels generalize payment channels by allowing parties to execute off-chain any application that is supported by the underlying blockchain, not just payments. 2-party state channels over Bitcoin are constructed in [16]. Most state channels constructions (e.g., [27–30]) function over Ethereum.

Commit-Chains. The original concept of a commit-chain was introduced by Plasma [11]. Many different plasma protocol variants such as MVP [31], Cash [32] Debit [33] and Snapp [34] were introduced thereafter. These have been mostly discussed at https://ethresear.ch without formal treatment.

Formal treatment of commit-chain/Plasma solutions was first presesnted by NOCUST and NOCUST-ZKP [35]. Their solution requires the underlying blockchain to support Turing-complete smart contracts. Another technique [36] achieves better efficiency in comparsion to preexisting solutions but relies on Trusted Execution Environments (which our work does not require). Liquid [37] is a centralized commit-chain that functions on top of Bitcoin: users need to trust a supermajority of a fixed federation of servers. Compared to channels, commit-chains avoid imbalance issues, payment routing, complex channel management and unsustainable collateral in exchange for instant finality.

Fast Finality Techniques. Snappy [38] and LDSP [39] speed up transactions and are optimized for a small set of merchants that receive payments from a large set of customers. A subset of the merchants (a.k.a *statekeepers*) guarantee fast payment finality using the customer's collateral, before the transaction becomes finalized on-chain. They only allow for unidirectional payments and put all transactions on-chain. We compare LN-based PCHs, NOCUST, Snappy, and the current work in Table 1. There, for Snappy it is epoch = latency period [38].

Rollups. Finally, a solution similar to commit-chains is called *rollups*. This approach aims at performing expensive computation (i.e., executing smart contracts) off-chain, while committing all (unprocessed) data to the blockchain, effectively using the latter as a *data availability layer* while the rollup is active, and as a *finality platform* once a party leaves the rollup. Rollups (e.g., [12,13,40–42]) are essentially a special case of commit-chains. They are of lesser interest for blockchains with restricted scripting capabilities such as Bitcoin, where the storage of L1, not its computation, corresponds to the lion's share of the cost.

Table 1. Comparison of PCHs based on LN [6], NOCUST [35], Bitcoin Clique, and Snappy [38] for n users. Ephemeral data is deleted after each epoch.

		PCH (LN)	NOCUST	Bitcoin Clique	Snappy (m statekeepers)
off-chain payment costs	Network (messages)	8	3	3	$3 + 2m$
	per-payment storage (user/operator)	$O(\log(\text{max pays}))$ / $O(\log(\text{max pays}))$	312b/841b (ephemeral)	1 sig + 5 pks/ 5 pks (ephemeral)	0 / 0
	fixed storage (user/operator)	2 ints + 2 pks/ $2n$ ints + $2n$ pks	529b/ $5n$ ints + n pks	n pks + n ints / n pks + n ints	0 / 0
on-chain overhead (txs)	startup	n	n	2	$n + m$
	pessimistic teardown	$2n$	$2n$	$2n$	$n + m$
	per epoch	—	1	1	0
	per payment	0	0	0	1
Works w/o Turing-complete SC		✓	✗	✓	✗
Allows any-to-any payments		✓	✓	✓	✗
user collateral (total payments of up to c coins/epoch)		—	0	0	c
operator collateral (c coins/user)		$n(n-1)c$	nc	nc	—
statekeeper collateral (insuring up to nc coins/epoch)		—	—	—	nc

Extensions to Adaptor Signatures. The technique of [43] extends adaptor signatures to two pre-signers, who collaborate to pre-sign. Given then a single adapted pre-signature, they can extract the witness. In contrast, in our technique a single pre-signer needs two adapted pre-signatures to extract the witness.

2   Preliminaries

A *digital signature scheme*, first formalized in [44], is an established cryptographic primitive that enables efficient message authentication. It provides (i) Gen, a *probabilistic polynomial time* (PPT) algorithm that generates a secret-public key pair, (ii) Sign, a PPT algorithm that, on input a secret key and an arbitrary message, produces a signature and (iii) *deterministic polynomial time* (DPT) Vrfy which, on input a public key, a message and signature, it returns whether the signature is valid. The security property ensures that, without knowledge of the secret key, one cannot forge a valid signature.

Consider next a security parameter $k \in \mathbb{N}$ and a *relation* $\mathcal{R}$, i.e., a set of statement-witness pairs (Y, y), where $Y, y \in \{0, 1\}^*$. Let $L_{\mathcal{R}}$, the *language* of the relation, be the set of statements for which a valid witness exists: $L_{\mathcal{R}} = \{Y \mid \exists y$ s.t. $(Y, y) \in \mathcal{R}\}$. We further say that $\mathcal{R}$ is a *hard* relation if: (i) there exists a PPT algorithm $\mathsf{RGen}(1^k)$ that produces new (Y, y) pairs in $\mathcal{R}$, (ii) one can check efficiently (i.e., in polynomial in k time) whether a given (Y, y) pair is in $\mathcal{R}$ (i.e., $\mathcal{R}$ is decidable) and (iii) there is no PPT algorithm that, given Y, produces a witness y such that $(Y, y) \in \mathcal{R}$ with more than negligible probability in k.

Adaptor Signatures (AS). This scheme, formalized in [45], is built on a digital signatures scheme and a hard relation $\mathcal{R}$. It enables the atomic exchange of (i) a valid signature on a message of interest $m \in \{0, 1\}^*$ with (ii) a valid witness of a pre-agreed statement. In addition to the 3 algorithms of the underlying signatures, adaptor signatures provide 4 new ones: pSign, pVrfy, Adapt and Ext. In this work we leverage a novel technique built on AS for a punishment mechanism at the heart of Bitcoin Clique.

The typical AS scenario involves two parties: Alice, who generates the pair $(Y, y) \in \mathcal{R}$, keeps the witness y secret, and publishes Y, and Bob, who controls the signing keypair (sk, pk). Initially, Bob calls $\mathsf{pSign}(sk, m, Y)$ in order to *pre-sign* m, then sends the resulting *pre-signature* $\tilde{\sigma}$ to Alice. She verifies that $\tilde{\sigma}$ is valid by checking that $\mathsf{pVrfy}(pk, m, \tilde{\sigma}, Y)$ returns 1. $\tilde{\sigma}$ is however *not* a valid signature (i.e., $\mathsf{Vrfy}(pk, m, \sigma) = 0$, where Vrfy is the verification algorithm of the underlying signature scheme). Nevertheless, Alice can call $\mathsf{Adapt}(pk, \tilde{\sigma}, y)$ (note the use of her witness y) to obtain the desired valid signature σ: now it is $\mathsf{Vrfy}(pk, m, \sigma) = 1$. Alice then broadcasts σ (usually on a blockchain). The adapted signature σ is special: Bob can *extract* Alice's witness y from it by running $\mathsf{Ext}(\sigma, \tilde{\sigma}, Y)$. The atomic exchange of σ for y is now complete.

The adapted signature σ thus serves a double role: It both proves that Bob indeed signed m and discloses Alice's witness to him.

A motivating application for this scheme is the atomic sale over a blockchain of a secret that satisfies a specific constraint, e.g., is the secret key of a specific public key: The seller Bob sends the statement (his public key) to the buyer Alice. She prepares a transaction that pays Bob, pre-signs it and sends him its pre-signature. Bob adapts it and publishes the transaction with the resulting signature. Lastly Alice extracts the witness (Bob's secret key) from the signature.

AS offer the following functional and security properties: (i) Bob cannot obtain a signature without adapting, (ii) if he adapts he will always obtain a valid signature and (iii) Alice can always extract the witness from an adapted signature. Thus, if Bob gets paid, then Alice learns the witness, ensuring atomicity.

CTV. We now provide some intuition on CTV, the proposed Bitcoin opcode [15] that we make heavy use of in this work. At a high level, it allows us to constrain the future use of coins. This new restriction ability enables complex ownership structures of coins, bringing to Bitcoin a large and useful subset of the smart contracts possible in blockchains with Turing-complete scripting languages [14] with a minimal, well-scrutinized modification to the Bitcoin Script.

Its mechanics are relatively simple: the CTV opcode is included in a transaction output and fully specifies every piece of data of the spending transaction, exept for the content of its inputs. At an intuitive level, it is enough to think that a CTV dictates the outputs of the next transaction.

For example, consider a transaction output θ' of c coins that is spendable by Alice, as well as another transaction output θ with $2c$ coins, encumbered only with a CTV that commits to a transaction with a single θ' output. This means that anyone can spend θ, as long as the spending transaction has a single output, θ'. The interpretation of this setup is that Alice has to pay a fee of c coins to the miners to gain c coins.

Let us examine a more useful example: Alice keeps her coins in an output encumbered with a CTV that specifies a single output. The latter is either spendable by her "hot wallet" key after a delay, or by her "cold wallet" key immediately. To pay, she first spends the CTV-encumbered output, then waits for the delay and finally uses the payment transaction. If however her hot wallet is compromised (which can presumably happen more easily than to her cold wallet), she still can salvage her coins with the cold wallet key within the delay window. Observe that in the common case of no compromise, her cold wallet secret key is never used. This way to secure funds is currently impossible in Bitcoin.

More complex applications of CTV, such as Bitcoin Clique, implicate multiple mutually distrustful parties. Without CTV, all involved outputs would have to be signed by all parties, otherwise any missing party could be cheated out of its coins by the rest. This however does not scale, as it requires the active participation of all parties for any state update. Even worse, a single inactive party can lead to the protocol stalling, effectively locking honest party coins forever. CTV removes these pitfalls by fixing where the coins of involved outputs will go without new signatures by all parties on every update.

With regards to notation, consider a transaction tx. We denote a CTV that commits to a transaction with the outputs of tx with CTV(tx): An output with spending condition CTV(tx) can only be spent by a transaction with the outputs of tx and no other transactions. For efficiency and privacy, a short commitment to the relevant tx data, generated with a hash function, is stored with CTV(tx).

3 Model

3.1 Blockchain and Transaction Model

In this work we focus on blockchains based on the Unspent Transaction Output (UTXO) model, such as Bitcoin. Under this model, coins are held in *outputs*. Formally, an output θ is a tuple (cash, φ), where cash denotes the amount of coins associated to the output and φ defines the conditions (also known as script) that need to be satisfied to spend the output. Our modeling is inspired by [16,46].

A *transaction* transfers coins across outputs, meaning that it consumes one or more existing outputs and creates a list of new outputs. A transaction has one *input* for each output it spends, which carries the *witness* that satisfies the script of the output being spent (typically one or more signatures). In other words, each transaction input is tied with exactly one previously unspent output of an older transaction. Thus, the transactions of a UTXO-based blockchain are organized in a directed, acyclic *transaction graph*. Formally, a transaction tx is a tuple of the form (txid, In, Out, Witness), where txid $\in \{0,1\}^*$ is the unique identifier of tx and is calculated as txid $:= \mathcal{H}(\mathsf{In}, \mathsf{Out})$, where $\mathcal{H}$ is a hash function, commonly modeled as a random oracle. In is a vector of pointers to the outputs being spent and Out $= (\theta_1, \ldots, \theta_n)$ is a vector of the new outputs. The sum of coins of the new outputs must not exceed the sum of coins of the spent outputs. Witness $\in \{0,1\}^*$ contains the witnesses that satisfy the scripts of the old outputs.

A valid transaction can be added to a single *block* of the blockchain (or *ledger*, $\mathcal{G}_{\mathrm{Ledger}}$). A block consists of a number of transactions. There is a unique block for each *height* $\in \mathbb{N}$ and new blocks are continuously created. As explained below, the height of the block in which it is included can be leveraged by the script(s) of a transaction via a *timelock*. The *liveness* property guarantees that an honest transaction has to wait for at most $u \in \mathbb{N}$ blocks from submission to inclusion. One can of course store a transaction locally (a.k.a. *off-chain*) along with (some of) its witnesses in order to publish it later on-chain if needed.

Let us now enumerate the five types of spending conditions of an output used in this work. The most common spending condition is a public key. To satisfy it, the spending transaction must be signed with the corresponding secret key. Two more spending conditions are *absolute* and *relative timelocks*. These conditions make the output unspendable *before* a certain point in time. An absolute timelock is a block height after which the output can be spent. A relative timelock is the number of blocks that the output must stay on-chain before it can be spent. All timelocks in this work last for strictly longer than the liveness parameter u. The fourth spending condition is the threshold signature, which allows a subset of specific size of a designated set of keys to spend the output (this functionality is implemented with the `OP_CHECKSIGADD` opcode[1]). The last spending condition type is CTV, which has been introduced in Sect. 2.

We introduce our notation through examples: The spending condition $pk_B \wedge \mathsf{CTV}(\mathsf{tx}_2) + t_1$ of an output of tx_1 can be spent by tx_2 signed by sk_B, only after tx_1 has been on-chain for t_1 blocks ("$+t$" denotes *relative timelock*). ($pk_C \wedge pk_D) \wedge t_2$ can be spent by a transaction signed by both sk_C and sk_D, only after block t_2 ("$\wedge t$" denotes *absolute timelock*).

3.2   Commit-Chain Model

A commit-chain protocol is executed among a set of users $\mathcal{P}$, an operator Op and $\mathcal{G}_{\text{Ledger}}$. We break the execution down into three phases: the *transaction*, the *exit*, and the *healing* phase. In the *transaction phase* users can transfer coins off-chain to one another and in the *exit phase* users can withdraw their rightful coins on-chain. Users that want to continue the Clique enter the *healing phase*.

Transaction Phase. During this phase each user $P_i \in \mathcal{P}$ can send a message of the form $(P_i, P_j, v, \mathsf{aux})$ to the operator Op indicating that P_i wants to send v coins to user $P_j \in \mathcal{P}$. At the end of this phase each user $P \in \mathcal{P}$ attempts to compute a tuple of the form (v, e, π), where v is P's balance in epoch e and π is a *balance proof*. The protocol should ensure that a user can send coins to and receive coins from multiple users during this phase. Balances are not updated immediately but only at the end of the transaction phase. This property is referred to as *late* or *eventual finality*. Due to late finality, it could indeed be the case that an honest user cannot calculate the latest π at every moment. In this case the user will use its previous balance proof to exit the system if she so wishes without loss of funds.

Op is tasked with processing payments and updating user balances. Some commit-chain protocols require Op to send one or more on-chain transactions to $\mathcal{G}_{\text{Ledger}}$ to commit to the latest state of the system at the end of each epoch.

Exit Phase. This phase can be triggered by any user $P \in \mathcal{P}$. It is carried out by submitting one or more suitable transactions to $\mathcal{G}_{\text{Ledger}}$. If Op misbehaves, P will detect it and exit in time, securely recovering all its coins on-chain.

Healing Phase. Some commit-chain protocols require a restoration process by the users and Op to revert to the transaction phase after an exit phase is completed.

3.3   Communication and Adversarial Assumptions

Let us now discuss the communication and adversarial assumptions in our modeling. A commit-chain protocol is executed in the presence of a PPT adversary who can corrupt up to all but one parties. The corrupted parties are then controlled by the adversary, i.e., they can deviate from the protocol description and act in an arbitrary and possibly coordinated fashion.

---

[1] `github.com/bitcoin/bips/blob/master/bip-0342.mediawiki#cite_note-5`.

We also assume that parties are connected via authenticated channels, i.e., the adversary can read, delay, replay or drop messages sent between parties but cannot modify their content. All parties have read and write access to $\mathcal{G}_{\text{Ledger}}$. The adversary cannot drop messages sent by an honest party to $\mathcal{G}_{\text{Ledger}}$, but it can delay them for up to a fixed period of time.

3.4   Security and Performance Guarantees

We here provide intuition for the intended guarantees of Bitcoin Clique.

Transaction Phase Correctness. We say that a transaction is valid if the sender owns in the commit-chain more coins than the amount to be paid. During the transaction phase, if Op, the sender $P_i \in \mathcal{P}$ and the receiver $P_j \in \mathcal{P}$ of a valid transaction $(P_i, P_j, v, \mathsf{aux})$ are honest, then either P_i's balance is reduced by v and P_j's balance is increased by v, or both balances remain unchanged (if the adversary drops or delays a message too much).

Exit Phase Correctness. If an honest user exits the commit-chain system, she is removed from the user set $\mathcal{P}$. For simplicity we assume that a user always exits with all her coins.

Balance Security. In the presence of *any number* of malicious parties, including Op, an honest user does not lose any coins at any stage of the protocol, i.e., an honest user is able to always exit with her entire balance. We note that due to late finality, this property essentially states that users will either be able to exit with their balance from the current or the previous epoch.

Operator Balance Security. An honest operator does not lose the collateral she deposited in the commit-chain, even in presence of *any number* of malicious users. Furthermore, she is able to exit the Clique at any time.

Formal security properties are given in Sect. 5 (Theorems 1 and 2).

Efficiency. Let t denote the duration of an epoch and c the per-epoch communication of Op with $\mathcal{G}_{\text{Ledger}}$. A commit-chain protocol is efficient if $t, c \in O(1)$, i.e., the duration of an epoch and the per-epoch communication of Op with $\mathcal{G}_{\text{Ledger}}$ independent of the number of both users and payments.

Efficiency is the reason why a commit-chain protocol is useful, as it guarantees that its payment fees are drastically lower than on-chain transaction fees.

4   Protocol Overview

In this section we go over the Bitcoin Clique protocol in an informal but detailed manner, providing the necessary intuition.

Consider users $\mathcal{P}$ with $|\mathcal{P}| = n$ and an operator Op running a Bitcoin Clique protocol. Under the current design, users can only own and exchange coins in a single, fixed denomination. Adding more denominations is relatively straight-forward, but left as future work – discussion to that direction can be found in Sect. 6. In the current section we limit the total number of coins to be a power of 2 and we assume that each user owns 1 coin for ease of exposition; these limitations are not present in the formal protocol.

This subsection is organized as follows: We start with the protocol flow during normal operation, which includes payments and *epoch* changes. We then explain the off-chain tree of transactions that is the core of the construction. Subsequently the exit phase is discussed. Afterwards we elaborate on the mechanism which guarantees that epoch changes respect balance security; this is where the extension of adaptor signatures and the need for operator collateral come into play. Then the Clique setup procedure is presented, tying everything together. Lastly we discuss the healing mechanism, which is formally presented in Appendix A.

Transaction Phase. During normal operation, Alice $\in \mathcal{P}$ can send her coin to Bob $\in \mathcal{P}$ by sending him a single signed message, who in turn generates some keys and sends them, together with Alice's message, to Op. The latter then signs and publishes these messages to all Clique users. In practice, this last step is efficient, as Op can simply post them on, e.g., its website. Honest users should check that their payments appear there and initiate the exit phase if they do not appear within a reasonable length of time.

Periodically, i.e., at the end of each *epoch*, Op publishes to $\mathcal{G}_{\text{Ledger}}$ a specially crafted step transaction with 1 input and 1 output that carries the sum of all Clique coins and commits to the latest coin distribution. This transaction spends a previous step transaction. This is efficient: a transaction of minimal, constant size safeguards all epoch payments, irrespective of their number or the amount of users. Looking ahead, in order to move its coins back on-chain, any user can unilaterally start the exit phase by spending on-chain the step transaction.

Transactions Structure. The central structure of a Clique is a binary tree of transactions with one leaf per coin, which exists entirely off chain during normal operation (i.e., until the exit phase). The root transaction of the tree has a single input that spends the step transaction and has two outputs, each with half the total coins. Each non-leaf transaction spends one of the two outputs of its parent and in turn provides two outputs, each with half the coins. Looking forward, a user can exit unilaterally by publishing to $\mathcal{G}_{\text{Ledger}}$ the branch of transactions that connect the root to its leaf, which contains $O(\log(n))$ transactions.

A parent transaction specifies its children using CTV. Crucially, CTV guarantees that Op can generate this tree locally, without interacting with the users, just by using their public keys. This avoids costly interactions and prevents a single user from stalling the protocol by inaction, ensuring the protocol is practical. Since CTV uses hashes, the resulting structure is a *Merkle tree* of transactions. This structure ensures logarithmic on-chain complexity for each user. An example Merkle tree can be seen in Fig. 1.

Exit Phase. If an honest user $P \in \mathcal{P}$ decides to move its coins back on-chain or detects misbehavior by Op, – slow response times, invalid responses, or an incorrect step transaction on-chain – it triggers the exit phase. As alluded to previously, P accomplishes this by publishing the root transaction that corresponds to the last valid step transaction, along with the $\log(n) + 1$ transactions that constitute its own branch of the Merkle Tree. In particular, each non-root transaction that P publishes spends one of the two outputs of its parent. This is the only way to spend this output without a timelock – the child transaction is specified via CTV.

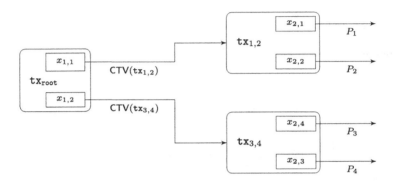

Fig. 1. Merkle tree for 4 users. The usage of CTV is exemplified.

The leaf transaction has 2 outputs as well, one of which concerns P. This output has a different spending condition: it requires an adaptor signature, pre-signed by Op and adapted by P — we will promptly explain why. P spends the leaf output using an out transaction, which finally gives P access to its coins after a timelock.

For example, if $n = 128$ and P is the only exiting user, it has to publish the root transaction, another 6 Merkle tree transactions and the out transaction to exit, i.e., 8 constant-size transactions in total.

Once the step transaction is spent by P, it prompts all other Clique users to either follow the same on-chain procedure to retrieve their coins on-chain within a fixed timeframe — this is the timelock of the Merkle tree transactions we alluded to before — or join the healing phase (discussed below), otherwise their coins can be confiscated by Op. The latter is required to guarantee operator balance security. Note that a user R exiting after P needs to publish less than $\log(n) + 1$ transactions on-chain, since part of the tree has already been published. More specifically, if R exits after P and shares $1 \leq m \leq \log(n)$ levels of the Merkle tree with P, then R only needs to publish $\log(n) - m + 1$ transactions to exit.

Some details that are omitted here for simplicity can be found in Sect. 5.

Updating Step Transactions. One crucial question has been left unanswered: How does Op securely supersede the step transaction at each epoch change? On the one hand, if Op can freely spend the step transaction, it can simply steal all Clique coins without recourse. On the other hand, future payments are not known when the step transaction is generated, thus CTV cannot be used. Of course, requiring signatures by all users for each epoch update is impractical.

To resolve this quandary, the following solution is employed: *Two* step transactions are active and unspent at each instant. Each carries the entirety of the Clique coins. The first set of coins is initially provided by the users, whereas the second is provided by Op as *collateral*. At the end of each epoch, a timelock on the older one expires and Op can freely spend it. If Op is honest, it will use the next step transaction, as discussed earlier. If however it steals the coins or stays inactive, users exit via the other active step transaction – the CTV spending method, which requires the root transaction, is not timelocked. Op cannot steal the newer step transaction, as it is still timelocked. This technique ensures *balance security* for the users.

This solution however creates yet another problem: What prevents the users from simply exiting via *both* step transactions? This would effectively double each user's coins by stealing Op's collateral. This is where our novel technique based on adaptor signatures is used. As alluded to above, $P \in \mathcal{P}$ has to publish an out transaction after the leaf transaction and wait for a timelock to access its coins. The out transaction needs a signature that P can only obtain by *adapting* a specially crafted pre-signature by Op using a specific AS witness. If Op learns *two* adapted signatures by P on out transactions of consecutive epochs, it can *extract* two AS witnesses, sum them to obtain a new AS witness and use the latter to confiscate the coins of one or both out transactions before P's timelock expires. Therefore P can claim its coins from either step transaction securely, but not from both. This technique provides *operator balance security*. We refer the reader to Fig. 2 for a complete illustration.

Special care needs to be taken when coins change hands between epochs. In order to maintain operator balance security, the payee needs an AS signature by the payer to spend its coin. This is so that Op can punish the payer if both payer and payee try to exit with the same coin.

Clique Setup. At last, all building blocks are in place. They are put together during the setup procedure as follows: Parties exchange keys and pre-signatures, then calculate the initial Merkle tree of transactions. Fixed conventions are used (e.g., lexicographic ordering of public keys) so that all parties agree on exactly the same tree. Each user then moves its c on-chain coins to the first step transaction, which exceptionally has n inputs. Its output commits to the Merkle root via CTV. Simultaneously Op moves its collateral (equal to the total Clique coins) to a step transaction that commits to the same Merkle root. As discussed before, Op can also spend them, but only after a timelock. The timelock of the second one is longer by t blocks. We say that t is the length of an epoch.

Observe that no user nor Op can lose coins during setup. Users only move their coins into the step transaction after ensuring that its output is the expected one and that they can spend their entire branch up to and including the out transaction (which needs the correct pre-signature). Likewise Op verifies that it can extract the required key and punish any user that attempts to take its coins from both step transactions.

Healing Phase. After one or more users exit, one or both step transactions are spent and part of the Merkle tree is on-chain. The remaining users need a mechanism to restore suitable unspent step transactions to carry on. We design a method by which the active users collaborate among them and with Op to consolidate the outputs of each Merkle tree into a new step transaction. This is achieved by including one more spending method to each output of each tree transaction. This method does not use a CTV, since the exiting users are not known when the tree is built and foreseeing all possible exit combinations leads to an exponential blowup. It instead needs a signature by Op and all users that have their coins in said output. At a high level, active users try to gather the needed signatures for the consolidating transaction. If some users that have not exited are inactive, the active users that share a tree output with them publish the minimum tree transactions needed to exclude the inactive users from the tree outputs and then try to consolidate again. Once the consolidating transaction is fully signed, it is published to $\mathcal{G}_{\text{Ledger}}$. The Clique is healed. A full description can be found in Appendix A.

Extension to Adaptor Signatures. As we saw in Sect. 2, an adaptor signature scheme (AS) [16] ties together the signature of a message (in our case a transaction) and the revelation of a secret value (a.k.a. witness). In a bit more detail, a pre-signer first generates a *pre-signature*, the publisher adapts this pre-signature using its witness, and upon publishing the resulting full signature the pre-signer can extract the publisher's witness using the pre- and full signatures. In order to ensure compatibility with Bitcoin, we instantiate AS with Schnorr adaptor signatures (we refer the reader to [16] for its details).

We extend this scheme to require *two* signatures for extraction. In particular, in our technique, the witness consists of two AS witnesses. A single signature only reveals one of the two AS witnesses, leaving the other (and the combined witness) secret. Our technique guarantees that extraction is impossible under a single valid signature and *prevention* of extraction is impossible under two valid signatures.

Sect. 5 describes our contribution in depth.

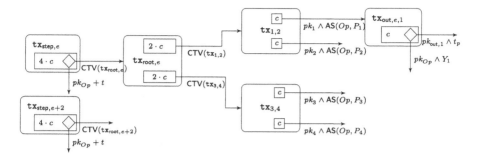

Fig. 2. Illustration of a Bitcoin Clique with 4 users, showing the transactions that can be published on-chain for the step transaction of epoch e, $\text{tx}_{\text{step},e}$. $\text{AS}(Op, P_j)$ represents a spending condition that requires a signature generated via an adaptor signature, where Op is the pre-signer and P_j the adapter. The diamond notation represents an OR spending condition, e.g., $\text{tx}_{\text{out},e,1}$ can be spent either by P_1 after block t_p or by Op if she knows y_1 such that $(Y_1, y_1) \in \mathcal{R}$. Op can learn y_1 only if P_1 maliciously publishes the tx_{out} of two consecutive epochs. The tx_{out} of *two* epochs are unspent at any point during a transaction phase, here only one is shown. The outputs of $\text{tx}_{\text{root},e}$, $\text{tx}_{1,2}$ and $\text{tx}_{3,4}$ can be spent by Op after a timelock, thus preventing a coalition of malicious users from indefinitely blocking Op's collateral. These timelocked spending methods however are omitted here for conciseness.

5   Bitcoin Clique Protocol

We now present our protocol in more detail. An illustration of the CTV-based Merkle tree can be seen in Fig. 2. Thanks to CTV, the root transaction is the only transaction that can spend the on-chain tx_{step}.

To update the balances of the users at the end of each epoch, this Merkle tree and the associated tx_{step} need to be updated by Op. As we saw earlier, after the end of the epoch Op has to be able to freely spend the current tx_{step} and replace it with the desired next tx_{step}. As discussed, to prevent Op from abusing this power and stealing all Clique coins, two step txs exist on-chain at any time. To protect Op from losing its collateral by a user that spends both step txs, the aforementioned AS extension is employed. In Fig. 2, P_1's secret y_1 is revealed if P_1 exits from both trees (i.e., by spending the tx_{step} of two consecutive epochs) and Op can use it on the $pk_{Op} \wedge Y_1$ spending condition of $\text{tx}_{\text{out},e,1}$ to punish P_1. Op is not in a race with P_1, since the latter cannot spend the coins immediately but needs to wait until block t_p (spending condition $pk_{\text{out},1} \wedge t_p$ of $\text{tx}_{\text{out},e,1}$).

In order for P to pay R, the latter generates two new statement-witness pairs for AS along with new keys for the tree and out txs. All users are informed by Op about the new keys, so that they can take them into account when computing the tree of the next epoch. Simply switching from P's to R's keys at the new epoch however would expose Op to an attack: P takes its output in the old epoch and R takes its output in the new epoch, thus Op loses an equal collateral. As alluded to earlier, the protection is as follows: When the current epoch ends, P receives a pre-signature from Op, adapts it, and gives the complete signature to R. R needs this extra signature to obtain its coins during the next epoch. Therefore, if both P and R try to obtain the same coin, Op will learn P's secret and retrieve its collateral from P's out tx in the current epoch.

To sum up, at any time there are two unspent $\mathsf{tx_{step}}$ on-chain, representing the last two epochs. Each can be spent by the corresponding tree of transactions, or by Op after a timelock. The two timelocks are staggered, so that Op cannot spend both $\mathsf{tx_{step}}$ simultaneously. At the end of the e-th epoch, Op spends one $\mathsf{tx_{step},e}$ with a new $\mathsf{tx_{step},e+2}$, alternating between the two series of step txs on every epoch. If some users exit, the rest can actively collaborate to heal the Clique by signing and publishing a single tx which moves all available coins to a new step output and carry on with the protocol.

We next provide the protocol pseudocode. We refer the reader to Appendix B of the full version [47] for the full protocol code, to Appendix C of the full version [47] for its security proof, and to Appendix A for the healing subprotocol.

Bitcoin Clique

Constants: N users with c coins each, operator Op, each epoch lasts t blocks.

Setup Phase.
1. Public keys distribution:
   – Op and users exchange normal and AS keys.
2. Initial transactions preparation:
   – $\mathsf{tx_{step},1}$ is funded by the N users and has a t-block timelock.
   – $\mathsf{tx_{step},2}$ is funded by Op with Nc collateral coins and has a $2t$-block timelock.
3. out transactions preparation:
   – Op pre-signs the two out txs of each user using as statement the AS keys of the user and sends the two pre-signatures to the user for verification.
4. Setup Finalization:
   – Users sign $\mathsf{tx_{step},1}$ and Op signs $\mathsf{tx_{step},2}$, the two txs are published to $\mathcal{G}_{\mathrm{Ledger}}$.

Payment Phase (P transfers an output to R).

1. P sends to R a signed message with the output, R's id and the next epoch.
2. R sends to Op new normal and AS keys, along with P's message.
3. Op generates a new AS key for this output and sends it to all N users, along with P's message and R's keys.
4. When the current epoch ends, P adapts the pre-signature by Op, gets a valid signature and sends it to R for verification, who needs this signature to spend the corresponding coins (see l. 1 of Epoch Finalization & l. 3 of User Exit).

Epoch Finalization Phase. When the timelock of $\mathsf{tx_{step},e}$ expires:

1. Op generates the $(e+2)$-th tx tree and $\mathsf{tx_{step},e+2}$ and publishes the latter, which spends $\mathsf{tx_{step},e}$. For each output that has been transferred during epoch e, Op uses the AS keys of both the sender and the receiver to build the new tx tree. This means that signatures from both parties are needed to spend the *leaf* tx of this output at epoch $e+1$.

2. *Op* pre-signs the new out tx of each user using as statement the AS key of the user and sends the pre-signature to the user.
3. Each user verifies that the epoch change has taken place in a timely manner, with the expected tx tree, and that the pre-signature is valid.

User Exit Phase. *P* must exit when it detects any dishonest behavior. The procedure below is repeated for each of *P*'s outputs.

1. *P* signs and publishes all txs that constitute the path from the root to its leaf of the latest Merkle tree, spending the latest unspent tx_{step}.
2. *P* adapts the relevant pre-signature and adds the resulting signature to $tx_{out,e}$.
3. If *P* received its output at the latest epoch, *P* also adds the previous owner's signature to $tx_{out,e}$ and publishes it.
4. *P* stops any action related to this output except for further use of its now on-chain coins. This prevents accidentally adapting another pre-signature and disclosing *P*'s secret keys to *Op*.

Operator Exit Phase. *Op* needs to receive *Nc* coins to recover its collateral.

1. *Op* tries to get the coins of a tx_{step} of which the timelock has expired.
2. If this fails (because both step txs are spent by the root tx of the corresponding tx tree), *Op* tries to take *c* coins per user:
   - If the timelock of any tx in the tx tree expires, *Op* gets its funds from it (thus receiving value equal to the sum of coins that are owned by the users that have tx in their path).
   - For every user *P* that has published both its out txs (and thus no timelock on either of its paths is left to expire), *Op* extracts both *P*'s AS secrets from the signatures using 2-Ext.
   - *Op* spends at least one of *P*'s two out txs using its own secret key and the sum of *P*'s two secrets, thus taking *c* coins from *P* as desired.

The two central balance security theorems follow, where an *environment* $\mathcal{E}$ may order any party to exit at any time:

Theorem 1 (User balance security). $\forall$ *honest* $P \in \mathcal{P}$ *that owns a set of outputs* O *in the protocol, if it is instructed by* $\mathcal{E}$ *to exit (Fig. 16 of the full version [47]), then it will eventually exclusively own all outputs in* O *on-chain.*

This theorem also covers any case of emergency exit or response to someone else's exit, since in such a case *P* must have already safeguarded or be in the process of safeguarding its outputs when it receives $\mathcal{E}$'s exit instruction. It holds because an honest user can retrieve its coins on-chain after a failed setup, it can unilaterally put exactly one out tx on-chain any time after a successful setup, and the timelock of the out tx will always expire, giving the user access to its funds on-chain.

Theorem 2 (Operator balance security). *If honest Op is instructed by* $\mathcal{E}$ *to exit (Fig. 18 of the full version [47]), then eventually Op will exclusively own at least the sum of all players' outputs (which is equal to Op's collateral).*

This theorem also implicitly covers any case in which a response to someone else's exit is needed. As discussed, it holds because Op can always claim the coins back, either from an expired timelock of a step or tree tx, or by punishing a user that published two out txs (and thus leaked its secret to Op).

Formal proofs for both theorems can be found in Appendix C of the full version [47]. Transaction and exit phase correctness as well as efficiency can be verified by simple inspection of the protocol.

6   Future Work

Several future work directions remain open. To begin with, only unilateral closure was considered. This however has a high aggregate on-chain cost and, in case of closure of a big Clique, could create on-chain congestion. Our protocol can be extended in a straightforward manner to efficiently handle cooperative exiting of a subset of the users. This is doable by moving the exiting users' outputs from the leaves of the Merkle tree to the next step transaction. This solution only needs the cooperation of Op, not of all Clique users, maintaining practicality.

Furthermore, the current construction is not privacy-preserving, as all parties learn all payments. Per-epoch mixing techniques can be used to bolster privacy.

Additionally, removing the fixed-denomination payment value limitation and the need for operator collateral would greatly improve usability and practicality. A simple extension of our protocol can provide multiple denominations by including one Merkle tree per denomination. Fiat cash exemplifies how this approach could be sufficient for practical use.

Operators introduce centralization concerns. Nevertheless, since many Cliques with different operators can coexist and compete, operators are dissuaded from providing poor service, and balance security ensures users only rely on the operator for quality of service, not for funds safety. Operator power can be further limited by (i) adding a voting mechanism among users to replace the operator and (ii) enabling inter-Clique payments. These are left as future directions.

Last but not least, the tree structure need not necessarily be binary. It is possible that other structures are in practice more efficient, e.g., tertiary trees. Complementarily, leaf transactions with more than 2 users can be leveraged, trimming a few levels from the tree. Such optimizations are left as a concern for a possible future production-level implementation.

Acknowledgements. This work was partly supported by the German Federal Ministry of Education and Research and the Hessen State Ministry for Higher Education, Research and the Arts within their joint support of the National Research Center for Applied Cybersecurity ATHENE.

A   Bitcoin Clique Healing

In its previously described form, Bitcoin Clique is vulnerable to a DoS attack: When the exit phase is initiated by any user, the entire Clique is torn down for everyone. We here propose an extension to the protocol, named *healing*, which allows active users to reinstate the Clique securely with minimal on-chain overhead.

At a high level, healing works by enabling a new way to spend tree txs which needs the active participation of all relevant users and Op. After some users exit, some tree tx outputs remain unspent. The users that want to stay in the Clique collaborate with each other and with Op to create a single transaction that spends all remaining tree tx outputs using the new spending method and produces a suitable step tx output. The protocol is resilient to inactive users.

A.1   Healing Extension Details

In more detail, the solution is as follows: Consider an output of an arbitrary tree tx, which is spendable by the subset of users $T \subset P$. We add an alternative spending method, named *healing*, to the tree tx. Its script is $\bigwedge_{P \in T} P \wedge Op$. This modification is done to every tree tx of every epoch.

$s + 1$ blocks after an exit phase is initiated, a user P that wishes to keep its coins in the Clique first initializes $C \subset P$ as the set of users that have not exited (i.e., the users of whom the out tx is not on-chain) and then repeats the following steps until either healing is complete (step 2) or the need for P to exit arises (discussed after the healing steps).

1. Generate and sign a new step tx that spends all currently unspent tree outputs using the *healing* spending method and has a single output with the coins and script of a step tx for users C (with the same b as the step tx that was exited from). See also Fig. 14 of the full version [47]. If the current block is within the epoch update period (Fig. 12 of the full version [47]) of the exited-from step tx, then produce the successor to the exited-from step tx instead (i.e., produce the step tx that would spend the exited-from step tx, two epochs later). Gossip signatures with other users and Op.
2. Wait for $t_{reconcile}$ blocks (a system-wide parameter, discussed in A.2). If all users in C and Op sign the new step tx as well within this period, then publish it to the ledger. Healing is complete.
3. Else:
   (a) Remove from C the users that have not provided the aforementioned signature.
   (b) Publish to the ledger the minimum set of tree txs on the path from the root to P's leaf so that all users that can spend the resulting tree output are in C. (This action ostracizes inactive users on P's path.)
   (c) Wait for $s + 1$ blocks (giving time to our and other branches to finalize on-chain).
   (d) Remove from C all users that can spend an unspent tx tree output that can also be spent by a user in $P \setminus C$. (This action ostracizes users that did not ostracize inactive users on other paths by following step 3b. This is needed because the healing spending method needs the signature of all relevant users.)

The procedure needs to be repeated potentially many times because previously active users may become uncooperative in the process.

The need for P to exit arises if the new step tx has not been published by block $t_{\mathsf{leave}} - s$. In that case, P exits by publishing its branch of the tx tree and out tx as usual. This scenario can happen if Op becomes malicious and does not sign the new step tx, or if the other users maliciously classify P as inactive and do not include its tree output in the step tx. This, together with the fact that all relevant users (including P) need to sign for the healing spending method to be used and the fact that P only uses it to return to a normal step tx, guarantees that the healing extension safeguards balance security.

Op follows the same procedure as the users, apart from step 3b. Since its signature is needed for all healing spending methods and it only uses it to return to a normal step tx, operator balance security is guaranteed.

It is possible for the protocol to be executed on both active step txs simultaneously — balance security and healing are maintained.

A.2   Discussion and Future Work

Note that $t_{\mathsf{reconcile}}$ does not appear in any timelock, as it only dictates off-chain communication timeouts. It could therefore be alternatively expressed in terms of time. We here however express $t_{\mathsf{reconcile}}$ in terms of blocks for homogeneity of notation. We recommend using the shortest $t_{\mathsf{reconcile}}$ value that ensures each user has enough time to do a communication round-trip with every other user.

During healing, users might end up being too quick to assume another user is inactive and publish a tree tx that is not strictly needed. This incurs unneeded on-chain fees. A practical system would need to experiment with concrete parameters to minimize such events while promoting quick healing. Users are encouraged to be online and share as many signatures as possible as early and widely as possible to minimize such events, as well as being Bitcoin peers with each other in order to minimize discrepancies in their ledger views. To further mitigate this effect, it is possible to design a more elaborate synchronization protocol that allows users that were erroneously assumed inactive in step 3d to be re-included in the set of active users during the subsequent signature gossip step 1. We leave this as future work.

The above shows that this is a best-effort mechanism and does not benefit from uniquely attributable faults, which would in turn enable exclusion of malicious users from the healed Clique. There are specific cases in which it is possible to uniquely attribute faults, such as when a user publishes the root tx and no subsequent tree tx. We leave detecting and punishing uniquely attribute faults as future work.

Nevertheless, the healing mechanism can save a lot of on-chain transactions in many realistic scenarios of DoS attempts and always leads to reinstating and continuing the Clique with all honest, active users irrespective of the number of malicious users if Op is honest and network delays are bounded.

Let us give us two example scenarios: In case a single user unilaterally exits and everyone else cooperates, then the on-chain footprint is $\log_2(N)$ transactions of the tree, 1 out tx, and 1 healing step tx. On the other hand, if at least one user of each leaf tx is malicious and publishes its entire branch of the tx tree, but not its out tx, then healing results in putting the entire tree tx on-chain and then recreating the exact same step tx output that was initially spent, for a total of $2N$ on-chain txs. The latter is the worst case scenario. We observe that even in this case, honest users can still successfully heal.

In a practical deployment, Op can facilitate the protocol by being the primary point of contact for users and leveraging its (presumably) better network connection to enhance coordination, collect and distribute signatures, and signal which users are inactive. Still, users must not rely solely on Op for message passing, lest they want to give it the ability to suppress an honest, active user.

References

1. Croman, K., et al.: On scaling decentralized blockchains. In: Clark, J., Meiklejohn, S., Ryan, P.Y.A., Wallach, D., Brenner, M., Rohloff, K. (eds.) FC 2016. LNCS, vol. 9604, pp. 106–125. Springer, Heidelberg (2016). https://doi.org/10.1007/978-3-662-53357-4_8
2. Nakamoto, S.: Bitcoin: A Peer-to-Peer Electronic Cash System (2008)
3. Gudgeon, L., Moreno-Sanchez, P., Roos, S., McCorry, P., Gervais, A.: SoK: layer-two blockchain protocols. In: Financial Cryptography and Data Security - 24th International Conference, FC 2020, Kota Kinabalu, Malaysia, February 10–14, 2020 Revised Selected Papers, pp. 201–226 (2020). https://doi.org/10.1007/978-3-030-51280-4_12
4. Bitcoin Wiki: Payment Channels (2022). https://tinyurl.com/y6msnk7u
5. Decker, C., Wattenhofer, R.: A fast and scalable payment network with bitcoin duplex micropayment channels. In: Pelc, A., Schwarzmann, A.A. (eds.) SSS 2015. LNCS, vol. 9212, pp. 3–18. Springer, Cham (2015). https://doi.org/10.1007/978-3-319-21741-3_1
6. Poon, J., Dryja, T.: The bitcoin lightning network: scalable off-chain instant payments (2016). https://tinyurl.com/q54gnb4
7. Update from the Raiden team on development progress, announcement of raidEX (2017). https://tinyurl.com/z2snp9e
8. Dziembowski, S., Eckey, L., Faust, S., Malinowski, D.: Perun: virtual payment hubs over cryptocurrencies. In: 2019 IEEE Symposium on Security and Privacy, pp. 106–123. IEEE Computer Society Press (2019). https://doi.org/10.1109/SP.2019.00020
9. Tairi, E., Moreno-Sanchez, P., Maffei, M.: A^{2}L: anonymous atomic locks for scalability in payment channel hubs. In: 2021 IEEE Symposium on Security and Privacy, pp. 1834–1851. IEEE Computer Society Press (2021). https://doi.org/10.1109/SP40001.2021.00111
10. Qin, X., et al.: BlindHub: bitcoin-compatible privacy-preserving payment channel hubs supporting variable amounts. In 2023 IEEE Symposium on Security and Privacy (SP), pp. 2462–2480. IEEE Computer Society, Los Alamitos, CA, USA (2023) https://doi.org/10.1109/SP46215.2023.10179427, https://doi.ieeecomputersociety.org/10.1109/SP46215.2023.10179427
11. Poon, J., Buterin, V.: Plasma: scalable autonomous smart contracts (2017)

12. Buterin V.: On-chain scaling to potentially 500 tx/sec through mass tx validation (2018). https://ethresear.ch/t/on-chain-scaling-to-potentially-500-tx-sec-through-mass-tx-validation/3477

13. Optimism: Optimistic rollup overview. https://github.com/ethereum-optimism/optimistic-specs/blob/0e9673af0f2cafd89ac7d6c0e5d8bed7c67b74ca/overview.md

14. Wood, G.: Ethereum: a secure decentralised generalised transaction ledger (2019)

15. Rubin J.: Bitcoin Improvement Proposal 119. https://github.com/bitcoin/bips/blob/master/bip-0119.mediawiki

16. Aumayr, L., et al.: Generalized channels from limited blockchain scripts and adaptor signatures. In: Tibouchi, M., Wang, H. (eds.) ASIACRYPT 2021. LNCS, vol. 13091, pp. 635–664. Springer, Cham (2021). https://doi.org/10.1007/978-3-030-92075-3_22

17. Eckey, L., Faust, S., Hostáková, K., Roos S.: Splitting payments locally while routing interdimensionally. IACR Cryptol. ePrint Arch., p. 555. https://eprint.iacr.org/2020/555 (2020)

18. Malavolta, G., Moreno-Sanchez, P., Schneidewind, C., Kate, A., Maffei, M.: Anonymous Multi-Hop Locks for Blockchain Scalability and Interoperability. In: 26th Annual Network and Distributed System Security Symposium, NDSS 2019, San Diego, California, USA, February 24–27, 2019: The Internet Society. https://www.ndss-symposium.org/ndss-paper/anonymous-multi-hop-locks-for-blockchain-scalability-and-interoperability/ (2019)

19. Tairi, E., Moreno-Sanchez, P., Maffei, M.: A^2L: anonymous atomic locks for scalability in payment channel hubs. In: 42nd IEEE Symposium on Security and Privacy, SP 2021, San Francisco, CA, USA, 24–27 May 2021, pp. 1834–185. IEEE. https://doi.org/10.1109/SP40001.2021.00111 (2021)

20. Thyagarajan, S.A.K., Malavolta, G., Schmidt, F., Schröder, D.: PayMo: payment channels For Monero. IACR Cryptol. ePrint Arch, p. 1441. https://eprint.iacr.org/2020/1441 (2020)

21. Malavolta, G., Moreno-Sanchez, P., Kate, A., Maffei, M., Ravi, S.: Concurrency and privacy with payment-channel networks. In: Thuraisingham, B.M., Evans, D., Malkin, T., Xu, D. (eds.) ACM CCS 2017, pp. 455–471. ACM Press. https://doi.org/10.1145/3133956.3134096 (2017)

22. Malavolta, G., Moreno-Sanchez, P., Schneidewind, C., Kate, A., Maffei, M.: Anonymous Multi-Hop Locks for Blockchain Scalability and Interoperability. In: NDSS 2019: The Internet Society (2019)

23. Avarikioti, Z., Thyfronitis Litos, O.S., Wattenhofer, R.: CERBERUS channels: incentivizing watchtowers for bitcoin. In: Bonneau, J., Heninger, N. (eds.) FC 2020. LNCS, vol. 12059, pp. 346–366. Springer, Cham (2020). https://doi.org/10.1007/978-3-030-51280-4_19

24. Avarikioti, Z., Litos, O.S.T.: Suborn channels: incentives against timelock bribes. In: Eyal, I., Garay, J.A. (eds.), Financial Cryptography and Data Security - 26th International Conference, FC 2022, Grenada, May 2–6, 2022, Revised Selected Papers: vol. 13411 of Lecture Notes in Computer Science, pp. 488–511. Springer, Cham. https://doi.org/10.1007/978-3-031-18283-9_24 (2022)

25. Kiayias, A., Litos, O.S.T.: A composable security treatment of the lightning network. In: IEEE CSF 2020, pp. 334–349 (2020)

26. Canetti, R.: Universally composable security: a new paradigm for cryptographic protocols. In: 42nd FOCS, pp. 136–145. IEEE Computer Society Press. https://doi.org/10.1109/SFCS.2001.959888 (2001)

27. Dziembowski, S., Faust, S., Hostáková, K.: General state channel networks. In: Lie, D., Mannan, M., Backes, M., Wang, X. (eds.) ACM CCS 2018, pp. 949–966. ACM Press. https://doi.org/10.1145/3243734.3243856 (2018)

28. Dziembowski, S., Eckey, L., Faust, S., Hesse, J., Hostáková, K.: Multi-party virtual state channels. In: Ishai, Y., Rijmen, V. (eds.) EUROCRYPT 2019. LNCS, vol. 11476, pp. 625–656. Springer, Cham (2019). https://doi.org/10.1007/978-3-030-17653-2_21

29. Miller, A., Bentov, I., Bakshi, S., Kumaresan, R., McCorry, P.: Sprites and state channels: payment networks that go faster than lightning. In: Goldberg, I., Moore, T. (eds.) FC 2019. LNCS, vol. 11598, pp. 508–526. Springer, Cham (2019). https://doi.org/10.1007/978-3-030-32101-7_30

30. Chakravarty, M.M.T., Coretti, S., Fitzi, M., Gazi, P., Kant, P., Kiayias, A., Russell, A.: Hydra: fast isomorphic state channels. Cryptology ePrint Archive, Report 2020/299. https://eprint.iacr.org/2020/299 (2020)

31. Buterin, V.: Minimal Viable Plasma. https://tinyurl.com/y2s9grpd (2018)

32. Floersch, K.: Plasma Cash Simple Spec. https://tinyurl.com/yxdp2rqr (2018)

33. Plasma Debit. https://tinyurl.com/yx936xzk (2018)

34. Plasma snapp. https://tinyurl.com/yxbza3pl (2018)

35. Khalil, R., Zamyatin, A., Felley, G., Moreno-Sanchez, P., Gervais, A.: Commit-Chains: Secure, Scalable Off-Chain Payments. Cryptology ePrint Archive, Report 2018/642. https://eprint.iacr.org/2018/642 (2018)

36. Erwig, A., Faust, S., Riahi, S., Stöckert, T.: CommiTEE: an efficient and secure commit-chain protocol using TEEs. In: 2023 IEEE 8th European Symposium on Security and Privacy (EuroS&P), pp. 429–448. IEEE Computer Society, Los Alamitos, CA, USA. https://doi.org/10.1109/EuroSP57164.2023.00033 (2023)

37. Nick, J., Poelstra, A., Sanders, G.: Liquid: A Bitcoin Sidechain (2020)

38. Mavroudis, V., Wüst, K., Dhar, A., Kostiainen, K., Capkun, S.: Snappy: fast on-chain payments with practical collaterals. In: 27th Annual Network and Distributed System Security Symposium, NDSS 2020, San Diego, California, USA, February 23–26, 2020: The Internet Society. https://www.ndss-symposium.org/ndss-paper/snappy-fast-on-chain-payments-with-practical-collaterals/ (2020)

39. Ng, L.K.L., Chow, S.S.M., Wong, D.P.H., Woo, A.P.Y.: LDSP: shopping with cryptocurrency privately and quickly under leadership. In: 2021 IEEE 41st International Conference on Distributed Computing Systems (ICDCS), pp. 261–271. https://doi.org/10.1109/ICDCS51616.2021.00033 (2021)

40. Whitehat B.: Roll up. https://github.com/barryWhiteHat/roll_up

41. Donno, L.: Optimistic and validity rollups: analysis and comparison between optimism and StarkNet. CoRR: vol. abs/2210.16610. https://doi.org/10.48550/arXiv.2210.16610 (2022)

42. Kalodner, H.A., Goldfeder, S., Chen, X., Weinberg, S.M., Felten, E.W.: Arbitrum: scalable, private smart contracts. In: Enck, W., Felt, A.P. (eds.) 27th USENIX Security Symposium, USENIX Security 2018, Baltimore, MD, USA, August 15–17, 2018, pp. 1353–1370. USENIX Association. https://www.usenix.org/conference/usenixsecurity18/presentation/kalodner (2018)

43. Erwig, A., Faust, S., Hostáková, K., Maitra, M., Riahi, S.: Two-party adaptor signatures from identification schemes. In: Garay, J.A. (ed.) PKC 2021. LNCS, vol. 12710, pp. 451–480. Springer, Cham (2021). https://doi.org/10.1007/978-3-030-75245-3_17

44. Katz, J., Lindell, Y.: Introduction to Modern Cryptography, 2nd edn. CRC Press: ISBN 9781466570269 (2014)

45. Dai, W., Okamoto, T., Yamamoto, G.: Stronger security and generic constructions for adaptor signatures. In: Progress in Cryptology - INDOCRYPT 2022: 23rd International Conference on Cryptology in India, Kolkata, India, December 11–14, 2022, Proceedings, pp. 52–77. Springer, Heidelberg. ISBN 978-3-031-22911-4. https://doi.org/10.1007/978-3-031-22912-1_3 (2023)
46. Erwig, A., Faust, S., Riahi, S., Stöckert, T.: CommiTEE: an efficient and secure commit-chain protocol using TEEs. Cryptology ePrint Archive, Report 2020/1486. https://eprint.iacr.org/2020/1486 (2020)
47. Riahi, S., Litos, O.S.T.: Bitcoin clique: channel-free off-chain payments using two-shot adaptor signatures. Cryptology ePrint Archive, Paper 2024/025. https://eprint.iacr.org/2024/025 (2024)

Programmable Payment Channels

Ranjit Kumaresan[1], Duc V. Le[1], Mohsen Minaei[1], Srinivasan Raghuraman[2],
Yibin Yang[3(✉)], and Mahdi Zamani[1]

[1] Visa Research, Palo Alto, USA
{rakumare,duc.le,mominaei,mzamani}@visa.com
[2] Visa Research and MIT, Cambridge, USA
[3] Georgia Institute of Technology, Atlanta, USA
yyang811@gatech.edu

Abstract. One approach for scaling blockchains is to create bilateral, offchain channels, known as payment/state channels, that can protect parties against cheating via onchain collateralization. While such channels have been studied extensively, not much attention has been given to *programmability*, where the parties can agree to *dynamically enforce arbitrary* conditions over their payments without going onchain.

We introduce the notion of a *programmable payment channel* (PPC) that allows two parties to do exactly this. In particular, our notion of programmability enables the sender of a (unidirectional) payment to *dynamically* set the terms and conditions for each individual payment using a smart contract. Of course, the verification of the payment conditions (and the payment itself) happens offchain as long as the parties behave honestly. If either party violates any of the terms, then the other party can deploy the smart contract onchain to receive a remedy as agreed upon in the contract. In this paper, we make the following contributions:

- We formalize PPC as an ideal functionality $\mathcal{F}_{PPC}$ in the universal composable framework, and build lightweight implementations of applications such as hash-time-locked contracts (HTLCs), "reverse HTLCs", and rock-paper-scissors in the $\mathcal{F}_{PPC}$-hybrid model;
- We show how $\mathcal{F}_{PPC}$ can be easily modified to capture the state channels functionality $\mathcal{F}_{SC}$ (described in prior works) where two parties can execute *dynamically chosen* arbitrary two-party contracts (including those that take deposits from both parties) offchain, i.e., we show how to efficiently realize $\mathcal{F}_{SC}$ in the $\mathcal{F}_{PPC}$-hybrid model;
- We implement $\mathcal{F}_{PPC}$ on blockchains supporting smart contracts (such as Ethereum), and provide several optimizations to enable *concurrent* programmable transactions—the gas overhead of an HTLC PPC contract is $< 100K$, amortized over many offchain payments.

We note that our implementations of $\mathcal{F}_{PPC}$ and $\mathcal{F}_{SC}$ depend on the CREATE2 opcode which allows one to compute the deployment address of a contract (without having to deploy it).

Keywords: Blockchain · Layer-2 channels · Programmable payments

Y. Yang— Work done in part while at Visa Research.

Supplementary Information The online version contains supplementary material available at https://doi.org/10.1007/978-3-031-54776-8_3.

C. Pöpper and L. Batina (Eds.): ACNS 2024, LNCS 14585, pp. 51–73, 2024.
https://doi.org/10.1007/978-3-031-54776-8_3

1   Introduction

With the rise of decentralized services, financial products can be offered on blockchains with higher security and lower operational costs. With its ability to run arbitrary programs, called smart contracts, and direct access to assets, a blockchain can execute complex financial contracts and settle disputes automatically. Unfortunately, these benefits all come with a major scalability challenge due to the overhead of onchain transactions, preventing the adoption of blockchain services as mainstream financial products.

Payment Channels. A well-known class of mechanisms for scaling blockchain payments are payment channels [2, 14]. Payment channels "off-load" transactions to an offchain communication channel between two parties. The channel is "opened" via an onchain transaction to fund the channel, followed by any number of offchain transactions. Eventually, by a request from either or both parties, the channel is "closed" via another onchain transaction. This design avoids the costs and the latency associated with onchain operations, effectively amortizing the overhead of onchain transactions over many offchain ones. While several proposals improve the scalability of payment channels [3, 16, 20–22, 27–29], they do not allow imposing arbitrary conditions on offchain payments, which prohibit fruitful applications requiring programmability.

State Channels. From a feasibility standpoint, the conditions on offchain payments can be achieved by a stronger notion called state channels. State channels [4, 11, 13, 15, 17, 25] allow two parties to perform general-purpose computation offchain by mutually tracking the current state of the program. The existing state channel proposals have two major drawbacks in practice.

First, with the exception of [13], state channel constructions require the parties to fix the program, which they wish to run offchain, at the time of channel setup. This means that no changes to the program are allowed after the parties go offchain. This is especially problematic in offchain scalability approaches based on the hub-and-spoke model [10, 16, 31], where each party establishes a general-purpose channel with a highly available (but untrusted) hub during setup to be able to later transact with many other parties without the need to establish an individual channel with each party (see Fig. 1 Left and Middle). In practice, parties usually have no a priori knowledge about the specific set of conditions required to transact with other (unknown) parties.

Second, the complexity of the existing state channel proposals could be overkill for simple, programmable payments. The authorization of an offchain transaction via a payment channel is significantly simpler as the flow of the payments is unidirectional while state channels need to track all state changes from both parties irrespective of the payment direction. Namely, the state channel is not a practical solution for achieving programmable payments.

Our Focus. In this paper, we introduce the notion of *programmable payment channels* (PPC) that allows the parties to agree offchain on the set of conditions (i.e., a smart contract) they wish to impose for each of their offchain payments

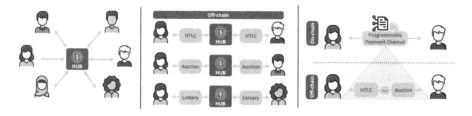

Fig. 1. Left: Hub-and-spoke model: Each party creates a single channel with the hub; **Middle:** Every pair of parties reuse their channels with the hub to execute different contracts; **Right:** PPC between two parties supporting any offchain application.

(see Fig. 1 Right). That is, we achieve lightweight offchain programmable payments denoted as *promises* where the logic can be determined *on-the-fly* after the channel has been opened.

A classic programmable payment covered by PPC is a hash-time-locked contract (HTLC) [1], which is foundational to the design of (multihop) payment channels [3,27]. Indeed, most current payment channels already embed HTLCs for routing. However, many useful applications remain difficult to build on top of payment channels using HTLCs. Consider the following example. Alice wants to reserve a room through an established payment channel with the hotel. Alice would like to send a payment under the following conditions: (1) Alice is allowed to cancel the reservation within 48 hours of booking to get back all of her funds, and (2) Alice can get back half of her funds if she cancels the reservation within 24 hours of the stay date. Achieving this simple real-life example of payment with PPC is simple and straightforward.

Full Version. The full version of this paper is [32].

1.1   Our Contributions

- We propose the notion of a *programmable payment channel* (PPC) that is a payment channel allowing two parties to transact offchain according to a collateral that they deposit onchain and a smart contract that they agree on offchain. PPC provides the following features:
  - *Scalability:* Only opening and closing the channel require Layer-1 access.
  - *Offchain Programmability*: The PPC protocol stays identical for new payment logic after the channel is opened.
- We formalize PPC and prove its correctness and security in the universal composable (UC) framework using a global ledger. In particular, we provide an ideal functionality $\mathcal{F}_{\mathsf{PPC}}$. We then show how to build lightweight implementations of simple applications such as HTLCs, "reverse HTLCs," on-chain betting (and also rock-paper-scissors) in the $\mathcal{F}_{\mathsf{PPC}}$-hybrid world.
- We show how PPC can be modified to capture the state channels functionality where two parties can execute *dynamically chosen arbitrary two-party contracts* (including those that take deposits from both parties) offchain, namely,

to realize $\mathcal{F}_{SC}$ in the $\mathcal{F}_{PPC}$-hybrid world. In particular, to launch an offchain contract, parties only need to make three calls to $\mathcal{F}_{PPC}$ to instantiate two programmable payments.

– We evaluate PPC by instantiating it on Ethereum. We show how the PPC contract deploys new contracts that embed the conditions of payments. Our results show that deploying the PPC contract needs about 3M gas, and that settling onchain in the optimistic case (honest parties) needs only 75K gas. In the pessimistic case (malicious parties), 700K more gas is needed for a simple logic such as HTLC.

We note that our implementations of $\mathcal{F}_{PPC}$ and $\mathcal{F}_{SC}$ depend on the CRE-ATE2 opcode which allow one to compute the deployment address of a contract (without having to deploy it). This opcode is available on any EVM (Ethereum Virtual Machine) based chain (including Ethereum, Polygon, etc.).

Compared to prior formalizations of payment and state channels, our work shows a practical way to implement a state channel that enables arbitrary offchain smart contract applications. Additionally, our abstractions of $\mathcal{F}_{PPC}$ and $\mathcal{F}_{SC}$ make it more natural to design protocols for applications whose states depend on the states of other contracts on the blockchain.

We also note that our implementations of $\mathcal{F}_{PPC}$ and $\mathcal{F}_{SC}$ allow for flexible reuse of established channels. Exploiting this fact, one can use the abstractions of $\mathcal{F}_{PPC}$ and $\mathcal{F}_{SC}$ to efficiently build complex multiparty applications. For instance, every pair of parties need not establish a PPC channel with each other, and can instead reuse their existing PPC channels with, say, an untrusted hub.

Similar to payment and state channels, relay nodes (in particular, hub nodes) in PPC also face scalability concerns, as the money has to be locked for several rounds. There are known incentivization techniques to mitigate similar issues that arise in DeFi lending protocols. The same techniques can be applied in our case as well.

1.2   Related Work

Payment Channels. The key idea behind a payment channel is an onchain contract: both parties instantiate this contract and transfer digital money to it. Whenever one party wants to pay another, they simply sign on the other party's monotonically-increasing credit. When the two parties want to close the channel, they submit their final signed credits to rebalance the money in the channel. No execution happens on the blockchain before closing the channel; the payment between two parties relies only on exchanging digital signatures. Payment channels have been heavily studied [2,14,17,23,25,26,29].

State Channels. A proposal for executing arbitrary contracts offchain is state channels [4,11,13,15,17,25]. The key idea is as follows: (1) the contract can be executed offchain by exchanging signatures, and (2) the contract can be executed onchain from the last agreed state to resolve any disagreements. For example, consider a two-party contract between Alice and Bob, whenever Alice wants to update the current state, she simply signs the newer state. Then, she forwards her signature and requests for Bob's signature. While Bob may not reply with his signature, Alice can submit the pre-agreed state to the blockchain with the contract and execute it onchain. This idea can be naturally extended to multi-party contracts (e.g., [12,15,25]).

The works of [13,17] are closest to ours. Unlike us, [13] do not provide any formal proofs or guarantees. As mentioned in [17], their work lacks features useful for practical implementation. Also, our protocols take advantage of the CREATE2 opcode which was introduced subsequent to the work of [13]. We follow [5,15–17] to formalize our channel using *universal composable* (UC) framework with a global ledger. However, these works focus on *channel virtualization*[1] , and are *not* directly related to this work.

Other Related Work. An excellent systematization of knowledge that explores offchain solutions can be found in [19]. See Appendix A for the comparison with rollups, another popular Layer-2 scaling solution [24,30,33]. See Appendix B for other works that use the CREATE2 opcode.

2   Preliminaries

Network and Time. We assume a synchronous complete peer-to-peer authenticated communication network. Thus, the execution of protocol can be viewed as happening in rounds. The round is also used as global timestamp. We use $msg \overset{t \leq T}{\leftrightharpoons} P$ to denote the message will be sent by party P before round T. Similarly, we use $msg \overset{t \leq T}{\hookrightarrow} P$ to denote that the message will be delivered to party P before round T.

GUC Model. We model and formalize PPC under *global universal composable* (GUC) framework [8,9]. UC is a general purpose framework for modeling and constructing secure protocols. The correctness and security of protocols rely on simulation-based proofs. We defer the formal description to Appendix C.1. We acknowledge that we restrict the distinguisher to a subclass of environments to simplify the formalizations. This restriction is standard (e.g., [16,17]) and can be easily removed using straightforward checks.

Cryptocurrency/Contract Functionalities. We follow [15,17] and model cryptocurrency as a global ledger functionality $\hat{\mathcal{L}}(\Delta)$ in the GUC framework (cf. Fig. 9 in Appendix C.2). Parties can move funds from/to the ledger functionality by invoking other ideal functionalities that can invoke the methods Add/Remove. Any operation on the global ledger will happen within a delay of Δ rounds, capturing that this is an onchain transaction.

Adversary. We consider an adversary who can corrupt one party in the two-party channel. The corrupted party is byzantine and can deviate from the protocol arbitrarily. As is standard in the GUC model, the objective of an adversary

---

[1] Virtual channels focus on designing protocols between parties who do not have a direct channel, but both have a channel with a (common) intermediary.

is to distinguish the real world from the ideal world. In applications such as ours, such behaviors could involve stealing funds from a party or a channel, violating channel restrictions, overriding application logic, state rollback, etc.

3   Programmable Payment Channels

3.1   Defining $\mathcal{F}_{\mathsf{PPC}}$

To incorporate programmability into a payment channel, one might hard-code the logic of an application inside the protocol as a template. However, this approach is not desirable as every new application requires a protocol update that would also include changes to the existing onchain contract. Motivated by this, our definition of $\mathcal{F}_{\mathsf{PPC}}$ allows for on-the-fly programmability as we explain below.

Recall that we call a programmable payment a *promise*. Concretely, our ideal functionality $\mathcal{F}_{\mathsf{PPC}}$ allows the following operations: (1) opening a payment channel, (2) creating a promise, (3) executing a promise, and (4) closing a payment channel. Our central observation is that a promise can be viewed as a smart contract. Specifically, the storage of the promise is captured by the storage of the contract, and the execution logic of the promise is captured by functions in the smart contract. The logic in different promises can be different or related, thereby capturing on-the-fly programmability. Also, importantly, the promise smart contract itself can be deployed from an appropriately designed payment channel contract.

Any number of promises can be created by an open channel and may be concurrently executed. Either party can create a promise to the other party. Since the payment is unidirectional, we refer to the creating party as the *sender* of a promise, and the other party as the *receiver* of a promise.

Promises can be related to each other in the sense that the state and the execution logic of a promise can depend on the state and execution logic of other promises. We capture this by allowing the functions of the promise have access to *its own storage,* read *access to the storage and functions of other promises in this channel, and more generally,* read *access to the storage and functions of other onchain contracts.*[2] Note that the *execution environment* of promises is quite rich, and we will show various examples of how to use this and certain caveats associated with what is implementable.

This type of dependence is common in onchain smart contracts especially in the *Decentralized Finance* applications. However, capturing this dependence (in the implementation of $\mathcal{F}_{\mathsf{PPC}}$) needs to be done carefully since promises executions are normally executed offchain, and may sometimes need to be executed onchain (and the dependence must be preserved even while the execution environment is changing). Care must be taken to ensure that this change of the execution environment (i.e., from offchain to onchain) does not affect function output.

---

[2] In Solidity (a high level language for EVM) parlance, promises can also call *pure* or *view* functions in onchain contracts or other promises.

Promises are executed onchain only if requested by the parties (following which, further executions related to that promise are carried out onchain).[3] Following prior work (e.g., [17]), we differentiate between onchain and offchain executions in $\mathcal{F}_{\mathsf{PPC}}$ by the amount of time it takes $\mathcal{F}_{\mathsf{PPC}}$ to respond to execution requests. That is, onchain executions are slower and take $O(\Delta)$ rounds where Δ is a blockchain parameter representing the amount of time it takes for the miners/validators to deliver a new block to the chain.

Each promise *resolves* to an unsigned integer value denoting the amount that needs to be transferred from the sender to the receiver. This resolved value is calculated at the time of payment channel closing, and then the resolved values of all promises are aggregated to determine the final settlements.

3.2 PPC Preliminaries

Contracts. We define *contracts* as in [17]. A *contract instance* consists of two attributes: *contract storage* (accessed by key storage) and *contract code* (accessed by key code). Contract storage σ is an attribute tuple containing at least the following attributes: (1) $\sigma.user_L$ and $\sigma.user_R$ denoting the two involved users; (2) $\sigma.locked \in \mathbb{R}_{\geq 0}$ denoting the total number of coins locked in the contract; (3) $\sigma.cash : \{\sigma.user_L, \sigma.user_R\} \to \mathbb{R}$ denoting the coins available to each user. A contract code is a tuple $C := (\Lambda, \mathsf{Construct}, f_1, \ldots, f_s)$ where (1) Λ denotes the admissible contract storage; (2) $\mathsf{Construct}$ denotes a constructor function that takes (P, t, y) as inputs and provides as output an admissible contract storage or $\perp$ representing failure to construct, where P is the caller, t is the current time stamp and y denotes the auxiliary inputs; and (3) each f denotes an execution function that takes (σ, P, t, z) as inputs and provides as output an admissible contract storage (could be unchanged) and an output message m, where $m = \perp$ represents failure.

PPC Parameters. A programmable payment channel is parameterized by an attribute tuple $\gamma := (\gamma.id, \gamma.\mathsf{Alice}, \gamma.\mathsf{Bob}, \gamma.cash, \gamma.\mathsf{pspace}, \gamma.duration)$ where (1) $\gamma.id \in \{0,1\}^*$ is the identifier for the PPC instance (think of this as the address of the PPC contract); (2) $\gamma.\mathsf{Alice}$ and $\gamma.\mathsf{Bob}$ denote the two involved parties; (3) $\gamma.cash : \{\gamma.\mathsf{Alice}, \gamma.\mathsf{Bob}\} \to \mathbb{R}_{\geq 0}$ denotes the amount of money deposited by each participant; (4) $\gamma.\mathsf{pspace}$ stores all the promise instances opened in the channel–it takes a promise identifier *pid* and maps it to a promise instance; and (5) $\gamma.duration \geq 0$ denotes the time delay to closing a channel.

Note that the attribute $\gamma.duration$ was not part of prior channel formalizations (e.g., [15,17]); we will further clarify it in Sect. 3.3. We further define two auxiliary functions: (1) $\gamma.\mathsf{endusers} := \{\gamma.\mathsf{Alice}, \gamma.\mathsf{Bob}\}$; and (2) $\gamma.\mathsf{otherparty}(x) := \gamma.\mathsf{endusers} \setminus \{x\}$ where $x \in \gamma.\mathsf{endusers}$.

Promises. We name a programmable payment a *promise*. Informally, a promise instance can be viewed as a special contract instance where only one party offers

---

[3] In our implementation, we make the simplifying assumption that once a promise is executed onchain, all the remaining promise executions happen onchain as well.

money. Formally, a *promise instance* consists of two attributes: *promise storage* (accessed by key storage) and *promise code* (accessed by key code). Promise storage σ is an attribute tuple containing at least the following attributes: (1) $\sigma.payer$ denotes the party who sends money; (2) $\sigma.payee$ denotes the party who receives money; and (3) $\sigma.resolve \in \mathbb{R}_{\geq 0}$ denotes the amount of money transferred from payer to payee. A promise code is a tuple $C := (\Lambda, \mathsf{Construct}, f_1, \ldots, f_s)$ similar to contract code with further restrictions: (1) the unique constructor function Construct will always set the caller to be the payer in the storage created; and (2) the constructor function's output is independent of input argument t, which is a time parameter capturing the current time of the blockchain. We add these restrictions to ensure that, even when the promise is registered onchain by CRE-ATE2, the initial state remains identical.

Diverging from [15,17], we assume that each f_i has access to the code and storage of other promises in the *same* channel, as well as the code and storage of all Layer-1 onchain contracts. Formally, we capture this by providing oracle access to the ideal functionalities. This is why we use the notation $f^{\mathcal{G},\gamma}$ in the definition of $\mathcal{F}_{\mathsf{PPC}}$ (see Fig. 2), i.e., f has oracle access to the storage and the functions of onchain smart contracts and to the promises in the channel.

3.3   Ideal Functionality $\mathcal{F}_{\mathsf{PPC}}$

We propose our PPC protocol under the UC framework following [15–17]. We first define the ideal functionality $\mathcal{F}_{\mathsf{PPC}}^{\hat{\mathcal{L}}(\Delta)}$ (with dummy parties) which summarizes all the features that our PPC protocol will provide. We use $\mathcal{F}_{\mathsf{PPC}}$ as an abbreviation in the absence of ambiguity. See Fig. 2 for the definition of $\mathcal{F}_{\mathsf{PPC}}$. The functionality will maintain a key-value data structure Γ to track all programmable payment channels between parties. $\mathcal{F}_{\mathsf{PPC}}$ contains the following 4 procedures.

(1) PPC *Creation.* Assume party P wants to construct a channel with party Q. Within Δ rounds, $\mathcal{F}_{\mathsf{PPC}}$ will take corresponding coins specified by the channel instance from P's account from $\hat{\mathcal{L}}$. If Q agrees to the creation, within another Δ rounds, $\mathcal{F}_{\mathsf{PPC}}$ will take Q's coins. Thus, the successful creation of a initial programmable payment channel takes at most 2Δ rounds. Note that if Q does not want to create the channel, P can take her money back after 2Δ rounds.
(2) *Promise Creation.* This procedure is used to create a programmable payment aka promise (offchain) from payer P to the payee Q. The promise instance is specified by payer's choice of channel γ, contract code C and arguments for the constructor function y, and a salt z that is used to identify this promise instance. Among other things, the ideal functionality ensures that $pid := (id, C, y, z)$ does not exist in $\gamma.\mathsf{pspace}$. Since payee always gains coins in any promise, we do not need an acknowledgment from the payee to instantiate a promise. Thus, the creation takes exactly 1 round.[4]

---
[4] Note that this does not hold for state channels as formalized in [17] where an instance requires coins from both parties.

Functionality $\mathcal{F}_{\mathsf{PPC}}^{\hat{\mathcal{L}}(\Delta)}$

Programmable payment channel opening

Upon $(\mathsf{open}, \gamma) \overset{t_0}{\hookleftarrow} P$ where γ is a valid initial programmable payment channel, i.e., $P \in \gamma.\mathsf{endusers}$, $\gamma.\mathsf{cash}(\cdot) \geq 0$, $\gamma.\mathsf{pspace} = \perp$, denote $Q := \gamma.\mathsf{otherparty}(P)$:

1. Within Δ rounds remove $\gamma.\mathsf{cash}(P)$ from P's account on $\hat{\mathcal{L}}$.
2. If $(\mathsf{open}, \gamma) \overset{t_1 \leq t_0 + \Delta}{\hookleftarrow} Q$, remove within another Δ rounds $\gamma.\mathsf{cash}(Q)$ coins from Q's account on $\hat{\mathcal{L}}$, set $\Gamma(\gamma.id) := \gamma$, and send $(\mathsf{opened}, \gamma) \hookrightarrow \gamma.\mathsf{endusers}$ and stop.
3. Else, upon $(\mathsf{refund}, \gamma) \overset{> t_0 + 2\Delta}{\hookleftarrow} P$, within Δ rounds add $\gamma.\mathsf{cash}(P)$ coins to P's account on $\hat{\mathcal{L}}$.

Promise initial instance creation

Upon $(\mathsf{create}, id, C\|y, z) \overset{t_0}{\hookleftarrow} P$, let $\gamma := \Gamma(id)$ and let $pid := (id, C, P, y, z)$. If $\gamma = \perp$ or $P \notin \gamma.\mathsf{endusers}$ or $\gamma.\mathsf{pspace}(pid) \neq \perp$ then stop. Else proceed as follows:

- Let $\nu := \perp$ and $\sigma := C.\mathsf{Construct}(P, t_0, y)$. Stop if $\sigma = \perp$. Set $\nu.\mathsf{code} := C$ and $\nu.\mathsf{storage} := \sigma$. Set $\Gamma(id).\mathsf{pspace}(pid) := \nu$ and $\Gamma(id).\mathsf{pspace}(pid).\mathsf{flag} := 0$. Send $(\mathsf{instance\text{-}created}, id, pid, \nu) \overset{t_0 + 1}{\hookrightarrow} \gamma.\mathsf{endusers}$.

Promise instance execution

Upon $(\mathsf{execute}, id, pid, f, z) \overset{t_0}{\hookleftarrow} P$, let $\gamma := \Gamma(id)$. If $P \notin \gamma.\mathsf{endusers}$ or $\gamma.\mathsf{pspace}(pid) = \perp$ or $f \notin \gamma.\mathsf{pspace}(pid).\mathsf{code}$ then stop. Else proceed as follows:

- If $\gamma.\mathsf{pspace}(pid).\mathsf{flag} = 0$, and both parties are honest, then set $T := t_0 + 5$ and $t := t_0$.
- Else if $\gamma.\mathsf{pspace}(pid).\mathsf{flag} = 0$, and one party is malicious, the simulator is allowed to specify a message msg.
  - If $\mathsf{msg} = \mathsf{continue}$, set $T := t_0 + 5$ and $t := t_0$. This captures the situation where the adversary wants to execute offchain.
  - If $\mathsf{msg} = \mathsf{onchain}$, set $T := t_0 + 4\Delta + 5$ and $\gamma.\mathsf{pspace}(\cdot).\mathsf{flag} := 1$. t is further specified by the simulator. This captures the situation where the adversary wants to execute onchain.
- Else if $\gamma.\mathsf{pspace}(pid).\mathsf{flag} = 1$, one party must be malicious, then set $T := t_0 + \Delta + 5$, t is set by the simulator.

Let $\nu := \gamma.\mathsf{pspace}(pid)$ and $\sigma := \nu.\mathsf{storage}$. Let $(\tilde{\sigma}, m) := f^{\mathcal{G}, \gamma}(\sigma, P, t, z)$. Set $\Gamma(id).\mathsf{pspace}(pid).\mathsf{storage} := \tilde{\sigma}$ and send $(\mathsf{executed}, id, pid, P, f, t, z, \nu) \overset{t_1 \leq T}{\hookrightarrow} \gamma.\mathsf{endusers}$. Note that the adversary can only postpone the execution but *cannot* block it.

Programmable payment channel closure

Upon $(\mathsf{close}, id) \overset{t_0}{\hookleftarrow} P$, let $\gamma := \Gamma(id)$. If $P \notin \gamma.\mathsf{endusers}$ then stop. Else block all future close invocations on γ. Wait at most $\gamma.duration + 7\Delta$ rounds and proceed as follows:

1. Calculate the following values (Note that either Alice or Bob could be P):
   (a) Set $total := \gamma.\mathsf{cash}(\gamma.\mathsf{Alice}) + \gamma.\mathsf{cash}(\gamma.\mathsf{Bob})$.
   (b) Set $credit_A := \sum_{\gamma.\mathsf{pspace}(pid).\mathsf{storage}.payer = \gamma.\mathsf{Bob}} (\gamma.\mathsf{pspace}(pid).\mathsf{storage}.resolve)$.
   (c) Set $credit_B := \sum_{\gamma.\mathsf{pspace}(pid).\mathsf{storage}.payer = \gamma.\mathsf{Alice}} (\gamma.\mathsf{pspace}(pid).\mathsf{storage}.resolve)$.
2. Within Δ rounds, add $min\{total, max\{0, \gamma.\mathsf{cash}(\gamma.\mathsf{Alice}) + credit_A - credit_B\}\}$ coins to $\gamma.\mathsf{Alice}$'s and $min\{total, max\{0, \gamma.\mathsf{cash}(\gamma.\mathsf{Bob}) + credit_B - credit_A\}\}$ coins to $\gamma.\mathsf{Bob}$'s account on $\hat{\mathcal{L}}$.
3. Send $(\mathsf{contract\text{-}close}, id) \overset{t_1 \leq t_0 + 8\Delta + \gamma.duration}{\hookrightarrow} \gamma.\mathsf{endusers}$.

Fig. 2. The ideal functionality $\mathcal{F}_{\mathsf{PPC}}^{\hat{\mathcal{L}}(\Delta)}$ achieved by the PPC protocol.

(3) *Promise Execution.* This procedure is used to update the promise instance's storage. Specifically, party P can execute the promise pid in channel id as long as P is one of the participants of the channel. Note that the existence of pid implies that this instance is properly constructed by the payer via the promise instance creation procedure. If both parties are honest, the execution completes in $O(1)$ rounds, inferring no onchain operation (i.e., *optimistic case*). Otherwise, if one of them is corrupt, it relies on onchain operations which takes $O(\Delta)$ rounds (i.e., *pessimistic case*). Note that, the adversary can postpone the function execution time, but it *cannot* block the honest party from executing it.

In particular, $\mathcal{F}_{\mathsf{PPC}}$ uses an attribute flag for each promise to trace the onchain/offchain status. Note that when the promise goes onchain for the first time, it takes at most 3Δ rounds to put the promise onchain. Once the promise is onchain, the execution will be taken on Layer-1 in Δ rounds. We follow [17] to break ties when both parties want to simultaneously execute the same promise, which includes at most 5 rounds delay.

(4) PPC *Closure.* When a party of the channel γ wants to close the channel, $\mathcal{F}_{\mathsf{PPC}}$ will wait for $\gamma.duration$ rounds to execute the remaining promises that have not been finalized. The corresponding procedure in the state channel functionality of [17] requires that all contract instances in the channel are finalized in order to close the channel. We cannot imitate this approach because in our case, the creation of a promise instance need only be authenticated by the payer, and so requiring finality will allow a malicious party to block closing by simply creating some non-finalizable promise instance. (Note that in this case it will be the malicious sender who is locking up its money.) Waiting for $\gamma.duration$ can be avoided if both parties agree to cooperatively close the channel.

3.4 Concrete Implementation of $\mathcal{F}_{\mathsf{PPC}}$

We show a pseudocode implementation of programmable payment channels contract in Fig. 3. In this subsection, we will detail the methods in the programmable payment channels contract, and along the way we will discuss the offchain protocol that is executed to implement $\mathcal{F}_{\mathsf{PPC}}$.

The programmable payment channel contract is initialized with a channel id id, the parties' public keys vk$_A$ and vk$_B$, and an expiry time claimDuration by which the channel settles the amounts deposited. We track the deposit amount and the credit amount (which will be monotonically increasing) for the two parties. We also track a *receipt* id (i.e., rid) and an accumulator value acc. We will describe what these are for below, but for now think of receipts as keeping track of received promises that have been resolved, and the accumulator as keeping track of received promises that have not yet resolved.

Remark. Since promise executions may take some time (e.g., HTLC, chess), it is important to support *concurrency*. Promises issued by a sender are immediately added to an accumulator associated with the sender (which is maintained by both parties), and then are removed from the accumulator when they get resolved.

PPC Contract

$\mathtt{Init}(\mathsf{id}', \mathsf{vk}'_A, \mathsf{vk}'_B, \mathsf{claimDuration}')$:

1. Set $(\mathsf{id}, \mathsf{claimDuration}) \leftarrow (\mathsf{id}', \mathsf{claimDuration}')$;

2. Set status ← "Active";   chanExpiry ← 0;   unresolvedPromises ← ⊥;

3. Set A ← {addr : vk'_A, deposit : 0, rid : 0, credit : 0, acc : ⊥, closed : F}

4. Set B ← {addr : vk'_B, deposit : 0, rid : 0, credit : 0, acc : ⊥, closed : F}

$\mathtt{Deposit}(\mathsf{amount})$:

1. Require status = "Active" and caller.vk ∈ {A.addr, B.addr};

2. If caller.vk = A.addr, then set A.deposit ← A.deposit + amount;

3. If caller.vk = B.addr, then set B.deposit ← B.deposit + amount.

$\mathtt{RegisterReceipt}(R)$:

1. Require status ∈ {"Active", "Closing"};

2. If status = "Active" then set chanExpiry ← now + claimDuration and status ← "Closing".

3. Require caller.vk ∈ {A.addr, B.addr};

4. If caller.vk = A.addr, then:
   (a) Require $\mathtt{SigVerify}(R.\sigma, [\mathsf{id}, R.\mathsf{idx}, R.\mathsf{credit}, R.\mathsf{acc}], B.\mathsf{addr})$;

   (b) Set A.rid ← R.idx, A.credit ← R.credit, and A.acc ← R.acc;
   Otherwise:
   (a) Abort if $\mathtt{SigVerify}(R.\sigma, [\mathsf{id}, R.\mathsf{idx}, R.\mathsf{credit}, R.\mathsf{acc}], A.\mathsf{addr})$;

   (b) Set B.rid ← R.idx, B.credit ← R.credit, and B.acc ← R.acc;

$\mathtt{RegisterPromise}(P)$:

1. Require status ∈ {"Active", "Closing"};

2. If status = "Active", then set chanExpiry ← now + claimDuration, and status ← "Closing".

3. Require caller.vk ∈ {A.addr, B.addr};

4. Require [P.addr, P.receiver] ∉ unresolvedPromises;

5. If P.sender = A.addr, set sender ← A and receiver ← B;
   Otherwise set sender ← B and receiver ← A;

6. Require $\mathtt{SigVerify}(P.\sigma, [\ \mathsf{id}, P.\mathsf{rid}, P.\mathsf{sender}, P.\mathsf{receiver}, P.\mathsf{addr}\ ], \mathsf{sender.addr})$;

7. If caller.vk = receiver.addr and P.rid < receiver.rid,
   Require ACC.VerifyProof(acc, P.addr, P.proof);

8. Invoke $\mathtt{Deploy}$ (P.byteCode, P.salt);

9. Set unresolvedPromises.push([P.addr, receiver])

$\mathtt{Close}()$:

1. Require caller.vk ∈ {A.addr, B.addr};

2. If caller.vk = A.addr, set A.closed ← T; Otherwise set B.closed ← T;

3. If A.closed and B.closed, set status ← "Closed";

4. If status = "Active", then set chanExpiry ← now + claimDuration, and status ← "Closing".

$\mathtt{Withdraw}()$:

1. Require status ∈ {"Closing", "Closed"};

2. If status = "Closing", Require now > chanExpiry;

3. For each (addr, receiver) ∈ unresolvedPromises:
   receiver.credit ← receiver.credit + addr.resolve();

4. Invoke $\mathtt{transfer}(A.\mathsf{addr}, min(total, max(0, A.\mathsf{deposit}\ +\ A.\mathsf{credit}\ -\ B.\mathsf{credit}))$ and
   $\mathtt{transfer}(B.\mathsf{addr}, min(total, max(0, B.\mathsf{deposit}\ +\ B.\mathsf{credit}\ -\ A.\mathsf{credit}))$,   where $total = $
   A.deposit + B.deposit.

Fig. 3. PPC Contract

Just as a regular payment channel, we also provide methods for the parties to deposit an amount (the pseudocode supports multiple deposits), and also for initiating the closing of a channel via the Close method. A call to the Close method will ensure that the channel status is set to "Closing" or "Closed", and further, sets the channel expiry time.

During the time that a channel is "Active" parties exchange any number of payment promises offchain. Each promise P is essentially the smart contract code describing the logic of the payment. Note that the promise contract logic may involve multiple steps and parties may concurrently send and receive any number of promises.

At a high level, the lifecycle of a promise is as follows: the sender sends the promise offchain, then the sender and the receiver execute the promise contract offchain. When both parties agree to the value of the final output of the resolve method on the promise, the sender of the promise signs a receipt signaling the fulfillment of the promise that reflects the updated credit balance of the receiver.

In more detail, a receipt from a sender consists of

- a monotonically increasing index, which keeps track of the number of fulfilled promises from the sender,
- a monotonically increasing credit, which keeps track of the sum of all resolved amounts in the fulfilled promises originating from the sender,
- an accumulator, which keeps track of all the pending promises issued by the sender, and
- a signature from the sender on all the above values with the channel id.

If the receiver obtains a faulty receipt (or did not receive the receipt, or is just malicious), then the receiver can deploy the promise onchain via the PPC contract. Note that in some cases (e.g., promises which involve multiple steps), it is possible that the sender (as opposed to the receiver) may need to deploy the promise onchain via the PPC contract.

This brings us to another important detail concerning the offchain execution of the promises that involve multiple steps (e.g., chess). In honest cases, parties will need to additionally exchange signatures with each other to commit to the storage of the promise contract after the offchain execution of individual steps. If some malicious behavior happens (e.g., some party aborts), to continue the promise execution onchain (we assume that the party also wishes to subsequently close the channel), the party calls RegisterReceipt with the latest receipt (along with the signature from the counterparty) that it possesses, and then calls RegisterPromise with the promise P.

Consistency Between Offchain and Onchain Executions. It is crucial to ensure that the switching between offchain and onchain is consistent. This is achieved by allowing parties to submit the latest state to the deployed promise (as a smart contract). Namely, the smart contract created by the PPC contract in Fig. 3 using CREATE2 needs to have a function interface to "bypass" its state to the latest one. This can be trivially realized by including a monotonically increasing version number to the state, which is signed by both parties during the offchain execution. (We remark that Item 8 in Fig. 3 will only deploy a smart contract (as a promise) on its initial state (e.g., an empty chess board).)

We now detail the components of a promise P:

- P.sender (resp. P.receiver) denotes the sender (resp. receiver) of a promise,
- P.byteCode denotes the smart contract corresponding to the payment logic,
- P.salt denotes a one-time salt chosen by the sender,
- P.addr denotes the address at which the promise will be deployed by the PPC contract; note that P.addr is derived deterministically from P.byteCode and P.salt using a collision resistant hash function (e.g., CREATE2 opcode),
- P.rid denotes the latest receipt index at the time of generating this promise,
- P.proof denotes the proof that the promise is contained in the accumulator (i.e., is unresolved at the time the latest receipt was generated), and
- P.σ denotes the signature of sender on (id, P.rid, P.sender, P.receiver, P.addr).

When `RegisterPromise` is called (when malicious behaviors happen) with a valid promise, the PPC contract deploys P.byteCode (i.e., the smart contract associated with the payment logic of promise P) at a predetermined address. The fact that the contract is deployed at a predetermined address is what makes it possible to have promises depend on each other (cf. Section 4). Here, we assume that the PPC contract uses CREATE2 opcode to deploy the contract. In Ethereum, using the CREATE2 opcode (EIP-1014), contracts can deploy contracts whose address is set by $\mathcal{H}(\texttt{0xFF}, sender, salt, bytecode)$ (where $\mathcal{H}$ is a collision resistant hash function). This capability implies that one can foresee the address of some yet-to-be-deployed contract.

Following deployment, parties can interact with the deployed promise independent of the PPC contract. (Again, they "bypass" to the last agreed state.) However, note that when a party calls the function `RegisterPromise`, the channel automatically goes into a closing state, and then after claimDuration time has passed, either party can withdraw funds. Thus, it is critical that the promises exchanged by the parties also meaningfully resolve within claimDuration time.

When a party calls the `Withdraw` method, the resolve method is called for each unresolved promise that is registered with the PPC contract. That is, these promises should be some onchain smart contracts. The value returned by the resolve method is then added to the credit of the corresponding receiver. Finally, each party gets transferred an amount that corresponds to its initial deposit and the difference of the credit that it is owed and the credit that it owes.

We formally state our theorem below. The formal protocols are described in the full version of our work.

Theorem 1 (Main). *Suppose the underlying signature scheme is existentially unforgeable against chosen message attacks. There exists a protocol working in $\mathcal{G}^{\hat{\mathcal{L}}(\Delta)}$-hybrid model that emulates $\mathcal{F}_{\textsf{PPC}}^{\hat{\mathcal{L}}(\Delta)}$ for every $\Delta \in \mathbb{N}$ such that (1) the creation of the initial promise instance takes 1 round, and (2) if both parties are honest, every call to instance execution procedure takes $O(1)$ rounds.*

3.5 Lightweight Applications of Programmable Payments

We use programmable payments on PPC to implement many lightweight applications and report the evaluations in Sect. 3.6. Here, we focus on discussing how PPC helps us implement these applications *as smart contracts*.

HTLC Contract

Init(amount′, hash′, expiry′):

   1. Set (amount, hash, expiry) ← (amount′, hash′, expiry′);

   2. Set secretRevealed ← F.

RevealSecret(secret):

   1. Require now < expiry and Hash(secret) = hash;

   2. Set secretRevealed ← T;

Resolve():

   1. If secretRevealed, then return amount, else return 0.

Fig. 4. HTLC Contract

HTLC. See Fig. 4 for an implementation of HTLC promises. The constructor specifies the amount this HTLC is for, and the hash image for which the preimage is requested, and the expiry time by which the preimage must be provided. Observe that these values are specified by the sender of the promise. On sending the preimage to the sender, the receiver will expect a receipt reflecting the updated credit (i.e., an increase by amount). If such a receipt was not provided, then the receiver will deploy the HTLC promise contract onchain[5] and then execute the RevealSecret function to lock the final resolved amount to the HTLC amount. On the other hand, if the secret was not revealed, then when the PPC channel closes (which we assume happens after the HTLC expiry), the resolve function will return zero.

Reverse HTLC. See Fig. 5 for an implementation of the reverse HTLC promise. In reverse HTLC, the sender commits to revealing a hash preimage within a given expiry time or else stands to lose the promise amount to the receiver. (Note that the roles are somewhat reversed in a regular HTLC promise.) This is a useful promise in, e.g., committing a reservation.

To implement reverse HTLC promise, the sender initializes the promise with the amount, the hash image, the expiry time, and the address of the receiver. Then the sender would reveal the hash preimage to the receiver offchain, and provide a receipt amount (reflecting a zero increase in credit). However, unlike a HTLC promise, here the sender additionally expects an acknowledgment from the receiver that they received the preimage (in the form of a signature on the preimage). If the acknowledgment is received, then the sender is assured that the promise will resolve to zero (since it can always call SubmitAck if the promise gets deployed onchain after the expiry time), and concludes the promise execution. Otherwise, the sender continues the promise execution onchain by deploying the reverse HTLC promise via the PPC contract, and then calling the RevealSecret method. This ensures that the promise will resolve to zero. Thus, reverse HTLC is an example (different from HTLC) where the sender might have to deploy the promise onchain.

---

[5] Note that the deployment byteCode already contains the constructor arguments hardcoded in it.

Reverse HTLC Contract

Init(amount′, hash′, expiry′, receiver′):
   1. Set(amount, hash, expiry, receiver) ← (amount′, hash′, expiry′, receiver′);
   2. Set (secretRevealed, ackSubmitted) ← (F, F).

RevealSecret(secret):
   1. Require now < expiry and Hash(secret) = hash;
   2. Set secretRevealed ← T;

SubmitAck(secret, sig):
   1. Require Hash(secret) = hash and SigVerify(sig, secret, receiver);
   2. Set ackSubmitted ← T;

Resolve():
   1. If secretRevealed or ackSubmitted, then return 0;
   2. Return amount.

Fig. 5. Reverse HTLC Contract

On-chain Event Betting

Init(amt′, threshold′, tMin′, tMax′):
   1. Set (amount, threshold, tMin, tMax) ← (amt′, threshold′, tMin′, tMax′);
   2. Set roundID ← 0

SetRoundID(roundID′):
   1. Require tMax ≥ getTimestamp(roundID′) ≥ tMin;
   2. Set roundID ← roundID′

Resolve():
   1. If roundID = 0, return 0
   2. (price, timestamp) ← eth-usd.data.eth.getRoundData(roundID)
   3. If price > threshold and timestamp > 0

Fig. 6. Onchain event betting

On-chain Event Betting. See Fig. 6 for an example promise where the sender is betting that the price of Ethereum will not go above a certain threshold (say, \$2,000) within a certain time period. In such a scenario, the party can send a promise that reads the price of Ethereum on-chain from an oracle (e.g., eth-usd.data.eth). This is an example of a promise that depends on the state of external onchain contracts. In such cases, it is important to design the promise carefully as the external contract may change state and cause offchain and onchain execution of promises to be different. Thus we use the function getRoundData (say, instead of latestPrice). This way, suppose the receiver does not send an acknowledgment that the price was indeed above the threshold (i.e., a receipt reflecting the updated credit), then the sender can deploy the promise onchain (without worrying about the exact block in which its promise will appear). In the example, we assume that the roundID values are calculated offchain and correspond to a time duration that both parties agree on.

Table 1. Gas prices for invoking PPC contract's functions.

Function	Gas Units	HTLC Specific	Gas Units
Deploy	3,243,988	Promise	611,296 (w/o. proof)
Deposit	43,010	Promise	626,092 (Merkle-100K txs)
Receipt	75,336	Reveal	66,340
Close	44,324	Withdraw	71,572

Table 2. The gas usage of the different functions of various applications. *:For Resolve functions we report the execution costs as these functions are view functions. +: The Reveal functions in the RockPaperScissor contracts need to be called twice to reveal the commitments for both parties.

HTLC		ReverseHTLC		OnchainBetting	
Deploy	222,795	Deploy	423,265	Deploy	442,479
Reveal	28,391	Reveal	28,413	checkPrice	48,093
Resolve*	4,582	SubmitAck	30,247	Resolve*	4,632
		Resolve*	2,499		
RockPaperScissor		RockPaperScissor-P1		RockPaperScissor-P2	
Deploy	534,167	Deploy	598,088	Deploy	381,537
Reveal$^+$	34,887	Reveal$^+$	34,773	Resolve*	16,937
Resolve*	9,571	Resolve*	6,573		

3.6 Implementation and Evaluation

PPC Gas Usage Costs. We implemented the PPC contract presented in Fig. 3 in Solidity. We evaluate our implementation in terms of Ethereum gas usage. The PPC contract requires 3, 243, 988 gas to be deployed on the Ethereum blockchain. While we did not aim to optimize gas costs. the PPC contract is already comparable to other simple payment channel deployments 2M+ and 3M+ gas for Perun [16] and Raiden [3][6] respectively. The gas usage for the remaining functions of the contract are reported in Table 1.

HTLC Application. In the optimistic case after a promise is sent from the sender, the receiver releases the secret for the HTLC and consequently, the sender sends a corresponding receipt to the receiver. In such a scenario, the receiving party will submit the receipt to the contract and close accordingly. However, in the pessimistic case, where the receiving party releases the secret but does not receive a receipt, it goes onchain and first submit its latest receipt. Next, it submits the promise for the HTLC which will be deployed by PPC where the party can reveal the secret of HTLC. Comparing the two scenarios (cf. Table 1), we see that the pessimistic case costs about 700K more gas to resolve the promise.

---

[6] https://tinyurl.com/etherscanRaiden.

We were able to achieve 110 TPS for the HTLC application end-to-end on a laptop running 2.6 GHz 6-Core Intel Core i7. The end-to-end process included random secret creation, hashing of secret, promise creation/verification, secret reveal/verification, and receipt creation/verification.

Other Applications. For the sake of completeness, we include gas usage costs for other applications presented in Sect. 3.5, i.e., reverse HTLC, onchain event betting, and rock-paper-scissors (cf. Appendix D) in Table 2. For the rock-paper-scissors, we provide two implementations: one using the compiler (cf. Sect. 4), and one without (i.e., the ad-hoc implementation in Appendix D). This is to emphasize that our SC from PPC compiler that we present next is highly efficient. Note that all this (i.e., gas cost) is relevant only when one of the parties is malicious. When both parties are honest, the executions are always offchain, and the application-specific onchain deployment costs are zero.

Comparing with Prior State Channels. Prior works on state channels (e.g., [4,17,25]) do not provide concrete implementations, performance numbers, or benchmarks. However, we note that, at the very least, state channel implementations typically require explicit signature verification on the application contract—something we avoid in most of our applications above. Furthermore, in multiparty applications where each party has a PPC channel with an untrusted hub, the onchain complexity in the worst case is only proportional to the number of malicious parties as opposed to the total number of parties as in the case with state channels.

4 State Channels from $\mathcal{F}_{\mathsf{PPC}}$

On the one hand, our programmable payment channel protocol subsumes regular payment channel protocols. A simple payment can be captured by payer P creating an initial promise instance directly constructed as finalized with the proper amount. On the other hand, it seems that our programmable payment channel protocol may not subsume protocols for state channels, i.e., execute a contract where two parties can both deposit coins in. In this section, we first formalize a variant of state channels that we call $\mathcal{F}_{\mathsf{SC}}$ that is very similar to PPC. Then we provide a construction that compiles a contract instance input to $\mathcal{F}_{\mathsf{SC}}$ into two promises that can be input to $\mathcal{F}_{\mathsf{PPC}}$. That is, we show how to efficiently realize $\mathcal{F}_{\mathsf{SC}}$ in the $\mathcal{F}_{\mathsf{PPC}}$-hybrid model.

4.1 Modifying $\mathcal{F}_{\mathsf{PPC}}$ to Capture State Channels

Our formalization of programmable payment channels is heavily inspired by the formalization of state channels in [17]. In fact, $\mathcal{F}_{\mathsf{PPC}}$ can be easily modified to yield a *variant* of state channel functionality $\mathcal{F}_{\mathsf{SC}}$, which can be used to execute any two-party contract offchain. We call these contracts *covenants*. Note that the ideal functionality for state channels $\mathcal{F}_{\mathsf{SC}}$ allows the following operations: (1) opening a (state) channel, (2) creating a covenant instance, (3) executing a covenant instance, and (4) closing the channel. Covenant instances, unlike promise instances, do not have a designated sender or receiver. Like $\mathcal{F}_{\mathsf{PPC}}$, any number of covenant instances can be created and executed using $\mathcal{F}_{\mathsf{SC}}$. Unlike $\mathcal{F}_{\mathsf{PPC}}$ though, the ideal functionality $\mathcal{F}_{\mathsf{SC}}$ accepts a covenant creation operation from a party only if the other party consents to it. The covenant instances allowed by $\mathcal{F}_{\mathsf{SC}}$ resolve to two integer values (that corresponds to the payout of each party). Again, this resolved value is calculated at the time of channel closing, and then the resolved values of all contract instances are aggregated to determine the final settlements.

4.2   Defining $\mathcal{F}_{\mathsf{SC}}$

Just as how $\mathcal{F}_{\mathsf{PPC}}$ creates and executes promise instances, we will have $\mathcal{F}_{\mathsf{SC}}$ create and execute *covenant* instances.

Covenant Instance. A covenant instance can be viewed as a special contract instance consisting of two attributes: *covenant storage* (accessed by key storage) and *covenant code* (accessed by key code). Covenant storage σ is an attribute tuple containing at least the following attributes: (1) $\sigma.resolve_A \in \mathbb{R}_{\geq 0}$ denotes the amount of money transferred from party B to party A; and (2) $\sigma.resolve_B \in \mathbb{R}_{\geq 0}$ denotes the amount of money transferred from party A to party B. Covenant code is a tuple $C := (\Lambda, \mathsf{Construct}, f_1, \ldots, f_s)$ similar to contract code. W.l.o.g., we assume Construct does not take caller as inputs but it can be incorporated into y. We note that we do not restrict the independence of the constructor.

See Fig. 7 for the definition of the ideal functionality that captures state channels. Like $\mathcal{F}_{\mathsf{PPC}}$, the functionality $\mathcal{F}_{\mathsf{SC}}$ contains the following 4 procedures.

(1) *State channel creation.* Similar to $\mathcal{F}_{\mathsf{PPC}}$, a party can instantiate a channel with another party by sending the channel creation information to $\mathcal{F}_{\mathsf{SC}}$. The operation of this procedure is identical to that of $\mathcal{F}_{\mathsf{PPC}}$.

(2) *Covenant Creation.* The covenant instance is specified by choice of channel γ, contract code C and arguments for the constructor function y, and a salt z that is used to identify this promise instance. Among other things, the ideal functionality ensures that $cid := (id, C, y, z)$ does not exist in $\gamma.$cspace. Note that unlike $\mathcal{F}_{\mathsf{PPC}}$, we need an acknowledgment from the counterparty before creating a covenant instance. Thus, the creation takes more rounds but optimistically remains $O(1)$.

(3) *Covenant Execution.* This procedure is used to update the covenant instance's storage. The operation of this procedure is identical to that of $\mathcal{F}_{\mathsf{PPC}}$.

(4) *State Channel Closure.* When a party of the channel instance γ wants to close the channel, $\mathcal{F}_{\mathsf{SC}}$ will wait for $\gamma.duration$ rounds to execute the remaining covenants that have not been finalized. The crucial difference from $\mathcal{F}_{\mathsf{PPC}}$ is in the way in which the credits are calculated (simply because of the difference in the final values of covenant instances vs. promise instances). We note that the closure requires extra $O(\Delta)$ rounds. Looking ahead, this is because

---

Functionality $\mathcal{F}_{\mathsf{SC}}^{\hat{\mathcal{L}}(\Delta)}$

State channel opening

Identical to programmable payment channel opening in $\mathcal{F}_{\mathsf{PPC}}^{\hat{\mathcal{L}}(\Delta)}$ but with a state channel of covenants (saved in cspace) as inputs.

Covenant creation

Upon $(\mathtt{create}, id, C\|y, z) \xhookleftarrow{t_0} P$, let $\gamma := \Gamma(id)$ and let $cid := (id, C, y, z)$. If $\gamma = \bot$ or $P \notin \gamma.\mathsf{endusers}$ or $\gamma.\mathsf{cspace}(pid) \neq \bot$ then stop. Else let $Q := \gamma.\mathsf{otherparty}(P)$.

- If $(\mathtt{create}, id, C\|y, z) \xhookleftarrow{t_0} Q$ and P, Q are honest or the the simulator behaves honestly, then let $\nu := \bot$ and $\sigma := C.\mathsf{Construct}(t_0, y)$. Stop if $\sigma = \bot$. Within 7 rounds, set $\nu.\mathsf{code} := C$ and $\nu.\mathsf{storage} := \sigma$. Set $\Gamma(id).\mathsf{cspace}(cid).\mathsf{flag} = 0$. Set $\Gamma(id).\mathsf{cspace}(cid) := \nu$. Send $(\mathtt{instance\text{-}created}, id, cid, \nu) \xhookrightarrow{t \leq t_0 + 7} \gamma.\mathsf{endusers}$.

- If $(\mathtt{create}, id, C\|y, z) \xhookleftarrow{t_0} Q$ and one party is malicious, then let $\nu := \bot$ and $\sigma := C.\mathsf{Construct}(t_0, y)$. Stop if $\sigma = \bot$. Within $4\Delta + 7$ rounds, set $\nu.\mathsf{code} := C$ and $\nu.\mathsf{storage} := \sigma$. Set $\Gamma(id).\mathsf{cspace}(cid).\mathsf{flag}$ by the simulator. Set $\Gamma(id).\mathsf{cspace}(cid) := \nu$. Send $(\mathtt{instance\text{-}created}, id, cid, \nu) \xhookrightarrow{t \leq t_0 + 4\Delta + 7} \gamma.\mathsf{endusers}$.

Covenant execution

Identical to promise instance execution in $\mathcal{F}_{\mathsf{PPC}}^{\hat{\mathcal{L}}(\Delta)}$ but with a state channel identity and a covenant identity as inputs.

State channel closure

Upon $(\mathtt{close}, id) \xhookleftarrow{t_0} P$, let $\gamma := \Gamma(id)$. If $P \notin \gamma.\mathsf{endusers}$ then stop. Else block all future close invocations on γ. Wait at most $2\gamma.duration + 11\Delta + 5$ rounds and proceed as follows: (Note that either Alice or Bob could be P)

1. Calculate

$$total := \gamma.\mathsf{cash}(\gamma.\mathsf{Alice}) + \gamma.\mathsf{cash}(\gamma.\mathsf{Bob})$$

$$credit_A := \sum(\gamma.\mathsf{pspace}(pid).\mathsf{storage}.resolve_A)$$

$$credit_B := \sum(\gamma.\mathsf{pspace}(pid).\mathsf{storage}.resolve_B)$$

2. Within Δ rounds, add $min\{total, max\{0, \gamma.\mathsf{cash}(\gamma.\mathsf{Alice}) + credit_A - credit_B\}\}$ coins to $\gamma.\mathsf{Alice}$'s and $min\{total, max\{0, \gamma.\mathsf{cash}(\gamma.\mathsf{Bob}) + credit_B - credit_A\}\}$ coins to $\gamma.\mathsf{Bob}$'s account.

3. Send $(\mathtt{contract\text{-}close}, id) \xhookrightarrow{t_1 \leq t_0 + 12\Delta + 2\gamma.duration + 5} \gamma.\mathsf{endusers}$.

Fig. 7. The ideal functionality $\mathcal{F}_{\mathsf{SC}}^{\hat{\mathcal{L}}(\Delta)}$.

we "compile" a covenant into two promises on $\mathcal{F}_{\mathsf{PPC}}$, and require an extra function call to settle down the resolved values of them.

Remarks. Our state channel ideal functionality differs from prior formalizations in many ways. Crucially, it makes explicit the dependence of covenant instances on other onchain contracts. Also, a covenant instance can depend on other covenant instances (this is something not considered in prior works).

4.3 Implementing $\mathcal{F}_{\mathsf{SC}}$ in the $\mathcal{F}_{\mathsf{PPC}}$-Hybrid World

Perhaps surprisingly, $\mathcal{F}_{\mathsf{PPC}}$ can be used to implement $\mathcal{F}_{\mathsf{SC}}$. In particular, a covenant can be compiled into two promises on $\mathcal{F}_{\mathsf{PPC}}$ that can be used to execute the covenant offchain.

To implement a covenant creation of a contract c in $\mathcal{F}_{\mathsf{SC}}$, we use two promises p_0, p_1, one from each endpoint of $\mathcal{F}_{\mathsf{PPC}}$. The promise p_0 contains all the logic of the covenant instance c. Note that c will resolve to either $(k, 0)$ or $(0, k)$ (or any other intermediate value), where k is non-negative. In particular, $(k, 0)$ denotes that the first party needs to pay k to the second party and $(0, k)$ denotes that the second party needs to pay k to the first party. Note that the resolved state of c will be saved in p_0 as well. Accordingly, p_0 will resolve to 0 in the case of $(0, k)$, otherwise as k. The resolve method of promise p_1 will instead read the state of p_0, and resolves in the opposite direction. That is, p_1 resolves to 0 in the case of $(k, 0)$, otherwise as k. That both parties consent to the contract instance is captured by requiring each party to provide its promise.

We illustrate this with an example of two-party contract for chess. We assume that each party puts in \$50, and the winner gets \$100. Assume that there exists a smart contract c that contains the entire logic of chess (i.e., checking validity of a move, checking whether the game has ended, who has won the game, and the payout to each party, etc.).

To play a game of chess offchain, parties each first create a promise. The promise from Bob contains all the logic in c and additionally has a resolve method which will depend on the payout logic in c in the following way: if the winner is Alice, then the resolve method returns \$50, else it returns zero. The promise from Alice is such that the resolve method invokes the resolve method of Bob's promise to get value v and returns \$50 − v as the resolved amount.

There exists a protocol that can implement $\mathcal{F}_{\mathsf{SC}}$ in the $\mathcal{F}_{\mathsf{PPC}}$-hybrid model. The essential step is to compile a covenant into two associated promises (cf. Figure 8) and then execute them on $\mathcal{F}_{\mathsf{PPC}}$. We present this formally as follows.

Theorem 2. *There exists protocol Π_{SC} working in $\mathcal{F}_{\mathsf{PPC}}$-hybrid model that emulates the ideal functionality $\mathcal{F}_{\mathsf{SC}}^{\hat{\mathcal{L}}(\Delta)}$ for every $\Delta \in \mathbb{N}$. Note furthermore that the the protocol Π_{SC} requires only three invocations of $\mathcal{F}_{\mathsf{PPC}}$ to create a covenant.*

Similar to Theorem 1, Theorem 2 can be formally proved by constructing straightforward simulators to translate between covenant and associated

---

Promise Code $C_{B \to A}$

Construct(P, t, z):

1. if $P \notin \{\sigma'.user_L, \sigma'.user_R\}$, return $\bot$.
2. $\sigma \leftarrow \sigma'$.
3. $\sigma.\mathsf{payer} := P, \sigma.expiry := t' + 2\Delta + 5, \sigma.\mathsf{payee} := \{\sigma'.user_L, \sigma'.user_R\} \setminus P,$ $\sigma.resolve := 0, \sigma.valid := 0$.
4. return σ.

Enable(σ, P, t, x):

1. if $P \neq \sigma.\mathsf{payer}$, return $(\sigma, \bot)$.
2. if $t > \sigma.expiry$, return return $(\sigma, \bot)$.
3. if $\sigma.valid = 1$, return $(\sigma, \bot)$.
4. $\sigma.valid := 1$.
5. return $(\sigma, 1)$.

Finalize(σ, P, t, x):

1. if $P \neq \sigma.\mathsf{payer}$ and $P \neq \sigma.\mathsf{payee}$, return $(\sigma, \bot)$.
2. if $\sigma.valid = 0$, return $(\sigma, \bot)$.
3. $\sigma.resolve := \sigma.resolve_A$.
4. return $(\sigma, 1)$.

$f_1, \cdots, f_s$.

Promise Code $C_{A \to B}$

Construct(P, t, pid, z):

1. $\sigma \leftarrow \bot$.
2. $\sigma.\mathsf{payer} := A, \sigma.\mathsf{payee} := B, \sigma.end := 0, \sigma.resolve := 0, \sigma.pid := pid$.
3. return σ.

Finalize(σ, P, t, x):

1. if $\sigma.pid$ does not exist, return $(\sigma, \bot)$, else let $\sigma_{B \to A}$ be the storage of contract $\sigma.pid$.
2. if $\sigma_{B \to A}.valid = 0$, return $(\sigma, \bot)$.
3. if $P \neq \sigma.\mathsf{payer}$ and $P \neq \sigma.\mathsf{payee}$, return $(\sigma, \bot)$.
4. $\sigma.resolve := \sigma_{B \to A}.resolve_B$.
5. return $(\sigma, 1)$.

(a) Promise $C_{B \to A}$ from Bob.   (b) Promise $C_{A \to B}$ from Alice.

Fig. 8. The compiled promises from a covenant code C at time t' and constructor inputs y, where $\sigma' := C.\mathsf{Construct}(t', y)$. $C_{B \to A}$ will hard-code σ'.

promises. Note that the crucial point is to argue the rounds taken by the two worlds are identical. Due to space limitations, we provide the formal description of the protocol and its analysis in the full version of our work.

5   Conclusions

In this paper we present programmable payment channels (PPC), a new abstraction that enables payment channels to support lightweight applications encoded in the form of smart contracts. We show the usefulness of PPC by constructing several example applications. Our gas cost estimates show us that the application implementations are indeed practical on Ethereum (or other EVM chains). Finally, we also present a modified version of state channels and show how PPC can also implement state channel applications efficiently.

Acknowledgments. We thank Pedro Moreno-Sanchez for many useful discussions and insightful comments.

References

1. Hash time locked contracts - bitcoin wiki. https://en.bitcoin.it/wiki/Hash_Time_Locked_Contracts. Accessed Oct 20 2023

2. Payment channels - bitcoin wiki. https://en.bitcoin.it/wiki/Payment_channels. Accessed Oct 20 2023
3. Raiden. https://raiden.network/. Accessed Oct 20 2023
4. State channels - ethereum.org. https://ethereum.org/en/developers/docs/scaling/state-channels/. Accessed Oct 20 2023
5. Aumayr, L., et al.: Bitcoin-compatible virtual channels. In: 2021 IEEE Symposium on Security and Privacy (SP), pp. 901–918. IEEE (2021)
6. Breidenbach, L.: libsubmarine. https://github.com/lorenzb/libsubmarine (2018)
7. Breidenbach, L., Daian, P., Tramèr, F., Juels, A.: Enter the hydra: towards principled bug bounties and exploit-resistant smart contracts. In: 27th USENIX Security Symposium (USENIX Security 18), pp. 1335–1352. USENIX Association, Baltimore, MD (Aug 2018). https://www.usenix.org/conference/usenixsecurity18/presentation/breindenbach
8. Canetti, R.: Universally composable security: A new paradigm for cryptographic protocols. In: Proceedings 42nd IEEE Symposium on Foundations of Computer Science, pp. 136–145. IEEE (2001)
9. Canetti, R., Dodis, Y., Pass, R., Walfish, S.: Universally composable security with global setup. In: Vadhan, S.P. (ed.) TCC 2007. LNCS, vol. 4392, pp. 61–85. Springer, Heidelberg (2007). https://doi.org/10.1007/978-3-540-70936-7_4
10. Christodorescu, M., et al.: Universal payment channels: An interoperability platform for digital currencies (2021). https://doi.org/10.48550/ARXIV.2109.12194, https://arxiv.org/abs/2109.12194
11. Close, T.: Nitro protocol. Cryptology ePrint Archive (2019)
12. Close, T., Stewart, A.: Forcemove: an n-party state channel protocol. Magmo, White Paper (2018)
13. Coleman, J., Horne, L., Xuanji, L.: Counterfactual: generalized state channels. Accessed. https://l4.ventures/papers/statechannels.pdf 4 2019 (2018)
14. Decker, C., Wattenhofer, R.: A fast and scalable payment network with bitcoin duplex micropayment channels. In: Pelc, A., Schwarzmann, A.A. (eds.) Stabilization, Safety, and Security of Distributed Systems, pp. 3–18. Springer International Publishing, Cham (2015)
15. Dziembowski, S., Eckey, L., Faust, S., Hesse, J., Hostáková, K.: Multi-party virtual state channels. In: Ishai, Y., Rijmen, V. (eds.) Advances in Cryptology – EUROCRYPT 2019: 38th Annual International Conference on the Theory and Applications of Cryptographic Techniques, Darmstadt, Germany, May 19–23, 2019, Proceedings, Part I, pp. 625–656. Springer International Publishing, Cham (2019). https://doi.org/10.1007/978-3-030-17653-2_21
16. Dziembowski, S., Eckey, L., Faust, S., Malinowski, D.: Perun: virtual payment hubs over cryptocurrencies. In: 2019 IEEE Symposium on Security and Privacy (SP), pp. 106–123. IEEE (2019)
17. Dziembowski, S., Faust, S., Hostáková, K.: General state channel networks. In: Proceedings of the 2018 ACM SIGSAC Conference on Computer and Communications Security, pp. 949–966 (2018)
18. Goldreich, O.: Foundations of cryptography: volume 2, basic applications. Cambridge University Press (2009)
19. Gudgeon, L., Moreno-Sanchez, P., Roos, S., McCorry, P., Gervais, A.: SoK: Layer-two blockchain protocols. In: Bonneau, J., Heninger, N. (eds.) Financial Cryptography and Data Security: 24th International Conference, FC 2020 , Kota Kinabalu, Malaysia, February 10–14, 2020 Revised Selected Papers, pp. 201–226. Springer International Publishing, Cham (2020). https://doi.org/10.1007/978-3-030-51280-4_12

20. Khalil, R., Gervais, A.: Nocust-a non-custodial 2nd-layer financial intermediary (2018)
21. Lind, J., Naor, O., Eyal, I., Kelbert, F., Sirer, E.G., Pietzuch, P.R.: Teechain: a secure payment network with asynchronous blockchain access. In: Brecht, T., Williamson, C. (eds.) Proceedings of the 27th ACM Symposium on Operating Systems Principles, SOSP 2019, Huntsville, ON, Canada, October 27–30, 2019, pp. 63–79. ACM (2019)
22. Malavolta, G., Moreno-Sanchez, P., Kate, A., Maffei, M., Ravi, S.: Concurrency and privacy with payment-channel networks. In: Proceedings of the 2017 ACM SIGSAC Conference on Computer and Communications Security, pp. 455–471 (2017)
23. Malavolta, G., Moreno-Sanchez, P., Schneidewind, C., Kate, A., Maffei, M.: Anonymous multi-hop locks for blockchain scalability and interoperability. In: NDSS (2019)
24. McCorry, P., Buckland, C., Yee, B., Song, D.: Sok: Validating bridges as a scaling solution for blockchains. Cryptology ePrint Archive (2021)
25. Miller, A., Bentov, I., Bakshi, S., Kumaresan, R., McCorry, P.: Sprites and state channels: payment networks that go faster than lightning. In: Goldberg, I., Moore, T. (eds.) Financial Cryptography and Data Security: 23rd International Conference, FC 2019, Frigate Bay, St. Kitts and Nevis, February 18–22, 2019, Revised Selected Papers, pp. 508–526. Springer International Publishing, Cham (2019). https://doi.org/10.1007/978-3-030-32101-7_30
26. Minaei Bidgoli, M., Kumaresan, R., Zamani, M., Gaddam, S.: System and method for managing data in a database (Feb 2023). https://patents.google.com/patent/US11556909B2/
27. Poon, J., Dryja, T.: The bitcoin lightning network: Scalable off-chain instant payments. https://lightning.network/lightning-network-paper.pdf (2016) Accessed Oct 20 2023
28. Roos, S., Moreno-Sanchez, P., Kate, A., Goldberg, I.: Settling payments fast and private: efficient decentralized routing for path-based transactions. In: 25th Annual Network and Distributed System Security Symposium, NDSS 2018, San Diego, California, USA, February 18–21, 2018. The Internet Society (2018). https://wp.internetsociety.org/ndss/wp-content/uploads/sites/25/2018/02/ndss2018_09-3_Roos_paper.pdf
29. Tairi, E., Moreno-Sanchez, P., Maffei, M.: a^2l: anonymous atomic locks for scalability in payment channel hubs. In: 2021 IEEE Symposium on Security and Privacy (SP), pp. 1834–1851 (2021). https://doi.org/10.1109/SP40001.2021.00111
30. Thibault, L.T., Sarry, T., Hafid, A.S.: Blockchain scaling using rollups: a comprehensive survey. IEEE Access **10**, 93039–93054 (2022). https://doi.org/10.1109/ACCESS.2022.3200051
31. Todd, P.: [bitcoin-development] near-zero fee transactions with hub-and-spoke micropayments. https://lists.linuxfoundation.org/pipermail/bitcoin-dev/2014-December/006988.html (2014). Accessed Oct 20 2023
32. Yang, Y., Minaei, M., Raghuraman, S., Kumaresan, R., Le, D.V., Zamani, M.: Programmable payment channels. Cryptology ePrint Archive, Paper 2023/347 (2023). https://eprint.iacr.org/2023/347
33. Yee, B., Song, D., McCorry, P., Buckland, C.: Shades of finality and layer 2 scaling. arXiv preprint arXiv:2201.07920 (2022)

Fair Private Set Intersection Using Smart Contracts

Sepideh Avizheh$^{(\boxtimes)}$ and Reihaneh Safavi-Naini

University of Calgary, Alberta, Canada
`sepideh.avizheh1@ucalgary.ca`

Abstract. A mutual private set intersection protocol (PSI) allows two parties to find the intersection of their private sets without leaking any other information. A mutual PSI protocol achieves complete fairness if a malicious party cannot disadvantage the honest party by using an early abort of the protocol. It has been proved that it is impossible to achieve complete fairness in plain two-party computation, and ensuring fairness needs the inclusion of a trusted third party (TTP). Smart contracts have been used to implement trusted computation in cryptographic protocols. In this paper, we consider fair mutual PSI protocols that use a smart contract as the TTP. We first show that it is impossible to achieve complete fairness by using a smart contract as a TTP in two-party mutual PSI, and consider the (weaker) goal of "fairness with coin compensation". We design two protocols, Π and Π^*, that achieve this notion of fairness using a smart contract as the TTP. The protocol Π is a redesign of a fair optimistic PSI protocol (Dong et al., DBSec 2013) that replaces TTP with a smart contract. The protocol Π^* is a more efficient protocol that replaces some of the zero-knowledge proofs of Π with *proof of misbehaviour* that enables the smart contract to correctly identify the dishonest party and compensate the honest party with coin. We prove the security and privacy of the protocols in an extension of the ideal/real paradigm for non-monolithic adversaries and provide a proof-of-concept implementation of the smart contract in both protocols in a local Ethereum network. We evaluate the performance of the protocols in terms of gas cost for optimistic and pessimistic executions, compare their performance, and discuss our results and directions for future work.

Keywords: Mutual PSI · Optimistic fairness · Smart contracts · Oblivious polynomial evaluation · Proof of misbehavior

1 Introduction

In a two-party *mutual private set intersection (PSI)* protocol Alice and Bob, each with a private set, engage in a protocol, at the end of which each party learns the intersection of the two sets and nothing else. In *unilateral (one-way)* PSI however, only one party learns the intersection, and the other party learns nothing. Mutual PSI protocols have diverse applications including in healthcare

© The Author(s), under exclusive license to Springer Nature Switzerland AG 2024
C. Pöpper and L. Batina (Eds.): ACNS 2024, LNCS 14585, pp. 74–104, 2024.
https://doi.org/10.1007/978-3-031-54776-8_4

systems, government and law enforcement applications, social networks, and e-commerce [7,11,17,41,42]. As a concrete example, consider a setting where two stores attempt to increase the number of their customers and agree to offer a discount to customers who have made purchases from both. Checking this information at the time of purchase will reveal the identity of customers of each store to the other. Using mutual PSI will allow the discount to be issued correctly, and no other information be leaked.

A mutual PSI protocol is *fair* if a malicious party cannot put the honest party in a disadvantaged position, for example, prevent the honest party from learning the intersection after learning it themselves. *Complete fairness* guarantees that if the malicious party learns the intersection, the honest party will also learn it. Most existing mutual PSI protocols [7,17,41,42] guarantee *security with abort*, and not complete fairness, allowing the corrupted party to abort without letting the honest party learning the result. For efficiency reasons, in this paper, we only consider protocols that achieve fairness in a constant number of rounds and exclude protocols such as [10,28,39,43] in which the number of rounds depends on the input size.

Cleve's [13] result on the impossibility of fair computation in two-party coin-tossing schemes, when applied to PSI, implies that full fairness is not achievable in the basic two-party setting. An alternative is to relax the notion of fairness to *partial fairness* where fairness fails with probability $1/p$ for an arbitrary polynomial p in security parameter [13,14,29,50], or *optimistic fairness* where a trusted third party (TTP) that is sometimes referred to as the *the arbiter,* ensures that the honest party always obtains the correct protocol result irrespective of the malicious party deviations from the protocol including early abort.

Using smart Contracts as TTP. A smart contract is a trusted program that runs on the consensus-based computer of a blockchain, and can be programmed to perform a trusted computation. Smart contracts have been widely used in cryptographic protocols [22,23,45,46,49] to implement a TTP. Smart contracts provide an attractive method of implementing TTP in optimistic protocols and can also serve to automate other processes when the protocol is deployed. For example, smart contracts can initiate negotiations between parties, store cryptographic values, as well as providing support for cryptocurrencies and transactions.

In this paper, we propose the first PSI protocol that uses a smart contract to implement the TTP. This however requires careful design because smart contracts are *transparent programs* that cannot hold secrets, and so all their stored data are public. A smart contract also cannot establish a private channel to any entity in the system. A smart contract also incurs costs, and so its execution and storage costs must be minimized. These constraints severely restrict the application of the smart contract as the TTP for providing fairness. Fair PSI protocols that use a TTP [7,18–21] and achieve complete fairness, crucially use the ability of TTP to hold private values which will be provided to the honest party if the protocol aborts. This will not be possible for a smart contract. The protocols in [36,37] use the TTP private computation for dispute resolution, and also use the TTP as a processor to help with the computation.

Our Work. We first provide an argument that shows that it is not possible to achieve complete fairness in two-party PSI by using a smart contract as the TTP, and propose to use *coin-compensated fairness* in which fairness is achieved by requiring an initial coin deposit from one (or more parties), and later compensating the honest party with coins when the dishonest party who learns the result and aborts is identified (e.g. by transferring to the honest party, the coins of the dishonest party together with the honest party's deposited coins, if any). We design a 4-round protocol Π, that achieves fairness by (always) correctly identifying the dishonest party using a dispute resolution phase. The protocol re-designs the PSI protocol of Dong et al. [21] (referred to as DCCR protocol) that achieves complete fairness using a TTP that can hold secrets. Noting that the dispute resolution phase is effectively an identification mechanism for the dishonest party, we improve the computational efficiency of the protocol by replacing ZKP in round 2 with the notion of Proof of Misbehavior (PoM) [22], and reducing a vector of m ZKPs in round 3 to only one ZKP with PoM. A PoM does not verify the correctness of each message but provides sufficient information to the honest party that can be used as evidence in the dispute-resolution phase, to prove the misbehavior of the dishonest party to the smart contract. Our PoM construction localizes the incorrect step of the computation that can be efficiently verified by the smart contract. The two protocols are the first protocols that ensure coin-compensated fairness using only smart contracts where the smart contract's computation complexity is $O(1)$ (i.e. constant number of modular exponentiations). The main challenge in designing Π and Π^* is to ensure privacy with respect to both parties *and* the publicly visible smart contract operations, in particular when PoM-based protocol is used to identify the dishonest party. We prove the security and privacy of both protocols using simulation-based security in the non-monolithic adversary framework of [3,36] that captures security and privacy against the malicious party, as well as privacy against the smart contract. We implemented the computation of the smart contract in Π and Π^* to estimate and compare the *gas* cost when the protocol runs on the Ethereum blockchain. More details are below.

Using a Smart Contract to Implement TTP. In Sect. 4.1, we outline an argument that shows that a smart contract that implements the TTP in a PSI protocol cannot provide any additional information to the parties after the protocol is completed, and so if complete fairness can be achieved by employing a smart contract, Cleve's result will be contradicted. This motivates us to use the notion of coin-compensated fairness that was introduced by Bentov-Kumaresan [6] for lottery protocols. Coin-compensated fairness has been widely used as a replacement for complete fairness [4,40,45–48]. Coin-compensated fairness uses blockchain's native coin to compensate the party that will be in a disadvantaged position and provides an attractive solution to overcome the impossibility of complete fairness. The approach assumes the compensation amount correctly reflects the potential losses of the honest party using factors such as the value of the lost data, and the costs of running the protocol.

Constructions. In Sect. 5, we propose protocol Π that starts with DCCR and modifies its messages assuming TTP is implemented as a smart contract, and achieves coin-compensated fairness while ensuring privacy for the input sets with respect to the SC (public). In Π, the party that starts the protocol is Alice, and the party that learns the result first is Bob. At the start of the protocol, Bob deposits the agreed amount of coins, p, to the smart contract. The coins will be used to compensate Alice if Bob aborts the protocol after learning the intersection. Honest execution of the protocol has four rounds and dispute resolution adds two more rounds to the protocol. The protocol uses Oblivious Polynomial Evaluation (OPE) for computing the intersection, and by using zero-knowledge proofs (ZKP) in the first three rounds, allows the parties to verify the correctness of the exchanged messages. In all rounds, the two parties store information in the smart contract, but the contract remains passive, it does not perform any computation. In the dispute resolution phase, Alice claims that Bob has aborted to reveal the required information. The smart contract verifies the claim using its stored information. It is also possible that Bob cannot reveal the required information because they did not receive Alice's message in its previous round. In both cases, the smart contract can correctly decide and identify the party that has misbehaved. The smart contract's computation will be a constant number of modular exponentiations.

In Π, the parties' computations are high as they have to generate and verify the zero-knowledge proofs in the first three rounds of the protocols. In Π^*, generating the ZKP in the second and third rounds is replaced by Proof of Misbehavior (PoM), hence improving the efficiency of parties P_1 and P_2. Using PoM also allows us to instantiate the commitment in the second round with hash-based commitments which further improve the computations of the parties. The protocol Π^* is described in Sect. 6.

PoM is a protocol between *two parties* P_1, P_2 where at least one of the two is honest, and an honest verifier. In a PoM, party P_1 provides a proof π_1 for the correctness of a statement to party P_2, and stores a *proof digest* with the verifier. The proof digest is *hiding* and leaks a negligible amount of information about the proof to the verifier. P_2 can verify the correctness of the proof, and if the verification fails, can generate a second proof π_2 that, together with the proof digest and the published values, will prove to the verifier that P_1 has not followed the protocol ("misbehaved"). PoM must satisfy *completeness* and *soundness*. Completeness ensures that an honest party *can always generate π_2 if there is a misbehavior,* and soundness requires that a cheating party can not generate a valid proof π_2 to frame an honest party.

We use two PoMs in Π^*, in both of which the two parties will be the provers and the SC will be the verifier. The first PoM will replace the ZKP in round 2 of Π. The proof π_1 will be constructed as the computation trace of the oblivious polynomial evaluation (OPE), and the proof digest is the root of a Merkle tree that will be constructed on the computation trace. The proof and the digest will be provided to P_1 and the SC, respectively. In the last round of the protocol, P_1 can verify the proof π_1 by replicating the computation, and if notices discrepancies, will generate a proof π_2 that allows the SC to verify the claim of P_1. The SC's computation will depend on the location of the error in the computation trace, and will consist of a single modular multiplication if the computation has been performed incorrectly, or will require verifying a ZKP if the input correctness is challenged. The second PoM is in round 3 and is used by P_1. We use one aggregate ZKP in round 3 of the protocol (instead of the original vector of m re-encryption ZKPs) to efficiently show the correctness of the re-encrypted ciphertexts. The aggregation will come together with a PoM that proves the correctness of the aggregate computation and is constructed using the trace of aggregate computation as described above. P_2 can verify the correctness of the aggregation, and prove to SC if P_1 has deviated from the protocol. Using PoMs does not add any additional rounds to the protocol. The complexity analysis of Π and Π^* are in Sect. 7.

Using PoM to delay the correctness proof to a later stage (i.e. dispute resolution), could potentially leak information, and this prevents us from replacing ZKP in the first message of Π (that proves the correct evaluation of coefficients of a polynomial) with PoM. This is because a dishonest P_1 can learn the items in the P_2's set by setting all coefficients of the polynomial to zero.

Simulation-Based Security. We prove the security and privacy of Π and Π^* using simulation-based security with non-monolithic adversaries [3] considering a Ledger ideal functionality to capture the transfer of coins. The non-monolithic adversary framework was introduced in [36] to capture the security of cryptographic protocols when there are two or more non-colluding adversaries with distinct goals. We consider two adversaries that capture, (i) the behavior of the dishonest party, and (ii) leakage to the public of the information that is seen by the smart contract. In DCCR, the TTP is assumed to be semi-honest and the protocol is designed to ensure that negligible information is leaked to the TTP. By using PoM, we modify the dispute resolution protocol and need to show our protocols still achieve the required privacy guarantee against the smart contract. We must show that by replacing the ZKP with PoM in the security proofs, the simulator (that has oracle access to the code of the cheating party) can still extract the input in all cases without using the extractability of ZKP. We achieve this by using the computation trace and the simulator's access to the random oracle ideal functionality. This approach was first used by [22] and later in [3]. Our security model uses a PSI ideal functionality that follows [21,36], an abstraction of blockchain that follows the approach of [22], and models coin-compensated fairness. Security proof is in the random oracle model and is done by designing a simulator for malicious parties, and an independent simulator for the smart contract to ensure both the security of the PSI, and privacy against the smart contract (and hence the public). The proof outline is in Sects. 5 and 6 and the complete proof is given in the full version of paper.

Implementation. We provide a proof-of-concept implementation of the smart contract in Protocols Π and Π^*. We have implemented a CryptoLib library in Solidity for the required cryptographic primitives of SC that implements the Elliptic Curve (EC) variant of Elgamal encryption, Pedersen commitment, the necessary zero-knowledge proofs of knowledge over curve $Secp256k1$, and the Merkle proof verification. The SC algorithms are given in the full version of the paper. We give the gas cost of SC in protocols Π and Π^*, for different set sizes n and m of party P_1 and P_2, respectively, for (i) *optimistic execution* where both parties are honest, and (ii) *pessimistic execution* where one party misbehaves. Our experiments show that as m increases, the gas cost of SC in Π^* is [17%-32%] higher than running SC in Π, and as n increases it is 29% higher than running SC in Π. The gas cost of running SC in Π is independent of n, but it grows linearly to $log(n)$ in protocol Π^*. The gas cost of the pessimistic execution in both protocols is dominated by the gas cost of the SC in the first four rounds of the protocol when m increases. Therefore, the storage cost of the SC limits the value of m to be much less than n.

Organization of the Paper. Section 2 gives the related work and Sect. 3 describes the preliminaries. Section 4 is model and security definitions. Sections 5 and 6 present protocol Π and Π^*, respectively. Section 7 is on the complexity analysis and comparison, Sect. 8 is on implementation, and Sect. 9 concludes the paper.

1.1   Other Coin-Compensated PSI

A recent online preprint [1] considers coin-compensated fairness for PSI and uses an SC for different functions, including verifying the correctness of messages. An external auditor is used to find the misbehaving parties in case the verification is not passed. We give an overview of the paper and compare it with our work. More details are in the full version of the paper.

The paper proposes two PSI schemes for two or more parties: (i) Justitia, and (ii) Anesidora. Justitia achieves coin-compensated fairness where the honest party either receives the set intersection result, or coins if there is an abort. The protocol is proven secure against malicious adversaries. Anesidora uses Justitia as a subroutine and is proven secure in a mixed model of malicious and rational adversaries, using an appropriate incentivization mechanism. We compare our work with Justitia which achieves coin-compensated fairness, when the number of parties is two.

Justitia uses a smart contract *and an external third-party auditor* (semi-honest) to correctly identify the cheating party and requires both parties to make deposits. The third-party auditor needs to learn the private (PRF) keys of parties to find the misbehaving party, and hence it cannot be directly implemented by the smart contract. Also, the smart contract *performs computation during the correct execution of the protocol.* Justitia follows the security model of [26] and achieves coin-compensated fairness and privacy in the presence of one active adversary, *or* a passive dealer (i.e. one of the two-party with the assigned role as a dealer), passive auditor, *or* passive public (which is the smart contract).

We use only a smart contract to achieve correctness and coin-compensated fairness, and smart contract computation is only during dispute resolution and is constant independent of the set sizes. We use the approach of [3] to define security and privacy of computation against parties, and privacy against smart contract in a unified framework, and obtain the security guarantee against an active adversary in both stages of the protocol: result computation, and dispute resolution.

2   Related Work

PSI Protocols. There is a vast amount of research in this area (e.g. [5,9,25,33,44, 52,53,56]). The main approaches are (i) protocols that are based on oblivious polynomial evaluation, OPE, [12,24,42] and (ii) protocols based on oblivious psuedorandom function evaluation, OPRF [15,16,30,34,35,44].

Mutual PSI Protocols. [7,11,17,32,41,42,51] ensure both parties receive the intersection result, but all the mentioned schemes assume that the adversary does not prematurely abort.

Fair PSI Protocols. The impossibility of fair PSI [13,27] implies that one has to use a relaxed notion of fairness such as partial fairness where fairness fails with a bounded probability [13,14,29,50], or optimistic fairness where the existence of a trusted third party (TTP) or arbiter is assumed (leading to what is known as *optimistic protocols*) [7]. In an optimistic PSI protocol [7,19–21], the TTP (or arbiter) ensures that the honest party obtains the correct protocol result when the malicious party deviates from the protocol, including the early abort.

Fair PSI Protocols that Use a TTP and proceed in a constant number of rounds have been considered in [1,7,18–21,36,37]. The TTP in these protocols can either participate *only* in the dispute resolution phase [7,18–21] and ensures optimistic fairness, or to participate in both the computation of PSI (a smart contract) and dispute resolution (a smart contract and an external third party auditor) [1] and achieves coin-compensated fairness, or the TTP participates in the computation of the intersection [36,37] and ensures complete fairness.

Coin-Compensated Fairness. The notion of coin-compensated fairness (aka. fairness with penalties) was introduced by [6] which allows an adversarial party to abort but in that case, it is forced to pay a predefined monetary penalty to every other party that did not receive the output. Coin-compensated fairness has been used in further research such as [4,40,46,48]. All the above protocols are symmetric, in that, all parties have to make a deposit and all parties achieve fairness with penalties. In a parallel work, [1] proposed coin-compensated multi-party PSI where all parties are required to make a deposit and it uses the smart contract and an external third-party auditor to ensure the correct transfer of funds. In contrast, our work is a two-party PSI and requires that only one party makes a deposit and ensures fairness with compensation assuming only an efficient smart contract as a TTP.

3   Preliminaries and Notations

We use P_1 and A interchangeably, where P_1 holds the set $X = \{x_1, ..., x_n\}$, and we use P_2 and B interchangeably, where P_2 holds set $Y = \{y_1, ..., y_m\}$. $|\cdot|$ represents the size of a set.

Commitment scheme has two algorithms $\{commit, open\}$. $commit$ is a probabilistic function that is used by the committer to commit to an input x and outputs $(c, d) \leftarrow commit(x)$ where c is the commitment to k, and d is the decommitment value. $open$ is a deterministic boolean function which is used by the receiver to verify that x is a correct opening for commitment c. We require the scheme to be hiding and binding.

Merkle trees are binary trees that are constructed over a sequence of data elements $x = (x_1, ..., x_n)$ using algorithm $Mtree$. The leaf nodes of a Merkle tree are the hash of the elements x. To commit to a sequence of elements we consider a randomized Merkle tree where each leaf node x_i is concatenated with unique uniformly sampled randomness $d_i \in \{0,1\}^\kappa$, i.e. $x'_i = x_i || d_i$. The commitment to x is comprised of $r_x = root(Mtree(x'))$ and $d = (d_1, ..., d_n)$. The randomized Merkle root commitment is computationally hiding in the random oracle model and is computationally binding assuming either the committer or receiver is honest.

Additive homomorphic encryption is a public key encryption scheme with the following properties: (1) given two ciphertexts $E_{pk}(m_1)$, $E_{pk}(m_2)$, $E_{pk}(m_1 + m_2) = E_{pk}(m_1) \cdot E_{pk}(m_2)$; where pk is the public key used to encrypt the messages m_1 and m_2. (2) given a ciphertext $E_{pk}(m_1)$ and a constant c, $E_{pk}(c \cdot m_1) = E_{pk}(m_1)^c$.

Symmetric encryption scheme consists of three algorithms: $k = Gen(\kappa)$ receives the security parameter κ and generates a key. The encryption algorithm takes the key k and the message m and returns the ciphertext $C = E_k(m)$. The decryption algorithm takes the key k and the ciphertext C and returns the message m, $m = D_k(C)$. We consider an IND-CPA secure encryption scheme.

Zero knowledge proof (ZK proof) allows a prover to prove the validity of a statement x to a verifier without leaking any other information. Prover shows that it knows a witness ω without revealing it such that $(x, \omega) \in \mathcal{R}$, where $\mathcal{R}$ is a relation. A ZK proof should satisfy correctness, soundness, and zero-knowledge properties.

The Freedman-Nissim-Pinkas protocol (FNP) [24] is a single output PSI protocol that is based on Oblivious Polynomial Evaluation (OPE). It uses an additively homomorphic encryption scheme (Paillier cryptosystem). The protocol proceeds as follows: (i) Party P_1 chooses a private public key pair (sk, pk) for an additive homomorphic scheme. (ii) P_1, constructs a polynomial $Q(y)$ whose roots are the elements in the set X, using the formula $Q(y) = \Pi_{i=1}^n(y - x_i) = \Sigma_{i=0}^n d_i y^i$, encrypts coefficients d_i for all $i \in \{0, n\}$, and sends all $E_{pk}(d_i)$ to P_2.

(iii) P_2 evaluates the polynomial $Q()$ on the elements of its set Y and computes $E_{pk}(r_j Q(y_j) + y_j)$ for each $y_j \in Y$ using the homomorphic properties of the underlying encryption scheme, where r_j is a random value. Note that if y_j is in the intersection $X \cap Y$ then it is the root of polynomial $Q(y)$ and hence $Q(y_j) = 0$. Otherwise, $Q(y_j)$ is a random value. (iv) P_1 decrypts each ciphertext $E_{pk}(r_j Q(y_j) + y_j)$ and obtains either $y_j \in X$ if y_j is in $X \cap Y$ or a random value otherwise. This protocol is secure against semi-honest adversaries.

The DCCR PSI protocol [21] is a mutual PSI protocol that ensures complete fairness assuming the existence of a semi-honest arbiter which can be involved if there is a dispute between parties. The protocol has two phases: intersection and dispute resolution. The intersection phase is run between parties P_1 and P_2 over a point-to-point channel. The dispute resolution is initiated by P_1 and used only if P_2 aborts in the fourth round of the protocol. Please see the details of the scheme in Fig. 2 (b). The protocol is based on the OPE scheme (based on Elgamal encryption) proposed by FNP with some subtle changes. They consider that (i) $|X| > |Y|$ to protect against leakage of the polynomial to party P_2 and require that P_1 ensures $|X| > |Y|$. (ii) The parties P_1 and P_2 are malicious (one of two). Therefore, ZK proof is used at each stage of the protocol to show that they are following the protocol correctly. (iii) The $E_{pk}(r_j Q(y_j) + y_j)$ is computed in the exponent of base g (a generator of a certain group), that is, $E_{pk}(g^{r_j Q(y_j)+y_j})$ to allow using efficient ZK proof and also obtaining additive homomorphic encryption using Elgamal encryption scheme. (iv) They consider a blinding factor r_j for each polynomial evaluation $E_{pk}(r'_j Q(y_j) + r_j + y_j)$ to hide the result temporarily from the party who has the public key Pk since it can decrypt the ciphertext and learn the result in an incorrect point of time.

Blockchain and Smart Contracts. Blockchain is a distributed ledger technology that stores transactions in a growing chain of blocks that are linked to each other through a cryptographic hash. Each block encapsulates a number of transactions (unit of operations performed in the system) [54]. If the number of honest parties who run the blockchain is more than 50 percent of the whole network, the ledger ensures immutability. Smart contract is a piece of computer program that is run on top of a blockchain. The nodes who are responsible for storing and updating the blockchain, execute the programs and reach agreement on their execution results.

4   Fair PSI Using Smart Contracts

In this section, we first show that complete fairness is impossible to be achieved in the smart contract-based setting where the smart contract is transparent and cannot hold any private key. Then we give the security model by capturing the notion of coin-compensated fairness.

4.1   Smart Contract as the TTP in Optimistic Mutual PSI

An important property of mutual PSI protocols is fairness. Cleve's results [13] show that complete fairness without honest majority is not possible and so it is impossible to achieve complete fairness in plain two-party mutual PSI. Optimistic PSIs however, provide correct output to the honest party by storing private values (e.g. the protocol output) that will be provided to the honest party if they are put in a disadvantaged position (because of the early abort of the dishonest party). Smart contracts however are transparent programs and cannot hold secrets. A smart contract can be seen as a third transparent processor that is connected transparently to the other two parties. Consider a mutual PSI protocol where P_1 and P_2 have their sets as their private inputs and the smart contract is used as the TTP. At the completion (or termination because of the early abort) of the protocol, P_1 and P_2 receive their corresponding private results and have *direct access to computation and stored values of the SC*. Thus, in the case of early abort, SC cannot provide any extra value to the honest party that was not known to them before. This informal argument can be formalized to prove that *it is impossible to achieve complete fairness for mutual PSI when using SC as the TTP* (see Full version of the paper).

The smart contract however can be used to verify statements and correct opening of commitments, and so detect malicious behaviour. This detection ability can be used to achieve *coin-compensated fairness* where the honest party who has not received the result will be compensated with coins. Coin-compensated fairness, although weaker than complete fairness, is an attractive approach in particular when one can estimate the value of the result to the parties. We use this notion of fairness in our protocols.

4.2   Security Model

We use the ideal world/real world paradigm [8] where the security proof simulates the behavior of real-world adversaries in the ideal world in which a trusted entity (ideal functionality) performs the task at hand. In the real world, each party is modeled by an interactive probabilistic polynomial time Turing machine (ITM) that interacts with other parties. The adversary $\mathcal{A}$ in the real world corrupts a set of parties and affects their execution. We consider a static adversary in which the parties are corrupted at the beginning of the protocol run. To capture the effects of the other protocols that coexist we assume the adversary receives an auxiliary input at the beginning of the protocol. In the ideal world the *ideal functionality* $\mathcal{F}$ interacts with dummy protocol parties and performs the task at hand. The ideal functionality captures the required security properties of the protocol π. The ideal adversary is called simulator Sim, which simulates the behavior of the real-world adversary in the ideal world and interacts with the ideal functionality through its interfaces. We consider an Environment $\mathcal{Z}$ which gives inputs to parties and receives their outputs.

Hybrid World. We use a hybrid real world where some of the cryptographic primitives/protocols are replaced by their corresponding ideal functionalities, $\mathcal{F}_1, ..., \mathcal{F}_n$, and using [8] still maintain security. We consider a stand-alone execution. We assume non-concurrent invocation of the subroutines.

Non-monolithic Adversary. In a standard simulation-based security framework the adversary is monolithic, a single entity can corrupt a set of parties and coordinate their attacks (i.e. parties can collude with each other). The need for modeling non-monolithic adversaries has been motivated by Kamara et al. [36] in the server-aided computation setting. In this paper, to define both security and privacy we need to use a non-monolithic adversarial model. We consider two adversaries, (i) an adversary $\mathcal{A}$ who corrupts one of the parties maliciously and gets access to its inputs and outputs and (ii) a semi-honest adversary, which is called smart contract adversary $\mathcal{A}_{sc}$, and models the observers of the SC. $\mathcal{A}_{sc}$ only sees the information that are made public to SC. We follow [3] that extends Kamara et al. model [36] to two non-monolithic adversaries and defines smart contract privacy.

Ledger Functionality $\mathcal{L}$ [22]. To transfer coins between parties and support contracts that lock coins, we consider the simplified ledger of [22] that provides the basic properties of a cryptocurrency. $\mathcal{L}$ has three interfaces: *update* that is called by the environment to update the balance of parties P_i; *freeze* is used to transfer p coins from one party to a contract where they are locked; *unfreeze* is used to transfer the coins from a contract to the balance of a party. In [22] this functionality is accessible to ideal functionalities only (i.e. the Judge ideal functionality), but in our protocol $\mathcal{L}$ is accessible to SC and ideal functionalities (Please see the full version of the paper for the details).

Random Oracle Functionality $\mathcal{H}$ [31]. $\mathcal{H}$ responds to all queries with uniformly random sampled values $r \leftarrow \{0,1\}^k$, and outputs the same value for the same query. All query-response pairs are stored in the set Q.

Communication Model. We consider a synchronous communication model the same as the one mentioned in [22] where the protocol proceeds in rounds and all parties are always aware of the current round [40] (synchrony can be emulated by allocating long enough round time considering bounded delay channels [38]).

Security and Privacy. The protocol execution has two cases. First, when both parties are honest, and the second, when one party is dishonest and the execution includes the dispute resolution protocol. Our security and privacy definition must capture security of computation against the party that can deviate from the protocol, and privacy of the input sets of parties, except the intersection, as well as privacy of both sets and the intersection against the smart contract in both types of execution. The parties' inputs/outputs and views are different from the smart contract's input/output and view and thus we follow [3] that the use Kamara et al. [36] framework of non-monolithic adversaries and model smart contract, and the participants as *non-colluding, non-cooperative independent* adversaries. The smart contract is modeled as a semi-honest entity, and the parties can deviate arbitrarily from the protocol (one of the two parties).

Definition 1. *Let Π be a protocol that realizes a smart contract based n-party functionality $\mathcal{F}$. Let $H \subseteq [n]$ be the set of honest parties, I_c and I_{nc} be the set of corrupted parties, where $I_{nc} \subseteq [n]$ denote the set of non-colluding parties, $I_c \subset [n]$ denote the set of colluding parties, and assume all subsets (H, I_c,* and I_{nc}) are pairwise disjoint, and let SC denote the semi-honest smart contract. Let ADV be an adversary structure that specifies the set of adversaries and their behaviors (e.g., semi-honest, non-cooperative, etc.). We say that Π (I_{nc}, I_c, ADV)-securely realizes $\mathcal{F}$, if for any PPT adversary $\mathcal{A}_i \in \{I_{nc}, I_c\}$ and smart contract adversary $\mathcal{A}_{sc}$, there exists PPT transformations Sim_i and Sim_{sc} respectively such that the following hold for negligible functions ϵ_1 and ϵ_2 in the security parameter.

Security: $|Pr[Real_{\Pi,\mathcal{A},Z}^{(i)}(\kappa, x) = 1] - Pr[Ideal_{\mathcal{F},Sim,Z}^{(i)}(\kappa, x) = 1]| \leq \epsilon_1$

Where $Real_{\Pi,\mathcal{A},Z}^{(i)}(\kappa, x)$ denotes the view of the adversary $\mathcal{A}_i$ and the output of the honest parties when running protocol Π; $Ideal_{\mathcal{F},Sim,Z}^{(i)}$ is the view of malicious parties and output of honest parties when running the ideal process computing $\mathcal{F}$; and $\mathcal{A} = \{\mathcal{A}_1, ..., \mathcal{A}_m\}$ and $Sim = \{Sim_1, ..., Sim_m\}$.

Smart Contract Privacy:

$|Pr[Real_{\Pi,\mathcal{A},\mathcal{A}_{sc},z}^{(j)}(\kappa, x) = 1] - Pr[Ideal_{\mathcal{F},Sim,Sim_{sc},z}^{(j)}(\kappa, x) = 1]| \leq \epsilon_2$

Where $Real_{\Pi,\mathcal{A},\mathcal{A}_{sc},z}^{(j)}$ denotes the view of the adversary $\mathcal{A}_{sc}$ and output of all other parties when running protocol Π in the presence of adversary $\mathcal{A}_j$; and $Ideal_{\mathcal{F},Sim,Sim_{sc},z}^{(j)}$ is the view of the semi-honest parties and output of all other parties when running the ideal process computing $\mathcal{F}$ in the presence of adversary Sim_j. Here κ is the security parameter, x is the set of outputs provided to all parties, and z is the set of auxiliary inputs provided to all parties.

4.3   Ideal Functionality for Coin-Compensated PSI

We consider an ideal functionality $\mathcal{F}_{PSI}^{\mathcal{L}}$ which ensures coin-compensated fairness for P_1 and complete fairness for P_2. $\mathcal{F}_{PSI}^{\mathcal{L}}$ captures the following properties:

Correctness. If parties P_1 and P_2 use their inputs X and Y respectively in the protocol, if they find the intersection $X \cap Y$, it is indeed correct.

Privacy. P_1 and P_2 do not learn anything beyond the intersection result[1].

Smart Contract Privacy. The smart contract does not learn anything about the elements in X and Y.

Fairness with Coin Compensation. Party P_1 either learns the intersection result or gets a monetary compensation, whereas P_2 receives the intersection result, or none of them learns anything.

Figure 1 shows the description of the ideal functionality $\mathcal{F}_{PSI}^{\mathcal{L}}$ which interacts with the ledger functionality $\mathcal{L}$. $\mathcal{F}_{PSI}^{\mathcal{L}}$ first freezes the p coins provided by P_2 in $\mathcal{L}$ and receives the inputs X' and Y' from both parties P_1 and P_2. The inputs X' and Y' can be equal to $\perp$ which means that one party aborts early in the protocol. In this case $\mathcal{F}_{PSI}^{\mathcal{L}}$ sends $\perp$ to everyone and terminates the protocol. If X' and Y' are not $\perp$ then $\mathcal{F}_{PSI}^{\mathcal{L}}$ informs everyone that it has received the

---

[1] We follow DCCR and consider the parties know the size of both sets and they can confirm $|x| > |y|$.

inputs from party P_1 and P_2. $\mathcal{F}_{PSI}^{\mathcal{L}}$ then computes the intersection denoted by O. We let the functionality send the result to the simulator Sim first and then send it to parties based on the decision made by Sim. This is to capture the fact that the malicious party who learns the intersection result can affect the protocol run. Sim returns b_1 and b_2, where $b_i \in \{\diamond, \perp\}$ and $\perp$ denotes abort and $\diamond$ denotes non-abort. $\mathcal{F}_{PSI}^{\mathcal{L}}$ distributes the coins based on b_1 and b_2 according to the conditions stated in Fig. 1. If both b_1 and b_2 are $\perp$, then none of the parties have learned anything, and the p coins are returned to P_2. If b_1 is $\perp$ which shows that P_1 should not receive the intersection result, $\mathcal{F}_{PSI}^{\mathcal{L}}$ unfreezes the coins in favor of P_1. Otherwise, P_1 receives the result and $\mathcal{F}_{PSI}^{\mathcal{L}}$ returns the p coins to P_2. In sum, P_2 always receives the intersection result no matter what the malicious party does after learning the output, but P_1 only learns the result if P_2 acts honestly. In all the above cases, we let SC learn the decision of the simulator Sim for party P_1 (which captures the fact that this information is public and can be learned by SC when the protocol is run).

Functionality $\mathcal{F}_{PSI}^{\mathcal{L}}$

Ideal functionality $\mathcal{F}_{PSI}^{\mathcal{L}}$ is available to P_1, P_2, and SC. P_1 has input X consisting of n distinct elements $X = \{x_1, ..., x_n\}$ where $x_i \in U$; P_2 has input Y consisting of m distinct elements $Y = \{y_1, ..., y_m\}$ where $y_i \in U$ and $n > m$ and it also has p coins. SC has no input. $\mathcal{F}_{PSI}^{\mathcal{L}}$ interacts with the global ledger functionality $\mathcal{L}$.

–Upon receiving $(Coins, \quad p)$ from P_2 send $(Coins, \quad p)$ to Sim_{SC}, send $(freeze, id, P_2, p)$ to $\mathcal{L}$ and wait to receive $(frozen, id, P_2, p)$ from $\mathcal{L}$. Otherwise, terminate.

– Upon receiving $(Input, id, X')$, where $X' \in \{X, \perp\}$, from P_1 store the message and if $X' \neq \perp$ send $(InputReceived, id, P_1)$ to everyone. Otherwise, terminate.

– Upon receiving message $(Input, id, Y')$, where $Y' \in \{Y, \perp\}$, from P_2 store Y and if $Y' \neq \perp$ send $(InputReceived, id, P_2)$ to everyone. Then compute $O = X' \cap Y'$, send $(Result, id, O)$ to Sim and $(Result, id)$ to Sim_{SC}. Upon receiving $(Output, id, b_1, b_2)$ from Sim, where $b_1, b_2 \in \{\diamond, \perp\}$ act as below:

- If $b_1 = b_2 = \perp$ send $\perp$ to both parties and $\perp$ to Sim_{SC}, unfreeze p coins in favor of P_2 by sending $(unfreeze, id, P_2, p)$ to $\mathcal{L}$. Upon receiving $(unfrozen, id, P_2, p)$ from $\mathcal{L}$ terminate.
- If $b_1 = \perp$ and $b_2 = \diamond$ send $\perp$ to P_1, O to P_2 and $\perp$ to Sim_{SC}, and unfreeze p coins to P_1 by sending $(unfreeze, id, P_1, p)$ to $\mathcal{L}$. Upon receiving $(unfrozen, id, P_1, p)$ from $\mathcal{L}$ terminate.
- If $b_1 = \diamond$ and $b_2 = \perp$ send O to both parties and $\diamond$ to Sim_{SC}, and unfreeze p coins to P_2 by sending $(unfreeze, id, P_2, p)$ to $\mathcal{L}$. Upon receiving $(unfrozen, id, P_2, p)$ from $\mathcal{L}$ terminate.
- If $b_1 = b_2 = \diamond$ send O to both parties and $\diamond$ to Sim_{SC}, and unfreeze p coins to P_2 by sending $(unfreeze, id, P_2, p)$ to $\mathcal{L}$. Upon receiving $(unfrozen, id, P_2, p)$ from $\mathcal{L}$ terminate.

Fig. 1. Ideal functionality for SC-aided PSI $\mathcal{F}_{PSI}^{\mathcal{L}}$

5   A Coin-Compensated Fair SC-Aided PSI

In the following, we outline the phases and messages of the protocol Π.

Protocol Π. The protocol Π follows the approach of DCCR and uses OPE as its core primitive. Π has the following steps: (i) P_2 sending p coins to SC which SC will freeze on the ledger $\mathcal{L}$. If P_1 sees enough coins deposited, P_1 continues the protocol with a message that is identical to the message in the first round of DCCR (See Fig. 2 for the details of the message). (ii) When P_2 receives round 1 message, it informs SC that it has received it. If SC does not receive the confirmation of P_2 within an allocated time, it will terminate the protocol and return the coins to P_2 (no-one obtains the intersection). In round 2, P_2 sends the message in round 2 of DCCR protocol to P_1 but omits the verifiable encryption of blinding factors. It sends the commitment to the blinding factors and the Merkle root r_e constructed on ciphertexts to SC. P_2 also sends to P_1 a zero-knowledge proof $Pk_{prop-new}$ that proves P_2 has correctly constructed its second round message (ciphertexts) with respect to committed blinding factors to SC. (iii) In round 3, P_2 sends the round 3 message of DCCR to SC. This is to prevent an unfair situation that can arise by P_1 aborting after they receive the message but blaming P_2 for aborting. (iv) In round 4, P_2 opens the commitments to the blinding factors. If P_2 does not abort in round 4, SC returns the coins to P_2. The correctness of the protocol messages of each round can be verified by the recipient using the associated ZK proof of that round. If any of the parties abort before round 4, SC returns the coins to P_2 and terminates the protocol as none of the participants have any information about the intersection result. In round 4, if any of the commitments is opened incorrectly by P_2, P_1 makes a proof which consists of the index of the incorrect commitment and its opening value published to SC for the first incorrectly opened commitment. SC verifies the proof in round 6 and sends the coins to the honest party if it is valid. If party P_2 finds that the round 3 messages, the zero-knowledge proofs of the re-encrypted polynomial evaluation, are not valid, then P_2 can abort opening the commitment in round 4 and rather sends a proof to the SC which shows the index of the invalid zero-knowledge proof for the re-encryption in round 3, the ciphertext under the public key Pk_1 that it computed itself in round 2 together with its Merkle proof with respect to root $r_e{}^2$. The SC verifies the Merkle proof and the zero-knowledge proof and if the zero-knowledge proof is invalid it returns the coins to P_2. Note that in this case if party P_1 complains that P_2 has aborted opening the commitment, its complaint will be rejected (see the full version of the paper for details).

5.1   Security Analysis

We show the security of our protocol using the model in Sect. 4.2. We consider two simulators, Sim and Sim_{SC} and consider 4 different corrupted cases.

---

[2] Party P_1 may attempt to send incorrect re-encryptions to party P_2 to force it to abort opening the commitments. In such case, P_2 aborts opening the commitment but it has to send a proof to prove to SC that P_1 is the cheating party.

Algorithm 1. Protocol Π

Input of P_1: $X = \{x_1, ..., x_n\}$, **Input of P_2:** $Y = \{y_1, ..., y_m\}$ and p coins **Input of SC:** n, m

Output of P_1: $X \cap Y$ or p coins, **Output of P_2:** $X \cap Y$, **Output of SC:** the identity of cheating party I

procedure INTERSECTION

    Round 0. $P_2 \to SC : p$ coins

    Round 1. $P_1 \to P_2 : E_{Pk_1}(g^{d_0}), ..., E_{Pk_1}(g^{d_n}), Pk_{poly}^{[1, n]}$

    Round 1. $P_2 \to SC : Received$

    Round 2. $P_2 \to P_1 : E_{Pk_1}(g^{r_1 Q(y_1)+r'_1+y_1}), ..., E_{Pk_1}(g^{r_m Q(y_m)+r'_m+y_m}), Pk_{prop-new}^{[1, m]}$

    Round 2. $P_2 \to SC : commit(g^{r'_1}), ..., commit(g^{r'_m}), r_e$

    Round 3. $P_1 \to SC : E_{Pk_2}(g^{r_1 Q(y_1)+r'_1+y_1}), ..., E_{Pk_2}(g^{r_m Q(y_m)+r'_m+y_m}), Pk_{re-enc}^{[1, m]}$

    Round 4. $P_2 \to SC : open(commit(g^{r'_1})), ..., open(commit(g^{r'_m}))$

procedure DISPUTE RESOLUTION

    if P_2 reveals an incorrect opening for $commit(g^{r'_j})$ **then**

        $P_1 \to SC :$ index j of commitment

        SC verifies opening of $commit(g^{r'_j})$

        if opening invalid **then**

            $SC \to P_1 : p$ coins

        else

            $SC \to P_2 : p$ coins

    if P_2 aborts opening the commitments **then**

        $SC \to P_1 : p$ coins

    if P_1 reveals an incorrect re-encryption where the ZKP is incorrect for index Pk_{re-enc}^j **then**

        $P_2 \to SC :$ index j of re-encryption, the encryption $E_{Pk_1}(g^{r_j Q(y_j)+r'_j+y_j})$ and its Merkle proof with respect to r_e

        SC verifies the Merkle proof and Pk_{re-enc}^j

        if Merkle proof valid but Pk_{re-enc}^j invalid **then**

            $SC \to P_2 : p$ coins

        else

            $SC \to P_1 : p$ coins

    if No PoM received **then**

        $SC \to P_2 : p$ coins

Theorem 1. *The coin-compensated PSI protocol Π securely realizes the $\mathcal{F}_{PSI}^{\mathcal{L}}$ functionality assuming the homomorphic encryption scheme E is semantically secure, the ZK proofs and the commitment scheme are secure (please see the full version of the paper for the proof).*

Proof Sketch. The environment Z sends input to parties and receives their outputs at the end of the protocol, it also sees the messages that are sent to the smart contract and has to distinguish ideal world from hybrid world. We consider the following cases:

Case 1. Party P_1 is Corrupted. We construct a simulator Sim_1 which has oracle access to the malicious code of P_1^* and interacts with the ideal functionality

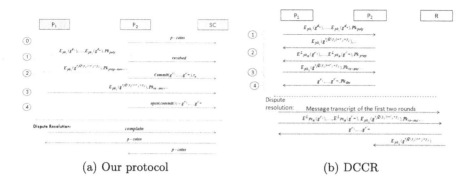

(a) Our protocol   (b) DCCR

Fig. 2. Coin-compensated fair PSI protocol vs. DCCR optimistically fair PSI protocol. In our protocol, each round is defined with respect to sending a message to the SC.

$\mathcal{F}^{\mathcal{L}}_{PSI}$. Sim_1 simulates the protocol transcript for messages that are sent to SC (because channels to SC are public and they can be seen by the environment Z) and simulates the protocol messages to the ideal functionality $\mathcal{F}^{\mathcal{L}}_{PSI}$. The honest party P_2 is dummy and sends the input it receives from Z to $\mathcal{F}^{\mathcal{L}}_{PSI}$. The important part of the proof is to show (1) how Sim_1 chooses the input of the corrupted P_1^* to send to $\mathcal{F}^{\mathcal{L}}_{PSI}$, (2) how Sim_1 chooses the input of the honest party to simulate the protocol transcript to SC, and (3) how Sim_1 identifies whether to simulate an abort and dispute resolution or not. For (1), Sim_1 extracts the input of P_1^* from Pk_{poly} in round 1 by rewinding P_1^*. For (2) Sim_1 chooses random values (in the input domain of the parties' set) as the elements in the set Y^* of the honest party P_2, and waits to receive the intersection result, O, from $\mathcal{F}^{\mathcal{L}}_{PSI}$. It replaces $|O|$ random values in Y^* with the elements in O and simulates the messages of P_2 in round 2. For (3), Sim_1 simulates generating the private/public key of the honest party at the beginning of the protocol, and later uses the private key of P_2 to decrypt the ciphertexts received from P_1^* in round 3, and checks whether the intersection result matches the intersection result O. If they match, it simulates round 4 (opening the commitments of blinding factors to SC) correctly and sends ($Output$, id, $\diamond$, $\diamond$) to $\mathcal{F}^{\mathcal{L}}_{PSI}$. Otherwise, if the intersection result computed based on the message of P_1^* does not match with O, Sim_1 sends ($Output$, id, $\bot$, $\bot$) to $\mathcal{F}^{\mathcal{L}}_{PSI}$, and simulates the dispute resolution, complaining about an incorrect re-encryption for one element to SC.

Case 2. Party P_2 is Corrupted. We construct a simulator Sim_2 which has oracle access to the malicious code of P_2^*. (1) To simulate the input of the corrupted party P_1^*, Sim_2 extracts the elements of the set Y of party P_2^* from $Pk_{prop\text{-}new}$ by rewinding it and sends Y to $\mathcal{F}^{\mathcal{L}}_{PSI}$. (2) Sim_2 chooses $n = |X|$ dummy elements for P_1, waits to receive the intersection O from $\mathcal{F}^{\mathcal{L}}_{PSI}$, and then replaces $|O|$ elements in X^* with the elements in O to get X', and uses X' to simulate the messages of P_1 including round 3 message. (3) If P_2^* does not abort, Sim_2 sends ($Output$, id, $\diamond$, $\diamond$) to $\mathcal{F}^{\mathcal{L}}_{PSI}$. Otherwise, if P_2^* initiates the dispute resolution (which is invalid), Sim_1 sends ($Output$, id, $\bot$, $\diamond$) to $\mathcal{F}^{\mathcal{L}}_{PSI}$.

Case 3. SC is Semi-honest and Party P_1 is Corrupted. We construct the simulator Sim_{sc}^1 which does not have access to X, Y, and $X \cap Y$. Sim_{sc}^1 simulates the protocol transcript from parties to SC by choosing random inputs taken from the input domain that are indistinguishable from the real inputs and generating the protocol messages using the random inputs. Since the cryptographic protocols are hiding and zero-knowledge, the environment cannot distinguish them from the real messages. The important part of the proof is that, if P_1 is corrupted it can reveal an incorrect message where P_2 has to complain about it. We only describe this part of the proof. Upon receiving $\diamond$ from $\mathcal{F}_{PSI}^{\mathcal{L}}$, Sim_{sc}^1 simulates round 3 message correctly using randomly chosen input values. Otherwise, if Sim_{sc}^1 receives $\perp$ from $\mathcal{F}_{PSI}^{\mathcal{L}}$, it simulates an incorrect round 3 message. In the next round, it simulates a dispute resolution from P_2 based on the corrupted message it has revealed.

Case 4. SC is Semi-honest and Party P_2 is Corrupted. We construct the simulator Sim_{sc}^2 which does not have access to X, Y, and $X \cap Y$. Sim_{sc}^2 simulates the protocol transcript from parties to SC by choosing random inputs taken from the input domain that are indistinguishable from the real inputs and generating the protocol messages using the random inputs. The important part of the proof is that, if P_2 is corrupted it may abort before learning the intersection which will not affect the fairness guarantee. However, if it aborts opening the commitment to blinding factors correctly, party P_1 has to complain and get compensated by coins; we only describe this part of the proof. To simulate this, Sim_{sc}^2 waits to receive either: $\diamond$ from $\mathcal{F}_{PSI}^{\mathcal{L}}$: In this case, it simulates opening the commitments to blinding factors on behalf of P_2 in round 4 correctly, and terminates. Else, if Sim_{sc}^1 receives $\perp$ from $\mathcal{F}_{PSI}^{\mathcal{L}}$, it incorrectly opens the commitments to blinding factors to SC and simulates the dispute resolution stage with a valid complaint on behalf of P_1.

Another Coin-Compensated PSI Protocol. Our approach to redesigning DCCR can be used for the PSI protocol [19], which is the most efficient existing mutual PSI with optimistic fairness. The protocol achieves linear computation and communication complexity. We give the outline of the redesigned protocol in the full version of the paper.

6   Improving the Efficiency of Π

We reduce the computation of parties by replacing ZKPs in round 2 and 3 by a more efficient protocol. Below, we give an outline of PoM and an overview of the protocol Π^*.

6.1   Our Technique for Optimizing the Protocol

We first define the PoM and then describe how ZKP can be replaced by PoM.

Proof of Misbehavior (PoM). We consider two provers $P_i, \forall i = \{1, 2\}$, where at most one can be dishonest, and a single honest verifier V. A function

$f()$ needs to be computed on input x. All parties know $f()$, provers know the input x and the verifier knows a commitment to x. Provers run the computation of $f(x)$ and the verifier has to decide which of the two is correct if they disagree.

Prover P_1 generates $(y = f(x),\ \pi_1,\ \zeta(\pi_1))$ where $\zeta(\pi_1)$ is a proof digest (i.e. a commitment to π_1), and sends $(y,\ \pi_1)$ to P_2 and $\zeta(\pi_1)$ to the verifier V over public channel. Here $y = f(x)$ denotes the computation of $f()$ on input x. π_1 can be verified by P_2 using the input x. P_2 runs $verify(x,\ f(),\ y,\ \pi_1)$ where the output is either 0 or 1. If $verify(x,\ f(),\ y,\ \pi_1) = 0$ then P_2 generates a PoM π_2 and sends it to the verifier. Verifier is able to run $Detect(\zeta(\pi_1),\ \pi_2) = P_i$ which verifies π_2 with respect to $\zeta(\pi_1)$ and outputs the identity of the cheating party P_i, $i \in \{1,\ 2\}$. We require the following properties:

- Correctness: If both provers are honest, then $verify(x,\ f(),\ y,\ \pi_1) = 1$ and $\pi_2 = \bot$ as well as $Detect(\zeta(\pi_1),\ \pi_2) = \bot$.
- Soundness: If prover P_1 is cheating then P_2 can always generate $\pi_2 \neq \bot$ such that $Detect(\zeta(\pi_1),\ \pi_2) = P_1$. If P_2 is cheating then $Detect(\zeta(\pi_1),\ \pi_2) = P_2$ for all possible π_2.

Replacing a ZKP with PoM. Consider a zero-knowledge proof of knowledge for the relation $R = \{x : y \in F_q, y = f(x)\}$ which states that the prover knows x such that x satisfies the statement $f(x)$. To remove ZKP we consider the computation of $f()$ by the circuit ϕ and design $(\pi_1,\ \zeta(\pi_1),\ \pi_2)$ as described above using this representation as follows:

- π_1 in its basic form consists of the wire values of circuit ϕ when run on the input x. We refer to this set as the *computation trace*. Computation trace has linear communication complexity in the size of the circuit. Reducing this size by using alternative encoding is an interesting direction for future work.
- $\zeta(\pi_1)$, in its simplest form is the root of the Merkle tree on the description of circuit ϕ, together with the root of the Merkle tree that is constructed on the computation trace. In our work, P_2 does not know the input x to $f()$ as it is blinded by random values. It however learns the input to $f()$ after completing the PSI computation with P_1. We include commitments to the blinding factors as part of $\zeta(\pi_1)$ that is later used for the verification of PoM.
- If P_1 is cheating, π_2 is the information of one gate in the computation trace (π_1) that has incorrect values (together with its corresponding Merkle proofs with respect to the Merkle root on the computation trace). If the gate is in the input layer, then π_2 is a zero-knowledge proof that shows the committed inputs are not correctly fed to the circuit. This is to ensure that the input is not revealed to the verifier (PSI privacy requirement).

We also replace the vector of m correct re-encryption ZKPs, Pk_{re-enc}, in round 3, with one aggregate ZKP of Pk_{re-enc}, together with the PoM (as mentioned above) for the aggregate computation.

In replacing ZKP with PoM, we must ensure that verifying the computation at the end of the interaction instead of verifying each message individually using ZKP, does not result in an unwanted leakage. For this reason, we do not replace

Pk_{poly} by PoM because, in the first round, we require that at least one coefficient be non-zero, otherwise, P_1 can learn the whole input set of P_2, which breaks the security of the PSI.

6.2   Overview of Π^*

Replacing ZK Proof $Pk_{prop-new}$ with a PoM. We express the computation of $E_{pk}(g^{r_j Q(y_j)+y_j})$ (in round 2) that its correctness needs to be proved, as a circuit ϕ consisting of high-level gates with two operations of $op_i \in \{\times, exp\}$ where $\times$ represents modular multiplication and exp is the modular exponentiation. We consider one output for each gate and a fan-in of 2. Each gate is described by $g_j = (j, op_i, I)$ where j is the index of the gate, op_i is the operation that it performs on its inputs and I is the indexes of the inputs to gate j. The indexes are set from the bottom layer and go up toward the output layer. In each layer, the wires are numbered from left to right. Figure 3 shows the graphical representation of this circuit when $n = 4$. The computation trace in this circuit is considered as the values carried by the wires marked with numbers 1 to 12 (note that these numbers are just markers not the indexes of the gates). We denote the computation trace with $CompTrace(y_j)$. Additionally, a circuit description ϕ is a set consisting of the description of all its gates. We define the Merkle root of circuit description as the Merkle root of the tree constructed on ϕ, i.e. $r_\phi = root(Mtree(\phi))$.

We change the protocol Π as below (c.f. Fig. 4):

- In round 2, P_2 performs the polynomial evaluation $E_{pk}(g^{r_j Q(y_j)+r'_j+y_j})$, encrypts each computation trace using key k_j and sends $E_{k_j}(CompTrace(y_j))$ to P_1. P_2 also sends the Merkle root constructed on the encrypted computation trace $r_{y_j} = root(Mtree(E_{k_j}(CompTrace(y_j))))$, the Merkle root on ciphertexts $r_e = root(Mtree(E_{pk_1}(g^{r_j Q(y_j)+r'_j+y_j})))$, $\forall j \in |Y|$, Merkle root on received coefficients $r_d = root(Mtree(E_{pk_1}(g^{d_0}), ..., E_{pk_1}(g^{d_n})))$, commitment to keys k_j, and commitment to blinding factors $g^{r'_j}$ to SC. P_1 verifies the Mekle roots match with the ones revealed to SC and it continues with the next message. Otherwise, it aborts. (Note that P_2 encrypts each computation trace to ensure P_1 does not learn the information about the values that are in the set Y. For instance, in Fig. 3, the wires marked with 1 to 4 can immediately leak information about y_j, so they cannot be revealed in plain).
- In round 5, after P_2 learns the intersection $X \cap Y$ result, it opens the commitments of the keys k_j for those indexes that their corresponding y_j is in the intersection. P_2 also reveals the blinding factors that he was committed in round 2 to SC. P_1 can remove the blinding factors from the result, obtains $X \cap Y$, decrypts the computation trace for the indexes that are in the intersection and verifies the computation trace for them. If there is any invalid value P_1 can generate a PoM.

Format of PoM. The format of PoM depends on the detected misbehavior. We need to consider all the possible cases in which one party can cheat and determine

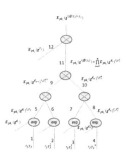

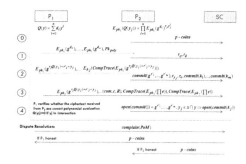

Fig. 3. The circuit representation of computing $E_{pk}(g^{r_jQ(y_j)+y_j})$

Fig. 4. Replacing Pk_{prop} and Pk_{re-enc} with PoM

how the honest party can prove to SC that the other party has cheated while keeping the SC computation minimal (the algorithm of each PoM is given in the full version of the paper).

We consider the following PoMs:

- $r_jQ(y_j) \neq 0$, which means that y_j is not in the intersection but the output of the circuit computation shows $r_jQ(y_j) = 0$ for the last gate: in this case, PoM is to show that the last multiplication gate in the circuit ϕ is not correct.
- P_2 uses random values for all the circuit values in the computation trace: PoM is to show that the computation is not correct for one (any) single gate in the circuit.
- P_2 uses different coefficients from what P_1 has sent to P_2: PoM is based on showing the computation of the gates that receive the coefficient and the input (which is in the form of $r_jy_j^i$) is not correct. Note that $r_jy_j^i$ does not reveal anything about y_j.
- P_2 does not reveal k_j for the execution trace of at least one element in the intersection: PoM is a ZK proof that shows P_1 knows an element y_j such that $r_jQ(y_j) = 0$ (which means it knows y_j such that $C_j = E_{pk_1}(g^{r_jQ(y_j)+y_j}) = E_{pk_1}(g^{y_j})$ but its corresponding key k_j has not been revealed.
- P_2 does not reveal (or reveal incorrectly) at least one g^{r_j}: PoM is asking SC to verify the commitment opening for one g^{r_j}.

Modifying ZK Proof Pk_{re-enc} to Construct PoM Efficiently. In round 3 of the protocol, Pk_{re-enc} is used to prove the correctness of re-encrypted ciphertexts. To enhance the efficiency of the scheme, we use the homomorphic property of the encryption scheme to aggregate the ciphertexts and compute ZK proof for one re-encryption which is the aggregate ciphertext (c.f. Fig. 4). Due to homomorphic property of the Elgamal encryption, P_1 can prove that the multiplication of all re-encrypted ciphertexts under key pk_2, $E_{pk_2}(\Pi e) = E_{pk_2}(e_1) \times ... \times E_{pk_2}(e_{|Y|})$ is a correct re-encryption for multiplication of the original ciphertexts under key pk_1 $E_{pk_1}(\Pi e) = E_{pk_1}(e_1) \times ... \times E_{pk_1}(e_{|Y|})$. Therefore, for such a proof one ZK proof, $(com,\ c,\ R)$, is constructed which can be published to SC. To ensure that if P_1 cheats in computing the aggregate ciphertexts, P_2 can detect it, we use PoM. We consider the circuit representation of $|Y| - 1$ ciphertext multiplications using multiplication gates of fan-in 2 and let ϕ be such a circuit. We define the computation trace of ϕ for computing $E_{pk_1}(\Pi e)$ and $E_{pk_2}(\Pi e)$ as $CompTrace(E_{pk_1}(\Pi e))$ and $CompTrace(E_{pk_2}(\Pi e))$ respectively. P_1 sends these two computation traces together with the ZK proof to SC. P_2 will check the correctness of multiplications using the computation traces $CompTrace(E_{pk_1}(\Pi e))$ and $CompTrace(E_{pk_2}(\Pi e))$ and the ZK proof, $Pk_{re-enc,new}$, (a non-interactive Sigma protocol $(com,\ c,\ R)$ which consists of one ZK proof for the aggregated ciphertexts) and make a PoM as below:

- One of the multiplications has not been computed properly: PoM is to reveal the description of the corresponding gate to SC, so that SC re-computes the multiplication and detects the cheating party.
- ZK proof is incorrect: PoM consists of the part of the ZK proof which is not verified (note that if R is more than one statement $R = (R_1,\ R_2)$ that needs to be verified, it is enough to let SC to verify only one of the incorrect statements).
- One of the inputs in the computation trace of $CompTrace(E_{pk_1}(\Pi e))$ is different from what P_2 has sent before: PoM is to show that the ciphertext in the computation trace is different from the ciphertext it has revealed at the previous round to P_1 which resides in the Merkle tree with root r_e (r_e is sent by P_2 to SC in round 2).

6.3   Security Analysis

We prove security of Π^* using the model in Sect. 4.2 with a slight change that we describe below:

In protocol Π^*, SC can learn the indexes and size of the intersection if the protocol terminates honestly. Therefore, we modify the ideal functionality of Sect. 4.2 and denote the new one with $\mathcal{F}'^{\mathcal{L}}_{PSI}$. In $\mathcal{F}'^{\mathcal{L}}_{PSI}$, if $b_1 = b_2 = \diamond$ or $b_1 = \diamond$ and $b_2 = \perp$, then both parties receive O and Sim_{sc} gets $(i, |O|)$ where i is the index of the element in the set of P_2 which is in the intersection, $|O|$ is the size of the intersection result. The other parts of $\mathcal{F}'^{\mathcal{L}}_{PSI}$ is the same as $\mathcal{F}^{\mathcal{L}}_{PSI}$.

Theorem 2. *The coin-compensated SC-aided PSI protocol Π^* securely realizes the $\mathcal{F}'^{\mathcal{L}}_{PSI}$ functionality in the random oracle model assuming the homomorphic encryption scheme E is semantically secure, the symmetric key encryption scheme E_k is IND-CPA secure, the associated ZK proofs and the commitment scheme are secure. Please see the full version of the paper for the proof.*

We highlight that by replacing the ZKP with PoM, We have to show that when P_2 is malicious (*Case 2*), the simulator can extract its input in all cases

Algorithm 2. Protocol Π^*

Input of P_1: $X = \{x_1, ..., x_n\}$, **Input of** P_2: $Y = \{y_1, ..., y_m\}$ and p coins **Input of** SC: n, m

Output of P_1: $X \cap Y$ or p coins, **Output of** P_2: $X \cap Y$, **Output of** SC: the identity of cheating party I and $|X \cap Y|$

procedure INTERSECTION

    Round 0. $P_2 \rightarrow SC$: p coins

    Round 1. $P_1 \rightarrow P_2$: $E_{Pk_1}(g^{d_0}), ..., E_{Pk_1}(g^{d_n}), Pk_{poly}^{[1, n]}$

    Round 1. $P_2 \rightarrow SC$: r_ϕ, r_d

    Round 2. $P_2 \rightarrow P_1$: $E_{Pk_1}(g^{r_1 Q(y_1)+r'_1+y_1}), ..., E_{Pk_1}(g^{r_m Q(y_m)+r'_m+y_m})$, $E_{k_1}(CompTrace(y_1)), ..., E_{k_m}(CompTrace(y_m))$

    Round 2. $P_2 \rightarrow SC$: $commit(g^{r'_1}), ..., commit(g^{r'_m}), r_{y_j}, r_e, commit(k_1), ..., commit(k_m)$

    Round 3. $P_1 \rightarrow SC$: $E_{Pk_2}(g^{r_1 Q(y_1)+r'_1+y_1}), ..., (com, c, R)$, $CompTrace(E_{pk_1}(\Pi e)), CompTrace(E_{pk_2}(\Pi e))$

    Round 4. $P_2 \rightarrow SC$: $open(commit(g^{r'_1})), ..., open(commit(g^{r'_m}))$, if $y_j \in X \cap Y \rightarrow open(commit(k_j))$

procedure DISPUTE RESOLUTION

    If(P_1 has not computed the multiplication in $CompTrace(E_{Pk_i}(\Pi e))$ correctly)

    – $P_2 \rightarrow SC$: the information of the multiplication gate in $CompTrace(E_{Pk_i}(\Pi e))$

    If(P_1 has not revealed a ZK proof of Pk_{re-enc}, (com, c, R))

    – $P_2 \rightarrow SC$: send the information of the statement R that is not verified

    If(P_1 has not used the correct encryption e_j (received from P_2) for computing $E_{pk_1}(\Pi e)$)

    – $P_2 \rightarrow SC$: reveal the correct e_j and the Merkle proof for that with respect to r_e

    SC **verifies the PoM**

    if valid PoM **then**

        $SC \rightarrow P_2$: p coins

    else

        $SC \rightarrow P_1$: p coins

    If(P_2 aborts opening the commitments of the blinding factors or at least one commitment $commit(g^{r'_j})$)

    – $P_1 \rightarrow SC$: the index j of the $commit(g^{r'_j})$

    If(P_2 reveals a computation trace that shows the output for $r_j Q(y_j) = 0$ which is not true)

    – $P_1 \rightarrow SC$: information of the output gate with the Merkle proofs with respect to $root_{y_j}$ and r_ϕ

    If(P_2 has used random values for all the circuit values)

    – $P_1 \rightarrow SC$: information of the one incorrect gate with the Merkle proofs with respect to $root_{y_j}$ and r_ϕ

    If(P_2 has used different coefficients d_j from what P_1 has sent)

    – $P_1 \rightarrow SC$: information of the incorrect input gate with the index of d_j and the Merkle proofs with respect to $root_{y_j}$ and r_ϕ

    If(P_2 has not revealed k_j for at least one element in the intersection)

    – $P_1 \rightarrow SC$: SK proof to show that P_1 knows y_j such that $r_j Q(y_j) = 0$ but k_j has not been revealed

    SC **verifies the PoM**

    if Valid PoM **then**

        $SC \rightarrow P_1$: p coins

    else

        $SC \rightarrow P_2$: p coins

    if No PoM received **then**

        $SC \rightarrow P_2$: p coins

without using the extractability of ZKP. We achieve this by using the computation trace of P_2 and the simulator's access to the random oracle ideal functionality (a similar approach is used by [3,22]).

Proof Sketch. We consider that environment Z only sends input to parties and receives the outputs from parties, it also sees the messages that are sent to the smart contract and it has to distinguish the ideal world from the hybrid world. Below we consider 4 different cases:

Case 1. Party P_1 is Corrupted. We construct a simulator Sim_1 which has oracle access to the malicious code of P_1^*. Sim_1 simulates the protocol messages from P_1 to the ideal functionality and also simulates the view of SC because channels to SC are public and they can be seen by the environment Z. The key techniques used for the simulation in this case are similar to the simulation of *Case 1* described in *Theorem 1*.

Case 2. Party P_2 is Corrupted. We construct a simulator Sim_2 which has oracle access to the malicious code of P_2^*. Sim_2 simulates the protocol messages that are sent from P_2^* to the ideal functionality and also simulates the view of SC because channels to SC are public and they can be seen by the environment Z. To simulate the honest party P_1, the simulation is similar to *Case 2* described in *Theorem 1*. In protocol Π^*, for a corrupted P_2^*, it is important to show how Sim_2 can extract the input set of the party P_2^*. Upon receiving the ciphertexts $E_{pk_1}(g^{r_j Q(y_j)+r_j'+y_j})$, the encrypted computation trace $E_{k_j}(CompTrace(g^{r_j Q(y_j)+r_j'+y_j})$, the commitments to blinding factors, and the commitments to the keys k_j (which are hash-based) from P_2^*, it extracts k_j's from the random oracle $\mathcal{H}$ and decrypts the ciphertexts $E_{k_j}(CompTrace(g^{r_j Q(y_j)+r_j'+y_j})$ using k_j. Then, it extracts y_j from the computation trace by computing $\frac{r_j y_j^i}{r_j y_j}$, then it decrypts $E_{pk_1}(g^{r_j Q(y_j)+r_j'+y_j})$ using the key sk_1. If the ciphertexts are not correctly formed or if it cannot extract the keys from the random oracle it sends $\perp$ to $\mathcal{F}_{PSI}^{\mathcal{L}}$. Else, it sends Y to $\mathcal{F}_{PSI}^{\mathcal{L}}$. The remaining part of the proof is the same as *Case 2* of *Theorem 1*.

Case 3. SC is Semi-honest and Party P_1 is Corrupted. Sim_{sc}^1 does not have access to X, Y, and $X \cap Y$, but it learns $(i, |O|)$ from the ideal functionality $\mathcal{F}_{PSI}^{\prime\mathcal{L}}$. Sim_{sc}^1 simulates the protocol transcript from parties to SC by choosing random inputs taken from the input domain that are indistinguishable from the real inputs and generating the protocol messages using the random inputs. When P_1 is corrupted, it is important to show the simulation for round 3 and we only describe this case. Upon receiving $\diamond$ from $\mathcal{F}_{PSI}^{\mathcal{L}}$, Sim_{sc}^1 correctly simulates the round 3 messages by using random inputs. Then, Sim_{sc}^1 opens the commitments to $g^{r_i'}$ and k_i to SC based on $(i, |O|)$ (and any other leaked information that it receives through the ideal functionality). Otherwise, if Sim_{sc}^1 receives $\perp$ from $\mathcal{F}_{PSI}^{\mathcal{L}}$, it incorrectly simulates the round 3 message. In the next round, it simulates a PoM (according to Π^*) from P_2 to SC based on the leaked information to that.

Case 4. SC is Semi-honest and Party P_2 is Corrupted. Sim_{sc}^2 does not have access to X, Y, and $X \cap Y$. As stated before, Sim_{sc}^2 simulates the protocol transcript from parties to SC by choosing random inputs taken from the input domain that are indistinguishable from the real inputs and generating the protocol messages using the random inputs. For a corrupted P_2, we have to show that Sim_{sc}^2 can correctly simulate the round 4 messages and a PoM from P_1, and we only describe this part of the proof. If Sim_{sc}^2 receives $\diamond$ from $\mathcal{F}_{PSI}^{\mathcal{L}}$, then it correctly opens the randomly generated commitments to $g^{r'_j}$ and k_j (based on the received $(i, |O|)$ from $\mathcal{F}_{PSI}^{\mathcal{L}}$) (and any other leaked information that it receives through the ideal functionality). Else, if it receives $\perp$ from $\mathcal{F}_{PSI}^{\mathcal{L}}$, it incorrectly opens the commitments in round 4 and simulates a valid PoM on behalf of P_1 based on the leaked information to that.

7 Complexity Analysis

In the following, we estimate the complexity of protocols Π and Π^*.

Computation Complexity. We give our concrete construction in the full version of the paper. Accordingly, we estimate the computation complexity of the full protocol Π and Π^* in terms of the number of exponentiations for each party in our scheme (see Table 1). Note that the computation and communication complexity of zero-knowledge proofs is linear in the number of statements that are needed to be proved: $O(PK_{poly})$ is $O(n)$, $O(PK_{prop-new})$ is $O(nm)$, $O(PK_{re-enc})$ is $O(m)$, and $O(PK_{re-enc,new})$ is $O(1)$. In the following, we estimate the complexity of messages other than zero-knowledge proofs.

In round 1 of both protocols, encrypting the coefficients requires $3n$ exponentiations. In round 2, evaluating the polynomial and computing the ciphertexts requires $2[nm + 2m]$ exponentiations. In round 3, decryption and re-encryption take $3m$ exponentiations. Therefore, the complexity of P_1 in both protocols are $O(n+m)$ and P_2 is $O(nm)$. Note that in Π^*, P_1 performs only 1 zero knowledge proof $Pk_{re-enc,new}$ which reduces the complexity of Pk_{re-enc} to $O(1)$ compared to DCCR which has complexity of $O(m)$. However, note that compared to DCCR, in protocol Π, P_2 does not need to compute (i) the verifiable encryption which has the complexity of $3m$ exponentiations, (ii) the zero-knowledge proof Pk_{dec} which is used to show that the blinding factors are correct decryptions of the verifiable encryption. Pk_{dec} has complexity of $O(m)$.

In protocol Π^*, compared to DCCR, P_2 does not need to compute (i) the verifiable encryption which has the complexity of $3m$ exponentiations, (ii) the Pk_{prop} which has the complexity of $O(nm)$, (iii) the zero-knowledge proof Pk_{dec} which is used to show that the blinding factors are correct decryptions of the verifiable encryption (see Table 2). Furthermore, in both of the protocols Π and Π^*, SC has to do $O(1)$ exponentiations if there is any dispute which is far less than the computation complexity of arbiter in DCCR which has to do $6m$ exponentiations to verify and decrypt the verifiable encryptions.

Communication Complexity. We estimate the communication complexity of Π and Π^* in terms of the number of group elements that should be sent between different parties (see Table 1). The total communication complexity of our protocols is close to DCCR, while it is less than DCCR in the dispute resolution stage for the interaction of parties to TTP.

Table 3 shows the comparison of our work with the existing fair PSI protocols. Our scheme is the only coin-compensated PSI that uses an SC as TTP efficiently.

Table 1. Computation and communication complexity of the proposed schemes compared to DCCR protocol.

		Protocols		
	Party	Protocol Π	Protocol Π^*	DCCR
Computation Complexity (exponentiations)	P_1	$O(n+m)$	$O(n+m)$	$O(n+m)$
	P_2	$O(nm)$	$O(nm)$	$O(nm)$
	TTP	$O(1)$	$O(1)$	$O(m)$
Communication Complexity (group elements, not counting ZKP)	P_1 to P_2 (and vice versa)	$2n+2m$	$2n+2m$	$2n+9m$
	Both parties to TTP	Intersection phase: $5m$ Dispute resolution: at most 2	Intersection phase: $5m$ Dispute resolution: at most 2	Intersection phase: 0 Dispute resolution: $5m+2n$

Table 2. Comparing computation complexity (number of modular exponentiations) in Π and Π^* for using PoM in lieu of ZKP.

	Protocols	
Party	Protocol Π	Protocol Π^*
$TTP(dispute resolution)$	$O(1)$	Incorrect input: $O(1)$ Incorrect computation: $-$
P_1	$nPk_{poly} + mVerifyPk_{prop-new} + mPk_{re-enc} + mVerifyCom_{pedersen}$	$nPk_{poly} + Pk_{re-enc}$
P_2	$nVerifyPk_{poly} + mPk_{prop-new} + mVerifyPk_{re-enc} + mCom_{pedersen}$	$nVerifyPk_{poly} + VerifyPk_{re-enc}$

8   Implementation

We provide a proof-of-concept implementation of the SC in Protocol Π and Π^* and evaluate the gas cost for running the smart contracts by each party P_1 and P_2 by increasing the set size of parties, i.e., m and n, in two scenarios: (i) optimistic execution: when both parties are honest, and (ii) pessimistic execution: when one party misbehaves and proof of misbehavior is needed (requires dispute resolution stage) (the definitions are based on [23]).

SCPSIEC implements the SC in Π and SCPSI2EC implements the SC in Π^* (see full version of the paper for the abstract of the contracts and pseudocodes). We have used solidity language to implement the SC and the required cryptographic primitives. We have implemented the CryptoLib library in solidity for cryptographic primitives, including Elliptic curve variant of Pedersen commitment, the Elgamal encryption, Zero-knowledge proof of knowledge for correct re-encryption, Zero-knowledge proof of knowledge for known plaintext, Merkle proof verification, and the necessary primitives for generating the message values that are sent to SC by parties P_1 and P_2. For zero-knowledge proofs, we followed the non-interactive Sigma protocols with Fiat-Shamir heuristic. All the cryptographic primitives are run over Elliptic curve $Secp256k1$ and we use the available libraries EllipticCurve, SafeMath, and EllipticCurveInterface and initial version of CryptoLib given in [55] for Elliptic curve operations. We used a contract called sharedStruct to define the data structures that are common in SCPSIEC, SCPSI2EC, and CryptoLib contracts. The smart contract codes are available in [2].

8.1   Evaluation

We used a Windows laptop computer with an Intel dual-core i7-7500 3.5 GHz system with 12 GB memory to run and execute the codes. We used Remix Ethereum IDE[3] to write and debug the smart contracts and deployed and evaluated them on the local Ethereum Blockchain network called Ganache using the Truffle suite[4]. Table 4 shows the gas cost of deploying each smart contract on Ganache.

Table 3. Comparing the existing fair PSI schemes that use a TTP (n is the set size of P_1, and m is the set size of P_2)

Scheme	Total Computation complexity	Total Communication complexity	Smart contract	External TTP	Computation complexity of TTP	Fairness
DCCR [21]	$O(mn)$	$O(m+n)$	–	×	$O(m)$	Optimistic
[19]	$O(m+n)$	$O(m+n)$	–	×	$O(m+n)$	Optimistic
[18]	$O(m+n)$	$O(m+n)$	–	×	$O(n)$	Optimistic
[20]	$O(m+n)$	$O(m+n)$	–	×	$O(m+n)$	Optimistic
[7]	$O(mn)$	$O(m+n)$	–	×	$O(m+n)$	Optimistic
[36, 37]	$O(m+n)$	$O(m+n)$	–	×	$O(m+n)$	Server-aided
[1]	$O(2hd^2)$	$O(2hd^2\zeta)$	×	×	$O(|S_\cap|(d + log_2|S|) + 2h \cdot d)$	Coin-compensated
Our work (based on DCCR)	$O(mn)$	$O(m+n)$	×	–	$O(1)$	Coin-compensated
Our work (based on [19])	$O(m+n)$	$O(m+n)$	×	–	$O(1)$	Coin-compensated

Table 4. Deployment cost of smart contracts

Contract	Gas cost	Eth cost[1]	USD cost[2]
SCPSIEC	2,494,793	0.049	$116.47
SCPSI2EC	4,894,379	0.097	$228.49
CryptoLib	3,662,609	0.073	$170.98
sharedStruct	96,322	0.0019	$4.50
Elliptic curve operation contracts	1,158,021	0.023	$54.1

[1] We set 1 Gas $= 20$ Gwei
[2] 1eth $= \$2334.19$ on January 1, 2024

Gas Cost vs Set Size of Party P_2. We compare the effect of increasing the set size m for $m = \{2^2, 2^3, 2^4, 2^7\}$ when $n = 2^{10}$ and show in Fig. 5 (left) the total

---

[3] https://remix.ethereum.org/.
[4] https://trufflesuite.com/.

gas cost of running both contracts, SCPSIEC and SCPSI2EC in the optimistic and pessimistic execution. The total gas cost is computed by adding the gas cost of the functions that are called by P_1 and P_2. The gas cost of pessimistic execution is the sum of the gas cost of the optimistic execution and the dispute resolution (PoM). For pessimistic executions, we have considered the mean of Judge function that is called in the dispute resolution stage for different types of complaints sent by P_1 and P_2, and also show the minimum and maximum of the gas cost of calling the Judge function.

For the SCPSIEC contract, the overhead of the gas cost for the pessimistic execution compared to the optimistic execution decreases from 16% to 2% when m increases, and the total gas cost is dominated by the gas cost of optimistic execution when $m = 128$ because the dispute resolution only varies with $log(m)$ (hash evaluations) but the optimistic execution increases linearly with m (storing $O(m)$ group elements). For SCPSI2EC contract, the overhead of the gas cost for the pessimistic execution compared to the optimistic execution decreases from 15% to 2% when m increases, and the total gas cost is dominated by the gas cost of optimistic execution when $m = 128$ because the dispute resolution only varies with $log(m)$ but the optimistic execution increases linearly with m. In total, the gas cost of running SCPSI2EC is approximately between 1.17 to 1.32 times higher than the gas cost of running SCPSIEC contract.

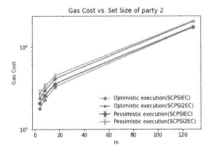 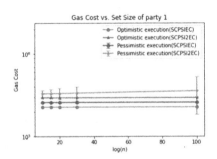

Fig. 5. Left: Total gas cost of running the smart contracts vs set size of party P_2 where $n = 2^{10}$. The overhead of gas cost for the pessimistic execution in SCPSIEC decreases from 16% to 2% and for SCPSI2EC decreases from 15% to 2%. The total gas cost is dominated by the optimistic execution when $m = 128$. **Right:** Total gas cost of running the smart contracts vs logarithm of the set size of party P_1 where $m = 8$. The overhead of gas cost for the pessimistic execution in SCPSIEC is 13% for all n and for SCPSI2EC increases from 12% to 21%.

Gas Cost vs Set Size of Party P_1. We compare the effect of increasing the set size of party P_1, n, for $n = \{2^{10}, 2^{15}, 2^{20}, 2^{30}, 2^{100}\}$ when $m = 8$ and show in Fig. 5 (right) the total gas cost of running both contracts, SCPSIEC and SCPSI2EC in the optimistic and pessimistic execution versus $log(n)$. The gas cost of SCPSIEC contract is independent of the n and its gas cost remains the same for both optimistic and pessimistic execution. The overhead of gas cost in the pessimistic execution versus the optimistic execution is 13%. The gas cost of the SCPSI2EC contract for the optimistic case is almost flat and the small changes are due to different input values that have been used in experiments. In the pessimistic case, however, the gas cost increases linearly with $log(n)$ (because of Merkle proof verification in the dispute resolution stage). The overhead of the gas cost in the pessimistic execution increases from 12% to 21% when n increases. In total, the gas cost of running SCPSI2EC is approximately 1.29 times higher than the gas cost of running SCPSIEC contract.

9   Concluding Remarks

We provided an argument that shows impossibility of achieving complete fairness in two-party mutual PSI when TTP is implemented by a smart contract, and redesigned DCCR to use a smart contract as the TTP, providing coin-compensated fairness. This is the first mutual PSI protocol that achieves fairness by replacing TTP with a smart contract for dispute resolution. We showed that using a smart contract allows us to significantly reduce the need for zero-knowledge proofs and use more efficient primitives. Our complexity analysis shows that compared to DCCR the computation complexity is reduced. We provided a proof-of-concept implementation for the SC and showed its gas cost as the set sizes were changed. Reducing communication complexity further and removing all zero-knowledge proofs in the protocol are interesting directions for future work.

References

1. Abadi, A., Murdoch, S.J.: Earn while you reveal: private set intersection that rewards participants. arXiv preprint arXiv:2301.03889 (2023)
2. Avizheh, S.: Implementation of fair private set intersection using smart contracts (2024). https://github.com/SepidehAvizheh/FairSC-PSI/tree/main
3. Avizheh, S., Haffey, P., Safavi-Naini, R.: Privacy-preserving fairswap: fairness and privacy interplay. Proc. Privacy Enhanc. Technolog. **2022**(1), 417–439 (2022)
4. Baum, C., David, B., Dowsley, R.: Insured MPC: efficient secure computation with financial penalties. In: Bonneau, J., Heninger, N. (eds.) FC 2020. LNCS, vol. 12059, pp. 404–420. Springer, Cham (2020). https://doi.org/10.1007/978-3-030-51280-4_22
5. Ben-Efraim, A., Nissenbaum, O., Omri, E., Paskin-Cherniavsky, A.: Psimple: practical multiparty maliciously-secure private set intersection. In: Proceedings of ACM Asia Conference on Computer and Communications Security, pp. 1098–1112 (2022)
6. Bentov, I., Kumaresan, R.: How to use bitcoin to design fair protocols. In: Garay, J.A., Gennaro, R. (eds.) CRYPTO 2014. LNCS, vol. 8617, pp. 421–439. Springer, Heidelberg (2014). https://doi.org/10.1007/978-3-662-44381-1_24
7. Camenisch, J., Zaverucha, G.M.: Private intersection of certified sets. In: Dingledine, R., Golle, P. (eds.) FC 2009. LNCS, vol. 5628, pp. 108–127. Springer, Heidelberg (2009). https://doi.org/10.1007/978-3-642-03549-4_7
8. Canetti, R.: Security and composition of multiparty cryptographic protocols. J. Cryptol. **13**(1), 143–202 (2000)

9. Chandran, N., Dasgupta, N., Gupta, D., Obbattu, S.L.B., Sekar, S., Shah, A.: Efficient linear multiparty psi and extensions to circuit/quorum psi. In: Proceedings of 2021 ACM Conference on Computer and Communications Security, pp. 1182–1204 (2021)

10. Chase, M., Miao, P.: Private set intersection in the internet setting from lightweight oblivious PRF. In: Micciancio, D., Ristenpart, T. (eds.) CRYPTO 2020. LNCS, vol. 12172, pp. 34–63. Springer, Cham (2020). https://doi.org/10.1007/978-3-030-56877-1_2

11. Cheon, J.H., Jarecki, S., Seo, J.H.: Multi-party privacy-preserving set intersection with quasi-linear complexity. IEICE Trans. Fundam. Electron. Commun. Comput. Sci. **95**(8), 1366–1378 (2012)

12. Cho, C., Dachman-Soled, D., Jarecki, S.: Efficient concurrent covert computation of string equality and set intersection. In: Sako, K. (ed.) CT-RSA 2016. LNCS, vol. 9610, pp. 164–179. Springer, Cham (2016). https://doi.org/10.1007/978-3-319-29485-8_10

13. Cleve, R.: Limits on the security of coin flips when half the processors are faulty. In: Proceedings of 18 Annual ACM Symposium on Theory of Computing, pp. 364–369 (1986)

14. Couteau, G., Roscoe, A.W., Ryan, P.Y.A.: Partially-fair computation from timed-release encryption and oblivious transfer. In: Baek, J., Ruj, S. (eds.) ACISP 2021. LNCS, vol. 13083, pp. 330–349. Springer, Cham (2021). https://doi.org/10.1007/978-3-030-90567-5_17

15. De Cristofaro, E., Jarecki, S., Kim, J., Tsudik, G.: Privacy-preserving policy-based information transfer. In: Goldberg, I., Atallah, M.J. (eds.) PETS 2009. LNCS, vol. 5672, pp. 164–184. Springer, Heidelberg (2009). https://doi.org/10.1007/978-3-642-03168-7_10

16. De Cristofaro, E., Kim, J., Tsudik, G.: Linear-complexity private set intersection protocols secure in malicious model. In: Abe, M. (ed.) ASIACRYPT 2010. LNCS, vol. 6477, pp. 213–231. Springer, Heidelberg (2010). https://doi.org/10.1007/978-3-642-17373-8_13

17. De Cristofaro, E., Tsudik, G.: Practical private set intersection protocols with linear complexity. In: Sion, R. (ed.) FC 2010. LNCS, vol. 6052, pp. 143–159. Springer, Heidelberg (2010). https://doi.org/10.1007/978-3-642-14577-3_13

18. Debnath, S.K., Dutta, R.: A fair and efficient mutual private set intersection protocol from a two-way oblivious pseudorandom function. In: Lee, J., Kim, J. (eds.) ICISC 2014. LNCS, vol. 8949, pp. 343–359. Springer, Cham (2015). https://doi.org/10.1007/978-3-319-15943-0_21

19. Debnath, S.K., Dutta, R.: New realizations of efficient and secure private set intersection protocols preserving fairness. In: Hong, S., Park, J.H. (eds.) ICISC 2016. LNCS, vol. 10157, pp. 254–284. Springer, Cham (2017). https://doi.org/10.1007/978-3-319-53177-9_14

20. Debnath, S.K., Dutta, R.: Towards fair mutual private set intersection with linear complexity. Secur. Commun. Netw. **9**(11), 1589–1612 (2016)

21. Dong, C., Chen, L., Camenisch, J., Russello, G.: Fair private set intersection with a semi-trusted arbiter. In: Wang, L., Shafiq, B. (eds.) DBSec 2013. LNCS, vol. 7964, pp. 128–144. Springer, Heidelberg (2013). https://doi.org/10.1007/978-3-642-39256-6_9

22. Dziembowski, S., Eckey, L., Faust, S.: Fairswap: how to fairly exchange digital goods. In: Proceedings of the 2018 ACM SIGSAC Conference on Computer and Communications Security, pp. 967–984 (2018)

23. Eckey, L., Faust, S., Schlosser, B.: Optiswap: fast optimistic fair exchange. IACR Cryptology ePrint Archive **2019**, 1330 (2019)
24. Freedman, M.J., Nissim, K., Pinkas, B.: Efficient private matching and set intersection. In: Cachin, C., Camenisch, J.L. (eds.) EUROCRYPT 2004. LNCS, vol. 3027, pp. 1–19. Springer, Heidelberg (2004). https://doi.org/10.1007/978-3-540-24676-3_1
25. Ghosh, S., Nilges, T.: An algebraic approach to maliciously secure private set intersection. In: Ishai, Y., Rijmen, V. (eds.) EUROCRYPT 2019. LNCS, vol. 11478, pp. 154–185. Springer, Cham (2019). https://doi.org/10.1007/978-3-030-17659-4_6
26. Goldreich, O.: Foundations of Cryptography, vol. 2. Cambridge Press, Cambridge (2004)
27. Gordon, S.D., Hazay, C., Katz, J., Lindell, Y.: Complete fairness in secure two-party computation. J. ACM (JACM) **58**(6), 1–37 (2011)
28. Gordon, S.D., Hazay, C., Le, P.H.: Fully secure psi via MPC-in-the-head. Proc. Privacy Enhanc. Technol. (2022)
29. Gordon, S.D., Katz, J.: Partial fairness in secure two-party computation. J. Cryptol. **25**(1), 14–40 (2012)
30. Hazay, C., Lindell, Y.: Efficient protocols for set intersection and pattern matching with security against malicious and covert adversaries. In: Canetti, R. (ed.) TCC 2008. LNCS, vol. 4948, pp. 155–175. Springer, Heidelberg (2008). https://doi.org/10.1007/978-3-540-78524-8_10
31. Hofheinz, D., Müller-Quade, J.: Universally composable commitments using random oracles. In: Naor, M. (ed.) TCC 2004. LNCS, vol. 2951, pp. 58–76. Springer, Heidelberg (2004). https://doi.org/10.1007/978-3-540-24638-1_4
32. Huberman, B.A., Franklin, M., Hogg, T.: Enhancing privacy and trust in electronic communities. In: Proceedings of 1st ACM Conference on Electronic Commerce, pp. 78–86 (1999)
33. Inbar, R., Omri, E., Pinkas, B.: Efficient scalable multiparty private set-intersection via garbled bloom filters. In: Catalano, D., De Prisco, R. (eds.) SCN 2018. LNCS, vol. 11035, pp. 235–252. Springer, Cham (2018). https://doi.org/10.1007/978-3-319-98113-0_13
34. Jarecki, S., Liu, X.: Efficient oblivious pseudorandom function with applications to adaptive OT and secure computation of set intersection. In: Reingold, O. (ed.) TCC 2009. LNCS, vol. 5444, pp. 577–594. Springer, Heidelberg (2009). https://doi.org/10.1007/978-3-642-00457-5_34
35. Jarecki, S., Liu, X.: Fast secure computation of set intersection. In: Garay, J.A., De Prisco, R. (eds.) SCN 2010. LNCS, vol. 6280, pp. 418–435. Springer, Heidelberg (2010). https://doi.org/10.1007/978-3-642-15317-4_26
36. Kamara, S., Mohassel, P., Raykova, M.: Outsourcing multi-party computation. IACR Cryptology ePrint Archive **2011**, 272 (2011)
37. Kamara, S., Mohassel, P., Raykova, M., Sadeghian, S.: Scaling private set intersection to billion-element sets. In: Christin, N., Safavi-Naini, R. (eds.) FC 2014. LNCS, vol. 8437, pp. 195–215. Springer, Heidelberg (2014). https://doi.org/10.1007/978-3-662-45472-5_13
38. Katz, J., Maurer, U., Tackmann, B., Zikas, V.: Universally composable synchronous computation. In: Sahai, A. (ed.) TCC 2013. LNCS, vol. 7785, pp. 477–498. Springer, Heidelberg (2013). https://doi.org/10.1007/978-3-642-36594-2_27
39. Kavousi, A., Mohajeri, J., Salmasizadeh, M.: Efficient scalable multi-party private set intersection using oblivious PRF. In: Roman, R., Zhou, J. (eds.) STM 2021. LNCS, vol. 13075, pp. 81–99. Springer, Cham (2021). https://doi.org/10.1007/978-3-030-91859-0_5

40. Kiayias, A., Zhou, H.-S., Zikas, V.: Fair and robust multi-party computation using a global transaction ledger. In: Fischlin, M., Coron, J.-S. (eds.) EUROCRYPT 2016. LNCS, vol. 9666, pp. 705–734. Springer, Heidelberg (2016). https://doi.org/10.1007/978-3-662-49896-5_25

41. Kim, M., Lee, H.T., Cheon, J.H.: Mutual private set intersection with linear complexity. In: Jung, S., Yung, M. (eds.) WISA 2011. LNCS, vol. 7115, pp. 219–231. Springer, Heidelberg (2012). https://doi.org/10.1007/978-3-642-27890-7_18

42. Kissner, L., Song, D.: Privacy-preserving set operations. In: Shoup, V. (ed.) CRYPTO 2005. LNCS, vol. 3621, pp. 241–257. Springer, Heidelberg (2005). https://doi.org/10.1007/11535218_15

43. Kolesnikov, V., Kumaresan, R., Rosulek, M., Trieu, N.: Efficient batched oblivious PRF with applications to private set intersection. In: Proceedings of 2016 ACM Conference on Computer and Communications Security, pp. 818–829 (2016)

44. Kolesnikov, V., Matania, N., Pinkas, B., Rosulek, M., Trieu, N.: Practical multi-party private set intersection from symmetric-key techniques. In: Proceedings of 2017 ACM Conference on Computer and Communications Security, pp. 1257–1272 (2017)

45. Kumaresan, R., Bentov, I.: How to use bitcoin to incentivize correct computations. In: Proceedings of 2014 ACM CCS, pp. 30–41 (2014)

46. Kumaresan, R., Bentov, I.: Amortizing secure computation with penalties. In: Proceedings of 2016 ACM CCS, pp. 418–429 (2016)

47. Kumaresan, R., Moran, T., Bentov, I.: How to use bitcoin to play decentralized poker. In: Proceedings of 22nd ACM CCS, pp. 195–206 (2015)

48. Kumaresan, R., Vaikuntanathan, V., Vasudevan, P.N.: Improvements to secure computation with penalties. In: Proceedings of 2016 ACM Conference on Computer and Communications Security, pp. 406–417 (2016)

49. Liu, J., Li, W., Karame, G.O., Asokan, N.: Toward fairness of cryptocurrency payments. IEEE Secur. Privacy 16(3), 81–89 (2018)

50. Maffei, I., Roscoe, A.: Optimally-fair exchange of secrets via delay encryption and commutative blinding. In: Baldimtsi, F., Cachin, C. (eds.) FC 2023. LNCS, vol. 13950, pp. 94–111. Springer, Cham (2024). https://doi.org/10.1007/978-3-031-47754-6_6

51. Meadows, C.: A more efficient cryptographic matchmaking protocol for use in the absence of a continuously available third party. In: 1986 IEEE Symposium on Security and Privacy, pp. 134–134. IEEE (1986)

52. Nevo, O., Trieu, N., Yanai, A.: Simple, fast malicious multiparty private set intersection. In: ACM Computer and Communications Security, pp. 1151–1165 (2021)

53. Raghuraman, S., Rindal, P.: Blazing fast psi from improved OKVS and subfield VOLE. In: ACM Conference on Computer and Communications Security, pp. 2505–2517 (2022)

54. Raikwar, M., Gligoroski, D., Kralevska, K.: SoK of used cryptography in blockchain. IEEE Access 7, 148550–148575 (2019)

55. SolGrined: Implementation of pedersen commitment in solidity (2023). https://github.com/18dew/solGrined/blob/master/contracts/

56. Zhang, E., Liu, F.H., Lai, Q., Jin, G., Li, Y.: Efficient multi-party private set intersection against malicious adversaries. In: Proceedings of the 2019 ACM SIGSAC Conference on Cloud Computing Security Workshop, pp. 93–104 (2019)

Powers-of-Tau to the People: Decentralizing Setup Ceremonies

Valeria Nikolaenko[1]($\boxtimes$), Sam Ragsdale[1], Joseph Bonneau[1,3], and Dan Boneh[2]

[1] A16Z Crypto Research Lab, St. Johns, USA
valeria.nikolaenko@gmail.com
[2] Stanford University, Stanford, USA
[3] New York University, New York, USA

Abstract. We propose several decentralized ceremonies for constructing a powers-of-tau structured reference string (SRS). Our protocols make use of a blockchain platform to run in a permissionless manner, where anyone can contribute randomness in exchange for paying the requisite transaction fees. The resulting SRS is secure as long as any single party participates honestly. We introduce several protocols optimized for different sized powers-of-tau setups and using an on-chain or off-chain data availability model to store the resulting string. We implement our most efficient protocol on top of Ethereum, demonstrating practical concrete performance.

1 Introduction

Many cryptographic protocols assume a *trusted setup ceremony*, a one-time procedure to generate public parameters which also generates an unwanted trapdoor as a byproduct. Perhaps the earliest example is the accumulator scheme of Benaloh and de Mare [11] which requires a public modulus N such that nobody knows its factorization $N = p \cdot q$, a trapdoor which allows forging a proof that any element is included in the accumulator.

In general, a setup ceremony consists of a randomized algorithm $\mathsf{Setup}() \xrightarrow{\$}$ (pp, τ). The *public parameters* (pp), also called a *structured reference string* (SRS), must be known to all users of the system, whereas the *trapdoor* (τ) must be discarded for the scheme to be secure. Such trapdoors have been called "toxic waste" due to the importance of destroying them after the setup is complete.

In the simplest case of a fully *trusted setup*, a single entity computes $\mathsf{Setup}()$ and is trusted to discard τ. Setup ceremonies have been conducted by several prominent cryptocurrency applications, which have pioneered the use of secure multiparty computation (MPC) ceremonies to avoid having any single party ever know the final trapdoor. These ceremonies have differed in the number of participants involved, the number of rounds, and the exact trust model, but so far all have been facilitated by a centralized coordinator. In particular, the coordinator has the ability to choose which parties are able to participate, making these protocols *permissioned*. We review setup ceremonies run in practice in Sect. 2.2.

C. Pöpper and L. Batina (Eds.): ACNS 2024, LNCS 14585, pp. 105–134, 2024.
https://doi.org/10.1007/978-3-031-54776-8_5

In this work, we endeavor to remove the coordinator and build the first truly *decentralized* and *permissionless* setup ceremony. This approach is appropriate given a multiparty computation which requires only one honest participant (sometimes called an "anytrust" or "dishonest majority" model). In this model, there is no downside (beyond computational overhead) of allowing additional participants to contribute to the protocol. We call this the *more-the-merrier* property. A more-the-merrier protocol can safely be opened to the general public, enabling an interesting new security property: any individual can participate and therefore they can trust the final result (at least to the extent that they trust themselves to have participated correctly), even if they make no assumptions about any of the other participants.

Powers-of-Tau. We focus on a common type of ceremony which constructs a powers-of-tau SRS. Working in elliptic curve groups $\mathbb{G}_1, \mathbb{G}_2$ of prime order p with generators B_1 and B_2 respectively and an efficiently computable pairing, the goal of the setup is to produce a public parameter string:

$$\mathsf{pp} := \left(\tau B_1, \tau^2 B_1, \ldots, \tau^n B_1 \; ; \quad \tau B_2, \tau^2 B_2, \ldots, \tau^k B_2\right) \in \mathbb{G}_1^n \times \mathbb{G}_2^k.$$

The value $\tau \in \mathbb{Z}_p$ is the trapdoor: it should be randomly generated and unknown to anybody. The structure of this string enables efficient *re-randomization*. Without knowing τ, it is possible to take an existing string pp and produce a new randomized string pp' by choosing a new random value τ' and multiplying each component of pp by an appropriate power of τ'. The new trapdoor will be $\tau \cdot \tau'$, which is secure as long as *either* τ or τ' are unknown and neither of them is zero.

This re-randomizability leads to a simple serial MPC protocol in which each participant in turn re-randomizes the string. Note that this can be done on an ongoing (or "perpetual") basis, as new participants can continue to join and re-randomize the string for future use. As long as each participant re-randomizes correctly and at least one participant destroys their local randomness, the cumulatively constructed string will be secure.

Applications. Powers-of-tau setup is required for many protocols:

- The KZG polynomial commitment scheme [44] requires a setup of n powers of tau in any one of the groups (e.g., $\mathbb{G}_1$), plus one power of tau in the other group (e.g., $\mathbb{G}_2$).
- SNARKs built from the KZG univariate polynomial commitment scheme, such as Sonic [54], Plonk [35], and Marlin [26], require a powers-of-tau string proportional in length to the size of the statement being proved.
- KZG commitments are also used in Verkle trees [47,50], a bandwidth-efficient alternative to Merkle trees. Unlike a binary Merkle tree, a Verkle tree is a b-ary tree, where each node is a vector commitment to up to b children. While Merkle trees have $O(\log_2 n)$ inclusion proof size, where n is the number of nodes, Verkle trees have $O(\log_b n)$ inclusion proof size. The most efficient Verkle trees, e.g. BalanceProofs [62], are based on KZG polynomial commitments requiring a powers-of-tau setup.

– Fast proofs of multi-scalar multiplication (MSM) over arbitrary groups of size $O(\log d)$ are possible using a powers-of-tau setup of length $O(\sqrt{d})$, where d is the number of scalars and group elements [16].
– The recent Danksharding proposal [20] for sharding Ethereum relies on a powers-of-tau string with 4096 elements in $\mathbb{G}_1$ and 64 in $\mathbb{G}_2$.

Challenges to Decentralization. Historically, ceremonies have been administered by a centralized coordinator which ensures several important properties, all of which we seek to achieve in a decentralized fashion:

– **Consensus:** All participants should agree on the final value of pp.
– **Validity:** Each participant should only be able to re-randomize the current string (and not simply replace it with one for which the trapdoor is known).
– **Data Availability:** The final string must be available for all to download, as well as the history of prior versions and participants for auditability.
– **Censorship Resistance:** Any willing participant should be able to contribute.

In this work we demonstrate how to replace the centralized coordinator with a smart contract, observing that blockchain platforms are designed to provide most or all of our desired properties. In particular, blockchains inherently provide consensus, previously done by fiat of the central coordinator, as well as censorship resistance, which has not been an explicit goal of centrally coordinated ceremonies. Validity and data availability are more interesting and provide several design options. For validity, we can rely on on-chain (Layer-1) verification of zero-knowledge proofs that each update is valid, or (to reduce costs) use a Layer-2 approach. We also show that it is possible (and even cheaper) to defer this task to users, who will verify the string before using it, which may be preferable in some settings. Similarly, for data availability we might post the full string pp on chain or, for efficiency, post only a commitment and rely on an external data-availability layer.

Contributions. We design ceremonies with two data-availability models: one with the entire string pp posted on-chain, and one with only a commitment to pp, namely $c = H(pp)$, posted on-chain and the full string stored in an external data-availability system. See Fig. 1 highlighting the properties of the two models that we develop. The latter can offer significant cost savings for large strings as on-chain data storage is expensive.

With data available on-chain, we present an efficient pairing-based proof construction for verifying each participant's contribution (Sect. 4). We implemented this protocol for the Ethereum blockchain, coding in Solidity and using the BN254 curve. We describe our implemention in Sect. 6; we have also released our open-source implementation (link). Participating in the ceremony costs 190,000 to 11,500,000 gas (about $5 to $315 at current Ethereum prices), depending on the size of the desired resulting parameters (in this case between 8 and 1024 powers-of-tau). The size of the setup is limited but can still be used to power

Verkle trees, data-availability sampling, and zero-knowledge SNARKs for small statements.

For larger strings, we develop methods that have on-chain verification, yet only store a short commitment to the full setup on-chain (see Sect. 5). We discuss how to make the data-availability solutions that can facilitate such setups light-weight. The data-availability service only needs to be able to produce a commitment over the data of an appropriate form and store at most two latest contributions.

Paper Organization. We discuss related work and some historical notes on setup ceremonies in Sect. 2. In Sect. 4, we present our fully on-chain protocol for powers-of-tau setup. In Sect. 5, we discuss several protocols for powers-of-tau setup with off-chain data availability, supporting larger structured reference strings. In Sect. 6, we describe our practical implementation and performance evaluation of the fully on-chain protocol on top of Ethereum. Finally we conclude in Sect. 7 by discussing various practical concerns and possible extensions, including censorship resistance, incentives and methods to lower on-chain cost through roll-ups, optimistic verification, batching, IVC and other techniques.

Data availability	Commitment scheme	Section	Proof size	Verifier time
On-chain	none	4	$O_\lambda(1)$	$O_\lambda(n)$
Off-chain	Any commitment	5.1	$O_\lambda(\log n)$	$O_\lambda(\log n)$
	AFGHO unstructured commitment	5.2	$O_\lambda(\log n)$	$O_\lambda(\log n)$

Fig. 1. Comparing on-chain powers-of-tau of length n to off-chain powers-of-tau with an on-chain commitment. On-chain storage requires linear on-chain work to verify an update. With off-chain storage we require only logarithmic on-chain work to verify an update. The AFGHO-based proof in the third row performs better in practice than the generic proof in the second row.

2   Related Work

2.1   Multiparty Setup Ceremonies

Generically, any trusted setup algorithm can be implemented via secure multiparty computation (MPC) to prevent any single entity from learning the trapdoor. Ben-Sasson et al. [10] proposed the first multi-party protocol to sample public parameters for a zero-knowledge proof scheme which was instantiated for Zcash Sprout. Although this ceremony was not instantiating the powers-of-tau, it paved the way for crowd-sourcing subsequent ceremonies.

Bowe et al. [14] designed a protocol for Groth16 [40], where constructing a powers-of-tau public string was part of one of two phases. The protocol however required a random beacon, an auxiliary process that produces publicly verifiable unpredictable and unbiasable randomness. Kohlweiss, Maller, Siim, and Volkhov [46] removed the need for a random beacon in the setup by proving that the setup remains secure for use with zero-knowledge proofs even if the public parameters have some degree of bias. Cohen et al. [28] demonstrated that the KZG commitments also remain secure in case the public parameters have bounded bias, thus similarly eliminating the need to use the random beacons for setups to be used for KZG commitments. Ganesh et al. [36] gave a UC secure protocol for Groth16 setup. The work of Groth, Kohlweiss, Maller, Meiklejohn, and Miers [41] introduced an updatable SRS model, they construct a SNARK where the SRS can be updated by anybody. The security is guaranteed as long as at least one of the contributors is honest. The generated setup string is different from the powers-of-tau, and the paper is not focusing on on-chain/off-chain deployments or optimizing the verification.

All of these protocols fall in a category of the more-the-merrier protocols, as they each require only a single one honest participant to be secure. However, all were built with the assumption of a central coordinator. Buterin [17] suggested a simple way to verify the update to the setup that, as we observe in this work, opens the possibility for a gas-efficient on-chain deployment which we base our on-chain protocol on.

Multiparty setup ceremonies have also been demonstrated for RSA-style parameter setup [13,34,37,42,53]. Chen et al. [25] demonstrated a multiparty protocol for sampling a 2,048 bit RSA modulus which can scale to thousands of participants and only requires a single honest participant for security.

2.2 Setup Ceremonies in Practice

Some of the most prominent ceremonies have been run by Zcash, a privacy-oriented blockchain project. Six participants carried out the first Zcash ceremony, Sprout, in 2016, and 90 participants built parameters for a Sapling upgrade in 2018.

The perpetual "powers-of-tau" ceremony was first run in a continuous mode, where contributions are still being accepted, by the team of the Semaphore project, a privacy preserving technology for anonymous signaling on Ethereum. The setup uses a BN254 elliptic curve and has had 71 participants so far. Other prominent projects later used this setup to run their own ceremonies on top, including Tornado.Cash [23], Hermez network [43], and Loopring [31]. Similar ceremonies on other curves were run by Aztec [6] for zkSync, a "layer two" Ethereum scaling solution that uses zero knowledge rollups; by Filecoin [32], a decentralized data storage protocol; by Celo [24], a layer-1 blockchain, for their light-client Plumo; Aleo [3], a blockchain for private applications.

Ethereum is currently running [33] a smaller trusted setup ceremony for its upcoming ProtoDankSharding and DankSharding upgrades: the targeted sizes are $2^{12}, 2^{13}, 2^{14}, 2^{15}$ powers in $\mathbb{G}_1$ and 64 powers in $\mathbb{G}_2$, over the BLS12 -381 curve. Those two upgrades will increase the amount of data that the Ethereum chain provides to clients for storage. This data will have a suggested expiry 30–60 days, it will not be accessible for the smart contracts in full, except for short KZG-commitments to the data. With around 95,000 contributions since its start in Jan 13th, 2023, it is the largest trusted setup ceremony to date in terms of participation.

2.3 Proof Systems with Transparent Setup

It is important to note that there has been considerable research effort aimed at building cryptographic systems with fully *transparent* setup; that is, setup in which there is no trapdoor at all and therefore no trust assumption is required for the setup ceremony. A notable effort in that direction comes from a partnership of Electric Coin Company, Protocol Labs, the Filecoin Foundation, and the Ethereum Foundation, who collaboratively work on the Halo2 proof-system [29] that does not require a trusted setup. Halo2 powers the ZCash cryptocurrency since Zcash Network Upgrade 5 (NU5) activated on mainnet on May 31, 2022.

Similarly, transparent setup is possible to replace RSA-style trusted setup, using *class groups* of imaginary quadratic order instead of the group $\mathbb{Z}_N^*$ for a large composite modulus N [52]. The Chia blockchain [27] utilizes class groups and randomly re-samples the group parameters periodically, avoiding the need for trusted setup.

However, known trustless systems don't match the efficiency of the ones based on a trusted setup: the zk-snarks have poly-logarithmic-time verification (e.g. Halo2 and STARKs) compared to constant-time (e.g. Groth16, Plonk, Marlin), and polynomial commitments have poly-logarithmic-size evaluation-opening proofs (e.g. FRI, Dory) compared to constant-size proofs (e.g. KZG). It remains to be an open problem and an impactful research direction to come up with a system for the aforementioned applications that does not require a trusted setup while providing constant-time verification, or alternatively prove an impossibility result in this regard. In the meanwhile, a unified framework for running setup ceremonies in a transparent, verifiable and censorship-resistant manner would help bootstrap more efficient cryptosystems.

3 A Powers-of-Tau System: Definitions

Our goal is to construct a "powers of τ" SRS of the following form:

$$\mathsf{pp} = (\tau B_1, \tau^2 B_1, \tau^3 B_1, \ldots, \tau^n B_1; \quad \tau B_2, \tau^2 B_2, \ldots, \tau^k B_2) \in \mathbb{G}_1^n \times \mathbb{G}_2^k , \quad (3.1)$$

where τ is unknown. We will show below that a computationally-limited verifier (e.g. a smart contract) can use the pairing to efficiently verify that pp is *well formed*, namely there exists a $\tau \in \mathbb{Z}_p^*$ such that pp satisfies (3.1).

Note that some applications require powers-of-τ strings in slightly different forms. Our techniques can generally be adapted and we focus on this simplest form. A notable case is "punctured" powers-of-τ strings which are missing a specific element. We discuss this case in Appendix D.

Our goal is to construct pp using a sequential multi-party computation between m contributors in m rounds, such that contributor number j contributes only in round number j, and does nothing in all other rounds. Each contributor can efficiently prove that their participation was correct. The main challenge is to ensure that the value of τ is unknown even if all but one of the contributors are malicious. In this way it is possible to conduct a permissionless setup in which any contributor is free to contribute, mediated by a smart contract which verifies each participant's contribution. Using a smart contract as the mediator ensures that anyone who wants to contribute can.

Notation. We use $\lambda \in \mathbb{Z}^+$ to denote the security parameter. We use $x \leftarrow y$ to denote the assignment of the value of y to x, and write $x \xleftarrow{\$} S$ to denote sampling an element from the set S independently and uniformly at random. For a positive integer p we use $\mathbb{Z}_p$ to denote the ring $\mathbb{Z}/p\mathbb{Z}$. We write $\mathbb{Z}_p^*$ for the set of non-zero elements in $\mathbb{Z}_p$. For a positive integer m we use $[m]$ to denote the set $\{1, \ldots, m\}$. We use $\mathrm{poly}(\lambda)$ and $\mathrm{negl}(\lambda)$ to denote a polynomial function and a negligible function in the security parameter λ, respectively.

Definition 1. *A Powers-of-Tau system is a triple of poly-time algorithms:*

- *GlobalSetup$(1^\lambda, n, k) \to$ par. The algorithm generates global parameters* par *that describe the three bilinear groups $\mathbb{G}_1, \mathbb{G}_2, \mathbb{G}_T$, each of prime order p, with generators B_1, B_2, B_T respectively, equipped with an efficiently computable non-degenerate bilinear pairing $e : \mathbb{G}_1 \times \mathbb{G}_2 \to \mathbb{G}_T$. These parameters are an implicit input to the remaining algorithms.*
- *Update$(\mathsf{pp}, r) \to (\mathsf{pp}', \pi)$. The algorithm uses the provided randomness $r \in \mathbb{Z}_p^*$ to update the powers-of-tau* pp *to* pp' *along with a proof π that the update was done correctly.*
- *Verify$(\mathsf{pp}, \mathsf{pp}', \pi) \to \{0, 1\}$. The algorithm checks the proof π and outputs 1 to accept the update.*

We require that for all supported (n, k), all par *output by GlobalSetup$(1^\lambda, n, k)$, all $\mathsf{pp} \in \mathbb{G}_1^n \times \mathbb{G}_2^k$ of the form (3.1), and all $r \in \mathbb{Z}_p^*$, we have*

$$\text{if } (\mathsf{pp}', \pi) \leftarrow \text{Update}(\mathsf{pp}, r) \text{ then Verify}(\mathsf{pp}, \mathsf{pp}', \pi) = 1.$$

The GlobalSetup algorithm need only be run once and can be reused for multiple powers-of-tau setups. It is not a trusted setup in that no secret randomness is required. GlobalSetup utilizes an algorithm GroupGen(1^λ) to generate the three additive pairing groups $\mathbb{G}_1, \mathbb{G}_2, \mathbb{G}_T$ and their generators.

The Verify algorithm runs on chain and must therefore be as efficient as possible to reduce transaction costs. We next define the initial state of the system and the security requirements.

Initialization. The Powers-of-Tau system begins with an initial state defined as:

$$\mathsf{pp}_0 := (B_1, B_1, B_1, \ldots, B_1; \quad B_2, B_2, \ldots, B_2) \in \mathbb{G}_1^n \times \mathbb{G}_2^k . \tag{3.2}$$

This is equivalent to an SRS with $\tau = 1$.

Security. We define security of a Powers-of-Tau system (Setup, Update, Verify) using a game that captures a setting where the adversary controls all the contributors except for one honest contributor. The game is stated with respect to some predicate

$$\Pi : \mathbb{Z}_p \times \mathcal{W} \to \{0,1\} .$$

At the end of the game the adversary outputs some $w \in \mathcal{W}$ and wins the game if $\Pi(\tau, w) = 1$, where τ is the secret exponent used to define the final powers-of-tau. This w represents some information that $\mathcal{A}$ was able to learn about τ. We give examples of some important predicates Π after the definition.

Since the prime p is determined by the security parameter, we define security with respect to a family of predicates $\Pi = \{\Pi_p : \mathbb{Z}_p \times \mathcal{W} \to \{0,1\}\}_{p \in \mathcal{P}}$ where $\mathcal{P}$ is the set of all integer primes. We say that Π is poly-time if there is an algorithm that for all p, τ, w evaluates $\Pi_p(\tau, w)$ in polynomial time in the security parameter λ.

Formally, Π-security is defined using a game between an adversary $\mathcal{A}$ and a challenger. The game is parameterized by (n, k) and proceeds as follows:

- The challenger runs GlobalSetup$(1^\lambda, n, k)$ and sends the resulting global parameters par to $\mathcal{A}$. This defines pp_0.
- $\mathcal{A}$ outputs a sequence of pairs $(\mathsf{pp}_1, \pi_1), \ldots, (\mathsf{pp}_\ell, \pi_\ell)$.
- The challenger samples $r \xleftarrow{\$} \mathbb{Z}_p^*$, runs Update$(\mathsf{pp}_\ell, r)$ to get $(\mathsf{pp}_{\ell+1}, \pi_{\ell+1})$, and sends $(\mathsf{pp}_{\ell+1}, \pi_{\ell+1})$ to $\mathcal{A}$. This emulates an honest contributor.
- Adversary $\mathcal{A}$ outputs a further sequence of pairs $(\mathsf{pp}_{\ell+2}, \pi_{\ell+2}), \ldots, (\mathsf{pp}_m, \pi_m)$ along with a guess $w \in \mathcal{W}$.

The adversary wins if Verify$(\mathsf{pp}_{i-1}, \mathsf{pp}_i, \pi_i) = 1$ for all $i \in [m]$, and either (i) $\Pi_p(\tau_m, w) = 1$, where τ_m is the secret exponent that defines pp_m, or (ii) pp_m is a malformed powers-of-tau.

We will show in Theorem 2 below how to use the pairing to efficiently test that pp_m is a *well formed* powers-of-tau. Hence, as long as Verify includes this test, the only way for $\mathcal{A}$ to win the game is to output some $w \in \mathcal{W}$ such that $\Pi_p(\tau_m, w) = 1$.

Definition 2. *Let* $\Pi = \{\Pi_p : \mathbb{Z}_p \times \mathcal{W} \to \{0,1\}\}_{p \in \mathcal{P}}$ *be a family of poly-time predicates. A Powers-of-Tau system is* Π*-secure if for all* n, k *that are* poly(λ), *and for all PPT adversaries* $\mathcal{A}$, *the probability that* $\mathcal{A}$ *wins the* Π*-security game is a negligible function of the security parameter* λ.

Remark 1. Definition 2 requires that the adversary cannot compute some information about the final τ_m. It does not require τ_m to be close to uniform in $\mathbb{Z}_p^*$ because that is not possible to achieve in our settings. If the last contributor is malicious, it could cause τ_m to become non-uniform in $\mathbb{Z}_p^*$ by repeatedly running the update procedure until the resulting pp satisfies some property (for example, the first ten bits of the first element in pp are zero).

Despite Remark 1, our definitional framework is sufficient for many applications. For example, suppose that the powers-of-tau is to be used in a KZG polynomial commitment scheme [44], and we need to ensure *evaluation binding*, meaning that a committed polynomial cannot be convincingly opened to two different values at one input. To do so, let us define the family of predicates Π_p^{SDH} where

$$\Pi_p^{\text{SDH}}\left(\tau \in \mathbb{Z}_p,\ (c, T) \in \mathbb{Z}_p \times \mathbb{G}_1\right) = 1 \quad \Longleftrightarrow \quad T = \left(\frac{1}{\tau+c}\right)B_1 \ . \tag{3.3}$$

Suppose that no PPT algorithm that takes a powers-of-tau string as input, can find a pair (c, T) that satisfies this predicate. Then it is not difficult to show that this implies evaluation binding for KZG. Hence, a powers-of-tau string that is generated by a Π^{SDH}-secure powers-of-tau system can be safely used to provide evaluation binding in KZG.

Note that the predicate Π_p^{SDH} can be checked in polynomial time using the element $Q_1 := \tau B_2$ from the powers-of-tau string because

$$\Pi_p^{\text{SDH}}\left(\tau,\ (c, T)\right) = 1 \quad \Longleftrightarrow \quad e(T,\ Q_1 + cB_2) = e(B_1, B_2) \ .$$

We will come back to this predicate when we analyze security of our powers-of-tau system. Other applications that require a powers-of-tau string can choose to use other predicates to argue security.

4 Powers-of-Tau Setup with Full Data On-Chain

We now describe the Update and Verify algorithms for our powers-of-tau system, when the entire string pp is stored on chain. This is the simplest construction, though may carry high costs for large powers-of-τ strings as it requires the verifier to do linear work (in n and k) for each update.

Let pp be the current SRS string which is assumed to be:

$$\begin{aligned}
\mathsf{pp} = (\ &P_1,\quad P_2, \ldots, \quad P_n;\quad Q_1, \ldots, \quad Q_k) \\
= (\ &\tau B_1, \tau^2 B_1, \ldots, \tau^n B_1;\quad \tau B_2, \ldots, \tau^k B_2)
\end{aligned} \tag{4.1}$$

for some (unknown) τ in $\mathbb{Z}_p^*$.

Let r be a random element in $\mathbb{Z}_p^*$. The Update(pp, r) algorithm begins by computing the updated SRS string pp' as

$$\begin{aligned}
\mathsf{pp}' := (\ &P_1',\quad P_2', \ldots, \quad P_n';\quad Q_1', \ldots, \quad Q_k') \\
= (\ &rP_1, r^2 P_2, \ldots, r^n P_n;\quad rQ_1, \ldots, r^k Q_k)
\end{aligned} \tag{4.2}$$

Observe that

$$\begin{aligned}
\mathsf{pp}' &= (r\tau B_1, r^2 \tau^2 B_1, \ldots, r^n \tau^n B_1;\quad r\tau B_2, \ldots, r^k \tau^k B_2) \\
&= (\tau' B_1, (\tau')^2 B_1, \ldots, (\tau')^n B_1;\quad \tau' B_2, \ldots, (\tau')^k B_2)
\end{aligned}$$

where $\tau' := r \cdot \tau$ is the secret exponent[1] for pp'. If an attacker knows τ but not r, and r was chosen uniformly at random from $\mathbb{Z}_p^*$ (meaning in particular that $r \neq 0$), then the attacker will have no information about τ. Consequently, if at least one of the contributors samples their update r randomly, and properly destroys it, then the final secret $\tau_m = r_1 \cdot r_2 \cdot \ldots \cdot r_m \in \mathbb{Z}_p^*$ is randomly distributed and unknown to anyone. This is assuming that none of the contributors set $r_i = 0$, which is easy to check for.

Update Proofs. Next, the Update(pp, r) algorithm needs to output a proof that the update was done correctly. In particular, the verify algorithm will need to convince itself of the following three claims:

Check #1 - the contributor knows r: this is needed to ensure that the latest update builds on the work of the preceding participants.

Check #2 - the new parameters pp' are well-formed: there is some $\tau' \in \mathbb{Z}_p$ such that pp' satisfies (3.1).

Check #3 - pp' is not degenerate, namely $r \neq 0$: defends against an update trying to erase the setup thus undermining the contributions of previous participants.

We will show that the verifier can efficiently check claims #2 and #3 on its own.

We first explain how to efficiently prove claim #1. To provide a zero-knowledge proof of knowledge of r, the Update(pp, r) algorithm has two options: it can use a Fiat-Shamir version of Schnorr's Σ-protocol [56,57] or it can use a BLS-style proof of possession [55] for r. The latter is more expensive to verify on-chain as it requires the verifier to compute pairings. We therefore focus on the former approach which works as follows:

Update(pp, r) samples a random $z \xleftarrow{\$} \mathbb{Z}_p^*$, computes

$$h \leftarrow \mathsf{HASH}(P_1' \,||\, P_1 \,||\, z \cdot P_1) \quad \text{and} \quad \pi \leftarrow (z \cdot P_1, \ z + h \cdot r) \in \mathbb{G}_1 \times \mathbb{Z}_p,$$

and outputs the proof $\pi \in \mathbb{G}_1 \times \mathbb{Z}_p$. Here HASH is a hash function that outputs elements in $\mathbb{Z}_p$. In the security proof we will model HASH as a random oracle.

The Verify(pp, pp', π) algorithm (an on-chain smart contract) verifies the proof $\pi = (\pi_1, \pi_2) \in \mathbb{G}_1 \times \mathbb{Z}_p$ by checking that:

Check # 1: $\pi_2 \cdot P_1 = \pi_1 + \mathsf{HASH}(P_1' \,||\, P_1 \,||\, \pi_1) \cdot P_1$

We next show how to verify claims #2 and #3.

Definition 3. *We say that the string* pp $= (P_1, P_2, P_3, \ldots, P_n; Q_1, Q_2, \ldots, Q_k)$ *is well-formed if there exists $\tau \in \mathbb{Z}_p$ such that $P_i = \tau^i B_1$ and $Q_\ell = \tau^\ell B_2$ for all $i = 1 \ldots n$ and $\ell = 1 \ldots k$.*

---

[1] Note that it is also possible to compute an additive update to the tau ($\tau' \leftarrow r + \tau$), however it would require the contributor to compute many multi-scalar multiplications making it less efficient.

To verify that pp is well-formed, the verifier samples two random scalars $\rho_1, \rho_2 \xleftarrow{\$} \mathbb{Z}_p^*$ and checks that:

Check # 2: (4.3)
$$e\left(\sum_{i=1}^{n} \rho_1^{i-1} P_i, \ B_2 + \sum_{\ell=1}^{k-1} \rho_2^{\ell} Q_\ell\right) = e\left(B_1 + \sum_{i=1}^{n-1} \rho_1^{i} P_i, \ \sum_{\ell=1}^{k} \rho_2^{\ell-1} Q_\ell\right)$$

For a well-formed string pp the check will always pass successfully, since:

$$e\left(\tau B_1 + \sum_{i=1}^{n-1} \left(\rho_1^i \cdot \tau^{i+1} B_1\right), \ B_2 + \sum_{\ell=1}^{k-1} \left(\rho_2^\ell \tau^\ell B_2\right)\right) =$$
$$e\left(B_1 + \sum_{i=1}^{n-1} \left(\rho_1^i \cdot \tau^i B_1\right), \ \tau \cdot \left(B_2 + \sum_{\ell=1}^{k-1} \left(\rho_2^\ell \tau^\ell B_2\right)\right)\right)$$

We prove that this check is sound in Theorem 2 below.

One complication is that an on-chain verifier does not have access to secure randomness. Instead, it will generate the scalars $\rho_1, \rho_2 \in \mathbb{Z}_p$ by hashing the string submitted by the contributor as $\rho_1 \leftarrow \mathsf{HASH}(\mathsf{pp}'\|1)$ and $\rho_2 \leftarrow \mathsf{HASH}(\mathsf{pp}'\|2)$.

Finally to ensure that the updated setup is non-degenerative, the verifier simply checks that the first element in pp' non-zero:

Check #3: $P_1' \neq 0$ (4.4)

Correctness: it is easy to check that the Update and Verify algorithms satisfy our correctness requirement.

4.1   Security

We now argue that the powers-of-tau system in the previous section satisfies the security definition (Definition 2). Recall that security is defined with respect to a poly-time predicate family $\Pi = \{\Pi_p : \mathbb{Z}_p \times \mathcal{W} \to \{0,1\}\}_{p \in \mathcal{P}}$. Let us first define the (n,k)-Π-DH assumption. The assumption says that no PPT adversary that takes a powers-of-tau string with secret exponent $\tau \in \mathbb{Z}_p$ as input, can find a $w \in \mathcal{W}$ such that $\Pi_p(\tau, w) = 1$.

Definition 4. *Let* $\Pi = \{\Pi_p : \mathbb{Z}_p \times \mathcal{W} \to \{0,1\}\}_{p \in \mathcal{P}}$ *be a poly-time predicate family. We say that the (n,k)-Π-**DH** assumption holds for the bilinear group generator* GroupGen *if for all PPT algorithms* $\mathcal{A}$,

$$\Pr\left[\Pi_p(\tau, \ \mathcal{A}(par, \ \tau B_1, \tau^2 B_1, \ldots, \tau^n B_1, \ \tau B_2, \tau^2 B_2, \ldots, \tau^k B_2) = 1)\right] \leq negl(\lambda),$$

where $par \xleftarrow{\$} $ GroupGen(1^λ) *and* $\tau \xleftarrow{\$} \mathbb{Z}_p^*$.

The (n,k)-Π-DH assumption encompasses a large class of standard cryptographic assumptions. For example, taking Π to be the predicate family Π^{SDH} from (3.3) gives the so called (n,k)-Strong Diffie-Hellman (SDH) assumption [12].

Definition 5. *We say that the predicate family* $\Pi = \{\Pi_p : \mathbb{Z}_p \times \mathcal{W} \to \{0,1\}\}_{p \in \mathcal{P}}$ *is **self reducible** if there is a PPT algorithm* Reduce *such that for all* $p \in \mathcal{P}$, *all* $\tau, r \in \mathbb{Z}_p^*$, *and all* $w \in \mathcal{W}$ *we have*

$$\Pi_p(\tau, w) = 1 \quad \Longrightarrow \quad \Pi_p(\tau \cdot r, \text{ Reduce}(r, w)) = 1 .$$

In other words, given a valid w for τ, algorithm Reduce outputs a valid w' for $\tau \cdot r$. For example, the predicate family Π^{SDH} from (3.3) is self reducible. To see why, observe that for all $p \in \mathcal{P}$ and $r \in \mathbb{Z}_p^*$ we have

$$\Pi_p^{\text{SDH}}(\tau, (c, T)) = 1 \quad \Longrightarrow \quad \Pi_p^{\text{SDH}}(\tau r, (cr, (1/r) \cdot T)) = 1$$

because

$$T = \tfrac{1}{\tau + c} \cdot B_1 \quad \Longrightarrow \quad \tfrac{1}{r} \cdot T = \tfrac{1}{\tau r + cr} \cdot B_1 .$$

With these definitions in place, we can now state the security theorem.

Theorem 1. *Let* $\Pi = \{\Pi_p : \mathbb{Z}_p \times \mathcal{W} \to \{0,1\}\}_{p \in \mathcal{P}}$ *be a poly-time self reducible predicate family. Then the powers-of-tau system in Sect. 4 is* Π-*secure, as in Definition 2, assuming the* (n, k)-Π-*DH assumption holds for* GroupGen *and the hash function* HASH *is modeled as a random oracle.*

We give the proof intuition and defer the proof to the full version of the paper.

Proof idea. For now, let us assume that the proof system used in the powers-of-tau system is zero knowledge and simulation extractable [38] even for a prover that proves multiple statements one after the other. We will justify these two assumptions later on.

We are given an adversary $\mathcal{A}$ that wins the attack game in Definition 2 with non-negligible probability. By Theorem 2 below, the only way for $\mathcal{A}$ to win the game is to output some $w_m \in \mathcal{W}$ such that $\Pi_p(\tau_m, w_m) = 1$. We use $\mathcal{A}$ to construct an adversary $\mathcal{B}$ that breaks the (n, k)-Π-DH assumption. Algorithm $\mathcal{B}$ is given as input an (n, k)-Π-DH challenge

$$\mathsf{pp}_{\text{chal}} := (P_1, \ldots, P_n; Q_1, \ldots, Q_k) \in \mathbb{G}_1^n \times \mathbb{G}_2^k .$$

It needs to find some $w \in \mathcal{W}$ such that $\Pi_p(\tau, w) = 1$, where $\tau \in \mathbb{Z}_p^*$ is the secret exponent used define this challenge. Algorithm $\mathcal{B}$ begins by running adversary $\mathcal{A}$ and the following happens:

- $\mathcal{B}$ receives from $\mathcal{A}$ a sequence of ℓ pairs $(\mathsf{pp}_1, \pi_1), \ldots, (\mathsf{pp}_\ell, \pi_\ell)$.
- $\mathcal{B}$ sends to $\mathcal{A}$ the pair $(\mathsf{pp}_{\text{chal}}, \pi)$ where π is a simulated proof that $\mathsf{pp}_{\text{chal}}$ is a valid update. Here we are using the zero knowledge property of the proof system.
- $\mathcal{B}$ receives from $\mathcal{A}$ an additional sequence of pairs $(\mathsf{pp}_{\ell+2}, \pi_{\ell+2}), \ldots, (\mathsf{pp}_m, \pi_m)$ along with a guess $w_m \in \mathcal{W}$.

Now $\mathcal{B}$ will use the extractor to extract from $\mathcal{A}$ all the randomizers $r_{\ell+2}, \ldots, r_m$ in $\mathbb{Z}_p^*$ that the adversary used to update the SRS in the second set of pairs that it output. To do so we are using the simulation extractability property of the proof system. Now, if all the extracted randomizers are correct, then

$$\tau_m = \tau \cdot (r_{\ell+2} \cdots r_m) \, ,$$

where τ_m is the exponent used to define pp_m. Moreover, if w_m output by $\mathcal{A}$ indeed satisfies $\Pi_p(\tau_m, w_m) = 1$, then by the self reducibility of Π, our $\mathcal{B}$ can efficiently find a w such that $\Pi_p(\tau, w) = 1$, as required.   □

It remains to argue that the proof system used in our powers-of-tau system is zero knowledge and simulation extractable. We first show that the verifier's Check #2 is sound, namely, a malformed string pp will fail the check with overwhelming probability.

Theorem 2. *Check #2 ensures the well-formedness of pp. In particular, let p be the size of the groups output by $\mathsf{GroupGen}(1^\lambda)$, and let n and k be polynomial in the security parameter λ. Then a malformed pp will pass Check #2 with probability at most $\frac{(n-1)(k-1)}{p}$, which is negligible in λ.*

The proof of this theorem can be found in Appendix A.

We next briefly argue that the proof system used in our powers-of-tau system is zero knowledge and simulation extractable. The proof output by algorithm $\mathsf{Update}(\mathsf{pp}, r)$ is a standard Schnorr proof of knowledge of discrete log that is made non-interactive using the Fiat-Shamir transform. This proof system is known to be zero-knowledge in the random oracle model, and simulation extractable in the random oracle model even for a prover that proves multiple such statements one after the other [36]. Moreover, Theorem 2 shows that a witness extracted from a convincing prover will correspond to a valid witness with overwhelming probability.

5   Powers-of-Tau Setup Protocol with Data Off-Chain

The required number of powers of tau for some applications can be as high as 2^{24}–2^{28}, resulting in public parameters of size in the range $0.5\,\mathrm{GB}$–$9\,\mathrm{GB}$. This rules out the possibility of storing the full parameters on chain, given limitations of today's Layer-1 smart contract platforms. However, it is still possible to take advantage of the anti-censorship properties of an L1 chain by posting a *commitment* to the parameters on chain, while storing the parameters off chain. Each contributor who updates the on-chain commitment proves that the update to the current off-chain parameters is well-formed by submitting a ZK proof to the smart contract. The contract accepts the contribution if the proof is valid.

In more detail, let Alice be the i-th contributor to the powers-of-tau. Let pp_i be the powers-of-tau before Alice's contribution and let pp_{i+1} be the powers-of-tau after. Prior to Alice's contribution, the smart contract holds a short binding commitment to pp_i, namely $c_i := H(\mathsf{pp}_i)$, for some collision resistant hash function H. Alice will send to the contract $c_{i+1} := H(\mathsf{pp}_{i+1})$ along with a succinct ZK proof π that the transition from c_i to c_{i+1} is well formed, as discussed in more detail in the next subsection. If the proof is valid, the contract updates the stored hash to c_{i+1} and erases c_i. Note that the contract places c_{i+1} in its storage array; however the proof π need only be sent to the contract as call data and does not need to be written to the contract's storage.

We describe three ways to produce the proof π: in Sect. 5.1 using a generic transparent SNARK; in Sect. 5.2 using the Dory polynomial commitment scheme; and in Appendix C using an inferior method of inner-pairing product argument.

Data Availability. If the L1 chain only holds a hash of the powers-of-tau, then the actual data must be kept elsewhere. One can use a centralized data-availability (DA) service, such as a cloud storage provider, or a decentralized one, such as EigenDA, Celestia, Polygon Avail, or Arweave. These data availability services vary in many respects, including the precise guarantees and pricing model, but they all commit to storing a large blob of data and making it publicly available, in exchange for fees. In the DA service the data is typically addressable by its hash-digest or a deterministic commitment. Updates can write a new copy of the data to the DA service and old versions will still exist. Regardless, of how the DA service is run, we only require it to attest to the availability of the data behind the on-chain commitment, we assume that the DA service is censorship-resistant and append-only. The DA service does not need to run any verification on the underlying data.

Note that the DA service can safely discard an old parameter set after the chain verifies a new parameter set, meaning that the DA service only needs to store at most two parameter sets at any given time, meaning it scales well to protocols with many participants.

5.1   Off-Chain Setup Using a Transparent Succinct Proof

Let pp be the current state of the powers-of-tau stored at some data availability service, and let $c := H(\mathsf{pp})$ be the commitment to pp stored in the smart contract on chain. Recall that

$$\mathsf{pp} = \left(P_1, P_2, P_3, \ldots, P_n; \quad Q_1, Q_2, \ldots, Q_k\right) =$$
$$= \left(\tau B_1, \tau^2 B_1, \tau^3 B_1, \ldots, \tau^n B_1; \quad \tau B_2, \tau^2 B_2, \ldots, \tau^k B_2\right) \in \mathbb{G}_1^n \times \mathbb{G}_2^k$$

for some secret $\tau \in \mathbb{Z}_p$ and public $B_1 \in \mathbb{G}_1$, $B_2 \in \mathbb{G}_2$.

Alice wants to re-randomize pp to obtain pp'. She chooses a random $r \in \mathbb{Z}_p$, computes

$$\mathsf{pp}' \leftarrow \left(rP_1, r^2 P_2, r^3 P_3, \ldots, r^n P_n; \quad rQ_1, r^2 Q_2, \ldots, r^k Q_k\right) =$$
$$= \left(P_1', P_2', P_3', \ldots, P_n'; \quad Q_1', Q_2', \ldots, Q_k'\right) \in \mathbb{G}_1^n \times \mathbb{G}_2^k$$

and sends pp' to the data availability service. Next, she computes the commitment $c' = H(\mathsf{pp}')$ and needs to convince the on-chain smart contract that the transition from c to c' is a valid transition. As explained in Sect. 4, Alice must produce a succinct zero-knowledge argument of knowledge (zk-SNARK) that the following relation holds, for random ρ_1, ρ_2 in $\mathbb{Z}_p$ chosen by the verifier:

public statement: c, c' and $\rho_1, \rho_2 \in \mathbb{Z}_p$,   witness: $\mathsf{pp}, \mathsf{pp}'$, and $r \in \mathbb{Z}_p$,

and the relation is satisfied if and only if

$$c = H(\mathsf{pp}), \quad c' = H(\mathsf{pp}'), \quad P_1' = rP_1, \quad P_1' \neq 0, \quad \text{and}$$

$$e\Big(\sum_{i=1}^{n} \rho_1^i P_i', \ \rho_2 B_2 + \sum_{j=1}^{k-1} \rho_2^{j+1} Q_j'\Big) = e\Big(\rho_1 B_1 + \sum_{i=1}^{n-1} \rho_1^{i+1} P_i', \ \sum_{j=1}^{k} \rho_2^j Q_j'\Big).$$

Note that the zero-knowledge property is needed to keep r secret.

The simplest, though not the most efficient, way to produce a succinct proof for this relation is to use a generic zk-SNARK system (we describe better approaches in the next subsection). To use a generic zk-SNARK, we need a proof system with the following properties: (i) *transparent*, namely the zk-SNARK requires no trusted setup, since we cannot assume the existence of a trusted setup in our settings; (ii) short, to reduce the cost of posting the proof on-chain; and (iii) fast to verify, to reduce the on-chain gas costs for verification. The STARK system [9] meets these requirements. In practice, the resulting proof is about 100KB which may be too expensive to post on chain for every update. In Sect. 7 we discuss batching proofs, namely supporting multiple updates using a single proof. This may make STARKs a viable option.

Once Alice constructs the proof π, she sends (c, c', π) to the on-chain contract. The contract verifies the proof, and if valid, it replaces c by c'.

5.2 Off-Chain Setup Using AFGHO Commitments On-Chain

In this section we describe a more efficient approach than the one in the previous section. We use the unstructured AFGHO commitments of Abe et al. [1] in combination with the Dory [49] inner-pairing product arguments. This leads to short and efficiently verifiable proofs on chain.

We again assume groups $\mathbb{G}_1, \mathbb{G}_2, \mathbb{G}_T$ of a prime order p and a bilinear operation $e : \mathbb{G}_1 \times \mathbb{G}_2 \to \mathbb{G}_T$. We adopt the product notation for pairing operations: for vectors $\mathbf{A} \in \mathbb{G}_1^n$ and $\mathbf{B} \in \mathbb{G}_2^n$ we write $\langle \mathbf{A}, \mathbf{B} \rangle = \sum_{i=1}^{n} e(A_i, B_i)$. Let $\boldsymbol{\Gamma}_2 \in \mathbb{G}_2^n$ be generators of $\mathbb{G}_2$ and $\boldsymbol{\Gamma}_1 \in \mathbb{G}_1^k$ be generators of $\mathbb{G}_1$, all randomly chosen in a transparent way.

Instead of the full parameters $\mathsf{pp} = (\mathbf{P}; \mathbf{Q}) = ((P_1, P_2, \ldots, P_n); (Q_1, Q_2, \ldots, Q_k))$, the chain only stores P_1 and AFGHO commitments $(C_1, C_2) \in \mathbb{G}_T \times \mathbb{G}_T$ on chain, where $C_1 = \langle \mathbf{P}, \boldsymbol{\Gamma}_2 \rangle \in \mathbb{G}_T$ and $C_2 = \langle \boldsymbol{\Gamma}_1, \mathbf{Q} \rangle \in \mathbb{G}_T$.

The contributor submits a proof-of-knowledge of the discrete log of the update to P_1 as explained in Check #1 of Sect. 4 and a logarithmic-size proof for the following inner-pairing product (IPP) relations:

$$C_1 = \langle \mathbf{P}, \mathbf{\Gamma}_2 \rangle \ \wedge \ C_2 = \langle \mathbf{\Gamma}_1, \mathbf{Q} \rangle \ \wedge$$
$$\rho_1^n P_n Q_1 - B_1 Q_1 = \langle \mathbf{P}, (1, \rho_1, \rho_1^2, \dots, \rho_1^{n-1}) \cdot (\rho_1 Q_1 - B_2) \rangle \ \wedge$$
$$\rho_2^k P_1 Q_k - P_1 B_2 = \langle (1, \rho_2, \rho_2^2, \dots, \rho_2^{k-1}) \cdot (\rho_2 P_1 - B_1), \mathbf{Q} \rangle \ \wedge \qquad (5.1)$$
$$P_n = \langle \mathbf{P}, (0, 0, \dots, 0, 1) \rangle \ \wedge \ P_1 = \langle \mathbf{P}, (1, 0, \dots, 0, 0) \rangle$$
$$Q_k = \langle \mathbf{Q}, (0, 0, \dots, 0, 1) \rangle \ \wedge \ Q_1 = \langle \mathbf{Q}, (1, 0, \dots, 0, 0) \rangle$$

We give further details on this construction in Appendix B.

6   Implementation and Evaluation on Ethereum

In this section, we analyse the practicality of our fully on-chain setup ceremony, presented in Sect. 4. We implemented our protocol on top of Ethereum [19], the most popular smart contract platform. Currently (as of May 2023), Ethereum natively supports only one group with bilinear pairing, BN254 (the initial EIP-197 [60] describes the curve equations). This group is foundational to multiple projects (e.g. Aztec, zkSync) although unfortunately its security has been lowered with recent attacks [7], and now estimated [45] to be at 100-bits level. Ethereum consensus layer uses BLS12-381, which is another pairing-friendly group, and also a popular choice for other projects (e.g. Aztec and Filecoin), has stronger security guarantees, however the precompiles for this curve are not available on Ethereum yet, though have been suggested (EIP-2537 [4]) alongside precompiles for other pairing-friendly curves BLS12-377 (EIP-2539 [61]) and BW6-761 (EIP-3026 [64]). The supported operations are scalar-multiplication and addition in $\mathbb{G}_1$ and a pairing precompile, which are priced as follows according to EIP-1108 [22]:

Name	Operation	Gas cost
ECADD	$A + B$ for $A, B \in \mathbb{G}_1$	150
ECMULT	αA for $\alpha \in \mathbb{Z}_p, A \in \mathbb{G}_1$	6,000
ECPAIR	$\sum_{i=1}^{k} e(A_i, B_i) = 0$ for $A_i \in \mathbb{G}_1, B_i \in \mathbb{G}_2$	$34,000 \cdot k + 45,000$

Each contribution is sent as calldata, which is a read-only byte array, currently priced at 16 gas per byte according to EIP-2028 [2].

Fully On-Chain Setup for $k = 1$. We first consider a setup with a single element in $\mathbb{G}_2$. The following pre-computation will reduce the cost of the Check #2 to $n + 3$ scalar multiplications and one ECPAIR, though the check will remain to dominate the verification cost:

Table 1. Estimates according to the Eq. 6.2 and actual costs. The pricing in USD is calculated based on rough numbers on 05/01/2023: 15 gwei per gas unit and 1 ETH = $1,850 (1 gwei = 10^{-9} ETH).

n	8	16	32	64	128	256	512	1024
compute in gas units	179,000	227,000	323,000	515,000	899,000	1,667,000	3,203,000	6,275,000
compute cost	$5	$6	$9	$14	$25	$46	$89	$174
storage in gas units	8,192	16,384	32,768	65,536	131,072	262,144	524,288	1,048,576
storage cost	$0	$0	$1	$2	$4	$7	$15	$29
Total (estimates)	187,192	243,384	355,768	580,536	1,030,072	1,929,144	3,727,288	7,323,576
	$5	$7	$10	$16	$29	$54	$103	$203
Total (actual)	192,162	272,217	432,702	755,340	1,406,185	2,731,526	5,474,920	11,341,136
	$5	$8	$12	$21	$39	$76	$152	$315

Check # 2 (more efficient): for $R := \sum_{i=1}^{n-1} \rho_1^{i-1} \cdot P_i$,

verify that $e(B_1 + \rho_1 R,\ Q_1)\ =\ e(R + \rho_1^{n-1} P_n,\ B_2)$ (6.1)

The contributor submits $64 \cdot n + 224$ bytes of calldata: n elements of $\mathbb{G}_1$ (64 bytes, uncompressed[2]), 1 element in $\mathbb{G}_2$ (128 bytes, uncompressed), and a proof which consists of one element in $\mathbb{Z}_p$ and one element in $\mathbb{G}_1$. The cost of the contribution is therefore comprised of compute and calldata storage:

$$\text{compute cost: } (n+3) \cdot 6,000 + 113,000 \text{ gas}$$
$$\text{storage cost: } n \cdot 1,024 + 3,584 \text{ gas} \qquad (6.2)$$

It is instructive to notice that the cost of compute is roughly 6x the cost of storage. The compute is dominated by the multi-scalar multiplication. Most likely it is inevitable for each element of the setup to have to be multiplied by a scalar or be directly inserted into a pairing, it is therefore unlikely to be able to reduce the compute cost for the fully on-chain setup. However, using techniques of Bellare et al. [8] the scalar-multiplications might be substituted by λ-random subset sums for λ-security, however for Ethereum this trick does not bring any savings. Table 1 shows estimated and concrete pricing per contribution with a check from Eq. 6.1 based on our open-sourced implementation[3].

---

[2] Our evaluations showed that recovering element from a compressed form would cost significantly more than sending them in an uncompressed form directly.
[3] github.com/a16z/evm-powers-of-tau.

Fully On-Chain Setup for $k > 1$. Since Ethereum does not support addition and scalar multiplication in $\mathbb{G}_2$ the following alternative method for Check #2 targeting Ethereum can be used, it does one additional pairing per each power in $\mathbb{G}_2$:

Check #2 (alternative):

For $R = \sum_{i=0}^{n-2} \rho^i \cdot P_{i+1,j} : e(B_1 + \rho R,\ Q_{1,j}) = e(R + \rho^{n-1} P_{n,j},\ B_2)$ (6.3)

For $t = 2..k\text{-}1 : \ e(P_{k-t,j}, Q_t) = e(P_{k,j}, B_2) \wedge e(B_1, Q_k) = e(P_{k,j}, B_2)$ (6.4)

Note that the right-hand part of the Eqs. 6.4 can be computed once. Note also that Eqs. 6.3 and 6.4 are each checking the equalities of pairings, these checks can be batched using pseudorandom scalars $\alpha_0, \alpha_1, \ldots, \alpha_D \in \left(\mathbb{Z}_p^*\right)^n$ sampled as $\alpha_i = \mathsf{HASH}(\mathsf{pp}_j, i)$ to transform into a check of the sum of pairings which is cheaper to do on Ethereum (Ethereum has an opcode that allows to verify $e(A_1, B_1) + \ldots + e(A_m, B_m) = 0$):

$$
\begin{aligned}
e(A_1, B_1) &= e(C_1, D_1) \\
e(A_2, B_2) &= e(C_2, D_2) \\
&\cdots \\
e(A_m, B_m) &= e(C_m, D_m)
\end{aligned}
\quad \Leftrightarrow \quad
\begin{cases}
e(\alpha_1 A_1, B_1) - e(\alpha_1 C_1, D_1) + \\
e(\alpha_2 A_2, B_2) - e(\alpha_2 C_2, D_2) + \\
\cdots \\
e(\alpha_m A_m, B_m) - e(\alpha_m C_m, D_m) = 0
\end{cases}
\quad (6.5)
$$

Note on the Use of Hash Functions for Generation of Scalars. For a 256-bits order groups, the hash function HASH needs to output 512-bits, should be given as inputs strings generated with invertible serialization method, and be domain-separated (i.e. the input should be prefixed with a fixed-length string indicating the step of the protocol and the purpose of hashing).

7   Concluding Discussion and Open Problems

In conclusion, we note that our work shows the practicality of *decentralized* setup ceremonies for the first time. These protocols can scale to support an unlimited number of participants as blockchain performance continues to improve. Our protocols inherit (and rely on) the ability of the underlying blockchain to support open participation while managing potential spam and denial-of-service.

Given the more-the-merrier property of our protocols, these represent a qualitative security advance over the state of the art. While practical trusted setup ceremonies have attempted to recruit a diverse and trustworthy group of participants to convince the public that the results of the ceremony can be trusted, decentralized setup ceremonies offer a stronger promise: if a participant doesn't trust the ceremony, they are free to contribute themselves. We hope that this model will inspire future setup ceremonies; it may also extend to other applications such as distributed randomness beacons which can be made decentralized and open to participation for all using blockchains.

We conclude with several open problems and directions for future work.

7.1   Incentives for Participation

Several options are available to subsidize gas costs to encourage additional participation. The simplest solution is to load funds into the setup contract and reward each user who successfully updates the structured reference string pp, although users will still need to first pay the requisite gas fees. Alternately, transaction relay services, such as the nascent Gas Station Network (GSN), can pay transaction fees for users sending data to the setup contract. The upcoming account abstraction, EIP 4337 [18], should also help build an ecosystem of paymasters that would sponsor transactions for other users. This makes it possible for an end user to participate in setup even if that user owns no crypto to pay for gas. Finally, we note that a setup ceremony might give users a non-monetary reward such as an NFT as a badge of participation. A challenge in all cases is that users might pseudonymously participate many times via Sybil accounts; while this doesn't undermine security of the setup (assuming there was at least one honest contributor) it may enable them to claim rewards multiple times or drain the available budget for covering transaction fees, preventing other users from participating cheaply.

7.2   Verifying Participation

Users may wish to see an authentic list of everyone who has contributed to the SRS. A lazy participant might see that enough participants that it trusts contributed, and choose to use the SRS without participating themselves. Fortunately, since every Ethereum transaction is signed by the party that initiates that transaction, any user can inspect the chain and construct a list of authenticated addresses that contributed to the ceremony since its inception.

7.3   Sequential Participation and Denial-of-Service

Our ceremonies are designed to run without any centralized coordination, but they do require contributions in a serial manner. The jth contributor must prove correctness of their update relative to the previous value pp_{j-1}. If two contributors independently submit transactions building on the same parameter set pp_{j-1}, only the one sequenced first will be executed successfully. The second will fail for referencing a stale parameter set. This means that, without off-chain coordination, at most one contribution per block is possible as contributors must first observe pp_{j-1}. For Ethereum this limits the ceremony to one contribution every 12 s or 219,000 contributions per month.

Worse, this also provides an avenue for denial-of-service and censorship: whenever an honest contribution arrives, an attacker can create an alternative contribution paying higher transaction fees, preempting the honest one. Such an attack could be detected off-chain via timing analysis. A stronger defense strategy against censorship could be to select one contribution among the conflicting ones in a random but publicly-verifiable way. To lower the transaction fees, a contributor could first register an intent to make a contribution, and only submit the actual data if it is selected. Alternatively, the setup contract can order the registered future contributors using a public randomness beacon, giving each user a random pre-assigned slot to contribute.

7.4   Verification with General-Purpose Roll-Ups

Verification costs can be decreased using a general Layer-2 compute platform such as a *rollup server*. ZK-Rollups (also called verifiable rollups) provide succinct proofs of execution (in our case, verifying a contribution) and hence provide equivalent security to execution on Layer-1. The two common constructions today are zero-knowledge rollups and optimistic rollups, each of which brings unique design challenges. Many (though not all) ZK-rollups themselves rely on a (centralized) trusted setup. However, our protocol can be seen as a way to perform new decentralized trusted setups given a single centralized one. Or we might use a ZK-rollup which relies on a transparent setup. Alternately, optimistic rollups require watchful observers to submit fraud proofs to detect incorrect execution. Given the serial nature of our ceremony, general optimistic rollups require caution as they naively require waiting for a *challenge period* before accepting correct execution.

Rollups might offer significant cost savings, given that execution costs are roughly $100\times$ cheaper on Layer-2, and execution costs (as opposed to storage) are over 75% of total transaction costs [48] in our evaluation. Combined with off-chain data availability, total costs can be greatly reduced. The result of a Layer-2 construction would be a 75% reduction in per transaction cost. The remainder of the transaction cost is due to the storage of elliptic curve points on Ethereum Layer-1. There are several proposals in process to decrease the cost of Layer-2 storage on Ethereum, potentially further decreasing setup cost (see EIP-4844 or EIP-4444). As of this writing, all production rollup servers rely on a single centralized sequencing server, undermining the censorship resistance benefits of an on-chain trusted setup. When these optimistic rollup Layer-2 s have decentralized their sequencing, we expect the costs outlined for a trusted setup can be decreased 75–95%. In the interim, one could also implement a hybrid design which allows updates via the rollup server (to save gas) but also directly on-chain in the event of a censoring rollup sequencer.

7.5   Protocol-Specific ZK Rollups via Proof Batching

Rather than relying on a general-purpose rollup server, we can design a specific one optimized for our application. In our ceremony, every contribution is accompanied by a proof of correctness, requiring a linear number of proofs in the number of updates. We can improve things using a coordinator which compiles a sequence of update proofs from multiple participants and aggregates them all into a single proof that all the received updates are valid. This can be done using proof recursion [59] or accumulation [8,15,21]. This coordinator will then post the aggregate proof on chain along with the aggregate update to the parameters.

This coordinator can censor particular participants by refusing to accumulate their proofs into the batch. However, since anyone can act as a coordinator, an affected participant can find another coordinator. In the worst case, if all coordinators are censoring, the participant can post their own update and proof directly on chain, bypassing the censoring coordinators.

7.6   Protocol-Specific Optimistic Verification and Checkpointing

Another mode of operation which may offer improved performance would have users post proofs (or even commitments to proofs with off-chain data availability), but not rely on on-chain verification in the optimistic case. Instead, users can post a fidelity bond which is forfeited (within a set challenge period) if another user determines off-chain that their proof is incorrect and challenges it on-chain. A caveat is that any invalidated update will also invalidate all subsequent updates due to the chained nature of the protocol. With this approach, users should verify recent contributions themselves before participating to avoid building on top of a contribution that is later invalidated.

To avoid requiring users to verify too many recent contributions before participating, it is possible to *checkpoint* certain updates by including a proof that all updates since the last checkpoint were valid. This checkpoint can be created via proof batching as discussed above. We note that, in our protocol in Sect. 4, only Check #1 needs to be repeated for each update since the last checkpoint; the more expensive Check #2 only needs to be done once on the latest version of the structured reference string.

7.7   Fully Off-Chain Verification via IVC/PCD

Another potential optimization is to conduct a ceremony with no on-chain proof verification, but where each update includes a succinct proof that *every* update since the start of the ceremony was well-formed. These proofs can be constructed using any incrementally verifiable computation scheme (IVC). In this case the parameters plus proof are an instantiation of proof-carrying data (PCD). With such a protocol, it is possible to execute the ceremony using a blockchain which only provides data availability and consensus (and no verification). Each user can verify the succinct proof of the latest parameters before using or updating them. The ceremony is only using the chain for its persistent storage and anti-censorship properties.

7.8   Forking/Re-starting

Throughout the paper we assumed that updates to the powers-of-tau are applied sequentially and each update is applied to the latest state. It is also possible that a project may build on an existing powers-of-tau string, but fork it for its own use. A forking community can continue to re-randomize their own powers-of-tau branch, while the rest of the world continues to re-randomize the main branch.

As such, the on-chain contract could be set up to handle forks in the update process, where multiple powers-of-tau are continuously updated independently of one another. Some powers-of-tau may even start afresh from scratch, perhaps to support different tower lengths and possibly different groups.

Acknowledgments. We would like to thank Lúcás Meier, Yashvanth Kondi, Mary Maller, and Justin Thaler for useful feedback on the early ideas underlying this work. The last author is supported by the Simons Foundation and NTT Research.

A   Proof of Theorem 2

In this section we prove Theorem 2 of Sect. 4 which guarantees that Check #2 guards the setup from malformed contributions.

Proof. Suppose the contributor generated a parameter set pp that passed Check #2. We write

$$\mathsf{pp} = (P_1, P_2, P_3, \ldots, P_n \; ; \; Q_1, \ldots, Q_k) =$$
$$= (a_1 B_1, a_2 B_1, \ldots, a_n B_1 \; ; \; b_1 B_2, b_2 B_2, \ldots, b_k B_2).$$

If check # 2 passed, then for two random scalars $x = \rho_1$ and $y = \rho_2$ in $\mathbb{Z}_p$ chosen by the verifier the following equation holds:

$$(1 + a_1 x + a_2 x^2 + \ldots + a_{n-1} x^{n-1}) \cdot (b_1 + b_2 y + \ldots + b_k y^{k-1}) -$$
$$(a_1 + a_2 x + \ldots + a_n x^{n-1}) \cdot (1 + b_1 y + b_2 y^2 + \ldots + b_{k-1} y^{k-1}) = 0 \quad (\text{A.1})$$

Let us define a 2-variate polynomial $f(x, y)$ to match the left-hand side of Eq. A.1. By the DeMillo-Lipton-Schwartz-Zippel (DLSZ) lemma [30,58,65], if f is a non-zero polynomial, then the number of zeros of f is bounded by $d \cdot p$ where $d = (n-1)(k-1)$ is the degree of $f(x, y)$. Equivalently, the probability that $f(x, y) = 0$ for x and y selected uniformly at random from $\mathbb{Z}_p$ is bounded above by d/p. Therefore, the probability that the polynomial f defined in Eq. A.1 is a zero polynomial is overwhelming: it is at least $1 - (k-1)(n-1)/p$. For a zero polynomial $f \equiv 0$, its coefficients are all zero. In particular the constant term $b_1 - a_1$ is 0 implying that $a_1 = b_1$, and we denote that by $\tau = a_1$. The rest of the coefficients being zero implies that

coefficient of x :	$a_1 b_1 - a_2 = 0$	$\Rightarrow$	$a_2 = \tau^2$
coefficient of x^2 :	$a_2 b_1 - a_3 = 0$	$\Rightarrow$	$a_3 = \tau^3$

. . .

coefficient of x^{n-1} : $a_{n-1} b_1 - a_n = 0$ $\Rightarrow$ $\&a_n = \tau^n$

Applying the same argument to the coefficients of y^i in Eq. A.1 we obtain:

coefficient of y :	$b_2 - a_1 b_1 = 0$	$\Rightarrow$	$b_2 = \tau^2$
coefficient of y^2 :	$\&b_3 - a_1 b_2 = 0$	$\Rightarrow$	$b_3 = \tau^3$

. . .

coefficient of y^k : $\&b_k - a_1 b_{k-1} = 0$ $\Rightarrow$ $b_k = \tau^k$

Therefore we obtain that a setup that successfully passes check #2 is well-formed with probability at least $1 - (k-1)(n-1)/p$, as required.

Note on Soundness for a Punctured Setup. At the end of Sect. 7 we explained how to modify Check # 2 to be able to handle powers-of-tau setups with one point missing. The soundness proof for this modified check is analogous: for random scalars $x = \rho_1, y = \rho_2$ in $\mathbb{Z}_p$ we define the polynomial $f(x, y)$ to match the left-hand side of Eq. D.3:

$$\left(\sum_{\substack{i=1 \\ i \neq N+1 \\ i \neq N+2}}^{2N} a_i x^{i-1} \right) \cdot \left(1 + \sum_{i=1}^{N-1} b_i y^i \right) - \left(1 + \sum_{\substack{i=1 \\ i \neq N \\ i \neq N+1}}^{2N-1} a_i x^i \right) \cdot \left(\sum_{i=1}^{N} b_i y^{i-1} \right) = 0$$

(A.2)

The probability that the polynomial f is zero is at least $1 - 2N^2/p$. For a zero polynomial all of its coefficients are zero, hence the constant term $b_1 - a_1 = 0$ (denote $\tau = a_1$) and analogously we get $b_i = \tau^i$ for $i = 1 \ldots N$ and $a_i = \tau^i$ for $i = 1 \ldots 2N$ where $i \neq N+1$. The only difference in the argument, is that we use the second pairing check (D.2) to get $a_{N+2} = a_N b_2$ which implies $a_{N+2} = \tau^{N+2}$.

B   Inner-Pairing Product Arguments for Sect. 5.2

We restate Eq. 5.1 of Sect. 5.2 again for convenience:

$$C_1 = \langle \mathbf{P}, \boldsymbol{\Gamma}_2 \rangle \tag{B.1}$$

$$C_2 = \langle \boldsymbol{\Gamma}_1, \mathbf{Q} \rangle \tag{B.2}$$

$$\rho_1^n P_n Q_1 - B_1 Q_1 = \langle \mathbf{P}, (1, \rho_1, \rho_1^2, \ldots, \rho_1^{n-1}) \cdot (\rho_1 Q_1 - B_2) \rangle \tag{B.3}$$

$$\rho_2^k P_1 Q_k - P_1 B_2 = \langle (1, \rho_2, \rho_2^2, \ldots, \rho_2^{k-1}) \cdot (\rho_2 P_1 - B_1), \mathbf{Q} \rangle \tag{B.4}$$

$$P_n = \langle \mathbf{P}, (0, 0, \ldots, 0, 1) \rangle \tag{B.5}$$

$$P_1 = \langle \mathbf{P}, (1, 0, \ldots, 0, 0) \rangle \tag{B.6}$$

$$Q_k = \langle \mathbf{Q}, (0, 0, \ldots, 0, 1) \rangle \tag{B.7}$$

$$Q_1 = \langle \mathbf{Q}, (1, 0, \ldots, 0, 0) \rangle \tag{B.8}$$

We first prove the soundness, namely we show that with an overwhelming probability a setup $\mathsf{pp} = (\mathbf{P}; \mathbf{Q})$ that satisfies the set of equations above for random scalars ρ_1 and ρ_2 chosen by the verifier has to be well-formed according to Definition 3. We denote by $x = \rho_1$, and we write $\mathbf{P} = (a_1 B_1, a_2 B_1, \ldots, a_n B_1)$ and $\mathbf{Q} = (b_1 B_2, b_2 B_2, \ldots, b_k B_2)$ for some $a_1, \ldots, a_n, b_1, \ldots, b_k \in \mathbb{Z}_p$ and we rewrite Eq. B.3 equivalently into the following equation:

$$x^n a_n b_1 - b_1 - (a_1 + x a_2 + x^2 a_3 + \ldots + x^{n-1} a_n) \cdot (x b_1 - 1) = 0 \iff$$
$$(a_1 - b_1) + (a_2 - a_1 b_1)x + (a_3 - a_2 b_1)x^2 + \ldots + (a_n - a_{n-1} b_1)x^{n-1} = 0$$

(B.9)

We denote the left-hand side of Eq. B.9 by $f(x)$, where f is a polynomial of degree $n - 1$ over $\mathbb{Z}_p$. We apply the DeMillo-Lipton-Schwartz-Zippel (DLSZ) lemma [30,58,65], if f is a non-zero polynomial, then the number of zeros of f is bounded by $d \cdot p$ where $d = n - 1$ is the degree of $f(x)$. Equivalently, the probability that $f(x) = 0$ for x selected uniformly at random from $\mathbb{Z}_p$ is bounded above by d/p. Therefore, the probability that the polynomial f defined in Eq. B.9 is a zero polynomial is overwhelming: it is at least $1 - (n - 1)/p$. For a zero polynomial $f \equiv 0$, its coefficients are all zero:

$$\text{free term} : a_1 - b_1 = 0 \Rightarrow a_1 = b_1 \text{we denote that by } a_1 = \tau$$
$$\text{coefficient of } x : a_2 - a_1 b_1 = 0 \Rightarrow a_2 = \tau^2$$
$$\text{coefficient of } x^2 : a_3 - a_2 b_1 = 0 \Rightarrow a_3 = \tau^3$$
$$\cdots$$
$$\text{coefficient of } x^{n-1} : a_n - a_{n-1} b_1 = 0 \Rightarrow a_n = \tau^n$$

With analogous analysis of Eq. B.4 we get that $b_i = \tau^i$ for all $i = 1..k$ with probability at least $1 - (k - 1)/p$. This proves Theorem 3:

Theorem 3. *A probabilistic polynomial-time contributor will satisfy Eq. B.3 and Eq. B.4 with a malformed setup string with probability at most $\frac{(n-1)+(k-1)}{p}$, which is negligible in the security parameter λ (where we assume $p \approx 2^{2\lambda}$ and n, k being polynomial-size in λ).*

The IPP Protocol. We now explain the interactive version of the protocol that can be made non-interactive with a Fiat-Shamir heuristic to be run with a verifier as an on-chain smart-contract.

1. The prover submits $C_1, C_2, P_1, P_n, Q_1, Q_k \in \mathbb{G}_T^2 \times \mathbb{G}_1^2 \times \mathbb{G}_2^2$ to the verifier.
2. The prover shows that it knows the discrete log to the update of P_1 (knowledge of discrete log of P_1 base the previous value of P_1 that is currently stored on-chain) as explained in Sect. 4, Eq. 4.
3. The verifier checks that the update is non-degenerative: $P_1 \neq 0$ and if so replies with two random scalars $\rho_1, \rho_2 \xleftarrow{\$} \mathbb{Z}_p$.
4. The prover sends $E_1 \in \mathbb{G}_1$ and $E_2 \in \mathbb{G}_2$ to the verifier, where $E_1 = \langle \mathbf{P}, (1, \rho_1, \rho_1^2, \ldots, \rho_1^{n-1}) \rangle$ and $E_2 = \langle \mathbf{Q}, (1, \rho_2, \rho_2^2, \ldots, \rho_2^{k-1}) \rangle$.
5. The prover runs six Dory-IPP arguments in batch to produce a proof π that it sends to the verifier. As we explain below.
6. The verifier checks that $E_1(\rho_1 Q_1 - B_2) = P_n \rho^n Q_1 - B_1 Q_1$, and $E_1(\rho_2 P_1 - B_1)E_2 = \rho_2^k P_1 Q_k - P_1 B_2$.
7. The verifier checks π and, if correct, updates the setup that it stores to $(C_1, C_2, P_1) \in \mathbb{G}_T^2 \times \mathbb{G}_1$.

We now show how to construct a succinct (logarithmic-size) proof π for Eq. B.1–B.8 using Dory inner product argument of Jonathan Lee [49]. Those arguments allow to prove the following general relation (where the vectors of scalars $\vec{s_1}$ and $\vec{s_2}$ are public and have multiplicative structure):

$$(D, C_1, C_2, E_1, E_2) \in \mathcal{L}_{n, \Gamma_1, \Gamma_2}(\vec{s_1}, \vec{s_2}) \in \mathbb{G}_T^3 \times \mathbb{G}_1 \times \mathbb{G}_2 \Longleftrightarrow$$

$$\text{Exists witnesses } \vec{v_1} \in \mathbb{G}_1 \text{ and } \vec{v_2} \in \mathbb{G}_2 : C_1 = \langle \vec{v_1}, \Gamma_2 \rangle \quad C_2 = \langle \Gamma_1, \vec{v_2} \rangle$$

$$E_1 = \langle \vec{v_1}, \vec{s_1} \rangle \quad E_2 = \langle \vec{v_2}, \vec{s_2} \rangle \quad D = \langle \vec{v_1}, \vec{v_2} \rangle$$

We invoke the argument six times (the arguments are batchable and allow to squash six proofs into a single one) to prove the following less general statements, we show two of those for Eq. B.3 and Eq. B.5 as the rest are analogous:

- For Eq. B.3: $(0, C_1, 0, E_1, 0) \in \mathcal{L}_{n, \Gamma_1, \Gamma_2}(\vec{s_1}, \vec{s_2})$ for scalars $\vec{s_1} = (1, \rho_1, \rho_1^2, \ldots, \rho_1^{n-1})$ and $\vec{s_2} = \vec{0}$ and witnesses $v_1 = \mathbf{P}$, $v_2 = \vec{0}$.
- For Eq. B.5: $(0, C_1, 0, P_n, 0) \in \mathcal{L}_{n, \Gamma_1, \Gamma_2}(\vec{s_1}, \vec{s_2})$ for scalars $s_1 = (0, 0, 0, \ldots, 0, 1)$, $s_2 = \vec{0}$ and witnesses $v_1 = \mathbf{P}$, $v_2 = \vec{0}$.

The verifier in [49] is set up with $4 \log(n) + 1$ pre-computed elements of $\mathbb{G}_T$. Those values are inner-products between subvectors of the vectors of generators Γ_1 and Γ_2 and can be pre-computed in linear-time.

Note that in this type of setup, the secret is only used to update the setup and prove knowledge of the discrete log of P_1. The bulk of the computation, namely proof generation, is independent of the secret chosen by the contributor. Thus, the contributor may outsource this computation to an untrusted helper.

C   Off-Chain Setup from IPP Arguments with a Smaller Setup

For completeness, we briefly explain the inner-product pairing (IPP) method of Bünz et al. [16]. It relies on a powers-of-tau SRS of a smaller size stored by the verifier in full:

$$\Gamma_1 = (\alpha B_1, \alpha^2 B_1, \ldots, \alpha^{2n} B_1), \qquad \Gamma_2 = (\beta B_2, \beta^2 B_2, \ldots, \beta^{2n} B_2)$$

The contributor can then commit to a larger setup of length $N = \eta \times n$ in $\mathbb{G}_1$ and $\mathbb{G}_2$ with structured AFGHO commitments of Abe et al. [1] as follows:

$$\text{For } \mathbf{P} = (\mathbf{P}_1, \ldots, \mathbf{P}_\eta) \in (\mathbb{G}_1^n, \ldots, \mathbb{G}_1^n) \text{ and}$$

$$\text{for } \mathbf{Q} = (\mathbf{Q}_1, \ldots, \mathbf{Q}_\eta) \in (\mathbb{G}_2^n, \ldots, \mathbb{G}_2^n) :$$

$$\mathbf{C}_1 = (\langle \mathbf{P}_1, \Gamma_{1,\text{even}} \rangle, \ldots, \langle \mathbf{P}_\eta, \Gamma_{1,\text{even}} \rangle) \in \mathbb{G}_T^\eta$$

$$\mathbf{C}_2 = (\langle \Gamma_{2,\text{even}}, \mathbf{Q}_1 \rangle, \ldots, \langle \Gamma_{1,\text{even}}, \mathbf{Q}_\eta \rangle) \in \mathbb{G}_T^\eta$$

The contributor submits commitments $\mathbf{C}_1, \mathbf{C}_2$ to the verifier and creates TIPP-proofs of a set of inner-pairing-product relations similar to the ones described in Sect. 5.2. The resulting proofs add up to be of cumulative size $O(\eta \log(n))$ and can be verified in $O(\eta \log(n))$ time.

This method leads to worse practical efficiency compared to the method described in Sect. 5.2, although it might yield better concrete costs if an on-chain setup is extended by a small multiple making the resulting length N be far from the power of two.

D Powers-of-Tau with a Punctured Point

Some systems require a powers-of-tau string where one power in the sequence is absent, namely

$$\mathsf{pp} = \left[(P_i)_{i=1, i \neq N+1}^{2N}, \ (Q_i)_{i=1}^{N} \right] = \left[(\tau^i B_1)_{i=1, i \neq N+1}^{2N}, \ (\tau^i B_2)_{i=1}^{N} \right],$$

where the point $P_{N+1} = \tau^{N+1} B_1$ is absent from pp. Example systems that use a punctured sequence include Groth'10 [39], Attema and Cramer [5], Lipmaa, Siim, and Zajac's Vampire scheme [51], and Waters and Wu [63]. The absence of the point P_{N+1} from pp is necessary for security. Check #2 in (4) can be modified to handle this case: the verifier will sample two random scalars ρ_1, ρ_2 in $\mathbb{Z}_p^*$ and carry out the following check that now consists of two equations:

Check # 2 for punctured setup:

$$e\left(\sum_{\substack{i=1 \\ i \neq N+1 \\ i \neq N+2}}^{2N} \rho_1^{i-1} P_i, \ B_2 + \sum_{\ell=1}^{N-1} \rho_2^{\ell} Q_\ell \right) =$$

$$= e\left(B_1 + \sum_{\substack{i=1 \\ i \neq N \\ i \neq N+1}}^{2N-1} \rho_1^{i} P_i, \ \sum_{\ell=1}^{N} \rho_2^{\ell-1} Q_\ell \right) \tag{D.1}$$

$$e\left(P_{N+2}, B_2 \right) = e\left(P_N, Q_2 \right) \tag{D.2}$$

It is not difficult to see that a well-formed setup will pass the check successfully. The soundness proof for this modified check is analogous: for random scalars $x = \rho_1, y = \rho_2$ in $\mathbb{Z}_p$ we define the polynomial $f(x, y)$ to match the left-hand side of Eq. D.3:

$$\left(\sum_{\substack{i=1 \\ i \neq N+1 \\ i \neq N+2}}^{2N} a_i x^{i-1} \right) \cdot \left(1 + \sum_{i=1}^{N-1} b_i y^i \right) - \left(1 + \sum_{\substack{i=1 \\ i \neq N \\ i \neq N+1}}^{2N-1} a_i x^i \right) \cdot \left(\sum_{i=1}^{N} b_i y^{i-1} \right) = 0$$

$$\tag{D.3}$$

The probability that the polynomial f is zero is at least $1 - 2N^2/p$. For a zero polynomial all of its coefficients are zero, hence the constant term $b_1 - a_1 = 0$ (denote $\tau = a_1$) and analogously we get $b_i = \tau^i$ for $i = 1 \ldots N$ and $a_i = \tau^i$ for $i = 1 \ldots 2N$ where $i \neq N+1$. The only difference in the argument, is that we use the second pairing check (D.2) to get $a_{N+2} = a_N b_2$ which implies $a_{N+2} = \tau^{N+2}$.

References

1. Abe, M., Fuchsbauer, G., Groth, J., Haralambiev, K., Ohkubo, M.: Structure-preserving signatures and commitments to group elements. In: Rabin, T. (ed.) CRYPTO 2010. LNCS, vol. 6223, pp. 209–236. Springer, Heidelberg (2010). https://doi.org/10.1007/978-3-642-14623-7_12
2. Akhunov, A., Sasson, E.B., Brand, T., Guthmann, L., Levy, A.: EIP-2028: Transaction data gas cost reduction (2019). https://eips.ethereum.org/EIPS/eip-2028
3. Aleo: Announcing aleo setup (2021). https://www.aleo.org/post/announcing-aleo-setup
4. Alex Vlasov, K.O.: EIP-2537: Precompile for bls12-381 curve operations (2020). https://eips.ethereum.org/EIPS/eip-2537
5. Attema, T., Cramer, R.: Compressed Σ-protocol theory and practical application to plug & play secure algorithmics. In: Micciancio, D., Ristenpart, T. (eds.) CRYPTO 2020. LNCS, vol. 12172, pp. 513–543. Springer, Cham (2020). https://doi.org/10.1007/978-3-030-56877-1_18
6. Aztec: Universal crs setup. https://docs.zksync.io/userdocs/security/#universal-crs-setup (2020)
7. Barbulescu, R., Duquesne, S.: Updating key size estimations for pairings. J. Cryptol. **32**(4), 1298–1336 (2019)
8. Bellare, M., Garay, J.A., Rabin, T.: Fast batch verification for modular exponentiation and digital signatures. In: Nyberg, K. (ed.) EUROCRYPT 1998. LNCS, vol. 1403, pp. 236–250. Springer, Heidelberg (1998). https://doi.org/10.1007/BFb0054130
9. Ben-Sasson, E., Bentov, I., Horesh, Y., Riabzev, M.: Scalable, transparent, and post-quantum secure computational integrity. IACR Cryptol. ePrint Arch. p. 46 (2018)
10. Ben-Sasson, E., Chiesa, A., Green, M., Tromer, E., Virza, M.: Secure sampling of public parameters for succinct zero knowledge proofs. In: IEEE Symposium on Security and Privacy (2015)
11. Benaloh, J., de Mare, M.: One-Way Accumulators: A Decentralized Alternative to Digital Signatures. In: Helleseth, T. (ed.) EUROCRYPT 1993. LNCS, vol. 765, pp. 274–285. Springer, Heidelberg (1994). https://doi.org/10.1007/3-540-48285-7_24
12. Boneh, D., Boyen, X.: Short signatures without random oracles. In: Cachin, C., Camenisch, J.L. (eds.) EUROCRYPT 2004. LNCS, vol. 3027, pp. 56–73. Springer, Heidelberg (2004). https://doi.org/10.1007/978-3-540-24676-3_4
13. Boneh, D., Franklin, M.: Efficient generation of shared RSA keys. In: Kaliski, B.S. (ed.) CRYPTO 1997. LNCS, vol. 1294, pp. 425–439. Springer, Heidelberg (1997). https://doi.org/10.1007/BFb0052253
14. Bowe, S., Gabizon, A., Miers, I.: Scalable multi-party computation for zk-snark parameters in the random beacon model. Cryptology ePrint Archive (2017)
15. Bünz, B., Chiesa, A., Mishra, P., Spooner, N.: Recursive proof composition from accumulation schemes. In: Pass, R., Pietrzak, K. (eds.) TCC 2020. LNCS, vol. 12551, pp. 1–18. Springer, Cham (2020). https://doi.org/10.1007/978-3-030-64378-2_1
16. Bünz, B., Maller, M., Mishra, P., Tyagi, N., Vesely, P.: Proofs for inner pairing products and applications. In: Tibouchi, M., Wang, H. (eds.) ASIACRYPT 2021. LNCS, vol. 13092, pp. 65–97. Springer, Cham (2021). https://doi.org/10.1007/978-3-030-92078-4_3

17. Buterin, V.: How do trusted setups work? (2022). https://vitalik.ca/general/2022/03/14/trustedsetup.html
18. Buterin, V., et al.: ERC-4337: Account abstraction using alt mempool. link (2021)
19. Buterin, V., et al.: Ethereum: a next-generation smart contract and decentralized application platform (2014). https://ethereum.org/669c9e2e2027310b6b3cdce6e1c52962/Ethereum_Whitepaper_-_Buterin_2014.pdf
20. Buterin, V.: What is Danksharding (2020)
21. Camenisch, J., Hohenberger, S., Pedersen, M.Ø.: Batch verification of short signatures. J. Cryptol. **25**(4), 723–747 (2012)
22. Cardozo, A.S., Williamson, Z.: EIP-1108: Reduce alt_bn128 precompile gas costs (2018). https://eips.ethereum.org/EIPS/eip-1108
23. Cash, T.: Tornado.cash trusted setup ceremony (2020). https://tornado-cash.medium.com/tornado-cash-trusted-setup-ceremony-b846e1e00be1
24. Celo: Plumo ceremony (2020). https://celo.org/plumo
25. Chen, M., et al.: Diogenes: lightweight scalable RSA modulus generation with a dishonest majority. In: IEEE Security and Privacy (2021)
26. Chiesa, A., Hu, Y., Maller, M., Mishra, P., Vesely, N., Ward, N.: Marlin: preprocessing zkSNARKs with universal and updatable SRS. In: Canteaut, A., Ishai, Y. (eds.) EUROCRYPT 2020. LNCS, vol. 12105, pp. 738–768. Springer, Cham (2020). https://doi.org/10.1007/978-3-030-45721-1_26
27. Cohen, B., Pietrzak, K.: The Chia Network Blockchain (2019). https://www.chia.net/wp-content/uploads/2022/07/ChiaGreenPaper.pdf
28. Cohen, R., Doerner, J., Kondi, Y., et al.: Guaranteed output in o(sqrt(n)) rounds for round-robin sampling protocols. Cryptology ePrint Archive (2022)
29. Company, T.E.C.: Halo2. https://github.com/zcash/halo2
30. DeMillo, R.A., Lipton, R.J.: A probabilistic remark on algebraic program testing. Technical report, Georgia Tech (1977)
31. Devos, B.: Loopring starts zkSNARK trusted setup multi-party computation ceremony. link (2019)
32. FileCoin: Trusted setup complete! (2020). https://filecoin.io/blog/posts/trusted-setup-complete/
33. Foundation, E.: Ethereum: Powers of tau specification (2022). https://github.com/ethereum/kzg-ceremony-specs
34. Frederiksen, T.K., Lindell, Y., Osheter, V., Pinkas, B.: Fast distributed RSA key generation for semi-honest and malicious adversaries. In: Shacham, H., Boldyreva, A. (eds.) CRYPTO 2018. LNCS, vol. 10992, pp. 331–361. Springer, Cham (2018). https://doi.org/10.1007/978-3-319-96881-0_12
35. Gabizon, A., Williamson, Z.J., Ciobotaru, O.: Plonk: permutations over lagrange-bases for oecumenical noninteractive arguments of knowledge. Cryptology ePrint Archive, Paper 2019/953 (2019)
36. Ganesh, C., Khoshakhlagh, H., Kohlweiss, M., Nitulescu, A., Zajac, M.: What makes fiat-shamir zksnarks (updatable srs) simulation extractable? Cryptology ePrint Archive, Paper 2021/511 (2021). https://eprint.iacr.org/2021/511, https://eprint.iacr.org/2021/511
37. Gilboa, N.: Two party RSA key generation. In: Wiener, M. (ed.) CRYPTO 1999. LNCS, vol. 1666, pp. 116–129. Springer, Heidelberg (1999). https://doi.org/10.1007/3-540-48405-1_8
38. Groth, J.: Simulation-sound NIZK proofs for a practical language and constant size group signatures. In: Lai, X., Chen, K. (eds.) ASIACRYPT 2006. LNCS, vol. 4284, pp. 444–459. Springer, Heidelberg (2006). https://doi.org/10.1007/11935230_29

39. Groth, J.: Short pairing-based non-interactive zero-knowledge arguments. In: Abe, M. (ed.) ASIACRYPT 2010. LNCS, vol. 6477, pp. 321–340. Springer, Heidelberg (2010). https://doi.org/10.1007/978-3-642-17373-8_19

40. Groth, J.: On the size of pairing-based non-interactive arguments. In: Fischlin, M., Coron, J.-S. (eds.) EUROCRYPT 2016. LNCS, vol. 9666, pp. 305–326. Springer, Heidelberg (2016). https://doi.org/10.1007/978-3-662-49896-5_11

41. Groth, J., Kohlweiss, M., Maller, M., Meiklejohn, S., Miers, I.: Updatable and universal common reference strings with applications to zk-SNARKs. In: Shacham, H., Boldyreva, A. (eds.) CRYPTO 2018. LNCS, vol. 10993, pp. 698–728. Springer, Cham (2018). https://doi.org/10.1007/978-3-319-96878-0_24

42. Hazay, C., Mikkelsen, G.L., Rabin, T., Toft, T., Nicolosi, A.A.: Efficient RSA key generation and threshold paillier in the two-party setting. J. Cryptol. **32**(2), 265–323 (2019)

43. Hermez, P.: Hermez zero-knowledge proofs (2020). https://blog.hermez.io/hermez-zero-knowledge-proofs/

44. Kate, A., Zaverucha, G.M., Goldberg, I.: Constant-size commitments to polynomials and their applications. In: Abe, M. (ed.) ASIACRYPT 2010. LNCS, vol. 6477, pp. 177–194. Springer, Heidelberg (2010). https://doi.org/10.1007/978-3-642-17373-8_11

45. Kim, T., Barbulescu, R.: Extended tower number field sieve: a new complexity for the medium prime case. In: Robshaw, M., Katz, J. (eds.) CRYPTO 2016. LNCS, vol. 9814, pp. 543–571. Springer, Heidelberg (2016). https://doi.org/10.1007/978-3-662-53018-4_20

46. Kohlweiss, M., Maller, M., Siim, J., Volkhov, M.: Snarky ceremonies. In: Tibouchi, M., Wang, H. (eds.) ASIACRYPT 2021. LNCS, vol. 13092, pp. 98–127. Springer, Cham (2021). https://doi.org/10.1007/978-3-030-92078-4_4

47. Kuszmaul, J.: V(ery short m)erkle trees. verkle trees (2018). https://math.mit.edu/research/highschool/primes/materials/2018/Kuszmaul.pdf

48. "l2 fees" (2022). https://l2fees.info/

49. Lee, J.: Dory: efficient, transparent arguments for generalised inner products and polynomial commitments. In: Nissim, K., Waters, B. (eds.) TCC 2021. LNCS, vol. 13043, pp. 1–34. Springer, Cham (2021). https://doi.org/10.1007/978-3-030-90453-1_1

50. Libert, B., Yung, M.: Concise mercurial vector commitments and independent zero-knowledge sets with short proofs. In: Micciancio, D. (ed.) TCC 2010. LNCS, vol. 5978, pp. 499–517. Springer, Heidelberg (2010). https://doi.org/10.1007/978-3-642-11799-2_30

51. Lipmaa, H., Siim, J., Zajac, M.: Counting vampires: from univariate sumcheck to updatable zk-snark. Cryptology ePrint Archive (2022)

52. Long, L.: Binary Quadratic Forms (2019). https://github.com/Chia-Network/vdf-competition/blob/main/classgroups.pdf

53. Malkin, M., Wu, T.D., Boneh, D.: Experimenting with shared generation of RSA keys. In: Proceedings of the Network and Distributed System Security Symposium, NDSS 1999, San Diego, California, USA. The Internet Society (1999)

54. Maller, M., Bowe, S., Kohlweiss, M., Meiklejohn, S.: Sonic: zero-knowledge snarks from linear-size universal and updatable structured reference strings. In: Proceedings of the 2019 ACM SIGSAC Conference on Computer and Communications Security, pp. 2111–2128 (2019)

55. Ristenpart, T., Yilek, S.: The power of proofs-of-possession: securing multiparty signatures against rogue-key attacks. In: Naor, M. (ed.) EUROCRYPT 2007.

LNCS, vol. 4515, pp. 228–245. Springer, Heidelberg (2007). https://doi.org/10.1007/978-3-540-72540-4_13

56. Schnorr, C.P.: Efficient identification and signatures for smart cards. In: Brassard, G. (ed.) CRYPTO 1989. LNCS, vol. 435, pp. 239–252. Springer, New York (1990). https://doi.org/10.1007/0-387-34805-0_22

57. Schnorr, C.P.: Efficient signature generation by smart cards. J. Cryptol. **4**(3), 161–174 (1991)

58. Schwartz, J.T.: Fast probabilistic algorithms for verification of polynomial identities. J. ACM (JACM) **27**(4), 701–717 (1980)

59. Valiant, P.: Incrementally verifiable computation or proofs of knowledge imply time/space efficiency. In: Canetti, R. (ed.) TCC 2008. LNCS, vol. 4948, pp. 1–18. Springer, Heidelberg (2008). https://doi.org/10.1007/978-3-540-78524-8_1

60. Vitalik Buterin, C.R.: EIP-197: Precompiled contracts for optimal ate pairing check on the elliptic curve alt_bn128 (2017). https://eips.ethereum.org/EIPS/eip-197

61. Vlasov, A.: EIP-2539: Bls12-377 curve operations (2020). https://eips.ethereum.org/EIPS/eip-2539

62. Wang, W., Ulichney, A., Papamanthou, C.: BalanceProofs: Maintainable Vector Commitments with Fast Aggregation. Cryptology ePrint Archive, Paper 2022/864 (2022)

63. Waters, B., Wu, D.: Batch arguments for NP and more from standard bilinear group assumptions. In: Dodis, Y., Shrimpton, T. (eds.) CRYPTO 2022. LNCS, vol. 13508, pp. 433–463. Springer, Cham (2022)

64. Youssef El Housni, Michael Connor, A.G.: EIP-3026: Bw6-761 curve operations (2020). https://eips.ethereum.org/EIPS/eip-3026

65. Zippel, R.: Probabilistic algorithms for sparse polynomials. In: Ng, E.W. (ed.) Symbolic and Algebraic Computation. LNCS, vol. 72, pp. 216–226. Springer, Heidelberg (1979). https://doi.org/10.1007/3-540-09519-5_73

Smart Infrastructures, Systems and Software

Self-sovereign Identity for Electric Vehicle Charging

Adrian Kailus[1], Dustin Kern[2(✉)], and Christoph Krauß[2]

[1] DB Systel GmbH, Frankfurt, Germany
`a@kailus.dev`
[2] Darmstadt University of Applied Sciences, Darmstadt, Germany
`{dustin.kern,christoph.krauss}@h-da.de`

Abstract. Electric Vehicles (EVs) are more and more charged at public
Charge Points (CPs) using Plug-and-Charge (PnC) protocols such as the
ISO 15118 standard which eliminates user interaction for authentication
and authorization. Currently, this requires a rather complex Public Key
Infrastructure (PKI) and enables driver tracking via the included unique
identifiers. In this paper, we propose an approach for using Self-Sovereign
Identities (SSIs) as trusted credentials for EV charging authentication
and authorization which overcomes the privacy problems and the issues
of a complex centralized PKI. Our implementation shows the feasibility
of our approach with ISO 15118, meaning that existing roles/features
can be supported and that existing timing/size constraints of the ISO
standard can be met. The security and privacy of the proposed approach
is shown in a formal analysis using the Tamarin prover.

Keywords: Electric Vehicle · Privacy · Plug and Charge ·
Self-Sovereign Identity · ISO 15118

1 Introduction

Plug-and-Charge (PnC), e.g., using the standard ISO 15118, enables Electric
Vehicles (EVs) to charge without user interaction at public Charge Points (CPs)
operated by a Charge Point Operator (CPO). The EV stores relevant data such
as contract credentials and automatically performs all necessary steps to start a
charging session, e.g., authentication, authorization, and negotiation of charging
parameters. No RFID cards or smartphone apps are required anymore. To enable
this, ISO 15118 defines a complex Public Key Infrastructure (PKI) and uses a
unique identifier to identify the user or actually the user's personal charging
contract. The charging contract is the basis for billing of PnC sessions and is
concluded between an EV user and an e-Mobility Service Provider (eMSP).

The complex PKI architecture of ISO 15118 requires all entities to operate central (sub-) Certificate Authorities (CAs). These entities include CPOs
and eMSPs but also Original Equipment Manufacturers (OEMs) and a Contract Clearing House (CCH). OEMs produce EVs and the CCH enables roaming

C. Pöpper and L. Batina (Eds.): ACNS 2024, LNCS 14585, pp. 137–162, 2024.
https://doi.org/10.1007/978-3-031-54776-8_6

services for charging at CPs from different operators. Furthermore, the Root CAs are possible single points of failure. The unique identifier of the charging contract, called e-Mobility Account Identifier (eMAID), enables user tracking which raises privacy issues. By analyzing movement profiles, user habits or even the health status may be deduced, e.g., if the vehicle is regularly charged at a hospital.

To overcome the issues of centralized systems such as PKIs or identity providers, Self-Sovereign Identities (SSIs) gained a lot of attention in the last years. SSI provides a digital identity and enables users to control the information they disclose to prove their identity and to protect their privacy.

In this paper, we propose an approach for using SSIs as trusted credentials for EV charging authentication and authorization. Our approach solves the issues of complex centralized PKI and protects against linking multiple authentication processes. The contributions of this paper are as follows: (i) Concept for the secure integration of SSI into ISO 15118 with privacy-preserving charging authentication/authorization. (ii) Proof-of-concept implementation showing minor additional overhead and easy integration into existing systems. (iii) Formal security and privacy analysis in the symbolic model using the Tamarin prover [35]. (iv) Publishing the used Tamarin models (cf. Sect. 7.2) for reproducibility of the automated proofs and reusability of used modeling concepts in related work.

The remainder of the paper is structured as follows: Sect. 2 describes necessary background to understand our approach. Related work is discussed in Sect. 3. In Sect. 4, we present identified requirements for our concept which is introduced in Sect. 5. Our prototypical implementation is described in Sect. 6, followed by the security, privacy, and practical evaluations in Sect. 7. Finally, we conclude the paper and discuss future work in Sect. 8.

2   Background

In this section, we describe background on e-mobility and SSI. The focus is on the certificate-based authentication which we replace with SSI credentials.

2.1   E-mobility

Figure 1 shows a simplified e-mobility architecture for AC and DC charging according to the ISO 15118 standard. There exist two editions of the standard, the first edition ISO 15118-2 [21] and the second edition ISO 15118-20 [22] which brings some security improvements. Our solution can be applied to both versions. Other methods for charge control/authentication are out-of-scope, e.g., basic Pulse-Width Modulation (PWM) signaling based on IEC 61851-1 [20] for AC charging, high-level communication via DIN 70121 [4] (which can be seen as a simpler/early version of ISO 15118-2 that only supports DC charging and does not include PnC authorization), or charge authorization via Autocharge [39] (i.e., insecure authorization via the vehicle's MAC address).

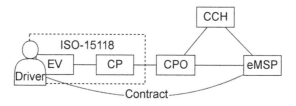

Fig. 1. Architecture Overview (cf. [6])

An OEM manufactures the EV (not shown), provides some initial credentials to the EV, and sells it to the new owner. The owner concludes a contract with an eMSP for charging at public CPs which are operated by a CPO. The initial credential from the OEM are used by the EV to request contract credentials from the eMSP. A Certificate Provisioning Service (CPS) establishes trust in the contract credentials provided by the eMSP. The EV stores and uses the contract credentials for PnC authorization and billing during a charging session with a CP. The communication between EV and CP is secured with TLS. The first edition of ISO 15118 uses unilateral TLS authentication of the CP and challenge-response-based authentication of the EV inside the TLS channel. The second edition uses mutual authentication with a vehicle certificate installed by the OEM in addition to the challenge-response-based EV authentication.

ISO 15118 requires multiple certificates and defines a rather complex PKI. The PKI consists of four[1] parts for CPO, OEM, eMSP, and CPS. All PKIs consist of up to two sub-CAs below a root CA. The root CA for CPO- and CPS-PKI is the V2G root CA which usually also certifies the sub-CAs of eMSP and OEM via cross-signing. The eMSP-PKI and OEM-PKI are always certified by their own root CAs.

The CPO-PKI is used for issuing certificates for CPs which are used for CP authentication in the TLS handshake.

The OEM-PKI is used to issue the OEM provisioning certificate which includes the unique identifier Provisioning Certificate Identifier (PCID). The OEM provisioning certificate is used as initial trust anchor for installing the contract credentials. In case the second edition ISO 15118-20 is used, additionally, a vehicle certificate is issued for EV authentication in the TLS handshake.

The eMSP-PKI is used to generate the contract certificate after concluding a contract with an EV owner. The eMSP generates contract certificate data which consists of a private key and the contract certificate (including the corresponding public key, a unique identifier called eMAID, and additional information). This data is installed when the EV is first connected to a public CP. The private key is encrypted with the public key of the OEM provisioning certificate to ensure that only the specific EV can access this key.

Finally, the CPS-PKI is used for generating certificates which are used by a CPS to sign contract certificate data generated by the eMSP. An EV can verify

---

[1] We omit the part for private environments since it is not relevant for our work.

the signature and the certificate chain up to the known V2G root CA. Thus, the verifier does not need to know the eMSP root CA.

The custom ISO 15118 PKI (with its required trust relations and certificate handling etc.) incurs a high level of complexity, which resulted in critique by relevant stake holders [2] and an importance for complexity-reducing measures [7]. Additionally, as backend communication is out-of-scope for ISO 15118, the PKI definition leaves many open issues such as certificate revocation handling, contract validation, or the handling of contract certificate requests/responses. Addressing these open issues requires proprietary solutions or additional standardization (e.g., the German VDE guideline for ISO 15118 certificate handling [46]), which further increases complexity.

In addition to the complexity of the PKI, there is another issue in ISO 15118 namely the lack of privacy protection. Currently, a lot of information, arguably not required for operation, is disclosed to entities such as CPOs, CCHs, and eMSPs [27]. For example, it would not be necessary to send the exact time and CP location of a charging session to the eMSP or the eMAID to the CPO.

2.2   Self-Sovereign Identity (SSI)

A Self-Sovereign Identity (SSI) allows a user to create and fully control a digital identity without requiring centralized infrastructures or identity providers. The user can also control how personal data is shared and used by another party via a decentralized path. After an information is verified by an issuer (e.g., a university verifying a degree), a verifier (e.g., a company) can always trust that information to be true. Subsequently, the information holder (e.g., a student) does not need to provide the full information to the verifier to prove its identity. This is achieved using verifiable credentials (standardized by the W3C [44]), the distributed identity protocol, and a distributed ledger technology (which is mostly a blockchain). The information holder registers an information identifier at a ledger, which is verified by an issuer, and the verifier can trust this information. In the following, we introduce the most relevant terms for our work.

Verifiable Claims. In SSI, the essence is that a counterpart can rely on a claim without having control over the content of the claim. Here, a distinction must be made between a Claim and a Verifiable Claim. First, a claim is simply a statement about a fact that anyone could make and without being verifiable. For example, it could be stated that Alice is a graduate of a certain university. However, for this statement to become a Verifiable Claim, the signature of an issuer may be added to it. Alternatively, zero-knowledge cryptography may be used in a privacy-preserving manner to indirectly prove that a claim is covered by a valid verifiable credential [44].

Verifiable Credentials. A collection of claims together with an identifier and metadata such as the issuer, expiration date, terms of use, and keys form a credential. Credentials are comparable to conventional ID documents, which likewise bundle a number of statements. Multiple credentials can be combined into one profile.[2]

Decentralized Identifiers. Identifiers that can be resolved to a Distributed Identifier (DID) Document[3] and do not require a central registration authority to be created. The DID Document, which can only be modified by the DID Controller, can contain information about public keys, verification methods, the controller, and authentication methods, among other things. The DID Controller also defines the subject of the DID, e.g., a person or organization. Specific sections in a DID document can be referenced by the respective DID URL. Both the DID and the DID Document are stored in a *Verifiable Data Registry* (e.g., a distributed ledger) and their combination is called a DID Record. The public keys of a DID enable encrypted communication with the owner of the DID. To do this, a communication partner can either use a DID Record they got from the other party or look up the public keys in the *Verifiable Data Registry* [41].

DID Auth. There are 10 different architectures to authenticate an identity holder using different transports for the challenge-response cycle [43]. The main focus is to let an identity holder prove to have control over a DID. Authentication can be unilateral or bilateral, with both parties demonstrating control over their own DID. This may also involve the exchange of Verifiable Credentials if required by the use case. There are three ways to combine DID Auth with Verifiable Credentials: DID Auth and the Verifiable Credentials are exchanged separately (in that order); The Verifiable Credentials are part of DID Auth and represent an optional field in the authentication protocol or finally, DID Auth can be considered a special case of a Verifiable Credential, with a claim "I am me". The authentication process is based on a challenge-response cycle where the relying party authenticates the identity holder using, for example, a cryptographic signature.

3   Related Work

The increasing integration of information and communication technology into vehicles enables automated tracking of vehicles which threatens the privacy of drivers and passengers [1]. [30] discusses privacy issues for electric mobility and [17] privacy challenges for EV charging.

Several approaches for security and/or privacy in EV charging have been proposed. In [31,32], an EV authentication protocol for contactless charging (i.e., using charging pads integrated into the road) using pseudonyms is proposed. An architecture for privacy-preserving contract-based charging and billing of EVs using ISO 15118 is presented in [19]. A formal analysis and improvements of this architecture are presented in [9]. A privacy-preserving solution for roaming EV charging and billing based on smart cards is proposed in [37]. The solutions

---

[2] Combining credentials, 2018, https://github.com/w3c/vc-data-model/issues/112.

[3] DID resolution, W3C, 2021, https://w3c-ccg.github.io/did-resolution/.

presented in [27,49,50] all require a Trusted Platform Module (TPM) to realize a Direct Anonymous Attestation (DAA) scheme for EV authentication. In [26], an approach for quantum-secure EV charging is presented. Using a TPM for protecting credentials but without privacy protection is proposed in [13–16]. All approaches still require a complex PKI.

Some work exists that seeks to address the issues around privacy and user profiling when charging EVs via the implementation of a new, anonymous payment channel. This often involves a blockchain solution that promises anonymous payment processing and a decentralized infrastructure. The authors of [10], for example, present a solution where payment for charging electricity is handled through multiple blockchains. A main blockchain negotiates transactions between the operator and the CPs, and on sub-blockchains, multiple customers join together to form credit sharing groups in which individual payments cannot be linked to the buyer of the credits. Here, the degree of anonymity is measured using K-anonymity, which quantifies the group size from which a user is indistinguishable. The main blockchain is connected to the sub-blockchains via a *bridge* role that communicates with credit buyers. The authors of [48] also present a blockchain-based solution for charging EVs, which is also based on *K-Anonymity*. Their approach uses a distributed PKI that separates user registration and verification across two blockchains. Payment here is handled via smart contracts. In [29], a blockchain-based approach for privacy-preserving selection of a CP based on tariff options and travel distance is presented. The authors of [47] propose the implementation of a blockchain-based PKI for Internet of Things (IoT) and demonstrate the feasibility and efficiency of such an IoT PKI through a prototype implementation and experiments. The PKI network is based on Emercoin 15 and uses a proof-of-stake consensus algorithm.

Some work already considers the use of SSI for EV charging. The authors of [42] provide a high-level analysis of the potential benefits that an SSI solution can bring to EV charging. However, no detailed concept is proposed and details on, e.g., the integration into existing EV charging processes or the resulting overhead are not analyzed. Similar to our work is the approach of [18], which also uses SSI for decentralized eRoaming. However, this concept differs from our ISO 15118 extension and makes use of the user's smartphone instead of allowing for PnC-based EV authentication without user interaction. Also, no implementation is developed and a detailed analysis of performance overhead and security is provided.

In contrast to related work, our work presents a novel solution for the integration of SSI into the EV charging ecosystem. We consider the integration into existing protocols and process to enhance the potential usability of the solution as much as possible. Additionally, we provide a performance analysis based on a proof-of-concept implementation as well as a formal security and privacy analysis using the Tamarin prover [35].

4 System Model and Requirement Analysis

The following section outlines the scope of this work, defines an attacker model, and discusses the concept requirements, which are grouped into three categories: Functional Requirements (FR), Security Requirements (SR), and Privacy Requirements (PR). We derive our requirements under consideration of the state of the art (cf. Sect. 2) in combination with the attacker model (cf. Sect. 4.2) and considering relevant threat/requirement analyses from related work (cf. Sect. 3).

4.1 Scope

Among other things, the PnC process maps a bidirectional authentication between CP and EV to trust the existence of a contractual relationship and to rule out malicious actors. These authentications in ISO 15118 are based on a common PKI, which is used, among other tasks, to authorize a vehicle for a charging process, to authenticate the charging infrastructure, or to establish the TLS connection. In an all-encompassing extension of traditional authentication via PKI and its certificates, both authentications would therefore be replaced, including their use for the TLS connection and the *metering* messages during the charging loop. The scope of this work, however, is limited to the proprietary application-layer-based authentication process of the contract information provided by the EV to the CP. Since the CP's authentication towards the EV uses generic TLS-based methods and has (based on our analysis) no special privacy requirements, we argue that the CP's authentication could be replaced with generic SSI-based methods (cf. *DID Auth* in Sect. 2.2) in a straight-forward manner. This would also address the CP-related PKI requirements. Thus, we do not consider further details of the CP's authentication in this work and instead focus on the EV's side.

4.2 Attacker Model

A successful attack in the EV charging context could lead to financial damages, cause safety issues or privacy violations, and may (if large-scale enough) even cause power grid stability issues [8,24,25]. Thus, in order to make the concept viable against possible attacks and vulnerabilities, an attacker model is set up in the following.

Classic attacker models, such as the Dolev-Yao Model [5], outline malicious network participants capable of intercepting network communications, sending and modifying messages. However, we assume that basic cryptographic primitives and implementations hold [36].

Additionally, we consider threats to the system's privacy. The centralized approach to certificate validation makes users traceable and their personal data vulnerable to attack by any of the actors. This threat is increased in case one of the actors is compromised by an attacker or stops following the agreed protocol to obtain additional information. While such *malicious operators* pose a major threat, the danger posed by such *malicious operators* is limited [40]. This is mainly due to the fact that operators have to comply with legal regulations and maintain their image to the public. Taking this into account, the *Honest-but-Curious Operator* is described below (cf. [27]).

Above all, the *Honest-but-Curious Operator* does not want to create a malicious impression to the outside world by deviating from the agreed protocols. Since involved in the process, such operators use all information available to them to ultimately derive additional benefit from it. In the PnC context, potentially *Honest-but-Curious Operators* can include the CPOs, eMSPs and the CCH. At this point it is assumed that several operators do not accumulate their available information to draw a more comprehensive data picture, since this is opposed to the competition relationship among operators and should additionally be prevented by regulations. Ultimately, the regulation of operators is beyond the control of this concept.

4.3   Functional Requirements

In order to ensure user-friendliness and to allow for an easy integration of the solution into existing protocols and processes, we define several functional requirements. The requirements ensure that features of the original ISO 15118 can be supported by the new concept. For example, in order for the vehicle to authenticate itself at the charging stations with its contract information, a process must be defined for contract installations which provide the vehicle with the necessary information. In order to uniquely associate a driver's contract with the vehicle, the vehicle must be uniquely identifiable during the installation process. In order to ensure that the solution is user-friendly, any additional overhead should remain acceptable. Functional Requirements (FR) are listed in the following:

FR1 Vehicle charging as well as contract installation should still be possible without further user interaction, since this is the concept of PnC.

FR2 Contract authentication via SSI should be negotiable as an option to the existing authentication methods.

FR3 All SSI roles should be able to be taken by an actor from the ISO 15118 ecosystem. In SSI, the credential verification process principally covers three roles: the Issuer, the Holder and the Verifier, which must be uniquely applied to an entity in the PnC context for each authentication.

FR4 The vehicle should continue to manage the necessary authentication information itself (in a wallet).

FR5 All contract issues from all issuers should fit an agreed schema baseline.

FR6 As in ISO-15118, it should be possible to delay the installation of the contract information until the first charging process.

FR7 The charging station should relay communication from the vehicle to the other actors in case the vehicle cannot use cellular.

FR8 The additional computational- and communication overhead of a SSI-based solution should be minor.

4.4   Security and Privacy Requirements

The non-functional requirements for the concept are listed and explained below. This includes Security Requirements (SR) and Privacy Requirements (PR). The security requirements focus on providing secure authentication for the actors involved in relevant processes (setup, credential installation, charging, billing):

SR1 The setup proceeds of the solution should be secure (e.g., the setup of EVs with provisioning credentials or the setup of eMSPs as issuers of verifiable credentials). That is, all relevant parties should be securely authenticated to enable trust between the parties.

SR2 During the contract credential installation the eMSP should be able to trust in the originality of the vehicle, similarly to the OEM provisioning certificate in ISO 15118, which is installed during vehicle production. That is, the EV should securely authenticate itself towards the eMSP during the credential installation process.

SR3 The CP/CPO should be able to trust the EV's provided contract information. That is, the EV should securely authenticate itself towards a CP before the start of a charging process.

SR4 The contract information should allow the eMSP to associate an invoice from a CPO with a contract. That is, the EV's charge authentication data should securely authenticate the EV's contract towards the eMSP for billing.

The privacy requirements focus non-traceability and non-linkability of EV users:

PR1 During the authentication process no information should be exchanged that makes the user traceable to either a CPO, CCH or an eMSP, preventing the creation of a user's movement profile (*non-traceability*).

PR2 A specific CPO, CCH or eMSP should not be able to associate multiple charging operations with individual users (*non-linkability*).

Notably, traceability and linkability of EV users by their eMSP is feasible due to payment processing via traditional payment methods. This problem may be solved by using smart contracts (cf. [48]), which is out-of-scope for this paper.

5   SSI Concept

In the following, our concept for integrating an SSI-based solution into the ISO 15118-2 authentication process is developed, including an architectural overview and the message sequences of the communication between the actors. The main challenge is in the specific combination of the different SSI concepts (cf. Sect. 2.2) such that actors, processes, and features of the existing EV charging architecture can still be supported while also designing the concept in a way that enables the (Tamarin-based) symbolic verification of the strong security and privacy requirements (cf. Sect. 4.4). Additionally, we discuss the applicability of the proposed solution to ISO 15118-20.

5.1   Concept Overview

In this specific scenario, the already existing parties of ISO 15118 are sufficient to map all three roles *Holder*, *Verifier*, and *Issuer* of the SSI process.

The Holder and the Verifier of the contract authentication process are easy to identify in the PnC context: The Holder is the actor in possession of the contract information. This data could be stored either in a wallet on the driver's smartphone, along with other credentials, or in the EV in the form of an on-board wallet. The first option would require driver consent each time information is accessed from the wallet, similar to [34]. Since the main goal of PnC is to enable vehicle charging without further user interaction, it is preferable to install the wallet in the EV. This also eliminates the need to communicate with the driver's smartphone. Since the verifier needs to authenticate the contracts, this role is taken by the CP, which is already performing this task in ISO 15118.

The issuer first needs access to the original contracts to authenticate them as credentials. This condition applies only to the eMSP, with each eMSP having access solely to the contracts of its clients. Furthermore, the verifiers, i.e., the CPs, should be able to trust the issuer. Since the CPs already had to trust the eMSPs in the conventional ISO 15118, this condition is also met.

To grant multiple issuers write permissions on the Ledger to create documents like *Credential Definitions* or *Credentials*, an additional instance is needed that can give these permissions to the different issuers - the *Steward*.

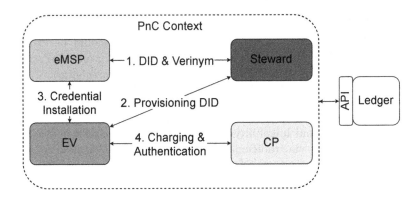

Fig. 2. Architecture Overview

Figure 2 shows how these four actors interact for charging authentication in the overall system. Initially, only the steward is authorized to write to the ledger which reduces the number of first-level write permissions. The steward grants second-level write permissions to new eMSPs later on. The steward writes these permissions to the ledger in the form of a verinym (step 1), which enables the eMSP to authenticate its contracts. A verinym is associated with the legal identity of the identity holder [11]. Thus, the legal entity of the eMSP that enters into the contracts with the customers is associated with the identity on the ledger that has write permissions for the credentials of those same contracts.

In step 2, a *Provisioning DID* is created for the vehicle. This is done before the vehicle is sold. This *Provisioning DID* is necessary to be able to link a specific vehicle to a contract later on. Furthermore, with the help of the public key of a DID, it is always possible for other actors to communicate with its owner in an encrypted way, which will also be helpful later on. Of course, this also applies to all other DIDs used in the PnC context.

Then, in order for the necessary contract information to be authenticated during a charging process, the information must be transferred to the vehicle. This third step can happen once a contract is established and the vehicle has connected to the internet (directly or via a CP). Since the vehicle may have wireless, but this is optional, this step can take place sometime after the *Provisioning DID* has been created between the conclusion of the contract and the charging process. For this, the vehicle requests the credentials from the respective eMSP, which authenticates them on the ledger.

The vehicle can then authenticate itself to the CP during the charging process in the final step 4. Authentication uses *Anoncreds*,[4] i.e., zero-knowledge proofs with Camenisch-Lysyanskaya (CL)-based credentials and paring-based revocation [28]. In short, the EV proofs to the CPs that it possesses valid contract credentials and that these credentials have not been revoked by the issuer (without revealing the actual credentials).

The following sections describe the changes made to the message sequence of ISO 15118 in order to create a working infrastructure for the transition to SSI authentication.

5.2   Provisioning DID Creation

Prior to any charging process, the issuer, in this case the eMSP, must be authorized to issue credentials. That is, the eMSP needs write permission to the ledger, which requires publishing its DID (containing a public key) to the ledger. Such a DID is often called a *Verinym*. The eMSP makes a request to the steward, which is authorized to write to the ledger. This process is secured based on pre-negotiated secret or public keys. Since both communication partners are legal entities, it can be assumed that there is an agreement between the two in which a secret or public key can be exchanged.

Anther setup process is the creation of a *Provisioning DIDs* (cf. Fig. 3), which is a prerequisite for linking the contract and the vehicle. This process is described in the following paragraphs:

Step 1. The EV provisioning process, starts with the production of the vehicle. During this process, the EV creates a *Provisioning DID*, which enables encrypted communication with the EV using the corresponding public key (shared via the ledger; without requiring a traditional PKI). A part of the DID is the *DID*

---

[4] https://github.com/hyperledger/indy-sdk/tree/main/docs/design/002-anoncreds.

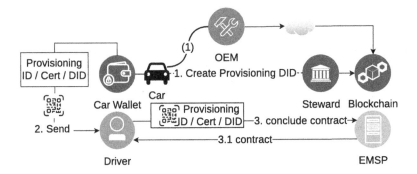

Fig. 3. Provisioning *DID* Creation

record, which contains the public information for a given DID and must be written to the ledger. In order to write an EV's *Provisioning DID record* on the ledger, communication towards the steward is handled by the EV's OEM on behalf of the EV. After connecting to the steward, the OEM starts with sending an *InitNymReq* with a nonce, answered by the steward with an *InitNymRes,* containing a DID for a key of the steward, the OEM's nonce, a fresh nonce from the steward and the OEM's ID. The *InitNymRes* is signed by the steward (with the key corresponding to the DID) and encrypted with a public key of the OEM. The steward's DID allows the OEM to encrypt future messages to the steward, and the nonces are used to ensure replay-protection and subsequently a proof of possession for the EV's *Provisioning DID.* The OEM creates a *Provisioning DID* (on behalf of the EV and for a provisioning key pair that is provided to the EV), decrypts the steward message, verifies the signature, and signs the steward's nonce with the private key of the *Provisioning DID.*[5] The *Provisioning DID* (including the corresponding public key) and the signature are sent back to the steward, encrypted with the public key from the steward's DID.

Steps 2 and 3. When the vehicle is purchased, the *Provisioning DID,* is passed to the user so that the user can pass the *Provisioning DID* to the eMSP and negotiate a contract. The handover at the time of concluding a contract with the eMSP could be via a QR code sent to the user, who then activates the contract by passing on the DID, but other ways are not excluded. Since a potential co-reader does not have the private keys of the DID, he cannot prove their possession and cannot succeed in a challenge. This completes the process until the first charging session.

---

[5] While it would be possible to generate the *Provisioning DID* key pair in the EV (similar to [13,16]) and have the OEM only collect a signature over the steward's nonce from the EV (which would prevent the EV's private key material from ever leaving the EV), we believe that this method may result in scalability issues. Additionally, one may assume a secure OEM to EV relation during production (in a controlled environment), which limits the security benefit of exclusive key possession by the EV.

5.3   Contract Credential Installation

The following is an explanation of the general process steps for installing the Contract Credential (cf. Fig. 4), which requires a *Provisioning DID* and an existing contract with an eMSP. This process is modeled on the Issue Credential Protocol from [12].

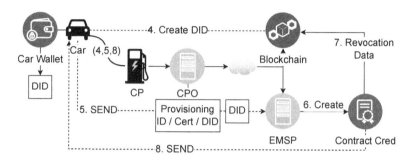

Fig. 4. Contract Credential Installation

Step 4 and 5. Contract credentials are required in the vehicle during a charging process. To do this, they must first be created and installed in an EV. Similarly to the current installation process in ISO 15118, we tunnel the necessary communication between the EV and the backend via the CP. This method enhances usability as the vehicle may not be able to connect to the Internet, and thus to the ledger and other services, until it is plugged into a CP for the first time. Once the connection is established, the EV starts by sending its *Provisioning DID* to the eMSP. The eMSP responds with its DID and a *Credential Offer*, which includes a nonce and a *Credential Definition ID*. The latter identifies a credential schema, which specifies the structure of all issued credentials (of a certain contract type) by this eMSP with all necessary and optional fields, with public keys, and a *Revocation Registry*. The eMSP's response is encrypted for the EV based on the *Provisioning DID* (i.e., based on the respective *Provisioning DID* public key).

Steps 6, 7, and 8. If the EV agrees to this *Credential Offer*, it generates a master secret for the credential. The EV then creates a blinded master secret for the *Credential Offer* and a correctness proof (as per *Anoncreds* definition). Afterwards, the EV builds a *Credential Request* with the blinded master secret and correctness proof and encrypts this request based on the eMSP's DID.

The eMSP decrypts this *Credential Request* and uses it to create the *Contract Credentials* that an EV needs in order to authenticate itself at CPs. Additionally, the eMSP updates the revocation information, i.e., the public tails files and the accumulator[6] on the ledger to include the new credential. This step can optionally include the revocation of old credentials in case a contract has been terminated or the terms of the contract have changed.

The *Contract Credentials* need to be authenticated by an authorized issuer, which can be the eMSP, and contain all billing-relevant information as attributes. This billing-relevant information, is at least, the eMSP's ID, which is needed by CPs/CPOs to identify the EV user's eMSP for billing purposes. Additionally, the credential attributes can include any tariff information that may be useful to CPs/CPOs (e.g., pricing thresholds or if Vehicle to Grid (V2G) power transfer is supported). The EV user can always decide which attributes from a *Contract Credential* they want to reveal during a zero-knowledge proof.

The EV receives the signed *Contract Credentials* along with the credential revocation information from the eMSP encrypted with the public key of the *Provisioning DID* via the existing connection in a *CreateContractCredentialRes*. The eMSP's response additionally includes a symmetric contract key, which is later used to securely authenticate the EV's contract towards the eMSP for billing purposes. The EV decrypts and verifies the received data and stores it for later authentication during charge sessions.

5.4 Charging Process and Credential Validation

The following section will outline the changes to the charging process (cf. Fig. 5). Specifically, the message sequence *Identification, Authentication, and Authorization* from ISO 15118 is considered.

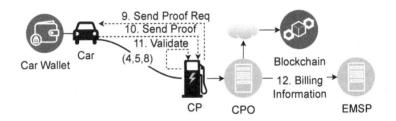

Fig. 5. Credential Validation during the Charging Process

Step 9. Figure 5 shows the authentication of the vehicle by the CP. In ISO 15118, service parameters such as the payment method are negotiated in the *Service-DiscoveryReq/-Res*. The authentication method now becomes another service parameter, making *Contract Proof Identification Mode* a third option besides the

---

[6] https://hyperledger-indy.readthedocs.io/projects/hipe/en/latest/text/0011-cred-revocation/README.html.

existing modes (e.g., PnC). In this *Contract Proof* message sequence, *Identification, Authentication, and Authorization* messages from ISO 15118 are changed after the *PaymentServiceSelectionRes*.

By sending a *RequestProofReq/-Res* the EV receives a proof request from the CP. The CP's proof request includes a nonce and specifies which individual credential attributes the CP expects in its role as verifier, not necessarily all the credentials/attributes issued to the EV by the eMSP.

Step 10. From the proof request, the EV then creates a zero-knowledge proof for the requested attributes and a proof of non-revocation using its credential master secret and the CP's nonce. The proofs guarantee to a verifier that the EV possesses valid non-revoked credentials for the identified attributes. The EV additionally uses its symmetric contract key to authenticate its contract towards the eMSP by generating an HMAC over a hash of the CP's *proof request*, a contract identifier, and a timestamp. The hashed *proof request* is used to bind the contract authentication data to the current CP/session, the contract identifier is used by the eMSP to identify the correct contract and symmetric contract key, and the timestamp is used to prevent replays. The contract authentication data is encrypted for the eMSP and sent together with the proofs to the CP in a *ValidateContractProofReq* message.

Step 11. The CP can validate the zero-knowledge proof for the credential attributes by using the eMSP's public key and can validate the revocation status of the corresponding credential by using the eMSP's public tails file and the corresponding accumulator value from the ledger. If all verifications are successful, the CP responds with a *ValidateContractProofRes* to the EV. Thereupon, the charging process can continue as described in ISO 15118.

Step 12. Finally, the encrypted contract authentication data (along with other billing relevant data, e.g., meter values) is sent from the CP to its CPO, who can forward this data to the corresponding eMSP. The eMSP can decrypt the contract authentication data and identify the correct contract. Hence, the usual billing relations are still possible, i.e., the CPO can bill the eMSP and the eMSP can bill the EV user. However, the CP/CPO can no longer identify the specific EV user and the eMSP can no longer identify the specific charging location.

5.5   Integration into ISO 15118-20

While ISO 15118-2 is still the prominent edition of the protocol today, we already consider the integration of our solution into ISO 15118-20, which can be expected to gain increased adoption in the future. We identify several relevant changes to the credential installation and charge authorization processes with ISO 15118-20 as follows: *(i)* updated cipher suites (e.g., from 128 bit AES to 256 bit AES), *(ii)* mutual authentication during the TLS handshake (instead of unilateral CP authentication), and *(iii)* the option to install multiple different contract credentials into one EV (e.g., for different eMSP charging contracts).

We argue that the proposed solution is also applicable for ISO 15118-20 as follows: *(i)* our solution is independent of specific cryptographic algorithms, *(ii)* the generic TLS based authentication (without application-specific requirements unlike the EV's application-layer authentication) can be replaced with generic DID-based approaches (to prevent the need for a conventional PKI) whereby the EV's authentication should again use *Anoncreds* (to not undermine the gained application-layer privacy), and *(iii)* the installation of multiple contract credentials is possible by repeating the process of Sect. 5.3.

6   Implementation

To demonstrate the feasibility of the concept, the contract authentication described therein was implemented during the charging process together with all preceding initiation steps such as the creation of the DIDs or the installation of contract credentials. Our implementation is based on the ISO 15118 reference implementation *RISE-V2G* [45]. In order to compare the concept with the actual state of the standard, we compare our implemented methods with the default *RISE-V2G* implementation.

The reference implementation covers all necessary features to establish comparability to the status quo and at the same time serve as a basis for the implementation of the concept. The project Hyperledger Indy[7] provides an implementation for all necessary SSI-operations, thus the Indy SDK[8] was chosen to be integrated into our prototype. The reference implementation was extended by the steward and the eMSP in addition to the existing services EV and CP. They are responsible for the detailed handling of the schemas, credential definitions, and credentials and interact with the other actors. Our prototypical implementation focuses on the message sequence *Identification, Authentication, and Authorization* and the associated communication between EV and the other services as described in the concept. The actual accounting and communication between the secondary actors is not part of the implementation, as this is not in the scope of ISO 15118. Additionally, the eMSP onboarding, its creation of the three data structures *Credential Schema, Credential Definition*, and *Revocation Registry* for the credentials of its customers' contracts and installation of *Provisioning DID* are also realized in the implementation.

The concept provides for the eMSP to use the secure channel established by the exchanged DID to create a *WriteVerinymReq*. In the prototype implementation, however, communication is still secured via the old certificate infrastructure, as this has only been extended to include the EV authentication. The CP continues to authenticate itself via certificates.

7   Evaluation

In this section, we evaluate the proposed/implemented solution. Specifically, in Sect. 7.1 we discuss the performance results based on our implementation

---

[7] Hyperledger, 2021, https://www.hyperledger.org.

[8] Indy SDK, 2021, https://github.com/hyperledger/indy-sdk#libindy-wrappers.

from Sect. 6, in Sect. 7.2 we describe our Tamarin-based symbolic security and privacy proofs, and in Sect. 7.3 we discuss how the concept addresses the defined requirements from Sect. 4.

7.1   Performance Measurements

Regarding performance, we evaluate the computational- and communication overhead of the proposed solution in comparison to the default ISO 15118 processes as implemented by *RISE-V2G*. Additionally, we verify that the incurred overhead remains within the existing timing and size constraints of the ISO 15118 standard (relevant constraints are the same for ISO 15118-2 and ISO 15118-20). For both types of overhead, the main changes are within the credential installation and charge authorization processes. Details are shown in Table 1.

Table 1. Duration and Size of Charging Session Messages for both Implementations

Message Name	RISE-V2G		SSI Impl.	
	time [ms]	size [byes]	time [ms]	size [byes]
Credential Installation				
CertificateInstallationReq	296.0	811	-	-
CertificateInstallationRes	32.8	3638	-	-
GetCredOfferReq	-	-	4.0	106
GetCredOfferRes	-	-	44.613	6710
CreateContractCredentialReq	-	-	134.429	2185
CreateContractCredentialRes	-	-	2603.864	5961
Charge Authorization				
PaymentDetailsReq	649.8	1452	-	-
PaymentDetailsRes	73.6	37	-	-
AuthorizationReq	129.6	13	-	-
AuthorizationRes	7.5	15	-	-
RequestProofReq	-	-	65.3	58
RequestProofRes	-	-	3.6	266
ValidateContractProofReq	-	-	282.302	7281
ValidateContractProofRes	-	-	136.3	55

The communication overhead of the proposed solution for credential installation messages is 14,962 bytes in total. The default *RISE-V2G* method requires 4,449 bytes for credential installation. Regarding charge authorization, the messages of the proposed solution are 7,660 bytes in total and the messages of the default *RISE-V2G* method are 1,517 bytes. For comparison, based on our measurements, the total communication overhead of a full 1-h default *RISE-V2G* charge session with a credential installation and a charge status message interval of 10 s is roughly 20,000 bytes. Notably, the only limit on message sizes of the ISO 15118 standard is a result of its 4 byte payload length field and is 4,294,967,295 bytes ([21], Sect. 7.8.3). Hence, we argue, that the increased overhead of the proposed solution is still acceptable.

For computational overhead, all measurements were performed 1000 times[9] and we report the respective average times (always including processing and message transfer). Regarding credential installation, the mean time of the proposed solution was 2786.9 ms compared to 328.8 ms with the default *RISE-V2G* method. Regarding charge authorization, the mean time of the proposed solution was 487.502 ms compared to 860.5 ms with the default *RISE-V2G* method (mostly due to certificate path validations). The results show good performance for the proposed method, especially considering that credential installation is rarely performed (only if a new contract is concluded or old credentials renewed). Notably, ISO 15118 defines relevant timeouts as: 40 s for generating a certificate installation request, 5 s for receiving a certificate installation response, 40 s for requesting a charge authorization, and 2 s for verifying the authorization ([21], Sect. 8.7.2). Hence, the proposed solution can still meet all relevant limits.

7.2 Security and Privacy Analysis with Tamarin

We analyze the security of the proposed solution in the symbolic model using the Tamarin prover [35] and the corresponding files are provided online.[10] Tamarin is a state-of-the-art tool for automated security protocol analysis. By default, analysis is performed in the symbolic model, i.e., assuming a Dolev-Yao adversary [5] with full control over the network who cannot break cryptographic primitives without knowing the respective private key (cf. adversary model in Sect. 4.2).

With Tamarin, protocols are specified using a set of *rules*, which define all relevant communication and processing steps of the protocol. Additionally, security requirements are defined as trace properties (lemmas), which need to hold for all possible execution traces of the protocol, i.e., all traces that can be built with the defined rules. Tamarin performs an exhaustive search for a trace that violates the defined requirements. If a trace is found, this trace serves as a counterexample (a specific attack path that violates the requirement). If no trace is found, the security requirement is proven to be satisfied by the defined protocol.

Furthermore, Tamarin enables the verification of observational equivalence properties, which can be used to show that an adversary cannot distinguish between two protocol runs. Observational equivalence is especially useful in order to verify privacy properties, e.g., by proving anonymity in EV charging by showing that an adversary cannot distinguish between two charge authorizations of different EVs.

---

[9] The measurements were performed on a Lenovo Thinkpad T480 with Intel® Core™ i5-8250U CPU @ 1.60 GHz × 8, 15.5 GiB Ram, running Ubuntu 20.04.3 LTS 64-bit.
[10] https://code.fbi.h-da.de/seacop/SSI-PnC-Tamarin.

Security Proofs.
The security requirements from Sect. 4.4 require authentication between different actors over different data. The most commonly used notion to prove strong authentication properties is defined in [33], namely *injective agreement* (preventing spoofing, replay, etc.). This property is defined as follows:

Definition 1 (Injective Agreement [33]). *A protocol guarantees to an initiator A* injective agreement *with a responder B on a set of data items ds if, whenever A (acting as initiator) completes a run of the protocol, apparently with responder B, then B has previously been running the protocol, apparently with A, and B was acting as responder in his run, and the two agents agreed on the data values corresponding to all the variables in ds, and each such run of A corresponds to a* unique *run of B.*

Using our defined Tamarin model, (See footnote 10) we successfully verify the following security properties based on the notion of injective agreement (cf. Definition 1). For this, we assume one steward and the ledger is modeled as a secure storage, where only authorized entities can write but everyone can read. Communication with the ledger is assumed to be a secure channel as specifics of this communication are not part of our concept, but instead standardized by the respective ledger specification. Additionally, we assume that the long-term key of all actors in a specific protocol run are secure since otherwise, attacks are trivially possible (e.g., if an EV's private provisioning key is leaked to an adversary, this adversary can spoof the affected EV towards an eMSP for contract credential installation). However, in order to keep the needed assumptions as weak as possible, other entities of the same types that are not directly involved in the protocol run can be compromised. For normal signatures/encryptions we use the built-in Tamarin functions. The EV zero-knowledge credential proofs are modeled with custom functions, whereby the EV can create a zero-knowledge proof based on the installed credential and its master secret, which the CP can verify with the eMSP's public key and revocation can be verified via a simple request over an accumulator in the ledger. However, zero-knowledge proofs are modeled without specific cryptographic details, since, in the symbolic model, cryptographic functions are anyway assumed to be secure. Besides the injective agreement-based lemmas to proof the desired security properties, our Tamarin files (See footnote 10) also includes lemmas to verify the correctness of the defined model. That is, correctness lemmas are included to verify that the intended processes can be implemented with the defined rules and without adversary intervention in order to prevent the security properties from being trivially met by an incorrect model (e.g., all possible authentications are trivially secure if no authentication is possible at all). In the following, we describe the verified security properties. Note that the following paragraphs only provide intuitive descriptions of the verified properties as the full proofs are automatically generated with the Tamarin tool based on the defined models. The full formal definitions are part of our Tamarin models (provided online (See footnote 10) for reproducibility).

```
1   lemma auth_emsp_steward_verinym:
2   "All Steward S_DID EMSP Verinym_DID #i .
3      CommitStewardVerinym(Steward, S_DID, EMSP, Verinym_DID) @
         i
4   ==> ( Ex #j .
5        RunningEMSPVerinym(EMSP, S_DID, Verinym_DID) @j
6      & (#j #i )
7      & not( Ex Steward2 EMSP2 S_DID2 #i2 .
8          CommitStewardVerinym(Steward2, S_DID2, EMSP2,
            Verinym_DID) @ i2
9        & not(#i2 #i) ) )
10   | ( Ex RevealEvent Entity #kr .
11        KeyReveal(RevealEvent, Entity) @ kr
12        & Honest(Entity) @ i)"
```

Listing 1.1. Injective Agreement Lemma in Tamarin

Secure Setup (eMSP to Steward). Regarding the secure setup (SR1), we verify that an eMSP and a steward (identified by their DID) injectivly agree on the eMSP's verinym DID (and corresponding public key) during the onboarding process. That is, whenever a steward S accepts an DID for writing on the ledger, apparently from an eMSP E, E has previously sent this DID to S and both actors agree on the content of the DID. Additionally, each accepted DID by S corresponds to a unique request from E. The only allowed exception is, if the long-term key of one of the parties involved in a specific protocol run was leaked.

The Tamarin lemma, which models the *Secure Setup (eMSP to steward)* security property is shown as an example in Listing 1.1. Hereby, lines 2–6 indicate that for every accepted eMSP verinym DID by as steward (identified by S_DID) at time i, there exists an event where the same eMSP has sent this verinym DID to the same steward at time j and j was before i. Lines 7–9 models the uniqueness property of the acceptance by the steward, i.e., it says that there cannot exist another protocol run between the same or different actors (steward2 and EMSP2) where the same verinym DID is accepted. Lines 10–12 model the exception, that the security property can be broken if the long-term keys of one of the actors involved in the protocol (i.e., the actor was assumed honest at time i; line 12) run was revealed.

Secure Setup (Cont.) Regarding the secure setup (SR1), we additionally verify that a steward and an eMSP injectivly agree on the steward's DID public key during the onboarding process. Furthermore, we verify mutual injective agreement between OEM and steward during the onboarding process of an OEM (see the full Tamarin models (See footnote 10) for details).

Secure Contract Credential Installation. Regarding the secure credential installation (SR2), we verify that an EV and an eMSP (identified by their DID) injectivly agree on a contract credential request and response respectively during the installation process (see the full Tamarin models (See footnote 10) for details). The only allowed exceptions are: *(i)* if the long-term key of one of the parties involved in a specific installation protocol run was leaked or *(ii)* if the long-term keys of a previous OEM to steward setup were leaked.

Secure Charge Authentication and Authorization. Regarding the secure charge authentication (SR3), we verify that an EV and a CP injectivly agree on an EV's charge request during the authentication process. Additionally, for secure charge authorization/billing (SR4), we verify that an EV and an eMSP injectivly agree on an EV's charge authorization data for the billing process (see the full Tamarin models(See footnote 10) for details). The only allowed exceptions are: *(i)* if the long-term key of one of the parties involved in a specific installation protocol run was leaked or *(ii)* if the long-term keys of a previous OEM to steward setup were leaked or *(iii)* if the long-term keys of a previous credential installation were leaked.

Privacy Proofs.

For our privacy analysis, we mainly focus on the verification of symbolic unlinkability properties. Formally, unlinkability is commonly defined as the adversary's inability to distinguish between a scenario in which the same user is involved in multiple protocol runs with a scenario that involves different users per protocol run [3]. This kind of unlinkability definition has been shown as usable for an automated analysis with Tamarin (based on Tamarin's observational equivalence feature) in the EV charging context by [27]. Specifically, we use Tamarin to prove observational equivalence for a scenario with two protocol runs that may be initiated by the same EV or by different EVs. Our models assume *Honest-but-Curious Operators* (cf. adversary model in Sect. 4.2) and we use separate Tamarin models per property for simplicity. The following descriptions provide an intuitive description of the verified properties and full formal definitions can be found as part of the provided Tamarin models. (See footnote 10)

Non-traceability. Regarding preventing the creation of a movement profiles (PR1), we verify unlinkability of EVs/users based on their billing relevant data (as received by the backend). Specifically, we show that for two honest EVs EV_1 and EV_2, the (*Honest-but-Curious*) adversary cannot distinguish between the scenario where charge billing data is received for an (authorized) session of EV_1 and EV_2 each and the scenario where charge billing data is received for two (authorized) session of EV_1. Charge session may be at the same or different locations to show that linkability across locations (i.e., traceability) is not possible.

Non-linkability. Regarding the non-linkability of EV users (PR2), we verify unlinkability of EVs/users based on their authentication/authorization data (as generated by the EV). Analogously to non-traceability, we show that the

(*Honest-but-Curious*) adversary cannot distinguish between a scenario with two authorizations of different EVs and a scenario with two authorizations of the same EV.

7.3   Discussion of Requirements

The functional requirements are addressed by the concept design as follows: Credential installation and charge authorization are still possible without user interaction FR1, which ensures user-friendliness. Contract authentication via SSI can be negotiated via the *ServiceDiscoveryReq/-Res* messages FR2. All SSI roles are covered by actors from the ISO 15118 ecosystem as discussed in Sect. 5.1 FR3. Vehicles manage their contract credential in their own wallet FR4. All contract credentials contain the same core elements as discussed in Sect. 5, which allows a CP to authenticate the contract of different eMSPs FR5. Credential installation can be delayed until the first charging session FR6 using the messages described in Sect. 5.3. Communication of the EV (e.g., for credential installation or reading data of the ledger) can still be tunneled via the CP FR7 using the same concepts as for the default ISO 15118 method (e.g., credential installation messages are simply forwarded to the backend in Base64 encoding via OCPP 2.0 [38]). We judge the additional overhead to be acceptable FR8 as discussed in Sect. 7.1.

The security requirements SR1–SR4 are addressed as discussed in Sect. 7.2. In short, the security requirements are shown to be met via symbolic proofs using the Tamarin tool. The corresponding models for automated proof generation are provided online. (See footnote 10) All properties are verified in roughly 30 min on a standard laptop.[11] The published repository includes the defined model/lemmas, the used oracles (for performance such that the model analysis terminates within a reasonable time frame), and instructions on running the models (for reproducibility of the formal analysis).

Analogously, the privacy requirements PR1 and PR2 are addressed as discussed in Sect. 7.2 and the models for automated proof generation are provided online. (See footnote 10) The concept primarily prevents linkability/traceability through the authentication process at the CPO/CP. However, since traditional payment channels are still supported and thus charging sessions must be associated by the eMSP with the respective customers, the eMSP can still link them. This could be fixed via anonymous payment methods, which is out-of-scope for this paper. Additionally, since we focus on the application layer authorization mechanism, linkability based on communication meta data is not addressed by the presented solution. For example, a CPO/CP could potentially track specific EVs based on their MAC addresses, which could be prevented by generic solutions such as MAC address randomization (which is already used by some EV OEMs such as Volkswagen Group [23]). Furthermore, since colluding operators are excluded in the adversary model (cf. Sect. 4.2), the privacy guarantees can be violated if the respective actors collude (e.g., collusion between an eMSP and a CPO to link charge sessions to a location). Colluding operators are outside

---

[11] Using a Lenovo ThinkPad T14 Gen 1 with 16GB RAM.

the scope of this paper (which focuses on a privacy-by-design solution for charge authorization to minimize privacy risks) but may for example be enforced by regulations.

8   Conclusion

In this paper, we propose an approach for using SSIs as trusted credentials for EV charging authentication and authorization in ISO 15118. By using verifiable credentials with zero-knowledge proofs, our solution addresses the privacy problems of ISO 15118 providing unlinkability of charging sessions. Furthermore, our solution uses a decentralized distributed ledger and does not require a complex centralized PKI anymore. Our prototypical implementation and performance evaluation show that the computational and communication overhead of our solution is relatively low and should be acceptable for a real-world implementation. Our formal analysis using Tamarin shows that all required security and privacy properties hold, i.e., still guarantee authentication properties between different actors while preserving the EV user's privacy to the highest possible extent (only eMSP can link a user's charging events for billing purposes). Future work could expand our concept to the authentication of all PnC actors, especially CPs.

Acknowledgements. This research work has been partly funded by the German Federal Ministry of Education and Research and the Hessian Ministry of Higher Education, Research, Science and the Arts within their joint support of the National Research Center for Applied Cybersecurity ATHENE and the Deutsche Forschungsgemeinschaft (DFG, German Research Foundation) - project number 503329135.

References

1. Bradbury, M., Taylor, P., Atmaca, U.I., Maple, C., Griffiths, N.: Privacy challenges with protecting live vehicular location context. IEEE Access **8**, 207465–207484 (2020)
2. ChargePoint, DigiCert, Eonti: Practical considerations for implementation and scaling iso 15118 into a secure ev charging ecosystem, May 2019. https://www.chargepoint.com/files/15118whitepaper.pdf
3. Delaune, S., Hirschi, L.: A survey of symbolic methods for establishing equivalence-based properties in cryptographic protocols. J. Log. Algebraic Methods Programm. **87**, 127–144 (2017)
4. DIN Standards Committee Road Vehicle Engineering: Electromobility - Digital communication between a d.c. EV charging station and an electric vehicle for control of d.c. charging in the Combined Charging System. DIN SPEC 70121:2014–12, Deutsches Institut für Normung (DIN) (12 2014)
5. Dolev, D., Yao, A.: On the security of public key protocols. IEEE Trans. Inf. Theory **29**(2), 198–208 (1983)
6. ElaadNL: EV related protocol study, January 2017. https://www.elaad.nl/research/ev-related-protocol-study/

7. ElaadNL: Exploring the public key infrastructure for iso 15118 in the ev charging ecosystem, November 2018. https://www.elaad.nl/news/publication-exploring-the-public-key-infrastructure-for-iso-15118-in-the-ev-charging-ecosystem/

8. Falk, R., Fries, S.: Electric vehicle charging infrastructure security considerations and approaches. In: Proceedings of INTERNET, pp. 58–64 (2012)

9. Fazouane, M., Kopp, H., van der Heijden, R.W., Le Métayer, D., Kargl, F.: Formal verification of privacy properties in electric vehicle charging. In: Piessens, F., Caballero, J., Bielova, N. (eds.) ESSoS 2015. LNCS, vol. 8978, pp. 17–33. Springer, Cham (2015). https://doi.org/10.1007/978-3-319-15618-7_2

10. Firoozjaei, M.D., Ghorbani, A., Kim, H., Song, J.: EVChain: a blockchain-based credit sharing in electric vehicles charging. In: 2019 17th International Conference on Privacy, Security and Trust (PST). IEEE, August 2019. https://doi.org/10.1109/PST47121.2019.8949026

11. Foundation, H.: Getting started with libvcx. https://github.com/hyperledger/indy-sdk/blob/master/vcx/docs/getting-started/getting-started.md   (2021). Accessed 28 Feb 2023

12. Foundation, H.: Hyperledger aries rfc 0036 (2021). https://github.com/hyperledger/aries-rfcs/blob/main/features/0036-issue-credential/README.md. Accessed 28 Feb 2023

13. Fuchs, A., Kern, D., Krauß, C., Zhdanova, M.: HIP: HSM-based identities for plug-and-charge. In: Proceedings of the 15th International Conference on Availability, Reliability and Security, ARES 2020, Association for Computing Machinery, New York (2020). https://doi.org/10.1145/3407023.3407066. https://doi.org/10.1145/3407023.3407066

14. Fuchs, A., Kern, D., Krauß, C., Zhdanova, M.: Securing electric vehicle charging systems through component binding. In: Casimiro, A., Ortmeier, F., Bitsch, F., Ferreira, P. (eds.) SAFECOMP 2020. LNCS, vol. 12234, pp. 387–401. Springer, Cham (2020). https://doi.org/10.1007/978-3-030-54549-9_26

15. Fuchs, A., Kern, D., Krauß, C., Zhdanova, M.: TrustEV: trustworthy electric vehicle charging and billing. In: Proceedings of the 35th ACM/SIGAPP Symposium on Applied Computing SAC 2020. ACM (2020). https://doi.org/10.1145/3341105.3373879

16. Fuchs, A., Kern, D., Krauß, C., Zhdanova, M., Heddergott, R.: HIP-20: Integration of vehicle-HSM-generated credentials into plug-and-charge infrastructure. In: Computer Science in Cars Symposium. CSCS '20, Association for Computing Machinery, New York (2020). https://doi.org/10.1145/3385958.3430483, https://doi.org/10.1145/3385958.3430483

17. Han, W., Xiao, Y.: Privacy preservation for V2G networks in smart grid: a survey. Comput. Commun. **91**, 17–28 (2016)

18. Hoess, A., Roth, T., Sedlmeir, J., Fridgen, G., Rieger, A.: With or without blockchain? towards a decentralized, ssi-based eroaming architecture. In: Hawaii International Conference on System Sciences (2022)

19. Höfer, C., Petit, J., Schmidt, R., Kargl, F.: Popcorn: privacy-preserving charging for emobility. In: Proceedings of the 2013 ACM Workshop on Security, Privacy & Dependability for Cyber Vehicles, pp. 37–48 (2013)

20. IEC: Electric vehicle conductive charging system - Part 1: General requirements. IEC Standard 61851–1:2017, International Electrotechnical Commission (2017)

21. ISO/IEC: Road vehicles - Vehicle-to-Grid Communication Interface - Part 2: Network and application protocol requirements. ISO Standard 15118–2:2014, ISO, Geneva, Switzerland, April 2014

22. ISO/IEC: Road vehicles - vehicle-to-grid communication interface - part 2: Network and application protocol requirements. ISO/DIS 15118–2:2018, International Organization for Standardization, Geneva, Switzerland, December 2018
23. Kaiser, C.: Plug in and charge aka autocharge aka plug & charge (2022). https://www.linkedin.com/pulse/plug-charge-aka-autocharge-chris-kaiser. Accessed 26 Sept 20213
24. Kern, D., Krauß, C.: Analysis of e-mobility-based threats to power grid resilience. In: Proceedings of the 5th ACM Computer Science in Cars Symposium, pp. 1–12 (2021)
25. Kern, D., Krauß, C.: Detection of e-mobility-based attacks on the power grid. In: 2023 53rd Annual IEEE/IFIP International Conference on Dependable Systems and Networks (DSN), pp. 352–365. IEEE (2023)
26. Kern, D., Krauß, C., Lauser, T., Alnahawi, N., Wiesmaier, A., Niederhagen, R.: Quantumcharge: Post-quantum cryptography for electric vehicle charging. In: International Conference on Applied Cryptography and Network Security, pp. 85–111. Springer (2023).https://doi.org/10.1007/978-3-031-33491-7_4
27. Kern, D., Lauser, T., Krauß, C.: Integrating privacy into the electric vehicle charging architecture. Proc. Privacy Enhancing Technol. **3**, 140–158 (2022)
28. Khovratovich, D., Lodder, M.: Anonymous credentials with type-3 revocation (2018). https://github.com/hyperledger/indy-crypto/blob/master/libindy-crypto/docs/AnonCred.pdf
29. Knirsch, F., Unterweger, A., Engel, D.: Privacy-preserving blockchain-based electric vehicle charging with dynamic tariff decisions. Comput. Sci.-Res. Dev. **33**(1–2), 71–79 (2018)
30. Langer, L., Skopik, F., Kienesberger, G., Li, Q.: Privacy issues of smart e-mobility. In: IECON 2013–39th Annual Conference of the IEEE Industrial Electronics Society, pp. 6682–6687. IEEE (2013)
31. Li, H., Dan, G., Nahrstedt, K.: Portunes: privacy-preserving fast authentication for dynamic electric vehicle charging. In: 2014 IEEE International Conference on Smart Grid Communications (SmartGridComm), pp. 920–925. IEEE (2014)
32. Li, H., Dán, G., Nahrstedt, K.: Portunes+: privacy-preserving fast authentication for dynamic electric vehicle charging. IEEE Trans. Smart Grid **8**(5), 2305–2313 (2016)
33. Lowe, G.: A hierarchy of authentication specifications. In: Proceedings 10th Computer Security Foundations Workshop, pp. 31–43. IEEE (1997)
34. Lux, Z.A., Thatmann, D., Zickau, S., Beierle, F.: Distributed-Ledger-based Authentication with Decentralized Identifiers and Verifiable Credentials. In: 2020 2nd Conference on Blockchain Research & Applications for Innovative Networks and Services (BRAINS). IEEE, Sept 2020. https://doi.org/10.1109/BRAINS49436.2020.9223292
35. Meier, S., Schmidt, B., Cremers, C., Basin, D.: The TAMARIN prover for the symbolic analysis of security protocols. In: Sharygina, N., Veith, H. (eds.) CAV 2013. LNCS, vol. 8044, pp. 696–701. Springer, Heidelberg (2013). https://doi.org/10.1007/978-3-642-39799-8_48
36. Monteuuis, J.P., Petit, J., Zhang, J., Labiod, H., Mafrica, S., Servel, A.: Attacker model for connected and automated vehicles. In: ACM COMPUTER SCIENCE IN CARS SYMPOSIUM (2018)
37. Mustafa, M.A., Zhang, N., Kalogridis, G., Fan, Z.: Roaming electric vehicle charging and billing: an anonymous multi-user protocol. In: 2014 IEEE International Conference on Smart Grid Communications (SmartGridComm), pp. 939–945. IEEE (2014)

38. OCA: Open Charge Point Protocol 2.0.1 - Part 2 - Specification. Open standard, Open Charge Alliance, Arnhem, Netherlands, March 2020. https://www.openchargealliance.org/protocols/ocpp-201/
39. Open Fastcharging Alliancey: Autocharge (2017). https://github.com/openfastchargingalliance/openfastchargingalliance/blob/master/autocharge-final.pdf. Accessed 27 Sept 2023
40. Paverd, A., Martin, A., Brown, I.: Modelling and automatically analysing privacy properties for honest-but-curious adversaries. Technical report (2014)
41. Reed, D., Sporny, M., Longley, D., Allen, C., Grant, R., Sabadello, M.: Decentralized Identifiers (DIDs) v1.0 W3C Candidate Recommendation Draft, May 2021
42. Richter, D., Anke, J.: Exploring potential impacts of self-sovereign identity on smart service systems: an analysis of electric vehicle charging services. In: Business Information Systems, pp. 105–116 (2021)
43. Sabadello, M., et al.: Introduction to DID Auth. Rebooting the Web of Trust VI, July 2018
44. Sporny, M., Longley, D., Chadwick, D.: Verifiable Credentials Data Model v1.1. (2021). https://w3.org/TR/vc-data-model/. Accessed 23 Nov 2021
45. V2G Clarity: RISE-V2G (2017). https://github.com/SwitchEV/RISE-V2G. Accessed 29 Nov 2021
46. VDE: Handling of certificates for electric vehicles, charging infrastructure and back-end systems within the framework of iso 15118. VDE-AR-E 2802–100-1:2019–12, December 2019
47. Won, J., Singla, A., Bertino, E., Bollella, G.: Decentralized public key infrastructure for internet-of-things. In: MILCOM 2018–2018 IEEE Military Communications Conference (MILCOM), pp. 907–913. IEEE (2018)
48. Xu, S., Chen, X., He, Y.: EVchain: an anonymous blockchain-based system for charging-connected electric vehicles. Tsinghua Sci. Technol. **26**(6), December 2021. https://doi.org/10.26599/TST.2020.9010043
49. Zelle, D., Springer, M., Zhdanova, M., Krauß, C.: Anonymous charging and billing of electric vehicles. In: Proceedings of the 13th International Conference on Availability, Reliability and Security, pp. 1–10 (2018)
50. Zhao, T., Zhang, C., Wei, L., Zhang, Y.: A secure and privacy-preserving payment system for electric vehicles. In: 2015 IEEE International Conference on Communications (ICC), pp. 7280–7285. IEEE (2015)

"Hello? Is There Anybody in There?" Leakage Assessment of Differential Privacy Mechanisms in Smart Metering Infrastructure

Soumyadyuti Ghosh[1]([✉]), Manaar Alam[2], Soumyajit Dey[1], and Debdeep Mukhopadhyay[1,2]

[1] Indian Institute of Technology Kharagpur, Kharagpur, India
`soumyadyuti.ghosh@iitkgp.ac.in`, `{debdeep,soumya}@cse.iitkgp.ac.in`
[2] New York University, Abu Dhabi, United Arab Emirates
`alam.manaar@nyu.edu`

Abstract. Smart meters provide fine-grained power usage profiles of consumers to utility providers to facilitate various grid functionalities such as load monitoring, real-time pricing, etc. However, information leakage from these usage profiles can potentially reveal sensitive aspects of consumers' daily routines and their home absence, as state-of-the-art metering strategies lack adequate security and privacy measures. Among various privacy-preserving mechanisms, Differential Privacy (DP) is widely adopted in the literature due to its solid mathematical foundation. Nevertheless, the privacy-utility trade-off problem in smart metering systems limits the amount of privacy protection various instances of DP mechanisms can provide. We demonstrate that the constraints imposed by the privacy-utility trade-off make it possible to launch empirical statistical attacks on the differential private metering data. In this paper, we propose a novel statistical methodology, constructed using the principles of *t-test* based hypothesis testing, to *discover the absence of a consumer in their household upon observing real-time differentially private output traces of sensitive meter readings over successive sampling windows*. Additionally, we formally establish that this trade-off is an inherent characteristic of the smart metering problem, implying that any mechanism adhering to this trade-off is susceptible to our attack. We conduct an extensive experimental evaluation using a real-world metering dataset to validate our proposed methodology. We evaluate our scheme against six state-of-the-art DP mechanisms employed in metering infrastructure. Our results demonstrate that the proposed approach attains a success rate exceeding 90% within a mere six-hour observation interval, highlighting its effectiveness in revealing vulnerabilities within established DP implementations.

Keywords: Differential Privacy · Laplacian Mechanism · Gaussian Mechanism · Privacy-Utility Trade-off · *t-test* based Hypothesis Testing

1   Introduction

The smart grid, as a prominent Cyber-Physical System (CPS), encompasses power generation and distribution networks, facilitated by a bi-directional communication infrastructure. The real-time consumption profiles provided by the network are communicated to various entities in the grid to perform diverse operations such as automated demand-response, real-time billing, failure detection, etc. Such primitives require advanced metering infrastructures that sample and transmit the power consumption data of consumers using smart meters [23]. Though these fine-grained consumption data are crucial for metering-enabled grid dispatch and control systems, it has been revealed that analyzing meter reading streams can provide significant insights into appliances' usage patterns, running time, "ON/OFF" status [2,29]. This analysis can potentially result in significant privacy breaches, exposing sensitive information about customers' daily life behaviors and home absences [2]. In such scenarios, Differential Privacy (DP) has received much attention as it provides a solid mathematical foundation for establishing and protecting the privacy of individual user [12–15,17]. One of the fundamental reasons for the appeal of DP is its ability to provide privacy guarantees regardless of the background knowledge or auxiliary information available to the attackers, thereby offering strong and robust privacy protection in different applications of the smart metering infrastructure. Recent studies have highlighted the versatile applications of DP, addressing concerns such as load monitoring, renewable energy resource privacy, and user data protection in decentralized settings [4,19,26,27,43,46,49]. However, differential privacy is not a one-size-fits-all solution. Its efficacy hinges on meticulous implementation and parameter optimization to strike a balance between privacy and utility [20,30], a concept often referred to as the *privacy-utility trade-off*. This trade-off is very common in smart grids where small input or control signal modifications can hamper the system performance [42]. Within the realm of DP-protected metering systems, this trade-off introduces a constraint on the degree of privacy protection that different instances of DP mechanisms can afford. Among various works, the authors of [43] propose a hybrid scheme integrating differential privacy and cryptography to address privacy issues in smart meters, achieving an efficient balance between privacy and utility. On the other hand, the authors of [46] employ the compressive sensing framework to establish theoretical bounds on the impact of differential privacy parameters on Non-Intrusive Load Monitoring (NILM) performance. Additionally, some existing works explore various differential privacy variants (Laplace, Gaussian, Uniform, Geometric) in blockchain-based smart metering, highlighting their performance under different parameters and their effectiveness in preserving privacy [26]. *In contrast to the aforementioned studies, Our work, presented in this paper, demonstrates how the privacy-utility trade-off constraint exposes potential vulnerabilities to empirical statistical attacks on differential private metering data, and we substantiate this assertion through formal proof, affirming the pivotal role played by this inherent trade-off.* We introduce a novel attack methodology, leveraging the principles of t-test based hypothesis testing to infer the consumer's home absence based on observed DP-induced metering data that adhere to this trade-off. To the best of our knowledge, our work is the first proposal in the domain of DP-protected metering systems where we aim to identify consumers' home absence from the DP-protected output traces. However, there has been a significant amount of research that has examined potential vulnerabilities and information leakage associated with DP mechanisms.

Related Work

We categorize these existing works into five distinct classes, each shedding light on different aspects of information leakage and attacks on DP implementations. Our objective is to emphasize the distinctions between these prior approaches and the novel contribution presented in our paper.

Correlated Data Records. In DP, the conventional assumption of independent records in datasets can pose significant privacy risks, especially when dealing with real-world datasets [36,45]. In the context of smart metering infrastructure, though the meter readings are not explicitly correlated, they may exhibit auto-correlation due to temporal dependencies. Current DP solutions for smart meters frequently neglect this auto-correlation, thereby exposing vulnerabilities that may result in significant privacy breaches. *To address this, we incorporate Group Differential Privacy [8,15] into the metering data streams across all the targetted DP mechanisms before assessing our proposed attack scheme.* This addition is pivotal in mitigating information leakages arising from auto-correlated readings and is instrumental in detecting privacy breaches (by determining consumers' home absence) within DP implementations that adhere to the privacy-utility trade-off.

Lower Local Sensitivity Value. Sensitivity quantifies the maximum potential change in the output of a DP scheme, resulting from the addition or removal of a single data record. However, the noise calibrated by the Local Sensitivity is small, leading to information leakages [37]. Our methodology, however, diverges from this by not relying on the small sensitivity values of the DP schemes; rather DP mechanisms having high sensitivity values that satisfy the privacy-utility trade-off are susceptible to our attack.

Sequential Query Composition. Sequential query composition involves consecutively querying a dataset to maintain DP guarantees and assessing their collective impact on privacy. This line of work discusses privacy degradation due to sequential query composition of DP techniques [33]. However, our proposal diverges from this line of work as we do not employ sequential querying to highlight potential data leakages. Rather, we consider a distinct query with respect to each DP mechanism during the construction of our methodology and apply the DP scheme on the secret meter readings only once at each time instance.

Timing and Floating-Point Attacks. This line of work discusses timing and floating-point attacks on DP techniques. The authors of [32] highlight that the Gaussian mechanism of DP suffers from a side channel attack due to floating-point arithmetic error. Simultaneously, discrete methods developed to protect against such floating-point attacks for both the Laplacian and Gaussian mechanisms also suffer from timing side channels. However, we perform an empirical attack on the DP streams that doesn't require any knowledge regarding the floating point computation errors due to the DP computation.

Data Poisoning Attacks. Data poisoning attacks manipulate Local differential privacy protocols by inserting fake users in the original datasets, with the goal of manipulating the data analytic results according to the attacker's intentions [7,9]. Our proposed attack scheme doesn't require the insertion of fake consumers into the differentially private metering systems to obtain the necessary information regarding consumer's home absence.

Unique Feature of our Approach: Our proposed approach represents an innovative contribution within the field of DP-protected metering systems. It effectively harnesses the privacy-utility trade-off, offering a novel perspective on information leakages from DP implementations, *by identifying consumer's home absence with a very high accuracy upon observing DP metering data.* Importantly, our approach achieves this without the need for sequential query composition, consideration of data correlation, low sensitivity values, or the insertion of fake data. Next, we provide a concise overview of our proposed *t-test* based attack scheme that delineates how the DP metering streams are utilized to determine the consumer's household status.

Brief Overview of Proposed Approach

In scenarios where a consumer's household remains unoccupied during successive sampling periods, the absence of peak power consumption levels from household appliances is apparent, as illustrated in a prior study [2]. However, certain appliances, like refrigerators, exhibit intermittent power consumption patterns, leading to consumption values that slightly exceed the minimum aggregate power consumption of all appliances. This results in the meter readings falling within a confined range of power consumption values. We signify this range as the *minimal power consumption range*, denoted as $[R_{min}, R_{max}]$. In this context, the

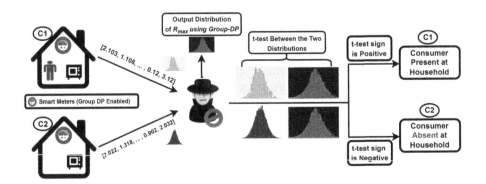

Fig. 1. Overview of Our Proposed Attack Scheme.

lower bound of this range (R_{min}) represents a scenario where all appliances are switched off, resulting in zero total aggregate power consumption during the sampling window. However, due to intermittent consumption patterns, R_{max} is slightly higher than R_{min}, though not significantly since peak power consumption values from appliances are absent during these continuous sampling periods [2]. We leverage this observation to determine the absence of the targetted consumer from their household. In Fig. 1, we present an illustration of our proposed approach involving two consumers, each implementing group DP to safeguard against information leakage arising from auto-correlation within meter readings. Here, consumer $C2$ is identified as absent from their household, while $C1$ is present at home. However, their DP-protected meter readings, shown in Fig. 1, were successfully able to hide such classification. The adversary collects these DP output traces from the consumers and tries to identify the consumer $C2$'s home absence using our proposed scheme. Our attack methodology, having access to the black box DP implementation, generates a candidate DP trace utilizing the value R_{max}. This process involves passing R_{max} through the group DP mechanism, with the number of iterations matching the size of the output stream, to generate a candidate DP trace. The attacking scheme then conducts a statistical *t-test* between the DP-protected profile of the targetted consumer and the computed trace associated with R_{max}. It is evident that the *sign* of the *t-test* results depend on the mean values of the two input distributions. Here, a negative *t-test* result suggests that the mean of the original data stream is bounded by R_{max}, signifying that the original meter readings fall within the *minimal power consumption range* of the household. This indicates the household's unoccupied status at those specific timing periods, which is the case for consumer $C2$. Conversely, if the *t-test* result is positive, we infer that the consumer is currently at home, as exemplified by consumer $C1$.

Contributions. The summary of our major contributions is as follows:

- ***Novel t-test Based Attack Methodology.*** We propose an innovative attack methodology based on *t-test* based hypothesis testing to determine consumers' home absence. This method analyzes DP-induced metering data that conforms to the privacy-utility trade-off while satisfying group DP to conceal information leakages arising from auto-correlated meter readings. The scheme collects differentially private output traces from consecutive sampling windows, aiming to determine consumers' household absence.
- ***Formal Proof.*** We present formal proof establishing that the privacy-utility trade-off criteria is fundamental in facilitating the success of our proposed attack and any DP mechanism constrained by the utility requirements will invariably remain susceptible to our scheme.
- ***Empirical Evaluation.*** We conducted an empirical evaluation of our attack methodology against six distinct state-of-the-art DP implementations in smart metering systems [3, 6, 18, 22, 24, 28]. We experimentally validated that the final estimation of our attack methodology matches the original state of the consumer's household with high accuracy thus highlighting its feasibility and capability.

2   Preliminaries

2.1   Differential Privacy

Differential Privacy [12] is a state-of-the-art privacy concept known for its efficient implementation and robust privacy assurances based on a solid mathematical foundation. *Regardless of the adversary's prior knowledge*, it provides strong privacy by ensuring the indistinguishability of whether or not a record is in the database upon observing the revealed information. Below, we introduce some definitions for DP, which are used for the rest of the paper.

Definition 1. *Adjacency of two datasets [31]. A pair of datasets denoted as $D_1, D_2 \subset \mathcal{D}$, where $\mathcal{D}$ is the domain of databases and $D_i = \{d_1^i, d_2^i, d_3^i, \cdots\}$, is called Adjacent datasets if they differ at most by a single entry. In other words, there exists an m such that $d_m^1 \neq d_m^2$ and $d_j^1 = d_j^2, \forall j \neq m$.*

Definition 2. *Sensitivity [16]. A multidimensional query function q is a mapping $\mathcal{D} \to \mathcal{R}^n$, where n is dimension of the output given a database $D \in \mathcal{D}$. The query output for a database D can be represented as $q(D) = (q_1(D), \cdots, q_n(D))$, for $q_i(D) \in \mathcal{R}, \forall i$. The sensitivity of q, denoted as $\Delta_{q,s}$, where s indicates the type of norm, can be computed as $\Delta_{q,s} = \max_{Adj(D_i, D_j)} \|q(D_i) - q(D_j)\|$. In simpler words, given a query function, the largest possible difference between the query outputs of two adjacent datasets is referred to as sensitivity.*

Definition 3. *Differential Privacy [16]. A randomized mechanism $\Pi : \mathcal{D} \times \Gamma \to \mathcal{P}$ guarantees (ϵ, δ)-differential privacy if for all the adjacent datasets D_i, D_j and for all the subsets of possible answers $P \subset \mathcal{P}$, $Pr[\Pi(D_i) \in P] \leq e^\epsilon Pr[\Pi(D_j) \in P] + \delta$. The probability is taken over the randomness of the privacy mechanism Π and the randomized noisy signals are drawn from the set Γ. Here, ϵ and δ are the privacy parameters. The parameter ϵ can be considered as an upper bound on the amount of leakage in the output and the approximation parameter δ is used to relax the DP definition. In case δ is not considered for approximation, then the mechanism Π preserves ϵ-differential privacy.*

Laplacian Mechanism. *For a dataset D and a query function q, a Laplacian mechanism preserves ϵ-differential privacy if the DP-noises are sampled from a Laplace distribution with zero mean and scale parameter $\beta = \frac{\Delta_{q,1}}{\epsilon}$. With a decreasing value of ϵ, the value of the scale parameter increases, resulting in a higher magnitude of noisy signals, which guarantees greater privacy protection.*

Gaussian Mechanism. *For a dataset D and a query function q, a Gaussian mechanism preserves (ϵ, δ)-differential privacy if the DP-noises are sampled from a zero mean Gaussian distribution with standard deviation $\sigma \geq \sqrt{2ln(\frac{1.25}{\delta})}\frac{\Delta_{q,2}}{\epsilon}$.*

Definition 4. *Group Differential Privacy [8, 15]. In correlated settings, allocating stronger privacy protection to groups of correlated records, each of size k, is essential to address the increased privacy risks resulting from data* *correlations. This implies that a privacy-preserving mechanism that achieves $\frac{\epsilon}{k}$-differential privacy in the non-correlated setting is sufficient to give ϵ-differential privacy over a database with a correlation parameter k. In the case of the Laplacian group DP, the noises are sampled from a Laplacian distribution with zero mean and scale parameter $\beta = \frac{\Delta_{q,1} \times k}{\epsilon}$. Similarly, for the Gaussian mechanism, the standard deviation of the zero mean Gaussian noises is $\sigma \geq \sqrt{2ln(\frac{1.25}{\delta})} \frac{\Delta_{q,2} \times k}{\epsilon}$.*

2.2   Statistical *t-test* Analysis

The Welch's test is the most often used method for determining if two distributions of data differ substantially. Because the samples in both distributions were taken from the same population, a *t-test* is likely to assess whether the two distributions are distinguishable. Significantly higher $|t|$-values in the *t-test* signify that the distributions are indistinguishable [21,39,40]. Let us consider two samples S_1 and S_2 having sample mean and sample variance as μ_1 (resp. μ_2) and σ_1^2 (resp. σ_2^2) respectively. Then, *t-test* statistic *t-value* is calculated as:

$$t = \frac{\mu_1 - \mu_2}{\sqrt{\left(\frac{\sigma_1^2}{n_1} + \frac{\sigma_2^2}{n_2}\right)}}$$

The sign of this *t-value* indicates whether the sample mean of S_1 is greater (positive) or smaller (negative) than the sample mean of S_2, offering insights into their relative means and central tendencies.

3   System and Threat Model

We consider a smart grid infrastructure with privacy-enabled smart meters that generate DP-protected output streams by adding controlled noises with the original meter readings while satisfying the desired privacy-utility trade-off criteria. This utility metric is bounded by a predefined threshold, and the privacy level is selected accordingly so that the utility bound is satisfied. Depending on the nature of the query function, the differential privacy mechanism implemented at the respective smart meters aims to conceal either the power consumption details of individual appliances, the maximum power consumption by a consumer, or the aggregate power consumption over a defined sampling window [3,6,18,22,24,28]. The resulting DP-induced meter readings are then sent to the Data Concentrator Units (DCU), which aggregate the consumers' power profiles and send the aggregated profile to the data servers located at the Utility Provider (UP). The DCUs, however, refrain from introducing additional DP noises to the aggregated power consumption profiles obtained from multiple consumers. These DCUs and UP are usually considered honest but curious (semi-honest) adversaries that can collect and potentially analyze consumers' power consumption information. In the literature, these security models for DCUs and UPs are highly utilized in the domain of smart metering systems [5,10,11,25,44]. Keeping this in mind, in this section, we elaborate on our threat model by describing the threat surfaces along with the goals and capabilities of the adversaries.

3.1 Threat Surfaces

The threat surfaces can be categorized into two classes, as elaborated below.

– *Honest but curious DCU and UP.* The DCUs and UP are semi-honest adversaries that want to learn critical information, such as a consumer's home presence, with the intention of potentially disclosing or selling this data to marketing firms for personal gain.
– *Collusion of malicious consumers with UP.* The DCUs aggregate the DP-induced readings before sending them to UP for operational purposes. In such scenarios, involving m consumers, UP can collude with the $(m-1)$ number of consumers to obtain the DP outputs of the targeted household. This can be achieved by subtracting the total power consumption of the compromised $(m-1)$ consumers from the aggregated power profile received from the DCU. Conversely, the UP can directly collude with the DCUs to obtain individual consumers' power consumption profiles. *It is important to note that the DP makes no assumptions about the prior knowledge available to attackers. Hence, our assumption does not violate the security settings of DP and a strong and correct DP implementation should ensure privacy in such settings.*

3.2 Capabilities of the Adversary

We assume that the adversaries have access to the black box DP implementation and the DP output traces of the targetted consumer before performing the attacking scheme. Being semi-honest entities, UPs and DCUs are capable of storing the preceding year's non-DP power consumption data, during a period when DP was not implemented in the consumer's metering setup. Upon the introduction of DP in the metering setup, DCUs can only collect the obfuscated DP-protected metering streams from individual consumers. Hence, DCUs are restricted from accessing the non-DP/original meter readings once DP is implemented. However, the DCUs and UP can analyze the accumulated historical non-DP measurements to obtain the *minimal power consumption range* of the targetted consumer, when the user's home is usually unoccupied.

3.3 Goal of the Adversary

Upon obtaining these differentially private output traces and having access to the black box DP mechanism, the adversaries aim to obtain the range of original meter readings, thus exposing the consumer's sensitive consumption pattern at the associated sampling periods. If the original power consumption stream lies in the *minimal power consumption range*, then the correct range estimation from the differentially private output traces can indicate the adversary about the consumer's home absence.

4 Formal Analysis of Leakage Due to Privacy-Utility Trade-Off in Smart Metering Systems

Incorporating differential privacy into smart metering systems introduces a subtle yet critical privacy-utility trade-off. On one hand, it enhances the protection of consumers' sensitive data by injecting controlled noise and obfuscating individual consumption patterns, thereby ensuring robust privacy preservation. However, this heightened privacy comes at the cost of compromised data accuracy and information quality, posing a significant challenge to the effective utilization of smart meter data in technical applications. As smart metering systems must satisfy the privacy-utility trade-off criteria, privacy levels need to be bounded against utility requirements. Our research aims to demonstrate that any mechanism offering acceptable utility is susceptible to our attacking scheme. Let us consider a smart meter reading stream $\vec{R} = \langle R_{in}(1), \cdots, R_{in}(i), \cdots, R_{in}(L) \rangle$ of length L. This metering stream, when processed through a DP mechanism Π with a privacy parameter ϵ_1, yields a DP-protected output stream, $\mathcal{T}_R^1 = \langle R_{out}^1(1), \cdots, R_{out}^1(i), \cdots, R_{out}^1(L) \rangle$. In the realm of smart metering systems, utility metrics are often framed around the disparity between the original meter readings and their differentially private counterparts. To assess the utility of this DP-protected data, we employ a utility metric, $U(\vec{R}, \mathcal{T}_R^1)$, which quantifies the overall quality between the original metering stream $\vec{R}$ and the corresponding DP trace $\mathcal{T}_R^1$. Without loss of generality, we define this utility metric as $U(\vec{R}, \mathcal{T}_R^1) = \sum_{i=1}^{L} ||R_{in}(i) - R_{out}^1(i)||_N$, where N represents the norm of the operation [38,41]. We denote the resulting value as $U(\vec{R}, \mathcal{T}_R^1) = \tau_1$. We further employ the same DP mechanism Π, but with a distinct privacy parameter ϵ_2, applied to the same input stream $\vec{R}$. This results in a different DP-protected output stream, $\mathcal{T}_R^2 = \langle R_{out}^2(1), \cdots, R_{out}^2(i), \cdots, R_{out}^2(L) \rangle$, such that $U(\vec{R}, \mathcal{T}_R^2) = \tau_2$. Our objective is to establish the relationship between these privacy parameters ϵ_1 and ϵ_2, and their utility counterparts τ_1 and τ_2. Here, if $\tau_1 > \tau_2$ holds true, our forthcoming analysis will show that $\epsilon_1 < \epsilon_2$. This observation highlights that a lower utility value is indicative of relatively weaker privacy protection of the DP mechanism. We further demonstrate how this clear distinction between the privacy levels employed in the DP mechanisms, can be leveraged to execute our proposed *t-test* based attack methodology to identify consumers' home absence. In summary, our approach shows the underlying vulnerability of DP mechanisms striving to reconcile the privacy-utility trade-off in smart metering systems.

Lemma 1. *In the context of DP-enabled metering systems, when $\tau_1 > \tau_2$, it signifies that a DP mechanism with privacy level ϵ_1 offers a heightened utility value while preserving more stringent privacy protection than ϵ_2. In essence, this infers that $\epsilon_1 < \epsilon_2$, implying a diminished level of privacy for the data stream $\mathcal{T}_R^2$ characterized by stricter utility requirements.*

Proof. By assumption, two data streams $\mathcal{T}_R^1$ and $\mathcal{T}_R^2$, generated to conform to the utility constraints τ_1 and τ_2 respectively, ensure that $U(\vec{R}, \mathcal{T}_R^1) = \tau_1$ and $U(\vec{R}, \mathcal{T}_R^2) = \tau_2$. In light of the utility function, these constraints are expressed as $\sum_{i=1}^{L} ||R_{in}(i) - R^1_{out}(i)||_N = \tau_1$ and $\sum_{i=1}^{L} ||R_{in}(i) - R^2_{out}(i)||_N = \tau_2$. In the context of DP, the terms $\langle R_{in}(i) - R^1_{out}(i)\rangle$ and $\langle R_{in}(i) - R^2_{out}(i)\rangle$ represent the respective magnitudes of noise introduced during the ith sampling period. We denote these noise streams associated with $\mathcal{T}^1_R$ and $\mathcal{T}^2_R$ as $\langle \delta^1_1, \ldots, \delta^1_i, \ldots, \delta^1_L\rangle$ and $\langle \delta^2_1, \ldots, \delta^2_i, \ldots, \delta^2_L\rangle$ respectively. These noise streams represent the perturbations applied to the original meter readings $\vec{R}$ by the DP mechanisms. Considering the cumulative noise introduced by the differential privacy mechanisms for the two streams, it follows that $\sum_{i=1}^{L} ||\delta^1_i||_N = \tau_1$ and $\sum_{i=1}^{L} ||\delta^2_i||_N = \tau_2$. Given the initial assumption $\tau_1 > \tau_2$, it is apparent that $\sum_{i=1}^{L} ||\delta^1_i||_N > \sum_{i=1}^{L} ||\delta^2_i||_N$. Since all the values of δ^1_i exhibit the same statistical properties and all the values of δ^2_i are sampled from a same distribution, then given $\sum_{i=1}^{L} ||\delta^1_i||_N > \sum_{i=1}^{L} ||\delta^2_i||_N$, we can conclude that $|\delta^1_i| \geq |\delta^2_i|$, $\forall i \in [1, L]$. In fact, there exists a set of possible values $m \in [1, L]$ for which $|\delta^1_m| > |\delta^2_m|$, $\exists m \in [1, L]$. Moreover, it is well-established that the magnitude of DP noise is inversely proportional to the privacy parameter (Sect. 2.1). Therefore, if $\mathcal{T}^1_R$ attains a higher level of privacy compared to $\mathcal{T}^2_R$ due to $|\delta^1_m| > |\delta^2_m|$, $\exists m \in [1, L]$, it follows that $\epsilon_1 < \epsilon_2$.

According to the principles of DP, if $\epsilon_1 < \epsilon_2$ holds true, the magnitude of noise introduced at each instance of $\mathcal{T}^1_R$ will be equal or higher than of $\mathcal{T}^2_R$. Consequently, the resulting means of $\mathcal{T}^1_R$ and $\mathcal{T}^2_R$, denoted as μ_1 and μ_2, can be compared, such that $\mu_1 > \mu_2$.

Corollary 1. *This observation implies the existence of a candidate reading* x^{est}, *for which the resulting differentially private output trace* $\mathcal{T}_{x^{est}}$ *has a mean denoted as* μ_{est}, *satisfying the condition* $\mu_1 > \mu_{est} > \mu_2$. *This signifies that the DP-protected streams* $\mathcal{T}^2_R$ *and* $\mathcal{T}_{x^{est}}$ *will have a negative t-value. If the candidate reading* x^{est} *is same as the upper bound of minimal power consumption range,* R_{max}, *i.e.* $x^{est} = R_{max}$, *then this negative t-value implies the consumer's home absence. On the other hand, the streams* $\mathcal{T}^1_R$ *and* $\mathcal{T}_{x^{est}}$ *will have a positive t-value indicating consumers home presence.*

This underscores that a privacy level of ϵ_1 can effectively safeguard the privacy of a consumer's home absence, which a privacy level of ϵ_2 can not achieve. Consequently, it is evident that higher privacy levels, i.e., lower utility thresholds, are more susceptible to our proposed attack approach. This strengthens our argument that the inherent privacy-utility trade-off is a fundamental problem in the metering system and any mechanism that seeks to balance this constraint is vulnerable to our proposed attack methodology.

5   Proposed Attack Methodology

In this section, we describe our robust *t-test* based attack methodology to infer the potential range of secret meter readings from the DP output traces, allowing the adversary to determine the consumer's household absence. These DP traces are obtained from the same consumer but in successive sampling windows. Let $\vec{R} = \langle R_{in}(1), \cdots, R_{in}(i), \cdots R_{in}(L)\rangle$ denote a L length original meter reading stream obtained over a time interval of length Lh ($k \in \mathbb{N}$), where h is the sampling period of the metering system. Under a group DP mechanism Π with correlation parameter k ($\leq L$) and privacy level ϵ, the corresponding differentially private output trace is denoted by $\mathcal{T}_R = \langle R_{out}(1), \cdots, R_{out}(i), \cdots, R_{out}(L) \rangle$. This output trace maintains a privacy guarantee of $\frac{\epsilon \times L}{k}$-DP, as each DP-protected reading individually complies with $\frac{\epsilon}{k}$-DP (Sect. 2.1). It is possible that meter readings of $\vec{R}$ may belong to the *minimal power consumption range* of the associated consumer, thus suggesting their home absence. The DP mechanism Π is supposed to generate $\mathcal{T}_R$ in such a manner that conceals this critical information regarding the original stream. Our proposed *t-test* based assessment methodology aims to validate the security claims of these DP mechanisms in a practical implementation where the privacy-utility trade-off is satisfied. This necessitates ensuring that the utility metric $U(\vec{R}, \mathcal{T}_R)$ does not exceed predefined thresholds. However, it is essential to obtain the *minimal power consumption range* specific to the targeted consumer in order to identify their home absence. With this objective in mind, we incorporate a precomputation phase into our attack methodology. During this phase, the adversary determines the *minimal power consumption range* by analyzing non-DP consumption profiles from the preceding years, particularly focusing on periods when the consumer's household is typically unoccupied. Next, we provide a thorough description of the precomputation phase and our proposed algorithm.

5.1   Precomputation Phase

In the precomputation phase, the adversary first computes the overall power consumption range of the targetted consumer by utilizing the historical non-DP power profile of the associated consumer. Here, the lower (x^{min}) and upper (x^{max}) bounds on the power consumption range are usually consumer-dependent and obtained by computing the minimum and maximum possible non-DP power consumption values of the targetted consumer. Moreover, if the knowledge of the available appliances present in a household is known to the adversary, the value of x^{max} can be calculated by accumulating the individual power consumption usage of all the appliances.

Partitioning. Upon obtaining x^{min} and x^{max}, we divide the overall power consumption range of the consumer's original power profile, denoted as $[x^{min}, x^{max}]$ into multiple partitions (referred to Z) such that meter readings within a specific interval will belong to a single partition. The interval length for these partitions is obtained based on the minimal power consumption of the consumers after carefully analyzing the historical non-DP profiles. We define these intervals as:

$$\Psi_1 = [x^{min}, x^1], \Psi_2 = (x^1, x^2], \cdots, \Psi_Z = (x^{max-1}, x^{max}]$$

such that $x^1 = \beta$, $|x^{max} - x^{max-1}| \leq \beta$ and $|x^{j+1} - x^j| = \beta$, $\forall j \in [1, max - 2]$. Here, we consider $[x^{min}, x^1]$ as the *minimal power consumption range* and β is the upper bound of the minimal consumption. The *minimal power consumption range* indicates that in that specific time period, the consumer's household is unoccupied as no peak power consumption from the appliances' is present.

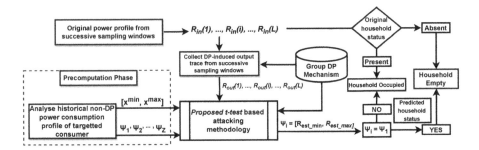

Fig. 2. Overview of the proposed attack methodology.

5.2   *t-test* Based Attack Methodology

Our proposed *t-test* based attack algorithm takes the protected group DP mechanism Π with correlation parameter k and privacy level ϵ, the output traces $\mathcal{T}_R$ and the set of partitions $\Psi_1, \cdots, \Psi_Z$ as inputs (as shown in Fig. 2) in order to provide a range estimation of $\vec{R}$, denoted as $[R_{est\_min}, R_{est\_max}]$. If the estimated range $[R_{est\_min}, R_{est\_max}]$ is same as Ψ_1, then the output trace $\mathcal{T}_R$ signifies the consumer's home absence. The attacking scheme also takes the minimum (x^{min}) and maximum (x^{max}) possible values of any smart meter reading associated with the household as inputs.

Algorithm Search Space. Our methodology illustrated through Algorithm 1 traverses from this minimum possible value of the corresponding meter readings to the maximum possible value in order to determine the partition Ψ_i in which the estimation for the mean (denoted as x^{est}) of $\vec{R}$ belongs. Algorithm 1 first calculates the minimum (x_{min}^{out}) and maximum (x_{max}^{out}) values of the output trace $\mathcal{T}_R$ and compares them against the input parameters x^{min} and x^{max} in order to compute an initial range for $\vec{R}$. It is possible that for a smart meter reading stream, $x_{min}^{out} < 0$; however, we do not need to consider readings less than zero during the estimation as meter readings can not be negative. In such scenarios, the algorithm should consider x^{min} as the probable lower bound for the input range. On the other hand, it is possible that x_{max}^{out} for a meter reading stream is higher than x^{max} due to the higher magnitude of the DP noises. In such cases, our proposed methodology considers x^{max} as the upper bound for the corresponding meter profile. The algorithm considers the maximum among x_{min}^{out} and x^{min} as the lower bound of $\vec{R}$ and the minimum between x_{max}^{out} and x^{max} as the upper bound of $\vec{R}$. Here, the information regarding x_{min}^{out} and x_{max}^{out} is obtained from the output traces and is independent of the system's design. However, x^{min} and x^{max} are consumer-dependent inputs to the algorithm.

Algorithm 1. *t-test* based Assessment Algorithm

1: **Inputs:**
   Protected DP mechanism: Π, Number of traces: L, Increment: δ.
   Differentially private smart metering output trace: $\mathcal{T}_R = \langle R_{out}(1), \cdots, R_{out}(i), \cdots, R_{out}(L) \rangle$.
   Minimum and maximum possible values of reading: x^{min} and x^{max}.
   Partitions: $\Psi_1 = [x^{min}, x^1], \Psi_2 = (x^1, x^2], \cdots, \Psi_Z = (x^{max-1}, x^{max}]$

2: **Output:** Estimated input range: $\Psi_i = [R_{est\_min}, R_{est\_max}]$.

3: $x_{min}^{out} \leftarrow min(\mathcal{T}_R)$

4: $x^{min} \leftarrow max(x_{min}^{out}, x^{min})$ ▷ Maximum between x_{min}^{out}, x^{min}

5: $x_{max}^{out} \leftarrow max(\mathcal{T}_R)$

6: $x^{max} \leftarrow min(x_{max}^{out}, x^{max})$ ▷ Minimum between x_{max}^{out}, x^{max}

7: **for** $x^{est} = x^{min}; x^{est} \leq x^{max}; x^{est} = x^{est} + \delta$ **do**

8:     $T_{x^{est}} \leftarrow L$ independent computations of group DP mechanism Π with correlation parameter k and privacy level ϵ on estimation x^{est}

9:     $t^{x^{est}} \leftarrow$ *t-test*$(\mathcal{T}_R, T_{x^{est}})$ ▷ *t-test* between $\mathcal{T}_R, T_{x^{est}}$

10:     **if** $t^{x^{est}} < 0$ **then**

11:        Obtain $\Psi_i = [R_{est\_min}, R_{est\_max}]$, such that $x^{est} \in \Psi_i$

12:        break

13: **Return** $\Psi_i = [R_{est\_min}, R_{est\_max}]$

Algorithm Traversal. In each step, our algorithm considers a possible candidate reading x^{est} and generates a L length differentially private output trace (denoted as $T_{x^{est}}$) using the black box DP implementation Π. Here, the group DP mechanism Π with correlation parameter k provides $\frac{\epsilon}{k}$-DP to the estimation x^{est}, independently L times in order to generate $T_{x^{est}}$. Being a randomized algorithm, Π generates different noises for each independent run to randomize the output trace $T_{x^{est}}$. Here, both $\mathcal{T}_R$ and $T_{x^{est}}$ satisfies $\frac{\epsilon \times L}{k}$-differential privacy. Upon obtaining $T_{x^{est}}$, Algorithm 1 performs a *t-test* with the distribution $\mathcal{T}_R$. As discussed in Sect. 2.2, the value of the *t-test* depends on the means of the two distributions. If the mean of the first distribution (in our case $\mathcal{T}_R$) is higher, then the *t-value* will be positive. On the other hand, a negative *t-value* signifies that the mean of $\mathcal{T}_R$ is comparatively lower. Based on this observation, we utilize the sign of the *t*-value in order to converge to *an estimation* x^{est} for which the resulting *t*-value < 0. The algorithm then identifies the partition $\Psi_i = [R_{est\_min}, R_{est\_max}]$, such that the final estimation $x^{est} \in \Psi_i$ and subsequently outputs the range $[R_{est\_min}, R_{est\_max}]$. If this estimated input range of $[R_{est\_min}, R_{est\_max}]$ matches the minimal power consumption range of $\Psi_1 = [x^{min}, x^1]$, then the adversary can deduce that the timing period associated with the original power profile $\vec{R}$ indicates consumer's home absence. This procedure has been illustrated in Fig. 2.

6 Evaluation of the Proposed Attack Methodology

6.1 Experimental Setup

Dataset. We analyze our attack model using the UK-DALE [35] (U.K. Domestic Appliance Level Electricity) dataset provided by Kelly *et. al.*. This open-access dataset describes the amounts of power demanded by home appliances over five houses in the U.K. during the period from 2012 to 2016. The sampling periods for mains and appliances were 1 second and 6 seconds, respectively. It is available for academic purposes and has been used for smart meter research in many existing works [34,48]. For our experimental purposes, we examine the metering data of consumer C_1 and consider the datasets of 2012 and 2013 as the non-DP metering streams. Simultaneously, we utilize the 2014 dataset to generate DP-induced power profiles and subsequently validate our attack methodology. We derive the ground truth regarding the consumer's home absence by observing individual appliances' power consumption profiles. We choose C_1 as it contains all the appliances' (total of 52) power consumption information, such as the kettle, fridge and dishwasher. The adversary utilizes these fine-grained power profiles of consumer C_1 to obtain the upper bound on the minimal power consumption range and identify C_1's usual daily life behavior such as work routine or home absence. The data streams from the year 2014 are passed through six well-studied DP mechanisms [3,6,18,22,24,28] in order to generate DP output streams. We have incorporated *group differential privacy* while implementing these six DP mechanisms, considering the auto-correlation property of the metering streams. We utilize *Google's differential privacy library* [1] to generate the Laplacian and Gaussian noises having varying sensitivity and privacy levels.

Choice of Privacy Levels and Sensitivity. In the literature, mostly the privacy levels of $\epsilon = 0.1$ and $\epsilon = 1$ are considered [3,18,22,24] with comparatively smaller sensitivity values. However, in the presence of large sensitivity values, the differential privacy mechanism with privacy levels of $\epsilon = 0.1$ or 1 produces a significantly higher magnitude of DP noises which are not suitable for smart grid applications. For our experiments, we consider different privacy levels (ϵ) from the range $\epsilon = 0.1$ to $\epsilon = 100$ having group sizes $k = 10, 20, 30, 40, 50, 60$ such that k successive meter readings provide the desired ϵ-DP guarantee. However, to determine the group size and privacy level pairs that satisfy the utility requirements of the metering system, we consider the *average distance distortion function* between the original and the perturbed streams as the utility metric. This distortion metric mainly computes the Root Mean Square Error (RMSE) between these two associated streams. We consider an upper bound of $3KW$ for the utility metric, which is significantly higher than the permitted system limit, and identify the group size and privacy level pairs that satisfy this bound. Based on these settings, we present the experimental evidence of leakage through six DP implementations using a real-life smart metering dataset by determining the consumer's home absence. Out of these, 3 methods use Laplacian noise [6,24,28], 2 utilizes gamma distribution to produce DP noises [3,18], and the remaining one generates Gaussian noises to obfuscate the meter readings [22]. Different values of sensitivity are considered during the noise generation of these methodologies following the six DP mechanisms, as highlighted below:

- *Maximum power consumption of an appliance.* In this case, the sensitivity of the query function, i.e. $\Delta_{q,1}$ is the maximum possible difference in values between a pair of profiles that differ on only one appliance. The query function considered here is the addition of individual appliances' power consumption value, and the DP mechanism proposed in [6] wants to hide the presence of individual appliances from the DP-induced output stream. Hence, as per the definition of sensitivity, $\Delta_{q,1}$ can be considered as the maximum variation caused by the appliance with the highest wattage. In the literature, Barbosa *et. al.* [6] uses this sensitivity value during noise generation. We assume that the appliance "laundry dryer" consumes the highest wattage i.e. 5 KW, among all the appliances in our use case so that $\Delta_{q,1} = 5$ KW. The UK-DALE dataset of $2012-13$ used during our experiments has the highest power consumption value of around 8 KW. Considering this, the sensitivity value of 5 KW is significantly large to hide the appliance's usage patterns.
- *Maximum allowed error in readings.* Here, the scale parameter of the Laplacian distribution is calculated using the maximum allowed error at each instance. We consider a 10% maximum error in each reading during the DP obfuscation phase. Based on this, the standard deviation and variance (σ^2) of the induced noises are computed so that the probability of obtaining the desired privacy level is significantly high, e.g. 98%. The magnitude of the scale parameter (denoted as b) of the Laplacian noise is calculated using the variance and the total number of measurements (denoted as $N=1$ for one sample): $b = \sqrt{\frac{\sigma^2}{2}}$. The authors of [28] use this methodology for noise generation. This mechanism provides a low sensitivity value; however, a lower value of ϵ can be used in the DP mechanism to provide higher privacy guarantees.
- *Maximum power reading of the consumer.* Out of the remaining 4 DP mechanisms examined in our paper, we consider the same sensitivity value for three of the DP mechanisms [3,22,24] that try to hide the sensitive power consumption value of individual households before their aggregation by the DCU. However, these three DP mechanisms follow different noise-generation techniques i.e. the methodology of [24] uses Laplacian noises, the scheme of [3] uses noises generated from the gamma distribution and the DP mechanism of [22] uses Gaussian noises to hide individual consumer's (in our case $\mathcal{C}_1$) power consumption usage. The query function tries to aggregate meter readings from multiple consumers. In order to hide the power usage of consumer $\mathcal{C}_1$, the maximum possible power consumption value of $\mathcal{C}_1$ is considered as the sensitivity value. Simultaneously, for the DP mechanism of [18], the query function computes the total power consumption for all the consumers over k sampling windows. For the consumer $\mathcal{C}_1$, let the vector $\vec{R} = \langle r_1^i, \cdots, r_j^i, \cdots, r_k^i \rangle$ denotes a k length original meter reading stream obtained over a time interval of length kh ($k \in \mathbb{N}$), where h is the sampling period of the metering system. The DP mechanism tries to hide the overall

power consumption over these k sampling windows. Here, the sensitivity is the sum of the maximum smart meter values at these k windows. It is clear that the sensitivity value considered during the mechanism of [18] is the highest among all the six mechanisms considered in our work. As a result, the magnitude of noise generated from the mechanism of [18] is also significantly higher.

6.2   Experimental Evaluation

In this section, we describe our experimental platform and elaborate on the significance of our proposed *t-test* based attack methodology in the context of determining consumers' absence in the household. We utilize the same UK-DALE dataset mentioned in Sect. 6.1 and consider the six DP mechanisms with the previously discussed sensitivity values to show the efficiency of our methodology.

Precomputation Phase

As discussed in Sect. 5, our proposed attacking scheme consists of a precomputation phase, where the adversary aims to acquire the *minimal power consumption range* specific to the targeted consumer, that indicates its home absence. Simultaneously, we try to obtain the group size and privacy level pairs that satisfy the privacy-utility trade-off criteria for all the aforementioned DP mechanisms.

Obtaining the Minimal Consumption Range Ψ_1. The adversary leverages the original smart metering dataset from the years 2012 and 2013 to derive the *minimal power consumption range*, denoted as Ψ_1, for consumer C_1. Figure 3 illustrates the power consumption patterns of consumer C_1 on November 28, 2012, and December 29, 2012. Notably, Fig. 3(a) clearly demonstrates the presence of the consumer at home on the specified day, despite very low power consumption (less than 400 W) during specific time intervals, such as from 4:30 AM to 12:00 PM. This pattern suggests minimal household activity during that period, possibly indicating the consumer's absence or sleeping duration. Similar consumption patterns are observed on different days, implying that this pattern reflects the consumer's typical routine. With the availability of appliance-level power consumption data, we can unveil the truth behind these power profiles. Figure 4 depicts the power profile of the kitchen lights appliance on November 28, 2012, highlighting the consumer's activity during the same time interval as in Fig. 3(a). Simultaneously, the dataset reveals that other appliances, such as the TV and dryer, are also active at different timing intervals, indicating C_1's home presence. However, the power profile on December 29, 2012 (Fig. 3(b)), indicates very little household activity throughout the day, suggesting the possibility of consumer's home absence. The power profile related to the kitchen lights appliance shows zero power consumption throughout the day, indicating that the consumer did not enter the kitchen to perform their daily activities. The consumption patterns observed in Fig. 3(b) are primarily attributed to the appliance fridge, which remained on throughout the day but did not exhibit peak power

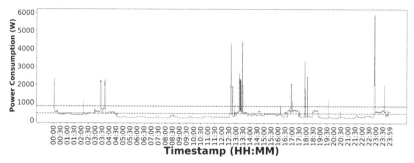

(a) Power consumption profile on November 28, 2012.

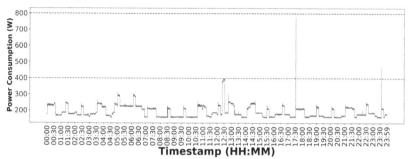

(b) Power consumption profile on December 29, 2012.

Fig. 3. Usual power consumption patterns of consumer C_1 during their home absence throughout the day (December 29, 2012) and their usual daily life routine (November 28, 2012). The blue and black line indicates the power consumption values of 400 W and 800 W respectively. (Color figure online)

consumption. In contrast, on November 28, 2012, peak power consumption from the appliance fridge can be observed. The variation in a fridge's power consumption between these days can be attributed to factors such as the fridge's cooling cycle. The appliance fridge performs cycles on and off regularly to maintain the desired temperature. On some days, the fridge may need to run longer and more frequently, especially if it's filled with warm items or if the ambient temperature is high. This increased cooling demand results in peak power consumption patterns (e.g. November 28, 2012). In contrast, on days when the fridge is less loaded or the ambient temperature is lower, it follows a more regular and energy-efficient pattern, which was the case on December 29, 2012. Consequently, the ground truth regarding the consumer's home absence can be reliably deduced by monitoring the power consumption patterns of individual appliances. This is particularly feasible, given that a majority of appliances remain inactive throughout the day, with exceptions such as appliances with periodic power consumption cycles (e.g., the cooling cycle of the fridge). Considering this, the overall power consumption for consumer C_1 is mostly confined within a minimal consumption range, specifically $[0, 400]$ W. Power profiles falling within this range can be readily identified as indicative of the consumer's home absence. The periodic

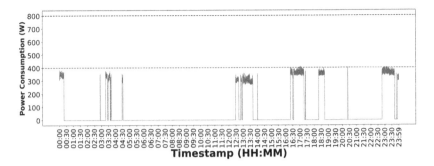

Fig. 4. Power consumption of appliance *kitchen lights* on November 28, 2012 which indicates consumer presence in the household during specific timing windows.

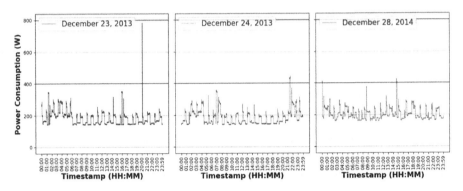

Fig. 5. Power consumption patterns of consumer C_1 during their home absence throughout the day on December 23, 2013, December 24, 2013, and December 28, 2014. Almost all of the power consumption readings from these three distinct days are bounded by the minimal consumption range of $\Psi_1 = [0, 400]$ W.

and predictable nature of household appliance activities, along with the defined minimal consumption range, facilitates the accurate estimation of consumer's home absence. Meter readings can also fall within the minimal consumption range of $[0, 400]$ during the consumer's sleeping duration. However, during consumer home absence, meter readings mostly belong to partitions Ψ_1 and Ψ_2, with a maximum of 2% of readings falling outside partition Ψ_1. If consumers are simply idle, such as during sleep, peak power consumption from some household appliances may be observed, with high power consumption values in the range of 1.5 kW to 2 kW. Figure 3 illustrates these scenarios by displaying the power consumption patterns on two different days for consumer C_1. The power profile from December 29 clearly indicates the consumer's absence throughout the day, with less than 0.02% of meter readings belonging to partition Ψ_2 and the rest falling into partition Ψ_1. In contrast, the power profile from November 28 depicts consumer C_1's typical daily routine, where idle periods mostly occur from 4:30 AM to 12:00 PM. The remaining time intervals include high power consumption

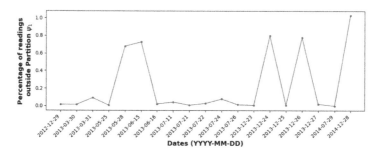

Fig. 6. Percentage of original meter readings outside partition Ψ_1 for consumer C_1 under different days when C_1's household is unoccupied.

values of up to 6 kW, including the time period from 12:00 AM to 2:00 AM (around 2 kW).

One important thing to note is that the minimal consumption range Ψ_1 remains consistently within the specified region of $[0, 400]$ W for consumer C_1 throughout the years 2012-2014. Figure 5 illustrates this scenario by showing the power consumption patterns of consumer C_1 during their absence from home throughout the day on specific dates, namely December 23, 2013, December 24, 2013, and December 28, 2014. During these periods, only a negligible percentage of power consumption readings deviate from the defined partition $\Psi_1 = [0, 400]$, with only $0.01\%, 0.80\%$, and 1.03% of readings falling outside this range, respectively. Similarly, the percentage of power consumption readings exceeding the boundaries of partition Ψ_1 for C_1 during the home absence is provided in Fig. 6, emphasizing the marginal nature of such occurrences. This clearly indicates throughout the years 2012–2014, on various unoccupied days, the percentage of readings surpassing the confines of Ψ_1 remains minimal. This consistent behavior implies that the minimal consumption range for C_1 does not deviate from the specified range of $\Psi_1 = [0, 400]$ W during these years. Consequently, it is established that the power readings during the absence of C_1 from home are predominantly confined within the range of $\Psi_1 = [0, 400]$ W. Building upon these empirical observations, we define the minimal consumption range Ψ_1 as $[0, 400]$ W for our experimental purposes. Thus, for our proposed Algorithm 1, we consider $\beta = 0.4\,KW$ and create the set of partitions $\Psi_1, \cdots, \Psi_Z$ and set a fixed increment $\delta = 0.1$ KW. With these considerations in mind, we conduct a real-time daywise assessment of the consumer's differentially private readings to determine their absence or presence at home throughout a 24-hour period.

Obtaining Privacy Parameters. It is evident that for a fixed privacy level ϵ, the magnitude of noises introduced to the meter readings increase monotonically with increasing group sizes (denoted as k) as each meter reading over the group size k satisfies $\frac{\epsilon}{k}$-differential privacy. Figure 7 illustrates the Root Mean Square Error (RMSE) between the original readings from December 28, 2014, and the DP-induced meter readings generated using the DP mechanism of [6] for a few selected k and ϵ pairs. The utility threshold is chosen as 3 KW, and indicated

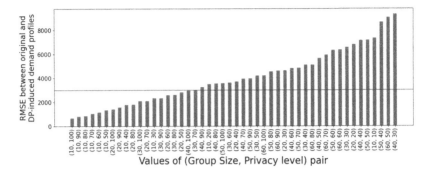

Fig. 7. Root Mean Square Error (RMSE) between the original and DP-induced meter readings generated using DP mechanism of [6] with respect to different group size and privacy level pairs. The blue line indicates the utility threshold of 3 KW. (Color figure online)

with a blue line in Fig. 7. All the k and ϵ pairs having RMSE values less than the threshold of 3 KW can be considered for further experiments. This is because the rest of the pairs will never be used in a smart metering setting as they may completely destabilize the system and assign abruptly high pricing signals to the consumers. We execute our proposed *t-test* based attack algorithm against these preferred k and ϵ pairs and subsequently highlight the lack of privacy protection these DP-induced readings provide in the context of determining a consumer's home absence. In a similar way, we obtain the k and ϵ pairs for the remaining five DP mechanisms considered in our paper. The k and ϵ pairs that produce the *most distortion* against the original streams of December 28, 2014, and satisfy the utility criteria under the DP mechanisms [3, 6, 18, 22, 24, 28] are $(40, 100)$, $(10, 20)$, $(40, 0.3)$, $(40, 10)$, $(20, 4)$ and $(60, 10)$ respectively. Note that if the *t-test* based assessment methodology requires L continuous metering traces to successfully execute the attacking scheme, the overall trace satisfies $\frac{\epsilon \times L}{k}$-differential privacy, which decreases the desired privacy protection. However, it is not feasible to reduce the privacy level ϵ even further as the RMSE values will increase drastically, resulting in a violation of privacy-utility trade-off criteria.

Evaluation of *t-test* Based Attack Methodology

We leverage Algorithm 1 to estimate the original range of meter readings from the DP-protected output streams as discussed in Sect. 5 and identify consumers' home absence under the group size and privacy level pairs obtained from the precomputation phase. To assess the efficacy of our proposed attack scheme, we select five distinct dates, namely July 29, August 23, August 24, December 28, and December 29, 2014, as the evaluation dates, during which consumer $\mathcal{C}_1$'s residence remains unoccupied throughout the day. Our determination of $\mathcal{C}_1$'s home absence is derived by employing the same steps outlined in the *Precomputation Phase* discussed in Sect. 6.2. In this context, we emphasize that during the consumer's home absence, the power consumption readings are almost

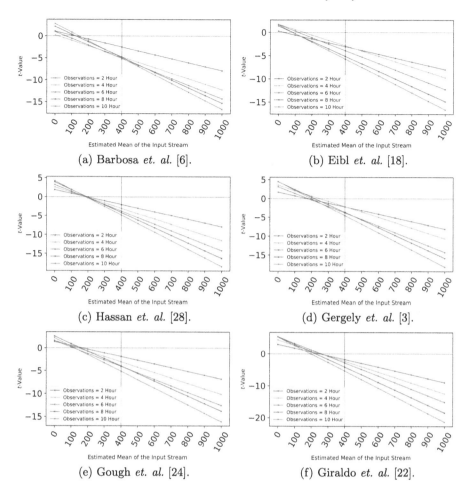

Fig. 8. Stepwise iteration for obtaining correct input range from DP traces under different DP mechanisms with an increasing observation window. The black line indicates the estimation of 400 and *t-value* of 0 through *x*-axis and *y*-axis respectively.

entirely bounded by Ψ_1, and no peak power consumptions from the appliances' are observed. As detailed in Sect. 6.1, we possess access to the power consumption patterns of all 52 appliances belonging to $\mathcal{C}_1$. Upon analyzing the non-DP power measurements from the 2014 dataset, we observed the absence of peak consumption by the appliances on these targeted dates. This is more evident from the fact that merely 1% of the readings fall outside the partition Ψ_1. Out of these dates, the power consumption profile of December 28, has the highest percentage of readings outside the range of partition $\Psi_1 = [0, 400]$ with a value of 1.03%. The slight fluctuations in power consumption outside of Ψ_1 can be attributed to the cooling cycle of the fridge, as previously discussed. Based on these observations, we establish the ground truth regarding the household

Table 1. Success rate of our proposed attack methodology (Algorithm 1) against the DP-induced streams of December 28 under six differential private mechanisms with increasing observation window.

Differential Private Mechanism	Success Rate of Proposed Attack Methodology											
	Observation Window											
	2 h	4 h	6 h	8 h	10 h	12 h	14 h	16 h	18 h	20 h	22 h	24 h
Barbosa *et al.* [6]	70%	76%	92%	96%	98%	98%	98%	100%	100%	100%	100%	100%
Eibl *et al.* [18]	74%	82%	84%	94%	96%	98%	98%	100%	100%	100%	100%	100%
Hassan *et al.* [28]	68%	86%	90%	90%	92%	94%	96%	96%	98%	100%	100%	100%
Gergely *et al.* [3]	68%	92%	92%	98%	98%	100%	100%	100%	100%	100%	100%	100%
Gough *et al.* [24]	72%	82%	94%	94%	94%	98%	98%	100%	100%	100%	100%	100%
Giraldo *et al.* [22]	74%	98%	100%	100%	100%	100%	100%	100%	100%	100%	100%	100%

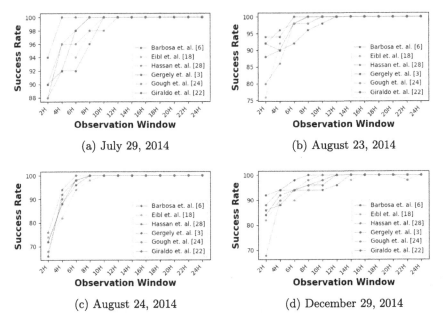

(a) July 29, 2014   (b) August 23, 2014

(c) August 24, 2014   (d) December 29, 2014

Fig. 9. Success Rate of our proposed *t-test* based attack methodology against six differential private mechanisms with increasing observation window under four different days when C_1's household is unoccupied.

status of C_1, affirming that C_1's home was indeed unoccupied on these dates. Subsequently, we gather the DP output traces from these specific dates under previously obtained group size and privacy level pairs and execute our attack scheme by incrementally increasing the number of output traces. Figure 8 represents the step-wise iteration of our proposed *t-test* based algorithm to estimate the original range of the meter reading stream under all six DP implementations from the DP-induced output traces of December 28. As discussed in Sect. 5, we try to identify the first reading for which the resulting *t-value* between the original DP-induced output trace and estimated trace is negative and subsequently obtain Ψ_i such that the estimation lies in partition Ψ_i. Figure 8 clearly illustrates that the resulting *t-value*s are producing negative signs on/before the estimation reaches the value of $400 \in \Psi_1$ starting from a two-hour observation period to ten-hour duration. Here, for all the scenarios and DP implementations, the proposed Algorithm 1 is able to successfully deduce the range of consumers' power profiles and subsequently indicate their home absence. In this paper, we conducted a comprehensive assessment of the aforementioned six differential privacy mechanisms. Our evaluation consisted of 50 independent runs, during which we applied our attacking scheme to distinct DP-induced output traces, all generated using the same precomputed group size and privacy level pairs. As depicted in Table 1, our analysis centers on the success rate of our attack methodology against the DP profiles of December 28 as the observation window size increases. It is a matter of significant concern that, with just an 8-hour observation window, the adversary can ascertain a consumer's home absence with an accuracy of more than 90%. Furthermore, this accuracy steadily rises with longer observation periods. Comparable results are observed on July 29, August 23, August 24, and December 29, as depicted in Fig. 9, which illustrates the success rates of our *t-test* based attack methodology against six differential private mechanisms. The success rates escalate proportionally with increasing observation window sizes across the four distinct days when C_1's household is unoccupied. In an alternative perspective, one can infer that the more extended the nighttime observation, the more confidently the adversary can conclude that the household is unoccupied. This vulnerability creates an ideal opportunity for potential burglaries or break-in attempts. Our observations across various dates when the consumer's household remained unoccupied consistently revealed similar patterns and highly accurate range estimations. This underscores the effectiveness of our methodology and highlights the limitations of prevailing state-of-the-art DP implementations in the context of smart metering infrastructure. Nonetheless, our proposed attacking scheme successfully identifies a consumer's home absence with exceptional accuracy, thereby ensuring the robustness and practical applicability of our approach.

7   Discussion

In addition to our proposed *t-test* based attack algorithm, we also conducted another statistical analysis utilizing Maximum Likelihood Estimation (MLE) on the differential private output traces with the objective of discerning the absence or presence of a consumer. MLE aims to determine the mean of input stream $\vec{R}$ based on the observable output distribution $T_R = \langle R_{out}(1), \cdots, R_{out}(i), \cdots, R_{out}(L) \rangle$. The value that maximizes the log-likelihood function (log of probability density function) is considered the final estimated mean (x^{est}). We compared our proposed attack method against the MLE scheme across all six DP mechanisms mentioned earlier while varying the number of output traces. Under the DP mechanisms [3,18,24,28], the performance of the MLE scheme closely parallels that of our proposed methodology. In contrast, when we delve into the Gaussian mechanism of [22], it becomes apparent that an accuracy level exceeding 90% is achieved following a 12-hour observation window. Conversely, when applying the MLE approach to the Laplacian mechanism of [6], the highest attained success rate is limited to a mere 84%. It is also important to highlight the presence of a potential countermeasure against the MLE based scheme, which can significantly reduce its accuracy to as low as 0%. As previously demonstrated in the literature [30, 47], DP mechanisms that incorporate non-zero mean can still satisfy the desired DP guarantees. When these DP mechanisms take into consideration a non-zero mean, which is intentionally concealed from potential adversaries, the resulting DP-induced output profile serves as a robust safeguard for sensitive information concerning the mean of the input data stream. This concealment effectively keeps the adversary in the dark regarding the precise mean of the DP mechanism in use. For instance, if the introduced mean corresponds to a specific value, such as $\beta = 400$ W, then even though the true mean of the input data stream lies within a minimal consumption range Ψ_1, the output of the MLE scheme provides an inaccurate estimation of the mean as being outside the Ψ_1 range. This discrepancy arises due to the MLE scheme's lack of knowledge regarding the mean of the DP mechanisms. On the other hand, our proposed approach operates under the assumption that the DP mechanism functions as a black box, a presumption well-founded in light of the security guarantees afforded by the principles of DP. As a result, the accuracy of determining the consumer's home presence remains the same for our proposed attack methodology. These fundamental distinctions highlight the superior effectiveness and robustness of our attack scheme in comparison to the MLE based method, concerning its ability to accurately determine the household status of the consumer.

8   Conclusion and Future Work

In this work, we proposed a simple albeit effective *t-test* based statistical attack methodology to detect consumers' home absence from the DP metering traces. All the six very well-studied DP mechanisms considered in our work try to protect the appliance's usage patterns, and original meter readings from adversaries; but fail to achieve their goal in a practical setting by leaking consumers' home absence through DP-induced output streams. Correct estimation of the consumer's home absence helps the adversaries bound the original power usage of the appliances and subsequently predict appliances' usage patterns as the high-wattage appliances will be switched off. As a result, leakage regarding consumers' home absence guarantees a serious breach of consumers' daily life privacy. The group DP mechanism to hide the auto-correlation between meter readings also could not prevent such privacy breaches due to the privacy-utility trade-off problem of the metering systems. As a possible future work direction, we plan to make a new privacy-preserving streaming algorithm that obscures the appliance's usage patterns to mitigate such attacks without incurring any aggregation and billing error which the current instance of DP fails to achieve.

Acknowledgement. The authors would like to thank the anonymous reviewers for their insightful comments and suggestions for improving the paper. They would also like to thank the Department of Science and Technology (DST), Govt of India, IHUB NTIHAC Foundation, C3i Building, Indian Institute of Technology Kanpur, and Centre on Hardware-Security Entrepreneurship Research and Development, Meity, India, for partially funding this work.

References

1. Google's differential privacy libraries (2022). https://github.com/google/differential-privacy
2. Naperville Smart Meters Keep Track of Household Activities (2022). https://smartgridawareness.org/2013/10/03/smart-meter-data-reveals/
3. Ács, G., Castelluccia, C.: I have a DREAM! (DiffeRentially privatE smArt Metering). In: Filler, T., Pevný, T., Craver, S., Ker, A. (eds.) IH 2011. LNCS, vol. 6958, pp. 118–132. Springer, Heidelberg (2011). https://doi.org/10.1007/978-3-642-24178-9_9
4. Avula, R.R., Oechtering, T.J.: Privacy-enhancing appliance filtering for smart meters. In: ICASSP 2022–2022 IEEE International Conference on Acoustics, Speech and Signal Processing (ICASSP), pp. 9042–9046. IEEE (2022)
5. Bao, H., Lu, R.: A new differentially private data aggregation with fault tolerance for smart grid communications. IEEE Internet Things J. **2**(3), 248–258 (2015). https://doi.org/10.1109/JIOT.2015.2412552
6. Barbosa, P., Brito, A., Almeida, H.: A technique to provide differential privacy for appliance usage in smart metering. Inf. Sci. **370** (2016)
7. Cao, X., Jia, J., Gong, N.Z.: Data poisoning attacks to local differential privacy protocols. In: 30th USENIX Security Symposium (USENIX Security 21), pp. 947–964 (2021)
8. Chen, R., Fung, B.C., Yu, P.S., Desai, B.C.: Correlated network data publication via differential privacy. VLDB J. **23**, 653–676 (2014)
9. Cheu, A., Smith, A., Ullman, J.: Manipulation attacks in local differential privacy. In: 2021 IEEE Symposium on Security and Privacy (SP), pp. 883–900. IEEE (2021)
10. Clark, M.R., Hopkinson, K.M.: Towards an understanding of the tradeoffs in adversary models of smart grid privacy protocols. In: 2013 IEEE Power and Energy Society General Meeting, pp. 1–5 (2013). https://doi.org/10.1109/PESMG.2013.6672334
11. Dimitriou, T.: Secure and scalable aggregation in the smart grid. In: 2014 6th International Conference on New Technologies, Mobility and Security (NTMS), pp. 1–5 (2014). https://doi.org/10.1109/NTMS.2014.6814048
12. Dwork, C.: Differential privacy. In: Bugliesi, M., Preneel, B., Sassone, V., Wegener, I. (eds.) ICALP 2006, Part II. LNCS, vol. 4052, pp. 1–12. Springer, Heidelberg (2006). https://doi.org/10.1007/11787006_1
13. Dwork, C.: Differential privacy: a survey of results. In: Agrawal, M., Du, D., Duan, Z., Li, A. (eds.) TAMC 2008. LNCS, vol. 4978, pp. 1–19. Springer, Heidelberg (2008). https://doi.org/10.1007/978-3-540-79228-4_1
14. Dwork, C.: A firm foundation for private data analysis. Commun. ACM **54**(1), 86–95 (2011)
15. Dwork, C., McSherry, F., Nissim, K., Smith, A.: Calibrating noise to sensitivity in private data analysis. In: Halevi, S., Rabin, T. (eds.) TCC 2006. LNCS, vol. 3876, pp. 265–284. Springer, Heidelberg (2006). https://doi.org/10.1007/11681878_14

16. Dwork, C., Roth, A., et al.: The algorithmic foundations of differential privacy. Found. Trends® Theor. Comput. Sci. (2014)
17. Dwork, C., Smith, A.: Differential privacy for statistics: What we know and what we want to learn. J. Priv. Confidentiality (2009)
18. Eibl, G., Engel, D.: Differential privacy for real smart metering data. Comput. Sci.-Res. Dev. **32**(1), 173–182 (2017)
19. Farokhi, F.: Review of results on smart-meter privacy by data manipulation, demand shaping, and load scheduling. IET Smart Grid **3**(5), 605–613 (2020)
20. Geng, Q., Ding, W., Guo, R., Kumar, S.: Tight analysis of privacy and utility trade-off in approximate differential privacy. In: International Conference on Artificial Intelligence and Statistics, pp. 89–99. PMLR (2020)
21. Gilbert Goodwill, B.J., Jaffe, J., Rohatgi, P., et al.: A testing methodology for side-channel resistance validation. In: NIST Non-invasive Attack Testing Workshop, vol. 7, pp. 115–136 (2011)
22. Giraldo, J., Cardenas, A., Kantarcioglu, M., Katz, J.: Adversarial classification under differential privacy. In: Network and Distributed Systems Security (NDSS) Symposium 2020 (2020)
23. Goel, S., Hong, Y.: Security challenges in smart grid implementation. In: Smart Grid Security. SC, pp. 1–39. Springer, London (2015). https://doi.org/10.1007/978-1-4471-6663-4_1
24. Gough, M.B., Santos, S.F., AlSkaif, T., Javadi, M.S., Castro, R., Catalão, J.P.: Preserving privacy of smart meter data in a smart grid environment. IEEE Trans. Ind. Inform. (2021)
25. Gough, M.B., Santos, S.F., AlSkaif, T., Javadi, M.S., Castro, R., Catalão, J.P.S.: Preserving privacy of smart meter data in a smart grid environment. IEEE Trans. Ind. Inf. **18**(1), 707–718 (2022). https://doi.org/10.1109/TII.2021.3074915
26. Hassan, M.U., Rehmani, M.H., Chen, J.: Performance evaluation of differential privacy mechanisms in blockchain based smart metering. arXiv preprint arXiv:2007.09802 (2020)
27. Hassan, M.U., Rehmani, M.H., Kotagiri, R., Zhang, J., Chen, J.: Differential privacy for renewable energy resources based smart metering. J. Parallel Distrib. Comput. **131**, 69–80 (2019)
28. Hassan, M.U., Rehmani, M.H., Kotagiri, R., Zhang, J., Chen, J.: Differential privacy for renewable energy resources based smart metering. J. Parallel Distrib. Comput. **131**, 69–80 (2019
29. Hong, Y., Liu, W.M., Wang, L.: Privacy preserving smart meter streaming against information leakage of appliance status. IEEE Trans. Inf. Forensics Secur. **12**(9) (2017). https://doi.org/10.1109/TIFS.2017.2704904
30. Huang, W., Zhou, S., Liao, Y., Zhuo, M.: Optimizing query times for multiple users scenario of differential privacy. IEEE Access **7**, 183292–183299 (2019)
31. Huang, Z., Mitra, S., Dullerud, G.: Differentially private iterative synchronous consensus. In: Proceedings of the 2012 ACM Workshop on Privacy in the Electronic Society, pp. 81–90 (2012)
32. Jin, J., McMurtry, E., Rubinstein, B.I., Ohrimenko, O.: Are we there yet? timing and floating-point attacks on differential privacy systems. In: 2022 IEEE Symposium on Security and Privacy (SP), pp. 473–488. IEEE (2022)
33. Kairouz, P., Oh, S., Viswanath, P.: The composition theorem for differential privacy. In: International Conference on Machine Learning, pp. 1376–1385. PMLR (2015)

34. Kelly, J., Knottenbelt, W.: Neural NILM: deep neural networks applied to energy disaggregation. In: Proceedings of the 2nd ACM International Conference on Embedded Systems for Energy-Efficient Built Environments, pp. 55–64 (2015)
35. Kelly, J., Knottenbelt, W.: The UK-dale dataset, domestic appliance-level electricity demand and whole-house demand from five UK homes. Sci. Data $2(1)$, 1–14 (2015)
36. Liu, C., Chakraborty, S., Mittal, P.: Dependence makes you vulnberable: differential privacy under dependent tuples. In: NDSS, vol. 16, pp. 21–24 (2016)
37. Nissim, K., Raskhodnikova, S., Smith, A.: Smooth sensitivity and sampling in private data analysis. In: Proceedings of the Thirty-Ninth Annual ACM Symposium on Theory of Computing, pp. 75–84 (2007)
38. Rajagopalan, S.R., Sankar, L., Mohajer, S., Poor, H.V.: Smart meter privacy: a utility-privacy framework. In: 2011 IEEE International Conference on Smart Grid Communications (SmartGridComm), pp. 190–195. IEEE (2011)
39. Randolph, M., Diehl, W.: Power side-channel attack analysis: a review of 20 years of study for the layman. Cryptography $4(2)$, 15 (2020)
40. Saha, S., Kumar, S.N., Patranabis, S., Mukhopadhyay, D., Dasgupta, P.: Alafa: automatic leakage assessment for fault attack countermeasures. In: Proceedings of the 56th Annual Design Automation Conference 2019, pp. 1–6 (2019)
41. Sankar, L., Rajagopalan, S.R., Mohajer, S., Poor, H.V.: Smart meter privacy: a theoretical framework. IEEE Trans. Smart Grid $4(2)$ (2012)
42. Tan, R., Badrinath Krishna, V., Yau, D.K., Kalbarczyk, Z.: Impact of integrity attacks on real-time pricing in smart grids. In: Proceedings of the 2013 ACM SIGSAC conference on Computer and communications security (2013)
43. Tran, H.Y., Hu, J., Pota, H.R.: Smart meter data obfuscation with a hybrid privacy-preserving data publishing scheme without a trusted third party. IEEE Internet Things J. $9(17)$, 16080–16095 (2022)
44. Wagh, G.S., Gupta, S., Mishra, S.: A distributed privacy preserving framework for the smart grid. In: 2020 IEEE Power and Energy Society Innovative Smart Grid Technologies Conference (ISGT), pp. 1–5 (2020). https://doi.org/10.1109/ISGT45199.2020.9087730
45. Wang, H., Xu, Z., Jia, S., Xia, Y., Zhang, X.: Why current differential privacy schemes are inapplicable for correlated data publishing? World Wide Web $24(1)$, 1–23 (2021)
46. Wang, H., Zhang, J., Lu, C., Wu, C.: Privacy preserving in non-intrusive load monitoring: a differential privacy perspective. IEEE Trans. Smart Grid $12(3)$, 2529–2543 (2020)
47. Xu, D., Yuan, S., Wu, X.: Achieving differential privacy and fairness in logistic regression. In: Companion Proceedings of the 2019 World Wide Web Conference, pp. 594–599 (2019)
48. Zhang, C., Zhong, M., Wang, Z., Goddard, N., Sutton, C.: Sequence-to-point learning with neural networks for non-intrusive load monitoring. In: Proceedings of the AAAI Conference on Artificial Intelligence, vol. 32 (2018)
49. Zheng, Z., Wang, T., Bashir, A.K., Alazab, M., Mumtaz, S., Wang, X.: A decentralized mechanism based on differential privacy for privacy-preserving computation in smart grid. IEEE Trans. Comput. $71(11)$, 2915–2926 (2021)

Security Analysis of BigBlueButton and eduMEET

Nico Heitmann$^{(\boxtimes)}$, Hendrik Siewert, Sven Moog, and Juraj Somorovsky

Paderborn University, Paderborn, Germany
heitnico@mail.upb.de

Abstract. Video conferencing systems have become an indispensable part of our world. Using video conferencing systems implies the expectation that online meetings run as smoothly as in-person meetings. Thus, online meetings need to be just as secure and private as in-person meetings, which are secured against disruptive factors and unauthorized persons by physical access control mechanisms.

To show the security dangers of conferencing systems and raise general awareness when using these technologies, we analyze the security of two widely used research and education open-source video conferencing systems: BigBlueButton and eduMEET. Because both systems are very different, we analyzed their architectures, considering the respective components with their main tasks, features, and user roles. In the following systematic security analyses, we found 50 vulnerabilities. These include broken access control, NoSQL injection, and denial of service (DoS). The vulnerabilities have root causes of different natures. While BigBlueButton has a lot of complexity due to many components, eduMEET, which is relatively young, focuses more on features than security. The sheer amount of results and the lack of prior work indicate a research gap that needs to be closed since video conferencing systems continue to play a significant role in research, education, and everyday life.

1 Introduction

The COVID-19 pandemic forced millions of people worldwide to stay at home [19]. As a result, meetings, classrooms, and private events were held online, and the demand and interest for online video conferencing systems increased [42]. In April 2020, Zoom Video Communications reported that their number of users had significantly increased due to the pandemic. While Zoom had 10 million daily users in December 2019, it had 200 million daily users in March 2020. Besides Zoom, there are numerous other video conferencing services, such as Microsoft Teams, Webex by Cisco, Google Meet, Skype, Zoho Meeting, BlueJeans, LifeSize, Whereby, and many others [30].

Security of Video Conferencing Systems. With the rise of video conferencing systems, security and privacy concerns grew. In April 2020, Google, SpaceX, and others banned Zoom over privacy concerns regarding its end-to-end encryption (E2EE) [22,38,45]. To eliminate vulnerabilities and increase security, several

C. Pöpper and L. Batina (Eds.): ACNS 2024, LNCS 14585, pp. 190–216, 2024.
https://doi.org/10.1007/978-3-031-54776-8_8

video conferencing providers, such as Zoom Video Communications, Inc. (Zoom) and 8x8, Inc. (Jitsi Meet), started bug bounty programs [1,48]. This measure bears fruit; Zoom received 401 reports and awarded $1.8 million in 2021 [12].

The demand for security and privacy in conferencing technologies also led to open-source video conferencing systems gaining popularity. Open-source software allows one to analyze the source code and self-host conferencing servers, which requires know-how but has the advantage that data remains on known servers. This is especially important in deployments that need to comply with European regulations for the protection of personal data. For example, in 2022, Germany's federal state Rhineland-Palatinate forbade the usage of Microsoft Teams in schools because it is not compliant with the General Data Protection Regulation (GDPR) [16].

Towards Systematic Security Analysis of Video Conferencing Systems. Despite the importance of security and privacy in video conferencing systems, there is, to our knowledge, no systematic research on the security of video conferencing systems yet. To gain insights into the attack surface associated with video conferencing systems, we selected two open-source systems widely used in research and education: BigBlueButton and eduMEET.

BigBlueButton has been developed since 2007 with the goal of giving teachers and researchers the ability for a new style of hybrid teaching where BigBlueButton should serve as an online classroom [27]. Similarly to other video conferencing systems, BigBlueButton gained popularity during the COVID-19 pandemic. It has, for example, become the primary mode of communication and learning in schools in France [7]. The recommendation was issued by the French Ministry of Education, which is responsible for 65,000 schools serving 12 million students. Even after the pandemic, BigBlueButton remained the recommended education tool in France [5] and several German federal states [16,46].

eduMEET was released in April 2020 by GÉANT, a European research network [15]. According to GÉANT, the release was rapidly accelerated due to lockdown measures and the need for an alternative and trustworthy video conferencing solution [26]. GÉANT's main arguments for having their video conferencing system were that it is from their community, self-hosted, and therefore the traffic stays within their network. Thus, they consider the tool trustworthy and cost-efficient compared to commercial alternatives [15].

To analyze the security of the chosen video conferencing systems, we must first understand how both systems are composed and which features they provide. This leads us to our research questions:

RQ1 *Which architecture concepts do BigBlueButton and eduMEET follow?*
RQ2 *What are the common features and user roles, and how are permissions assigned to individual features?*
RQ3 *What types of attacks result from the given architecture, features, and user roles?*

Our Approach. To perform a systematic analysis of a video conferencing system, we need to know how it is structured. That includes its components, as well as their responsibilities and tasks. Therefore, we break down the complex structures of each system to form shared components with their main tasks. Furthermore, we examine the connection between features, permissions, and user roles that are common to video conferencing systems. Using this information, we define our attacker model and use it to perform a source code analysis, for which we follow the data flow within and between components. Thus, we can check whether the components adhere to their responsibilities and correctly enforce user permissions as assigned by the user roles.

Results. Besides both being web video conferencing systems with similar user roles, the architectures of BigBlueButton and eduMEET differ drastically. BigBlueButton has many features with a very complex structure, while eduMEET is more minimal in comparison. Our architecture analyses laid the groundwork for the systematic security analyses of both conferencing systems; we found 7 vulnerabilities and 7 bugs. Among them are classic security flaws like broken access control, NoSQL injection, and DoS, but also vulnerabilities that are feature-specific and could be detected due to our in-depth architecture analyses.

Contributions. In summary, we make the following contributions:

- We provide a structured security analysis of two modern open-source video conferencing systems: BigBlueButton and eduMEET.
- We present a common structure of both systems and introduce their main components, features, and user roles.
- With our security analyses, we were able to identify 57 vulnerabilities and bugs. These range from attacks targeting confidential meeting chats, participant lists, and streams to impersonation and DoS attacks.

Responsible Disclosure. We responsibly disclosed all vulnerabilities and bugs to the developers of BigBlueButton and eduMEET.

2   Background

In this section, we cover WebRTC, which both analyzed video conferencing systems use as their method for real-time audio and video transfer.

2.1   WebRTC

WebRTC [8] is a suite of protocols for real-time communication (RTC) over the Internet. For web applications, it defines a JavaScript API to access media devices and to manage WebRTC connections. WebRTC supports media streams and message-based transfer of arbitrary data. It supports peer-to-peer (P2P) connections, where two users exchange data directly, without the data flowing over a server.

Before two peers can establish a direct WebRTC connection, they need to exchange information using a signaling server. They negotiate the initial media streams, with configuration such as codecs and bitrate, in the form of a Session

Description Protocol (SDP) offer and answer [6]. These also contain the information needed for opening the direct connection, including NAT traversal (Interactive Connectivity Establishment (ICE) candidates). Once a direct connection has been established, the peers can transfer the negotiated streams. WebRTC currently supports only one media transport protocol, DTLS-SRTP [25].

2.2 WebRTC Architectures in Conferencing Systems

In a typical conferencing setting, a group of users exchanges media data, for example, audio and camera streams. Using a P2P architecture for broadcasting media streams minimizes latency and avoids server bandwidth overhead. However, this approach does not scale well due to the limited bandwidth of end users. Therefore, using a P2P architecture is often infeasible for conferences.

Instead of using a P2P architecture, conferencing systems implement servers that can receive and redistribute the media streams for each user. There are two types of architectures a WebRTC server can follow. In the Selective Forwarding Unit (SFU) architecture, the server distributes incoming streams unmodified. If the server processes and combines incoming media streams, the architecture is called Multipoint Control Unit (MCU). This lowers the bandwidth requirements for the clients in exchange for processing on the server.

3 Analysis Method

Due to the lack of systematic analyses of video conferencing systems, there is no methodology for us to use and adapt. Thus, we started developing an approach that was further refined during our analysis. The structure of our paper reflects the steps of our analysis.

In the first part of this section, we outline the procedure for analyzing the architecture and user roles of the chosen systems. The second part of this section deals with the structured source code analysis. We assume attackers can reach a conferencing server over the network, with the server operator being a trustworthy party. The source code analysis requires a detailed attacker model based on the architecture, so we defer the detailed attacker model to Sect. 6.

3.1 High-Level Analysis

In the primary analysis, we use the respective documentation and the publicly available source code to get a broad overview of the respective system. Getting an overview helps to assess the complexity of the system, as well as understanding the functionality and use case for the video conferencing system (e.g., education). We divide the primary analysis into the following steps.

Architecture and Components (RQ1). The first step contains the architecture of the respective system (see Sect. 4). Next to the main components of the architectures, such as web client and server, we are especially interested in the WebRTC components and the messaging between components since these aspects facilitate the understanding of the systems the most.

Conferencing Features (RQ2). Then, we look at the features that each system offers (see Sect. 5.1). The features are needed for our analysis because each feature interacts with a meeting in a certain way (e.g., removing users from a meeting). These interactions are mostly limited to certain groups of users, such as moderators, and therefore require access control.

User Roles (RQ2). Finally, we check the user roles and permissions (see Sect. 5.2). We map these to the features that we gathered in the previous step. This allows us to get an overview and understanding of the system, which facilitates a more detailed source code analysis.

3.2 Source Code Supported Security Analysis

In our source code analysis, we chose a manual approach since automation does not work in our case (see Sect. 8.3). As the first step, we perform a detailed analysis of the implementation. This shares commonalities with the primary architecture analysis, but we now focus on the internal implementation of each component. We manually validate that the implementation matches the documentation and our understanding of the features. This step also results in the identification of internal assumptions, for example, which parts of internal messages the components treat as trustworthy. All components have the responsibility to satisfy these often implicit internal assumptions.

Because almost all server logic gets triggered by user actions, we perform a data flow analysis on each possible user action. We confirm the overall behavior in practice, for example, via the browser's developer tools. During this data flow analysis, we consider the responsibilities of each component (e.g., access control on the conferencing server). Whenever it is not certain that an aspect of the conferencing system correctly adheres to the responsibilities, we need to investigate further.

When investigating a potential vulnerability, we may move directly to building a proof of concept. Otherwise, we may also re-evaluate whether it is handled elsewhere than expected. In either case, we conclude when we have either demonstrated an exploit or have complete reasoning for the behavior to be correct.

4   Architectures of the Analyzed Open-Source Conferencing Systems (RQ1)

We answer **RQ1** by analyzing the architectures of BigBlueButton and eduMEET. From both systems, we first derive a shared architecture that gives a high-level overview of common components and outlines their main tasks, which not only helps understanding the analyzed video conferencing systems, but also might facilitate future work. Then, we describe the implementation specifics of BigBlueButton and eduMEET. Finally, we compare the feature sets they offer to users.

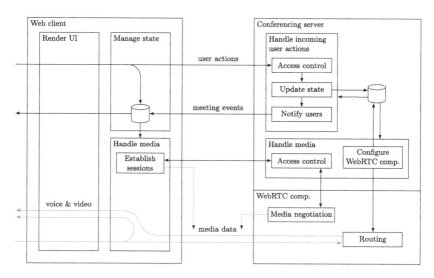

Fig. 1. Shared architecture of the analyzed video conferencing systems, showing the three components "web client", "conferencing server", and the "WebRTC component" with their main tasks. Arrows represent communication, and media streams are marked in green. The dotted arrows mark the creation of the WebRTC connection. The cylinders represent data storage.

4.1   Shared Architecture

We first focus on commonalities of the analyzed video conferencing systems by deliberately abstracting from specific features of BigBlueButton and eduMEET. This results in the architecture of a video conferencing system with minimal features. Figure 1 shows a summary of the components of such a video conferencing system. In the following, we describe the main components of the shared architecture. Then, we describe how each analyzed system implements each component with its uniqueness.

Web Client. The web client is responsible for three main tasks. The first main task, closest to the user, is rendering the user interface (UI). The UI allows users to interact with the meeting. The web client updates the UI in response to interactions triggered both by the local user and actions by other users in the meeting. Such actions include a user enabling their camera or sending a chat message. The web client is also responsible for displaying the conferencing system's features, such as video chat. The features depend on the conferencing system (see Sect. 5.1).

The second main task of the web client is handling media streams. This includes establishing a WebRTC connection (see Sect. 2.1), where one peer is the web client and the other peer is the WebRTC component. Once a streaming session has been established, the peers can start sending and receiving media data. On the client side, incoming media streams are connected to the UI, where the videos are displayed. The client also displays its outgoing video streams.

The third main task is processing and sending meeting state updates. When a user performs actions in the UI, the client sends *user actions*, i.e., intended changes to the meeting state, to the server. If the user's intended change is valid, the server notifies the web clients of the changes to the meeting state, which we refer to as an *event*. When a web client receives an event, it processes it and updates the local state in near real-time. Possible events include receiving new chat messages, changes to permissions, muting audio, or starting and stopping a video. The possible events depend on the features of the conferencing system.

Server-Side Components. The analyzed conferencing systems consist of two server-side components: the conferencing server and a WebRTC component.

Conferencing Server. The first task of the conferencing server is processing incoming user actions. This involves three main steps. First, the server performs access control by checking whether the user may perform the requested user action. Second, if the action is valid, the conferencing server executes it. This may involve additional processing by the server and results in changes to the meeting state. Finally, the server publishes events to the clients.

The second task of the conferencing server is managing streaming sessions. For this purpose, it controls the WebRTC component, which may be an external media server or embedded in the conferencing system as a library. The conferencing server participates in establishing streaming sessions by creating them in the WebRTC component and providing communication between the client and WebRTC component for the initial negotiation. The conferencing server is responsible for access control by mediating the initial communication. After the negotiation, the WebRTC component and client establish a direct communication channel, and the conferencing server can no longer mediate. If the permissions of a user get revoked, the conferencing server is responsible for closing streaming sessions via the WebRTC component's management interface.

WebRTC Component. Finally, there is a WebRTC component with loose coupling to the conferencing server. The WebRTC component relies on commands by the conferencing server for management and has the task to establish streaming sessions. The second task of the WebRTC component is to route media streams. The conferencing systems covered here use the SFU architecture for all video streams, so the server redistributes media streams unmodified (see Sect. 2.2).

4.2   Implementation of BigBlueButton

In this section we show how BigBlueButton's components implement their tasks.

Web Client. BigBlueButton uses the frontend framework React[1] for its UI. React does not provide any communication between the server and client. The server and client of BigBlueButton use the web framework Meteor.js to facilitate communication, which provides remote procedure call (RPC) and publish/subscribe capabilities. Internally, if possible, Meteor.js uses a WebSocket for communication. Using the publish/subscribe capabilities of Meteor.js, the client mirrors the meeting state of the server and receives state changes triggered by user actions. Therefore, the web client of BigBlueButton only needs to perform limited state management.

Server-Side Components. The server side of BigBlueButton is split into a conferencing server and two standalone servers for WebRTC.

Conferencing Server. The conferencing server of BigBlueButton is internally split into several individual components. It receives user actions on the WebSocket connection provided by Meteor.js and routes them within the conferencing server. At the destination, a handler performs access control checks and updates the meeting state. These updates to the meeting state are propagated internally. The conferencing server keeps a copy of the meeting state in a MongoDB database and uses the publish/subscribe mechanism of Meteor.js to pass change events to the clients, with access control in the publishing step.

For managing media streams, BigBlueButton interacts with its two media servers. The web client has the initiative to open media streams for its outgoing and incoming streams. For the audio conference, BigBlueButton does not mediate signaling between the client and the WebRTC component but instead relies on the client's knowledge of a five-digit voice conference number for access control. For video streams, the server performs a permission check when clients want to open a stream. When clients get removed from the meeting, the server component reacts to the event by closing their video streams.

WebRTC Component. BigBlueButton 2.3.3, the version analyzed here, uses two media servers: FreeSWITCH, and Kurento Media Server (Kurento).[2] The voice conference of meetings is handled by FreeSWITCH, with clients directly connecting to FreeSWITCH to perform media negotiation. The video streams are handled by Kurento, with the conferencing server mediating media negotiation. BigBlueButton also uses Kurento to relay the voice conference to participants who only listen. The conferencing server communicates with both media servers for access control and necessary configuration, for example, media routing.

Extensions to the Shared Architecture. BigBlueButton does not provide user management but instead relies on external software to integrate BigBlue-

---

[1] https://reactjs.org/.

[2] BigBlueButton 2.4 introduces the media server mediasoup, which replaces Kurento as the default as of 2.5, with a modified media topology.

Button's meeting functionality, for example, Greenlight[3] or Moodle.[4] The 3rd-party application performs authentication and access control for joining meetings. For this purpose, BigBlueButton provides a custom HTTP management API. A shared secret between BigBlueButton and 3rd-party server applications controls access to the API.

For processing uploaded presentation slides, BigBlueButton uses several external programs, depending on the file type. The resulting files are made available to other clients from disk. BigBlueButton allows users to record the meetings. If a meeting is recorded, it stores audio and video recordings and the internal messages of the entire meeting as files. BigBlueButton embeds an instance of the collaborative text editor Etherpad[5] to implement its shared notes.

The media negotiation between the client and FreeSWITCH extends our general model as it is not mediated by the conferencing server. This allows server operators to connect FreeSWITCH to an external telephony provider via Session Initiation Protocol (SIP), allowing users to join the conference by telephone.

4.3   Implementation of eduMEET

Web Client. For its web client, eduMEET uses the frontend framework React. For maintaining the meeting state on the client, eduMEET uses Redux,[6] a JavaScript library for state management in web applications. It uses a store that holds the application state. The application state gets updated when user actions or events are dispatched. User-triggered actions can either modify the meeting room (e. g., locking the room) or change the user settings. The client may pass these user actions to the server using a WebSocket. To establish and manage a WebRTC streaming session, the client uses the mediasoup client library.

Server-Side Components. The server side of eduMEET is split into a conferencing server, which consists of an Express[7] web server with WebSocket support, and the Node.js library mediasoup for WebRTC.

Conferencing Server. The conferencing server handles all incoming connections and user authorization. Because of the WebSocket support in the Express web server, WebSocket handlers and HTTP request handlers share access to a session object for all requests from the same client. The WebSocket are attached to a *peer* object representing a user. The peer object contains relevant information such as user roles, a unique peer ID, a room ID, and a socket. Any modification to a peer object is done via the peer ID, which references the peer object in a dictionary.

---

[3] https://github.com/bigbluebutton/greenlight.
[4] https://moodle.org/.
[5] https://etherpad.org/.
[6] https://redux.js.org/.
[7] https://expressjs.com/.

WebRTC Component. For media handling on the server, eduMEET uses the Node.js library mediasoup, a layer of JavaScript that communicates with a set of C/C++ subprocesses. The internal architecture of mediasoup has its own terminology, which contains workers, routers, transports, producers, and consumers [11]. When a new user joins, the client and the conferencing server create a producer instance. The conferencing server then notifies the other peers and creates a consumer instance for each. The notified peers create local consumer instances for themselves.

Extensions to the Shared Architecture. The first additional component in eduMEET is a torrent tracker for its file sharing feature (see Sect. 5.1). It keeps track of users participating in upload and download, helping users to connect to each other. In the web client, eduMEET uses the WebTorrent[8] library, which uses WebRTC for peer-to-peer communication. Furthermore, eduMEET uses the Passport[9] module for external authentication strategies. Depending on the authentication strategy, new components might arise, for example, an Identity Provider for OpenID Connect (OIDC) [29].

5 Features and User Roles (RQ2)

In this section, we first compare features the analyzed conferencing systems offer. We then present user roles shared by both analyzed conferencing systems. Finally, we go into detail on how each of the analyzed video conferencing systems handles user roles, permissions, and the mapping to features.

5.1 Comparison of Features

Table 1 shows an overview of the features of both systems. While there is some overlap, there are also several features specific to BigBlueButton or eduMEET. Features specific to BigBlueButton are, for example, polls or shared notes. On the other hand, eduMEET offers file sharing, which is not implemented in BigBlueButton.

Some features require additional libraries or application logic. Other features require extending the conferencing system with new components, which are either controlled by the server operator or an external entity. Components can be additional servers or important libraries that play a vital role in the video conferencing system (e. g., mediasoup in eduMEET). A component controlled by the server operator is, for example, a WebRTC media server. A torrent tracking server for file sharing would be an example of a component that is controlled by an external entity (see Sect. 4.3). Importantly, additional features and components introduce a new level of complexity and a broader attack surface.

---

[8] https://webtorrent.io/.
[9] https://www.passportjs.org/.

Table 1. Conferencing features supported by BigBlueButton and eduMEET, with their required roles. Several features are present both in BigBlueButton and eduMEET, while others are only supported by one. The table lists which role a user needs to actively use a feature, where the role "everyone" includes users without access to the meeting. Note that some features are accessible by multiple user groups.

Feature	BigBlueButton support	roles	eduMEET support	roles
🎤 Voice conference	●	$\mathcal{V}$	●	$\mathcal{V}$
📷 Video conference	●	$\mathcal{V}$	●	$\mathcal{V}$
🖵 Screen sharing	●	$\mathcal{P}$	●	$\mathcal{V}$
💬 Text chat	●	$\mathcal{V}$	●	$\mathcal{V}$
👥 Role management	●	$\mathcal{M}$	●	$\mathcal{M}^{*}$
🛡 External authentication	◐	Ω	◐	Ω
⧗ Waiting room	●	$\mathcal{M}$	●	$\mathcal{V}^{*}, \mathcal{M}$
⮕ Breakout rooms	●	$\mathcal{M}$	○	–
✋ Hand raise	●	$\mathcal{V}$	●	$\mathcal{V}$
📋 Shared notes	●	$\mathcal{V}$	○	–
📊 Polls	●	$\mathcal{P}$	○	–
💬 Text captions	●	$\mathcal{M}$	○	–
↱ File sharing	○	–	●	$\mathcal{V}$
🗎 Slide upload	●	$\mathcal{P}$	○	–
🖊 Whiteboard	●	$\mathcal{V}^{*}, \mathcal{P}$	○	–
🔴 Recordings	●	$\mathcal{M}$	●	$\mathcal{V}$
📞 Telephone dial-in	◐	Ω^{*}	○	–

○ not supported   ● supported   ◐ requires additional configuration
Ω everyone   * additional requirements $\mathcal{V}$ viewers $\mathcal{M}$ moderators $\mathcal{P}$ presenters

5.2   User Roles

Common User Roles. BigBlueButton and eduMEET use user roles combined with permissions for their access control; users who participate in meetings have different roles, which give them permission to access or use certain features. Such permissions allow users to share their audio or video, or give users access to moderation features.

The analyzed conferencing systems have two main user roles in common: "viewer" and "moderator". The viewer role, also referred to as "normal" in eduMEET, gives users basic permissions and allows them, for example, to send and receive media streams. The moderator role allows for managing the meeting room, the users, and access to other features. Furthermore, depending on the features of the respective conferencing system, we can differentiate between users in a waiting room (or lobby) and users in a meeting. Oftentimes, restrictions like this are not implemented by creating new user roles, but rather using properties or flags that are part of the user objects. Thus, two viewers might have different permissions or access to different features. For example, one user with the viewer role might be in a waiting room and cannot receive audio and video streams from other users, while other users with the same role do not have these restrictions because they are already in the meeting.

Because user roles and the associated permissions are heavily influenced by features and the current meeting state, access control is a complex topic. The following sections explain the details of each analyzed conferencing system. Table 1 gives an overview of the requirements to access individual features. Some features have additional requirements besides the user role; for example, regular users in BigBlueButton may only draw on the whiteboard if the presenter has given them permission.

BigBlueButton-Specific User Roles. In addition to the viewer and moderator role, every meeting has at most one presenter, who gets permissions related to a presentation area in the meeting. These additional permissions are limited to the presenter; other users, including moderators, cannot affect the presentation area.

Permissions may depend on context. Within breakout rooms, there is no distinction between moderators and viewers, and all users can interact with the meeting as viewers. BigBlueButton has a guest waiting room, allowing moderators to limit access to the meeting until they approve new users. Users calling in via telephone do not have access to the web interface of BigBlueButton and thus only have access to a very limited set of user actions.

BigBlueButton also allows moderators to "lock" viewers and presenters, to take away specific permissions. One may use this to aid in the moderation of large meetings or for specific use cases, like online exams, where participants should not see each other.

eduMEET-Specific User Roles. In eduMEET, one can use a configuration file to define new roles and to assign specific permissions. This also permits changing existing assignments of roles and permissions. The default configuration contains the roles "normal" (here referred to as "viewer"), "moderator", and "admin". A user can have multiple roles.

A moderator can kick users, disable audio, video, and screen sharing for users (which the user can activate again), take down raised hands, clear the chat, and end the meeting. Furthermore, a moderator can use the role manager to give and remove roles during a meeting. Each role has a "promotable" flag, which determines whether moderators can give and take the role. In addition, each role has a configurable level. The level of a moderator must be at least equal to the role of the target user to modify the target user role. The admin role, which has the highest level, allows users to enter a full room or a locked room, which normally sends users to the room's lobby to wait for approval. As long as no moderator is in the meeting, viewers can also lock and unlock the room. The permission is revoked as soon as a user with the moderator role joins.

6   Attacker Model

After performing the primary analysis, as mentioned in Sect. 3, we developed an attacker model that fits the setting of a video conferencing system.

We assume an attacker may send arbitrary network requests. They do not have access to any private information regarding the server or the users. The attacker cannot read or interfere with the network traffic of other users. The server operator is assumed to be entirely trustworthy. We do not impose conditions on the surrounding situation because conferencing systems are used to host various types of events. The attacker may be a viewer, presenter, or even moderator in a meeting. The attacker may also be a non-participant with no roles at all or be in the waiting room. The attacker may create their own meetings. During a meeting, users' roles may change, so we also consider cases where a moderator revokes an attacker's permissions.

We consider an attack successful if the attacker breaks any of the aspects of the CIA triad. The attacker breaks confidentiality guarantees if, for example, they join a locked meeting and retrieve sensitive streams or public chat content. The integrity of the meeting state is broken when an attacker oversteps the permissions of their role, by performing any action that modifies the meeting state in a way that they are not allowed to. This includes an attacker joining a meeting without permission. For availability, we consider an attack successful if the attacker performs DoS against any feature in any meeting, affecting any user other than the attacker themselves. We exclude DoS by resource exhaustion and only consider cases of DoS in the application logic, for example, an attacker blocking seats in a meeting.

We limit the scope of our analysis to the first-party code of BigBlueButton and eduMEET, respectively. External components and libraries are out of scope and thus deemed to be safe for the purpose of our evaluation. They are expected to conform to their documentation with configuration files as distributed with the conferencing systems. With our analysis, we target the server-side code because it implements the main application logic. For eduMEET, however, all clients take an active role in maintaining the meeting state, so we consider both the server and client side of eduMEET. BigBlueButton relies on the external framework Meteor.js to maintain the client state, which is out of the scope of this analysis. Since the server operator is fully trustworthy, we assume that additional configurations made by the server operator are secure.[10]

7   Evaluation (RQ3)

We performed the evaluation on BigBlueButton 2.3.3 and eduMEET 3.5.0-beta.1, the most recent versions at the time of analysis.[11] Because our attacker model is relatively broad, we identified not only high-impact vulnerabilities but also several smaller vulnerabilities without significant impact on the meeting. To not overestimate their impact, we explicitly classify such vulnerabilities as "bugs". Hereafter, we refer to vulnerabilities and bugs as "findings".

Our evaluation resulted in 45 findings in BigBlueButton (38 vulnerabilities and 7 bugs) and 12 findings in eduMEET (12 vulnerabilities). Table 2 gives a

---

[10] This mainly applies to eduMEET, as it allows flexible configuration of the user roles and permissions.

[11] We analyzed commit bb46e2d of https://github.com/edumeet/edumeet (branch "develop"), which was later merged into eduMEET 3.5.0-beta.1.

Table 2. Summary of all findings in BigBlueButton (BXX) and in eduMEET (EXX). The final two columns denote which role a legitimate user needs to access the feature, and the role an attacker needs to perform the attack. The role "everyone" includes users without access to the meeting.

Description	Type (CIA)	Feature (see Table 1)	Legit.	Attacker
B1 Read other meetings' public chat	C		−	Ω^*
B2 Read arbitrary private chats	C		−	Ω^*
B3 Write into chat when lock setting changes	I		$\mathcal{V}^*$	$\mathcal{V}$
B4 Retain access to shared notes after leaving	CIA		−	Ω^*
B5 Bypass read-only shared notes	I		$\mathcal{M}$	$\mathcal{V}$
B6 Impersonate users in shared notes	I		−	$\mathcal{V}$
B7 Write captions (mechanism 1)	I		$\mathcal{M}$	$\mathcal{V}$
B8 Write captions (mechanism 2)	I		$\mathcal{M}$	$\mathcal{V}$
B9 View individual poll responses	C		$\mathcal{P}$	$\mathcal{V}$
B10 View free-form answers before poll ends	C		$\mathcal{P}$	$\mathcal{V}$
B11 Bug: Submit multiple free-form poll answers	I		−	$\mathcal{V}$
B12 View names of all waiting guests	C		$\mathcal{M}$	$\mathcal{V}$
B13 Get confidential meeting info as waiting guest	C		−	Ω^*
B14 Block seats in the meeting	A		−	$\mathcal{V}$
B15 Bypass participant limit when joining	CI		$\mathcal{M}$	$\mathcal{V}^*$
B16 View user list while locked	C		$\mathcal{V}^*$	$\mathcal{V}$
B17 Read information about previous users	C		Ω^*	$\mathcal{V}$
B18 Bypass getting banned	CIA		−	$\mathcal{V}$
B19 Receive meeting state updates after leaving	C		−	Ω^*
B20 Receive list of all users on the server	C		−	Ω^*
B21 Bug: Add emoji status to other users	I		−	$\mathcal{M}$
B22 Impersonate users in breakout rooms	I		−	$\mathcal{V}^*$
B23 Access all breakout rooms	CI		$\mathcal{M}$	$\mathcal{V}^*$
B24 Run moderator actions in breakout rooms	IA		−	$\mathcal{V}^*$
B25 Bug: Access breakout room data after demotion	C		−	$\mathcal{V}^*$
B26 View unshown slides in current meeting	C		−	$\mathcal{V}$
B27 View slides in other meetings	C		−	Ω^*
B28 Give others access to the whiteboard	I		$\mathcal{P}$	$\mathcal{V}^*$
B29 Run whiteboard actions after losing access	IA		−	$\mathcal{V}^*$
B30 Add pencil annotations to whiteboard	I		$\mathcal{P}, \mathcal{V}^*$	$\mathcal{V}$
B31 Impersonate users towards FreeSWITCH	CIA		−	Ω^*
B32 Impersonate users towards bbb-webrtc-sfu	CIA		−	Ω^*
B33 Access meeting voice conferences	CIA		$\mathcal{V}$	Ω^*
B34 Receive audio and screen share after leaving	C		−	Ω^*
B35 Bypass locked webcam viewing (mechanism 1)	C		$\mathcal{M}$	$\mathcal{V}$
B36 Bypass locked webcam viewing (mechanism 2)	CI		$\mathcal{M}$	$\mathcal{V}$
B37 Bypass locked webcam sharing	IA		$\mathcal{M}$	$\mathcal{V}$
B38 Manipulate shared camera	CI		−	$\mathcal{V}^*$
B38.1 Activate participants' webcams	CI		−	$\mathcal{V}^*$
B38.2 View webcams in other meetings	C		−	Ω^*
B39 Replace others' webcam streams	I		−	Ω^*
B40 Abort running screen shares	A		$\mathcal{P}, \mathcal{M}$	Ω^*
B41 Bug: Receive metadata on shared videos	C		$\mathcal{V}$	Ω^*
B42 Access recordings by meeting ID	C		Ω^*	Ω^*
B43 Bug: Exclude own camera from recording	I		−	$\mathcal{V}$
B44 Bug: See limited camera streams (via recordings)	C		$\mathcal{M}$	Ω^*
B45 Bug: See contents of shared notes (via recordings)	C		$\mathcal{V}, \Omega^*$	Ω^*
E1 Forge malicious chat objects	IA		−	$\mathcal{V}$
E1.1 Write chat message as a different user	I		−	$\mathcal{V}$
E1.2 Send chat message in the past or future	I		−	$\mathcal{V}$
E1.3 DoS meeting via chat message	A		−	$\mathcal{V}$
E1.4 Manipulate link display via markup	I		−	$\mathcal{V}$
E2 Rejoin after kick, bypassing locked room	CIA		$\mathcal{V}$	$\mathcal{V}$
E3 Overwrite peer reference	CIA		−	$\mathcal{V}$
E3.1 Participate in meeting invisibly	CI		−	$\mathcal{V}$
E3.2 Being untargetable by moderator actions	CI		−	$\mathcal{V}$
E3.3 Block new media streams for victim	IA		−	$\mathcal{V}$
E4 DoS meeting with overlong display names	A		−	$\mathcal{V}$
E5 Hijack WebSockets cross-site	CI		−	Ω
E6 DoS meeting by manipulating the peer ID	A		−	$\mathcal{V}$
E7 Inject arbitrary data in logs	I		−	$\mathcal{V}$
E8 Impersonate via display name and picture	I		−	$\mathcal{V}$
E9 Bypass permission checks after role change	I		−	Ω^*
E10 Prevent getting muted	IA		$\mathcal{V}$	$\mathcal{V}$
E11 Client DoS via inconsistent media config	A		−	$\mathcal{V}$
E12 Read shared files	C		$\mathcal{V}$	Ω^*

C: confidentiality   I: integrity   A: availability   ● vulnerability   ● bug
− not a feature Ω everyone   * additional requirements $\mathcal{V}$ viewer $\mathcal{M}$ moderators $\mathcal{P}$ presenters

short description of each finding, provides the type of violation of the CIA triad (see Sect. 6), and assigns to each finding the features it affects (see Table 1). A finding may affect multiple features because some features share parts of their implementation, for example, the voice and video conference. If a finding is not related to any specific feature but the core implementation for meeting state and communication of the respective conferencing system, we use ⚙. The last two columns of Table 2 show the user roles needed to perform the actions associated with the findings. Some of these actions are available as features to specific user roles, shown in the column *legitimate roles*, while others are not intended to be accessible.

As can be seen in Table 2, most of the findings in BigBlueButton are in the core implementation and in the video conferencing feature. The rest of the findings are distributed across the other features. In eduMEET, most of the findings are also in the core implementation and in the text chat feature.

7.1   BigBlueButton

In this section, we present five representative findings out of the 45 findings in BigBlueButton.

B1: Read Other Meetings' Public Chat. This finding allows an attacker to access sensitive data from other meetings hosted on the same server.

To transfer chat messages from the conferencing server to the web client, BigBlueButton uses the publish/subscribe mechanism of Meteor.js (see Sect. 4.2). In particular, the client subscribes to a publisher called *group-chat-msg*, which always publishes public chat messages in their meeting and messages in private chats. The client establishes the subscription with a WebSocket message to the server. Listing 1.1 shows how the server restricts its responses in the publisher. In this query, the server inserts the `meetingId` of the meeting. The first branch only matches messages where the `chatId` value is set to `"MAIN-PUBLIC-GROUP-CHAT"`, which means that the client is subscribed to the public messages in their particular meeting. The second branch matches all messages with a chat ID in the `chatsIds` array, which is a parameter sent by the client. However, missing validation of `chatsIds` resulted in the fact that the server can leak public chats of *every* meeting hosted on the server.

For the attack description, we assume an attacker who participates in any meeting hosted on a BigBlueButton server. The attacker has access to the public chat in their particular meeting. Using a modified client or browser developer tools, the attacker can modify the parameters their client sends to the server for the subscription. If the attacker adds `"MAIN-PUBLIC-GROUP-CHAT"` into the `chatsIds` list, intended for private chats (see Listing 1.2), their clients' subscription applies to the public chat of every meeting hosted by the server; the publisher on the server provides the messages from the public chats of all meetings. The attacker thus gains access to all messages from the public chat of every meeting hosted on the particular server.

```
[
  { "meetingId": meetingId,
    "chatId": "MAIN-PUBLIC-GROUP-CHAT"
  },
  { "chatId":
    { "$in": chatsIds }
  }
]
```

```
[
  { "meetingId": meetingId,
    "chatId": "MAIN-PUBLIC-GROUP-CHAT"
  },
  { "chatId":
    { "$in": [ "MAIN-PUBLIC-GROUP-CHAT" ] }
  }
]
```

Listing 1.1. The publisher's server-side MongoDB query (simplified). When a chat message matches either one of the two branches, the server publishes it to the client.

Listing 1.2. By adding the string "MAIN-PUBLIC-GROUP-CHAT" to the list intended for private chats, an attacker subscribes to public chat messages of all meetings on the server.

B2: Read Arbitrary Private Chats. This finding interacts with B1, increasing the impact of this finding. The publisher *group-chat-msg* is also vulnerable to NoSQL injection. The parameter `chatsIds` can contain arbitrary values supported by EJSON, an extension of JSON used by Meteor.js. The server does not check the value's type. An attacker can modify the parameters their client sends to the server like in the previous attack. In particular, the attacker can set the publisher's parameter `chatsIds` to [/.*/], causing it to provide all messages from all public and private chats in all meetings on the server.[12]

B4: Retain Full Access to Shared Notes After Leaving. This finding affects shared notes. BigBlueButton relies on the external server component Etherpad for shared notes. Thus, the conferencing server needs to ensure access control, including revoking access when a user loses access to the meeting. For this, the conferencing server includes checks when users make HTTP requests to Etherpad which reject all users without a BigBlueButton session and check whether the Etherpad pad belongs to the meeting that the user is in.

However, there is an issue with this process as Etherpad uses a long-running WebSocket connection for communication between the server and client. When a user leaves or gets kicked from a meeting, the conferencing server cannot close the WebSocket to Etherpad; an attacker can continue reading and editing the shared notes. In addition, the session used for the server-side check stays valid after leaving the meeting, so the server also allows new WebSocket connections to Etherpad.

B26: View Unshown Presentation Slides in Current Meeting. BigBlue-Button relies on a client's knowledge of a presentation ID for the client to download presentation slides for each uploaded presentation. However, the server leaks the presentation IDs.

---

[12] This is an array, containing a native JavaScript regular expression object for `.*`. In EJSON, it is serialized as [{ "$regexp": ".*", "$flags": "" }].

The server sends the presentation IDs to clients so they can can display the slides, but inadvertently reveals them for all presentations in the meeting due to incomplete filtering. This allows an attacker in the meeting to view all slides that have been uploaded, including future slides in the currently chosen presentation and the slides of presentations that were uploaded but never shown to the viewers.

B34: Receive Audio and Screen Share After Leaving. The final finding described here affects the voice and video conference and the screen share feature of BigBlueButton. It allows the attacker to listen to audio and watch screen shares secretly, even after they leave the meeting.

We assume the attacker is a viewer in a meeting and leaves or gets kicked. While still in the meeting, the attacker can open multiple viewing sessions for each media stream with a modified client that sends additional requests. For the screen share and listen-only audio, the conferencing server only closes one of the sessions when the attacker leaves the meeting. The remaining sessions stay valid in the WebRTC component and only get closed when the screen share or meeting ends, respectively.

7.2   eduMEET

We explain three representative findings in eduMEET. In Sect. A.1, we cover an additional interesting yet more complex finding in depth (E3).

E1: Forge Malicious Chat Objects. This finding points to one of the root causes of several findings in eduMEET and allows a multitude of attacks. A client can send a chat message to the server as a chat message object in its WebSocket connection to the server. The server forwards this object to all other participants in the same room as long as the sender has the SEND_CHAT permission. An attacker can manipulate fields in messages they send to perform several attacks. In the following, we describe three possible attacks. First, the attacker can manipulate the **name** field, which is used to display the name of the sender. The attacker can abuse it to impersonate other users by changing the content. Second, the attacker can also manipulate the **time** field, allowing them to manipulate the chat conversation and send messages in the past or future. Third, the attacker can also set the **name** field to **null** or other invalid objects. This leads to a DoS attack against the receiving clients because the client does not expect other data types, and the errors are not handled, which leads to a crash in the application. Interestingly, when users affected by such a DoS attack try to rejoin the meeting, they are usually redirected to the index page instead of joining the meeting. This happens because joining users receive the chat and file history, which automatically repeats the attack. The attacker can stay in the room to prevent the room from resetting, effectively blocking the room indefinitely.

E2: Rejoin After Kick, Bypassing Locked Room. This finding allows an attacker to bypass the room lock, which can be used as a security mechanism to prevent other users from joining the room without approval. In this attack scenario, a moderator kicks the attacker from the room. Afterward, the moderator locks the room, which prevents users from joining the room without approval. The attacker is now not able to rejoin the meeting without further actions because the client generates a new peer ID and the server prevents new users from joining a locked room. However, the attacker can set their client's peer ID to any value, for example, by overwriting the client-generated value with the browser developer tools. If the attacker sets their peer ID to their old peer ID when they were in the meeting, the server treats the attacker as a returning user, which allows bypassing a locked or even a full room. Therefore, the attacker can rejoin the locked room after getting kicked by changing the peer ID to the old peer ID.

E10: Prevent Getting Muted. This finding allows an attacker in a meeting to disrupt it without others being able to mute them. Moderators can mute participants for everyone (global mute). The affected user can still unmute themselves, so this is not a security mechanism. Participants can also decide to mute another participant for themselves (local mute). However, an attacker can circumvent getting muted by sending a request to create a second microphone producer and muting their first microphone producer. Other participants cannot globally or locally mute the attacker's second microphone producer.

7.3   Responsible Disclosure

We reproduced all findings on unmodified instances of BigBlueButton 2.3.3 and eduMEET 3.5.0-beta.1. We worked in local environments to not affect real video conferencing deployments with their users. We reported the findings to the developers of BigBlueButton and eduMEET between July 2021 and May 2022. The developers of eduMEET thanked us for the findings but have not released fixed versions as of December 2023. The developers of BigBlueButton acknowledged the findings and started publishing fixes with BigBlueButton 2.3.9. As of December 2023, the developers have fully addressed 37 of the 45 findings and assigned CVEs to 14 of them (see Table 3). The remaining issues are still to be fixed.

8   Discussion

We discuss our findings from Sect. 7 by considering the potential root causes in the respective conferencing system. For this, we identify commonalities between the findings. Finally, we discuss the limitations of our evaluation.

8.1   BigBlueButton

BigBlueButton offers a lot of features, making it the more complex of the two conferencing systems. Because of this breadth of features, the attack surface is naturally larger when compared to eduMEET. In addition, the interplay between features makes correct implementation more difficult. We observed that our findings in BigBlueButton have two major types of root causes, both of which relate to the complexity of the software.

Several vulnerabilities came up as a result of subtle logic bugs in the internal server logic. We can see this in the situation arising when an attacker opens multiple media streams B35, but also in several other findings: B1, B3, B10, and B18, among others. These can, to some extent, be traced back to the internal logical complexity of BigBlueButton, which results from a large set of features and evolution over time.

For several other vulnerabilities, one can see a commonality of incomplete or missing security considerations in the design. For example, in B33, the ability of an attacker to join voice conferences without legitimate access can be traced back to reliance on a 5-digit voice conference ID for access control. When users leave, the server cannot revoke this ID to revoke access, as it is identical for all participants. In this case, there is a mitigation in place, but it is not sufficient to prevent attacks. There are also some more subtle cases, for example, in B27, where guessable secrets allow an attacker to gain read access to uploaded slides.

8.2 eduMEET

The root causes in most of our findings for eduMEET. are of a different nature. Oftentimes, the server trusts the client and forwards its messages without properly checking the input, for example, in E1, E4, and E6.

While the technical details of the other findings differ, they may stem from a similar root cause. For example, E2, which results from an implementation error, can also be seen as a missing feature because the moderator cannot effectively ban the attacker from the meeting. The same applies to E10 where the moderator cannot force an attacker to stop sharing audio. Here, it would be helpful to have a more fine-grained permission system, like the "lock settings" feature in BigBlueButton. This feature could allow the moderator to withdraw permissions of viewers, for example, to share audio.

In summary, most findings in eduMEET are either because there is too much trust in the client or because of missing moderation features. Both factors result in a lack of security and measures to eliminate disruptive factors within a meeting. Consequently, these findings show that filtering client messages and moderation features are critical measures to ensure secure meetings.

8.3 Limitations

Scope. To understand the architecture and behavior of conferencing systems, we analyzed the functionality and interaction of both conferencing systems. We examined server-side and client-side components in eduMEET. In BigBlueButton, we concentrated on the server-side components since these implement most of the logic and functionality. BigBlueButton's client delegates state management to the third-party framework Meteor.js, which is out of scope for our analysis. For this reason, we did not examine the BigBlueButton client, which could bring new findings regarding web security.

Automation. For comparison with our manual approach, we used SonarCloud[13] to scan for bugs automatically. While it found code snippets that could be improved, it did not find any vulnerabilities. This result is expected because most of the bugs can be classified as logical flaws and require user interactions and a certain meeting state. Such conditions cannot be automatically applied by a static code analysis tool. BigBlueButton has publicly used SonarCloud as part of their quality control since June 2021.[14]

Architecture of Conferencing Systems. Comparing two architectures as different as those of eduMEET and BigBlueButton was not a trivial task. Thus, we agreed on a shared architecture by breaking down the architecture of the respective conference systems. Certainly, the shared architecture can be used for future work. However, depending on the conferencing system and architecture, it may be necessary to extend the model. Our model uses the SFU WebRTC architecture, while other systems may use P2P or other WebRTC architectures, which allow for direct communication between the clients. Furthermore, other conferencing systems may communicate differently, for example, by using Extensible Messaging and Presence Protocol (XMPP).

Analysis of Further Conferencing Systems. We limited the scope of our analysis to allow us to cover the chosen conferencing systems and their architectures in detail. Further analyses of open-source conferencing systems may be performed using a similar process, applied to their respective architectures. Our analysis process is not directly applicable to closed-source software. Nevertheless, the detected logical flaws can provide inspiration for new vulnerabilities in other closed-source conferencing systems supporting the affected features.

9   Related Work

Although various vulnerabilities have been found in web conferencing systems in the past, there is little exhaustive scientific research in the general area of video conferencing systems. Thus, we consider previous research, vulnerability reports, and talks regarding conferencing systems to get a grasp of the attack surface.

Most of the vulnerabilities found in web conferencing systems are related to classic web security vulnerabilities such as cross-site scripting (XSS) [43, 44], server-side request forgery (SSRF) [9], SQL injection via custom URI

---

[13] https://www.sonarsource.com/products/sonarcloud.
[14] https://github.com/bigbluebutton/bigbluebutton/pull/10737#issuecomment-860211455.

scheme [18], and different types of misconfigurations [40,41]. Also common are vulnerabilities resulting from missing checks [40,41], flawed role management [4,40,47], missing security considerations [2,47], and image or document conversions leading to vulnerabilities [2,10]. While all these vulnerabilities are interesting, we wanted to focus more on factors that extend our attack surface.

Among the previously mentioned reports, some stand out in particular because the described vulnerabilities are located in the client, but the client differs from our architecture. In our architecture, the client is a web browser. In some reports [3,20,28,43], the client is an Electron[15] app. These applications are made with web technologies and use Chromium and Node.js. Vulnerabilities in these applications are critical since they can lead to client-side remote code execution (RCE) [3,20,28,43]. Other kinds of conferencing clients are classic executables on Windows, Mac, or Linux, which extend the attack surface as well, for example, due to memory-related issues [31,37]. Thus, different types of clients introduce different types of attacks, and the more types of clients the conferencing system offers, the larger the attack surface. The same applies to other components, such as Zoom's Multimedia Router (MMR), which is responsible for transmitting audio and video between Zoom clients; this component was affected by a buffer overflow found by Google Project Zero [37].

Another interesting component used in conferencing systems is the login mechanism. Sudhodanan and Paverd found an attack related to Single Sign-On (SSO), where an attacker creates a Zoom account with the victim's email (before the victim creates an account) [39]. When the victim now uses an identity provider with the same email to create a Zoom account, Zoom merges the accounts, which allows the attacker to log in to the victim's account with the attacker's password.

Natalie Silvanovich from Google Project Zero released articles in 2018, where she analyzed and fuzzed the WebRTC implementation in Chrome and closed-source video conferencing applications such as FaceTime and WhatsApp [32–36]. Four years later, she found one memory-related vulnerability in Zoom's client and another one in Zoom's MMR [37]. In the end, she pointed out that the closed-source software comes with a lot of challenges for researchers, which prevents further progress in verifying security properties [37]. She recommended making closed-source software available to security researchers [37]. In the same year, Ivan Fratric from Google Project Zero presented at Black Hat USA a 0-click RCE vulnerability in Zoom [14]. Fratric found out that different components use different XML parsers, which allowed him to smuggle XMPP messages (stanza smuggling) [14].

In the last years, cryptographic vulnerabilities in Matrix clients and libraries became public [13,24]. In 2021, Kasak et al. drew attention to two vulnerabilities where vulnerable clients may be tricked into disclosing encryption keys [13]. In 2022, Albrecht et al. presented six attacks that affected the Matrix standard and its flagship client Element [24]. These attacks break authentication and confidentiality but require the cooperation of the homeserver, which is responsible

---

[15] https://www.electronjs.org/.

for storing communication history and account information and relaying messages [23,24].

While we mentioned vulnerabilities in conferencing systems from a technical point of view, Ling et al. focused on the attacker as a person who is responsible for disruptions in a meeting, i. e., Zoombombing [21]. Their results indicate that such attackers often have help from an insider within the meeting. Therefore, password protections and meeting IDs are a rather ineffective mechanism to prevent Zoombombing; they argue that unique join links would be an effective security mechanism.

In summary, there are lots of reports and findings in different fields regarding video conferencing systems and their components. However, there is a gap in scientific approaches, especially regarding open-source video conferencing systems. Our work is a first step to approach this problem.

10   Conclusions and Future Work

In our work, we systematically analyzed two open-source conferencing systems and detected 57 vulnerabilities and bugs. While the root cause for vulnerabilities in BigBlueButton mostly lies in the complexity of the system and the interplay between the features, in eduMEET, they mainly resulted from missing strict authorization checks and excessive trust in client messages. We want to highlight that our findings do not imply that BigBlueButton and eduMEET are less secure than commercial closed-source alternatives. The high number of findings was largely enabled by the open-source implementations, which facilitated our in-depth evaluations. On the negative side, it needs to be mentioned that both systems lack a swift vulnerability patching process. In the case of eduMEET, none of the reported vulnerabilities have been fixed. This is not acceptable for systems processing security-critical data.

The high number of findings shows that there is indeed a research gap in the security of video conferencing systems. With our systematic security analyses, we want to draw attention to this topic and want to stress that video conferencing systems offer a large attack surface due to their large number of components and used technologies. This is also confirmed by many related vulnerabilities, mostly found in non-systematic analyses by bug bounty hunters in recent years.

Our work can be extended in different directions. XML parsers within XMPP implementations are underexplored and are an interesting attack vector since XMPP is often used in video conferencing systems [14]. Other than that, the systematic approach that we applied to BigBlueButton and eduMEET could be applied to other open-source conferencing systems. Closed-source software is often more difficult to analyze if it is not freely and openly available [37]. Commercial providers should consider facilitating further security research and we hope there will be more future work that helps to improve the security of video conferencing systems.

Acknowledgements. We thank our anonymous reviewers for their insightful comments and detailed suggestions. We are also grateful to Sven Hebrok for helpful discussions and contributions in the early stage of this research.

This research was funded by the PRISMA Elite Program of the Department of Computer Science of Paderborn University, and by the research project "North Rhine-Westphalian Experts in Research on Digitalization (NERD II)", sponsored by the state of North Rhine-Westphalia – NERD II 005-2201-0014.

A   Appendix

A.1   eduMEET

E3: Overwrite Peer Reference. This finding leads to multiple high-impact issues in eduMEET. When a user connects to a room, the server creates a JSON Web Token (JWT) [17], bound to a peer ID generated by the client. The JWT is stored on the server and referenced by a cookie-based session. When a user connects to a room, eduMEET performs two checks. First, the server checks if there is a JWT for the session and if the peer ID is already used by a connected user. The server rejects the connecting peer if the peer ID is already used, but no JWT exists. Otherwise, the server verifies the JWT, i.e., the server checks if the peer ID matches the JWT. In case of a valid JWT, the server treats the user as returning and closes the old connection.

The vulnerability stems from the fact that the server creates a new peer object regardless of whether the JWT matches the peer ID. The peer object (see Sect. 4.3) represents a meeting participant and contains, among other things, a unique peer ID, a room ID, a list of user roles, and a socket for communication. Despite the importance of the JWT validity, in the first step, the server only checks if a peer ID and a JWT exist. Therefore, the peer ID does not have to match the JWT. When an attacker connects to a room with an existing peer ID and a valid session referencing a JWT that does not match the peer ID, the server still creates a new peer object. The server keeps a list of peer objects referenced by their peer IDs. Since the peer ID exists, the server overwrites the existing peer reference. However, the old connection stays open, and the old peer can still participate in the meeting.

To perform an attack, the attacker first joins any meeting. The attacker has a valid peer ID generated by the client and a valid session from the server. The attacker now joins the targeted meeting. Instead of having their client generate a new random peer ID for this connection, the attacker chooses an existing peer ID (see below). To achieve this, they may use the browser developer tools to overwrite the JavaScript variable holding the peer ID their client generated and then join the meeting. The new peer ID does not match the attacker's JWT anymore. The WebSocket connection of the old peer with the same peer ID is not closed but not referenced anymore. That means the old peer cannot be targeted by moderator actions (E3.2). If the new peer with the same peer ID now leaves the meeting, the UI of all participants changes, and peers with the target peer ID are not visible anymore, but the connection of the old peer is still open. The old peer is invisible in the meeting but can still participate (E3.1), for example, listen to existing streams and read the chat. To exploit the first two scenarios (E3.1 and E3.2), the attacker needs to be the old and new peer at the same time, which they can achieve using two browser instances. In the last scenario (E3.3), the attacker uses the victim's peer ID to prevent the victim from receiving new media streams. The peer IDs of all participants are known because the server broadcasts them when joining.

A.2   Status of Fixes in BigBlueButton

Table 3. All findings in BigBlueButton (BXX) with their status as of December 2023. The latest version at this time was BigBlueButton 2.7.3. In total, 37 of the 45 findings were fully fixed and the impact of one additional finding was significantly reduced.

Description	Fixed?	CVE
B1 Read other meetings' public chat	●	CVE-2022-29232
B2 Read arbitrary private chats	●	(none)
B3 Write into chat when lock setting changes	●	CVE-2022-29234
B4 Retain access to shared notes after leaving	●	(none)
B5 Bypass read-only shared notes	●	(none)
B6 Impersonate users in shared notes	●	(none)
B7 Write captions (mechanism 1)	●	(none)
B8 Write captions (mechanism 2)	●	CVE-2022-29231
B9 View individual poll responses	●	CVE-2022-23490
B10 View free-form answers before poll ends	●	(none)
B11 Bug: Submit multiple free-form poll answers	●	(none)
B12 View names of all waiting guests	●	(none)
B13 Get confidential meeting info as waiting guest	●	(none)
B14 Block seats in the meeting	●	(none)
B15 Bypass participant limit when joining	●	(none)
B16 View user list while locked	○	(none)
B17 Read information about previous users	●	(none)
B18 Bypass getting banned	●	CVE-2022-41961
B19 Receive meeting state updates after leaving	●	CVE-2022-41959
B20 Receive list of all users on the server	●	(none)
B21 Bug: Add emoji status to other users	●	CVE-2022-41962
B22 Impersonate users in breakout rooms	●	(none)
B23 Access all breakout rooms	●	CVE-2022-29233
B24 Run moderator actions in breakout rooms	◐	(none)
B25 Bug: Access breakout room data after demotion	●	(none)
B26 View unshown slides in current meeting	○	(none)
B27 View slides in other meetings	○	(none)
B28 Give others access to the whiteboard	●	(none)
B29 Run whiteboard actions after losing access	●	CVE-2022-41963
B30 Add pencil annotations to whiteboard	●	CVE-2022-29236
B31 Impersonate users towards FreeSWITCH	○	(none)
B32 Impersonate users towards bbb-webrtc-sfu	●	(none)
B33 Access meeting voice conferences	○	(none)
B34 Receive audio and screen share after leaving	●	(none)
B35 Bypass locked webcam viewing (mechanism 1)	●	CVE-2022-23488
B36 Bypass locked webcam viewing (mechanism 2)	●	(none)
B37 Bypass locked webcam sharing	●	(none)
B38 Manipulate shared camera	●	CVE-2022-23489
B38.1 Activate participants' webcams		
B38.2 View webcams in other meetings		
B39 Replace others' webcam streams	●	CVE-2022-23489
B40 Abort running screen shares	●	(none)
B41 Bug: Receive metadata on shared videos	●	CVE-2022-29235
B42 Access recordings by meeting ID	○	(none)
B43 Bug: Exclude own camera from recording	○	(none)
B44 Bug: See limited camera streams (via recordings)	●	(none)
B45 Bug: See contents of shared notes (via recordings)	●	(none)

○ unfixed   ◐ partially fixed   ● fixed

References

1. 8x8, Inc., Vulnerability Disclosure Program Policy (2023). https://hackerone.com/8x8
2. Ahmed, M.: Hacking Zoom: Uncovering Tales of Security Vulnerabilities in Zoom (2020). https://mazinahmed.net/blog/hacking-zoom/
3. Altpeter, B.: RCE in Jitsi Meet Electron prior to 2.3.0 due to insecure use of shell.openExternal() (CVE-2020-25019) (2020). https://benjamin-altpeter.de/jitsi-meet-electron-rce-shell-openexternal/
4. Anthony, T.: Zoom Security Exploit - Cracking private meeting passwords (2020). https://www.tomanthony.co.uk/blog/zoom-security-exploit-crack-private-meeting-passwords/
5. Thévenet, A.: France digital strategy for education supports the use of digital commons (2023). https://joinup.ec.europa.eu/collection/open-source-observatory-osor/news/france-digital-strategy-education-2
6. Begen, A.C., Kyzivat, P., Perkins, C., Handley, M.J.: SDP: Session Description Protocol. RFC 8866 (Proposed Standard) (2021). https://www.rfc-editor.org/rfc/rfc8866.txt
7. BigBlueButton. French Ministry of Education chooses BigBlueButton (2023). https://bigbluebutton.org/2023/01/11/french-ministry-of-education-chooses-bigbluebutton/
8. Boström, H., Jennings, C., Castelli, F., Bruaroey, J-I.: WebRTC: Real-time communication in browsers. W3C recommendation, W3C (2023). https://www.w3.org/TR/2023/REC-webrtc-20230306/
9. Bräunlein, F.: MS Teams: 1 feature, 4 vulnerabilities (2021). https://positive.security/blog/ms-teams-1-feature-4-vulns
10. Böck, H.: File Exfiltration via Libreoffice in BigBlueButton and JODConverter (2020). https://blog.hboeck.de/archives/902-File-Exfiltration-via-Libreoffice-in-BigBlueButton-and-JODConverter.html
11. Castillo, I.B.: mediasoup v3 Design (2020). https://mediasoup.org/documentation/v3/mediasoup/design/
12. Davis, R.: Zoom's Bug Bounty Program: 2021 in Review (2022). https://blog.zoom.us/zoom-bug-bounty-program-2021/
13. Kasak, D., Callahan, D., Hodgson, M.: Practically-exploitable Cryptographic Vulnerabilities in Matrix (2022). https://matrix.org/blog/2021/09/13/vulnerability-disclosure-key-sharing
14. Fratric, I.: XMPP Stanza Smuggling or How I Hacked Zoom (2022). https://i.blackhat.com/USA-22/Thursday/US-22-Fratric-XMPP-Stanza-Smuggling.pdf
15. GÉANT. Build Your Own eduMEET Service (2020). https://web.archive.org/web/20200416162612/https://edumeet.org/build/
16. heise online. Rheinland-Pfalz: Schulen dürfen Microsoft-Software Teams nicht mehr nutzen [Rhineland-Palatinate: Schools no longer allowed to use Microsoft Teams] (2022). https://www.heise.de/news/Rheinland-Pfalz-Schulen-duerfen-Microsoft-Software-Teams-nicht-mehr-nutzen-7154309.html
17. Jones, M.B., Bradley, J., Sakimura, N.: JSON Web Token (JWT). RFC 7519 (Proposed Standard) (2015). https://www.rfc-editor.org/rfc/rfc7519.txt. Updated by RFCs 7797, 8725
18. Keegan, R.: Patched Zoom Exploit: Altering Camera Settings via Remote SQL Injection (2020). https://medium.com/@keegan.ryan/patched-zoom-exploit-altering-camera-settings-via-remote-sql-injection-4fdf3de8a0d

19. Kelly, S.M.: Zoom's massive 'overnight success' actually took nine years. CNN (2020). https://edition.cnn.com/2020/03/27/tech/zoom-app-coronavirus/index.html

20. Kinugawa, M.: Discord Desktop app RCE (2020). https://mksben.l0.cm/2020/10/discord-desktop-rce.html

21. Ling, C., Balci, U., Blackburn, J., Stringhini, G.: A first look at Zoombombing. In: 2021 IEEE Symposium on Security and Privacy (SP), pp. 1452–1467 (2021). https://ieeexplore.ieee.org/document/9638984

22. Marczak, B., Scott-Railton, J.: Move fast and roll your own crypto - a quick look at the confidentiality of zoom meetings (2020). https://citizenlab.ca/2020/04/move-fast-roll-your-own-crypto-a-quick-look-at-the-confidentiality-of-zoom-meetings/

23. Martin, T., Radzio, M., Sharma, K.: Matrix concepts (2023). https://matrix.org/docs/matrix-concepts

24. Albrecht, M.R., Celi, S., Dowling, B., Jones, D.: Practically-exploitable Cryptographic Vulnerabilities in Matrix (2022). https://nebuchadnezzar-megolm.github.io/static/paper.pdf

25. McGrew, D., Rescorla, E.: Datagram Transport Layer Security (DTLS) Extension to Establish Keys for the Secure Real-time Transport Protocol (SRTP). RFC 5764 (Proposed Standard) (2010). https://www.rfc-editor.org/rfc/rfc5764.txt. Updated by RFCs 7983, 9443

26. Meyer, K.: GÉANT eduMEET service launched early to support communication needs during the COVID-19 lockdown (2020). https://connect.geant.org/2020/06/16/geant-edumeet-service-launched-early-to-support-communication-needs-during-the-covid-19-lockdown

27. Nettleton, R.: BigBlueButton (2010). https://web.archive.org/web/20100814003302/https://edc.carleton.ca/blog/index.php/2010/06/04/bigbluebutton/

28. s1r1us and TheGrandPew. Remote Code Execution on Element Desktop Application using Node Integration in Sub Frames Bypass - CVE-2022-23597 (2022). https://blog.electrovolt.io/posts/element-rce/

29. Sakimura, N., Bradley, J., Jones, M.B., de Medeiros, B., Mortimore, C.: OpenID Connect Core 1.0. OpenID Foundation (2014). https://openid.net/specs/openid-connect-core-1_0-final.html

30. Schreiber, P., Hoffman-Andrews, J., Grauer, Y.: Videoconferencing Guide (2020). https://videoconferencing.guide/

31. Sector7. Zoom RCE from Pwn2Own 2021 (2021). https://sector7.computest.nl/post/2021-08-zoom/

32. Silvanovich, N.: Adventures in Video Conferencing Part 1: The Wild World of WebRTC (2018). https://googleprojectzero.blogspot.com/2018/12/adventures-in-video-conferencing-part-1.html

33. Silvanovich, N.: Adventures in Video Conferencing Part 2: Fun with FaceTime (2018). https://googleprojectzero.blogspot.com/2018/12/adventures-in-video-conferencing-part-2.html

34. Silvanovich, N.: Adventures in Video Conferencing Part 3: The Even Wilder World of WhatsApp (2018). https://googleprojectzero.blogspot.com/2018/12/adventures-in-video-conferencing-part-3.html

35. Silvanovich, N.: Adventures in Video Conferencing Part 4: What Didn't Work Out with WhatsApp (2018). https://googleprojectzero.blogspot.com/2018/12/adventures-in-video-conferencing-part-4.html

36. Silvanovich, N.: Adventures in Video Conferencing Part 5: Where Do We Go from Here? (2018). https://googleprojectzero.blogspot.com/2018/12/adventures-in-video-conferencing-part-5.html
37. Silvanovich, N.: Zooming in on Zero-click Exploits (2022). https://googleprojectzero.blogspot.com//2022/01/zooming-in-on-zero-click-exploits.html
38. Reuters Staff. Google bans Zoom software from employee laptops. REUTERS (2020). https://www.reuters.com/article/us-google-zoom-idUSKCN21Q32V
39. Sudhodanan, A., Paverd, A.: Pre-hijacked accounts: an empirical study of security failures in user account creation on the web. In: Proceedings of the 31st USENIX Security Symposium (USENIX Security 2022), pp. 1795–1812, Boston, MA (2022). USENIX Association. https://www.usenix.org/conference/usenixsecurity22/presentation/sudhodanan
40. Thodupunoori, R.: Part-1 Dive into Zoom Applications (2021). https://rakesh-thodupunoori.medium.com/part-1-dive-into-zoom-applications-d70f3de53ec5
41. Thodupunoori, R.: Part 2: Dive into Zoom Applications (2021). https://rakesh-thodupunoori.medium.com/part-2-dive-into-zoom-applications-1b01091345c1
42. Tudor, C.: The Impact of the COVID-19 pandemic on the global web and video conferencing SaaS market. Electronics 11, 2633 (2022)
43. Vegeris, O.: "Important, Spoofing" - zero-click, wormable, cross-platform remote code execution in Microsoft Teams (2020). https://github.com/oskarsve/ms-teams-rce
44. Vela, E.: Zoom: XSS in Zoom.us Signup Flow (2020). https://github.com/google/security-research/security/advisories/GHSA-fpgp-vrmv-v8f2/
45. Vengattil, M., Roulette, J.: Elon Musk's SpaceX bans Zoom over privacy concerns -memo. REUTERS (2020). https://www.reuters.com/article/us-spacex-zoom-video-commn-idUSKBN21J71H
46. Website of the conference of ministers of education (Kultusministerkonferenz). Digitale Lernangebote [Digital Learning Tools] (2023). https://www.kmk.org/themen/bildung-in-der-digitalen-welt/distanzlernen.html
47. Wittmann, L.: Visavid - Datensicherheit im Warteraum [Visavid - Data Security in the Waiting Room]. Medium (2021). https://lilithwittmann.medium.com/visavid-datensicherheit-im-warteraum-77c184c1d58a
48. Zoom Video Communications, Inc., Vulnerability Disclosure Policy (2021). https://www.zoomgov.com/docs/en-us/vulnerability-disclosure-policy.html

An In-Depth Analysis of the Code-Reuse Gadgets Introduced by Software Obfuscation

Naiqian Zhang, Zheyun Feng, and Dongpeng Xu[✉]

University of New Hampshire, Durham, NH 03824, USA
{Naiqian.Zhang,Zheyun.Feng,Dongpeng.Xu}@unh.edu

Abstract. Software obfuscation techniques are commonly employed to resist malicious reverse engineering. However, recent studies indicate that obfuscation introduces potential vulnerabilities susceptible to code-reuse attacks because the number of code-reuse gadgets in obfuscated programs significantly increases. Understanding how different obfuscation techniques contribute to the emergence of these code-reuse gadgets is crucial for developing secure obfuscation schemes that minimize the risk of code-reuse attacks, but no existing study has investigated this problem.

To address this knowledge gap, we present a comprehensive study on the impact of software obfuscation on code-reuse gadgets in programs. Firstly, we collect and analyze metrics data of gadgets obtained from a benchmark of programs obfuscated using various techniques. By examining the statistical results, we establish quantitative and qualitative relationships between each obfuscation technique and the resulting gadgets. Our key findings reveal how obfuscation techniques introduce significant code-reuse attack risks to a gadget set from different measurement schemes. Secondly, we delve into the underlying mechanisms of each obfuscation technique and elucidate why they contribute to generating specific types of gadgets. Lastly, we propose a mitigation strategy that combines low-risk obfuscation methods. Evaluation results demonstrate that our mitigation strategy effectively reduces the risks associated with code-reuse attacks without compromising obfuscation strength.

Keywords: Software Obfuscation · Code-reuse Attack · Gadget

1 Introduction

Software obfuscation has become increasingly important in defending against malicious reverse engineering, with various obfuscation methods being designed and implemented in both academic prototypes and industrial tools [12,20,24, 25,33]. Despite their widespread usage, the security aspects of these obfuscation techniques have received limited attention. One significant risk arises from the insertion of opaque code by obfuscators, which is often treated as a black box due to its lack of comprehensibility from the users' perspective. Previous research has shown that obfuscation can increase the number of gadgets in obfuscated binaries [18,19]. However, the underlying mechanisms of obfuscation and the reasons behind the surge of these gadgets have not been extensively explored.

In this paper, we conduct an in-depth examination of selected popular obfuscation methods and their impacts on introducing code-reuse gadgets. We first apply various obfuscation techniques to a program benchmark and measure different characteristics of the code-reuse gadgets within the obfuscated programs. To compare, we focus on three aspects: the code-reuse gadget set's quantity, type, and risk. We assign scores to each obfuscation method based on these metrics and generate a prioritized list. Consequently, we propose a mitigation strategy that combines one low-risk obfuscation method with another for the protected programs. Through evaluation, we demonstrate that this strategy significantly reduces the number of exploitable code-reuse gadgets while maintaining the same level of obfuscation complexity.

In our study, we obfuscate 900 programs from an obfuscation benchmark [3] with four well-known obfuscators in academia and industry, namely Tigress [12], Obfuscator LLVM [20], VMProtect [33] and Code Virtualizer [24]. These obfuscators collectively implement a wide range of prevalent obfuscation methods. Each program is built with a unique obfuscation configuration to facilitate our incremental analysis. By comparing gadget metrics between the unobfuscated programs and obfuscated programs employing a specific obfuscation technique, we gain insights into the inner mechanisms of each obfuscation method and their impacts on code-reuse gadgets. Our findings reveal that different obfuscation techniques pose varying levels of code-reuse attack risks to the original program. To summarize, our contributions are as follows:

- First, we conduct a systematic study that sheds light on how obfuscation techniques introduce code-reuse gadgets. Our study employs a combined measurement scheme encompassing quantitative, qualitative, exploitable metrics and code-reuse attack risk assessment.
- Second, we conduct an in-depth analysis of each obfuscation method, unveiling the key factors that influence the presence of code-reuse gadgets and gadget sets. We develop a comprehensive assessment mechanism that ranks the obfuscation methods based on their code-reuse risks.
- Third, we propose a mitigation strategy to minimize the risk of code-reuse attacks without compromising the complexity and strength of obfuscation. Evaluation results demonstrate that employing low-risk obfuscation techniques, or multiple instances of them on the original program, reduces the code-reuse attack risk compared to high-risk obfuscation methods, all while preserving the complexity of obfuscation.

2   Background

To provide a better understanding of our work, we begin by introducing the background of code obfuscation techniques and the fundamentals of code-reuse attacks.

2.1   Code Obfuscation

Code obfuscation involves transforming a normal program into a semantically equivalent but more complex form. This transformation makes it challenging to comprehend the obfuscated code, and as a result, obfuscation techniques are widely employed to protect proprietary code from reverse analysis by hackers. Popular obfuscation tools, such as Tigress, Obfuscator-LLVM, VMProtect, and Code Virtualizer, incorporate a range of obfuscation schemes, as shown in Table 1.

Table 1. Obfuscation schemes in popular obfuscation tools.

Type	Description
Control Flow Flattening	Transform a program's control flow into a flat dispatch structure inside a loop, where a variable decides the program's next step [22]. The code inside the loop is in a linear style without any branches.
Instruction Substitution	Replace one instruction with a more complex but equivalent form, which may bring additional instructions to perform intermediate steps. For example, $x \mid y \Rightarrow (x \wedge y) \mid (x \oplus y)$
Bogus Control Flow	Insert dummy path conditions without changing the original program semantics. Usually, the dummy branch is randomly filled up with garbage codes.
Virtualization	Create a custom virtual machine (VM) and then translate the original program into the VM's bytecode, so the program's behaviors hide in the complicated VM execution. Virtualization has been recognized as one of the most complex obfuscation methods [23, 26].
Just-In-Time Dynamic	Translate the program into a sequence of customized intermediate representative instructions. This new code part will be dynamically compiled into machine code at run-time.
Self-Modification	Insert special code patterns into the program, which can change other parts with the same functionality of the program during run-time.
Encode Components	Replace integers, integer variables, integer arithmetic, and string literal to more complicated and complex expressions and opaque representations. It looks similar to Instruction Substitution but has a wider range of action objects

2.2 Code-Reuse Attack

In recent years, code-reuse attacks have emerged as a highly dangerous attacking technique [9]. In such attacks, attackers search for short code snippets, known as gadgets, within a normal program, which are combined to achieve malicious objectives. This technique originated from traditional return-to-libc attacks. Shacham demonstrated that a gadget set used in code-reuse attacks is Turing-complete, which is theoretically capable of performing any malicious behavior [31]. Subsequent research has further extended code-reuse attacks from various perspectives. For instance, gadgets can involve complex control flow structures [4], and dispatch gadgets [16,17], multiple architectures [8,13], call-preceded [9], and jump-preceded [11] gadgets have been introduced.

Practical code-reuse attacks typically aim to gain control of the victim's machine (root) or tamper the permissions of specific files. Table 2 lists commonly triggered system calls during malicious activities. Furthermore, exploiting code-reuse attacks necessitates the presence of at least one known memory write vulnerability in the victim program, allowing the attacker to write the payload to the stack. Attackers leverage these vulnerabilities as starting points for code-reuse attacks, which can exist in the original, obfuscated, or library code. Several existing tools [2,5,6,10,15,27,34] aid in the identification of these memory vulnerabilities. However, the focus of this work does not include the process of locating these memory vulnerabilities.

Table 2. The system calls commonly used in code-reuse attacks.

Syscall	Description
execve	Trigger a shell-like /bin/bash on the victim machine.
mmap mremap	Map a file controlled by attackers as executable and then redirect the execution to that tampered file.
mprotect	Mark a page that includes content controlled by an attacker as executable and then redirects the program counter toward that tampered page.
fchown fchmod	Change permissions of a file

3 Code-Reuse Gadgets Introduced by Obfuscation

Characterizing the impact of obfuscation on code-reuse attack gadget sets presents a considerable challenge. While modern obfuscation methods introduce a large number of gadgets into the code-reuse attack gadget sets, there is a lack of prior research that offers precise analysis and conclusions in this field. Therefore, a detailed investigation of the gadgets introduced by obfuscation is necessary.

In this section, we thoroughly examine the listed obfuscation methods and analyze the principles and implementation details behind each. Subsequently, we apply these methods to the programs within an obfuscation benchmark, generating code-reuse gadget sets for each program. We then observe and compare the number and types of gadgets in each set before and after applying the obfuscation method. Furthermore, we conducted in-depth research on existing works and discovered that they primarily focused on analyzing the number of gadgets in the gadget set resulting from obfuscation. However, to better reflect the true potential risk, combining this analysis with qualitative assessments of the gadget sets and the searching strategies employed by existing code-reuse generation tools is essential. To provide a comprehensive measurement of the impact of obfuscation, we implemented a standardized measurement system that examines the code-reuse gadget sets before and after obfuscation. This system analyzes the gadget sets from multiple perspectives, including quantitative assessment, qualitative assessment, and identification of exploitable gadgets. This comprehensive analysis enables us to assess whether a gadget set carries a higher risk of code-reuse attacks.

3.1 Benchmark and Obfuscation Selection

We carefully selected 100 C programs from an obfuscation benchmark [3], ensuring diversity in program size, complexity, and functionality. When choosing the benchmark and programs, we considered the aspects of Ground Truth and Applicability. This benchmark encompasses a wide range of C programs and includes scripts that allow us to obfuscate the programs using our selected obfuscators. Notably, the "basic algorithm" and "small programs" sets within the benchmark consist of simple and basic programs that align well with the ground truth. Hence, we utilize them as the benchmark for our analysis.

We employed four popular obfuscation tools mentioned in the previous section to conduct our study. We follow three criteria to pick the obfuscation variants to make the study comprehensive:

1. The variant is offered by at least one of the selected tools.
2. The variant can be successfully performed on all the benchmark programs without errors or run-time crashes.
3. The variant can transform any snippets inside the program rather than only specific ones.

We select seven obfuscation techniques introduced at Table 1 based on these criteria. For virtualization, we performed both the source and binary code obfuscation. We generated 900 distinct obfuscation variants for the benchmark programs by integrating each chosen technique from the selected obfuscators. Our analysis did not consider the programs as statically or dynamically linked libraries. Generally, attackers can utilize gadgets included in library code when mapping the program's memory address at runtime.

To examine the impact of each obfuscation method on code-reuse attack gadget sets, we compared the different obfuscation variants against the original binary without any obfuscation applied. We applied only one obfuscation method to the original program strictly adhering to the default configurations at a time and did not consider overlapping multiple obfuscation methods. For each original program and obfuscation variant, we scanned the gadget set of each binary and conducted a detailed analysis. We categorized all gadgets from each gadget set into two groups: useful and useless gadgets. The classification was based on whether existing code-reuse exploitation construction tools could utilize a gadget. Useful gadgets refer to those utilized by existing exploitation tools to form valid gadget chains for code-reuse attacks, while useless gadgets have never been incorporated into gadget chains by any existing exploitation tools.

3.2   Gadget Measurement

Increment Rate. This quantitative metric assesses how the number of gadgets increases as a result of different obfuscation methods. We identify and calculate the new gadgets introduced by obfuscation that are not in the original binary. A code-reuse gadget refers to a binary code sequence ending with a control-flow transfer instruction such as `ret`, `jmp`, `call`, `syscall`, etc. The `jmp` instruction can further be categorized into conditional and unconditional jumps. After obfuscation, we count the number of gadgets and calculate the rate of increase for each gadget set. It is important to note that gadgets which remain semantically unchanged but are relocated to a new memory address after obfuscation are not considered as increased.

Exploitability. To better assess the code-reuse attack risk of a gadget set, we introduce the exploitable metric, which measures whether a gadget can be considered useful or if it poses a code-reuse attack risk to the gadget set. This metric determines the number of gadgets within a gadget set that automated search tools can utilize. Generally, more exploitable gadgets in a gadget set indicate a greater risk of code-reuse attacks.

To investigate existing code-reuse exploitation tools as well as their implementation details and search efficacy, we categorize them based on different searching methods into three aspects, as shown in Table 3. To guarantee the comprehensiveness of our exploitable metric, we select the code-reuse attacks searching tools following three criteria:

1. The tool is publicly available and easily used in the original and obfuscated programs.
2. The tool can generate valid chains that can perform at least one type of attack shown in Table 2.

Table 3. Methods of searching code-reuse attacks and representative tools.

Method	Description
Pattern matching and hard-coded searching	ROPGadget [28] and Ropper [29] both apply this strategy. They search for a bunch of known gadget patterns and require hard-coded rules based on built-in exploitation templates to chain gadgets together.
Symbolic execution and exploration	Angrop [1] and ROPium [32] identifies gadgets via symbolic execution. They maintain an intermediate representation of gadgets, which matches the symbolic execution result with the pre- defined semantic rules of the gadgets and chains of those gadgets together based on the attacker's specifications.
Program Synthesis	As the state-of-the-art exploitation technique, SGC [30] synthesizes logical formulas to represent the gadget chains between the starting and ending program states. Then it uses an SMT solver to verify the gadget chain is feasible

3. The tool can clearly show all gadgets in a human-readable format in the attack chains.

We considered these criteria on each type of searching method in Table 3 and selected the representative tools from each category: ROPGadget, Angrop, and SGC. Then, we conducted analysis on the programs within the obfuscation benchmark using these selected tools, examining the chaining results. By counting the number of gadgets comprising the gadget chains found by each existing tool within each unobfuscated program, we identified the types of gadgets contributing more effectively to the code-reuse exploitation process. Figure 1 illustrates representative gadget chains discovered by each type of existing automated search tool. We observed that many of these gadget chains included gadgets performing assignments, such as those with **pop** and **mov** instructions. Therefore, gadgets with these instructions are considered exploitable gadgets.

Expressivity and Quality. In measuring the quality and expressivity of a gadget set, we selected a method proposed by Brown et al. [7]. For gadget set expressivity, this method evaluates the power of gadget set expressivity based on three aspects: practical ROP exploits, ASLR-proof practical ROP exploits, and Turing completeness. At a specific level of expressivity, a gadget set must contain at least one gadget that fulfills the required computational criteria for each of these aspects. For example, achieving practical ROP exploits necessitates the presence of gadgets that assign targeted values to specific registers, store values to memory, and trigger system calls, among others.

Regarding gadget set quality, the metric from Brown et al. focuses on the functionality of each gadget. This qualitative measurement assesses whether a

```
Gadget 1: 0x483635:
mov qword ptr[rsi],rax
ret
Gadget 2: 0x4106fe:
pop rsi
ret
Gadget 3: 0x452f37:
pop rax
ret
Gadget 4: 0x447d19:
xor rax, rax
ret
Gadget 5: 0x478ca0:
add rax, 1
ret
Gadget 6: 0x401752:
pop rdi
ret
Gadget 7: 0x4106fe:
pop rsi
ret
Gadget 8: 0x40165f:
pop rdx
ret
Gadget 9: 0x401213:
syscall
```

```
Gadget 1: 0x4f235d:
pop rax
ret
Gadget 2: 0x628f79:
pop rcx
ret
Gadget 3: 0x4c02ab:
mov dword ptr[rcx-0x7f],rax
ret
Gadget 4: 0x4f235d:
pop rax
ret
Gadget 5: 0x628f79:
pop rcx
ret
Gadget 6: 0x4c02ab:
mov dword ptr[rcx-0x7f],rax
ret
Gadget 7: 0x5be23e:
pop rdi
ret
Gadget 8: 0x514f31:
pop rdx
ret
Gadget 9: 0x74f9ff:
pop rsi
ret
Gadget 10: 0x401213:
syscall
```

```
Gadget 1: 0x48b0c6:
pop rbx
pop rbp
pop r12
pop r13
ret
Gadget 2: 0x418f47:
mov rax,r12
pop rbx
pop rbp
pop r12
pop r13
ret
Gadget 3: 0x473cbe:
mov rdx,r12
mov rsi,rbp
mov rdi,rbx
call qword ptr[r13+0x38]
```

(a) ROPGadget   (b) Angrop   (c) SGC

Fig. 1. Gadget chains built by existing code-reuse chain searching tools.

gadget exhibits side effects, such as conditional branches, additional memory or register operations, or stack pointer-related manipulations, which can affect exploit construction. For example, consider the gadget {add eax, 1; ret;}; it contains no intermediate instructions and thus has no side effect. On the contrary, the gadgets {add esi, ecx; xor eax, eax; mov dword ptr[edx], r si; ret;} have side effects. The instruction xor eax, eax; overwrites the value in eax, impacting the result set up by the attacker. Thus, gadgets without side effects and with single functionality are easier to exploit.

For our work, we employed the Gadget Set Analyzer (GSA) [7], a state-of-the-art tool for measuring gadget set properties. GSA calculates the gadget set expressivity by inspecting the first instruction of each gadget to determine if it satisfies the computational criteria for any of the three aspects mentioned earlier. The expressivity is then expressed as the total number of satisfied classes for each aspect. If the expressivity of a gadget set increases in one or more aspects, it is considered a potentially risky outcome. Regarding gadget set quality, GSA assigns a score to each gadget based on the presence of intermediate instructions that introduce side effects. The average quality score of the entire gadget set is then computed. If the score of the transformed gadget set surpasses that of the original gadget set, it indicates a potentially risky outcome.

Overall Risk. Lastly, in our gadget set measurement, we combine the aforementioned three measurement standards to derive a summarized metric for assessing the code-reuse attack risk of a gadget set resulting from different obfuscation transformations. We propose a formula

$$Risk_{CRA} = \frac{N_{(Chain\_Related)}}{N(Gadgets)} + V_{Expressivity} + V_{Quality}$$

that considers several statistical values related to the measurement variables of a gadget set. The risk value of the code-reuse attack gadget set is defined as the sum of three components: the expressivity value (sum of all three aspects), the quality value, and the ratio of the number of exploitable gadgets to the total number of gadgets in the set. This formula enables us to measure the code-reuse attack risk introduced by an obfuscation method to the gadget set.

4   Study Results

4.1   Gadget Quantity

We observed a substantial increase in the number of gadgets after obfuscation, as depicted in Fig. 2. A comparison of gadget sets between the original program and obfuscated programs of various transformation types revealed an average increase of approximately 43 times in the number of gadgets. ROPGadget was used to calculate the gadget count due to its superior gadget-searching capabilities among existing tools. This highlights the significant impact of obfuscation methods on gadget sets' quantity and composition, introducing numerous different kinds of exploitable gadgets into the original programs.

4.2   Gadget Exploitability

We employed existing exploitation tools, as mentioned in Sect. 3, to search for code-reuse gadget chains in both the original and obfuscated programs. Subsequently, we analyzed which gadgets were frequently used in the gadget chains. Notably, for specific obfuscation methods, there was an apparent increase in the number of commonly used gadgets in the chains. Successful code-reuse attacks often involve triggering system-level calls such as *execve, mprotect, fchown*, and *mmap*. Exploitation tools must find appropriate gadgets to assign parameter values for these system calls. For instance, assuming the attacker intends to call *execve* to spawn a shell, the x86-64 calling convention requires assigning the system call number $0 \times 3b$ to the `rax` register, followed by assigning values to `rsi`, `rdi` and `rdx` as the arguments of *execve*.

By running existing tools for gadget chain searching on our test set, we collected over 300 chains, most of which exhibited similar patterns frequently used in gadget compositions mentioned in Sect. 3. The common exploit objective was to trigger the `execve` system call and spawn a shell.

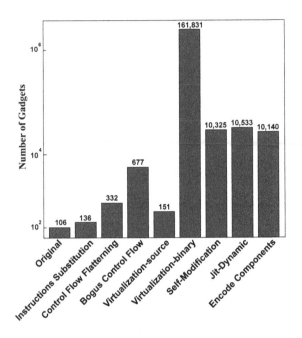

Fig. 2. Comparison of the number of gadgets from the original program and different types of obfuscated programs.

To gain a better understanding of the gadgets involved in the gadget chains, we tallied the number of exploitable gadgets in each gadget set and calculated their proportion within the set. This metric served as a crucial aspect for evaluating changes in gadget sets before and after obfuscation, as shown in Table 4. Most obfuscation methods led to an increase in the number of exploitable gadgets, indicating a worrisome sign for program protection against code-reuse attacks.

4.3   Gadget Quality

Our experiments revealed that specific obfuscation methods, particularly those involving opaque predicates or complex expression modifications like *Encode Components*, tended to increase the expressivity and quality value of a gadget set. The complete results are presented in the second and third columns of Table 5. Higher values in expressivity and quality indicate a greater range of gadget utility but an elevated risk of code-reuse attacks.

4.4   Code-Reuse Attack Risk

Based on the metric formula we defined for measuring the risk of code-reuse gadget sets and the results from our experiments, we ranked the risk value of each obfuscation method from low to high. A higher value indicates a greater risk posed by the respective obfuscation technique. The detailed risk values for each method are displayed in the fourth column of Table 5.

Table 4. The exploitable gadgets' number and the rates included in each gadget set of the original program and different obfuscated transformations. If the number of exploitable gadgets increases, this is considered a risk-increasing result.

Obfuscation	#Exploitable Gadgets	Rates
Original	36.25	30.5%
Instructions Substitution	41.47	31.4%
Control Flow Flattening	87.37	28.2%
Bogus Control Flow	101.25	16.1%
Virtualization-Source	58.45	38.9%
Virtualization-Binary	44625.36	27.6%
Self-Modification	2769.68	26.7%
Jit-Dynamic	2768.30	26.2%
Encode Components	2731.88	26.9%

Table 5. The second and third columns represent each gadget set's average expressivity and quality values for the original program and different obfuscated transformations. An obfuscation method that increases the expressivity value and decreases the quality value signifies an increase in risk. The fourth column presents the code-reuse attack risk value for each obfuscation method.

Obfuscation	Expressivity	Quality	Risk Value
Original	(4.125 / 6.125 / 2.175)	1.399	14.129
Instructions Substitution	(4.125 / 6.500 / 2.275)	1.322	14.536
Control Flow Flattening	(4.125 / 6.275 / 2.125)	1.263	14.070
Bogus Control Flow	(4.725 / 7.250 / 4.475)	1.068	17.679
Virtualization-Source	(4.950 / 8.450 / 3.025)	1.274	18.088
Virtualization-Binary	(44.950 / 78.450 / 53.025)	9.883	186.584
Self-Modification	(7.750 / 26.525 / 12.150)	1.786	48.460
Jit-Dynamic	(7.950 / 27.8 / 12.775)	1.798	50.585
Encode Components	(7.975 / 27.025 / 12.50)	1.809	49.578

5   The Anatomy of the Obfuscations and Gadgets

In light of the experimental results, this section offers an in-depth exploration and analysis of the varying gadget sets that correspond to each type of obfuscation method. We conducted a meticulous differential analysis of the binary code and the associated gadget sets, comparing singularly obfuscated variants against their original program counterparts. In addition, our investigation delves deeper into the implementation mechanisms of selected obfuscation techniques to comprehend the ways in which these techniques reshape the composition of gadget sets and the resulting impact on program security.

5.1   Instructions Substitution

Implementation Details. Instructions Substitution replaces binary operators with more complex sequences of instructions that have equivalent functionalities, such as arithmetic or Boolean operators. In Obfuscator-LLVM, this obfuscation technique supports integer operations including addition and subtraction, along with Boolean operators such as AND, OR, and XOR. For any given operator, there exist multiple equivalent expressions. The detailed implementation rules are shown in Table 6. The random selection of one of these equivalent expressions introduces a desirable diversity in the resulting binary instruction substitution. Moreover, instructions substitution significantly complicates the task of automatically searching for specific machine instruction patterns which are commonly used in symmetric ciphers such as XOR more difficult [20].

Table 6. The implementation rules of Instructions Substitution in Obfuscator-LLVM. X, Y, Z, and K are all integers.

Operator	Modified Equivalent Instructions
x = y + z	x = y - (-z)
	x = -(-y + (-z))
	x = y + k; x += z; x -= k;
	x = y - k; x += z; x += k;
x = y - z	x = y + (-z)
	x = y + k; x -= z; a -= k;
	x = y - k; x -= z; x += k;
x = y & z	x = (y ^!z) & y
x = y | z	x = (y & z) | (y ^z)
x = y ^z	x = (!y & z) | (y & !z)

Root Causes and Discussion. *Instructions Substitution* resulted in an increase of nearly 30% in new gadget generation compared to the original program. Those freshly introduced gadgets barely affected the number of exploitable gadgets but slightly increased the value of gadget quality and expressivity. We observed that a majority of the newly introduced gadgets are tied to arithmetic or logic operators. It introduces novel operators at the assembly level as it replaces one binary operator with a sequence of instructions. For instance, an obfuscated program that substitutes the expression {x = y + z} with {x = -(-y + (-z))}. This operation not only utilizes addition but also subtraction to accomplish the operation. As a result, a new gadget {add al, 0 × 3d; sbb al, 0 × 30; ret} is added to the gadget set. Gadgets of this nature can significantly increase the expressivity of the gadget set, but they do not contribute to the generation of gadget chains.

5.2 Control Flow Flattening

Implementation Details. Control Flow Flattening manipulated the principal structure of the source code into a format that conceals the targets of branches. Initially, each function was broken up into basic blocks. These blocks, regardless of their original nesting levels, are then arrayed in parallel within a switch-case statement. Each basic block resides in a distinct case structure, and the entire switch structure is encapsulated within a loop statement. The order of control flow is guaranteed by a control variable, which is assigned at the termination of each basic block as the predicates of the finishing the loop and selection of switch statement. Figure 3b illustrates the obfuscated program that has applied the control flow flattening method to the original program shown in Fig. 3a. As can be observed, all basic blocks from the original program are at the same level in the obfuscated program, thus effectively concealing the loop structure of the original program.

Root Causes and Discussion. As demonstrated in Sect. 4, *Control Flow Flattening* contributed to a 213% increase in the introduction of new gadgets compared to the original program. Those newly introduced gadgets subtly impact the gadget set's exploitable gadgets, quality, and expressivity. The count of exploitable gadgets doubles, whereas the values of expressivity and quality remain unchanged or even decrease. We observed a substantial number of gadgets ending with a direct jump being introduced into the gadget set, these gadgets account for almost all of the newly introduced gadgets, even serving as the ending instructions for the exploitable gadget. The situation is directly related to the implementation mechanism of this transformation. *Control Flow Flattening* generally employs a Switch-Case structure to flatten an entire function's control flow graph. At the assembly level, a Switch-Case statement usually relies on a jump table and fills in the case names. It requires direct jumps with conditions to decide the control flow's direction. Consequently, the gadget set

```
1   int main()
2   {
3       int Var = 1;
4       while(Var != 0){
5           switch(Var){
6           case 1:{
7               int a = 1, b = 0;
8               Var = 2;
9               break;
10              }
11          case 2:{
12              if(a <= 50){
13                      Var = 3;
14              } else{
15                      Var = 0;
16              }
17              break;
18              }
19          case 3:{
20              b += a;
21              a ++;
22              Var = 2;
23              break;
24              }
25          }
26      }
27  }
```

```
1   int main()
2   {
3       int a = 1;
4       int b = 0;
5
6       while(a <= 50){
7               b += a;
8               a ++;
9       }
10  }
```

(a)   (b)

Fig. 3. The sample programs before and after using Control Flow Flattening.

with this transformation introduces many gadgets ending with a direct jump. However, drawing upon our experience and corroborated by the state-of-the-art exploitation tools, we find that these newly introduced gadgets cannot be harnessed for constructing gadget chains for code-reuse attacks.

5.3 Bogus Control Flow

Implementation Details. *Bogus Control Flow* involves the insertion of spurious control flows within a function to reconstruct its corresponding control flow graph. The outcome is a chaotic control flow graph encompassing three irrelevant types of branches, all of which are shielded by opaque predicates. (1). The dead branch that is never engaged; (2). The superfluous branches that are invariably engaged; (3). The branches that are sporadically engaged. The first type involves the inclusion of a counterfeit block (which could be arbitrary code) within a basic block, giving the impression that it might be executed later, but in reality, it is never executed. The second type involves the insertion of a true predicate midway through a basic block, creating the illusion that the original block is only intermittently executed. The third type involves the insertion of a variable predicate which occasionally directs the execution left or right, with the resulting paths being identical regardless of the direction chosen by the predicate.

Root Causes and Discussion. *Bogus Control Flow* resulted in a 538% increase in new gadgets compared to the original program. Those newly introduced gadgets augment the count of exploitable gadgets as well as the value of expressivity. However, most of those gadgets end with direct jumps, which cannot be used to generate a gadget chain and thus have no impact on the quality value. Furthermore, this transformation also brings tons of Control Flow Graph (CFG) nodes to the original CFG. These spurious CFG nodes necessitate a significant number of direct jumps with conditions to facilitate their integration into the original CFG. Consequently, the gadgets introduced via *Bogus Control Flow* scarcely contribute to increasing the code-reuse attack risk.

5.4   Virtualization

Implementation Details. *Virtualization* involves the conversion of selected portions of code into bytecode, defined by a specialized virtual instruction set architecture. The bytecode is then emulated by an embedded interpreter on the actual machine during runtime. More specifically, the original code of a program is initially transformed into bytecode as per a custom virtual instruction set. Subsequently, the bytecode interpreter carries out execution following a Fetch-Decode-Dispatch procedure. The fetch step involves the retrieval of the next bytecode instruction, the decode step is responsible for decoding the instruction and its operands (if any), and the dispatch sets up the execution environment and calls the correct handlers.

Root Causes and Discussion. The *Virtualization* offered by Tigress led to the introduction of nearly 50% more new gadgets than the original program, meanwhile, the quality and the expressivity of the gadget sets remained unaltered. Given that Tigress implements the transformation at the source code level, we carefully examined the obfuscated source code and found that the bytecode and handlers are appended to the source code prior to compilation. Figure 4 provides an example of the bytecode in the obfuscated source file. Subsequently, a `switch-case` based dispatch structure is utilized to interpret the bytecode and map the bytecode to corresponding handlers. Aside from introducing a few gadgets with direct jumps following the dispatch process, this transformation in Tigress neither alters the control flow of the original program nor complicates the operation of individual instruction. As a result, no gadgets with practical functions are introduced.

For comparison, we also performed binary-level virtualization on the same benchmark using Code Virtualizer [24], a commercial software obfuscation product developed by Oreans Technologies. The binary-level virtualization brings tons of new gadgets, resulting in an increase of 1500 times more new gadgets than the original program. This tremendous increase is attributable to the binary-level virtualization embedding the entire virtual machine, its handler set, and the translated bytecode from the original code into the obfuscated program. Those components are equivalent to adding a complete virtual machine program to the original program, which greatly boosts the number of gadgets as well as the expressivity and quality values of the gadget sets. Therefore, binary-level virtualization poses greater code-reuse attack risks compared to source-code-level virtualization.

```
1   enum ops {
2     Return = 249, Store = 242, Formal = 183,
3     Plus = 178, Goto = 62, Load = 89, Local = 126
4   };
5
6   unsigned char bytecode[31]  = {
7     Formal,1,0,0,0,Load,Formal,0,0,0,0,Load,Plus,
8     Local,0,0,0,0,Store,Goto,4,0,0,0,Local,8,0,0,0,
9     Load,Return };
```

Fig. 4. The bytecode in Tigress-obfuscated source file.

5.5 Just-In-Time Dynamic

Implementation Details. Tigress incorporated the *Just-In-Time* (JIT) dynamic techniques for obfuscation, which is implemented atop the MyJit library [21]. This transformation converts a function F into a new function F' by integrating a sequence of intermediate code instructions. Upon execution of F', it dynamically compiles function F into machine code. Essentially, this technique generates machine code during run-time and then executes it. Figure 5 illustrates an example of an obfuscated program, which we utilize to describe the JIT dynamic procedure. Initially, the program constructs a new instance of the JIT compiler by invoking jit_init() on line 6. It then adds the intermediate code by calling jit_add_op(). Next, the JIT compiler translates the intermediate code into actual machine code by calling jit_generation_code(). Ultimately, the control flow is redirected to the code generated just now and the execution begins.

Root Causes and Discussion. *JIT Dynamic* results in a hundredfold increase in new gadgets compared to the original program, marking a substantial rise. The value of expressivity and quality also experience a significant rise. The implementation of JIT Dynamic id is dependent on a third-party library, with several functions in the library being called during the compilation and execution phases. This is equivalent to adding another new program into the original one, analogous to binary-level virtualization, thereby increasing the code-reuse attack surface of the original program. As a consequence, the gadget set contains a larger quantity of gadgets that can be used to construct gadget chains after transformation. Additionally, the gadget set exhibits higher expressivity and includes a greater number of gadgets with side effects.

```
 1  int obf_target(int x, int y) {
 2      ...
 3      //First, initialization
 4      static int (*_obf_target)(int x , int y) ;
 5      int result;
 6      p = jit_init();
 7      jit_add_prolog(p, & _obf_target, 0);
 8      jit_add_op();
 9      jit_add_op();
10      ...
11      //Second, compilation
12      jit_generate_code(p);
13      ...
14      //Third, execution
15      result = (*_obf_target)(x, y);
16      return (result);
17  }
```

Fig. 5. JIT Dynamic implementation example in Tigress.

5.6   Self-modification

Implementation Details. *Self-Modification* aims to render functions self modifying during runtime. Typically, *Self-Modification* can be achieved by encrypting, encoding, or embedding certain parts of the code pattern into the original program, or by altering the program's execution path when it's running. Tigress amalgamates self-modification templates with two different types of transformations. One is the binary arithmetic expressions and comparisons, which inserts a binary code template at the top of the function and uses the template for modification. The other combines code virtualization and flattening, proving particularly effective after the introduction of indirect branches. Those indirect branches are transformed into other byte sequences that correspond to the direct jumps during runtime. This modification effectively thwarts deobfuscation methods that solely search for indirect branches, which have been removed from the original code.

Root Causes and Discussion. *Self-Modification* also results in an increase of new gadgets by a factor of 100 compared to the original program, with the value of quality and expressivity of the gadget set also increasing. This transformation inserts abundance of pre-defined code patterns into the obfuscated source code. Although these patterns are randomly employed during compilation, they remain attached, thereby enhancing the diversity of the original code and bringing more gadgets and higher risks.

5.7   Encode Components

Implementation Details. *Encode Components* comprises three components: encode literals, encode arithmetic, and encode data. The encode literals obfuscates integer literals (such as 100) and string literals (such as "100"), replacing them with opaque expressions or a function that is generated during runtime. The encode arithmetic substitutes integer arithmetic with more intricate and convoluted expressions based on certain fixed patterns. This means that for each operator, there are numerous possible encoding styles within this transformation, which are selected randomly. For example, Fig. 6 shows how an expression of integer addition can be replaced with a random Mixed Boolean-Arithmetic (MBA) expression of higher complexities, yielding the same arithmetic results. The encode data targets integer variables, altering them to a non-standard data representation with the aim of concealing a variable's real value until it needs to be displayed. Moreover, if a variable is encoded, all variables associated with it will also be encoded. For instance, a random integer variable v can be replaced

```
1  int main(int x, int y) {
2      int x = 0;
3      int y = 5;
4      int z = x + y;
5      return 0;
6  }
```

(a) Before

```
1   int main(int x, int y) {
2       int x ;
3       int y ;
4       int z ;
5       x = 0;
6       y = 5;
7       z = ((x | y) << 1)
8           - (x ^ y);
9       return (0);
10  }
```

(b) After

Fig. 6. Encode Arithmetic Transformation.

with $v' =$ a * v + b. Figure 7 demonstrates the difference before and after this transformation. It can be observed that the real values of variable x and z are both obscured.

```
1  int main(int x, int y) {
2    int x = 5;
3    int z = x;
4    return 0;
5  }
```

```
1  int main(int x, int y) {
2    int x ;
3    int z ;
4    ...
5    x = 1583543192U;
6    z = (int )(1509654933U
7      * x - 2053070707U);
8    ...
9  }
```

        (a) Before   (b) After

Fig. 7. Encode Data Transformation.

Root Causes and Discussion. *Encode Components* results in the introduction of new gadgets at a rate 100 times greater than the original program, also escalating the quality and expressivity values of the gadget set. This transformation is analogous to *Instructions Substitution* in general, but its implementation is more advanced. Our observation of the obfuscated source code revealed the inclusion of some Just-In-Time (JIT) techniques, indicating that the entire JIT library is attached to the obfuscated binary post-compilation. This explains why *Encode Components* generates more chain-related gadgets and exhibits higher expressivity and quality values, even though it operates on the same transformation principle as *Instructions Substitution*.

6 Mitigation

In light of the code-reuse attack risk associated with each obfuscation scheme, we propose mitigation strategies in this section to counter-measure and minimize the risk without significantly compromising the obfuscation strengths. Our proposed solution is to limit the use of obfuscation schemes associated with high-risk values as much as possible while increasing the use of those with low-risk values. Additionally, to ensure the effectiveness of obfuscation while maintaining the complexity of obfuscated programs, we recommend repeated application of one low-risk obfuscation scheme or a combined use of multiple low-risk schemes.

6.1   Strategy

To this end, we designed a set of experiments to verify the correctness of our proposed solution. We first categorized the obfuscation schemes into two groups based on the risk values ranking obtained from Table 5. One group consists of low-risk value schemes: *Instructions Substitution, Control Flow Flattening, Bogus Control Flow, Virtualization(source)*; The other group includes high-risk value schemes: *Jit-Dynamic, Self-Modification, Encode Components*.

For the low-risk value group, we applied each obfuscation method to the same source program once, twice, and three times respectively, and then combined the three methods from Obfuscator-LLVM on the source program as another variant. We determined the number of times an obfuscation method was applied to the source code by adjusting the command-line parameters. For the high-risk value group, obfuscation methods were applied individually.

6.2   Evaluation

To gauge how effective our mitigation strategy restrains the growth of the code-reuse attack risk, we applied our metrics to the obfuscated programs shown in Table 7 column one. By calculating the risk values for each obfuscation variant, we evaluated the outcomes of our mitigation strategy.

The evaluation results revealed that our mitigation strategy is highly effective at diminishing the code-reuse attack risk. Applying low-risk obfuscation methods multiple times to the same original program can effectively curb the growth of the risk values of the gadget set compared to those high-risk methods, which typically have risk values nearing 50.

While focusing on the code-reuse attack risk value, we also assessed the effect of applying one obfuscation method multiple times. We used IDA Pro [14] to analyze the CFG of each variant binary based on the number of CFG nodes and verified whether the obfuscated variant could maintain the same obfuscation complexity. A program with more CFG nodes can be considered as one with higher obfuscation complexity. The results indicated that applying the low-risk obfuscation method (Control Flow Flattening used as an example here) multiple times does not diminish the complexity of the obfuscation results. The number of CFG nodes is 35, 37, and 36, respectively, corresponding to applying the obfuscation method once, twice, and three times. The original program only has 7 CFG nodes. Therefore, after multiple obfuscation iterations, the obfuscated program possesses more CFG nodes and a complex control flow, thereby better protecting it against reverse engineering. Meanwhile, the code-reuse attack risk values are 14.070, 17.567, and 14.534, respectively, corresponding to applying the obfuscation once, twice, and three times to the original program. These risk values are not as high as those of other high-risk obfuscation methods, indicating the efficacy of our mitigation strategy.

Table 7. The gadget-set-related data for each type of obfuscation method with low-risk and high-risk values. The number after the method name indicates how often this method has been applied to the original program.

Obfuscation	#Gadgets	#Exploitable	Expressivity	Quality	Risk Value
Original Program	106	36.25	(4.125/6.125/2.175)	1.399	14.129
Instructions Substitution (1)	136	41.47	(4.125/6.500/2.275)	1.322	14.536
Instructions Substitution (2)	290	44.00	(4.125/6.500/2.275)	1.093	14.144
Instructions Substitution (3)	650	114.00	(4.750/14.500/7.500)	1.028	27.953
Control Flow Flattening (1)	332	87.37	(4.125/6.275/2.125)	1.263	14.070
Control Flow Flattening (2)	455	91.50	(4.500/8.525/3.000)	1.341	17.567
Control Flow Flattening (3)	460	87.50	(4.500/6.500/2.075)	1.269	14.534
Bogus Control Flow (1)	677	101.25	(4.725/7.250/4.475)	1.068	17.679
Bogus Control Flow (2)	2,469	229.21	(5.025/8.500/6.075)	0.946	20.638
Bogus Control Flow (3)	8,573	427.27	(5.125/15.500/7.275)	0.943	28.892
Virtualization-source	151	58.45	(4.950/8.450/3.025)	1.274	18.088
Virtualization-Binary	161,831	44,625.36	(44.950/78.450/53.025)	9.883	186.584
Jit-Dynamic	10,533	2768.30	(7.950/27.8/12.775)	1.798	50.585
Self-Modification	10,325	2769.68	(7.750/26.525/12.150)	1.786	48.460
Encode Components	10,140	2731.88	(7.975/27.025/12.50)	1.809	49.578

We also conducted a comparison between applying a high-risk obfuscation method once and applying a low-risk obfuscation method multiple times. We selected the *Jit-Dynamic*, which has the highest risk value among all methods as the representative of the high-risk value group, and *Bogus Control Flow* as the representative of the low-risk value group. The comparison results showed that, despite each CFG node of the Jit-Dynamic obfuscated program having numerous instructions, it only has three nodes on its CFG. On the contrary, a program obfuscated three times with the Bogus Control Flow method has over 1,000 CFG nodes. The low-risk obfuscation method evidently contributes more obfuscation complexity than the high-risk method. Moreover, using the low-risk obfuscation method multiple times results in a code-reuse attack risk value of 14.534, which is significantly less than the risk value of 50.585 associated with applying a high-risk obfuscation method once.

From the results of our evaluation, we noticed that our mitigation strategy not only curbs the growth trend of code-reuse attack risk on obfuscated programs but also significantly increases the complexity and intensity of them. Therefore, we conclude that when applying obfuscation techniques, it is preferable to choose a method with low-risk value and apply it multiple times to the original programs, while avoiding high-risk value methods.

7   Related Work

Concerning code-reuse attacks in obfuscated programs, our research demonstrated each obfuscation method's key factors that influence the presence of code-reuse gadgets and gadget sets. One recent work Gadget-Planner [35], also sheds light on code-reuse attacks on obfuscated code, but our work differs from it.

Gadget-Planner simply compares the gadget chains before and after obfuscation and then focuses on building more complex attack chains from the obfuscated programs. However, the key point of our work is to investigate the underlying causes behind the variations in gadget chains introduced by different obfuscation methods. Our work fully exposes the attack risk by measuring the quantity, quality, and expressivity of gadget sets.

Comparatively, other similar works [18, 19] focus solely on the number of gadgets within the gadget set, using the increase in gadget count to imply potential attack risks. Our analytical approach is more comprehensive and employs a reasonable risk metric, extending beyond a simple quantitative analysis. Our work ranks the risk levels associated with different obfuscation methods and reveals the root cause of each method. Additionally, we offer solutions to mitigate these risks, making it a complete and comprehensive research endeavor.

8   Conclusion

Software obfuscation techniques have become increasingly popular for protecting the logic of programs by introducing complex data and control flow structures that make the code difficult to comprehend. However, existing research predominantly focuses on cracking and reversing obfuscated programs, neglecting the potential security risks associated with these obfuscations. To address this gap, our study provides a comprehensive analysis of popular obfuscation techniques, specifically examining their impacts on code-reuse attack vulnerabilities. We have developed a measurement framework to assess the code-reuse attack risks introduced by different obfuscation methods. Our analysis reveals that each obfuscation method introduces varying levels of code-reuse attack risks, underscoring the need for a meticulous selection of obfuscation techniques. To mitigate these risks, we propose a mitigation strategy that combines low-risk obfuscation methods, effectively reducing the code-reuse attack vulnerabilities while maintaining strong obfuscation. In conclusion, our research highlights the importance of considering the code-reuse attack risks associated with obfuscation techniques and provides valuable insights for developing secure obfuscation schemes. By adopting our proposed mitigation strategy, users can enhance the security of their software while maintaining robust obfuscation protection.

Acknowledgments. We would like to thank the anonymous reviewers and shepherd for their valuable feedback. This work was supported by NSF grants CNS-2022279 and CNS-2211905.

References

1. Angr-team: Angrop - a ROP gadget finder and chain builder. https://github.com/angr/angrop (2021)
2. Avgerinos, T., Cha, S.K., Rebert, A., Schwartz, E.J., Woo, M., Brumley, D.: Automatic exploit generation. Commun. ACM **57**(2), 74–84 (2014)
3. Banescu, S., Collberg, C., Pretschner, A.: Predicting the resilience of obfuscated code against symbolic execution attacks via machine learning. In: Proceedings of the 26th USENIX Conference on Security Symposium (USENIX Security 2017) (2017)
4. Bletsch, T., Jiang, X., Freeh, V.W., Liang, Z.: Jump-oriented programming: a new class of code-reuse attack. In: Proceedings of the 6th ACM Symposium on Information, Computer and Communications Security (AsiaCCS) (2011)
5. Böhme, M., Pham, V.T., Nguyen, M.D., Roychoudhury, A.: Directed Greybox fuzzing. In: Proceedings of the 2017 ACM SIGSAC Conference on Computer and Communications Security (2017)
6. Böhme, M., Pham, V.T., Roychoudhury, A.: Coverage-based Greybox fuzzing as markov chain. IEEE Trans. Softw. Eng. **45**(5), 489–506 (2017)
7. Brown, M.D., Pande, S.: Is less really more? towards better metrics for measuring security improvements realized through software debloating. In: 12th USENIX Workshop on Cyber Security Experimentation and Test (CSET 19) (2019)
8. Buchanan, E., Roemer, R., Shacham, H., Savage, S.: When good instructions go bad: generalizing return-oriented programming to RISC. In: Proceedings of the 15th ACM Conference on Computer and Communications Security (CCS 2008) (2008)
9. Carlini, N., Wagner, D.: ROP is still dangerous: breaking modern defenses. In: Proceedings of the 23rd USENIX Conference on Security Symposium (2014)
10. Cha, S.K., Avgerinos, T., Rebert, A., Brumley, D.: Unleashing mayhem on binary code. In: IEEE Symposium on Security and Privacy. IEEE (2012)
11. Checkoway, S., Davi, L., Dmitrienko, A., Sadeghi, A.R., Shacham, H., Winandy, M.: Return-oriented programming without returns. In: Proceedings of the 17th ACM Conference on Computer and Communications Security (2010)
12. Collberg, C.: The Tigress C Obfuscator. https://tigress.wtf
13. Francillion, A., Castelluccia, C.: Code injection attacks on harvard-architecture devices. In: CCS 2008: Proceedings of the 15th ACM Conference on Computer and Communications Security. ACM (2008)
14. Hex-Rays: IDA Pro. https://www.hex-rays.com/products/ida/
15. Hu, H., Chua, Z.L., Adrian, S., Saxena, P., Liang, Z.: Automatic generation of data-oriented exploits. In: 24th USENIX Security Symposium (USENIX Security 15) (2015)
16. Hu, H., Shinde, S., Adrian, S., Chua, Z.L., Saxena, P., Liang, Z.: Data-oriented programming: on the expressiveness of non-control data attacks. In: IEEE Symposium on Security and Privacy (SP) (2016)
17. Ispoglou, K.K., AlBassam, B., Jaeger, T., Payer, M.: Block oriented programming: automating data-only attacks. In: Proceedings of the ACM SIGSAC Conference on Computer and Communications Security (2018)
18. Joshi, H.P., Dhanasekaran, A., Dutta, R.: Impact of software obfuscation on susceptibility to return-oriented programming attacks. In: 36th IEEE Sarnoff Symposium (2015)

19. Joshi, H.P., Dhanasekaran, A., Dutta, R.: Trading off a vulnerability: does software obfuscation increase the risk of ROP attacks. J. Cyber Secur. Mobility 4(4), 305–324 (2015)
20. Junod, P., Rinaldini, J., Wehrli, J., Michielin, J.: Obfuscator-LLVM - software protection for the masses. In: Proceedings of the IEEE/ACM 1st International Workshop on Software Protection, SPRO (2015)
21. Krajca, P.: MyJit Library. http://myjit.sourceforge.net/
22. László, T., Kiss, Á.: Obfuscating C++ Programs via Control Flow Flattening. Annales Universitatis Scientarum Budapestinensis de Rolando Eötvös Nominatae, Sectio Computatorica (2009)
23. Manikyam, R., McDonald, J.T., Mahoney, W.R., Andel, T.R., Russ, S.H.: Comparing the effectiveness of commercial obfuscators against MATE attacks. In: Proceedings of the 6th Workshop on Software Security, Protection, and Reverse Engineering (SSPREW) (2016)
24. Oreans Technologies: Code Virtualizer: Total Obfuscation against Reverse Engineering. http://oreans.com/codevirtualizer.php
25. Oreans Technologies: Themida: Advanced Windows Software Protection System. https://www.oreans.com/themida.php
26. Polychronakis, M.: Reverse Engineering of Malware Emulators. (2011)
27. Rawat, S., Jain, V., Kumar, A., Cojocar, L., Giuffrida, C., Bos, H.: VUzzer: application-aware evolutionary fuzzing. In: Network and Distributed Systems Security Symposium (2017)
28. Salwan, J.: ROPgadget (2011). http://shell-storm.org/project/ROPgadget/
29. Schirra, S.: Ropper (2019). https://scoding.de/ropper/
30. Schloegel, M., Blazytko, T., Basler, J., Hemmer, F., Holz, T.: Towards automating code-reuse attacks using synthesized gadget chains. In: European Symposium on Research in Computer Security (2021)
31. Shacham, H.: The geometry of innocent flesh on the bone: return-into-libc without function calls (on the x86). In: Proceedings of the 14th ACM Conference on Computer and Communications Security (2007)
32. Souchet, A.: Ropium (2018). https://github.com/Boyan-MILANOV/ropium
33. VMProtect Software: VMProtect software protection. http://vmpsoft.com
34. Wang, Y., et al.: Revery: from proof-of-concept to exploitable. In: Proceedings of the 2018 ACM SIGSAC Conference on Computer and Communications Security (2018)
35. Zhang, N., Alden, D., Xu, D., Wang, S., Jaeger, T., Ruml, W.: No free lunch: on the increased code reuse attack surface of obfuscated programs. In: 53rd Annual IEEE/IFIP International Conference on Dependable Systems and Networks (DSN) (2023)

ProvIoT: Detecting Stealthy Attacks in IoT through Federated Edge-Cloud Security

Kunal Mukherjee[1] (ORCID), Joshua Wiedemeier[1] (ORCID), Qi Wang[2], Junpei Kamimura[3], John Junghwan Rhee[4], James Wei[1], Zhichun Li[3], Xiao Yu[3], Lu-An Tang[5],

Jiaping Gui[6], and Kangkook Jee[1]([✉]) (ORCID)

[1] The University of Texas at Dallas, Richardson, TX, USA
{kunal.mukherjee,josh.wiedemeier,james.wei,kangkook.jee}@utdallas.edu
[2] University of Illinois at Urbana-Champaign, Champaign, IL, USA
qiwang11@illinois.edu
[3] Stellar Cyber, San Jose, CA, USA
jkamimura@stellarcyber.ai, zhichun@gmail.com, yuxiaoinf@gmail.com
[4] University of Central Oklahoma, Edmond, OK, USA
jrhee2@uco.edu
[5] NEC Labs America Inc., Princeton, NJ, USA
ltang@nec-labs.com
[6] Shanghai Jiao Tong University, Shanghai, China
jgui@sjtu.edu.cn

Abstract. Internet of Things (IoT) devices have increased drastically in complexity and prevalence within the last decade. Alongside the proliferation of IoT devices and applications, attacks targeting them have gained popularity. Recent large-scale attacks such as Mirai and VPNFilter highlight the lack of comprehensive defenses for IoT devices. Existing security solutions are inadequate against skilled adversaries with sophisticated and stealthy attacks against IoT devices. Powerful provenance-based intrusion detection systems have been successfully deployed in resource-rich servers and desktops to identify advanced stealthy attacks. However, IoT devices lack the memory, storage, and computing resources to directly apply these provenance analysis techniques on the device.

This paper presents ProvIoT, a novel federated edge-cloud security framework that enables on-device `syscall`-level behavioral anomaly detection in IoT devices. ProvIoT applies federated learning techniques to overcome data and privacy limitations while minimizing network overhead. Infrequent on-device training of the local model requires less than 10% CPU overhead; syncing with the global models requires sending and receiving ~2MB over the network. During normal offline operation, ProvIoT periodically incurs less than 10% CPU overhead and less than 65MB memory usage for data summarization and anomaly detection. Our evaluation shows that ProvIoT detects fileless malware and stealthy APT attacks with an average F1 score of 0.97 in heterogeneous real-world IoT applications. ProvIoT is a step towards extending provenance analysis to resource-constrained IoT devices, beginning with well-resourced IoT devices such as the RaspberryPi, Jetson Nano, and Google TPU.

© The Author(s), under exclusive license to Springer Nature Switzerland AG 2024
C. Pöpper and L. Batina (Eds.): ACNS 2024, LNCS 14585, pp. 241–268, 2024.
https://doi.org/10.1007/978-3-031-54776-8_10

Keywords: Provenance graph analysis · anomaly detection · dynamic malware analysis · federated learning · deep learning · privacy

1 Introduction

The Internet of Things (IoT) revolution established a radical new computing paradigm that traditional security protocols have failed to comprehensively cover. With the recent development of small and powerful devices [8, 39, 65], increased network connectivity [70] has allowed IoT devices, including wearables, drones, and autonomous vehicles, to be deployed at an unprecedented scale [31]. These IoT devices are not only independently security critical [1, 78], but they are also entry points into a network to perform data theft, surveillance, and denial-of-service [21, 22, 83] attacks. As IoT technology's attack surface increases, so will the prevalence of attacks targeting IoT devices.

Traditional stealthy attack techniques are quickly being adapted to threaten IoT devices and cyber-physical systems [15, 42]. Various security solutions for IoT devices have been proposed to defend against these attacks, but they are limited in their capability to defend against skilled adversaries [60, 71]. Beyond the legacy approach to defense, several provenance-based security approaches [14, 41, 43, 82] have been proposed to protect conventional IT infrastructure (*e.g.,* server and desktop computers) against sophisticated malicious actors. Instead of a naïve dependence on static signatures, provenance-based solutions analyze the runtime behavior of known programs to detect anomalies.

Provenance-based defenses provide a promising approach for IoT devices as well. These defenses first capture the benign behavior of the program by aggregating auditing data to show causal relations between system events. These causal events are represented as a provenance graph, which is then vectorized so that machine-learning (ML) techniques can model the typical (*i.e.,* benign) behavior of the program. Provenance graphs are rising in popularity alongside advances in graph-based learning approaches [29]. However, the overhead incurred by graph techniques that digest an entire provenance graph is unacceptably high for most IoT devices.

Since most IoT devices run on limited resources, system components such as the CPU, memory, and storage are engineered to serve a single dedicated task, leaving scarce resources for security. Network bandwidth is likewise constrained in mobile IoT situations. These limitations severely hinder the data processing efforts required to support graph-based ML security solutions for IoT systems. Since the quality of the data deteriorates, the detection accuracy of ML models using the data also deteriorates. Additionally, the often scattered nature of IoT deployment makes the task of consistent and stable data collection challenging.

To address these issues, we propose ProvIoT, a novel federated edge-cloud collaborative security architecture for IoT that extends the detection capability of IoT security against sophisticated and stealthy attacks. ProvIoT aims to provide a system-wide behavioral graph analysis framework for the IoT domain. To overcome the IoT specific data collection and privacy constraints, ProvIoT uses a federated edge-cloud collaborative framework with two major components: *(1)* A *Local Brain* for system event collection, summarization, model training and anomaly detection in an edge device, and *(2)* a *Cloud Brain* for performing federated averaging [55] on these local models to produce a global model and orchestrating the distribution of the global model.

Our work extends a path-based graph summarization approach for system provenance analysis [41,43,82] that reduces computational overhead by extracting subgraphs (*i.e.,* causal paths) from the whole provenance graph. We design a novel federated anomaly detection framework using Local Brains and a Cloud Brain in the context of IoT. Our prototype runs Local Brains on multiple IoT platforms — ARM-based IoT, edge GPU devices [39,65], and x86-based Linux hosts. For a long term evaluation, we deployed Local Brains to 33 devices and collected low-level system events over twelve months.

The Cloud Brain established global behavioral models for the twenty commonly installed programs listed in Table 3 and the five major IoT use cases listed in Table 2. We evaluated ProvIoT against real-world IoT malware designed to impersonate long-running and trusted software which included both natively fileless malware and malware [20] that uses a fileless wrapper [36]. We also used realistic testbeds to reproduce prominent attacker tactics, techniques, and procedures (TTPs) that comprise the essential components of advanced persistent threat (APT) campaigns following the MITRE ATT&CK framework. Our evaluation results in Sect. 7 show that ProvIoT efficiently constructs behavioral models that can accurately detect stealthy attacks, including fileless IoT malware and APT-style attack campaigns.

In summary, our work brings in the following contributions:

- To the best of our knowledge, ProvIoT is the first proposed provenance based security detection approach in the context of IoT that counters stealthy attacks using federated learning and on-device detection.
- ProvIoT provides a new design choice for federated edge-cloud collaborative security learning by streamlining computationally expensive graph-based behavioral security in the IoT context.
- We extensively evaluated the efficiency and effectiveness of ProvIoT with realistic deployments. Adversarial cases are carefully designed using realistic attack cases and fileless malware samples.
- We will publish the complete IoT provenance dataset and tools required for our data analysis pipeline [61] as open artifacts.

2   Background

In this section, we first introduce fileless attacks, their operations, and their application to the IoT domain. We then provide insights for using in-host system provenance graphs to build behavioral models in IoT devices.

2.1   Fileless Attacks on IoT Devices

In this paper, *fileless attack* refers to a group of attack techniques with no footprint in the file system. Alternative terms used in the field include "zero-footprint", or "living off the land" [26].

Fileless attacks are characterized by the impersonation of trusted off-the-shelf applications and pre-installed system utilities. Since many of these trusted applications are commonly used by users and system administrators, it is harder for defenses to block access to them to prevent such attacks completely. Such impersonation techniques have seen rising popularity in recent cyberattacks [26,51]. Instead of storing the malware payload directly onto the disk before executing it, this malware uses the strategy of "living off the land" by injecting it into benign running processes (*e.g.,* trusted applications) and avoiding detection by executing only in process memory. During runtime, the malware may also rename itself to a seemingly benign process name using a `prctl(PR_SET_NAME)` call. These impersonation approaches have diverged and evolved in multiple ways in IoT systems [33,34]. Some possible impersonation approaches are highlighted below.

Process Injection. `ptrace()` is a system API used to support code injection to another process for development purposes. However, attackers have abused `ptrace()` to inject malicious code into the memory of legitimate processes [13].

In-Memory Execution. The `memfd_create()` system API family creates an anonymous file in memory-mounted file systems. Using `memfd_create()`, an attacker can directly load malware from the memory space without writing a payload to the filesystem. This attack enhances the traditional attack strategy of storing malware in transient storage (*e.g.,* `/tmp`, `/var/run`, `/dev/shm`). With `memfd_create()`, the malware further reduces its footprint, preventing users from locating it with standard filesystem access even during runtime. Multiple loader frameworks [36] exist that are able to encode regular file-based malware into different fileless variants.

Case Study: FritzFrog. In January 2020, a security group discovered and reported FritzFrog [42], a sophisticated peer-to-peer (P2P) malware botnet. FritzFrog is a crypto mining worm that breaks into and spreads through SSH servers. Written in Golang to natively target different architectures, FritzFrog uses fileless techniques to leave no traces on the filesystems of the infected devices. We specifically consider FritzFrog in the context of IoT devices.

FritzFrog performs file operations in memory to impersonate a regular benign system process's identity. After the initial break-in, FritzFrog masquerades as the `nginx` web server or the `ifconfig` process. The infected IoT device connects to a command and control (C&C) server via encrypted sessions to seemingly benign beacons. Then, the malware infects other IoT devices to mine cryptocurrencies by exploiting a weakness in SSH services. Figure 1 compares the behavior of the original `nginx` process and that of FritzFrog impersonating `nginx`. Although FritzFrog leaves no filesystem footprint, provenance-based intrusion detection

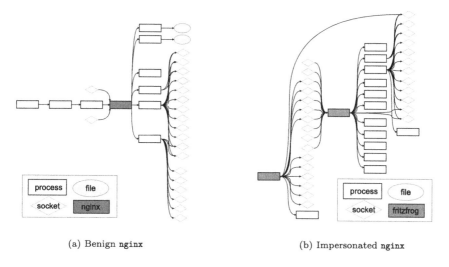

(a) Benign nginx   (b) Impersonated nginx

Fig. 1. FritzFrog malware impersonating nginx web-server.

systems can detect and defend against it as the behavior of benign nginx and FritzFrog are distinct.

2.2 System Provenance and Graph Learning

ProvIoT extends system provenance analysis [53], originally proposed by King et al. [45], to implement on-device edge IoT behavior monitoring system. System provenance operates through the installation of a data collection agent on each host to collect syscall level system events. These events are then sent to an in-memory database to build a causality graph by associating data and control dependencies between processes, files, and network resources. The events that system provenance collects are as follows: (1) process events, such as process create and destroy; (2) file events, including file read, write, and execute; and (3) network events, including socket create, destroy, read, and write.

With the increased deployment of provenance-based security solutions in the last decade [35], the output of system provenance, the *provenance graph*, forms the foundation for graph-based learning and detection approaches. In this regard, provenance graphs best represent the runtime characteristics of system entities and have quickly become an essential source of input to model a program's runtime behavior. Along with recent developments in graph-based learning approaches [46,67], research on behavioral modeling and its application for anomaly detection has gained considerable momentum [43,82].

While Graph Neural Network (GNN)-based learning analysis techniques have exploded in popularity, they often struggle to digest provenance graphs, which are large and extremely dense. Typically, system provenance graphs contain many nodes and edges that store the different labels and detailed attributes system events. For instance, our graph dataset produced nodes and edges with an average of 10 ~ 15 attributes for node and edge types. In our attempt to evaluate a GNN-based framework on our data, we encountered many limitations with the open-sourced framework [76,84] especially in regard to the processing power needed to process provenance graphs.

Works such as [43,82] have addressed the challenge of data processing overhead in general Neural Network (NN) approaches by implementing efficient path selection to build behavior models for detecting anomalous deviations. To adapt this design for use in IoT devices, we collect system-level events on the IoT devices and summarize them using the path selection approach. Recent advances in IoT machine learning frameworks have also made significant strides in executing sophisticated neural architectures in low-resource IoT environments [10,52]. The Local Brain locally trains a model on local data and shares only the model weights with the Cloud Brain. The Cloud Brain aggregates the model weights in a federated way [27] to build behavioral profiles that integrate global perspectives across multiple devices while preserving each device's privacy.

3   Threat Model

Our threat model assumes that the data collection and summarization pipeline on the IoT device is trusted *i.e.,* the integrity of the provenance records are guaranteed by existing secure provenance systems [41,43,62,82]. This assumption is consistent with existing provenance research that requires end-host data collection and reporting [43,53,82]. Securing and verifying the trustworthiness of the end-host data reporting is an important research topic that is orthogonal to our research [19]. Procedural dataset poisoning is outside the scope of our work. We consider the use of distributed consensus protocols [49] or attestation approaches that extend the root of trust with hardware level support [79].

Attacks targeting the IoT platform, communication infrastructure [18], or the analysis process running in the cloud are outside the scope of this paper. We further assume that the reporting agents are honest and restrict our target IoT devices to those with at least 375MB of RAM [60,71] to support provenance summarization. Many modern commodity IoT devices (*e.g.,* smart thermostats [3], smart watches [2], smart fridges [16], smart doorbells [11], and smart home devices [5]) are equipped with 512MB or more of RAM.

ProvIoT attempts to detect malicious behavior in IoT systems by learning the distribution of expected benign behaviors and reporting significant deviations from that expectation. We primarily consider APT scenarios [62] and fileless malware [42,58,80] that impersonates one or more of a set of whitelisted programs to evade traditional IDS [41] mechanisms.

4   System Overview

Figure 2 presents the architecture of ProvIoT, that is composed of two collaborating subsystems: *Local Brains* and a *Cloud Brain*. Each Local Brain gathers host-level monitoring data from the IoT device into an in-memory database. It

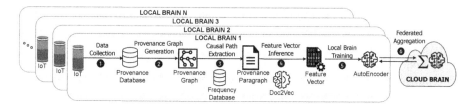

Fig. 2. The federated training pipeline of ProvIoT.

then summarizes the data and converts it to neural embeddings for ML model training. Data summarization only incurs 10% CPU usage and 65MB of RAM overhead. We can set the relevant local events and model training to run infrequently during low-load periods. After the local training, the Local Brain sends the updated neural weights to the Cloud Brain.

The Cloud Brain uses federated averaging [55] to combine the weights received from the Local Brains into a global model, which is sent back to each Local Brain for use in detection. The Local Brain can then perform detection directly on the IoT device using the federated global model. Periodically, the Local Brain will synchronize with the Cloud Brain, pushing up its local weights and fetching the updated global model. The *only* communication that the Local Brains have with the Cloud Brain is the communication of model weights during training. The Local Brains are fully capable of defending the IoT devices even when disconnected from the network.

4.1   Local Brain

We deploy a Local Brain to each IoT device to collect host-level monitoring data including process creations, file operations and network socket interactions. The Local Brain's training has the following major steps: *(1)* data collection, *(2)* provenance graph generation, *(3)* causal path extraction, *(4)* feature vector inference and *(5)* model training.

The first step in doing provenance analysis in IoT is data collection ❶, where we collect system monitoring data and create system event records. Similar to [41,43,53,62,82], we collect monitoring data for the following types of system entities: processes, files, and Unix domain sockets. Each entity type is associated with a set of attributes. For example, the attributes of a process are its creation time, command used to invoke, executable path and other relevant information. We use these entities and the interactions between them (*e.g.*, creation, reading, writing) to represent the system behaviors of the IoT device.

The collected data consists of raw syscall sequences which are translated into meaningful system information (*e.g.*, file descriptors are translated into file paths and PIDs are translated into process names) and stored in the provenance database. After translation, the data collection module processes the information into system events, which embodies the interaction between two system entities. Formally, we define a system event as $e_R(n_s, n_d, t)$ where n_s is the source entity,

n_d is the destination entity, t is the time when e occurs, and R is the relationship (*e.g.*, read, write, create). For example, `Process A opens (with write permission) File B` at time T is $e_w(A, B, T)$.

System events are queried from an in-memory database to generate ❷ the provenance graphs, $G(p)$, for a particular program. The generated provenance graphs are decomposed into subgraphs (*i.e.*, provenance paths). Formally, we define a causal path λ in a provenance graph $G(p)$ as an ordered sequence of system events (or edges) $\{e_1, e_2, \ldots, e_n\}$ in $G(p)$, where $\forall e_i, e_{i+1} \in \lambda$, $e_i.dst ==$ $e_{i+1}.src$ and $e_i.time < e_{i+1}.time$. The time constraint enforces that an event can only be dependent on events in the past, which prevents infinite loops.

After causal paths are extracted from provenance graphs, the relevant causal paths are extracted ❸ using a frequency database. Relevant causal paths during training are the common causal paths since we want to train the behavioral model with common provenance paths, but during anomaly detection relevant causal paths are the rare, since we want to detect these rare behaviors.

The frequency database stores historical behavior information for a particular program and is used during the ranking process, including how many times the system has seen a particular system event in the past. For example, if an entry in the frequency database is `</bin/bash|CREATE|/bin/cat, [1000]>`, it means in the past `/bin/bash` created `/bin/cat` one thousand times. False positives due to benign program evolution is an important issue for ML-based detectors. Therefore, ProvIoT updates the frequency database at run-time using benign behavior to capture the evolution of program behavior.

The relevant causal paths are converted ❹ to feature vectors using *doc2vec* [50]. The local model is then trained ❺ on the feature vectors, and the model weights are sent ❻ to the Cloud Brain to update the global model and propagate the localized information to the other connected Local Brain instances. After the Local Brain receives the aggregated global model weights, it starts the anomaly identification process. The Local Brain model uses the new model weights to detect anomalous behavior and raises an alert if any anomalous events are found. The pipeline is visualized in Fig. 3 and explained in Sect. 5.

Since the only connection with the Cloud Brain host is for sending and receiving model weights, the network overhead is constant and independent of the amount of data processed on each IoT device. Additionally, since the global models are stored on the device itself, the Local Brain can still operate even if the network connectivity is lost. This gives ProvIoT an advantage over other IoT behavioral anomaly detectors [32,69] as it does not require the transmission of the data to a centralized server for detection to occur. This also preserves the privacy of the device. We describe the detection models in more detail in Sect. 5.

4.2   Cloud Brain

Since the Cloud Brain resides in the cloud, it has sufficient computing power to aggregate ❻ the model updates from multiple Local Brain instances to build the global detection models and to synchronize the aggregated global weights with the Local Brain instances. This architecture scales more efficiently than

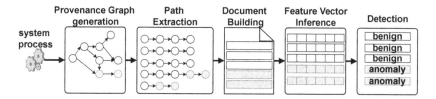

Fig. 3. The detection pipeline of the Local Brain.

centralized off-device detection schemes because federated averaging is infrequent and is less intensive than performing anomaly detection for an entire fleet of IoT devices, so expanding the fleet does not dramatically increase the computational requirements of the Cloud Brain.

Federated Aggregation. Device specific anomaly detection models are aggregates them using the `FederatedAveraging` algorithm described in [55]. Because each device gathers data only from the information it encounters, the data from a single device represents a slice of all the potential benign behaviors. The aggregation that takes place in the Cloud Brain improves the detection accuracy by combining the different pieces of information from all the connected clients.

5   Federated Detection

A core component of ProvIoT is its ability to perform detection autonomously on the IoT device without a centralized server. The local detection module raises alerts when suspicious events occur.

While a centralized server is used to keep the detection module up to date, it is not necessary for detection. The detection pipeline in the Local Brain use the same data collection and preprocessing steps as the training pipeline, but selects rare paths for detection instead of common paths for training.

The detection pipeline, shown in Fig. 3, works in the following manner: first, the Local Brain will generate provenance graphs for each target program and extract rare causal paths for consideration. These causal paths are converted into causal sentences [82], which are combined to form a causal document. Next, we use an NLP model, *doc2vec* [50], to embed the causal document as set of k-dimensional feature vectors. Finally, we use the trained *autoencoder* [40] model to detect the malicious causal paths as done by recent studies [41,62]. The intuition is that when feature vectors are inferred using the *doc2vec* model, benign causal paths will generate feature vectors that would be clustered separately from anomalous feature vectors.

It is possible that there is no anomaly in a process, but a combination of processes can lead to the anomaly, even still ProvIoT would be able to identify these anomalies. Since, during the graph building phase we capture both the forward dependencies (*e.g.*, creating new interactions with different system artifacts or modifying system artifacts) and backward dependencies (*e.g.*, capturing the malware payload deployment event that started the attack as well

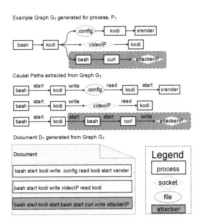

Fig. 4. Example causal paths extracted from a provenance graph, G_1, generated for process, P_1. Using the extracted causal paths the sentences are formed for a document, D_1.

as different program and data dependencies), we obtain a holistic system snapshot. Because malicious activities contain previously unseen behavior, their corresponding causal paragraphs will contain rare sentences, which will be inspected during the detection process.

5.1 Graph Building and Path Selection

For each target program, the Local Brain will generate provenance graphs from system events gathered in the data collection module. Causal paths are extracted from the provenance graphs through a series of random walks. We consider the rarest 15 % of the causal paths using [43]; 15 % was empirically determined in our training phase. Following [43,62,82], the rarity of a causal path is calculated using the frequency database introduced in Sect. 4.1. The regularity of an event is $R(e = (u, v, r)) = \frac{|Freq(u,v,r)|}{|Freq(u,*,r)|}$, and the regularity of a causal path is $R(P = (e_1, e_2, \ldots, e_n)) = \Pi_{e \in P} R(e) \cdot \alpha$, where α is a correction factor to prevent the regularity of long paths from trending towards zero. The rarity of a path is simply the complement of its regularity, $1 - R(P)$.

The information embedded in the provenance graph needs to be extracted to be used as features. One naïve approach may be to use the whole provenance graph for detection. However, using the entire graph will result in a lot of benign noise (events) being mixed into the overall data and the overhead needed to digest the entire graph for ML purposes are unreasonable in an IoT context. Many stealthy malware writers use this property to attempt to blend in with the surrounding benign noise in the graph. Thus, we use a frequency database, as defined in [43] to extract *rare* causal paths from the whole provenance graph. An example of causal paths extracted from a provenance graph in Fig. 4.

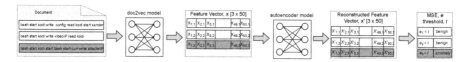

Fig. 5. Example detection workload for graph G_1 in Fig. 4. After the document D_1 is formed, the causal sentences in the document are converted into feature vectors (fv) using doc2vec model. Then the fv are fed into the autoencoder to get the reconstructed fv. Sentences are flagged as anomalous if the mean squared error between the original fv and the reconstructed fv is above a threshold determined during training.

For each selected path, ProvIoT removes the host/entity-specific features, such as host name and identifier, from each node and edge. This process ensures that the extracted representation is general for the subsequent learning tasks.

5.2   Document Embedding Model

The extracted causal paths need to be vectorized before they can be processed by the local detection model. As illustrated in Fig. 4, we first translate the causal paths into causal sentences, a process detailed in [82]. These causal sentences collectively form a document. Following recent methodologies [62,82], we employ the *doc2vec* Natural Language Processing (NLP) model [50] to transform these causal sentences into their corresponding feature vectors, as depicted in Fig. 5. Our *doc2vec* model, trained using data from benign deployments, ensures that causal sentences common in benign contexts yield neural embeddings that are more similar to each other compared to embeddings from rare causal sentences.

5.3   Federated Autoencoder

In ProvIoT, each Local Brain trains autoencoder models on the feature vectors from 5.2 and shares the model weights with the Cloud Brain for aggregation using federated averaging [55]. After fetching the global autoencoder models from the Cloud Brain, the Local Brain is ready to independently detect anomalies.

The Cloud Brain is distinct from the central server in the current state-of-the-art (SOTA) provenance system for IoT [32,69], which collects all the device data over the network and performs anomaly detection serverside. ProvIoT's on-device detection approach affords several advantages: *(1)* sending only the model weights over the network both reduces network overhead and preserves the privacy of activities on the IoT device; *(2)* on-device detection allows the IoT device to remain protected even when disconnected from the network; and *(3)* distributing the detection workload to the edge devices allows ProvIoT to scale horizontally with the size of the IoT device fleet, rather than requiring a vertically scaling central server.

The Local Brain's autoencoder models follow a typical structure for anomaly detection. The autoencoder has an encoder, which maps the benign feature vectors to a latent space representation that captures behavioral patterns, and a decoder, which reconstructs the original input. To detect anomalies, we measure the Mean Squared Error (MSE) of the reconstructed input and the original input; the input is flagged as anomalous if the MSE is higher than an experimentally determined threshold, which for our implementation was the 99th percentile. The intuition behind this detection scheme is that the autoencoder can effectively reconstruct benign samples similar to the ones it was trained on, but should struggle to reconstruct samples that are substantially different (*i.e.,* anomalies).

6   Implementation

Our ProvIoT prototype was written in C++, Java, and Python. The system level data collection agent was written in C++ with the provenance graph generator and path selection module implemented in Java. The document embedding and ML model were implemented in Python. The Local Brain's data pipeline modules communicate using the Unix domain socket.

System Level Data Collection. In a Local Brain, our prototype's data collection module uses the Linux audit framework to collect a subset of system calls relevant to our interested system entities (*i.e.,* files, processes, and network sockets), which include system calls for *(1)* file operations (*e.g.,* read(), write(), unlink()), *(2)* network socket operations (*e.g.,* connect(), accept()), *(3)* process operations (*e.g.,* fork(), exec(), exit()). We used SQLite as an in-memory database where system level data are stored. The in-memory database is computationally lightweight and executes queries quickly. Therefore, our provenance graph generation can be done without putting too much strain on the IoT device's resources. The primary workload of the IoT device is taken into consideration as well as the limited onboard resources, such that the Local Brain will pause data collection and subsequent processes (*e.g.,* graph generation, path extraction, training and detection) if the resource usage exceeds a present threshold, set at 30% CPU time or 1024MB memory by default.

Data Processing and Summarization. We use the NLP *doc2vec* model in the Gensim Library [9] for document embedding. The Keras library with Tensorflow [77] backend was used to implement the *autoencoder* model. The autocoder model has four fully connected layers with 50, 10, 10, and 50 neurons respectively. The first two layers are used for encoding, and the last two are used for decoding. The Adam optimizer with L1 regularization is used to prevent overfitting.

7   Evaluation

In this section, we evaluate ProvIoT's efficacy in detecting stealthy attacks in IoT devices. To this end, we seek answers for the following three research questions (RQs):

RQ1: Detection Accuracy. How effective is ProvIoT at detecting stealthy attacks (*e.g.,* fileless IoT malware impersonating trusted system programs) and APT campaigns? (Sects. 7.3, 7.4)

RQ2: Benefit of Federated Architecture. What benefits does the collaborative architecture have over a centralized approach? (Sect. 7.5)

RQ3: Resource Efficiency. What CPU and memory overhead does ProvIoT incur? (Sect. 7.6)

7.1   Dataset

In this section, we introduce the provenance datasets that consist of provenance graphs generated by capturing the benign and malicious IoT system's behavior.

Dataset Components. Our datasets consist of three major components: forward graphs, backward graphs and causal paths. The forward graphs consist of all the system events that are caused by the process associated with a Point of Interest (POI) event, *e.g.,* process creation, file and socket reads/writes. The backward graphs consist of the system events that created the POI event. We merge the forward and the backward graphs to get a unified graph that captures all the system events associated with the POI event. We then extract causal paths from this unified graph; the size statistics for the graphs and causal paths are shown in Table 3 in the appendix. To generate a graph dataset for a given program, we use all process creations for the given program name as POI events to build forward and backward graphs.

Benign Dataset. We consulted our university's Institutional Review Board (IRB) to develop an ethical experimental protocol for selecting volunteers for benign data collection. Once the volunteers were chosen, they received information about how their data would be used and securely stored to ensure confidentiality. The benign data collection took place over a period of twelve months, from January 2021 to December 2021, and resulted in the collection of over 30 TB of data. The benign profile for the programs was constructed by gathering system events from a diverse set of 33 devices, including ARM-based IoT devices such as Raspberry Pi, Google TPU, and NVIDIA Jetson Nano boards [8,39,65]. The device platforms consist of 1 Google TPU, 1 NVIDIA Jetson Nano, 3 Raspberry Pi 4, 5 Raspberry Pi 3B+, 5 desktops, 5 laptops, and 13 servers. Importantly, the provenance graphs that capture the behavior of a given system program exhibit a relative consistency across different IoT devices and platforms.

The IoT devices in our benign testbeds performed various IoT tasks and common system operations categorized as *IoT Applications* and *System Programs* respectively in Table 3. Using this system event data, we generated provenance graphs for popular IoT applications [25] and common system programs [33,34] that are frequently targeted for impersonation. We chose 1000 benign process instances for each of the 20 programs and 150 instances for each of the 5 IoT applications to create the benign dataset. The provenance graphs generated from the benign IoT applications consisted of 237,923.84 causal paths, 1,046.97 vertices, and 1,534.66 edges (IoT Application in Table 3) on average. Similarly, the provenance graph generated from the Linux system processes had an average of 168,652.11 causal paths, 332.49 vertices, and 398.48 edges (System Program in Table 3). For readers interested in further details about the statistics of the benign dataset and how it was generated, please refer to Sect. A.

Malicious Dataset. We created two isolated testbeds to run the malicious workloads. Firstly, we launched publicly known IoT malware using a fileless wrapper [36] to impersonate the identities of the popular IoT applications in Table 2. Second, we conducted a typical APT scenario by carefully coordinated the APT attack vector with the MITRE ATT&CK [59] framework to comprise the end-to-end attack [59] campaign. We launched a stealthy attack campaign that contains five kill-chain [12] stages (Table 5) — *(S1) gain access* by injecting a malicious payload into an active benign process; *(S2) establish a foothold* by communicating back to a C&C server over HTTPS (port 443); *(S3) deepen access* using a privilege escalation exploit [57], *(S4) move laterally* by scanning the local network for vulnerable hosts with open ports; and *(S5) look, learn, and remain* by exfiltrating sensitive user data to the C&C server. Each attack stage was conducted by different attack TTPs using Metasploit [57].

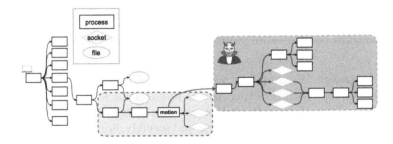

Fig. 6. Attacker injects and creates fileless malware as a child process of `motion` process. The provenance graph captures the attacker's behavior which can be used for detection.

We injected each attack TTP into five common IoT applications listed in Table 2 using a fileless wrapper [36]. Therefore, the IoT application's behavior captured in the provenance graph would contain additional nodes and edges (*i.e.*, malicious subgraphs) corresponding to the malicious behavior due to the injected attack TTPs. Because the malicious payload behaves differently than the benign application behavior, those malicious subgraphs are likely to contains rare and anomalous paths that will be detected by the Local Brain. In Fig. 6, we render the simplified provenance graph where we injected one of the attack TTPs to `motion`. It adds a subgraph whose size is proportional to the number of malicious activities performed.

We performed the program impersonation experiment five times for each of the four fileless IoT malware samples, with a total of twenty impersonation targets (Table 1), resulting in a total of 400 experiments. We conducted the APT

Table 1. ProvIoT is highly effective in distinguishing IoT malware impersonating as benign system process as evident from high F1 scores. Grey cells contain low F1 score to indicate indistinguishable malware behavior for system process, discussed in Sect. 7.3.

Impersonation target	Malware			
	BASHLITE	FritzFrog	ransomware	lizkabab
bash	0.98	0.96	0.96	0.98
cat	0.93	0.99	1.00	0.97
cp	0.92	0.97	0.92	0.95
cron	0.97	0.98	0.98	0.97
dash	0.95	0.96	1.00	0.98
dbus-daemon	0.94	0.95	0.92	0.98
dd	0.96	0.97	0.98	0.99
firefox	0.97	0.96	0.99	1.00
grep	0.96	0.97	0.94	0.95
java	0.96	0.96	0.96	0.98
ls	0.99	0.96	0.94	0.98
nginx	0.97	0.98	0.98	0.96
perl	0.96	0.96	0.95	0.97
ps	0.98	0.97	0.95	0.97
python	0.93	0.97	0.93	0.99
rm	0.92	0.96	0.93	0.98
service	0.93	0.95	0.90	0.99
sh	0.96	0.97	0.91	0.98
smbd	0.96	0.96	0.99	0.99
sshd	0.97	0.96	0.97	0.98
Average	**0.96**	**0.97**	**0.96**	**0.98**

scenario seven times on each of the five APT attack stages for five IoT applications (Table 5), totaling 175 experiments to build the APT dataset. Combining all our experiments, we conducted a total of 575 experiments (175 APT + 400 malware) to create the anomalous dataset. The provenance graphs collected from the malware evaluation have an average of 11,726.98 causal paths, 207.25 vertices, and 211.35 edges. The provenance graphs for the APT Kill chain scenario have an average of 19,716.37 causal paths, 435.49 vertices, and 481.40 edges. Interested readers can refer to Appendix Sect. A for further details.

7.2   Experimental Protocol

To generate the training and validation sets, we extract all the causal paths from the provenance graphs generated during benign deployment, reserving 90% of the data for training and 10% for validation. To generate the test set, we extract the rarest 15% of causal paths from the malicious testbeds, which simulates a real environment that has been attacked [43,82] and includes a mix of benign and anomalous paths. The Local Brain instances train on the benign training data and propagate their model weights to the Cloud Brain. The Cloud Brain then performs federated aggregation on those models to generate a global model, then propagates the global model back to the Local Brain instances. Each Local Brain tunes its detection threshold using its own validation set. In intrusion detection, we emphasize the importance of *unsupervised* learning because the defender should not make strong a priori assumptions about the attacker's behaviors.

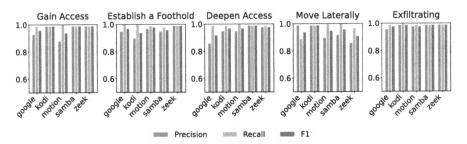

Fig. 7. High detection accuracy of ProvIoT against APT attacks using federated learning, some rare exceptions which are discussed in Sect. 7.4.

7.3 IoT Malware Detection

To represent a wide variety of malware, we selected two popular IoT malwares from [37], a natively fileless IoT malware [42], and a typical ransomware that would target an IoT system. We injected these well-known IoT malwares into trusted system processes using a fileless wrapper [36] to impersonate them. The detection results, summarized in Table 1, demonstrate that ProvIoT achieves high F1 scores for the majority of combinations, ranging from 0.96 to 0.98. This indicates that even when IoT malware is fileless and impersonates benign programs, its behavior remains distinct from the original system behavior.

However, some (impersonation target, malware) pairs, highlighted in Table 1, proved challenging for ProvIoT to reliably detect: BASHLITE was able to effectively masquerade as cp and rm because it primarily performs file copy and delete operations on the local device while preparing to participate in the botnet; ransomware effectively impersonated cp with large amounts of file copy operations, dbus-daemon with significant inter-process communication for cryptographic exchanges, service with manipulation of antivirus services, and sh with command execution.

7.4 APT Detection

The consistently high detection accuracy [41,82] of ProvIoT, as measured by precision, recall, and F1 score, is showcased in Fig. 7. Outside some rare exceptions, which will be discussed in more depth, the precision ranges from 0.93 to 0.99, the recall ranges from 0.97 to 1, and F1 scores range from 0.95 to 0.99. The results show that ProvIoT can reliably detect APT attacks while limiting the number of false alarms.

ProvIoT generates more false positives than false negatives, evidenced by its higher average recall (99%) than average precision (95%). This trend is also seen in other anomaly detection systems [41,82]. The high F1 score shows that the threshold is chosen in such a way that the actual anomalous behaviors (true positives) are detected rather than reducing FPs. Therefore, ProvIoT does not compromise on its detection ability to address false positive rates.

False Negative Cases. Even with path-based behavioral modeling, certain attack cases (*e.g., move laterally (S4)* attack for `google`) are hard to detect because the attacker's behavior is extremely similar to the application's benign behavior. The precision is 0.99 and the recall is 0.89, which is much lower than the second-lowest recall rate of 0.97. The *move laterally (S4)* stage scans for vulnerable ports to exploit, which is behaviorally similar to `google` scanning ports for available IP cameras.

False Positive Cases. ProvIoT has delivered steady and robust detection performance across our various APT workloads (Table 2). Against some APT stages, ProvIoT had a relatively high false positive rate such as *Deepen Access (S3)* for `google` has precision of 0.86 and recall of 0.99, *Establishing a Foothold (S2)* for `kodi` has precision of 0.90 and recall of 1, *Gain Access (S1)* for `motion` has precision of 0.88 and recall of 1; *Move Laterally(S4)* for `samba` has precision of 0.86 and recall of 0.99 and `zeek` has precision of 0.86 and recall of 0.97.

These instances of high false positive rates are due to system interactions with high behavioral variance. We investigated these cases and outlined the explanations based on the ground truth:`kodi` often reads hidden configuration files, downloads files containing streaming links from the internet and writes them to temporary locations; `google` creates and stops many short-lived threads; `motion` changes directory and file permission configuration for camera video storage; `samba` and `zeek` both scan and listen to different IPs and ports, which generates noisy provenance graphs (high variance). We see a high rate of false positives surrounding the creation and modification of temporary files and directories; since these behaviors are rare and not well-represented in the benign dataset, so they are marked as anomalous even when the actions are not malicious. The majority of the malicious paths were marked correctly as anomalous even though the precision score was below 0.90, the recall score was above 0.96. These results show that ProvIoT is very effective in detecting stealthy malware.

7.5   Federated Learning Benefits

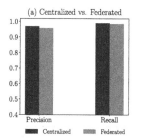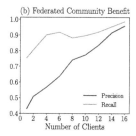

Fig. 8. (a) Federated performance is similar to centralized performance on the same data. (b) Increasing the number of clients increases performance by increasing the amount of data in the system.

We evaluate ProvIoT's federated approach against a traditional centralized architecture using `kodi` as a representative application. Figure 8(a) shows that ProvIoT trades just 1% precision for the scalability, privacy, and reliability benefits of the federated architecture. The centralized model was trained on the full dataset and achieved 0.97 precision and 0.99 recall. For ProvIoT, we used the 16 clients from our benign deployment that had `kodi` installed for training, then evaluated those models in our malicious testbeds. In this experiment, ProvIoT achieved 0.96 precision and 0.99 recall, performing almost identically to the centralized approach.

To demonstrate how ProvIoT is able to overcome the data view limitation of provenance-based anomaly detection on IoT devices, we visualize the average performance of the Local Brains as more clients are incorporated into the system in Fig. 8(b). By adding new Local Brains that see different data, the Cloud Brain is able to aggregate the incoming models to export a global model that better understands the full benign distribution. These model improvements manifest in improved recall and precision as new clients are introduced.

ProvIoT's federated approach provides critical benefits for IoT in data localization and privacy. The primary security benefit is localized detection, which reduces network overhead, allows detection in the absence of a network connection, and distributes the global detection workload across the federated devices. Further, because we only share model weights, specific system events are not shared with the network, which preserves the privacy of the data.

7.6   ProvIoT Overhead

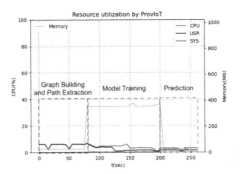

Fig. 9. On RaspberryPi 4B, Local Brain's processing and prediction uses <10% CPU and 65MB memory. Model training takes about 375MB memory and <10% CPU.

We experimentally demonstrate the overhead imposed by ProvIoT using an event database containing 7,085 process creation events, 56,587 file interactions, and 3,608 network interactions. This is typical for 24 h of execution. We experimented using different ARM IoT devices such as RaspberryPi 4B board [8] with four CPU cores and 8 GB memory for CPU only device; Jetson Nano [65] with four CPU cores, 4 GB memory and NVIDIA gpu; and Google Edge TPU [39] with single core, 512 MB memory, and edge TPU ML accelerator. To train a reliable model for kodi, ProvIoT requires two weeks worth of data, which results in 5.46 GB of data and four weight synchronizations.

To accurately characterize the overhead imposed on the edge IoT devices, we need to consider two different modes of execution: training and detection. Training occurs infrequently (approximately once per week) and requires less than 10% of the CPU processing power and less than 375MB of memory for less than four minutes as shown in Fig. 9. Detection occurs frequently (approximately once per day) and requires less than 10% of the CPU processing power and less than 65MB of memory for less than two minutes as shown in Fig. 9. Even during peak resource utilization (*i.e.,* during training), ProvIoT does not monopolize the IoT resources. Many home IoT devices, such as smart fridges, thermostats, and doorbells [2,3,5,11,16] contain sufficient memory to support on-device training.

8   Limitations

Hardware Constraints. The most prominent limitation of ProvIoT is the memory utilization of 375 MB during local training phase as measured in Sect. 7.6. Therefore, ProvIoT cannot be used for IoT which do not have at least 512 MB of RAM, such as ESP32 boards. ProvIoT is suitable for mid to large scale IoT devices. Real world vendors need to ensure that their products posses the required resources before deploying our system.

To reduce memory overhead, it is possible to train the local models on smaller batches of data, but train more frequently. This approach "flattens the curve" of resource usage, requiring more total computation, but reducing the peak memory usage. Increasing the training frequency may also increase the models' vulnerability to incremental dataset shifting attacks. The Local Brain training frequency can be modulated independently of the Cloud Brain synchronization frequency.

Privacy of Federated Learning. Recent advancements have shown that attackers can use model weights to infer statistics about the training dataset. These statistics can then be used to craft targeted payloads and APT stages that blend in with the typical behavior of the system to evade detection. To protect the confidentiality and ensure the integrity of the model weights, communication between the Local Brains and the Cloud Brain should be encrypted and signed using public/private key pairs, which can be distributed by the vendor during manufacturing. To further improve the privacy preservation, the communication of model weights and computation of federated averaging can leverage recent advancements in fully homomorphic encryption for IoT devices [17,54], which shifts the heavy computational workload to the resource-rich Cloud Brain; this method would preserve the privacy of the IoT devices even against an attacker with full read access to the Cloud Brain and the capacity to recover private data from model weights alone.

Poisoning on Federated Learning. In ProvIoT, the design tradeoff between false positives due to benign software evolution and vulnerability to malicious incremental model shifting attacks is parameterized by the frequency of training and synchronization between the Local Brains and the Cloud Brain. In the real world, this tradeoff is of critical importance and will require careful consideration by experts on the security requirements of the specific application of ProvIoT.

9   Related Work

IoT Security. With the growth of IoT, a significant number of vulnerabilities have been identified in IoT devices [58,74,80], protocols [86], applications, and platforms [38]. In response to IoT attacks, diverse detection and prevention approaches have been proposed, such as network-based solutions [75], platform-based solutions [32,69,72,73] and application-based solutions [44,82]. Our work defends against stealthy attacks including fileless malware and APTs.

Cosson et al. [32] and Rieger et al. [69] has proposed a centralized node-level monitoring system for IoT using network traffic. However, it requires the local devices to send their local data to a centralized server where the detection occurs. ProvIoT has a major advantage over [32] because the users' data does not leave the local device and detection occurs on the local device without a network connection. [60,63,71] have showed how to do federated anomaly detection on IoT, but solely focused on network data. While the network data is important, stealthy attacks can easily circumvent those defenses with specially crafted network packets. To the best of our knowledge, we are the first to propose a federated, privacy preserving, collaborative learning framework using host-level provenance data for IoT.

IoT Defenses. General intrusion detection [37,81] approaches have been extensively studied. For example, [28] and [68] designed defenses to detect routing attacks. However, their work focuses on the 6LoWPAN protocol. Our work focuses on creating a generalized federated framework for IoT.

Recently, several anomaly-based solutions have been proposed to detect different IoT attacks. SDN-based approaches [66], signature-based approaches [48] and machine learning based approaches [24,30,56,63,64] have been proposed to detect IoT botnet attacks such as Mirai. However, these approaches only focus on analyzing network traffic, limiting their capability in detecting attacks with minimal network footprints. The most directly related previous work is [32,69], which forwards telemetry data for the entire IoT fleet to a central server for anomaly detection; ProvIoT improves upon the privacy and scalability of [32,69] by enabling on-device detection with federated learning and provenance analysis.

10   Discussion and Future Work

Real-Time Prevention. Although we focus on a detection system in this paper, ProvIoT can be easily extended to provide real-time prevention [23] (*e.g.*, blocking or killing anomalous processes). ProvIoT can also be augmented with other kinds of defenses (*e.g.*, dynamic quarantine or deep inspection) when it raises alerts. ProvIoT supports online forensic analysis including backtracking analysis and data query by leveraging its extensive system event collection.

Applicability to IoT Devices with Other OSes. While our current implementation and evaluation mainly focuses on Linux-based IoT devices, our approach is general and applicable to the devices with other operating systems, such as Windows, TinyOS, or Riot. For example, the Windows OS also has a system to log system events [4] that ProvIoT can use to generate provenance graphs for training and anomaly detection.

Trends in IoT Capacity and ML Overhead. As a step towards bringing powerful provenance-based threat detection to IoT devices, ProvIoT synergizes both with advancements in increasing hardware power in IoT devices and low-resource ML [10]. Indeed, recent work [52] has demonstrated training a 43-layer CNN in less than 256KB of RAM. We envision new works that combine ProvIoT's federated architecture with innovations in memory-constrained provenance analysis to extend on-device protection to the general IoT space.

11   Conclusion

In this paper, we present ProvIoT, a novel end-to-end edge-cloud collaborative security framework for IoT security. ProvIoT adapts modern provenance graph-based anomaly detection to IoT devices. ProvIoT is the first anomaly detection framework to perform on-device provenance analysis with federated learning in IoT devices. ProvIoT preserves the privacy of local system events and achieves high detection accuracy while incurring low overhead and enabling localized detection. We extensively evaluated ProvIoT with a realistic provenance dataset against real-world IoT malware and APT attack campaigns. ProvIoT detects fileless malware and APT attacks with an average F1-score of 0.97 and 0.99, respectively. During periodic detection cycles, ProvIoT incurs less than 10% CPU overhead, 65MB memory overhead, and does not require network connectivity. The detection with infrequent training cycles incurs similar CPU overhead, less than 375MB memory overhead, and up to 2MB network bandwidth consumption for model updates.

Acknowledgments. We thank the anonymous reviewers for their helpful feedback.

A Appendix

A.1 IoT Workload.

The Table 2 shows the typical usage for the IoT applications. Typical usage for media center (*e.g.*, kodi [47]) is to browse different streams to find playable and downloadable content. kodi was used to download different medias from the wed along with browsing different steams. A voice assistant such as Google Assistant [6] was used for answering common questions such as "what is the weather like?". An IP camera (*e.g.*, motion [7]) was used to stream our lab setting from our home. We used a network attached storage unit to access files from remote locations as well as to modify the files. Finally, we used a network security monitoring tool (*e.g.*, zeek [85]) to sniff and inspect at the network traffic that was generated in our lab environment.

Table 2. The IoT applications chosen for evaluation as well as their usage examples.

Usages	Application	Scenario
Voice Assistant	google	Inquired general knowledge and everyday household questions to Google Assistant.
Media Center	kodi	Updated media streams and played media during different parts of the day.
IP Camera	motion	Started streaming multiple live camera streaming server and watched them.
Network Attached Storage	samba	Performed network storage action such as list all the files, delete a file, or add a file.
Network Security Monitor	zeek	Investigated the network traffic coming from IoT using Zeek

A.2 Dataset Statistics.

This section contains the data set details shown in Tables 3 and 4. In Table 3 the benign dataset is represented where we experimented with five commonly used IoT programs [33] and twenty prevalent Linux system programs [53]. Table 4 shows the malicious data set which consists of two parts: four IoT malware which impersonated the twenty Linux system programs and APT kill chain scenarios conducted using the five IoT programs.

Table 3. Number of vertices and edges used to create a benign profile for IoT applications and system programs

	Avg. # of causal paths	Avg. # of total vertices / edges	Avg. # of forward vertices / edges	Avg. # of backward vertices / edges
IoT Application				
google	571,052.33	159.0 / 314.0	95.67 / 216.0	63.33 / 98.0
kodi	29,946.89	210.33 / 273.78	149.33 / 176.89	61.0 / 96.89
motion	9,113.0	179.0 / 504.0	5.0 / 4.0	174.0 / 500.0
samba	85,347.0	2,537.0 / 2,857.0	76.4 / 120.8	2,460.6 / 736.2
zeek	494,160.0	2,149.5 / 3,724.5	1,032.5 / 1,124.5	1,117.0 / 2,600.0
average	**237,923.84**	**1,046.97 / 1,534.66**	**271.78 / 328.44**	**775.19 / 1,206.22**
System Program				
bash	166,355.43	454.25 / 510.76	10.57 / 9.31	443.68 / 501.45
cat	184,346.43	310.51 / 210.9	9.0 / 6.99	301.51 / 203.91
cp	175,636.86	193.42 / 212.7	179.09 / 184.69	14.33 / 28.01
cron	214,827.71	327.16 / 241.85	10.27 / 9.96	316.89 / 231.89
dash	153,808.57	371.87 / 381.97	211.61 / 206.44	160.26 / 175.53
dbus-daemon	156,713.0	20.16 / 20.04	9.02 / 6.42	11.14 / 13.62
dd	213,601.29	995.5 / 1,003.6	551.68 / 501.81	443.82 / 501.79
firefox	176,843.86	194.22 / 504.56	15.84 / 18.78	178.38 / 485.78
grep	212,413.86	191.51 / 502.32	13.51 / 16.43	178.0 / 485.89
java	169,180.71	133.94 / 222.4	17.44 / 19.63	116.5 / 202.77
ls	179,185.86	213.62 / 356.47	10.25 / 9.3	203.37 / 347.17
nginx	258,367.17	514.27 / 514.13	500.76 / 501.26	13.51 / 12.87
perl	809.0	25.01 / 23.22	11.95 / 12.05	13.06 / 11.17
ps	181,846.43	834.01 / 998.14	369.21 / 501.77	464.8 / 496.37
python	161,755.57	365.71 / 348.31	11.51 / 8.14	354.2 / 340.17
rm	174,590.43	452.89 / 440.38	15.06 / 18.5	437.83 / 421.88
service	231.43	18.32 / 21.24	15.32 / 18.55	3.0 / 2.69
sh	208,367.43	445.01 / 851.27	4.16 / 357.78	440.85 / 493.49
smbd	201,559.57	355.37 / 371.15	9.69 / 3.39	345.68 / 367.76
sshd	182,601.57	233.04 / 234.15	9.35 / 6.6	223.69 / 227.55
average	**168,652.11**	**332.49 / 398.48**	**99.26 / 120.89**	**233.23 / 277.59**

Table 4. Number of vertices and edges used to create IoT Malware and APT attack profile

	Avg. # of causal paths	Avg. # of total vertices / edges	Avg. # of forward vertices / edges	Avg. # of backward vertices / edges
IoT Malware				
BASHLITE	110.5	21.0 / 21.0	4.0 / 3.0	17.0 / 18.0
FritzFrog	46,253.8	751.0 / 747.4	248.6 / 246.8	502.4 / 500.6
lizkebab	293.2	29.0 / 33.0	6.0 / 4.0	23.0 / 29.0
randomware	250.4	28.0 / 44.0	8.0 / 12.0	20.0 / 32.0
average	**11,726.98**	**207.25 / 211.35**	**66.65 / 66.45**	**140.6 / 144.9**
APT Kill Chain Scenario				
Gain Access (S1)	2,789.6	510.6 / 554.8	495.2 / 537.6	15.4 / 17.2
Establish a Foothold (S2)	46,763.75	470.25 / 550.12	398.38 / 429.5	71.88 / 120.62
Deepen Access (S3)	1,192.4	171.0 / 202.6	164.0 / 195.0	7.0 / 7.6
Move Laterally (S4)	27,314.33	97.5 / 116.0	70.17 / 84.83	27.33 / 31.17
Look, Learn and Remain (S5)	20,521.75	928.12 / 983.5	897.38 / 929.62	30.75 / 53.88
average	**19,716.37**	**435.49 / 481.40**	**405.03 / 435.31**	**30.47 / 46.09**

Table 5. APT TTPs for cyber-killchain stages

Cyber-killchain Stages	Techniques (ATTCK TTP)	Scenarios
Gain Access (S1)	Exploitation for Client Execution (T1203)	Attackers modify a benign looking executable, but once the user opens the application it can be used by the attacker for arbitrary code execution
	File and Directory Permissions Modification (T1222)	Attacker modifies objects in the system so that it can be copied by lower privilege users that the attacker has hijacked
Establish a Foothold (S2)	Data from Local System (T1005)	Attacker moves around the file system, finding files that contain valuable information
	Exfiltration Over C2 Channel (T1041)	Attacker downloads valuable files into a local directory
Deepen Access (S3)	Create and Modify system process (T1543)	Attacker creates a system process that can run in the background and do reconnaissance or mine information
	Service Stop (T1489)	Attacker stops firewall or external IDS services so that they cannot detect the APT
Move Laterally (S4)	Process injection (T1055)	Attacker injects a vulnerable process such as a trojan into a benign application so that IDS cannot differentiate
Look, Learn, and Remain (S5)	System Information Discovery (T1082)	Attacker discovers system hardware information so that they can craft better exploits or exploit hardware vulnerabilities
	Network Service Scanning (T1046)	Attackers scan network services to find services they can use as backup or use as a secondary mode of connections
	Network Sniffing (T1040)	Attackers sniff the network to find insecure SSL connections or any other connections to extract valuable information

A.3 APT Scenarios

The advanced Persistent Threat (APT) scenario was established in our malicious testbed by loading APT kill-chain components using fileless wrapper (Table 5). The APT attack vectors were coordinated to comprise the end-to-end attack campaign referring to MITRE ATT&CK framework.

References

1. Insteon hub 2242–222 - lack of web and API authentication (2013). https://www.exploit-db.com/exploits/27284. Accessed 26 May 2023
2. Apple watch ram size comparison chart: how much ram does apple watch have? (2015). https://www.knowyourmobile.com/wearable-technology/apple-watch-ram-size/. Accessed 26 May 2023
3. Google nest - support (2015). https://support.google.com/googlenest/answer/9230098. Accessed 26 May 2023
4. Auditing security events (2017). https://goo.gl/FkaDCa
5. Google home mini teardown, comparison to echo dot, and giving technology a voice (2017). https://tinyurl.com/ykbay2fu. Accessed 26 May 2023
6. Google Assistant, your own personal Google (2018). https://assistant.google.com/
7. Motion (2018). https://motion-project.github.io/

8. Raspberry Pi - Teach, Learn, and Make with Raspberry Pi (2018). https://www.raspberrypi.org
9. Gensim: Topic modelling for humans (2019). https://radimrehurek.com/gensim/index.html
10. Tinyml foundation (2019). https://www.tinyml.org/. Accessed 25 May 2023
11. Inside amazon's ring alarm system (2020). https://tinyurl.com/yck5jm4m. Accessed 26 May 2023
12. Cyber kill chain® — lockheed martin (2021). https://www.lockheedmartin.com/en-us/capabilities/cyber/cyber-kill-chain.html. Accessed 24 Jul 2021
13. Process injection: Ptrace system calls, sub-technique t1055.008 - enterprise — mitre att&ck® (2021). https://attack.mitre.org/techniques/T1055/008/. Accessed 23 Jul 2021
14. Cloud-based data platform for cybersecurity, it operations and devops — splunk (2022). https://www.splunk.com/. Accessed 23 Jul 2021
15. Iot is a gold mine for hackers using fileless malware for cyberattacks - techrepublic (2022). https://tek.io/30dBnIU. Accessed 23 Jul 2021
16. Smart refrigerator with family hub (2022). https://tinyurl.com/4kz6z6z5. Accessed 26 May 2023
17. Acar, A., Aksu, H., Uluagac, A.S., Conti, M.: A survey on homomorphic encryption schemes: Theory and implementation. ACM Comput. Surv. **51**(4), 1–35 (2018). https://doi.org/10.1145/3214303
18. Acar, A., et al.: Peek-a-boo: I see your smart home activities, even encrypted! In: Proceedings of the 13th ACM Conference on Security and Privacy in Wireless and Mobile Networks, pp. 207–218. WiSec 2020, Association for Computing Machinery, New York, NY, USA (2020). https://doi.org/10.1145/3395351.3399421
19. Ahmad, A., Lee, S., Peinado, M.: HARDLOG: practical tamper-proof system auditing using a novel audit device. In: 2022 IEEE Symposium on Security and Privacy (SP), pp. 1791–1807 (2022)
20. Alrawi, O., et al.: The circle of life: a large-scale study of the IoT malware lifecycle. In: USENIX Security Symposium, pp. 3505–3522 (2021)
21. Antonakakis, M., et al.: Understanding the Mirai botnet. In: 26th USENIX Security Symposium (USENIX Security 17), pp. 1093–1110. USENIX Association, Vancouver, BC (2017). https://www.usenix.org/conference/usenixsecurity17/technical-sessions/presentation/antonakakis
22. Armis Security: Blueborne: Bluetooth exposes android, linux, windows and iOS devices to airborne attacks (2017). https://www.armis.com/research/blueborne/
23. Babun, L., Celik, Z.B., McDaniel, P., Uluagac, S.: Real-time analysis of privacy-(un)aware IoT applications. Proc. Priv. Enhancing Technol. **2021**, 145–166 (2021). https://doi.org/10.2478/popets-2021-0009
24. Bahşi, H., Nõmm, S., La Torre, F.B.: Dimensionality reduction for machine learning based IoT botnet detection. In: 2018 15th International Conference on Control, Automation, Robotics and Vision (ICARCV), pp. 1857–1862. IEEE (2018)
25. Bansal, A., Kandikuppa, A., Chen, C.Y., Hasan, M., Bates, A., Mohan, S.: Towards efficient auditing for real-time systems. In: Atluri, V., Di Pietro, R., Jensen, C.D., Meng, W. (eds.) Computer Security – ESORICS 2022. ESORICS 2022. Lecture Notes in Computer Science, vol. 13556, pp. 614–634. Springer, Cham (2022). https://doi.org/10.1007/978-3-031-17143-7_30
26. Barr-Smith, F., Ugarte-Pedrero, X., Graziano, M., Spolaor, R., Martinovic, I.: Survivalism: systematic analysis of windows malware living-off-the-land. In: IEEE symposium on security and privacy (SP). In: IEEE Symposium on Security and Privacy (SP), pp. 1557–1574 (2021). https://doi.org/10.1109/sp40001.2021.00047

27. Bonawitz, K., et al.: Towards federated learning at scale: system design. arXiv.org (2019)
28. Bostani, H., Sheikhan, M.: Hybrid of anomaly-based and specification-based IDS for internet of things using unsupervised OPF based on MapReduce approach. Comput. Commun. **98**, 52–71 (2017)
29. Chaudhary, A., Mittal, H., Arora, A.: Anomaly detection using graph neural networks. In: 2019 International Conference on Machine Learning, Big Data, Cloud and Parallel Computing (COMITCon), pp. 346–350 (2019). https://doi.org/10.1109/COMITCon.2019.8862186
30. Chawathe, S.S.: Monitoring IoT networks for botnet activity. In: 2018 IEEE 17th International Symposium on Network Computing and Applications (NCA), pp. 1–8. IEEE (2018)
31. Chen, J., et al.: Iotfuzzer: Discovering memory corruptions in IoT through app-based fuzzing. In: NDSS (2018)
32. Cosson, A., Sikder, A.K., Babun, L., Celik, Z.B., McDaniel, P., Uluagac, A.S.: Sentinel: a robust intrusion detection system for IoT networks using kernel-level system information. In: Proceedings of the International Conference on Internet-of-Things Design and Implementation, pp. 53–66 (2021)
33. Costin, A., Zaddach, J.: IoT Malware: comprehensive survey, analysis framework and case studies. BlackHat Briefings (2019). https://bit.ly/3DFrCBA
34. Cozzi, E., Graziano, M., Fratantonio, Y., Balzarotti, D.: Understanding Linux malware. In: 2018 IEEE Symposium on Security and Privacy (SP), pp. 161–175. IEEE (2018)
35. CrowdStrkie: Endpoint Detection and Response (EDR), Tech. rep., CrowdStrkie (2020)
36. Cybersecurity, A.: Malware using new Ezuri memory loader — at&t alien labs (2021). https://cybersecurity.att.com/blogs/labs-research/malware-using-new-ezuri-memory-loader. Accessed 23 Jul 2021
37. Ding, F., et al.: DeepPower: non-intrusive and deep learning-based detection of IoT Malware using power side channels. In: Proceedings of the 15th ACM Asia Conference on Computer and Communications Security, pp. 33–46 (2020)
38. Fernandes, E., Jung, J., Prakash, A.: Security analysis of emerging smart home applications. In: IEEE S&P (2016)
39. Google: Edge TPU - run inference at the edge — google cloud (2021). https://cloud.google.com/edge-tpu. Accessed 23 Jul 2021
40. Google: Intro to autoencoders (2021). https://www.tensorflow.org/tutorials/generative/autoencoder
41. Han, X., et al.: {SIGL}: Securing software installations through deep graph learning. In: 30th USENIX Security Symposium (USENIX Security 21), pp. 2345–2362 (2021)
42. Harpaz, O.: FritzFrog: a new generation of peer-to-peer botnets - guardicore (2020). https://bit.ly/3mJzyeq. Accessed 23 Jul 2021
43. Hassan, W.U., et al.: NoDoze: combatting threat alert fatigue with automated provenance triage. In: NDSS (2019)
44. Jia, Y.J., et al.: ContexIoT: towards providing contextual integrity to appified IoT platforms. In: NDSS (2017)
45. King, S.T., Chen, P.M.: Backtracking intrusions. ACM SIGOPS Oper. Syst. Rev. **37**, 223–236 (2003). https://doi.org/10.1145/945445.945467
46. Kipf, T.N., Welling, M.: Variational graph auto-encoders. arXiv preprint arXiv:1611.07308 (2016)

47. Kodi — Open source home theater software (2018). https://kodi.tv/
48. Kumar, A., Lim, T.J.: Early detection of mirai-like IoT bots in large-scale networks through sub-sampled packet traffic analysis. arXiv preprint arXiv:1901.04805 (2019)
49. Lamport, L., Shostak, R., Pease, M.: The byzantine generals problem. ACM Trans. Program. Lang. Syst. **4**(3), 382–401 (1982). https://doi.org/10.1145/357172.357176
50. Le, Q., Mikolov, T.: Distributed representations of sentences and documents. In: International Conference on Machine Learning, pp. 1188–1196 (2014)
51. Li, Z., Chen, Q.A., Yang, R., Chen, Y., Ruan, W.: Threat detection and investigation with system-level provenance graphs: a survey. Comput. Secur. **106**, 102282 (2021)
52. Lin, J., Zhu, L., Chen, W.M., Wang, W.C., Gan, C., Han, S.: On-device training under 256KB memory. In: Advances in Neural Information Processing Systems, vol. 35, pp. 2941–2295 (2022)
53. Liu, Y., et al.: Towards a timely causality analysis for enterprise security. In: NDSS (2018)
54. Matsumoto, M., Oguchi, M.: Speeding up encryption on IoT devices using homomorphic encryption. In: 2021 IEEE International Conference on Smart Computing (SMARTCOMP), pp. 270–275 (2021). https://doi.org/10.1109/SMARTCOMP52413.2021.00059
55. McMahan, B., Moore, E., Ramage, D., Hampson, S., y Arcas, B.A.: Communication-efficient learning of deep networks from decentralized data. In: Artificial Intelligence and Statistics, pp. 1273–1282. PMLR (2017)
56. Meidan, Y., et al.: N-Baiot: network-based detection of IoT botnet attacks using deep autoencoders. arXiv preprint arXiv:1805.03409 (2018)
57. metasploit: metasploit (2021). https://www.metasploit.com/. Accessed 29 Nov 2021
58. Mirai Attacks (2016). https://goo.gl/QVv89r
59. MITRE: Mitre att&ck® (2023). https://attack.mitre.org/. Accessed 23 Jul 2021
60. Mothukuri, V., Khare, P., Parizi, R.M., Pouriyeh, S., Dehghantanha, A., Srivastava, G.: Federated-learning-based anomaly detection for IoT security attacks. IEEE Internet Things J. **9**(4), 2545–2554 (2021)
61. Mukherjee, K.: ProvIoT: detecting stealthy attacks in IoT through federated edge-cloud security (2023). https://github.com/syssec-utd/proviot
62. Mukherjee, K., et al.: Evading provenance-based ML detectors with adversarial system actions. In: USENIX Security Symposium (SEC) (2023)
63. Nguyen, T.D., Marchal, S., Miettinen, M., Dang, M.H., Asokan, N., Sadeghi, A.R.: Diot: a crowdsourced self-learning approach for detecting compromised IoT devices. arXiv preprint arXiv:1804.07474 (2018)
64. Nõmm, S., Bahşi, H.: Unsupervised anomaly based botnet detection in IoT networks. In: 2018 17th IEEE International Conference on Machine Learning and Applications (ICMLA), pp. 1048–1053. IEEE (2018)
65. NVIDIA: Nvidia jetson nano developer kit — nvidia developer (2022). https://developer.nvidia.com/embedded/jetson-nano-developer-kit. Accessed 23 Jul 2021
66. Ozcelik, M., Chalabianloo, N., Gur, G.: Software-defined edge defense against IoT-based DDOs. In: 2017 IEEE International Conference on Computer and Information Technology (CIT), pp. 308–313. IEEE (2017)
67. Pan, S., Hu, R., Long, G., Jiang, J., Yao, L., Zhang, C.: Adversarially regularized graph autoencoder for graph embedding. arXiv preprint arXiv:1802.04407 (2019)

68. Raza, S., Wallgren, L., Voigt, T.: Svelte: real-time intrusion detection in the internet of things. Ad Hoc Netw. **11**(8), 2661–2674 (2013)
69. Rieger, P., Chilese, M., Mohamed, R., Miettinen, M., Fereidooni, H., Sadeghi, A.R.: Argus: context-based detection of stealthy IoT infiltration attacks. arXiv preprint arXiv:2302.07589 (2023)
70. Shafi, M., et al.: 5G: a tutorial overview of standards, trials, challenges, deployment, and practice. IEEE J. Sel. Areas Commun. **35**(6), 1201–1221 (2017). https://doi.org/10.1109/JSAC.2017.2692307
71. Shahid, O., Mothukuri, V., Pouriyeh, S., Parizi, R.M., Shahriar, H.: Detecting network attacks using federated learning for IoT devices. In: 2021 IEEE 29th International Conference on Network Protocols (ICNP), pp. 1–6. IEEE (2021)
72. Sikder, A.K., Aksu, H., Uluagac, A.S.: 6thSense: a context-aware sensor-based attack detector for smart devices. In: 26th USENIX Security Symposium (USENIX Security 17), pp. 397–414. USENIX Association, Vancouver, BC (2017). https://www.usenix.org/conference/usenixsecurity17/technical-sessions/presentation/sikder
73. Sikder, A.K., Aksu, H., Uluagac, A.S.: A context-aware framework for detecting sensor-based threats on smart devices. IEEE Trans. Mob. Comput. **19**(2), 245–261 (2020). https://doi.org/10.1109/TMC.2019.2893253
74. Sikder, A.K., Petracca, G., Aksu, H., Jaeger, T., Uluagac, A.S.: A survey on sensor-based threats and attacks to smart devices and applications. IEEE Commun. Surv. Tutorials **23**, 1125–1159 (2021). https://doi.org/10.1109/COMST.2021.3064507
75. Sivaraman, V., Gharakheili, H.H., Vishwanath, A., Boreli, R., Mehani, O.: Network-level security and privacy control for smart-home IoT devices. In: WiMob, pp. 163–167 (2015)
76. Team, D.: Deep graph library: easy deep learning on graphs (2022). https://www.dgl.ai/. Accessed 21 Sep 2021
77. Team, K.: Keras: the Python deep learning API (2021). https://keras.io/
78. Trend Micro: Brickerbot malware permanently bricks IoT devices (2017). https://tinyurl.com/2wc4vw5b
79. Introducing Arm TrustZone (2018). https://developer.arm.com/technologies/trustzone
80. VPNFilter (2018). https://blog.talosintelligence.com/2018/05/VPNFilter.html
81. Wang, J., et al.: IoT-praetor: undesired behaviors detection for IoT devices. IEEE Internet Things J. **8**(2), 927–940 (2020)
82. Wang, Q., et al.: You are what you do: Hunting stealthy malware via data provenance analysis. In: NDSS (2020)
83. Williams, M.: A new philips hue security patch keeps hackers from taking control of your network (2019). https://tinyurl.com/yejh839k
84. Ying, R., Lou, Z., You, J., Wen, C., Canedo, A., Leskovec, J.: Neural subgraph matching. CoRR abs/2007.03092 (2020), https://arxiv.org/abs/2007.03092
85. Zeek (2021). https://zeek.org/
86. Critical flaw identified in Zigbee smart home devices (2015). https://goo.gl/BFBa1X

Attacks

A Practical Key-Recovery Attack on LWE-Based Key-Encapsulation Mechanism Schemes Using Rowhammer

Puja Mondal[1]([✉])[ID], Suparna Kundu[2][ID], Sarani Bhattacharya[3][ID], Angshuman Karmakar[1,2][ID], and Ingrid Verbauwhede[2][ID]

[1] Department of Computer Science and Engineering, IIT Kanpur, Kanpur, India
{pujamondal,angshuman}@cse.iitk.ac.in
[2] COSIC, KU Leuven, Kasteelpark Arenberg 10, BUS, 2452, B-3001
Leuven-Heverlee, Belgium
{suparna.kundu,ingrid.verbauwhede}@esat.kuleuven.be
[3] Department of Computer Science and Engineering, IIT Kanpur, Kharagpur, India
sarani@cse.iitkgp.ac.in

Abstract. Physical attacks are serious threats to cryptosystems deployed in the real world. In this work, we propose a microarchitectural end-to-end attack methodology on generic lattice-based post-quantum key encapsulation mechanisms to recover the long-term secret key. Our attack targets a critical component of a Fujisaki-Okamoto transform that is used in the construction of almost all lattice-based key encapsulation mechanisms. We demonstrate our attack model on practical schemes such as Kyber and Saber by using Rowhammer. We show that our attack is highly practical and imposes little preconditions on the attacker to succeed. As an additional contribution, we propose an improved version of the plaintext checking oracle, which is used by almost all physical attack strategies on lattice-based key-encapsulation mechanisms. Our improvement reduces the number of queries to the plaintext checking oracle by as much as 39% for Saber and approximately 23% for Kyber768. This can be of independent interest and can also be used to reduce the complexity of other attacks.

Keywords: Post-quantum cryptography · Key-encapsulation mechanism · micro-architecture attacks · Rowhammer · Saber · Kyber

1 Introduction

Post-quantum cryptography (PQC) refers to cryptographic protocols and algorithms designed to be secure against attacks by both classical and quantum computers. A large quantum computer can *easily* subvert the security assurance

---

Supplementary Information The online version contains supplementary material available at https://doi.org/10.1007/978-3-031-54776-8_11.

of our current widely used public-key cryptographic (PKC) schemes based on integer factorization [52] and elliptic curve cryptography [40] using Shor's [55] and Proos-Zalka's [46] algorithm respectively. Therefore, it is imperative that we replace our existing PKC cryptographic with PQC schemes. However, the transition to post-quantum cryptography is a complex process that involves careful evaluation, standardization, and implementation of new cryptographic algorithms. A watershed moment in this process is the recently concluded standardization procedure by the National Institute of Standards and Technology (NIST) [1]. NIST proposed the key-encapsulation mechanism (KEM) Kyber [14] and digital signature schemes Dilithium [22], Falcon [25] and SPHINCS+ [6] as PQC standards.

Nevertheless, a pivotal step before a cryptosystem can be deployed for widespread public use is the assessment of its physical security. It is not a rare instance when the security of a mathematically secure cryptosystem is completely compromised by physical attacks [4,7,12]. During the standardization process, NIST also highlighted resilience against physical attacks as one of the important criteria in the selection of standards. For physical security assessments, usually, two primary types of attacks are considered. First, passive side-channel attacks (SCA), that work by exploiting flaws in the implementation and using leakage of secret information through physical channels such as power consumption, electromagnetic radiation, acoustic channels, etc. Second, active fault attacks (FA), that work by disrupting the normal execution of a cryptographic scheme through laser radiation, power glitches, etc., and then manipulate the result of the faulty execution to extract the secret key. There exists another type of physical attack known as microarchitectural (MA) attacks. This type of attack exploits the vulnerabilities or imperfections in the architecture of the platform where the cryptographic scheme executes. A strong motivation for studying MA attacks is that while traditional side-channel and fault attacks primarily target small, low-power devices such as microcontrollers e.g. Cortex-M devices and Internet of Things (IoT) devices, MA attacks can affect a much broader range of platforms such as enterprise servers, cloud platforms where multiple honest processes share the same hardware with a potentially hostile process. The two former physical attacks require the attacker to have physical access to the target device, but MA attacks can be performed remotely. Also, there are some relatively simpler methods like constant-time coding techniques that can help defend against some side-channel attack vectors like simple-power analysis, but for MA attacks e.g. Rowhammer-induced bit-flips [43] cannot be easily mitigated through coding practices alone. In the past, successful MA attacks on classical cryptographic schemes such as elliptic-curve discrete signature algorithms and symmetric schemes such as AES [20] have been demonstrated before [5,24,44,54].

Currently, there exist studies on physical attacks on PQC using SCA and FA [30,41,45,49] and some generic countermeasures such as masking and shuffling [15,35,58]. At this moment there exists only a handful of MA attacks on PQ schemes such as digital signature schemes Dilithium and LUOV [31,42] and key-encapsulation mechanism (KEM) Frodo [23]. Among these only Dilithium is a PQC standard. Therefore, we can safely admit that currently there is a huge gap in the literature regarding the assessment and countermeasures of MA attacks. As PQC seems to be prevalent in the near future it is crucial to study MA attacks in the context of PQC schemes. Hence, in this work, we focus on mounting efficient MA attacks on PQC schemes. We briefly summarize our contributions below.

- We study MA attacks or specifically Rowhammer attacks on KEMs based on hard lattice problem learning with errors (LWE). Most LWE-based KEMs share a generic framework Lyubashevsky et al. [38] to first create public-key encryption and then convert it to key-encapsulation mechanism using a version of Fujisaki-Okamoto transform [27]. We sketch an outline of how such generic constructions can be attacked using a Rowhammer-based MA attack. In Rowhammer attacks an attacker repeatedly accesses the memory rows adjacent to the victim process's memory row. Such repeated access can result in bit-flips in the victim process's memory row. Rowhammer can be single-sided when the attacker accesses memory rows only on one side of the target memory row or more aggressively double-sided, where the attacker accesses memory rows above and below the target memory row. This happens due to imperfections in the dynamic random-access memory (DRAM). For interested readers, we have provided more details of Rowhammer in Appendix A.
- Physical attacks on chosen-ciphertext attack (CCA) secure KEMs [30,41,45, 49] work by running the decapsulation procedure or the plaintext checking oracle multiple times with different ciphertexts. At each run side-channel traces are captured or faults are induced which reveal some part of the key. Therefore, reducing the number of invoking the plaintext checking oracle can make the attack more practical. The work in [47] proposed a method to reduce the number of times the plaintext checking oracle is invoked. Here, we further reduced the number of times the oracle is invoked by as much as 39% for Saber and approximately 23% for Kyber768 compared to the previous work using some offline computations. The advantage of our method is not limited to this work only and can be of independent interest in the context of physical attacks on lattice-based KEMs.
- We choose two PQ KEMs Kyber [14] and Saber [21] to demonstrate the practicality of our attack. Kyber is a PQ KEM standard proposed by NIST and Saber was a finalist of the NIST PQC standardization procedure. We tailor our attack according to the design choices and parameters of Saber and Kyber.
- We show an end-to-end key-recovery method on Saber and Kyber based on remote software-induced faults only without using electromagnetic radiation, voltage glitch, laser radiation, etc. Our attack is very realistic as our conditions of attack are very relaxed compared to the previous works.
- Finally, we discuss the effect of existing physical attack countermeasures on our attack.

1.1 Paper Organization

The structure of this paper is organized as follows. The paper is organized as follows: Sect. 2 provides an overview of the necessary background information and introduces the notation and definitions used throughout the paper. Section 3 reviews the previous research conducted in the field. Section 4 presents the generic fault model of LPR schemes and explains its application to Kyber and Saber. Section 5 focuses on the practical realization of the fault model.

2 Preliminaries

Notations: We denote $\mathbb{Z}_q$ to represent the ring of integers modulo q. We use lowercase letters, lowercase letters with a bar, and uppercase letters to denote an element in $\mathbb{Z}_q$, vectors containing elements in $\mathbb{Z}_q$, and matrices with elements in $\mathbb{Z}_q$ respectively. Let $x \in \mathbb{Z}_q$, then x^i represents the i-th bit of x. Bold lowercase letters are used to denote elements in R_q where R_q is the polynomial ring $\mathbb{Z}_q[x]/(x^n + 1)$. For $i \in \{0, 1, \ldots, n-1\}$, $\mathbf{x}[i]$ represents the i-th coefficient of the polynomial $\mathbf{x} \in R_q$. R_q^l represents the ring with vectors of l polynomials of R_q and the ring with matrices of $l \times k$ polynomials of R_q is presented by $R_q^{l \times k}$. We use bold lowercase with a bar and bold uppercase letters to denote elements in R_q^l and $R_q^{l \times k}$, respectively. For $\bar{\mathbf{x}} \in R_q^l$ and $\mathbf{X} \in R_q^{l \times k}$, $\bar{\mathbf{x}}_i$ denotes the i-th polynomial of the vector $\bar{\mathbf{x}}$ and $\mathbf{X}_{i,j}$ denotes the (i, j)-th polynomial of the matrix $\mathbf{X}$. The product of two polynomials $\mathbf{x}$ and $\mathbf{y}$ is denoted by $\mathbf{xy}$. The inner product of $\bar{\mathbf{x}}$ and $\bar{\mathbf{y}}$ in R_q^l is equal to $\sum_{i=0}^{l-1} \bar{\mathbf{x}}_i \bar{\mathbf{y}}_i$ is denoted by $\langle \bar{\mathbf{x}}, \bar{\mathbf{y}} \rangle$. If x is sampled from the set S according to the distribution $\mathcal{X}$, then we denote it as $x \leftarrow \mathcal{X}(S)$. We use $\mathcal{U}$ to represent uniform distribution and β_ν to indicate centered binomial distribution (CBD) with the standard deviation $\sqrt{\nu}/2$. $\lfloor x \rfloor$ outputs the largest integer, which is less than or equal to x. $\lfloor x \rceil$ represents the rounding of x to the nearest integer, which is equal to $\lfloor x + \frac{1}{2} \rfloor$. $r \gg x$ and $r \ll x$ denotes r shifted by x bit positions towards right and left respectively. All these operations can be extended to the polynomials, vectors, and matrices by applying them coefficient-wise. The cardinality of a set S is denoted by $|S|$.

2.1 Learning with Errors (LWE) Problem and Its Variants

LWE Problem: Let us assume $A \leftarrow \mathcal{U}(\mathbb{Z}_q^{l \times k})$, error $\bar{e} \leftarrow \chi(\mathbb{Z}_q^l)$, secret $\bar{s} \leftarrow \chi(\mathbb{Z}_q^k)$, $\bar{b} = A\bar{s} + \bar{e} \in \mathbb{Z}_q^l$, and $\bar{b}' \leftarrow \mathcal{U}(\mathbb{Z}_q^l)$, where l, k, n are positive integers and χ is a distribution. Then, the decision version of the LWE problem states that distinguishing between $(A, \bar{b})$ and $(A, \bar{b}')$ is hard. This hardness depends on the parameter (n, l, k, q, χ) [51].

Ring-LWE (RLWE) Problem: If we use the polynomial ring $R_q = \mathbb{Z}_q[X]/(x^n + 1)$ instead of $\mathbb{Z}_q$ and $l = k = 1$, then we call the problem as Ring learning with error problem (RLWE) [38]. So, in the RLWE problem, given $\mathbf{a} \leftarrow \mathcal{U}(R_q)$, $\mathbf{e}$, $\mathbf{s} \leftarrow \chi(R_q)$, $\mathbf{b} = \mathbf{as} + \mathbf{e} \in R_q$, and $\mathbf{b}' \leftarrow \mathcal{U}(R_q)$, it is hard to distinguish between $(\mathbf{a}, \mathbf{b})$ and $(\mathbf{a}, \mathbf{b}')$. This hardness depends on the parameter (n, q, χ).

Module-LWE (MLWE) Problem: In the MLWE problem [37], $\mathbf{A} \leftarrow \mathcal{U}(R_q^{l \times l})$ and $\bar{\mathbf{e}}$, $\bar{\mathbf{s}} \leftarrow \chi(R_q^l)$, $\bar{\mathbf{b}} = \mathbf{A}\bar{\mathbf{s}} + \bar{\mathbf{e}} \in R_q^l$, and $\bar{\mathbf{b}}' \leftarrow \mathcal{U}(R_q^l)$. The MLWE problem states that it is hard to distinguish between $(\mathbf{A}, \bar{\mathbf{b}})$ and $(\mathbf{A}, \bar{\mathbf{b}}')$. Here, the hardness depends on the parameter (n, l, q, χ).

Learning with Rounding (LWR) Problem: In this problem, the error sampling is replaced by the rounding operation. Let us assume $\mathbf{A} \leftarrow \mathcal{U}(\mathbb{Z}_q^{l \times k})$, $\mathbf{s} \leftarrow \chi(\mathbb{Z}_q^k)$, $\mathbf{b} = \lfloor \frac{p}{q}(\mathbf{As}) \rceil \in \mathbb{Z}_p^l$, and $\mathbf{b}' \leftarrow \mathcal{U}(\mathbb{Z}_p^l)$, where $q > p > 0$. Then the LWR problem states that distinguishing between $(\mathbf{A}, \mathbf{b})$ and $(\mathbf{A}, \mathbf{b}')$ is hard. This hardness depends on the parameter (n, l, k, q, χ) [10].

The ring-LWR (RLWR) problem and the module-LWR (MLWR) problem can be defined from the LWR problem in a similar way as the RLWE problem and the MLWE problem are defined from the LWE problem.

2.2 LPR Public-Key Encryption

Lyubashevsky, Peikert, and Regev proposed the LPR public-key encryption (PKE) scheme based on the RLWE problem [38] as shown in Fig. 2. Throughout this paper, we call this scheme as LPR.PKE. Here all the polynomials are elements of R_q, where q is a prime number and n is a power of two. In LPR.PKE.KeyGen, the secret $\mathbf{s} \leftarrow \chi(R_q)$ and the error $\mathbf{e} \leftarrow \chi(R_q)$. Here, χ is the Gaussian distribution, which is replaced by CBD in Kyber and Saber. $\mathbf{a} \leftarrow \mathcal{U}(\mathbb{Z}_q)$ and $\mathbf{b} = \mathbf{as} + \mathbf{e} \in R_q$. This algorithm declares $pk = (\mathbf{a}, \mathbf{b})$ as public key and saves $sk = (\mathbf{a}, \mathbf{s})$ as private key. In the LPR.PKE.Enc algorithm, a part of the ciphertext $\mathbf{u}$ is computed similarly to the public key $\mathbf{b}$. The other part of the ciphertext $\mathbf{v}$ contains message m and is computed as $\mathbf{v} = \mathbf{br} + \mathbf{e_2} + \text{Encode}(m)$. Here the Encode function is defined as $\text{Encode}(m) = m \cdot \lfloor \frac{q}{2} \rfloor$ i.e. multiplication of each message coefficient $m[i]$ with $\frac{q}{2}$. Then this algorithm outputs $c = (\mathbf{u}, \mathbf{v})$ as the ciphertext of the message m. The LPR.PKE.Dec algorithm takes the ciphertext c, and the secret key $\mathbf{s}$ as input, and then computes $\mathbf{m}' = \mathbf{v} - \mathbf{us}$. Now,

$$\mathbf{m}' = \mathbf{v} - \mathbf{us} = (\mathbf{br} + \mathbf{e_2} + \text{Encode}(m)) - (\mathbf{ar} + \mathbf{e_1})\mathbf{s}$$
$$= (\mathbf{as} + \mathbf{e})\mathbf{r} + \mathbf{e_2} + m \cdot \lfloor q/2 \rfloor - (\mathbf{ar} + \mathbf{e_1})\mathbf{s} = m \cdot \lfloor q/2 \rfloor + \mathbf{er} + \mathbf{e_2} - \mathbf{e_1 s}$$

Here, $\mathbf{d} = \mathbf{er} + \mathbf{e_2} - \mathbf{e_1 s}$ is known as decryption noise. The LPR.PKE.Dec algorithm uses the Decode function to remove the decryption noise from the message polynomial $\mathbf{m}'$ and recovers the message $m \in \{0, 1\}^n$.

Fujisaki-Okamoto (FO) Transformation: The LPR.PKE scheme provides security against chosen-plaintext attacks (CPA) but does not offer protection against chosen-ciphertext attacks (CCA). FO transform is a generic transform to transform a CPA-secure PKE to CCA-secure KEM. Due to the presence of noise in the LPR-based scheme, a variant of FO transformation proposed by Jiang et al. [32] is generally used. The algorithms of this KEM are shown in Fig. 1. A more detailed discussion regarding this FO transformation is provided in Appendix B.

2.3 Kyber

Kyber [14] is an LPR-based KEM with MLWE as its underlying hard problem. In the key generation algorithm of Kyber, the secret $\bar{\mathbf{s}} \leftarrow \beta_{\eta_1}(R_q^l)$ and error $\bar{\mathbf{e}} \leftarrow \beta_{\eta_1}(R_q^l)$. One part of the public key $\mathbf{A} \leftarrow \mathcal{U}(R_q^{l \times l})$ and the another part of the public key is $\bar{\mathbf{b}} = \mathbf{A}\bar{\mathbf{s}} + \bar{\mathbf{e}}$. The secret key is $sk = (\mathbf{A}, \bar{\mathbf{s}})$. In the encryption algorithm, the errors $\bar{\mathbf{r}} \leftarrow \beta_{\eta_1}(R_q^l)$ and the errors $\bar{\mathbf{e}}_1 \leftarrow \beta_{\eta_2}(R_q^l)$ and $\mathbf{e_2} \leftarrow \beta_{\eta_2}(R_q)$. A part of the ciphertext $\bar{\mathbf{u}}$ is computed similarly to the public key $\bar{\mathbf{b}}$ generation. Another part of the ciphertext $\mathbf{v} = \langle \bar{\mathbf{b}}, \bar{\mathbf{r}} \rangle + \mathbf{e_2} + \texttt{Encode}(m)$, where $\texttt{Encode}(m) = \lfloor m \cdot \frac{q}{2} \rfloor$. Then this algorithm uses $\texttt{compress}_q$ to compress each coefficient of $\bar{\mathbf{u}}$ to d_u bits and $\mathbf{v}$ to d_v bits. $c = (\bar{\mathbf{c}}_1, \mathbf{c_2}) = (\texttt{compress}_q(\bar{\mathbf{u}}), \texttt{compress}_q(\mathbf{v}, d_v))$ serves as the ciphertext associated with the message m. The decryption algorithm first

---

LPR.PKE.KeyGen()

1. $\boldsymbol{a} \leftarrow \mathcal{U}(R_q)$
2. $\boldsymbol{s}, \boldsymbol{e} \leftarrow \chi(R_q)$
3. $\boldsymbol{b} = \boldsymbol{as} + \boldsymbol{e}$
4. **return** $(pk = (\boldsymbol{a}, \boldsymbol{b}), sk = (\boldsymbol{a}, \boldsymbol{s}))$

LPR.PKE.Dec($sk = (\boldsymbol{a}, \boldsymbol{s}), c = (\boldsymbol{u}, \boldsymbol{v})$)

1. $\boldsymbol{m}' = \boldsymbol{v} - \boldsymbol{us}$
2. $m = \texttt{Decode}(\boldsymbol{m}')$
3. **return** m

LPR.PKE.Enc($pk = (\boldsymbol{a}, \boldsymbol{b})$, message $m \in \{0, 1\}^n$)

1. $\boldsymbol{r}, \boldsymbol{e}_1, \boldsymbol{e}_2 \leftarrow \chi(R_q)$
2. $\boldsymbol{u} = \boldsymbol{ar} + \boldsymbol{e}_1$
3. $\boldsymbol{v} = \boldsymbol{br} + \boldsymbol{e}_2 + \texttt{Encode}(m)$
4. **return** $c = (\boldsymbol{u}, \boldsymbol{v})$

Fig. 1. CCA secure KEM based on LPR.PKE using FO transformation [32]

Table 1. Parameter set of Kyber and Saber corresponding to different security levels

Scheme Name		Parameters						Post-quantum Security	Failure Probability	NIST Security Level
		l	n	q	p	T	CBD parameters			
Kyber					$p = 2^{d_u}$	$T = 2^{d_v}$	η_1 η_2			
	Kyber512	2	256	3329	2^{10}	2^4	3 2	2^{107}	2^{-139}	1
	Kyber768	3			2^{10}	2^4	2 2	2^{166}	2^{-164}	3
	Kyber1024	4			2^{11}	2^5	2 2	2^{232}	2^{-174}	5
Saber				$q = 2^{\epsilon_q}$	$p = 2^{\epsilon_p}$	$T = 2^{\epsilon_T}$	μ			
	LightSaber	2	256	2^{13}	2^{10}	2^3	5	2^{107}	2^{-120}	1
	Saber	3				2^4	4	2^{172}	2^{-136}	3
	FireSaber	4				2^6	3	2^{236}	2^{-165}	5

decompresses both components $\bar{c}_1$ and c_2 of the ciphertext c with $\mathtt{Decompress}_q$ function. Suppose $\bar{u}' = \mathtt{Decompress}_q(\bar{c}_1,\ d_u)$ and $v' = \mathtt{Decompress}_q(c_2,\ d_v)$. Then it computes $\mathtt{Decode}(v' - \langle \bar{s},\ \bar{u}' \rangle) = \mathtt{Compress}_q((v' - \langle \bar{s},\ \bar{u}' \rangle),\ 1)$ to recover the message m. There are three security versions of Kyber based on the parameter set, and we include them in Table 1. In this paper, unless otherwise specified we refer to the parameter set of Kyber768 with Kyber. For more details, we refer the interested reader kindly to the original paper [14] for further details.

KEM.KeyGen()   KEM.Encaps(pk)

1. $(pk,\ sk) = $ PKE.KeyGen()   1. $m \leftarrow \mathcal{U}(\{0,\ 1\}^n)$
2. $z \leftarrow \mathcal{U}(\{0,\ 1\}^n)$ 2. $(K',\ r) = \mathcal{G}(m,\ \mathcal{H}(pk))$
3. **return** $(pk,\ sk' = (sk\|pk\|\mathcal{H}(pk)\|z)$ 3. $ct = $ PKE.Enc($pk,\ m,\ r$)
                                                    4. $K = \mathcal{F}(K',\ \mathcal{H}(ct))$
                                                    5. **return** $(ct,\ K)$

KEM.Decaps($sk' = (sk\|pk\|\mathcal{H}(pk)\|z),\ ct$)

1. $m' = $ PKE.Dec($sk,\ ct$)
2. $(K'',\ r') = \mathcal{G}(m',\ \mathcal{H}(pk))$
3. $c = $ LPR.PKE.Enc($pk,\ m',\ r'$)
4. **if:** $ct = c$ **return** $K = \mathcal{F}(K'',\ \mathcal{H}(ct))$
5. **else: return** $K = \mathcal{F}(z,\ \mathcal{H}(ct))$

Fig. 2. CPA secure LPR.PKE [38]

2.4   Saber

Saber [21] is a KEM based that also follows the LPR model. Saber is based on the hard problem MLWR. Here q in R_q is power-of-two. In the key generation algorithm of Saber, the secret $\bar{s} \leftarrow \beta_\mu(R_q^l)$. The public key here is $(\mathbf{A},\ \bar{b})$ where $\mathbf{A} \in R$ is an element of $R_q^{l \times l}$ and is sampled uniformly and $\bar{b} = (\mathbf{A}\bar{s} + \bar{h}) \gg (\epsilon_q - \epsilon_p) \in R_p^l$. The vector $\bar{h}$ is needed for rounding, and it consists of constant polynomials with each coefficient equal to $2^{\epsilon_q - \epsilon_p - 1}$. In the case of the encryption algorithm, $\bar{s}'$ is also sampled from the CBD distribution β_μ. The key contained part of the ciphertext $\bar{u}$ is computed similarly to the public key $\bar{b}$. The message contained part of the ciphertext v is computed as $(\langle \bar{b},\ \bar{s}' \rangle + h_1 - \mathtt{Encode}(m) \bmod p) \gg \epsilon_p - \epsilon_T \in R_T$. h_1 is a constant polynomial with each coefficient equal to $2^{\epsilon_q - \epsilon_p - 1}$. It is required for rounding. Let $c = (\bar{u},\ v)$ is the ciphertext corresponding to the message m. Then, the decryption algorithm takes the ciphertext $c = (\bar{u},\ v)$ and secret $\bar{s}$ as inputs. It computes $(\langle \bar{u},\ \bar{s} \rangle \bmod p - 2^{\epsilon_p - \epsilon_T} v + h_2) \bmod p \gg (\epsilon_p - 1) \in R_2$ to find the decrypted message. h_2 is also a constant polynomial with each coefficient equal to $2^{\epsilon_p - 2} - 2^{\epsilon_p - \epsilon_T - 1}$. Like Kyber, Saber also has three security versions depending on the parameter set, and we present them in Table 1. Similar to Kyber, in this paper, we refer to the parameter set of Saber with $l = 3$ with Saber, and we refer to the original paper [21] for further details.

2.5   Related Works

Lattice-based post-quantum KEMs are vulnerable to side-channel attacks. A timing attack on the KEM.Decaps has been shown in [29], it targets the non-constant time implementation of the ciphertext equality checking (Line 4 in KEM.Decap algorithm of Fig. 1). [49], proposed a generic and practical Electromagnetic (EM) power analysis assisted CCA on LWE-based KEMs. They also target the KEM.Decaps in their attack. They have constructed a plaintext-checking oracle $\mathcal{O}$ with the help of an EM power attack, which can distinguish two particular messages $m_1 = 00\ldots0$ (all zeros) and $m_2 = 00\ldots01$ (all zeros except the LSB). This oracle provides single-bit information related to one coefficient of the secret key. Continuing the same methods, the attacker can find the whole secret key. This paper has shown that 2000 to 4000 queries are required to retrieve the complete secret key for Kyber. [56] reduced the query requirements by creating a multiple-valued plaintext-checking oracle. Here, the attacker acquires information regarding multiple secret key coefficients from a single query. In [47], the authors further reduced the number of queries required to recover the whole secret keys by improving the model of plaintext-checking oracle. One significant area of research in this domain revolves around improving the efficiency of attacks by minimizing the number of required quires. This reduction enables a more precise evaluation of the cost of an optimal attack. Our attack contributes in this direction by improving the process of using the parallel plaintext checking oracle model of the paper [47].

Rowhammer has been used to successfully attack many cryptographic primitives. In the paper [50], researchers demonstrated a Rowhammer attack on RSA signatures. Additionally, in [36], the authors illustrate the direct reading of

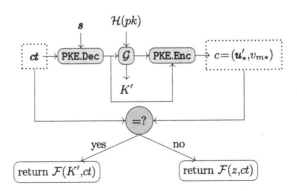

Fig. 3. Decapsulation algorithm of KEM based on LPR.PKE (Fig. 1). Here z is a random number generated in the KEM.KeyGen() algorithm (Fig. 1). The fault location is marked in red.

RSA key bits from the memory address. However, there is limited research on Rowhammer attacks targeting post-quantum schemes. The current state-of-the-art in this domain focuses on a single work involving Rowhammer attacks on the PQC KEM Frodo [13]. This research primarily targets the key-generation procedure, which is known to be relatively easy to protect. In this work, we will demonstrate an end-to-end Rowhammer attack on the decapsulation algorithm of the targeted schemes.

3   Our Attack Using Binary Decision Tree on the LPR-Based Schemes

Attack Surface: The KEM based on LPR.PKE shown in Fig. 1 is resistant to CCA. In such schemes, the secret key is generated using the KEM.KeyGen is *non-ephemeral i.e.* stored and used for the long term. The key generation and encapsulation processes are executed only once. Therefore, the attacker needs to recover the secret key or the shared key from a single execution. However, the secret key remains fixed in the decapsulation algorithm for a long time and is used to derive the shared secret key K from multiple users. This is done to remove the huge overhead of running the key generation process and distributing the public key each time two communicating parties want to establish the shared secret K. However, this convenience also helps an attacker. An attacker can now execute the decapsulation operation multiple times and collect multiple traces or induce faults at different locations. This helps the attacker to refine its attack strategy and increase the probability of success manifold. This is why attacking the decapsulation operation is mostly chosen by attackers to mount physical attacks [30, 41, 45, 49]. So, we also choose the decapsulation method as our target. The structure of the KEM.Decaps given in Fig. 1 is shown in Fig. 3. Here we also assume the attacker can invoke the victim's decapsulation procedure by submitting any ciphertexts of its preference.

We assume the general Rowhammer threat model, where the attacker and victim use two different processes in the same operating system or two virtual machines on the same server [59]. This threat model is also used in most of the micro-architectural attacks work [60]. Here the attacker shares the same hardware responsible for performing the victim's decapsulation procedure of LPR-based KEM. The attacker can also invoke the victim's decapsulation procedure by submitting any ciphertexts of its preference.

3.1   Implementing a Parallel Plaintext Checking (PC) Oracle

In the KEM.Decaps procedure in Fig. 1, the decrypted message m undergoes a hashing operation G with the public key. The resulting hash, denoted as (K', r), where r is combined with the message m and is used as input for the subsequent re-encryption procedure using LPR.PKE.Enc algorithm. The generated key K' is employed to create a valid shared key K. It is crucial to note that the hash function G is deterministic and solely relies on the decrypted message m and public key pk. Considering 2^t messages where a fixed chunk of t bits are changed while keeping all other $n - t$ bits fixed, such as

$$m^{(0)} = \underbrace{000\ldots0}_{t\ bits}\,\underbrace{000\ldots0}_{(n-t)\ bits}$$

$$m^{(1)} = \underbrace{100\ldots0}_{t\ bits}\,\underbrace{000\ldots0}_{(n-t)\ bits}$$

$$m^{(2)} = \underbrace{010\ldots0}_{t\ bits}\,\underbrace{000\ldots0}_{(n-t)\ bits}$$

$$\ldots$$

$$m^{(2^t-1)} = \underbrace{111\ldots1}_{t\ bits}\,\underbrace{000\ldots0}_{(n-t)\ bits}$$

A variation of t bits in these messages leads to substantial variations in the computations performed during the hash $\mathcal{G}$ operation. Consequently, the ciphertexts generated by the LPR.PKE.Enc algorithm will differ for each of the 2^t messages.

In our attack scenario, we require the output to be dependent on the decrypted message. However, if we use artificially constructed ciphertext ct (which is not generated from LPR.PKE.Enc), then with high probability, the re-encrypted ciphertext c and ct will be unequal. The current implementation always returns $\mathcal{F}(z,\ \mathcal{H}(ct))$ as the shared key, which is independent of the decrypted message. In order to distinguish the potential 2^t decrypted messages of the ciphertext ct, we need the output to be message-dependent. By omitting this equality checking condition, we ensure that the hash value $\mathcal{F}(K',\ \mathcal{H}(ct))$ is consistently returned, which is decrypted message dependent. That allows us to differentiate between the possible decrypted messages of ct. Our goal is to reliably acquire the shared key $\mathcal{F}(K',\ \mathcal{H}(ct))$ by employing a physical attack.

In the KEM.Decaps, both Saber and Kyber use a variable named "fail". Compare the ciphertexts ct and c by calling the function verify(c, ct, BYTES_CCA_DEC) and storing the return value of this function in the "fail" variable. If the value of fail is 0, then it returns the shared key $\mathcal{F}(K',\ \mathcal{H}(ct))$, which depends on the decrypted message. Otherwise, it returns the random shared key. Our aim is to flip the value of the variable "fail" by introducing fault even when the ciphertexts are not equal.

3.2   Generic Attack Model Using PC Oracle

The first stage of our attack is to carefully craft ciphertexts c to reduce the number of invocations of the KEM.Decaps procedure. Here, we target to recover t secret coefficients of the secret key s at a time. We introduce a notation $s_i^{(t)}$ to represent a block of consecutive t coefficients of s, where $i \in \{0,\ 1,\ \ldots, \lfloor \frac{n}{t} \rfloor - 1\}$ and the last block $s_{\lfloor \frac{n}{t} \rfloor}^{(t')}$ consists $t' = n - (\lfloor \frac{n}{t} \rfloor \times t)$ secret coefficients. This ciphertext c is then transmitted to the oracle $\mathcal{O}_\mu$. Here the oracle $\mathcal{O}_\mu$ defined as follows:

$$\mathcal{O}_\mu(c; \ x^{(0)}, \ x^{(1)}, \ldots, \ x^{(\mu-1)}) = r, \ \text{if PKE.Dec}(c) = x^{(r)}, 0 \leq r \leq \mu - 1.$$

This oracle $\mathcal{O}_\mu$ takes a ciphertext c and μ number of messages $x^{(i)}$ and returns the value r such that the decrypted message of c is $x^{(r)}$. Upon receiving the ciphertext, the oracle $\mathcal{O}_\mu$ processes c along with a set of potential messages $x^{(0)}, \ x^{(1)}, \ldots, \ x^{(\mu-1)}$. Then, the oracle provides a response r such that LPR.PKE.Dec($sk, \ c$) $= x^{(r)}$. By analyzing the decrypted message $x^{(r)}$, we gain knowledge about the secret block $s_i^{(t)}$. As each secret coefficient is intricately tied to the decrypted message, this process gradually reduces the dimension of the secret coefficients within the targeted block. This reduction process involves considering the relationship between the decrypted message and the secret coefficients. After successfully reducing (not fully recovering) the dimension of the secret block, we construct another new ciphertext c_α that exploits the potential secret block $s_i^{(t)}$. Then, repeating the aforementioned process, we further reduce the cardinality of the secret set corresponding to each coefficient of the secret block to get our desired secret. The challenge lies in determining how many iterations of this process are necessary to effectively reduce the dimension of the secret block $s_i^{(t)}$. One possible approach is to repeat until the entire secret block $s_i^{(t)}$ is obtained. In the paper [47], the authors used this approach. In this method, we need to query the oracle $\mathcal{O}_\mu$ $\lceil \log |S_0| \rceil$ times to find each of the secret blocks $s_i^{(t)}$ and $s_{\lfloor \frac{n}{t} \rfloor}^{(t')}$, where $i \in \{0, \ 1, \ \ldots, \ \lfloor \frac{n}{t} \rfloor - 1\}$ and $t' = n - (\lfloor \frac{n}{t} \rfloor \times t)$. Here, S_0 represents the set of all possible values of a coefficient of the secret key. However, each iteration incurs a cost regarding the number of injected faults. Since each fault is resource-intensive, the objective is to find the secret with the minimum number of faults.

In our approach, we reduce the number of queries to the oracle $\mathcal{O}_\mu$ to find the all secret blocks $s_i^{(t)}$ and $s_{\lfloor \frac{n}{t} \rfloor}^{(t')}$, where $i \in \{0, \ 1, \ \ldots, \lfloor \frac{n}{t} \rfloor - 1\}$ and $t' = n - (\lfloor \frac{n}{t} \rfloor \times t)$. Here, the previous approach is repeated $\lfloor \log |S_0| \rfloor$ times to progressively reduce the cardinality of the secret set corresponding to each coefficient of each secret block. Since we query $\lfloor \log |S_0| \rfloor$ times to the oracle $\mathcal{O}_\mu$ for each block, there will be some secrets that have not been determined yet. So, after reducing the dimension of each secret block, an index set, denoted as Index [], is created to track the indices of the secret coefficients that have not been determined yet. A new ciphertext c_α is then constructed based on the Index [] set, and the values of the secret coefficients corresponding to the indices in Index [] are updated accordingly. For simplicity, we describe this attack template step by step for a parallelization factor t, which is a divisor of n, to unveil the secret block gradually. The process will be similar for other parallelization factor t.

Constructing the Ciphertext c. Here, we present a method to construct a dummy ciphertext $ct = (\mathbf{u}, \ \mathbf{v}) \in R_q \times R_q$. This method helps to decrease the number of queries required to retrieve all the secrets of the block $s_0^{(t)}$, which contains $\{\mathbf{s}[0], \ \mathbf{s}[1], \ \ldots, \ \mathbf{s}[t-1]\}$ first t coefficients of the secret polynomial $\mathbf{s}$. To construct the ciphertext ct, first we set $\mathbf{u}[0] = k_u$ and $\mathbf{v}[j] = k_{v_j}$, $\forall 0 \leq j \leq t-1$ are non zero and others coefficients of $\mathbf{u}$ and $\mathbf{v}$ are zero. Then

$$(\mathbf{v} - \mathbf{us}) = \sum_{j=0}^{t-1} k_{v_j}.x^j - \sum_{j=0}^{n-1} k_u \mathbf{s}[j].x^j$$

$$\text{So } (\mathbf{v} - \mathbf{us})[j] = \begin{cases} (k_{v_j} - k_u \mathbf{s}[j]) & \text{if } 0 \leq j \leq t-1 \\ (-k_u \mathbf{s}[j]) & \text{Otherwise .} \end{cases}$$

Hence the coefficients of the decrypted message m will be

$$m^j = \begin{cases} \texttt{Decode}(k_{v_j} - k_u \mathbf{s}[j]) & \text{if } 0 \leq j \leq t-1 \\ \texttt{Decode}(-k_u \mathbf{s}[j]) & \text{Otherwise .} \end{cases}$$

We choose the value $(k_u, k_{v_0}, k_{v_1}, \ldots, k_{v_{t-1}})$ such that

$$m^j = \begin{cases} \text{Depends on } \mathbf{s}[j] & \text{if } 0 \leq j \leq t-1 \\ 0 & \text{Otherwise} \end{cases}$$

We construct a binary decision tree shown in Fig. 4 to distinguish the secrets. We select each value k_{v_j} from the tree accordingly. Initially, all the values k_{v_j} will be the root value d_0. Then, depending on the decrypted message, we update the value k_{v_j} from the tree. Also, the value of k_u will be fixed in an iteration because we are constructing the dummy ciphertext to get t bits of information at a time.

To recover j'-th secret block, $\mathbf{s}_{j'}^{(t)}$ that contains the secret coefficients $\mathbf{s}[j']$, $\mathbf{s}[j'+1]$, $\ldots$, $\mathbf{s}[j'+t-1])$, where $j' > 0$ we have to construct the dummy ciphertext $ct = (\mathbf{u}, \mathbf{v}) \in R_q \times R_q$, where $\mathbf{u}[n - j'] = k_u$ and $\mathbf{v}[j] = k_{v_j}$, $\forall 0 \leq j \leq t-1$ are non zero and others coefficients of $\mathbf{u}$ and $\mathbf{v}$ are zero. Then

$$(\mathbf{v} - \mathbf{us}) = \sum_{j=0}^{t-1} k_{v_j}.x^j + \sum_{j=j'}^{n-1} k_u \mathbf{s}[j].x^{j-j'} - \sum_{j=0}^{j'-1} k_u \mathbf{s}[j].x^{n-j'+j}$$

Here, the decrypted message m will be

$$m^j = \begin{cases} \texttt{Decode}(k_{v_j} + k_u \mathbf{s}[j'+j]) & \text{if } 0 \leq j \leq t-1 \\ \texttt{Decode}(-k_u \mathbf{s}[j]) & \text{Otherwise} \end{cases} \tag{1}$$

Similarly, the value of k_{v_j} will be taken from the binary decision tree pictured in Fig. 4. We also present the algorithm to create ciphertext in Algorithm 1.

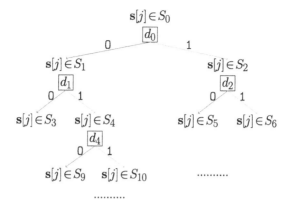

Fig. 4. Binary tree to select the value of $k_{v_j} = d_i$ for each $v[j]$

Parallel PC Oracle for $s_i^{(t)}$ by Pruned Binary Decision Tree: We construct a binary decision tree with two types of nodes; one is the $(S_y,\ d_y)$ where secret set S_y with $|S_y| > 1$ and the constant values d_y which helps us to split the secret set S_y into two disjoint sets S_{2y+1} and S_{2y+2}. The other one is S_y with $|S_y| = 1$ as shown in Fig. 4. We construct the tree such that the tree will be almost complete and the distance of node $(S_y,\ d_y)$ from the root node $(S_0,\ d_0)$ will be longer if the set S_y contains the secret coefficients with comparatively lower probability. Let h be the maximum height of the node of format $(S_y,\ d_y)$ from the root node $(S_0,\ d_0)$. Without loss of generality, assume that this maximum height node is $(S_w,\ d_w)$ i.e., the distance of the node $(S_w,\ d_w)$ from the root node is h and the height of the tree is $h + 1$ which is the distance from the node $(S_0,\ d_0)$ to the node S_{2w+1}. We have distinguished the secrets from the tree as follows:

Algorithm 1. Ciphertext creation I

Input: The index i of secret block $s_i^{(t)}$ and the current secret set S_{r_k} corresponding to the block.

Output: Ciphertext ct such that the decrypted message of c will be zero except the first t positions.

1: **for** $k = 0; k < n; k{+}{+}$ **do**
2:     $u[k] = 0;\ v[k] = 0$
3: **end for**
4: $u[(n - i)\%n] = k_u$
5: **for** $k = 0; k < t; k{+}{+}$ **do**
6:     **if** $s[i + k] \in S_{r_k}$ **then**
7:         $v[k] = d_{r_k}$
8:     **end if**
9: **end for**

First, we will query to the oracle $\mathcal{O}_\mu$ with the constructed ciphertext ct and 2^t messages $m^{(0)}, m^{(1)}, \ldots, m^{(2^t-1)}$ described before. Let $m^{(r)}$ be the decrypted message of the ciphertext ct, which is received from the oracle $\mathcal{O}_\mu$. If the j-th secret coefficient of the block $\mathbf{s}_i^{(t)}$, $\mathbf{s}[i+j] \in S_y$ and $|S_y| > 1$, then we will distinguish $\mathbf{s}[i+j] \in S_{2y+1}$ or $\mathbf{s}[i+j] \in S_{2y+2}$ according to the value of the corresponding j-th message bit of $m^{(r)}$ which is $\texttt{Decode}(d_y - k_u \mathbf{s}[i+j]) = 0/1$ i.e., observing the current secret set S_y in which the secret coefficient belongs and the decrypted bit $\texttt{Decode}(d_y - k_u \mathbf{s}[i+j])$, we reduce the possible values of the secrets from S_y to S_{2y+1} or S_{2y+2}. In each iteration of the block $\mathbf{s}_i^{(t)}$, each value of k_{v_j} will traverse this tree from the root node (S_0, d_0) (with height 0). In our attack, we traverse each value k_{v_j} from the tree up to the height $h-1$, i.e., We pruned the highest heighted node (S_w, d_w) from this tree. In this way, we reduce the cardinality of the secret set corresponding to each secret. Since we ignore the highest height node (S_w, d_w), only secret coefficients that belong to the secret set S_w will still be undetected.

Construction of Index[] Set. As we discussed before, only secret coefficients belonging to the secret set S_w will still be undetected. Now, we will search the indexes of the secret coefficients that are still not decided and store them in a set named "Index[]". Then, we apply the parallel checking oracle $\mathcal{O}_\mu$ on this Index[] set. We describe the detailed process in the following section.

Construction of Ciphertext c_α from Index[]: Before arriving at this stage, we found most secrets except the Index[] set secrets. Without loss of generality, assume that $\mathbf{s}[i] \in S_w \ \forall i \in \texttt{Index[]}$, where S_w contains the values with a low probability occurrence and d_w is the corresponding value of ciphertext selection in the Fig. 4.

Let Index[] $= \{\alpha_0, \alpha_1, \ldots, \alpha_r\}$. Construct the dummy ciphertext $ct = (\mathbf{u}, \mathbf{v}) \in R_q \times R_q$ to reduce the cardinality of the secret set corresponding to each coefficient of the secret coefficients $\mathbf{s}[\alpha_0], \ldots, \mathbf{s}[\alpha_{t-1}]$ (we called it secret block $\mathbf{s}_{\alpha_0, \ldots, \alpha_{t-1}}^{(t)}$ of size t). We choose $\mathbf{u}[0] = k_u$ and $\mathbf{v}[\alpha_j] = d_w, \forall 0 \le j \le t-1$, as each $\mathbf{s}[\alpha_j] \in S_w$. All the remaining coefficients of $\mathbf{u}$ and $\mathbf{v}$ will be zero. Then

---

Algorithm 2. Cardinality reduction of the secret set of the block $\mathbf{s}_i^{(t)}$

Input: The decrypted message m of the ciphertext c such that m is non-zero at most in the first t positions.

Input: The value r_k such that $\mathbf{s}[i+k] \in S_{r_k}$, $0 \le k \le t-1$.

Output: Update $[i+k]$ where $0 \le k \le t-1$.

1: **for** $l = 0; l < t; l{+}{+}$ **do**
2:     **if** $m^l = 0$ **then**
3:         $\mathbf{s}[i+l] \in S_{2r_l+1}$
4:     **else**
5:         $\mathbf{s}[i+l] \in S_{2r_l+2}$
6:     **end if**
7: **end for**

Algorithm 3. Ciphertext creation II

Input: The index $\alpha_0, \ldots, \alpha_{t-1}$ of those we want to find actual secret.

Output: Ciphertext ct such that the decrypted message of c will be zero except the positions $\alpha_0, \ldots, \alpha_{t-1}$.

1: **for** $k = 0; k < n; k++$ **do**
2:     $\mathbf{u}[k] = 0;\ \mathbf{v}[k] = 0$
3: **end for**
4: $\mathbf{u}[0] = k_u$
5: **for** $k = 0; k < t; k++$ **do**
6:     $\mathbf{v}[\alpha_k] = d_w$
7: **end for**

---

the decrypted message will be

$$m^j = \begin{cases} \text{Decode}(d_w - k_u \mathbf{s}[j]) & \text{if } j = \alpha_0, \ \ldots, \ \alpha_{t-1} \\ \text{Decode}(-k_u \mathbf{s}[j]) & \text{Otherwise} \end{cases} \tag{2}$$

So, the message will depend on all the α_j-th secret coefficient $\mathbf{s}[\alpha_j]$, where $0 \leq j \leq t-1$, which is followed by the construction of our binary decision tree shown in the Fig. 4.

We query the oracle $\mathcal{O}_\mu$ with the forged ciphertext c_α and the 2^t messages $m^{(0)'}, m^{(1)'}, \ldots, m^{(2^t-1)'}$ to get t bits of information with location $\alpha_0, \ldots, \alpha_{t-1}$ simultaneously. Here, we take each message $m^{(i)'}$ such that α_j-th bit of the message $m^{(i)'}$ is the j-th bit of i and the others bits are zero. Here, we use Algorithm 3 to create forged ciphertexts.

Updating the Secret Coefficients Whose Index Lies in Index[]: We divide the sampling set into two distinct parts: $S_{2w+1} = \{s : \text{Decode}(d_w - k_u s) = 0\}$ and $S_{2w+2} = \{s : \text{Decode}(d_w - k_u s) = 1\}$, where d_w is a predefined constant. Since S_w contains the values such that the highest distance from the root node with $|S_w| > 1$, therefore $|S_{2w+1}|$ and $|S_{2w+2}|$ must be 1. Otherwise, it violates our assumption of the set S_w. So, querying the oracle $\mathcal{O}_\mu$ with one ciphertext c_α and the above messages $m^{(0)'}, m^{(1)'}, \ldots, m^{(2^t-1)'}$, we will get a decrypted message as a response. This decrypted message decides the t number of secret coefficients $\mathbf{s}[\alpha_0], \mathbf{s}[\alpha_1] \ldots, \mathbf{s}[\alpha_{t-1}]$ at a time. So, running the process $\lceil \frac{|\text{Index}[]|}{t} \rceil$ times, we will find the whole secret with mixed signs and in a different order. We described the process of finding the secret in actual order. Also, from Eq. 1, we can see that for the secret block $\mathbf{s}_{j'}^{(t)}$, each j-th message m^j will depend on the secret coefficient $-s[j' + j], 0 \leq j' \leq t-1$. So basically, we are decreasing the dimension secret coefficients $\mathbf{s}[0], \ldots, \mathbf{s}[t-1], -\mathbf{s}[n-t], -\mathbf{s}[n-t+1] \ldots, -\mathbf{s}[n-1], -\mathbf{s}[n-2t], \ldots, -\mathbf{s}[n-t-1], \cdots - \mathbf{s}[t], -\mathbf{s}[t+1], \ldots, -\mathbf{s}[2t-1]$. We transformed it into the actual secret block using the Algorithm 4.

Number of Queries: Here (S_w, d_w) is the most distanced node from the root node with $|S_w| > 1$ and containing secrets occurring with comparatively lower probability.

Algorithm 4. Rotating secret coefficients

Input: The secret $\mathbf{s}$ is in the sequence $\mathbf{s}[0]$, ..., $\mathbf{s}[t-1]$, $-\mathbf{s}[n-t]$, $-\mathbf{s}[n-t+1]$, ..., $-\mathbf{s}[n-1]$, $-\mathbf{s}[n-2t]$, ..., $-\mathbf{s}[n-t-1]$, $\cdots = \mathbf{s1}$

Output: The secret $\mathbf{s}$ with actual order i.e.,($\mathbf{s}[0]$, $\mathbf{s}[1]$, ..., $\mathbf{s}[n-1]$)

1: **for** $j = 0; j < t; j++$ **do**
2:     $\mathbf{s}[j] = \mathbf{s1}[j]$;
3: **end for**
4: **for** $j = 1; j < \lfloor \frac{n}{t} \rfloor; j++$ **do**
5:     **for** $k = 0; k < t; k++$ **do**
6:         $\mathbf{s}[t*j+k] = -\mathbf{s1}[(n-t*j+k)\%n]$;
7:     **end for**
8: **end for**
9: Return $\mathbf{s}$

---

1. Best case: If all the secret values lie in $S_0 - S_w$, then the number of queries will be minimum because, in this case, we need $\lfloor \log |S_0| \rfloor$ queries to find each block of secrets $\mathbf{s}_i[j]$, $\mathbf{s}_i[j+1]$, ..., $\mathbf{s}_i[j+t-1]$ of blocksize t. The total number of queries will be: $\lceil \frac{n}{t} \rceil \times \lfloor \log |S_0| \rfloor$.
2. Average case: Let E_1 be the expected number the secret coefficients those belongs to S_w. Then the total number of queries will be: $(\lceil \frac{n}{t} \rceil \times \lfloor \log |S_0| \rfloor) + (\lceil \frac{E_1}{t} \rceil)$.

With our method, the number of queries for the average case decreases compared to the state-of-the-art works [47,56].

3.3 Model for Kyber and Saber

Kyber and Saber are based on the module-LWE and module-LWR problems, respectively i.e., here, the modules R_q^l are used for the secret and the ciphertext $\bar{\mathbf{b}}'$ instead of the ring R_q. But if we construct $c = (\bar{\mathbf{b}}', \mathbf{v})$ as follows:

$$\bar{\mathbf{b}}'_i[j] = \begin{cases} k_u, \text{ if } i = 0, j = 0 \\ 0, \text{ otherwise} \end{cases} \quad \text{and} \quad \mathbf{v}[j] = \begin{cases} k_{v_j}, \text{ if } 0 \le j \le t-1 \\ v, \text{ otherwise}, \end{cases}$$

where k_u, k_{v_j} are constants. Then the problem reduces to the generic LPR problem, i.e., to the ring problem. Therefore, here the total number of queries will be $l \times$ **the number of queries for LPR**. We use the corresponding d_i from Table 2 and 3 for Kyber768 and the Saber, respectively. We will construct the corresponding binary decision tree from Table 2 and 3 and construct our ciphertext accordingly. For Kyber768, we have seen that for $k_u = 38$, $v = 14$ and $k_{v_j} = d_i$. From Table 2, we can recover the secret by a similar process mentioned in the previous section.

Number of Queries for Kyber768 and Saber: According to Table 2, for Kyber768 S_4 will be the highest distanced node from the root node containing

Table 2. For Kyber768

S	$d_0 = 12$	$d_1 = 4$	$d_2 = 13$	$d_4 = 3$
-2	0	1	0	1
-1	0	1	0	0
0	0	0	0	0
1	1	0	0	0
2	1	0	1	0

Table 3. For Saber

S	$u = 0x3c8$							$u = 7$
	d_0 =4	d_2 =2	d_5 =3	d_6	d_1 =6	d_3 =7	d_4 =5	d_7 =12
-4	0	0	0	0	0	0	0	0
-3	0	0	0	0	0	1	0	0
-2	0	0	0	0	1	1	0	0
-1	0	0	0	0	1	1	1	0
0	1	0	0	0	1	1	1	0
1	1	0	1	0	1	1	1	0
2	1	1	1	0	1	1	1	0
3	1	1	1	1	1	1	1	0
4	1	1	1	1	1	1	1	1

secrets with comparatively low probability and $|S_4| > 1$. Also, Table 3 shows that for Saber, S_7 will be that specified node above. For Kyber768 and Saber, $l = 3$, we consider our best case and average cases of both the algorithms for $l = 3$.

1. Best case: In case of Kyber768, if all the secret values lie in $S_0 - S_4$, then the number of queries will be minimum because, in this case, we need 2 queries to find each block of secrets $\bar{s}_i[j]$, $\bar{s}_i[j+1]$, ..., $\bar{s}_i[j+t-1]$ of blocksize t. The total number of queries will be: $\lceil \frac{n}{t} \rceil \times 3 \times 2$. For Saber this number will be $\lceil \frac{n}{t} \rceil \times 3 \times 3$.
2. Average case: In the case of Kyber768, if E_1 is the expected number of the secret coefficients of each polynomial that lie in the set S_4, the total number of queries will be: $3 \times ((\lceil \frac{n}{t} \rceil \times 2) + \lceil \frac{E_1}{t} \rceil)$. Similarly, for Saber, if E_1 is the expected number of the secret coefficient of each polynomial that lies in S_7, then the total number of queries will be: $3 \times ((\lceil \frac{n}{t} \rceil \times 3) + \lceil \frac{E_1}{t} \rceil)$.

3.4 Comparing Our Attack with the State-of-the-Art

In this section, we compare the total number of ciphertexts required to retrieve the whole secret key for the average case in Kyber768 and Saber with our attack and the work by Rajendran et al. [47], which also proposed methods to reduce the number of ciphertexts using parallel plaintext checking oracle model. Even though we need to use the same number of ciphertext as [47] to recover the whole secret key when the parallelization factor $t = 1$, our attack model requires less number of ciphertexts than [47] to recover the whole secret key in the average case when the parallelization factor $t > 1$. If $t = 10$ or 12 or 16, for Kyber768 we use approximately 22% less number of ciphertext than [47]. Also, in Saber, if we take $t = 10$, we require $\approx 39\%$ less number of ciphertext than the paper [47] to recover the key. However, we require 57 number of ciphertext to recover the whole secret key of Kyber768 in the average case when the parallelization factor $t = 32$. We observe that increasing the parallelization factor t will reduce the number of required ciphertexts. However, in this case, the process of finding the decrypted message from the shared key (offline calculation) will be more costly (takes 2^t comparison). For this reason, we take the value of the parallelization factor t up to 32. But, with a more powerful computer that can do 2^{40} comparison, then we can take the parallelization factor $t = 40$. In this case, the number of queries will be 48.

Frequency of Fault Induction in the Attack for Kyber768: We have discussed earlier that to recover the whole secret of the algorithm Kyber768, we require 57 faulted shared keys i.e., 57 many times, we often have to introduce the bit-flip faults at the location of the variable "fail" (Table 4).

Table 4. Number of queries required to recover the key for Kyber768 and Saber in total

Scheme		Parallelization factor t					
		1	10	12	16	32	40
Kyber768	This work $3 \times ((\lceil \frac{256}{t} \rceil \times 2) + \lceil \frac{80}{t} \rceil)$	1776	**180**	**153**	**111**	**57**	**48**
	Rajendran et al. [47]	1776	232	197	144	72	63
Saber	This work $3 \times ((\lceil \frac{256}{t} \rceil \times 3) + \lceil \frac{9}{t} \rceil)$	2331	**237**	201	147	75	66
	Rajendran et al. [47]	–	390	–	–	–	–

4   Realization of the Fault Model

In this section, we are going to illustrate an end-to-end strategy to demonstrate the fault model in practice.

4.1   Nature of the Fault in the Attack

In the previous sections, we discuss that our objective is to obtain the output $\mathcal{F}(K', \mathcal{H}(ct))$ by exploiting a fault, where K' is derived from the decrypted message m of the ciphertext ct. This fault uses the plaintext checking oracle $\mathcal{O}_\mu$. To achieve this, it is crucial to neutralize the effectiveness of comparing two ciphertexts, denoted as c and ct, in terms of equality checking. For all security levels of Saber and Kyber, the design employs a `verify` function that takes two ciphertexts, c and ct, along with their lengths and returns 0 if they are equal or 1 otherwise. The result is stored in a variable called "fail". In our attack, we construct ciphertexts in a particular pattern, ensuring that the ciphertexts c and ct are highly likely to be unequal. As a result, the variable "fail" will always be set to 1. This allows us to perform a bit-flip or get stuck at zero at the location of the "fail" variable, thus obtaining our desired output $\mathcal{F}(K', \mathcal{H}(ct))$. If we observe that for our constructed ciphertext ct, the value of the shared key is different from $\mathcal{F}(z, \mathcal{H}(ct))$. At this time, we are ensured that the value of the "fail" variable has changed to 0, and this value is our essential shared key $\mathcal{F}(K', \mathcal{H}(ct))$.

A stuck-at-zero fault is where a signal or a specific bit within a circuit is constantly held at logic zero. This fault can occur due to manufacturing defects, electrical shorts, environmental factors, or other physical issues. In contrast, a bit-flips fault involves the unintentional change of a single bit within a circuit or memory location from its intended value to the opposite value. Both stuck-at-zero and bit-flip faults can have various causes and implications. It is important to note that the specific type and cause of these faults can vary depending on the context, such as the hardware or software implementation, the cryptographic scheme used, and the fault injection techniques employed. Stuck-at-zero and bit-flip faults can lead to unexpected behaviour, data corruption, security vulnerabilities, or system crashes. To ensure system reliability and data integrity, detecting and mitigating these faults often involves employing error detection and correction techniques, such as error-correcting codes, redundant storage methods, or fault-tolerant designs.

Table 5. Model details of our target devices

	Model name	RAM size
1	Intel (R) Core (TM) i7-4770 CPU	4 GB
2	Intel (R) Core (TM) i7-3770 CPU	8 GB
3	Intel (R) Core (TM) i5-3330 CPU	4 GB

In this paper, we choose Dynamic Random Access Memory (DRAM) reliability issue *Rowhammer* to introduce a software-driven hardware fault attack to induce a bit-flip ($1 \rightarrow 0$) at the address of the "fail" variables. We also present a series of steps that could be followed to incorporate this fault at a precise location in realistic timeframes.

4.2   Our Target Devices

To demonstrate our attack, we employ a deliberate technique of inducing bit-flips during the decapsulation process of Kyber. In our model, the attacker is assumed to be colocated in the same server as the victim, which performs the decapsulation process of Kyber and Saber. This scenario can also be extended to multiple virtual machines operating on a shared server. In this model, the primary assumption is that the victim and the attacker are co-located on the same physical piece of memory hardware, typically a DRAM and the vulnerable locations are neighbors to each other. This model exists in the current research field of row hammer [16,23] and is also consistent with most microarchitectural attacks [17]. Furthermore, since Kyber and Saber are designed as a CCA-secure scheme, our attack assumes that the attacker can often query the decapsulation process with the constructed ciphertext. We demonstrate our attack against the machines listed in Table 5.

4.3   Probabilities of Incorporating Precise Fault Using Random Rowhammer

The task of incorporating bit-flips in random locations in memory is common and is very well studied in literature after Rowhammer has been reported in practice, but the hard part is to precisely induce the faults in the location of one's choice. In this paper, considering the target example, if we run the target code of Kyber/Saber multiple times in one process and an unsupervised row hammer code in another process, the address of the variable "fail" coinciding with one of the vulnerable locations, the probability of such event occurrence is considerably low. Suppose there are a total N number of vulnerable locations after hammering randomly among N_1 locations present on a device. Then, the possibility of the variable "fail" being vulnerable = Pr(the location of "fail"=X) × Pr("fail" coincide in a vulnerable location |the location of "fail" = X) = $\frac{1}{N_1} \times \frac{N}{N_1} = \frac{N}{N_1^2}$, which is very low as $N_1 \gg N$. In our system, we randomly access $N_1 = 2^{30}$ bytes of memory; we discovered $N < 10$ vulnerable locations by accessing the memory randomly. Notably, the number of vulnerable locations (N) is considerably smaller than the total memory access. In order to make this process deterministic, we follow the steps described below.

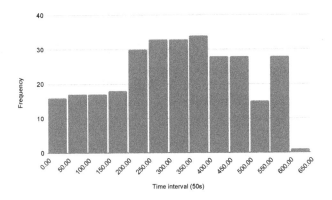

Fig. 5. Frequency of bit-flips in every 50 s

Using the Deterministic Process of Rowhammer: We have used the *hammertime* code[1] available at [57] to execute row hammering operations. Through our exploration, we have observed that *hammertime* is a valuable simulator, offering a convenient approach to deterministically evaluate vulnerable locations. This versatile tool is purpose-built for testing, profiling, and simulating the Rowhammer DRAM attack, providing a comprehensive suite of capabilities for assessing the outcomes of exploits.

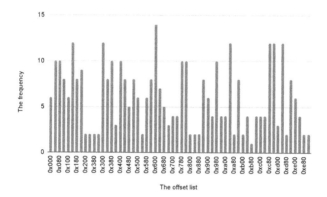

Fig. 6. Frequency of the bit-flips in the corresponding offset.

The provided code presents two types of row hammering techniques: single-sided row hammering and double-sided row hammering. We have employed the single-sided row hammering process outlined in their code for our implementation. In each iteration of this approach, our target is to find the vulnerable rows from an aggressive row's upper or lower rows. Also, in our victim machine, the bit-flip occurs considerably frequently. Figure 5 shows the bit-flip frequency in every 50 s. In the hammertime code, we observe that this code deterministically selects an aggressive row, then fills up the memory with values all 1's ("0xff") in the aggressive row and its neighbouring rows, and repeatedly flushes the corresponding portions of cache memory allocation. Iteratively, it only accesses the addresses with offsets $A = \{a_i\}_i$, where $a_0 = 0$ and $a_{i+1} - a_i = $ 0x020, for all i to check the bit-flip result. So, we can get the vulnerable address with the offset lie in A by running the hammering code. Figure 6 shows the offsets of the bitflip addresses and their frequency observed in our experiments. We perform a first-level templating of main memory using the *hammertime* code as shown in Fig. 6, identifying locations that are vulnerable to Rowhammer. This templating step also aids us in identifying trigger rows so that we can replicate Rowhammer deterministically by re-accessing those aggressor rows again over time. By using the hammering code, we get the vulnerable addresses having different offsets and construct the set A. In this particular attack algorithm, we

---

[1] "https://github.com/vusec/hammertime.git".

want the adversary to induce a bit-flip to a known vulnerable location. In order to achieve that, the variable in the decapsulation process (target "fail" variable) must coincide with atleast one offset in the set A of vulnerable addresses in order to precisely induce the fault. In order to increase the reproducibility of the attack over multiple runs, we have assigned the datatype of the variable "fail" in our implementation to "static int" rather than simply using "int". Doing so guarantees that the offset of the "fail" variable remains unchanged throughout the execution. Without loss of generality, if our attack methodology is implemented on any other target secret, then a similar technique could be applied to any global variable or a local variable with a static flag for the sake of the reproducibility of our attack. We consider the offset 0x040 of the "fail" variable, which was observed on our executable. This offset can be any value without loss of generality in Kyber/Saber's implementation, and the appropriate matching offset of the Rowhammer fault can also be selected from the templating phase. In our attack scenario, we select the vulnerable locations offset of 0x040 to show the vulnerability. We construct the following template shown in Fig. 7.

Process 1	Process 2
1. Run the "hammertime code" until we get the bit-flip $(1 \rightarrow 0)$ at the location A	
2. Unmap the page of A	3.Run the decapsulation code of Kyber/Saber
4. Run the "hammertime code" for the same location A	

Fig. 7. Template of generating oracle $\mathcal{O}_\mu$ using Rowhammer

The templating method in Rowhammer provides a method that induces a bit-flip from 1 to 0 at the "fail" variable. First, we run the *hammertime* code and observe a bit-flip $(1 \rightarrow 0)$ at an address with the offset 0x040. In this phase, we proceed to unmap the corresponding page of that address and emit a signal, enabling us to execute the victim code in process 2. With a high likelihood, the victim code gets mapped to the unmapped page just being freed by the *hammertime* executable. This will allow the "fail" variable to be sitting in the Rowhammer vulnerable location of the unmapped page. The scenario of page reallocation of the recently unmapped page is commonly encountered using the Page Frame Cache during page allocations involving the buddy allocator [16].

After successfully aligning the "fail" variable with the vulnerable location of Rowhammer, our objective is to actually induce the fault in the target location to change its value to "0". To accomplish this, we need to continue performing row hammering on the same aggressive row that inflicted the Rowhammer in the templating phase. This ensures that the bit-flip occurs at the same vulnerable address, which is now unmapped from the hammering code, but possessed by the target executable of the victim. To achieve this, we made some modifications to the *hammertime* tool, and iterated through the following processes.

An extra *loop* is added inside the *profile_singlesided* function. Once the target page is unmapped, only then this *loop* will run. The *loop* contains minor modifications to the following functions *fill_rows* and *c->hamfunc*. This modification involves a checking condition that inside the function *fill_rows*, we ignore the addresses lying on the unmapped page. This function activates aggressive rows and neighbor rows and as a result, the vulnerable address is affected, leading to a change in its bit from "1" to "0".

After unmapping the page, we run the victim code (decapsulation process with our constructed ciphertext) parallel to the *hammertime code* until we observe the faulty shared key. If we observe a different shared key, then the Rowhammer attempt has been successful and we stop this process. We summarize the whole process as follows:

1. By running the hammering code, vulnerable addresses with offsets from set A are identified, and the "fail" variable is positioned to coincide with one of these vulnerable addresses. A suitable vulnerable location is selected and the corresponding page is unmapped from the code.
2. After unmapping the page, we run the victim code until we do not get the faulty shared key. If we get a different shared key, then we are done.
3. To achieve a bit-flip from "1" to "0" at the "fail" variable, row hammering is continued on the same aggressive row, modifying the fill_row function to fill memory with "0xff" and performing a memory flush on all addresses except the unmapped page corresponding to the vulnerable address.

Figure 8 illustrates the distribution of timings observed for the Rowhammer bit-flip to occur at the vulnerable location through the *hammertime* code after unmapping the vulnerable page.

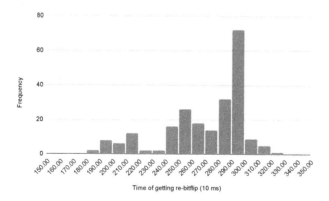

Fig. 8. The value of an interval $[a, b]$ is the number of bit-flips which takes the time $t \in [a, b]$, to make re-bitflip at the same address

In order to estimate the total time to recover the whole secret key we need 57 independent queries to the oracle. This translates to 57 independent fault occurrences on the "fail" variable in the implementation of the decapsulation algorithm. One such occurrence can be estimated to happen in $< 350ms$ with a significantly high probability. So this attack can be realised using an additive progression of timing on respective queries and can be observed in a linear timescale.

5   Discussion and Future Direction

In this paper, we show an end-to-end software-driven hardware fault on PQ LWE-based KEMs. We choose Saber and Kyber key encapsulation schemes and perform the fault analysis with as much as 39% reduced number of queries for Saber and approximately 23% for Kyber768 on the existing literature. This was achieved by pruning selected leaves of the decisional binary search tree used in the attack. The fault induction using the Rowhammer has been known in the literature to appear in random locations of memory due to the reliability issues of commercial DDR RAMs. We follow some precise steps by first templating the memory space, listing out vulnerable addresses of a system, and then precisely locating the target KEM implementation in that vulnerable location. In this context, we use publicly available *Hammertime* code to template the memory space, then make minor modifications to re-induce Rowhammer using the selected aggressor rows on that same location deterministically. This semi-deterministic process is highly useful in conjunction with the paging policies of the Buddy allocator, and then inflicting these bit-flips on the publicly available target implementation.

Though there has been recent work on Frodo KEM [23], where the authors incorporate fault in the key generation phase using Rowhammer. As discussed in Sect. 3, the key generation of a CCA-secure KEM is a one-time operation and is invoked rarely. Hence, if necessary the key generation can even be done offline in an isolated environment. On the other hand, the decapsulation of a CCA-secure KEM is invoked multiple times to generate the shared secret key from multiple sources. Therefore, in a practical scenario for the sake of performance, the decapsulation cannot run in an isolated environment. Therefore the attack described in [23] is far less realistic than our attack methodology. Further, the authors assume that they can slow down the execution by slowing down components of the target executable. This is already a strong assumption. Additionally, the authors have disabled ASLR (Address Space Layout Randomization) for their experiments which makes the assumptions even stronger and the attack more unrealistic.

5.1   Shuffling and Masking:

Previous attacks [47,56] based on parallel plaintext checking oracle have used side-channel analysis such as EM power analysis. So, these attacks can be prevented using masking countermeasures [48]. Our attack can be conducted on the masked or shuffled implementation of the LWE-based KEMs. Because here, we do not use any side-channel assistance to perform the attack. We induce a bitflip fault to the "fail" variable, which stores the result of the comparison between the public ciphertext and the re-encrypted ciphertext. As a result of this fault, the value of the "fail" variable always remains 0, and that causes decapsulation success. When applying side-channel countermeasures such as masking and shuffling on the decapsulation algorithm of LWE-based KEMs [15,35,58], this fail variable remains unaffected and unmasked, since it is not dependent on the secret. Therefore, the success of our attack does not get affected by generic side-channel countermeasures such as masking or shuffling.

5.2   Extension of Our Attack on Other PQC Schemes

The parallel plaintext checking oracle used in our attack model can be applicable to any LWE-based KEMs. It is not specific to Saber and Kyber. It can be applicable to other LWE-based schemes such as NewHope [3], Lizard citeCheon-KLS18, Round5 [9], Frodo [13], Smaug [18](proposed in the ongoing Korean PQC [34] competition), etc. The Rowhammer methodology we propose in this work to introduce fault can also be applicable to other fault attack models where a single or multi-bit fault is required. Popular side-channel countermeasures such as masking and shuffling are ineffective to protect against this attack.

5.3   Combining of Lattice Reduction Techniques with Our Attack

There can be some cases when the attacker only has a limited number of accesses to the decapsulation procedure. Then, the attacker can use our attack to recover some of the coefficients of the secret key and then use lattice reduction techniques to recover the rest of the secret key [28]. The LWE-estimator toolbox [2,19] can provide an estimate on the computation effort required to recover the secrets using the lattice reduction techniques. It is up to the attacker to determine the optimum point till when our attack should be stopped and the lattice reduction methods should be used. However, more investigation is needed to combine our attack results with these LWE-estimators to efficiently recover the secret key. We would like to investigate it in the future.

5.4   Possible Countermeasures

Although masking or shuffling countermeasures are unable to prevent our attack, there are a few countermeasures that can be useful to thwart our attack. Below, we list these countermeasures in two categories.

– Fault attack countermeasure on the LWE-based schemes: Recently, Berthet et al. [11] propose a countermeasure named quasi-linear masking on Kyber to prevent fault injection attacks together with side-channel attacks. This countermeasure might be used to prevent our attack.

- Rowhammer Countermeasures: There have been various countermeasures of RowHammer attacks proposed in the literature. The authors in the paper [33] proposed Probabilistic Adjacent Row Activation (PARA), where the memory controller is designed to refresh its adjacent rows with probability p (typically 1/2). The memory controller being probabilistic, the approach does not require a complex data structure for counting the number of row activations. Earlier in [53], it was shown that doubling the refresh rate and removing access to clflush instruction are potential prevention techniques to RowHammer. An interesting countermeasure to rowhammer has been proposed in Anvil [8]. If the cache misses over a time interval is observed to be significantly high, then the software module triggers sampling of the DRAM accesses. ANVIL selectively performs a row refresh if the software module detects repeated accesses to particular rows in the same bank. Another process, Target Row Refresh (TRR), believed to be a definitive solution, can prevent RowHammer bit flips [39] [1]. However, in the paper [26], the authors also find that consumer CPUs rely on in-DRAM TRR and are vulnerable to many-sided RowHammer attacks. They introduce TRRespass, which can autonomously discover intricate hammering patterns to launch real-world attacks on numerous DDR4 DRAM modules available in the market. Till now, there is no concrete solution that can prevent the RowHammer bit flip problem. [1] J.-B. Lee, "Green Memory Solution," in Samsung Electronics, Investor's Forum, 2014.

Acknowledgements. This work was supported in part by Horizon 2020 ERC Advanced Grant (101020005 Belfort), CyberSecurity Research Flanders with reference number VR20192203, BE QCI: Belgian-QCI (3E230370) (see beqci.eu), and Intel Corporation.

Angshuman Karmakar is funded by FWO (Research Foundation - Flanders) as a junior post-doctoral fellow (contract number 203056/1241722N LV). Puja Mondal and Angshuman Karmakar are also supported by C3iHub, IIT Kanpur.

References

1. Alagic, G., et al.: Status Report on the third round of the nist post-quantum cryptography standardization process (2022). https://nvlpubs.nist.gov/nistpubs/ir/2022/NIST.IR.8413-upd1.pdf. Accessed 26 Jun 2023
2. Albrecht, M.R., Player, R., Scott, S.: On the concrete hardness of Learning with Errors. Cryptology ePrint Archive, Report 2015/046 (2015). https://eprint.iacr.org/2015/046
3. Alkim, E., Ducas, L., Pöppelmann, T., Schwabe, P.: Post-quantum key exchange - a new hope. In: Holz, T., Savage, S. (eds.) 25th USENIX Security Symposium, USENIX Security 16, Austin, TX, USA, August 10–12, 2016, pp. 327–343. USENIX Association (2016). https://www.usenix.org/conference/usenixsecurity16/technical-sessions/presentation/alkim
4. Aranha, D.F., Fouque, P.-A., Gérard, B., Kammerer, J.-G., Tibouchi, M., Zapalowicz, J.-C.: GLV/gls decomposition, power analysis, and attacks on ECDSA signatures with single-bit nonce bias. In: Sarkar, P., Iwata, T. (eds.) ASIACRYPT 2014. LNCS, vol. 8873, pp. 262–281. Springer, Heidelberg (2014). https://doi.org/10.1007/978-3-662-45611-8_14

5. Aranha, D.F., Novaes, F.R., Takahashi, A., Tibouchi, M., Yarom, Y.: LadderLeak: breaking ECDSA with less than one bit of nonce leakage. In: Proceedings of the 2020 ACM SIGSAC Conference on Computer and Communications Security. CCS 2020, New York, NY, USA, pp. 225–242, Association for Computing Machinery (2020). https://doi.org/10.1145/3372297.3417268

6. Aumasson, J.P., et al.: SPHINCS+: stateless hash-based signatures. https://sphincs.org/. Accessed 28 Jun 2023

7. Aumüller, C., Bier, P., Fischer, W., Hofreiter, P., Seifert, J.-P.: Fault attacks on RSA with CRT: concrete results and practical countermeasures. In: Kaliski, B.S., Koç, K., Paar, C. (eds.) CHES 2002. LNCS, vol. 2523, pp. 260–275. Springer, Heidelberg (2003). https://doi.org/10.1007/3-540-36400-5_20

8. Aweke, Z.B., et al.: ANVIL: software-based protection against next-generation rowhammer attacks. ACM SIGPLAN Notices **51**(4), 743–755 (2016)

9. Baan, H., Bhattacharya, S., Fluhrer, S., Garcia-Morchon, O., Laarhoven, T., Rietman, R., Saarinen, M.-J.O., Tolhuizen, L., Zhang, Z.: Round5: compact and fast post-quantum public-key encryption. In: Ding, J., Steinwandt, R. (eds.) PQCrypto 2019. LNCS, vol. 11505, pp. 83–102. Springer, Cham (2019). https://doi.org/10.1007/978-3-030-25510-7_5

10. Banerjee, A., Peikert, C., Rosen, A.: Pseudorandom functions and lattices. In: Pointcheval, D., Johansson, T. (eds.) EUROCRYPT 2012. LNCS, vol. 7237, pp. 719–737. Springer, Heidelberg (2012). https://doi.org/10.1007/978-3-642-29011-4_42

11. Berthet, P., Tavernier, C., Danger, J., Sauvage, L.: Quasi-linear Masking to Protect Kyber against both SCA and FIA. IACR Cryptol. ePrint Arch. p. 1220 (2023). https://eprint.iacr.org/2023/1220

12. Biehl, I., Meyer, B., Müller, V.: Differential fault attacks on elliptic curve cryptosystems. In: Bellare, M. (ed.) CRYPTO 2000. LNCS, vol. 1880, pp. 131–146. Springer, Heidelberg (2000). https://doi.org/10.1007/3-540-44598-6_8

13. Bos, J.W., et al.: Frodo: take off the ring! practical, quantum-secure key exchange from LWE. In: Weippl, E.R., Katzenbeisser, S., Kruegel, C., Myers, A.C., Halevi, S. (eds.) Proceedings of the 2016 ACM SIGSAC Conference on Computer and Communications Security, Vienna, Austria, October 24–28, 2016, pp. 1006–1018. ACM (2016). https://doi.org/10.1145/2976749.2978425

14. Bos, J.W., et al.: CRYSTALS - Kyber: a CCA-secure module-lattice-based KEM (2017). http://eprint.iacr.org/2017/634

15. Bos, J.W., Gourjon, M., Renes, J., Schneider, T., van Vredendaal, C.: Masking kyber: first- and higher-order implementations. IACR Trans. Cryptogr. Hardw. Embed. Syst. **2021**(4), 173–214 (2021). https://doi.org/10.46586/tches.v2021.i4.173-214

16. Chakraborty, A., Bhattacharya, S., Saha, S., Mukhopadhyay, D.: ExplFrame: exploiting page frame cache for fault analysis of block ciphers. In: 2020 Design, Automation & Test in Europe Conference & Exhibition, DATE 2020, Grenoble, France, March 9–13, 2020, pp. 1303–1306. IEEE (2020). https://doi.org/10.23919/DATE48585.2020.9116219

17. Chakraborty, A., Bhattacharya, S., Saha, S., Mukhopdhyay, D.: Rowhammer Induced Intermittent Fault Attack on ECC-hardened memory (2020). https://eprint.iacr.org/2020/380

18. Cheon, J.H., Choe, H., Hong, D., Yi, M.: SMAUG: Pushing Lattice-based Key Encapsulation Mechanisms to the Limits. Cryptology ePrint Archive, Paper 2023/739 (2023). https://eprint.iacr.org/2023/739

19. Dachman-Soled, D., Ducas, L., Gong, H., Rossi, M.: LWE with Side Information: Attacks and Concrete Security Estimation. Cryptology ePrint Archive, Report 2020/292 (2020). https://eprint.iacr.org/2020/292
20. Daemen, J., Rijmen, V.: Rijndael for AES. In: The Third Advanced Encryption Standard Candidate Conference, April 13–14, 2000, New York, New York, USA, pp. 343–348. National Institute of Standards and Technology (2000)
21. D'Anvers, J., Karmakar, A., Roy, S.S., Vercauteren, F.: Saber: module-LWR based key exchange, CPA-secure encryption and CCA-secure KEM (2018). http://eprint.iacr.org/2018/230
22. Ducas, L., Lepoint, T., Lyubashevsky, V., Schwabe, P., Seiler, G., Stehlé, D.: CRYSTALS - Dilithium: Digital Signatures from Module Lattices (2017). http://eprint.iacr.org/2017/633
23. Fahr, M., et al.: When frodo flips: end-to-end key recovery on frodokem via rowhammer. In: Proceedings of the 2022 ACM SIGSAC Conference on Computer and Communications Security. CCS 2022, New York, NY, USA, pp. 979–993. Association for Computing Machinery (2022). https://doi.org/10.1145/3548606.3560673
24. Fan, H., Wang, W., Wang, Y.: Cache attack on MISTY1. IACR Cryptol. ePrint Arch. p. 723 (2021). https://eprint.iacr.org/2021/723
25. Fouque, P.A., et al.: Falcon: fast-fourier lattice-based compact signatures over NTRU (2018). https://falcon-sign.info/falcon.pdf. Accessed 28 June 2023
26. Frigo, P., et al.: TRRespass: exploiting the many sides of target row refresh. In: 2020 IEEE Symposium on Security and Privacy, SP 2020, San Francisco, CA, USA, May 18–21, 2020, pp. 747–762. IEEE (2020). https://doi.org/10.1109/SP40000.2020.00090
27. Fujisaki, E., Okamoto, T.: Secure integration of asymmetric and symmetric encryption schemes. J. Cryptol. **26**(1), 80–101 (2013). https://doi.org/10.1007/s00145-011-9114-1
28. Gama, N., Nguyen, P.Q.: Predicting lattice reduction. In: Smart, N. (ed.) EUROCRYPT 2008. LNCS, vol. 4965, pp. 31–51. Springer, Heidelberg (2008). https://doi.org/10.1007/978-3-540-78967-3_3
29. Guo, Q., Johansson, T., Nilsson, A.: A key-recovery timing attack on post-quantum primitives using the Fujisaki-Okamoto transformation and its application on FrodoKEM. In: Micciancio, D., Ristenpart, T. (eds.) CRYPTO 2020. LNCS, vol. 12171, pp. 359–386. Springer, Cham (2020). https://doi.org/10.1007/978-3-030-56880-1_13
30. Hermelink, J., Pessl, P., Pöppelmann, T.: Fault-enabled chosen-ciphertext attacks on Kyber. In: Adhikari, A., Küsters, R., Preneel, B. (eds.) INDOCRYPT 2021. LNCS, vol. 13143, pp. 311–334. Springer, Cham (2021). https://doi.org/10.1007/978-3-030-92518-5_15
31. Islam, S., Mus, K., Singh, R., Schaumont, P., Sunar, B.: Signature correction attack on Dilithium signature scheme. In: 7th IEEE European Symposium on Security and Privacy, EuroS&P 2022, Genoa, Italy, June 6–10, 2022, pp. 647–663. IEEE (2022). https://doi.org/10.1109/EuroSP53844.2022.00046, https://doi.org/10.1109/EuroSP53844.2022.00046
32. Jiang, H., Zhang, Z., Chen, L., Wang, H., Ma, Z.: Post-quantum IND-CCA-secure KEM without Additional Hash. Cryptology ePrint Archive, Report 2017/1096 (2017). https://eprint.iacr.org/2017/1096
33. Kim, Y., et al.: Flipping bits in memory without accessing them: an experimental study of DRAM disturbance errors. ACM SIGARCH Comput. Archit. News **42**(3), 361–372 (2014)

34. KpqC: Korean post-quantum cryptography competition (2022). https://www.kpqc.or.kr/competition.html. Accessed 28 Jun 2023

35. Kundu, S., D'Anvers, J., Beirendonck, M.V., Karmakar, A., Verbauwhede, I.: Higher-order masked saber. In: Galdi, C., Jarecki, S. (eds.) SCN 2022. Lecture Notes in Computer Science, vol. 13409, pp. 93–116. Springer, Cham (2022)

36. Kwong, A., Genkin, D., Gruss, D., Yarom, Y.: Rambleed: reading bits in memory without accessing them (2020). https://doi.org/10.1109/SP40000.2020.00020

37. Langlois, A., Stehlé, D.: Worst-case to average-case reductions for module lattices. Des. Codes Cryptogr. **75**(3), 565–599 (2015). https://doi.org/10.1007/s10623-014-9938-4

38. Lyubashevsky, V., Peikert, C., Regev, O.: On ideal lattices and learning with errors over rings. In: Gilbert, H. (ed.) EUROCRYPT 2010. LNCS, vol. 6110, pp. 1–23. Springer, Heidelberg (2010). https://doi.org/10.1007/978-3-642-13190-5_1

39. Micron: DDR4 SDRAM Datasheet (2016)

40. Miller, V.S.: Use of elliptic curves in cryptography. In: Williams, H.C. (ed.) CRYPTO 1985. LNCS, vol. 218, pp. 417–426. Springer, Heidelberg (1986). https://doi.org/10.1007/3-540-39799-X_31

41. Mujdei, C., Beckers, A., Bermundo, J., Karmakar, A., Wouters, L., Verbauwhede, I.: Side-Channel Analysis of Lattice-Based Post-Quantum Cryptography: Exploiting Polynomial Multiplication. IACR Cryptol. ePrint Arch. p. 474 (2022). https://eprint.iacr.org/2022/474

42. Mus, K., Islam, S., Sunar, B.: QuantumHammer: a practical hybrid attack on the luov signature scheme. In: Proceedings of the 2020 ACM SIGSAC Conference on Computer and Communications Security. CCS 2020, New York, NY, USA, pp. 1071–1084. Association for Computing Machinery (2020). https://doi.org/10.1145/3372297.3417272

43. Mutlu, O., Kim, J.S.: RowHammer: A Retrospective. IEEE Trans. Comput. Aided Des. Integr. Circuits Syst. **39**(8), 1555–1571 (2020). https://doi.org/10.1109/TCAD.2019.2915318

44. Osvik, D.A., Shamir, A., Tromer, E.: Cache attacks and countermeasures: the case of AES. In: Pointcheval, D. (ed.) CT-RSA 2006. LNCS, vol. 3860, pp. 1–20. Springer, Heidelberg (2006). https://doi.org/10.1007/11605805_1

45. Pessl, P., Prokop, L.: Fault attacks on CCA-secure lattice KEMs. IACR Trans. Cryptogr. Hardw. Embed. Syst. **2021**(2), 37–60 (2021). https://doi.org/10.46586/tches.v2021.i2.37-60

46. Proos, J., Zalka, C.: Shor's discrete logarithm quantum algorithm for elliptic curves. Quantum Inf. Comput. **3**(4), 317–344 (2003). https://doi.org/10.26421/QIC3.4-3

47. Rajendran, G., Ravi, P., D'Anvers, J., Bhasin, S., Chattopadhyay, A.: Pushing the limits of generic side-channel attacks on LWE-based KEMs - parallel PC oracle attacks on Kyber KEM and beyond. IACR Trans. Cryptogr. Hardw. Embed. Syst. **2023**(2), 418–446 (2023). https://doi.org/10.46586/tches.v2023.i2.418-446

48. Ravi, P., Chattopadhyay, A., Baksi, A.: Side-channel and Fault-injection attacks over Lattice-based Post-quantum Schemes (Kyber, Dilithium): Survey and New Results. IACR Cryptol. ePrint Arch. p. 737 (2022). https://eprint.iacr.org/2022/737

49. Ravi, P., Roy, S.S., Chattopadhyay, A., Bhasin, S.: Generic Side-channel attacks on CCA-secure lattice-based PKE and KEMs. IACR Trans. Cryptogr. Hardw. Embed. Syst. **2020**(3), 307–335 (2020), https://doi.org/10.13154/tches.v2020.i3.307-335

50. Razavi, K., Gras, B., Bosman, E., Preneel, B., Giuffrida, C., Bos, H.: Flip feng shui: hammering a needle in the software stack. In: Proceedings of the 25th USENIX

Conference on Security Symposium. SEC 2016, pp. 1–18. USENIX Association, USA (2016)

51. Regev, O.: Lecture notes: Lattices in computer science. https://cims.nyu.edu/regev/teaching/lattices_fall_2009

52. Rivest, R.L., Shamir, A., Adleman, L.M.: A method for obtaining digital signatures and public-key cryptosystems. Commun. ACM **21**(2), 120–126 (1978). https://doi.org/10.1145/359340.359342

53. Seaborn, M., Dullien, T.: Exploiting the DRAM rowhammer bug to gain kernel privileges. Black Hat **15**, 71 (2015)

54. Settana, M., Naila, A., Yaseen, H., Huwaida, T.: Cache-timing attack against AES crypto-systems countermeasure using weighted average masking time algorithm. J. Inf. Warfare **15**(1), 104–114 (2016). https://www.jstor.org/stable/26487484

55. Shor, P.W.: Algorithms for quantum computation: discrete logarithms and factoring. In: 35th Annual Symposium on Foundations of Computer Science, Santa Fe, New Mexico, USA, 20–22 November 1994, pp. 124–134. IEEE Computer Society (1994). https://doi.org/10.1109/SFCS.1994.365700

56. Tanaka, Y., Ueno, R., Xagawa, K., Ito, A., Takahashi, J., Homma, N.: Multiple-valued plaintext-checking side-channel attacks on post-quantum KEMs (2022). https://eprint.iacr.org/2022/940

57. Tatar, A., Giuffrida, C., Bos, H., Razavi, K.: Defeating software mitigations against rowhammer: a surgical precision hammer. In: Bailey, M., Holz, T., Stamatogiannakis, M., Ioannidis, S. (eds.) RAID 2018. LNCS, vol. 11050, pp. 47–66. Springer, Cham (2018). https://doi.org/10.1007/978-3-030-00470-5_3

58. Veyrat-Charvillon, N., Medwed, M., Kerckhof, S., Standaert, F.-X.: Shuffling against side-channel attacks: a comprehensive study with cautionary note. In: Wang, X., Sako, K. (eds.) ASIACRYPT 2012. LNCS, vol. 7658, pp. 740–757. Springer, Heidelberg (2012). https://doi.org/10.1007/978-3-642-34961-4_44

59. Xiao, Y., Zhang, X., Zhang, Y., Teodorescu, R.: One bit flips, one cloud flops: cross-VM row hammer attacks and privilege escalation. In: Holz, T., Savage, S. (eds.) 25th USENIX Security Symposium, USENIX Security 16, Austin, TX, USA, August 10–12, 2016, pp. 19–35. USENIX Association (2016). https://www.usenix.org/conference/usenixsecurity16/technical-sessions/presentation/xiao

60. Yarom, Y., Falkner, K.: FLUSH+RELOAD: a high resolution, low noise, L3 cache side-channel attack. In: Fu, K., Jung, J. (eds.) Proceedings of the 23rd USENIX Security Symposium, San Diego, CA, USA, August 20–22, 2014, pp. 719–732. USENIX Association (2014). https://www.usenix.org/conference/usenixsecurity14/technical-sessions/presentation/yarom

A Side-Channel Attack on a Higher-Order Masked CRYSTALS-Kyber Implementation

Ruize Wang[(⊠)], Martin Brisfors, and Elena Dubrova

KTH Royal Institute of Technology, Stockholm, Sweden
{ruize,brisfors,dubrova}@kth.se

Abstract. In response to side-channel attacks on masked implementations of post-quantum cryptographic algorithms, a new bitsliced higher-order masked implementation of CRYSTALS-Kyber has been presented at CHES'2022. The bitsliced implementations are typically more difficult to break by side-channel analysis because they execute a single instruction across multiple bits in parallel. However, in this paper, we reveal new vulnerabilities in the masked Boolean to arithmetic conversion procedure of this implementation that make the shared and secret key recovery possible. We also present a new chosen ciphertext construction method which maximizes secret key recovery probability for a given message bit recovery probability. We demonstrate practical shared and secret key recovery attacks on the first-, second- and third-order masked implementations of Kyber-768 in ARM Cortex-M4 using profiled deep learning-based power analysis.

Keywords: Public-key cryptography · Post-quantum cryptography · Kyber · LWE/LWR-based KEM · Side-channel attack

1 Introduction

CRYSTALS-Kyber is a key encapsulation mechanism (KEM) which is indistinguishable under an adaptive chosen-ciphertext attack (IND-CCA2-secure) in the classical and quantum random oracle models [3]. The security of Kyber relies on the hardness of the module learning with errors (M-LWE) problem that comes from inserting unknown noise into otherwise linear equations. Kyber has recently been selected for standardization by the National Institute of Standards and Technology (NIST) [23] and included in the National Security Agency (NSA) suite of cryptographic algorithms recommended for national security systems [1].

However, the theoretical IND-CCA2 security of Kyber KEM can potentially be bypassed by a side-channel attack of its implementation executed on a physical device. Side-channel attacks on software [5,6,28,32,33,35,37,38,41,42] and hardware [20,30] implementations of Kyber have been demonstrated. The discovered vulnerabilities promoted stronger mitigation techniques against side-channel attacks, e.g. [4,19,34], and helped strengthen Kyber implementations that were released later [7,9,10]. In the improved implementations, all known vulnerabilities are typically patched. Indeed, the experiments presented in this paper

C. Pöpper and L. Batina (Eds.): ACNS 2024, LNCS 14585, pp. 301–324, 2024.
https://doi.org/10.1007/978-3-031-54776-8_12

show that side-channel information extracted from the higher-order masked implementation of Kyber by Bronchain et al. [9] is more difficult to exploit using previous methods.

Contributions: We discovered new vulnerabilities in a higher-order masked implementation of Kyber by Bronchain et al. [9] that result in an effective message/shared key recovery attack. These vulnerabilities are located in the masked Boolean to arithmetic conversion procedure which is carried out during the re-encryption step of decapsulation.

We also present a new chosen ciphertext construction method which maximizes secret key recovery probability for a given message bit recovery probability. This method uses $3 \times k$ chosen ciphertexts to extract the secret key of Kyber from a masked implementation, where k is the module rank. While this number is the same as in the chosen ciphertext construction method of Ravi et al. [28], the new way of mapping message bits into the secret key coefficients can raise the likelihood of recovering the full secret key by up to 39% compared to the worst case.

We demonstrate practical shared and secret key recovery attacks on ω-order masked implementations of Kyber-768 in ARM Cortex-M4 using profiled deep learning-based power analysis, for $\omega \in \{1, 2, 3\}$. The training of neural networks is performed on traces captured from five profiling devices, which are different from the device under attack (DUA). The message recovery is carried out using the single-step method of Ngo et al. [24] which extracts the message directly, without extracting each share explicitly. For $\omega = 3$, we apply the recursive learning method of [13]; otherwise neural networks do not learn. Our experimental results show that, for the first-order masked implementation run on the DUA, we can recover the shared key from three traces with a close to 1 probability, and the secret key from 18 traces with 0.94 probability.

The rest of this paper is organized as follows. Section 2 reviews previous work on side-channel analysis of Kyber implementations. Section 3 gives a background on Kyber algorithm. Section 4 defines the adversary model. Section 5 describes the profiling and attack stages. Section 6 presents the equipment used in the experiments. Section 7 analyses side-channel leakage of three different implementations of Kyber and describes new vulnerabilities in the implementation of [9]. Section 8 presents neural network training strategy. Section 9 introduces the new chosen ciphertext construction method. Section 10 summarizes experimental results. Section 11 discusses possible countermeasures. Section 12 concludes the paper.

2   Previous Work

Since the beginning of the NIST post-quantum cryptography standardization process in 2016, many different side-channel attacks on software [6,33,35,37] and hardware [20,30] implementations of Kyber have been presented. In response, protected implementations have been developed such as [7,9–11,18,31].

In [28], near field EM based secret key recovery attacks on unprotected and protected implementations of Kyber are described. In these attacks, Hamming weight (HW)-based templates are constructed for the message decoding operation to recover the message bits. For secret key recovery, $3 \times k$ chosen ciphertexts are required to identify each key coefficient uniquely, where k is the rank of the module. It is also shown how a first-order masked implementation can be broken in two steps, by extracting each share individually.

In [17], a chosen ciphertext side-channel attack on a first-order masked software implementation Kyber combined with belief propagation is presented. The attack can recover the secret key from k traces captured during the inverse NTT step of decryption for a noise tolerance level $\sigma \leq 1.2$ based on the HW leakage on simulated data.

In [32] a chosen ciphertext side-channel attack is presented which uses codes for detecting faulty positions in the initially recovered secret key. These positions are further corrected with additional traces. An EM-based template attack on an unprotected software implementation of Kyber-512 is demonstrated which can recover the secret key using 1619 traces on average with 0.4 out of 512 faulty coefficients on average. Another chosen ciphertext construction method for Kyber, using low density parity check codes, is described in [15]. It targets masked message encoding using the implementation by Heinz et al [18].

Yet another interesting chosen ciphertext construction method is presented in [27]. The total number of queries required for the secret key recovery is reduced by using binary decision trees. However, the downside is that this method relies on an unbalanced distribution of the coefficients of the secret key. In contract, the chosen ciphertext construction method introduced in this paper is equally applicable to algorithms with a uniform distribution of secret key coefficients. Furthermore, it is applicable to masked implementations, whereas the method of [27] is not.

In [5], a chosen ciphertext side-channel attack on a first-order masked and shuffled software implementation of Kyber-768 on an ARM Cortex-M4 is demonstrated, which can extract the secret key from 38,016 power traces. The main idea is to recover shuffling indices 0 and 255, extract the corresponding two message bits, and then cyclically rotate the message by modifying the ciphertext. In this way, all message bits are extracted using 128 rotations.

In [37], a side-channel attack on the first-order masked implementation of CRYSTALS-Kyber targeting the message encoding vulnerability found in [33] is presented. In [6], side-channel attacks on two implementations of masked polynomial comparison are demonstrated on the example of CRYSTALS-Kyber.

In [13], a message recovery attack on the higher-order masked implementation of CRYSTALS-Kyber by Heinz et al. in [18] is presented. A new neural network training method called *recursive learning* is introduced which constructs the initial state for a neural network model based on the states of models trained for the attacks on lower-order masked implementations.

3 Background

This section describes notation and Kyber algorithm specification from [3].

KYBER.CPAPKE.KeyGen()
1: $(\rho, \sigma) \leftarrow \mathcal{U}(\{0,1\}^{256})$
2: $A \leftarrow \mathcal{U}(R_q^{k \times k}; \rho)$; $s, e \leftarrow B_{\eta_1}(R_q^{k \times 1}; \sigma)$
3: $t = \mathsf{Encode}_{12}(As + e)$; $s = \mathsf{Encode}_{12}(s)$
4: return $(pk = (t, \rho), sk = s)$

KYBER.CPAPKE.Enc($pk = (t, \rho), m, r$)
1: $t = \mathsf{Decode}_{12}(t)$
2: $A \leftarrow \mathcal{U}(R_q^{k \times k}; \rho)$; $r \leftarrow B_{\eta_1}(R_q^{k \times 1}; r)$
3: $e_1 \leftarrow B_{\eta_2}(R_q^{k \times 1}; r)$; $e_2 \leftarrow B_{\eta_2}(R_q^{1 \times 1}; r)$
4: $u = A^T r + e_1$
5: $v = t^T r + e_2 + \mathsf{Decompress}_q(\mathsf{Decode}_1(m), 1)$
6: $c_1 = \mathsf{Encode}_{d_u}(\mathsf{Compress}_q(u, d_u)$
7: $c_2 = \mathsf{Encode}_{d_v}(\mathsf{Compress}_q(v, d_v)$
8: return $c = (c_1, c_2)$

KYBER.CPAPKE.Dec(s, c)
1: $u = \mathsf{Decompress}_q(\mathsf{Decode}_{d_u}(c_1), d_u)$
2: $v = \mathsf{Decompress}_q(\mathsf{Decode}_{d_v}(c_2), d_v)$
3: $s = \mathsf{Decode}_{12}(s)$
4: $m = \mathsf{Encode}_1(\mathsf{Compress}_q(v - s \cdot u, 1))$
5: return m

KYBER.CCAKEM.KeyGen()
1: $z \leftarrow \mathcal{U}(\{0,1\}^{256})$
2: $(pk, s) = $ KYBER.CPAPKE.KeyGen()
3: $sk = (s, pk, \mathcal{H}(pk), z)$
4: return (pk, sk)

KYBER.CCAKEM.Encaps(pk)
1: $m \leftarrow \mathcal{U}(\{0,1\}^{256})$
2: $m = \mathcal{H}(m)$
3: $(\hat{K}, r) = \mathcal{G}(m, \mathcal{H}(pk))$
4: $c = $ KYBER.CPAPKE.Enc(pk, m, r)
5: $K = \mathsf{KDF}(\hat{K}, \mathcal{H}(c))$
6: return (c, K)

KYBER.CCAKEM.Decaps(sk, c)
1: $m' = $ KYBER.CPAPKE.Dec(s, c)
2: $(\hat{K}', r') = \mathcal{G}(m', \mathcal{H}(pk))$
3: $c' = $ KYBER.CPAPKE.Enc(pk, m', r')
4: if $c = c'$ then
5:     return $K = \mathsf{KDF}(\hat{K}', \mathcal{H}(c))$
6: else
7:     return $K = \mathsf{KDF}(z, \mathcal{H}(c))$
8: end if

Fig. 1. Kyber algorithms from [3] (simplified).

3.1 Notation

Let $\mathbb{Z}_q$ be the ring of integers modulo a prime q and R_q be the quotient ring $\mathbb{Z}_q[X]/(X^n + 1)$. We use regular font letters for elements in R_q, bold lower-case letters for vectors with coefficients in R_q, and bold upper-case letters for matrices. The transpose of a vector v (or matrix A) is denoted by v^T (or A^T). The ith entry of a vector v is denoted by $v[i]$. The polynomial multiplication is denoted by "$\cdot$". The Boolean XOR is denoted by "$\oplus$". The term $\lceil x \rfloor$ stands for rounding of x to the closest integer with ties being rounded up.

The term $x \leftarrow \mathcal{D}(S; r)$ stands for sampling x from a probability distribution $\mathcal{D}$ over a set S using seed r. The uniform distribution is denoted by $\mathcal{U}$. The centered binomial distribution with parameter μ is denoted by B_μ.

3.2 Kyber Algorithm

Kyber [3] consists of a chosen-plaintext attack (CPA)-secure PKE scheme, KYBER.CPAPKE, and a CCA-secure KEM scheme, KYBER.CCAKEM, which is built on the top of KYBER.CPAPKE using a version of the Fujisaki-Okamoto (FO) transform [14]. These schemes are described in Fig. 1.

Inputs and outputs to all API functions of Kyber are byte arrays. Kyber works with vectors of ring elements in R_q^k, where k is the rank of the module defining the security level. There are three versions of Kyber: Kyber-512, Kyber-768 and Kyber-1024, for $k = 2, 3$ and 4, respectively, see the specification [3] for details. In this paper, we focus on Kyber-768.

Kyber uses the number-theoretic transform (NTT) to perform multiplications in R_q efficiently. The NTT details are omitted from Fig. 1 to simplify the pseudocode.

The Decode$_l$ function decodes an array of $32l$ bytes into a polynomial with n coefficients in the range $\{0, 1, \cdots, 2^l - 1\}$. The Encode$_l$ function is the inverse of Decode$_l$. It first encodes each polynomial coefficient individually and then concatenates the output byte arrays.

The Compress$_q(x, d)$ and Decompress$_q(x, d)$ functions, for $x \in \mathbb{Z}_q$ and $d < \lceil \log_2(q) \rceil$, are defined by:

$$\text{Compress}_q(x, d) = \lceil (2^d/q) \cdot x \rfloor \bmod^+ 2^d,$$
$$\text{Decompress}_q(x, d) = \lceil (q/2^d) \cdot x \rfloor.$$

The functions $\mathcal{G}$ and $\mathcal{H}$ represent the SHA3-512 and SHA3-256 hash functions, respectively. The KDF is a key derivation function. It is realized by SHAKE-256.

4 Adversary Model

An adversary model is typically defined using three components: assumptions, goals and capabilities [12].

Assumptions: We assume that an adversary has a physical access to the DUA which runs the Kyber KEM decapsulation algorithm. We also assume that the adversary possesses fully controllable profiling devices that are similar to the DUA. In addition, we assume that the keys (pk, sk) are static.

Capabilities: The adversary is a clever outsider who has equipment and tools for power analysis, as well as expertise in side-channel attacks, Kyber KEM, and deep learning. The adversary is capable of eavesdropping on the channel between the DUA and the server and query the DUA with chosen ciphertexts.

Goals: The goal of the adversary is to extract the shared key K and/or the long-term secret key sk of Kyber from its implementation running on the DUA. Note that the long-term secret key recovery implies the shared key recovery, but not vice versa.

5 Attack Description

Figure 2 illustrates the main steps of the presented attack.

5.1 Profiling Stage

At the profiling stage, the adversary first uses KYBER.CCAKEM.KeyGen() to generate a key pair (pk_p, sk_p). Then he/she selects uniformly at random a message $m_p \in \{0, 1\}^{256}$ and uses KYBER.CCAPKE.Enc() to compute a ciphertext c_p encrypting m_p. Knowing the message contained in c_p is necessary for creating a labeled dataset for neural network training.

These steps are repeated multiple times until a profiling dataset of the desired size is gathered. Note that a labeled dataset can be created either using a static key pair, or a set of key pairs which is re-generated for each message m_p. This does not affect the success probability of the presented attack.

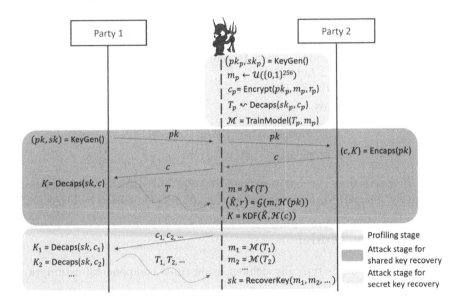

Fig. 2. Attack scenario.

Then, the adversary runs KYBER.CCAKEM.Decaps() on a profiling device to decapsulate each c_p in the dataset and measure the total power consumption of the device during the execution of the algorithm. The resulting power trace T_p is recorded.

Finally, the adversary uses the resulting labeled data set to train a neural network $\mathcal{M}$ which learns the leakage profile of KYBER.CCAKEM.Decaps() in order to predict message bit values from power traces.

5.2 Attack Stage

To recover the shared key K, the adversary eavesdrops on the communication channel between the two parties to obtain the public key pk and the ciphertext c containing the encapsulated K. The adversary also measures the power consumption of the DUA during the execution of the decapsulation algorithm with c as input. The segments of the resulting power trace T corresponding to the processing of the message m encrypted in c are extracted. These segments are given as input to the model $\mathcal{M}$ trained at the profiling stage to predict the bits of m. Once m is recovered, the pre-key $\hat{K}$ is derived as $(\hat{K}, r) = \mathcal{G}(m, \mathcal{H}(pk))$ and then the shared key K is computed as $K = \mathsf{KDF}(\hat{K}, \mathcal{H}(c))$.

To recover the secret key sk, the DUA is queried with chosen ciphertexts $c_1, c_2, \ldots$ and the power consumption of the DUA during the execution of the decapsulation algorithm is measured. We describe the method for constructing chosen ciphertexts in Sect. 9. The messages $m_1, m_2, \ldots$ are extracted from the recorded power traces $T_1, T_2, \ldots$ similarly to the case of shared key recovery

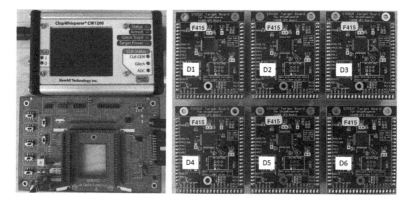

Fig. 3. The equipment used in the experiments. The devices D_1–D_5 are used for the profiling and D_6 is used for the attack.

attack. A difference between the two attacks is that chosen ciphertexts are mal-formed and thus do not pass the FO transform. This is however not important for the presented attack since it targets an earlier step of the decapsulation algo-rithm (re-encryption). Finally, the extracted messages $m_1, m_2, \ldots$ are mapped into the coefficients of the secret key according to the mapping table of the chosen ciphertexts construction method.

6   Experimental Setup

The equipment used in our experiments is shown in Fig. 3. It consists of the ChipWhisperer-Pro, the CW308 UFO main board and six CW308T-STM32F4 target boards. Each target board contains a STM32F415-RGT6 chip based on ARM Cortex-M4 32-bit RISC core operating at a frequency of 24 MHz. The traces are acquired with the sampling rate of 96 MS/s.

Three C implementations of Kyber are used in the experiments:

1. The unprotected implementation by Kannwischer et al. [21].
2. The first-order masked implementation by Heinz et al. [18].
3. The higher-order masked implementation by Bronchain et al. [9].

All implementations are compiled using `arm-none-eabi-gcc` with the highest optimization level `-O3` (recommended default).

7   Leakage Analysis

The presented attack targets the message encoding operation at the re-encryption step of the FO transform. In this section, we first analyse the unpro-tected implementation of the message encoding operation from the *pqm4* library for the ARM Cortex-M4 developed by Kannwischer et al. [21]. Then, we compare

```
void poly_frommsg(poly *r, unsigned char msg[32])
int i,j;
uint16_t mask;
1: for (i = 0; i < 32; i++) do
2:     for (j = 0; j < 8; j++) do
3:         mask = -((msg[i]>>j) & 1);
4:         r->coeffs[8 * i + j] = mask & ((KYBER_Q+1)/2);
5:     end for
6: end for
```

Fig. 4. The C code of `poly_frommsg()` procedure from [21].

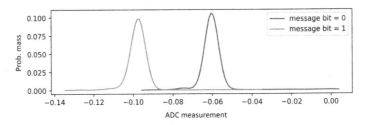

Fig. 5. Distributions of power consumption during the processing of a single message bit by `poly_frommsg()` procedure of the unmasked implementation of [21].

the realizations of message encoding in the implementations of Heinz et al. [18] and Bronchain et al. [9]. We show that in the implementation of [9], the leakage is significantly weaker than the one in [18]. Thus, the former implementation is more difficult to break than the latter. The presented attack would not be as effective if we would use only previously known leakage points. However, we discovered two new leakage points in the masked Boolean to arithmetic conversion procedure of the implementation of [9] that result in an effective attack.

7.1 Unprotected Message Encoding

The message encoding operation converts an array of 32 bytes representing a message m into a polynomial f in which each of the 256 coefficients, $f[j]$, is equal to $f[j] = \lceil q/2 \rfloor \cdot m[j]$, where $m[j]$ is the jth bit of m for $j \in \{0, 1, \cdots, 255\}$, see $\mathsf{Decompress}_q(\mathsf{Decode}_1(m), 1)$ at line 5 of KYBER.CPAPKE.Enc() in Fig. 1.

In the unprotected implementation of Kyber by Kannwischer et al. in [21], the message encoding is realized by the procedure called `poly_frommsg()` shown in Fig. 4. It contains two nested **for**-loops in which each polynomial coefficient is computed individually. The intermediate variable `mask` is used to replace the **if-then-else**-statement in order to guarantee a constant processing time regardless of the message bit value. Otherwise, a timing attack can be mounted to extract the message bit.

However, in a software implementation, the power consumption may differ if the Hamming weights of the two processed values differ. The intermediate variable `mask` is computed based on the message bit, see line 3 in Fig. 4. Its value

```
void masked_poly_frommsg(masked_poly *r, masked_u8_msgbytes *msg)
int i,j;
uint16_t mask;
 1: for (i = 0; i < 32; i++) do
 2:   for (j = 0; j < 8; j++) do
 3:     mask = -((msg->share[0].u8[i] >> j) & 1);
 4:     r->poly[0].coeffs[8*i+j] += (mask & ((KYBER_Q + 1)/2));
 5:   end for
 6: end for
 7: for (i = 0; i < 32; i++) do
 8:   for (j = 0; j < 8; j++) do
 9:     mask = -((msg->share[1].u8[i] >> j) & 1);
10:     r->poly[1].coeffs[8*i+j] += (mask & ((KYBER_Q + 1)/2));
11:   end for
12: end for
13: ...Further processing ...
```

Fig. 6. The C code of `masked_poly_frommsg()` procedure from [18].

is either 0 (0x0000) or -1 (0xFFFF). The corresponding polynomial coefficient computed from the `mask` in the next line takes values either 0 or $(q+1)/2$. Since in both cases the difference in the Hamming weights of two values is large, one can recover the message bits by analysing power consumption [2,28,33]. Such type of leakage is referred to as *determiner* leakage [33], because the `mask`/polynomial coefficient values are determined by the corresponding message bit.

Figure 5 shows the distributions of power consumption during the processing of a single message bit by `poly_frommsg()` procedure. The distributions are plotted based on 10K traces at the trace point with the maximum absolute t-test score. The overlap in the plots of message bits with values 0 and 1 determines the difficulty of distinguishing between these values. We can see that there is almost no overlap. This means that two values can be distinguished easily.

7.2   Masked Message Encoding

A common way to decorrelate a sensitive variable from the power consumption is to split the variable into multiple shares [7,11,25]. For the ω-order masked message encoding, the message m is split into $\omega + 1$ Boolean shares $\{m_0, m_1, \cdots, m_\omega\}$, such that $m = m_0 \oplus m_1 \cdots \oplus m_\omega$. For each Boolean share $m_i, i \in \{0, 1, \cdots, \omega\}$, the corresponding arithmetic share f_i is computed so that the jth coefficient of the polynomial f satisfies:

$$f[j] = \sum_{i=0}^{\omega} f_i[j] \bmod q = \lceil q/2 \rfloor \cdot m[j], \tag{1}$$

for all $j \in \{0, 1, \cdots, 255\}$, where "$\sum$" is the arithmetic addition.

Implementation of Masked Message Encoding in [18]. The first-order masked implementation of Heinz et al. [18] adopts the masking strategy of [25]. The message m is split into two Boolean shares $\{m_0, m_1\}$ and the corresponding arithmetic shares $\{f_0, f_1\}$ are computed separately. If both Boolean shares have

```
void masked_poly_frommsg(StrAPoly y, uint8 m[32 * NSHARES], size_t stride) /* stride is the
byte distance between each share */
int i,j,k;
uint32_t t1[NSHARES]; /* Boolean shares */
int16_t t2[NSHARES]; /* Arithmetic shares */
 1: for (i = 0; i < 32; i++) do
 2:    for (j = 0; j < 8; j++) do
 3:        for (k = 0; k < NSHARES; K++) do
 4:            t1[k] = (m[i+k*stride]>>j) & 1; /* Bit extraction from byte */
 5:        end for
 6:        secb2a_1bit(NSHARES, t2, t1); /* Masked B2A */
 7:        for (k = 0; k < NSHARES; k++) do
 8:            y[k][i*8+j] = (t2[k] * (KYBER_Q+1)/2) % KYBER_Q;
 9:        end for
10:    end for
11: end for

void secb2a_1bit(size_t nshares, int16_t *a, uint32_t *x)
 1: b2a_qbit(nshares, a, x);
 2: refresh_add(nshares, a);

void b2a_qbit(size_t nshares, int16_t *a, uint32_t *x)
int i;
 1: a[0] = x[0]; /* Copy the bit of the first share in x */
 2: for (i = 1; i < nshares; i++) do
 3:    secb2a_qbit_n(i+1, a, a, x[i]); /* Use the bit of share i in x */
 4: end for

void secb2a_qbit_n(size_t n, int16_t *c, int16_t *a, uint32_t x)
int j;
int16_t b[n];
int16_t r[2];
 1: ... Processing ...
 2: for (j = 0; j < n; j++) do
 3:    c[j] = b[j] + 2 * KYBER_Q;
 4:    c[j] -= 2 * b[j] * x; /* Compute polynomial value from bit value */
 5:    c[j] = c[j] % KYBER_Q;
 6: end for
 7: c[0] = (c[0] + x) % KYBER_Q;
```

Fig. 7. The C code of `masked_poly_frommsg()` procedure from [9].

value 1, then both resulting polynomial coefficients have value $\lceil q/2 \rceil$, which does not satisfy Eq. (1) due to the rounding. To fix this, an extra term is added[1].

The C code of the procedure `masked_poly_frommsg()` realizing the message encoding in the implementation of [18] is shown in Fig. 6. We can see that two nested **for**-loops of the procedure `poly_frommsg()` in Fig. 4 are repeated twice to compute the arithmetic shares $\{f_0, f_1\}$. Therefore, the leakage of each share is similar to the one of the unprotected version. Several attacks exploiting this leakage have been demonstrated recently [13,15].

Implementation of Masked Message Encoding in [9]. The higher-order masked implementation of Bronchain et al. [9] employs the masking strategy of [31]. It uses a masked Boolean to arithmetic conversion algorithm to transform the Boolean shares $\{m_0, m_1, \cdots, m_\omega\}$ into the arithmetic shares $\{f_0, f_1, \cdots, f_\omega\}$ such that $\sum_{i=0}^{\omega} f_i[j] \bmod q = m[j]$, for all $j \in \{0, 1, \cdots, 255\}$.

---

[1] We refer to [18,25] for details since our leakage analysis does not rely on that.

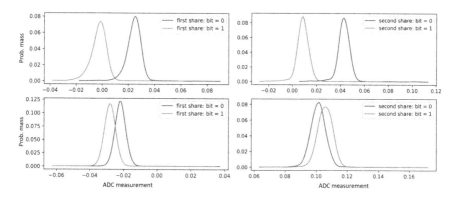

Fig. 8. Distributions of power consumption during the processing of a single bit of Boolean shares by `masked_poly_frommsg()` in the first-order masked implementations of [18] (top) and [9] (bottom).

Figure 7 shows the C code of the procedure `masked_poly_frommsg()` realizing the message encoding in the implementation of [9]. First, each Boolean share bit is extracted from the corresponding byte, see line 4 of `masked_poly_frommsg()` in Fig. 7. This is similar to the lines 3 and 9 of `masked_poly_frommsg()` procedure from [18] in Fig. 6. However, an essential difference is that, instead of computing the variable `mask`, the implementation of [9] only extracts each Boolean share bit and performs a masked Boolean to arithmetic conversion latter on. Hence, the difference in the Hamming weight of values computed in line 4 of Fig. 7 is only one, while the difference in the Hamming weight of `mask` values computed in lines 3 and 9 of Fig. 6 is 16. Consequently, it is more difficult to extract the Boolean share bits from the implementation of [9] by power analysis using the leakage related to the line 4 of Fig. 7.

The plots at the bottom of Fig. 8 show the distributions of power consumption during the processing of a single bit of Boolean shares by `masked_poly_frommsg()` procedure of the implementation of [9]. The distributions are plotted based on 10K traces captured from a profiling device running a first-order masked implementation with known masks at the trace point with the maximum absolute t-test score. Note that these traces are used for leakage analysis only. We do not use them for profiling, or in the attack.

The plots at the top of Fig. 8 show similar distributions for the implementation in [18]. One can see the significant difference in the overlapping areas of the plots of Boolean share bits with values 0 and 1. In the implementation of [18] there is almost no overlap, while in the implementation of [9] the overlap is large.

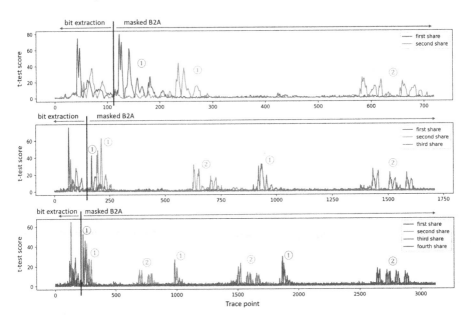

Fig. 9. T-test results for a single bit of each Boolean share of `masked_poly_frommsg()` procedure of the first- (top), second- (middle), third-order (bottom) masked implementations of [9]. Traces are acquired from a profiling device running implementations with known masks (used for leakage analysis only).

7.3   Finding New Leakage Points

The C code of masked Boolean to arithmetic conversion procedure `secb2a_1bit()` in Fig. 7 contains two operations that are directly related to the individual bits of each share. One is located in `b2a_qbit()` procedure, see lines marked in red. In line 1, the bit value of the first Boolean share `x[0]` is copied to the first arithmetic share `a[0]`. In line 3, all bit values of shares `x[i]`, $i \in \{1, \ldots, nshares - 1\}$, are given as input to `secb2a_qbit_n()`, one by one, where *nshares* is the number of shares.

Another operation related to individual bits of each share is located in `secb2a_qbit_n()` procedure. The bit value of the Boolean share `x[i]` is processed $i + 1$ times in the **for**-loop, see lines 2–6 of `secb2a_qbit_n()` in Fig. 7. In line 4, the value of `2*b[j]*x` is computed and subtracted from the intermediate value `c[j]`. Therefore, the Hamming weight of `c[j]` does not change if `x = 0`. Otherwise, for `x = 1`, it is likely to change[2].

To see if the two above-mentioned operations leak side-channel information, we performed t-test of `masked_poly_frommsg()` procedure for the first-, second- and third-order masked implementations with known masks captured from a profiling device. Figure 9 shows t-test results for a single bit of each Boolean

---

[2] The Hamming weight of an arithmetic share may remain the same if a non-zero value is subtracted.

share on 10K traces. The leakage points can be grouped into three types. Peaks on the left-hand side of the black vertical line are related to the extraction of a single Boolean share bit from a byte (line 4 of `masked_poly_frommsg()` in Fig. 7). Such a leakage is also present in the unprotected implementation of [21] (line 3 in Fig. 4) and the masked implementation of [18] (line 3 and 9 in Fig. 6).

Peaks on the right-hand side of the black vertical line, marked by "①" and "②", are related to the processing of individual Boolean share bits by the two above-mentioned operations (lines 1 and 3 of `b2a_qbit()` and line 4 of `secb2a_qbit_n()`). We call them the *direct-copy* leakage and the *additive* leakage, respectively. They are specific for the implementation of arbitrary-order masked Boolean to arithmetic conversion introduced in [9]. To the best of our knowledge, until now nobody has reported that these leakages are exploitable.

For direct-copy leakage, since the first Boolean share `x[0]` is assigned to the arithmetic share `a[0]` directly (line 1 of `b2a_qbit()`), the distance between the peaks corresponding to `x[0]` and `x[1]` is smaller than the distance between the peaks corresponding to `x[i]` and `x[i+1]`, for any $i > 0$.

For additive leakage, the number of peaks is equal to the number of times the share is processed in the **for**-loop (line 4 of `secb2a_qbit_n()`). For example, at the bottom plot of Fig. 9 representing the third-order masked implementation, there are two orange peaks (second share), three green peaks (third share), four red peaks (forth share) marked by '②'. There is no peak for the first share since `secb2a_qbit_n()` is not called to process it. The fact that a change of the Hamming weight of a Boolean share does not always lead to the change of the Hamming weight of the arithmetic share may explain why in Fig. 9 additive leakage is weaker than direct-copy leakage.

Next we compare distributions of power consumption of the direct-copy and additive leakages on the example of the first-order masked implementation, see Fig. 10. The distributions are plotted based on 10K traces at the trace point with the maximum absolute t-test score. These traces are acquired from a profiling device running the implementation with known masks during the execution of masked Boolean to arithmetic conversion. We can see that, for direct-copy leakage, the overlap in the plots is smaller than the one for additive leakage. This is consistent with t-test results in Fig. 9. Since the overlap is not complete, both types can be exploited for message recovery.

In the message recovery attack presented in Sect. 10.1, we use both direct-copy and additive leakages as well as the leakage in the bit extraction part.

8 Neural Network Training

This section describes our neural network training strategy. It is a combination of techniques employed in previous profiling deep learning-based side-channel attacks on PQC and symmetric cryptographic algorithms, with some differences which we highlight.

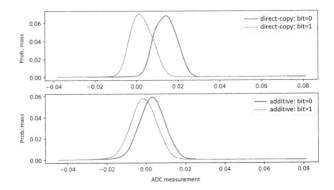

Fig. 10. Distributions of power consumption during the processing of a single bit of Boolean shares by `secb2a_1bit()` in the first-order masked implementation of [9] for the direct-copy (top) and additive (bottom) leakage.

Following [13], we train a single universal neural network model for message bit prediction on cut-and-joined and standardized traces. A multilayer perceptron (MLP) with an architecture similar to the one in [13] is used. A difference from [13] is that we use traces from five profiling devices in the training set. Such an approach is used in the side-channel attack on AES presented in [39]. Another difference from [13] is that we use three leakage points, so cut-and-join is a bit more tedious to perform.

8.1 Trace Acquisition and Pre-processing

Since `masked_poly_frommsg()` procedure processes the Boolean share bits one-by-one, it is possible to train a universal model for predicting all bits except the first and the last. The trace shape for the first/last bits typically differ from the rest because their previous/next instructions differ [24].

The complete execution of `masked_poly_frommsg()` procedure in the implementation of [9] does not fit into the buffer of ChipWhisperer-Pro which we use for trace acquisition. Therefore, for the first- and second-order masked implementation we capture traces containing the execution of the first 33 bits only and use a union of intervals corresponding to the bits 1–32 for training. For the third-order masked implementation, we capture traces containing the execution of the first 17 bits only and use a union of intervals corresponding to the bits 1–16 for training. In all cases, the interval is a concatenation of three segments covering the three leakage points described in Sect. 7.3.

Since the implementation of [9] uses a true random number generator (TRNG) with a range check for generating masks, the raw traces are misaligned. We synchronize the traces by cross-correlating with templates, one for each leakage point. We also apply standardization to traces.

To minimize the total number of traces required from the DUA, we perform profiling on different devices. We use five profiling devices, D_1–D_5, in order to

Table 1. MLP architecture used for message recovery. The input size is $size = 590, 1000$ and 1610 for the first-, second- and third-order masked implementations, respectively.

Layer type	Output shape
Batch Normalization 1	$size$
Dense 1	512
Batch Normalization 2	512
ReLU	512
Dense 2	256
Batch Normalization 3	256
ReLU	256
Dense 3	128
Batch Normalization 4	128
ReLU	128
Dense 4	2
Softmax	2

reduce the negative effect of inter-device variation on neural network's classification accuracy. The benefits of such a multi-source profiling are well-known [36].

8.2 Network Architecture and Training Parameters

The neural networks with the architecture listed in Table 1 are trained with a batch size of 1024 for a maximum of 100 epochs using early stopping with patience 10. We use Nadam optimizer with a learning rate of 0.01 and a numerical stability constant $epsilon = 1e-08$. Categorical cross-entropy is used as a loss function to evaluate the network classification error. 70% of the training set is used for training and 30% is left for validation. Only the model with the highest validation accuracy is saved.

9   New Chosen Ciphertext Construction Method

It is known that the secret key of an LWE/LWR KEM algorithm can be derived from messages recovered from chosen ciphertexts. Many different methods for constructing the chosen ciphertexts have been presented in the past, including [5, 24, 28, 29, 41]. These methods uniquely map each secret key coefficient into a b-bit binary vector composed from the message bits recovered from b chosen ciphertexts. Some methods, e.g. [5, 24], impose an additional requirement that b-bit binary vectors are codewords of some linear code with the code distance C_d. In the latter case, for each secret key coefficient, c errors in the recovered message bits can be corrected and d additional errors can be detected, where $2c + d + 1 \leq C_d$. The method [5] also minimizes the Hamming weight of the chosen ciphertexts.

However, none of the previous chosen ciphertext construction methods map the secret key coefficients into codewords so that the full secret key recovery probability is maximized for a given message bit recovery probability. We introduce such a method in this section.

First we explain the method of composing chosen ciphertexts and then derive a formula relating the probability of the secret key recovery to the probability of a message bit recovery. Using this formula, we select a best codeword for each key coefficient which maximizes the secret key recovery probability. Finally, we show that there is a considerable difference between secret key recovery probabilities of the best and the worst mappings.

9.1 Constructing Chosen Ciphertexts

In Kyber-768, the secret key s consists of three polynomials $s = (s_0, s_1, s_2)$, and the ciphertext (u, v) consists of three polynomials $u = (u_0, u_1, u_2)$ and one polynomial v. To recover 256 coefficients of s_i, one of the polynomials of u is set to a non-zero constant k_1 and the other two polynomials of u are set to zero:

$$u = \begin{cases} (k_1, 0, 0) \in R_q^{3 \times 1} & \text{for } i = 0, \\ (0, k_1, 0) \in R_q^{3 \times 1} & \text{for } i = 1, \\ (0, 0, k_1) \in R_q^{3 \times 1} & \text{for } i = 2. \end{cases}$$

All 256 coefficients of v are set to the same constant k_0:

$$v = k_0 \sum_{j=0}^{255} x^j \in R_q^{1 \times 1}.$$

The constants (k_1, k_0) inducing a given mapping between the secret key coefficients and message bits can be found by a brute-force search through all legal pairs (k_1, k_0) (if the solution exists). Next we derive a formula which helps select the best mapping that maximizes the secret key recovery probability.

9.2 Selecting Optimal Mapping

Let p be the probability of recovering a single message bit, and $d(x, x')$ be the Hamming distance between the codewords representing the secret key coefficients x and x', for $x, x' \in \{-2, -1, 0, 1, 2\}$.

Given a codeword composed from b recovered message bits, there are three possible outcomes:

1. The codeword is recovered correctly (*no errors*). We denote this probability by p_c.
2. The recovered codeword contains errors and matches the codeword representing another secret key coefficient (*undetected error*). We denote this probability by p_u.
3. The recovered codeword contains errors but does not match any codewords of another secret key coefficients (*detected error*). We denote this probability by p_d.

Table 2. Mappings which give the maximum (left) and the minimum p_{sk} (right).

$\mathcal{C}_{best}$: (k_1, k_0)	-2	-1	0	1	2	$\mathcal{C}_{worst}$: (k_1, k_0)	-2	-1	0	1	2
(1977,208)	1	1	0	1	0	(104,1040)	1	1	1	1	0
(627,208)	1	1	0	0	1	(419,416)	1	1	0	0	0
(731,1040)	0	1	1	0	0	(940,1040)	0	1	1	0	1

The secret key coefficients are generated using the centered binomial distribution, see line 2 of KYBER.CPAPKE.KeyGen() in Fig. 1. For Kyber-768, the probability of occurrence of $x \in \{-2, -1, 0, 1, 2\}$, p_x, is given by:

$$
p_x = \begin{cases}
1/16, & \text{for } x = -2 \\
4/16, & \text{for } x = -1 \\
6/16, & \text{for } x = 0 \\
4/16, & \text{for } x = 1 \\
1/16, & \text{for } x = 2
\end{cases} \tag{2}
$$

Thus, the expected probabilities of three outcomes listed above are given by:

$$
p_c = \sum_x p_x \cdot p^b = p^b \tag{3}
$$

$$
p_u = \sum_x p_x \cdot \sum_{x', x' \neq x} (1-p)^{d(x,x')} p^{b-d(x,x')} \tag{4}
$$

$$
p_d = 1 - p_c - p_u \tag{5}
$$

Let e be the maximum tolerable number of detected errors. Then, for Kyber-768, the probability of full secret key recovery is:

$$
p_{sk} = \sum_{i=0}^{e} \binom{768}{i} p_d^i \cdot p_c^{768-i} \tag{6}
$$

By a brute-force search through all possible codewords of the length $b = 3$ for each secret key coefficient, one can find a mapping $\mathcal{C}_{best}$ which results in the highest p_{sk} and a mapping $\mathcal{C}_{worst}$ which gives the lowest p_{sk}. Examples of such mapping are listed in Table 2. They are not unique. One can see that, for the optimal mapping $\mathcal{C}_{best}$, $d(0, x) \geq 2$ for all for $x \in \{-2, -1, 1, 2\}$, while for $\mathcal{C}_{worst}$, $d(0, x') = 1$, for $x' \in \{-1, 1, 2\}$. Thus, single-bit errors are more likely to be undetected in $\mathcal{C}_{worst}$ case.

Figure 11 plots p_{sk} as a function of p for the mappings $\mathcal{C}_{best}$ and $\mathcal{C}_{worst}$ (plots of other mappings would be in between the two) and a fixed $e = 16$. For $0 < p < 1$, $\mathcal{C}_{best}$ always results in a higher p_{sk}. The difference between the two mappings first grows as p increases, reaching the maximium of 39% at $p = 0.9991$. Then, it starts decreasing and the plots converge at $p = 1$.

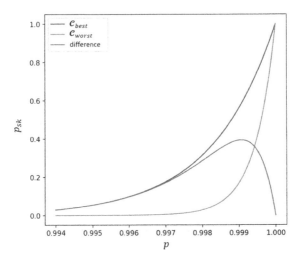

Fig. 11. Secret key recovery probability, p_{sk}, as a function message bit recovery probability, p, for the best and worst mappings.

10 Experimental Results

This section presents the results of message and secret key recovery attacks on the higher-order masked implementation of Kyber-768 [9] in ARM Cortex-M4.

10.1 Message Recovery Attack

Using the strategy described in Sect. 8, we trained neural network models for message bit recovery. For each ω-order masked implementation in the experiments, a single universal model was trained for recovering all bits. The models were trained using power traces captured from five profiling devices, D_i, $i \in \{1, 2, \ldots, 5\}$. For each implementation, one fifth of training traces were captured from each profiling device. As we mentioned in Sect. 8.1, the complete execution of `masked_poly_frommsg()` procedure in the implementation of [9] does not fit into the buffer of ChipWhisperer-Pro. For $\omega = 1$ and 2, we captured 2K traces from each D_i and trained the models based on the message bits 1–32. For $\omega = 3$, 4K traces were captured from each D_i and the models were trained based on the message bits 1–16. In all three cases, after the cut-and-join, the total number of training traces is 320K.

The models were tested on power traces captured from the DUA D_6 for 1000 ciphertexts encrypting messages selected at random. For each ciphertext, we repeated the decapsulation twenty times and recorded the corresponding power traces. We use N to denote the number of repetitions of the same decapsulation.

Table 3 summarizes the results of message recovery attacks on the first-order masked implementation. It lists the empirical average message bit recovery probability, p_{bit}, and the full message recovery probability, p_m, estimated as $p_m = (p_{bit})^{256}$, for different number of repetitions N.

Table 3. Empirical results of message recovery attack on the first-order masked implementation.

# Repetitions	$N = 1$	$N = 2$	$N = 3$
Avg. message bit recovery prob., p_{bit}	0.99928	0.99997	1
Est. full message recovery prob., p_m	0.83	0.99	1

Table 4. Empirical results of message recovery attack on the second-order masked implementation.

# Repetitions	$N = 1$	$N = 2$	$N = 4$	$N = 8$	$N = 16$
Avg. message bit recovery prob., p_{bit}	0.97203	0.99519	0.99953	0.99959	0.99994
Est. full message recovery prob., p_m	0	0.29	0.89	0.90	0.98

Table 5. Empirical results of message recovery attack on the third-order masked implementation.

# Repetitions	$N = 1$	$N = 2$	$N = 4$	$N = 8$	$N = 16$
Avg. message bit recovery prob., p_{bit}	0.95356	0.98219	0.99356	0.99819	0.99994
Est. full message recovery prob., p_m	0	0.01	0.19	0.63	0.98

We can see that the estimated full message recovery probability is 0.83 for a single-trace attack. When the number of repetitions increases to three, p_m reaches 1. As observed in [13], side-channel attacks of masked implementations benefit from the independence of errors in repeated measurements due to random mask update at each execution.

Table 4 and 5 show the results of message recovery attacks on the second- and third-order masked implementations. We increase the number of repetitions exponentially since higher-order masking is more difficult than first-order to break. One can see that, for both $\omega = 2$ and $\omega = 3$, the empirical full message recovery probability p_m reaches 0.98 for sixteen repetitions.

Note that the ChipWhisperer target board used in our experiments has a low noise. For the attacks in noisier conditions, convolutional neural networks [22,26], or transformers [8,16] may be more suitable neural network architectures. Noise reduction, e.g. by using autoencoders [22,40], may also be helpful.

10.2   Secret Key Recovery Attack

In order to evaluate the effectiveness of the new method of mapping message bits into secret key coefficients, we generated 100 different secret and public key pairs for $\omega = 1, 2$ and 50 different key pairs for $\omega = 3$ using KYBER.CCAKEM.KeyGen(), respectively. According to Tables 3, 4 and 5, three and 16 repetitions should give a close to 1 message bit recovery probability for $\omega = 1$ and $\omega = 2, 3$. Then, we captured from the DUA D_6 the corresponding

Table 6. Empirical results of secret key recovery attack on the first-order masked implementation.

# Repetition	$\mathcal{C}_{best}$ mapping			$\mathcal{C}_{worst}$ mapping		
	p_{bit}	p_{sk}	Enum	p_{bit}	p_{sk}	Enum
$N = 1$	0.99761	0.26	5^{16}	0.99746	0	$>5^{16}$
$N = 2$	0.99987	0.94	5^{4}	0.99989	0.84	5^{1}
$N = 3$	0.99995	0.98	5^{4}	0.99997	0.97	5^{1}

Table 7. Empirical results of secret key recovery attack on the second-order masked implementation.

# Repetition	$\mathcal{C}_{best}$ mapping			$\mathcal{C}_{worst}$ mapping		
	p_{bit}	p_{sk}	Enum	p_{bit}	p_{sk}	Enum
$N = 1$	0.97466	0	$>5^{16}$	0.97365	0	$>5^{16}$
$N = 2$	0.99600	0.10	5^{11}	0.99570	0	5^{3}
$N = 4$	0.99970	0.79	5^{2}	0.99960	0.60	5^{1}
$N = 8$	0.99975	0.81	5^{5}	0.99971	0.72	5^{1}
$N = 16$	0.99997	0.97	5^{1}	0.99996	0.92	5^{1}

Table 8. Empirical results of secret key recovery attack on the third-order masked implementation.

# Repetition	$\mathcal{C}_{best}$ mapping			$\mathcal{C}_{worst}$ mapping		
	p_{bit}	p_{sk}	Enum	p_{bit}	p_{sk}	Enum
$N = 1$	0.94794	0	$>5^{16}$	0.95095	0	$>5^{16}$
$N = 2$	0.98108	0	$>5^{16}$	0.98215	0	$>5^{16}$
$N = 4$	0.99290	0	$>5^{16}$	0.99297	0	$>5^{16}$
$N = 8$	0.99793	0.36	5^{7}	0.99781	0.02	5^{1}
$N = 16$	0.99977	0.82	5^{2}	0.99979	0.74	5^{1}

number of traces for each key pair during the decapsulation of chosen ciphertexts constructed for the mappings $\mathcal{C}_{best}$ and $\mathcal{C}_{worst}$ defined in Table 2.

Table 6 shows the results for the mappings $\mathcal{C}_{best}$ and $\mathcal{C}_{worst}$ for the first-order masked implementation. We can see that the difference in the average message bit recovery probabilities, p_{bit}, of $\mathcal{C}_{best}$ and $\mathcal{C}_{worst}$ for a fixed N is insignificant. However, due to the different mappings $\mathcal{C}_{best}$ and $\mathcal{C}_{worst}$, the difference in full secret key recovery probabilities, p_{sk}, is significant for $N = 1$. For $\mathcal{C}_{best}$, we get $p_{sk} = 0.26$ with the maximum enumeration of 5^{16}. In contract, for $\mathcal{C}_{worst}$, none of the 100 secret keys can be recovered. As N increases, the difference between $\mathcal{C}_{best}$ and $\mathcal{C}_{worst}$ decreases.

Table 7 shows the results of secret recovery attack on the second-order masked implementation. We can see that, for $\mathcal{C}_{best}$, 16 repetitions instead of three, are required to reach the full secret key recovery probability $p_{sk} = 0.97$. We can also see that, for $N = 4$, the difference in p_{sk} between $\mathcal{C}_{best}$ and $\mathcal{C}_{worst}$ is maximum, 19%.

Similarly, Table 8 shows the results of secret recovery attack on the third-order masked implementation. The probability of the full secret key recovery is $p_{sk} = 0.82$ using $\mathcal{C}_{best}$ when $N = 16$. The gap in p_{sk} between $\mathcal{C}_{best}$ and $\mathcal{C}_{worst}$ is maximum, 34%, for $N = 8$.

11   Countermeasures

The presented secret key recovery attack would not be possible if the decapsulating device could refuse decrypting the chosen ciphertexts. This can be realized by authenticating the ciphertexts e.g. using the Encrypt-then-Sign method proposed by Azouaoui et al. [4], or subjecting the ciphertexts to the minimal range check [41].

Another possibility is to update the keys (pk, sk) for each new shared key establishment session rather than keeping them static. In this scenario, the shared key becomes the primary attack target. Note, however, that the dynamic keys (pk, sk) make the likelihood of recovering the shared key less likely, but not impossible. For instance, for the first-order masking, the attacker is expected to recover the shared key from a single trace with the probability of 26% (see Table 6). Since the success probability grows quickly if the decapsulation can be repeated multiple times, designing a mechanism which prevents repeated decapsulations of the same ciphertext could be considered as an option.

The presented message recovery attack would be more difficult if the procedure `masked_poly_frommsg()` were bitsliced. Using a TRNG with a range check for generating masks is an excellent design choice because the resulting traces' misalignment creates an extra hurdle for the attacker.

12   Conclusion

We demonstrated practical shared and secret key recovery attacks on the higher-order masked implementation of Kyber by Bronchain et al. [9] by profiled deep learning-based power analysis.

We discovered new vulnerabilities in the implementation of arbitrary-order masked Boolean to arithmetic conversion introduced in [9]. Note that such an implementation is applicable not only to Kyber, but also to any algorithm using masked Boolean to arithmetic conversion. Our work shows that, to resist power analysis, the implementation needs to be further strengthened.

Another contribution is the chosen ciphertext construction method that maximizes the likelihood of recovering the secret key for a given message bit recovery probability. The new way of mapping message bits into the secret key coefficients can raise the probability of recovering the secret key by up to 39% compared to the worst case.

Acknowledgments. This work was supported in part by the Swedish Civil Contingencies Agency (Grant No. 2020-11632) and the Swedish Research Council (Grant No. 2018-04482).

References

1. Announcing the commercial national security algorithm suite 2.0. National Security Agency, U.S Department of Defense, September 2022. https://media.defense.gov/2022/Sep/07/2003071834/-1/-1/0/CSA_CNSA_2.0_ALGORITHMS_.PDF
2. Amiet, D., Curiger, A., Leuenberger, L., Zbinden, P.: Defeating NEWHOPE with a single trace. In: Ding, J., Tillich, J.-P. (eds.) PQCrypto 2020. LNCS, vol. 12100, pp. 189–205. Springer, Cham (2020). https://doi.org/10.1007/978-3-030-44223-1_11
3. Avanzi, R., et al.: CRYSTALS-Kyber algorithm specifications and supporting documentation (2021). https://pq-crystals.org/kyber/data/kyber-specification-round3-20210131.pdf
4. Azouaoui, M., Kuzovkova, Y., Schneider, T., van Vredendaal, C.: Post-quantum authenticated encryption against chosen-ciphertext side-channel attacks. IACR Trans. Crypt. Hardw. Embed. Syst. **2022**, 372–396 (2022)
5. Backlund, L., Ngo, K., Gartner, J., Dubrova, E.: Secret key recovery attacks on masked and shuffled implementations of CRYSTALS-Kyber and Saber. Cryptology ePrint Archive, Paper 2022/1692 (2022). https://eprint.iacr.org/2022/1692
6. Bhasin, S., D'Anvers, J.P., Heinz, D., Pöppelmann, T., Beirendonck, M.V.: Attacking and defending masked polynomial comparison for lattice-based cryptography. Cryptology ePrint Archive, Paper 2021/104 (2021). https://eprint.iacr.org/2021/104
7. Bos, J.W., Gourjon, M., Renes, J., Schneider, T., Van Vredendaal, C.: Masking Kyber: first-and higher-order implementations. IACR Trans. Crypt. Hardw. Embed. Syst. **2021**, 173–214 (2021)
8. Brisfors, M.: Advanced Side-Channel Analysis of USIMs, Bluetooth SoCs and MCUs. Master's thesis, School of EECS, KTH (2021)
9. Bronchain, O., Cassiers, G.: Bitslicing arithmetic/Boolean masking conversions for fun and profit: with application to lattice-based KEMs. IACR Trans. Crypt. Hardw. Embed. Syst. **2022**, 553–588 (2022)
10. D'Anvers, J.P., Beirendonck, M.V., Verbauwhede, I.: Revisiting higher-order masked comparison for lattice-based cryptography: algorithms and bit-sliced implementations. Cryptology ePrint Archive, Paper 2022/110 (2022). https://eprint.iacr.org/2022/110
11. D'Anvers, J.P., Heinz, D., Pessl, P., Van Beirendonck, M., Verbauwhede, I.: Higher-order masked ciphertext comparison for lattice-based cryptography. IACR Trans. Crypt. Hardw. Embed. Syst. **2022**, 115–139 (2022)
12. Do, Q., Martini, B., Choo, K.K.R.: The role of the adversary model in applied security research. Comput. Secur. **81**, 156–181 (2019)
13. Dubrova, E., Ngo, K., Gärtner, J., Wang, R.: Breaking a fifth-order masked implementation of crystals-kyber by copy-paste. In: Proceedings of the 10th ACM Asia Public-Key Cryptography Workshop, pp. 10–20 (2023)
14. Fujisaki, E., Okamoto, T.: Secure integration of asymmetric and symmetric encryption schemes. In: Wiener, M. (ed.) CRYPTO 1999. LNCS, vol. 1666, pp. 537–554. Springer, Heidelberg (1999). https://doi.org/10.1007/3-540-48405-1_34

15. Guo, Q., Nabokov, D., Nilsson, A., Johansson, T.: SCA-LDPC: a code-based framework for key-recovery side-channel attacks on post-quantum encryption schemes. Cryptology ePrint Archive (2023)
16. Hajra, S., Saha, S., Alam, M., Mukhopadhyay, D.: TransNet: shift invariant transformer network for side channel analysis. Cryptology ePrint Archive, Paper 2021/827 (2021). https://eprint.iacr.org/2021/827
17. Hamburg, M., et al.: Chosen ciphertext k-trace attacks on masked CCA2 secure Kyber. IACR Trans. Crypt. Hardw. Embed. Syst. **2021**, 88–113 (2021)
18. Heinz, D., Kannwischer, M.J., Land, G., Pöppelmann, T., Schwabe, P., Sprenkels, D.: First-order masked Kyber on ARM Cortex-M4. Cryptology ePrint Archive, Paper 2022/058 (2022). https://eprint.iacr.org/2022/058
19. Hoffmann, C., Libert, B., Momin, C., Peters, T., Standaert, F.X.: Towards leakage-resistant post-quantum CCA-secure public key encryption. Cryptology ePrint Archive, Paper 2022/873 (2022). https://eprint.iacr.org/2022/873
20. Ji, Y., Wang, R., Ngo, K., Dubrova, E., Backlund, L.: A side-channel attack on a hardware implementation of CRYSTALS-Kyber. Cryptology ePrint Archive, Paper 2022/1452 (2022). https://eprint.iacr.org/2022/1452
21. Kannwischer, M.J., Petri, R., Rijneveld, J., Schwabe, P., Stoffelen, K.: PQM4: post-quantum crypto library for the ARM Cortex-M4. https://github.com/mupq/pqm4
22. Maghrebi, H., Portigliatti, T., Prouff, E.: Breaking cryptographic implementations using deep learning techniques. In: Carlet, C., Hasan, M.A., Saraswat, V. (eds.) SPACE 2016. LNCS, vol. 10076, pp. 3–26. Springer, Cham (2016). https://doi.org/10.1007/978-3-319-49445-6_1
23. Moody, D.: Status Report on the Third Round of the NIST Post-Quantum Cryptography Standardization Process. NISTIR 8309, pp. 1–27 (2022). https://nvlpubs.nist.gov/nistpubs/ir/2022/NIST.IR.8413.pdf
24. Ngo, K., Dubrova, E., Guo, Q., Johansson, T.: A side-channel attack on a masked IND-CCA secure Saber KEM implementation. IACR Trans. Crypt. Hardw. Embed. Syst. **2012**, 676–707 (2021)
25. Oder, T., Schneider, T., Pöppelmann, T., Güneysu, T.: Practical CCA2-secure and masked ring-LWE implementation. IACR Trans. Crypt. Hardw. Embed. Syst. **2018**, 142–174 (2018)
26. Picek, S., Samiotis, I.P., Kim, J., Heuser, A., Bhasin, S., Legay, A.: On the performance of convolutional neural networks for side-channel analysis. In: Chattopadhyay, A., Rebeiro, C., Yarom, Y. (eds.) SPACE 2018. LNCS, vol. 11348, pp. 157–176. Springer, Cham (2018). https://doi.org/10.1007/978-3-030-05072-6_10
27. Rajendran, G., Ravi, P., D'Anvers, J.P., Bhasin, S., Chattopadhyay, A.: Pushing the limits of generic side-channel attacks on LWE-based KEMs-parallel PC oracle attacks on Kyber KEM and beyond. IACR Trans. Crypt. Hardw. Embed. Syst. **2023**, 418–446 (2023)
28. Ravi, P., Bhasin, S., Roy, S.S., Chattopadhyay, A.: On exploiting message leakage in (few) NIST PQC candidates for practical message recovery attacks. IEEE Trans. Inf. Forensics Secur. **17**, 684–699 (2021)
29. Ravi, P., Roy, S.S., Chattopadhyay, A., Bhasin, S.: Generic side-channel attacks on CCA-secure lattice-based PKE and KEMs. IACR Trans. Crypt. Hardw. Embed. Syst. **2020**, 307–335 (2020)
30. Rodriguez, R.C., Bruguier, F., Valea, E., Benoit, P.: Correlation electromagnetic analysis on an FPGA implementation of CRYSTALS-Kyber. Cryptology ePrint Archive, Paper 2022/1361 (2022). https://eprint.iacr.org/2022/1361

31. Schneider, T., Paglialonga, C., Oder, T., Güneysu, T.: Efficiently masking binomial sampling at arbitrary orders for lattice-based crypto. In: Lin, D., Sako, K. (eds.) PKC 2019. LNCS, vol. 11443, pp. 534–564. Springer, Cham (2019). https://doi.org/10.1007/978-3-030-17259-6_18

32. Shen, M., Cheng, C., Zhang, X., Guo, Q., Jiang, T.: Find the bad apples: an efficient method for perfect key recovery under imperfect SCA oracles - a case study of Kyber. IACR Trans. Crypt. Hardw. Embed. Syst. **2023**, 89–112 (2023)

33. Sim, B.Y., et al.: Single-trace attacks on message encoding in lattice-based KEMs. IEEE Access **8**, 183175–183191 (2020)

34. Tsai, T.T., Huang, S.S., Tseng, Y.M., Chuang, Y.H., Hung, Y.H.: Leakage-resilient certificate-based authenticated key exchange protocol. IEEE Open J. Comput. Soc. **3**, 137–148 (2022)

35. Ueno, R., Xagawa, K., Tanaka, Y., Ito, A., Takahashi, J., Homma, N.: Curse of re-encryption: a generic power/EM analysis on post-quantum KEMs. IACR Trans. Crypt. Hardw. Embed. Syst. **2022**, 296–322 (2022)

36. Wang, H., Forsmark, S., Brisfors, M., Dubrova, E.: Multi-source training deep learning side-channel attacks. In: IEEE 50th International Symposium on Multiple-Valued Logic, ISMVL 2020 (2020)

37. Wang, J., Cao, W., Chen, H., Li, H.: Practical side-channel attack on message encoding in masked Kyber. In: 2022 IEEE International Conference on Trust, Security and Privacy in Computing and Communications (TrustCom), pp. 882–889. IEEE (2022)

38. Wang, R., Ngo, K., Dubrova, E.: A message recovery attack on LWE/LWR-based PKE/KEMs using amplitude-modulated EM emanations. In: Seo, SH., Seo, H. (eds.) Information Security and Cryptology, ICISC 2022. LNCS, vol. 13849, pp. 450–471. Springer, Cham (2023). https://doi.org/10.1007/978-3-031-29371-9_22

39. Wang, R., Wang, H., Dubrova, E.: Far field EM side-channel attack on AES using deep learning. In: Proceedings of the 4th ACM Workshop on Attacks and Solutions in Hardware Security, pp. 35–44 (2020)

40. Wu, L., Picek, S.: Remove some noise: On pre-processing of side-channel measurements with autoencoders. IACR Trans. Crypt. Hardw. Embed. Syst. **2020**, 389–415 (2020)

41. Xu, Z., Pemberton, O.M., Roy, S.S., Oswald, D., Yao, W., Zheng, Z.: Magnifying side-channel leakage of lattice-based cryptosystems with chosen ciphertexts: the case study of Kyber. IEEE Trans. Comput. **71**, 2163–2176 (2021)

42. Yajing, C., Yan, Y., Zhu, C., Guo, P.: Template attack of LWE/LWR-based schemes with cyclic message rotation. Entropy **24**(10), 1489 (2022)

Time Is Money, Friend! Timing Side-Channel Attack Against Garbled Circuit Constructions

Mohammad Hashemi[1]([✉]), Domenic Forte[2], and Fatemeh Ganji[1]([✉])

[1] Worcester Polytechnic Institute, Worcester, MA 01609, USA
{mhashemi,fgangi}@wpi.edu
[2] University of Florida, Gainesville, FL 32611, USA
dforte@ece.ufl.edu

Abstract. With the advent of secure function evaluation (SFE), distrustful parties can jointly compute on their private inputs without disclosing anything besides the results. Yao's garbled circuit protocol has become an integral part of secure computation thanks to considerable efforts made to make it feasible, practical, and more efficient. For decades, the security of protocols offered in general-purpose compilers has been assured with regard to sound proofs and the promise that during the computation, no information on parties' input would be leaking. In a parallel effort, timing side-channel attacks have proven themselves effective in retrieving secrets from implementations, even through remote access to them. Nevertheless, the vulnerability of garbled circuit frameworks to timing attacks has, surprisingly, never been discussed in the literature. This paper introduces Goblin, the first timing attack against commonly employed garbled circuit frameworks. Goblin is a machine learning-assisted, non-profiling, single-trace timing side-channel attack (SCA), which successfully recovers the garbler's input during the computation under different scenarios, including various garbling frameworks, benchmark functions, and the number of garbler's input bits. In doing so, Goblin hopefully paves the way for further research in this matter.

Keywords: Grabled Circuits · Timing Side-channel Analysis · Clustering · Non-profiling Attack · Single-trace Attack

1 Introduction

Secure function evaluation (SFE) has had an immense impact on the field of cryptography. Practical implementations of general SFE have been proposed and flourished after the introduction of garbled circuits (GCs) by Yao [93]. It has found several applications including secure multi-party computation [6,22,23,57], functional encryption [27,28,80], key-dependent message security [2,3], homomorphic encryption [26,76], and recently, quantum circuits [9]. The key premise of GCs is that it allows two parties to evaluate any (known)

Code is available at https://github.com/vernamlab/Goblin.

C. Pöpper and L. Batina (Eds.): ACNS 2024, LNCS 14585, pp. 325–354, 2024.
https://doi.org/10.1007/978-3-031-54776-8_13

function on their respective inputs x and y without violating their privacy. Besides real-world applications foreseen for GCs traditionally (e.g., credit evaluation function, background- and medical history checking, privacy-preserving database querying, etc. [53,82]), nowadays GCs have found applications in privacy-preserving genome analysis [43], email spam filtering [36], image processing [12] and machine learning and statistical analysis [14,24,71,75], just to name a few. To face obstacles preventing further adoption of GCs in real-world systems, optimization techniques have been developed, aiming to reduce communication and computation costs. Here we focus on two of the most acknowledged methods, namely free-XOR [53] and half-gates [97]. Similar to other optimization mechanisms, the main argument put forward by these techniques is that security is not compromised for the sake of being efficient. However, the question is whether this holds true when implementing these protocols. This becomes even more critical since today's applications of GCs (or potential ones) encompass services run on distributed computing systems, cloud services, connected devices, etc.

Timing Side-Channel Analysis. Irrespective of what cryptographic functions are embedded in programmable instruction set processors, such systems can exhibit observable features and data-dependent behavior that leak information about users' data/keys from the implementation. As a prime example, timing side channels can be observed when the time taken to execute a piece of code depends on the secret variables [52,63,72,90]. In this regard, two broad categories of timing side channels can be identified: instruction-related and cache-related cf. [92]. The former refers to the number or type of instructions executed along a path that can differ depending on the values of secret variables. On the other hand, cache-related timing side channels correspond to the case, where the memory subsystem may behave differently based on the values of secret variables. In both categories, CPU instruction execution, specifically the branch prediction, memory access, and data caches, have been exploited to launch successful SCA on the cryptographic systems cf. [1,7,20,29,78]. Recently, the security of open-source cryptographic libraries and implementations of protocols (excluding GC) has just been evaluated in an extensive study [45], where the vulnerability of some of those libraries to timing SCA has been demonstrated. More interesting and inspiring from the perspective of this work is the gap between academic research and cryptographic engineering when it comes to timing SCA.

SCA Against GC Constructions. Despite the achievements made to prove the security of GC schemes, there is a gap between what theoretical findings have suggested and what observations can be made by parties involved in executing a GC protocol. The only example of studies addressing this gap is a recent attack proposed by Levi et al., which leverages the side-channel leakage as a result of using a secret, global value for free-XOR, correlated with the power consumption of the garbler's device [55]. Although multiple assumptions have been made to launch the attack, their attack has successfully disclosed the global value used to perform free-XOR optimization. Now the question is whether one can go even beyond this attack and perform timing SCA and whether some of the assumptions made in [55] can be relaxed in that case.

Generally speaking, timing attacks feature outstanding properties that make them more interesting [45]: first, timing attacks can be launched remotely, including cases of running code in parallel to the victim code without the need for local access to the target computer; second, timing attacks can be carried out covertly. In light of this state of affairs, this work attempts to answer the following question: *Is it possible to reveal parties' input by observing the timing information leaking when executing a GC protocol?* More specifically, we answer this question positively for free-XOR- and half-gates-optimized constructions. The contribution of our work is as follows.

Our **Contributions** are summarized as follows.

1. We introduce *Goblin*, the first non-profiling, single-trace timing SCA that successfully extract the user's input, which by definition, should have been kept secret. To better demonstrate the power of our attack, we compare it with the recent attack in [55]. The power SCA in [55] has successfully extracted the global secret used in free-XOR optimization, whereas Goblin focuses entirely on the recovery of the garbler's input. Needless to say that even with the help of the disclosed secret, the garbler's input could not be fully recovered. Moreover, in contrast to [55], Goblin's effectiveness is limited to neither circuits with a minimum number of input gates nor gate types (XOR or AND).
2. Goblin is machine-learning assisted in disclosing the garbler's input, regardless of its size. For this purpose, k-means clustering is applied, where no manual tuning or heuristic leakage models are needed. It is, of course, advantageous to the attacker and allows for scalable and efficient attacks.
3. Last but not least, our paper highlights the vulnerabilities of multiple available garbling tools to timing SCA. We believe that this constitutes a basis for studying the SCA with respect to GC.

2 Background and Adversary Model

Notations. We follow a standard notation typically used in SFE-related literature. $\in_R$ denotes uniform sampling, $\|$ is used to show concatenation of bit strings. $\langle a, b \rangle$ represents a vector with two components a and b, whereas $a \| b$ is its bit string representation. A *gate* is denoted by $W_c = g(W_a, W_b)$ with input wires W_a and W_b, output wire W_c and $g : \{0,1\}^2 \to \{0,1\}$.

2.1 Yao's Garbled Circuit (GC)

One of the most widely studied SFE approaches, designed to meet the needs of Boolean circuits, is garbling [56,58]. The first protocol within the context of GC is Oblivious transfer (OT). We consider 1-out-of-2 OT, which is a two-party protocol with the following definition. The sender P_1 possesses two secret messages m_0, and m_1, and the receiver P_2 has a selection bit $i \in \{0,1\}$. By executing the protocol, P_2 learns m_i, but not m_{1-i}, while the sender P_1 does not learn anything about i.

Garbling. The protocol execution begins with garbling the circuit C, where the garbler (P_1) randomly chooses secrets w_i^j with the garbled value of $j \in \{0, 1\}$ on each wire W_i. Needless to say that it is expected that w_i^j does *not* reveal any information about j. Practical implementations of Yao's GC, e.g., [86] considered in this paper, represent each of the logical "0" and "1" values with n-bit values, where n is often referred to as the security parameter. In this sense, w_i^j (so-called token) is the encryption of the concatenation of j and $(n-1)$-bit values drawn uniformly. After generating the tokens, the garbler creates a garbled table T_i for each gate G_i, where each row of the gate truth table is encrypted output with regard to the tokens, and the output of the gate is called a "ciphertext," illustrated in Fig. 1.(a) as the output of the operand $E(\cdot)$, i.e., the encryption operation (symmetric key operations, e.g., fixed-key block cipher). Since the table rows can reveal information about the internal wire values, they are permuted. The main property of T_i is that its output can be recovered given a set of garbled inputs, while this process does not leak any information about the garbler's and evaluator's (P_2) inputs. For this, along with T_i's, the token corresponding to the garbler's input value is obliviously transferred to P_2 through OT. P_2 is then able to obtain the garbled output by evaluating the garbled circuit gate by gate using the tables T_i and receiving j for the output wire from P_1 cf. [87]. Garbling of the output wires of the circuit can be skipped so that two parties learn (only) the output of the circuit [53].

Optimizations of Yao's GC. Reducing the computation and communication costs of SFE protocols has been an objective of numerous studies. Among optimization techniques introduced in the literature, **free-XOR** has attracted considerable attention since it reduces the cost on the garbler side effectively, namely by 25%. To reduce garbler's cost, the wire values are garbled as presented in Fig. 1.(b). For any gate G_i, $w_i^1 = w_i^0 \oplus R$ for some secret, global $R \in_R \{0, 1\}^{n1}$. Here, for the sake of simplicity, let $(A, A \oplus R)$ and $(B, B \oplus R)$ denote the wire labels. **half-gates** protocol complements the free-XOR protocol in the sense that not only are XOR gates evaluated for free, but also AND gates are garbled using only two ciphertexts (see Fig. 1.(c)). Since Goblin is interested in recovering the garbler's input, in Fig. 1.(c), we show how the half-gates are generated on the garbler's side, where garbler knows which inputs she wants to garble (for more information about the whole process, see [97]).

2.2 k-means Algorithm

The main goal of clustering algorithms, like k-means, is to group samples of a set with some common features into subsets, i.e., *clusters*. With regard to the pairwise distances, clusters are made around the mean vectors, which are called *centroids* [37,91]. k-means aims to partition N members of a set into k clusters in a way that each member of a cluster has a close value to the centroid of the cluster [91]. To be more specific, k-means finds partitions (clusters) $p = \{p_1, p_2, \cdots, p_k\}$ for the dataset $c = \{c_i\}_{i=1}^n$ to minimize

---

[1] For specifics of the encryption function in the free-XOR protocol, see [13,34].

Input	Garbled Input	XOR Output	Garbled XOR Output	AND Output	Garbled AND Output
0,0	w_a^0, w_b^0	0	$E_{w_a^0, w_b^0}(w_c^0)$	0	$E_{w_a^0, w_b^0}(w_c^0)$
0,1	w_a^0, w_b^1	1	$E_{w_a^0, w_b^1}(w_c^1)$	0	$E_{w_a^0, w_b^1}(w_c^0)$
1,0	w_a^1, w_b^0	1	$E_{w_a^1, w_b^0}(w_c^1)$	0	$E_{w_a^1, w_b^0}(w_c^0)$
1,1	w_a^1, w_b^1	0	$E_{w_a^1, w_b^1}(w_c^0)$	1	$E_{w_a^1, w_b^1}(w_c^1)$

(a)

Input	Garbled Input	XOR Output	Garbled XOR Output	AND Output	Garbled AND Output
0,0	A_i^0, B_i^0	0	$w_c^0 = A_i^0 \oplus B_i^0$	0	$E_{A_i^0, B_i^0}(w_c^0)$
0,1	$A_i^0, B_i^0 \oplus R$	1	$w_c^0 \oplus R$	0	$E_{A_i^0, B_i^0 \oplus R}(w_c^0)$
1,0	$A_i^0 \oplus R, B_i^0$	1	$w_c^0 \oplus R$	0	$E_{A_i^0 \oplus R, B_i^0}(w_c^0)$
1,1	$A_i^0 \oplus R, B_i^0 \oplus R$	0	w_c^0	1	$E_{A_i^0 \oplus R, B_i^0 \oplus R}(w_c^0 \oplus R)$

(b)

Known input	Other input	Garbled Input	XOR output	Garbled XOR output	AND Output	Garbled AND output
0	0	A_i^0, B_i^0	0	$w_c^0 = A_i^0 \oplus B_i^0$	0	$E_{B_i^0}(w_c^0)$
	1	$A_i^0, B_i^0 \oplus R$	1	$w_c^0 \oplus R$	0	
1	0	$A_i^0 \oplus R, B_i^0$	1	$w_c^0 \oplus R$	0	$E_{B_i^0 \oplus R}(w_c^0 \oplus R)$
	1	$A_i^0 \oplus R, B_i^0 \oplus R$	0	w_c^0	1	

(c)

Fig. 1. Garbled gates look-up table with (a) no optimization, (b) free-XOR optimization, and (c) half-gate optimization.

$$\min_{p,\{\mu_j\}_1^k} \sum_{j=1}^{k} \sum_{c_i \in p_j} ||c_i - \mu_j||^2,$$

where μ_j is the mean of all examples assigned to j^{th} centroid [39]:. Here the squared Euclidean distance is one of the commonly applied distance measures applied to minimize the total cluster variance [85].

2.3 Cache Architecture

Modern x86 processors comprise three cache layers: L1, L2, and L3, with data inclusively across all levels [25,74]. Figure 2 presents the Intel core-i7 cache architecture. Each CPU core has a dedicated L1 and L2 cache, with the former divided into data and instruction caches of 32KB each [74]. L2 cache is shared across CPU threads and has a larger capacity (256KB [74]). The largest cache, L3, is shared across all CPU cores with an 8MB capacity [74].

Processor instructions fall into three categories: memory read/write, control flow (data processing), and arithmetic/logic operations [15,25]. The execution time of the latter is determined by the type of operation and the number of arithmetic-logic unit (ALU) calls [15]. Memory access time, however, depends on whether the instruction is accessing RAM or cache [32,64,73,81,94].

For efficient memory access management, the CPU stores operation results in the cache hierarchy (L1, L2, L3) and an instantiation in RAM [54,98]. On data request, the CPU checks the data availability in this order: L1 cache, L2 cache, L3 cache, and finally RAM [54].

Cache Eviction Strategies. Four eviction strategies can be considered as highlighted in [31]. The first and second use static and dynamic eviction sets, respectively, with static access patterns. The third uses both dynamic eviction set and access pattern, enabling fully automated attacks. The fourth uses a static eviction set with a dynamic access pattern, but is less efficient [31].

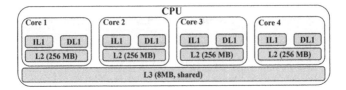

Fig. 2. Intel core-i7 cache architecture [74].

2.4 Adversary Model

The security of GCs has been considered in two main paradigms, namely honest-but-curious and malicious adversary models. The latter reflects the situation, where a party potentially adopts an arbitrary attack strategy. On the other hand, honest-but-curious parties follow the protocol honestly, although they may attempt to learn additional information from the execution, similar to the one launching SCA. This has also been well-formulated in [5], where it is suggested that Yao's GC reveals no side-information beyond the function being computed, i.e., no information about parties' inputs leaks. One closely relevant adversary model is devised for server-aided or cloud-assisted, where the standard SFE protocol is run with the help of a server (or a small set of them), which does not contribute to running the protocol by giving inputs, but by making their computational resources available to the parties cf. [8,10,11,16,17,48–50]. In the proposed setting, the server is instantiated by a public cloud service provider, where parties who need more computational power (e.g., the garbler) can outsource their computations. In such scenarios, the server can be honest-but-curious [51]. Our model goes one step further and take into account any -even unprivileged- access to the CPU during the execution of the protocol.

Our Adversary Model assumes that the parties and the server are independent, i.e., none of them collude [21,48,50]. In practice, given the consequences in terms of losing the reputation and legal actions, it is reasonable to assume that the server will not collude with the parties. The adversary is capable of performing local code execution, potentially even on the same core. Additionally, the adversary must possess the capability to evict data from the cache to the main memory. Note that although throughout the paper, we refer to the server as the entity collecting the timing information, this does not rule out the fact that any entity with the capabilities mentioned above can launch the attack.

3 Timing Side-Channel Leakage in Garbling Tools: An Observation

Broadly speaking, timing side-channels leak due to the dependency of the time taken to execute a piece of software code on the values of secret variables. Here, two types of timing side-channels are of interest, namely instruction-related and cache-related ones. The former indicates that the number or type of instructions executed along a path depends on the values of secret variables. In contrast, cache-related timing side channels refer to the difference due to the memory subsystem behavior depending on the values of secret variables, e.g., a cache hit takes a few CPU cycles. Still, a miss takes hundreds of cycles cf. [92]. By analyzing the code line-by-line, the adversary can find and further exploit such vulnerabilities. Nevertheless, manual analysis of the timing characteristics of a code is challenging as it requires thorough knowledge of the code and the platform on which it is executed. The broad range of existing tools for automatically checking timing side-channel leakage can help pinpoint such vulnerabilities. In doing so, we select a recent tool recommended in the literature [44], namely SC-Eliminator [92]. Among the most important features of SC-Eliminator is the fact that, in view of available garbling protocols, it can analyze codes written in C/C++. To this end, using an LLVM compiler performs static analyses to identify the sensitive variables and timing leakage associated with them, given a program and a list of secret inputs.

GC Tools. To explore whether GC frameworks would be vulnerable to timing SCA, we selected 5 open-source tools written in C/C++, which mostly support AES-NI (Advanced Encryption Standard New Instruction) instruction set (for more features of these tools cf. [38]). As a result, they have made computing AES encryptions on modern processors efficient, and consequently, the computation cost of GC is reduced drastically. **JustGarble** [4] is a library for garbling and evaluating circuits licensed under GNU GPL v3 license; however, JustGarble does not support communication or circuit generation and is, therefore, not a general-purpose framework. Nevertheless, it has become a cornerstone of various frameworks, e.g., [30,33,35,47,70,87]. The reason behind JustGarble's efficiency is its ability to make only one AES call per garbled-gate evaluation which makes it far faster than any prior reported results [4]. JustGarble exploits the cryptographic permutations realizable by fixed-key AES acting like a public random permutation [4]. Although this might be a strong assumption cf. [33,35], thanks to its efficiency and the theoretical foundation laid for JustGarble, it has been used in a wide variety of MPC and GC frameworks cf. [30,70].

Songhori et al. [86,87] extended JustGarble in **TinyGarble**, a highly compressed and scalable sequential GC, which is a self-contained framework that can directly be used in MPC applications [38]. Three steps are taken in TinyGarble, namely converting a function defined in Verilog to a netlist format, converting that netlist to a custom circuit description (SCD), and finally, securely evaluating the resulting Boolean circuit using a garbled circuit protocol. This flow has been considered a strict improvement over JustGarble as TinyGarble further includes recent protocol and circuit optimizations. Nevertheless, and irrespective of the flexibility of TinyGarble for producing hardware circuits, changes made to JustGarble have introduced timing side-channel leakage, as will be discussed in Sects. 5 and 6.

In contrast to TinyGarble, which is an extension of Verilog, **Obliv-C** is an extension of C that executes a GC protocol in a two-party setting [96]. The C language is extended by adding an obliv qualifier that is applied to C types and constructs. By enforcing typing rules, obliv types remain secret unless explicitly

Table 1. The number of leaky IF conditions (IF) in various frameworks. (for a detailed report, refer to Appendix 8)

Framework	IF
TinyGarble [86] (half-gate)	4
TinyGarble [86] (free-XOR)	7
JustGarble [42]	11
EMP-toolkit [67]	0
Obliv-C [95]	4
ABY [18]	0

revealed. In doing so, it is suggested that oblivious functions and conditionals could modify public data, if they are executed within a qualified obliv block, where the code is always executed cf. [95,96]. In addition to the data security achieved by means of these rules, modular libraries can be easily developed when using Obliv-C. Thanks to this property, Obliv-C has found application in, e.g., linear regression [24], decentralized certificate authorities [46], aggregated private machine-learning models [89], classification of encrypted emails [36] and stable matching [19].

Besides the frameworks mentioned above, we also took EMP-toolkit [67] and ABY [18], libraries developed in C++, into account. EMP-toolkit is composed of multiple MPC frameworks and allows for executing circuit-based protocols due to the available circuit generation and cryptographic libraries. ABY library offers a mechanism for mixing protocols, including optimized versions of Yao's garbled circuit protocol.

Our Observations. As mentioned earlier, as a first, we examined the possibility of mounting timing SCA against GC frameworks enumerated above. In such an attack scenario, the adversary attempt to take advantage of possible unbalance if-else statements (branches). The adversary can assume that different operations performed to generate garbled inputs in free-XOR and half-gate optimized Yao's GC protocols (see Fig. 1) can result in leakage if neither a constant-time implementation nor branch-less assignments are used for sensitive branches. To examine this, SC-Eliminator [92] is applied against TinyGarble [86], JustGarble [42], EMP-toolkit [67], Obliv-C [95], and ABY [18]. Table 1 contains the number of leaky IFs for this experiment. When taking a close look at the list of leaky IFs among the set of leaky IFs, we observed unbalanced IF statements in the garbled-input generation, i.e., garbled inputs were generated in a secret-dependent manner. The existence of these unbalanced IFs demonstrates the likelihood of timing attacks to be successfully mounted against them. According to the results in Table 1, EMP-toolkit [67] and ABY [18] do not have any leaky IFs. Nevertheless, we should stress that although SC-Eliminator does not find any vulnerability in terms of leaky IFs in these frameworks, this does not rule out the possibility of other attacks. Next, we introduce our attack, Goblin, to leverage the timing side-channel leaking from existing unbalanced IF statements.

4   Goblin and Its Building Blocks

The main steps in Goblin's flow are: (1) filling the cache with junk by using junk generator (JG) to evict the garbler secret from the cache. This step aims to maximize the CPU core's access time to the global secret (R) from the cache and capture the CPU cycles corresponding to each gate connected to input wires (i.e., gates in the input layer); It is noteworthy that for some GC frameworks, even without relying on timing variability due to cache effects, it is possible to successfully launch Goblin (see Appendix 8). (2) measuring the time on the CPU, including the time taken to generate garbler token, linked to the input size; (3) recovering the garbler's secret (i.e., garbler's input) after pre-processing the acquired CPU cycles and running a clustering algorithm.

4.1   Our Eviction Method: Junk Generator

We presume that the server and parties are independent (see Sect. 2.4), i.e., the adversary lacks knowledge of the cache slice function or the victim's physical addresses; hence, static eviction set and static access pattern strategies are impossible to employ [31]. As implementing a dynamic eviction set and static access pattern strategy requires informing the adversary about the target's replacement policy, it is not feasible [31]. Hence, our JG adopts the dynamic eviction set and dynamic access pattern strategy [31]. Our JG is, in fact, an enhancement of the dynamic eviction set and access pattern method in [31]. Our attack shares similarities with Evict+Time attacks presented in the literature [65]. Specifically, in our attack, JG accesses the memory frequently in the form of reading and writing from/to it similar to [77]. However, in their attack, the adversary should first determine which part of the critical information is accessed during the encryption. In contrast, Goblin does not require this as the time difference between garbling "1" and "0" reveals the input bit ("0/1") directly. To maximize this time difference, the JG algorithm recursively generates eviction sets and performs memory accesses randomly. Despite requiring many eviction tests, this approach needs minimal system information, enabling automated attacks on unknown systems. It is also considered more efficient than the static eviction set and dynamic access pattern strategy [31]. Cache eviction can also be achieved by reading the cache line [77]. Yet, we opted to generate junk on the fly to bypass CPU memory management [31]. Despite the simplicity of iterative For loops used in our JG (see Appendix 8), we chose the recursive function for JG to generate junk indefinitely, considering the unknown duration of a circuit garbling process.

4.2   Measuring Time on CPUs

After the JG boosts the difference between the input bit-dependent execution times, the time can be measured. According to Martin et al. [68], to measure the time without breaking the software, there are three main sources to take advantage of cf. [66]: (1) internal, hardware time sources, e.g., timestamp counters; (2)

external time sources, e.g., external interrupts; and (3) creating a virtual clock, for instance, the virtual clock implementation on multi-processor systems with shared memory [79]. Without loss of generality, we focus on how timing information can be retrieved using the first option, namely `rdtsc`. The Read Timestamp Counter `rdtsc` is an x86 instruction that returns the value of the CPU timestamp counter (TSC) register. In general, the TSC register is shared with every user with any level of privileged access [66]; therefore, it can be accessed by: (1) a privileged/non-privileged user who has complete control over the CPU; (2) a service provider who shares the processor with the victim, such as cloud servers [68]; (3) a virtual-machine user with a privileged/non-privileged access level, who runs a process on a shared processor with the victim (e.g., cross-virtual machine attacks) [66]. Hence, the adversary can have either privileged/non-privileged access to (1) the CPU on which the garbling scheme is running, (2) the CPU of the service provider's system, or (3) a cross-virtual machine to share the processor with the victim running the garbling scheme. What could make a difference is that an unprivileged attacker cannot precisely control the garbler's execution and interrupt it, unlike a privileged attacker. Nevertheless, if the attacker can figure out when the garbling process begins, or use a trigger signal such as a cache-based side channel [83], then the collected traces can be aligned based on that timing information [62]. Therefore, without loss of generality, we consider aligned timing measurements to mount the attack, similar to [41,69]. For the sake of demonstration, we have inserted the `rdtsc` before and after the garble gate function in the frameworks source code, which are all publicly available, and achieved the time stamps based on their difference.

Resolution of Timing Measurements. The timestamps provided by `rdtsc` often have a resolution between 1 and 3 cycles on modern CPUs cf. [61]. For example, on AMD CPUs until the Zen microarchitecture, a cycle-accurate resolution can be obtained; however, more recent generations come with a significantly lower resolution as the register is only updated every 20 to 35 cycles. Another example is Intel Core $i7-7700$ Processors, i.e., what has been used in this study, where the `rdtsc` register is updated every cycle [40]. Nevertheless, although it might be thought that lower resolutions might make performing attacks more challenging, Goblin is not affected since it requires mainly the difference between two readings with the same resolution (see Sect. 6 for more details). Therefore, in contrast to attacks requiring repetition when relying on `rdtsc`, it is not needed for Goblin to do so and use the average timing differences over all executions. We stress that Goblin is a single-trace attack, i.e., thanks to the gate-by-gate operation in GC frameworks, the time difference directly driven from `rdtsc` is a collection of time stamps associated with gates. We should also add that our attack is an example of a timing attack, meaning that we believe other methods for acquiring the timing information can definitely be applied.

4.3   Recovering Garbler's Input

Counting the Gates in the Input Layer. According to our adversary model, we assume that the adversary is neither the garbler nor the evaluator. Therefore, there is no information about the circuit, input size, and gate types in the input layer. Here we describe how this information is retrieved by Goblin when the garbler uses JustGarble, as an example of GC tools. This example is selected due to its broad applications (see Sect. 3) and its role as the core of other garbling frameworks, e.g., ones considered in our study [87,96]. Listing 1 illustrates a high-level description of JustGarble primary functions. In Listing 1, NF, LF, GT, IF, INL, WL, GC, and OL, denoted in Lines 1–9, refer to the number of fan-outs, location of fan-outs, gates' types, the value of filled input fan-out, initial input values, wire labels, Garbled circuit, and output labels, respectively.

According to the protocol flow of JustGarble (see, Listing 1), in the first step, the garbler's tokens for zero and one logical values (IL) are constructed through createNewWire (Listing 1 line 5). Then, the parser function (the label corresponding function createInputLabels Listing 1 line 3) starts parsing the simple circuit description (SCD) file and g_init files, which contain information about the circuit and the garbler's input values. The parser function learns about the circuit (GT) and locates the fan-in and fan-out of the input layer gates (LF and NF) that are connected to the garbler input based on g_init file information. For every input, the createInputLabels is called once for garbler label and once for the evaluator label of the input, twice per input in total. At this point, Goblin starts counting the number of createInputLabels calls and calculating the number of input layer gates as half of the total number of createInputLabels function calls. Afterward, the gates are garbled one by one by calling the garbleCircuit function (Listing 1 line 9), starting from the input layer gates, where the garbler's and evaluator's inputs are fed, before proceeding to the following layer gates. This allows Goblin to count the CPU cycle associated with each gate in the input layer by knowing the number of input gates.

Goblin Against Free-XOR Optimization. When the framework starts garbling the gates, output labels (OL) and garbled tables (GT) are generated in the order provided in the SCD file. As JustGarble, similar to various modern garbling frameworks, utilizes the free-XOR optimization to generate garbler tokens for input value 1, the garbler must access the R frequently. When free-XOR optimization is enabled, GarbleCircuit function (Listing 1 line 9) skips line 11 to line 14 of the Listing 1. Therefore, regardless of whether the input is known or secret, it checks the type of the input gate (GT) and treats all inputs as a secret. If the gate type is XOR, including all gates categories that are considered XOR in GC protocols (INV, XOR and XNOR gates), it generates the OL as the XOR results of labels 0 and 1 (Listing 1 line 16); otherwise, the OL is constructed through a series of encryptions, see, Listing 1, line 18 to 22. It is clearly observable that in the last part of the encryption, Listing 1 line 14 and between lines 25 and 28, if the garbler input value is "1", one more encryption, one memory access, and one XORing take place, which can result in the input dependency observable in the execution time of garbling process.

In other words, when garbling AND (non-XOR) gates (including (AND/NAND, OR/NOR, ANDN, ORN, NANDN, and NORN), there is an unbalanced if condition, which means a longer execution time for input value one. This is the point that Goblin

```
 1  def JustGarble(g_init, SCD):
 2      NF, LF, GT = createNewWire(g_init, SCD)     #Pasrses the circuit,
        locate the fan-outs, and generates wire labels.
 3      IF, INL = createInputLabels(NF, LF) #Fills tokens to input fan-
        outs (called twice per garbler input).
 4      GC, OL, TT = garbleCircuit(IF, IFS, WL, GT) #Generates garbled
        tables and Garbled output tokens.
 5  def createNewWire(g_init, SCD):
 6      for i in SCD[0]: #first line of SCD, which contains the
        information about input layer gates
 7          IF[i][0] = randomBlock();
 8          IF[i][1] = xorBlocks(R, IF[i][0]);
 9  def garbleCircuit(IFS, WL, GT):
10      R = AESEcbEncryptBlks(AES_Key)
11      if(IFS == known):
12          GC, OL = HalfGarbleGate(GT, IF)
13          return GC, OL
14      else: #(IFS == secret):
15          if(GT == XORGATE):
16              OL = XorBlock (IFS, R) #free-XOR optimization
17          else: #if(GT == ANDGATE)
18              mask1, mask2, mask3, mask4=AESEcbEncryptBlks(AES_Key,4)
19              #AND encryptions
20              OL = XorBlock(mask1 , mask2)
21              if (IFS == 1):
22                  OL = XorBlock(OL , R);
23              GC = [XorBlock(OL, mask3), XorBlock(OL, mask4)]
24          if(gate_location is in input_layer): #Generates associate
        garbler tokens to be transferred to Evaluator.
25              if(g_init == 0):
26                  TT = IF;
27              else:
28                  TT = xorBlocks(R, IF);
29      return GC, OL, TT
```

Listing 1. Protocol flow of primary functions of JustGarble.

takes advantage of differences in execution time of the garbling process for each gate due to their input value. If R is available in the L1 level of the cache, this difference is subtle and, in most cases, negligible to the time of the encryption process. Hence, to maximize the difference between the time taken to generate tokens for input 0 and 1, the JG (see Sect. 4.1) starts filling the cache with junks parallel to the execution of the **createNewWire** function (Listing 1 line 5) to enforce CPU to fetch R into L1 cache from RAM, which increases the execution time difference between 0 and 1 token generation. To boost the effect of JG, Goblin first finds the CPU core and thread on which the garbling process is happening by calling the **LSCPU** instruction; then asks the server to assign the JG task to the same thread, or if not possible, at least to the same core on which the garbling process is happening. It should be indicated that neither any privilege is needed nor any restriction on assigning the JG to the same core is posed as it fills the shared L3 cache level; nevertheless, assigning JG to the same core as the garbling process core will result in faster cache filling and fewer errors as JG first fills L1 and L2 level cache.

Goblin Against Half-gate Optimization. Though JustGarble doesn't support half-gate optimization, subsequent frameworks like TinyGarble and Obliv-C do. Despite this, Goblin remains effective against these frameworks. When half-gate optimization is enabled, **HalfGarbleGate** (see Listing 2) is called by

```
 1  def HalfGarbleGate(GT, IF):
 2      R = AESEcbEncryptBlks(AES_Key)
 3      mask1, mask2 = AESEcbEncryptBlks(AES_Key,2)
 4      if(IF[0] == 0):
 5          if(GT == ANDGATE):
 6              OL = mask1 #XorBlock(mask1, 0)
 7          else: #if(GT == XORGATE):
 8              OL = XorBlock(mask1, IF[1])
 9      if(IF[0] == 1):
10          if(GT == XORGATE):
11              OL = mask1 #XorBlock(mask1, 0)
12          else: #if(GT == ANDGATE):
13              OL = XorBlock(mask1, R)
14      GC = XorBlock(OL, mask2)
15      if(gate_location is in input_layer): #Generates associate
            garbler tokens to be transferred to Evaluator.
16          if(g_init == 0):
17              TT = IF;
18          else:
19              TT = xorBlocks(R, IF);
20      return GC, OL, TT
```

Listing 2. HalfGarbleGate function flow.

GarbleGate. When the input value (IF) is zero and the gate type (GT) is ANDGATE, the function bypasses the garbling process, assigning a constant to OL, thus reducing the execution time compared to the garbling process for input value one or other gate types. If the input value is one, encryption occurs (Listing 2 line 11), introducing an unbalanced if path and creating a dependency between the garbling process execution time and the input value. Just like with free-XOR optimization, Goblin capitalizes on these differences in execution times due to the unbalanced if conditions in Listing 2, lines 3 and 8.   The rest of the steps are not interesting for Goblin because they do not hold any information about the secret (garbler's input), and the above-mentioned information is adequate to launch the Goblin; therefore, from now on, Goblin can continue the attack from an offline phase.

Pre-processing the Acquired CPU Cycles. As explained before, when employing free-XOR optimization, the attacker expects to see a significant difference between the CPU cycle of INV, XOR, and XNOR gates and other gate types, including AND/NAND, OR/NOR, ANDN, ORN, NANDN, and NORN gates (refer to Sect. 5 for more information). This significant difference is because in the free-XOR optimization, as its name implies, an XOR-type gate is garbled by simply using the XORing operation that takes a few CPU cycles. On the other hand, garbling other types of gates, such as an AND gate, requires reading/writing from/to memory and cipher generation, which results in extra memory reads; hence, accumulating these leads to a drastic increase in CPU cycles. This is evident thanks to the definition of this optimization technique and the number of operands included in the computation of those gates, see Fig. 1.(b). When employing clustering to discover the garbler's input in a non-profiled manner, this difference causes the gate types to be dominant centroids of the clustering algorithm over the input values. To overcome this challenge, Goblin first divides the CPU cycle into the number of subgroups equal to the number of available gate types, i.e., AND (AND/NAND, OR/NOR, ANDN, ORN, NANDN, and NORN) and XOR

(INV, XOR and XNOR gates, hereafter called XOR gates) with regard to the median of the CPU cycles. Afterward, it normalizes each subgroup of CPU cycles by employing *z-score* normalization, and finally, concatenates the normalized data to form the CPU cycle array while maintaining the order of captured CPU cycles. Normalization minimizes the difference between the CPU cycle requirements of XOR and AND gate types, consequently improving the SR.

The first step is more complicated in a case where the half-gates optimization is enabled. Specifically, according to our observation, not only garbling the XOR gates exhibits a significantly larger number of CPU cycles compared to other gate types, but also there is a dramatic difference in the number of CPU cycles in the OR/NOR gates garbling process. There is, of course, a reason behind this, namely how gates with truth tables containing an odd number of ones (e.g., AND, NAND, OR, NOR, etc.) can be expressed and constructed. Generally speaking, these gate can be defined as $G : (v_a, v_b) \rightarrow (\alpha_a \oplus v_a) \wedge (\alpha_b \oplus v_b) \oplus \alpha_c$, where v_a and v_b are logical values and α_a, α_b, and α_c are constant values cf. [97]. For AND gate, α values are set to 0, whereas for OR gate, they are set to 1. Therefore, it is unsurprising that the CPU cycles collected when garbling OR/NOR gates compose a cluster different from the others.

In the same vein, one can also observe that it takes more time for the garbler to generate the garbled OR/NOR gate with input "0", as opposed to AND/NAND gates with input "1". Therefore, contrary to the case of free-XOR optimization, where AND/NAND and OR/NOR can be considered as belonging to the same type, it is challenging to make a distinction between AND/NAND gates with input "0" and OR/NOR gates with input "1". This overlap results in inaccurate clustering since the algorithm puts both into one cluster, although they should be put into two different clusters due to their inputs.

To counter this challenge, Goblin applies the following additional data scaling technique before the normalization to force the pattern to match other gate types (i.e., a larger number of CPU cycles for input 1). First, similar to the free-XOR case, the CPU cycle collected from the input gates $\{c_i\}_{i=1}^n$ should be partitioned into subsets corresponding to different gate types: XOR/XNOR, AND/NAND, and OR/NOR. For this, Goblin calculates 66th percentiles of elements in $\{c_i\}_{i=1}^n$ and assign the elements larger than that to the subset c_{OR}. The remaining elements of $\{c_i\}_{i=1}^n$ are assigned to AND and XOR subsets similarly as done in the free-XOR case: the larger elements are assigned to c_{AND} by considering the median of the $\{c_i\}_{i=1}^n \setminus c_{AND}$. The remaining elements are then assigned to the subset corresponding to the XOR/XNOR gates. Afterward, Goblin applies the transformation $t_i = ac_i + b$ for $c_i \in c_{OR}$, where a and b are calculated as

$$a = \frac{\text{Max}(c_{AND}) - \bar{c}_{AND}}{\text{Max}(c_{OR}) - \bar{c}_{AND}}, \quad b = \bar{c}_{AND} - a \cdot \bar{c}_{OR},$$

where $\text{Max}(\cdot)$ and $\bar{c}$'s denote the maximum and the average of the subsets, respectively. After this step, normalization is applied, similar to the free-XOR case.

Extracting garbler's input through clustering. After obtaining the pre-processed data, Goblin launches the clustering algorithm to determine each gar-bler's input bit. As Goblin applies normalization to the CPU cycle data, the gate types' dominance in the centroids has vanished; therefore, Goblin clusters CPU cycles into only two clusters corresponding to input zero and input one, regardless of the gate types. To disclose the input bits, Goblin keeps track of the $\text{Max}(\{c_i\}_{i=1}^{n})$ before normalization. When the clustering process is over, all cluster members that include the maximum element are labeled as "1", mean-ing that the garbler input bit is "1"; consequently, other cluster includes c_i's corresponding to garbler's input bit "0".

4.4   Performance Metric

Let $\mathbf{c}_i$ be a leakage measurement, i.e., the number of CPU cycles, for a garbler input $x = x_1 \cdots x_n$ with n-bits corresponding to n wires giving the garbler's input to the circuit. For instance, for a garbled 128-bit AES design, $n = 128$. To evaluate the effectiveness of our attack, we calculate its success rate of recovering the garbler's input given a *single* trace $\{c\}_i^n$. Note that Goblin is a non-profiling attack; hence, as opposed to profiled attacks, no leakage profile is made and used during the attack. k-means clustering algorithm is used as a distinguisher so that any observation c_i is assigned to either cluster p_0 or p_1 associated with input bit x_i being "0" or "1". Precisely, the success rate is defined as follows.

$$\text{SR} := \sum_{j \in \{0,1\}} \sum_{i=1}^{n} \Pr(c_i \in p_j \mid x_i = j).$$

To put this simply, SR indicates how many bits are correctly disclosed out of n bits in the garbler's input. Note that this definition aligns with the general case considered in SCA-related literature [88]. In this context, we consider the success rate of order 1, i.e., the probability that the correct key is ranked first.

5   Experimental Results

We ran the JustGarble, TinyGarble and Obliv-C frameworks, publicly available via GitHub repositories [42,86,95]. Garbler and evaluator codes ran on two sys-tems with Linux Ubuntu 20, 16 GB of memory, and an Intel Core $i7-7700$ CPU 3.60GHz CPU. Two systems were connected through a local area network (LAN) cable. As garbling process might access R anytime during garbling process, to force CPU to fetch R from RAM to L1 level cache in maximum possible cases, we started JG as soon as the garbling process begins. This can be easily determined by calling non-privileged CPU instructions showing which applications run on each core. Moreover, we assigned the JG to the same core that generates garbled circuits on the garbler system. To capture each trace, i.e., multiple time stamps, we used `rdtsc` as discussed before in Sect. 4.2. We have also used the k-means clustering algorithm implemented in Matlab 2021.

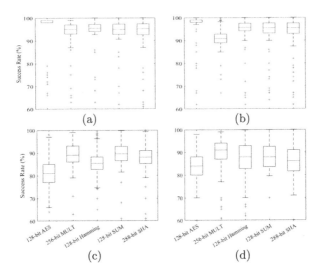

Fig. 3. SR of Goblin for 1000 randomly chosen inputs given to GC garbled by Tiny-Garble [87] with (a) free-XOR, (b) half-gate optimizations, (c) JustGarble [42], and (d) Obliv-C [95].

5.1 Results for Benchmark Functions

To evaluate the efficacy of Goblin, we have targeted the commonly-used benchmark functions, including 128-AES, 288-SHA3, 256-bit Multiplier, 128-bit Summation, and 128-bit Hamming garbled by JustGarble [42], TinyGarble [87], and Obliv-C [95] (results for the benchmark functions with various input sizes can be found in Sect. 5.3). For this purpose, to calculate the success rate (SR), we have applied various garbler's inputs and provided the statistics in this section. Launching Goblin against all combinations of inputs is impractical due to the massive number of input combinations (i.e., for a 256-bit Multiplier, the attack had to be launched 2^{256} times); therefore, we have chosen 1000 random inputs to run Goblin. For each of these inputs, a single trace is captured that has multiple time stamps. In the k-means algorithm setting, the centroids are chosen at 100 different starting values, and the algorithm returns the result for the least within-cluster sums of point-to-centroid distances.

Figure 3 shows the SR when free-XOR or half-gate optimization was enabled. The red lines in the boxes indicate the average SR of the attack against these benchmark functions. It is observable in Fig. 3.(a) that the attack achieved a better SR when launched against the AES benchmark compared to, e.g., the 256-bit Multiplier. The reason is three-fold. First, only 1000 inputs are tested; therefore, the results might vary. Second, the input layer of the 256-bit Multiplier contains more XOR gates than the AES, which are more challenging because of the subtle difference between the number of clock cycles taken for "1" and "0". Third, per input, notice that Goblin is a non-profiling, single-trace attack, meaning that it receives one timing measurement per gate (and per input bit, consequently); hence, the more input bits, the better Goblin determines them. This is further studied in Sect. 5.2.

Compared to Fig. 3.(a), Fig. 3.(b) corresponding to the half-gates optimization shows an overall reduced SR for the same benchmark functions. This is because of the increase in the number of gate types to be identified for the same number of input bits and observations, consequently. Needless to say, even for circuits with various gate types, such as AES, Goblin achieved an average SR of more than 90%, which means the effect of variation in the gate types does not affect Goblin's SR drastically (see Appendix 8). Imperfect process of filling the L3 level cache with junk accounts for the outliers in Fig. 3. The implication of this is that the availability of R in the L1 cache level of the garbler core decreases the execution time difference between garbler 0 and 1 token generation. However, these outliers happen barely, i.e., in 11 out of 1000 experiments, which means the JG has a small error. Note that even for the outliers, Goblin still revealed the garbler's input with a range of 60% to 100% SR.

5.2 Scalability of Goblin

To test Goblin's scalability, we have launched Goblin against three benchmark functions, including MULT, SUM, and Hamming, with a range of input sizes between 128 and 1024. Figure 4 illustrates the results, where Fig. 4.(a) and Fig. 4.(b) depict the free-XOR and half-gate optimization results. As shown in Fig. 4.(a), increasing the input size increases the minimum and average SR for virtually all cases. This SR increment is because Goblin has a broader range of data to cluster, which means it has more observations to compare with one another. Similar to previous experiments, outliers can be observed in Fig. 4. To reduce the number of outliers, the natural question to ask is whether it is possible to launch Goblin without JG. We conducted experiments to answer this questions and found out that for JustGarble [42] and Obliv-C [95], the SR could decrease dramatically (close to 50%) due to the small difference between the execution times for garbler's input "0" and "1." Nonetheless, for TinyGarble [86], it is indeed possible to mount the attack with high SR without using JG (see Appendix 8).

5.3 Impact of the Number of Traces

In previous experiments in this section, to evaluate the effectiveness of our attack, we selected 1000 random inputs since capturing CPU cycles for all inputs is impractical and infeasible. This can directly impact the variance in our results. To investigate this, we collected CPU cycles after feeding powers of tens (from 10-100,000) random inputs into the 128-bit SUM, Hamming, and MULT benchmark functions, i.e., the ones demonstrating a fairly high variance (see, Fig. 3). Figure 5 illustrates the SR of Goblin when being launched against a range of CPU cycle traces. As can be seen, increasing the number of CPU cycle traces results in increasing the SR of Goblin. We have observed that for a higher number of traces, SR exhibits less variance, and the average settles around 97% in all cases,

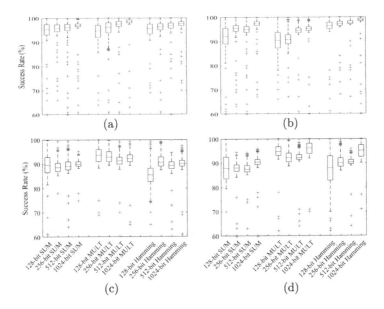

Fig. 4. SR of Goblin against benchmark functions for a range of input bits garbled by TinyGarble [86] with (a) only free-XOR optimization, (b) half-gate protocol, (c) JustGarble [42], and (d) Obliv-C [95] for 1000 randomly chosen inputs.

except for 128-MULT. The reason behind this is the variation in the gate types as discussed before. Note that since Goblin is a single trace attack, each trace is processed by Goblin individually. In other words, the increase in the number of traces does not impact each attack but reduces the variance of the overall results. Therefore, to judge the effectiveness of Goblin, it is recommended to use more traces. We could not do this in the first place due to the time-consuming process of collecting traces for all benchmark functions. Nonetheless, comparing the results for 1000 and 100,000 traces, the change in the average SR is subtle.

6   Discussion

Relative accuracy of rdtsc. For applications using rdtsc, successive calls must have a difference that accurately reflects the number of cycles between two calls. This is referred to as "relative accuracy" cf. [68], meaning that any measurement through rdtsc is accurate with regard to the previous call/measurement. The relative accuracy does not pose any constraint to the application since they must tolerate some variations as rdtsc instruction's number of cycles can vary due to the state of caches, DVFS, scheduling, etc. [68]. Similarly, Goblin is resilient against variations as long as the variation is smaller than the difference between the number of cycles spent on garbling the XOR and non-XOR gates (in order of tens of thousands of cycles).

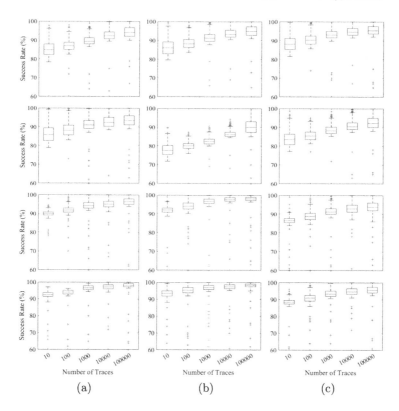

Fig. 5. SR of Goblin against (a) 128-bit SUM, (b) 128-bit Hamming, and (b) 128-bit MULT for a range of 10-100,000 randomly chosen inputs (first to last row: JustGarble [42], Obliv-C [95], TinyGarble [86] with free-XOR, and with half-gate optimizations).

Limited Resolution of rdtsc on Some Platforms. As introduced in Sect. 4.2, rdtsc can have various resolutions depending on the platform. In the same vein, as explained about the relative accuracy of the time read using rdtsc, the resolution cannot impact the effectiveness of Goblin. The point is that as long as the XOR gates can be distinguished from non-XOR ones, Goblin can successfully extract the garbler's input. For this purpose, it is necessary to have at least a resolution comparable to the number of cycles taken to garble the XOR gates (couples of tens cycles, e.g., 80 cycles as observed in our experiments).

6.1   Potential Countermeasures

To come up with a countermeasure against Goblin, one should first determine factors contributing to Goblin's success. Here we describe these factors and emphasize that if they are considered and encountered when proposing a framework, the likelihood of Goblin's success can decrease.

The Coding Style of the Framework. Frameworks like EMP-toolkit [67], Obliv-C [95], and ABY [18] securely tackle the vulnerability in unbalanced IF statements by generating both 0 and 1 garbler's tokens, although it's less optimized than one-token-per-input methods in TinyGarble [87] and JustGarble [42].

Memory Management. Assigning R to a fixed memory address reduces memory access time. Usage of registers can lead to overwrites, forcing the CPU to fetch R from RAM and causing time variation in token generation. Most frameworks like EMP-toolkit [67], Obliv-C [95], JustGarble [42], and ABY [18] fixed R's address, but TinyGarble [87] used registers in token generations, leading to possible overwrites when using JG.

Can Restricting Access Stop Goblin? Restricting high-resolution timer access can deter the Goblin attack, but also negatively impact certain unprivileged applications like adb, cargo, Docker [59]. It's noted that an attacker could still use a counting thread to establish a timestamp [60,61,84], which could even have higher resolution than the rdtsc instruction on Intel CPUs [84].

7   Conclusion

Nowadays, several applications, including multi-party computation, rely on the efficient implementations of GC. To achieve this efficiency, many optimizations, such as free-XOR and half-gates, have been presented to reduce the cost of garbling progress. This paper has introduced Goblin, the first machine learning-assisted, non-profiling, single-trace timing SCA against GC frameworks. Specifically, Goblin targets frameworks using free-XOR and half-gate by collecting and analyzing the time stamps of the garbling process by reading the time stamp counter, i.e., calling rdtsc. In doing so, the garbler's inputs that should have been kept secure can be disclosed without prior knowledge about the circuit being garbled. In this regard, Goblin can be run in parallel to the garbling framework without requiring any privileged access. Goblin has also been proven to be scalable when targeting large circuits. We have studied several cases, including various GC frameworks, benchmark functions, and the number of garbler's input bits. Under different scenarios, Goblin disclosed the garbler's input with high probability. Further, we have discussed Goblin's success factors and countermeasures against that.

8   Responsible Disclosure

Corresponding authors and/or owners of GitHub repositories of the affected frameworks [42, 86, 95] were contacted about their GC framework vulnerabilities presented in this paper.

Acknowledgments. This work has been supported partially by Semiconductor Research Corporation (SRC) under Task IDs 2991.001 and 2992.001 and NSF under award number 2138420. We also thank Mr. Saleh Khalaj Monfared and Mr. Caner Tol for their support.

Appendix A

Table 3 contains details of leaky IF conditions in each function of TinyGarble [86], EMP-toolkit [67], Obliv-C [96], and ABY [18].

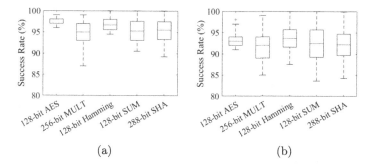

Fig. 6. SR of Goblin for 1000 randomly chosen inputs given to GC garbled by Tiny-Garble [87] when (a) only free-XOR or (b) half-gate optimization is enabled and JG is disabled.

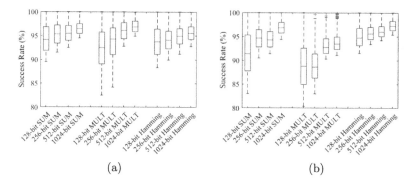

Fig. 7. SR of Goblin against MULT, SUM, and Hamming benchmark functions for a range of inputs garbled by TinyGarble [86] when (a) only free-XOR optimization, (b) half-gate protocol is enabled, and JG is disabled.

Appendix B

To study the impact of an implementation in which not all timing side-channel vulnerabilities are considered, we have launched Goblin against TinyGarble when the JG has been disabled.

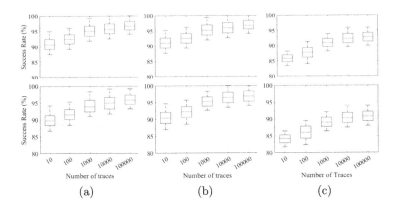

Fig. 8. SR of Goblin against 128-bit (a) SUM, (b) Hamming, and (c) MULT. CPU cycle traces captured from 10-100,000 randomly chosen inputs when JG is disabled. (Top: TinyGarble [86] with only free-XOR, Bottom: with half-gate optimization).

Table 2. Type of the gates in the input layer of the AES and 256-bit MULT modules.

	AES		256-bit MULT	
	Percentage (%)	Count	Percentage (%)	Count
AND gates in input layer	75	96	50	256
XOR gates in input layer	25	32	50	256

Fig. 6 illustrates the results of Goblin against TinyGarble when JG is disabled. It is observable in Fig. 6 that even without JG, Goblin can reveal the garbler's input with an average SR average of 95% or higher, slightly lower than the case when JG is enabled. To further investigate this, we launched Goblin against MULT, SUM, and Hamming benchmarks with input ranges between 128 and 1024 bits when JG was disabled. Figure 7 shows the results of launching Goblin against MULT, SUM, and Hamming benchmark functions for a range of inputs garbled by TinyGarble when (a) only free-XOR optimization, (b) half-gate protocol is enabled, and JG is disabled. Same as results in Sect. 5.2, one can observe a similar pattern of increasing SR of Goblin according to the increased size of benchmarks input. As another part of our investigations, we have launched Goblin against MULT, SUM, and Hamming modules without JG. Figure 8 illustrates SR of Goblin against 128-bit (a) SUM, (b) Hamming, and (b) MULT

Algorithm 1. Junk Generator pseudo code

```
Require: Size = size of cache/64
Ensure: Junk ← Array[size] and n ← 1
  function JG(n)
    while User Interrupt do
      if n == 1 then
        Seed ← t_time
        Junk[0...3] ← rand(Seed)
        n ← n + 1                                    ▷ Initiate recursive algorithm.
        return JG(2)
      else if n == (Size − 1) then
        return JG(1)
      else if n ≠ (Size − 1) and n ≠ 1 then
        i ← n
        Loop over i ≤ (Size − n − 1) :
          Junk[i + n + 1] ← Junk[i] + Junk[n]
        n ← n + 1
        return JG(2)
      end if
    end while
  end function
```

benchmarks for a range of CPU cycle traces captured from $10 - 100,000$ randomly chosen inputs when JG is disabled. These results prove that Goblin can reveal garbler information from an insecurely implemented framework even without the help of JG.

Appendix C

The JG, as in Algorithm 1, works as follows. The iteration's parameter n determines how many cell indexes in the array are summed and updates another array cell. This procedure repeats until it reaches the index of (Size-1). At this point, JG produces new random numbers and repeats the process indefinitely, resulting in cache disruption and potentially evicting critical data, like the global parameter R used for free-XOR [53]/Half-gates [97] optimizations.

Appendix D

To investigate the effects of the gate types in the input layer on the SR, we counted the number of XOR and AND gates in the input layer of the AES and 256-bit MULT since the results for these two benchmark functions vary largely as shown in Fig. 3. Table 2 contains the detail about the type of the gates in the AES and 256-bit MULT benchmark functions. Moreover, the category of AND gate contains AND/NAND, OR/NOR, ANDN, ORN, NANDN, and NORN gates, and the category of XOR gate includes NV, XOR, and XNOR gates as described in Sect. 4.3. It is observable that the AND gates are dominant in the AES input layer (75% input layer gates) while the portions of XOR and AND gates are equal in the input layer of 256-bit MULT. This can explain why the results for these two benchmark functions are different. In fact, it is because of the fact that it is more challenging to determine the inputs given to XOR gates.

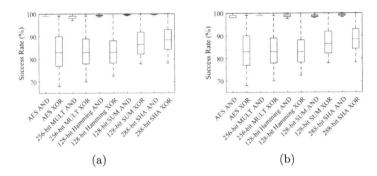

(a)   (b)

Fig. 9. SR of Goblin computed separately for AND and XOR input gates of 128-AES, 256-bit MULT, 128-bit Hamming, 128-bit SUM, and 288-bit SHA modules with (a) free-XOR and (b) half-gate optimization.

Table 3. A detailed report of leaky IF conditions (IF) of every function call in JustGarble [4], TinyGarble [86] with half-gate and free-XOR optimization, EMP-toolkit [67], Obliv-C [96], and ABY [18].

Framework	Function	IF	Framework	Function	IF
TinyGarble(half-gate) [86]	GarbledLowMem	0	JustGarble [42]	createNewWire	0
	GarbledGate	2		TRUNCATE	0
	ParseInitInputStr	0		TRUNC_COPY	0
	RemoveGarbledCircuit	0		getNextId	0
	HalfGarbleGateKnownValue	0		getFreshId	0
	NumOfNonXor	0		getNextWire	0
	HalfGarbleGate	2		createEmptyGarbledCircuit	0
	InvertSecretValue	0		removeGarbledCircuit	0
	XorSecret	0		startBuilding	0
	OutputBN2StrLowMem	0		finishBuilding	2
	RandomBlock	0		extractLabels	0
	Total	4		garbleCircuit	8
TinyGarble(free-XOR) [86]	GarbledLowMem	2		blockEqual	0
	GarbledGate	5		mapOutputs	0
	ParseInitInputStr	0		createInputLabels	0
	RemoveGarbledCircuit	0		randomBlock	0
	NumOfNonXor	0		xorBlocks	0
	XorSecret	0		findGatesWithMatchingInputs	1
	OutputBN2StrLowMem	0		Total	11
	RandomBlock	0	EMP-toolkit [67]	HalfGateGen	0
	Total	7		parse_party_and_port	0
Obliv-C [96]	yaoGenerateGate	3		NetIO	0
	yaoGenrRevealOblivBits	0		Total	0
	yaoGenrFeedOblivInputs	1	ABY [18]	YaoSharingInit	0
	yaoKeyNewPair	0		BooleanCircuit	0
	yaoSetBitAnd	0		init_aes_key	0
	yaoSetBitOr	0		ceil_divide	0
	yaoSetBitXor	0		clean_aes_key	0
	yaoFlipBit	0		EncryptWire	0
	yaoSetHashMask	0		EncryptWireGRR3	0
	yaoSetHalfMask	0		PrintKey	0
	yaoSetHalfMask2	0		PrintPerformanceStatistics	0
	yaoKeyDouble	0		XOR_DOUBLE_B	0
	Total	4		Total	0

To further analyze the reason behind this, we have separately calculated the SR of Goblin against applied against AND and XOR gates. Figure 9 illustrates the results for launching Goblin against 128-AES, 256-bit MULT, 128-bit Hamming, 128-bit SUM, and 288-bit SHA modules, similar to Fig. 3, where the results for AND and XOR gates are combined. As observable in Fig. 9, Goblin's average SR when launching against AND gates are always close to 100% while its average SR has a range between 100% and 65% when launching against XOR gates for the benchmark functions. This is aligned with the results presented in Fig. 3. In that figure, the difference between the mean values of CPU cycles collected for inputs "0" and "1" is larger for AND gates in comparison to XOR gates.

References

1. Acıiçmez, O., Koç, Ç.K.: Trace-driven cache attacks on AES (Short Paper). In: Ning, P., Qing, S., Li, N. (eds.) ICICS 2006. LNCS, vol. 4307, pp. 112–121. Springer, Heidelberg (2006). https://doi.org/10.1007/11935308_9

2. Applebaum, B.: Key-dependent message security: generic amplification and completeness. In: Paterson, K.G. (ed.) EUROCRYPT 2011. LNCS, vol. 6632, pp. 527–546. Springer, Heidelberg (2011). https://doi.org/10.1007/978-3-642-20465-4_29

3. Barak, B., Haitner, I., Hofheinz, D., Ishai, Y.: Bounded key-dependent message security. In: Gilbert, H. (ed.) EUROCRYPT 2010. LNCS, vol. 6110, pp. 423–444. Springer, Heidelberg (2010). https://doi.org/10.1007/978-3-642-13190-5_22

4. Bellare, M., Hoang, V.T., Keelveedhi, S., Rogaway, P.: Efficient garbling from a fixed-key blockcipher. In: 2013 IEEE Symposium on Security and Privacy, pp. 478–492. IEEE (2013)

5. Bellare, M., Hoang, V.T., Rogaway, P.: Foundations of garbled circuits. In: Proceedings of the 2012 ACM Conference on Computer and Communication Security, pp. 784–796 (2012)

6. Benhamouda, F., Lin, H.: k-round multiparty computation from k-round oblivious transfer via garbled interactive circuits. In: Nielsen, J.B., Rijmen, V. (eds.) EUROCRYPT 2018. LNCS, vol. 10821, pp. 500–532. Springer, Cham (2018). https://doi.org/10.1007/978-3-319-78375-8_17

7. Bernstein, D.J.: Cache-timing attacks on AES (2005)

8. Bogetoft, P., et al.: Secure multiparty computation goes live. In: Dingledine, R., Golle, P. (eds.) FC 2009. LNCS, vol. 5628, pp. 325–343. Springer, Heidelberg (2009). https://doi.org/10.1007/978-3-642-03549-4_20

9. Brakerski, Z., Yuen, H.: Quantum garbled circuits. In: Proceedings of the 54th Annual ACM SIGACT Symposium on Theory of Computing, pp. 804–817 (2022)

10. Carter, H., Lever, C., Traynor, P.: Whitewash: outsourcing garbled circuit generation for mobile devices. In: Proceedings of the 30th Annual Computer Security Applications Conference, pp. 266–275 (2014)

11. Carter, H., Mood, B., Traynor, P., Butler, K.: Outsourcing secure two-party computation as a black box. Secur. Commun. Netw. 9(14), 2261–2275 (2016)

12. Chen, D., Chen, W., Chen, J., Zheng, P., Huang, J.: Edge detection and image segmentation on encrypted image with homomorphic encryption and garbled circuit. In: 2018 IEEE International Conference on Multimedia and Expo (ICME), pp. 1–6. IEEE (2018)

13. Choi, S.G., Katz, J., Kumaresan, R., Zhou, H.-S.: On the security of the free-XOR technique. In: Cramer, R. (ed.) TCC 2012. LNCS, vol. 7194, pp. 39–53. Springer, Heidelberg (2012). https://doi.org/10.1007/978-3-642-28914-9_3

14. Cock, M.d., Dowsley, R., Nascimento, A.C., Newman, S.C.: Fast, privacy preserving linear regression over distributed datasets based on pre-distributed data. In: Proceedings of the 8th ACM Workshop on Artificial Intelligence and Security, pp. 3–14 (2015)

15. Conti, M., et al.: Losing Control: on the effectiveness of control-flow integrity under stack attacks. In: Proceedings of the 22nd ACM SIGSAC Conference on Computer and Communications Security, pp. 952–963 (2015)

16. Damgård, I., Ishai, Y.: Constant-round multiparty computation using a black-box pseudorandom generator. In: Shoup, V. (ed.) CRYPTO 2005. LNCS, vol. 3621, pp. 378–394. Springer, Heidelberg (2005). https://doi.org/10.1007/11535218_23

17. Damgård, I., Ishai, Y., Krøigaard, M., Nielsen, J.B., Smith, A.: Scalable multiparty computation with nearly optimal work and resilience. In: Wagner, D. (ed.) CRYPTO 2008. LNCS, vol. 5157, pp. 241–261. Springer, Heidelberg (2008). https://doi.org/10.1007/978-3-540-85174-5_14

18. Demmler, D., Schneider, T., Zohner, M.: Aby-a framework for efficient mixed-protocol secure two-party computation. In: NDSS (2015)

19. Doerner, J., Evans, D., Shelat, A.: Secure stable matching at scale. In: Proceedings of the 2016 ACM SIGSAC Conference on Computer and Communications Security, pp. 1602–1613 (2016)

20. Easdon, C., Schwarz, M., Schwarzl, M., Gruss, D.: Rapid prototyping for microarchitectural attacks. In: USENIX Security Symposium (2022)

21. Feige, U., Killian, J., Naor, M.: A minimal model for secure computation. In: Proceedings of the Twenty-Sixth Annual ACM Symposium on Theory of Computing, pp. 554–563 (1994)

22. Garg, S., Srinivasan, A.: Garbled protocols and two-round MPC from bilinear maps. In: 2017 IEEE 58th Annual Symposium on Foundations of Computer Science (FOCS), pp. 588–599. IEEE (2017)

23. Garg, S., Srinivasan, A.: Two-round multiparty secure computation from minimal assumptions. In: Nielsen, J.B., Rijmen, V. (eds.) EUROCRYPT 2018. LNCS, vol. 10821, pp. 468–499. Springer, Cham (2018). https://doi.org/10.1007/978-3-319-78375-8_16

24. Gascón, A., et al.: Privacy-preserving distributed linear regression on high-dimensional data. Proc. Priv. Enhancing Technol. **2017**(4), 345–364 (2017)

25. Ge, Q., Yarom, Y., Cock, D., Heiser, G.: A survey of microarchitectural timing attacks and countermeasures on contemporary hardware. J. Cryptogr. Eng. **8**, 1–27 (2018)

26. Gentry, C., Halevi, S., Vaikuntanathan, V.: i-hop homomorphic encryption and rerandomizable Yao circuits. In: Rabin, T. (ed.) CRYPTO 2010. LNCS, vol. 6223, pp. 155–172. Springer, Heidelberg (2010). https://doi.org/10.1007/978-3-642-14623-7_9

27. Goldwasser, S., Kalai, Y., Popa, R.A., Vaikuntanathan, V., Zeldovich, N.: Reusable garbled circuits and succinct functional encryption. In: Proceedings of the Forty-Fifth Annual ACM Symposium on Theory of Computing, pp. 555–564 (2013)

28. Gorbunov, S., Vaikuntanathan, V., Wee, H.: Functional encryption with bounded collusions via multi-party computation. In: Safavi-Naini, R., Canetti, R. (eds.) CRYPTO 2012. LNCS, vol. 7417, pp. 162–179. Springer, Heidelberg (2012). https://doi.org/10.1007/978-3-642-32009-5_11

29. Gras, B., Razavi, K., Bos, H., Giuffrida, C.: Translation leak-aside buffer: defeating cache side-channel protections with {TLB} attacks. In: 27th USENIX Security Symposium (USENIX Security 18), pp. 955–972 (2018)

30. Groce, A., Ledger, A., Malozemoff, A.J., Yerukhimovich, A.: CompGC: efficient offline/online semi-honest two-party computation. Cryptology ePrint Archive (2016)

31. Gruss, D., Maurice, C., Mangard, S.: Rowhammer.js: a remote software-induced fault attack in JavaScript. In: Caballero, J., Zurutuza, U., Rodríguez, R.J. (eds.) DIMVA 2016. LNCS, vol. 9721, pp. 300–321. Springer, Cham (2016). https://doi.org/10.1007/978-3-319-40667-1_15

32. Gruss, D., Maurice, C., Wagner, K., Mangard, S.: Flush+Flush: a fast and stealthy cache attack. In: Caballero, J., Zurutuza, U., Rodríguez, R.J. (eds.) DIMVA 2016. LNCS, vol. 9721, pp. 279–299. Springer, Cham (2016). https://doi.org/10.1007/978-3-319-40667-1_14

33. Gueron, S., Lindell, Y., Nof, A., Pinkas, B.: Fast garbling of circuits under standard assumptions. In: Proceedings of the 22nd ACM SIGSAC Conference on Computer and Communications Security, pp. 567–578 (2015)

34. Guo, C., Katz, J., Wang, X., Weng, C., Yu, Yu.: Better concrete security for half-gates garbling (in the multi-instance setting). In: Micciancio, D., Ristenpart, T. (eds.) CRYPTO 2020. LNCS, vol. 12171, pp. 793–822. Springer, Cham (2020). https://doi.org/10.1007/978-3-030-56880-1_28

35. Guo, C., Katz, J., Wang, X., Yu, Y.: Efficient and secure multiparty computation from fixed-key block ciphers. In: 2020 IEEE Symposium on Security and Privacy (SP), pp. 825–841. IEEE (2020)

36. Gupta, T., Fingler, H., Alvisi, L., Walfish, M.: Pretzel: email encryption and provider-supplied functions are compatible. In: Proceedings of the Conference of the ACM Special Interest Group on Data Communication, pp. 169–182 (2017)

37. Hastie, T., Tibshirani, R., Friedman, J.: The Elements of Statistical Learning. SSS, Springer, New York (2009). https://doi.org/10.1007/978-0-387-84858-7

38. Hastings, M., Hemenway, B., Noble, D., Zdancewic, S.: SoK: General purpose compilers for secure multi-party computation. In: 2019 IEEE Symposium on Security and Privacy (SP), pp. 1220–1237. IEEE (2019)

39. Hettwer, B., Gehrer, S., Güneysu, T.: Applications of machine learning techniques in side-channel attacks: a survey. J. Cryptogr. Eng. **10**(2), 135–162 (2020)

40. Intel Corporation: Intel Core i7 Processors. https://www.intel.com/content/www/us/en/products/details/processors/core/i7.html. Accessed 30 Jan 2023 (2017)

41. Irazoqui, G., Inci, M.S., Eisenbarth, T., Sunar, B.: Wait a minute! a fast, cross-VM attack on AES. In: Stavrou, A., Bos, H., Portokalidis, G. (eds.) RAID 2014. LNCS, vol. 8688, pp. 299–319. Springer, Cham (2014). https://doi.org/10.1007/978-3-319-11379-1_15

42. irdan: JustGarble framework. https://github.com/irdan/justGarble. Accessed 30 Jan 2023 (2014)

43. Jagadeesh, K.A., Wu, D.J., Birgmeier, J.A., Boneh, D., Bejerano, G.: Deriving genomic diagnoses without revealing patient genomes. Science **357**(6352), 692–695 (2017)

44. Jancar, J.: The state of tooling for verifying constant-timeness of cryptographic implementations. https://neuromancer.sk/article/26. Accessed 7 Feb 2023 (2021)

45. Jancar, J., et al.: They're not that hard to mitigate: what cryptographic library developers think about timing attacks. In: 2022 IEEE Symposium on Security and Privacy (SP), pp. 632–649. IEEE (2022)

46. Jayaraman, B., Li, H., Evans, D.: Decentralized certificate authorities. arXiv preprint arXiv:1706.03370 (2017)
47. Juvekar, C., Vaikuntanathan, V., Chandrakasan, A.: {GAZELLE}: a low latency framework for secure neural network inference. In: 27th USENIX Security Symposium (USENIX Security 18), pp. 1651–1669 (2018)
48. Kamara, S., Mohassel, P., Raykova, M.: Outsourcing multi-party computation. Cryptology ePrint Archive (2011)
49. Kamara, S., Mohassel, P., Raykova, M., Sadeghian, S.: Scaling private set intersection to billion-element sets. In: Christin, N., Safavi-Naini, R. (eds.) FC 2014. LNCS, vol. 8437, pp. 195–215. Springer, Heidelberg (2014). https://doi.org/10.1007/978-3-662-45472-5_13
50. Kamara, S., Mohassel, P., Riva, B.: Salus: a system for server-aided secure function evaluation. In: Proceedings of the 2012 ACM Conference on Computer and Communications Security, pp. 797–808 (2012)
51. Kamara, S., Mohassel, P., Riva, B.: Salus: a system for server-aided secure function evaluation. Cryptology ePrint Archive (2012)
52. Kocher, P.C.: Timing attacks on implementations of Diffie-Hellman, RSA, DSS, and other systems. In: Koblitz, N. (ed.) CRYPTO 1996. LNCS, vol. 1109, pp. 104–113. Springer, Heidelberg (1996). https://doi.org/10.1007/3-540-68697-5_9
53. Kolesnikov, V., Schneider, T.: Improved garbled circuit: free XOR gates and applications. In: Aceto, L., Damgård, I., Goldberg, L.A., Halldórsson, M.M., Ingólfsdóttir, A., Walukiewicz, I. (eds.) ICALP 2008. LNCS, vol. 5126, pp. 486–498. Springer, Heidelberg (2008). https://doi.org/10.1007/978-3-540-70583-3_40
54. Lai, C.H., Zhao, J., Yang, C.L.: Leave the cache hierarchy operation as it is: a new persistent memory accelerating approach. In: Proceedings of the 54th Annual Design Automation Conference 2017, pp. 1–6 (2017)
55. Levi, I., Hazay, C.: Garbled-circuits from an SCA perspective: free XOR can be quite expensive... Cryptology ePrint Archive (2022)
56. Lindell, Y., Pinkas, B.: A proof of Yao's protocol for secure two-party computation. ECCC report TR04-063. In: Electronic Colloquium on Computational Complexity (ECCC) (2004)
57. Lindell, Y., Pinkas, B.: An efficient protocol for secure two-party computation in the presence of malicious adversaries. In: Naor, M. (ed.) EUROCRYPT 2007. LNCS, vol. 4515, pp. 52–78. Springer, Heidelberg (2007). https://doi.org/10.1007/978-3-540-72540-4_4
58. Lindell, Y., Pinkas, B.: A proof of security of Yao's protocol for two-party computation. J. Cryptol. 22(2), 161–188 (2009)
59. Lipp, M., Gruss, D., Schwarz, M.: AMD prefetch attacks through power and time. In: USENIX Security Symposium (2022)
60. Lipp, M., Gruss, D., Spreitzer, R., Maurice, C., Mangard, S.: {ARMageddon}: cache attacks on mobile devices. In: 25th USENIX Security Symposium (USENIX Security 16), pp. 549–564 (2016)
61. Lipp, M., Hadžić, V., Schwarz, M., Perais, A., Maurice, C., Gruss, D.: Take a way: exploring the security implications of AMD's cache way predictors. In: Proceedings of the 15th ACM Asia Conference on Computer and Communications Security, pp. 813–825 (2020)
62. Lipp, M., et al.: PLATYPUS: software-based power side-channel attacks on x86. In: 2021 IEEE Symposium on Security and Privacy (SP), pp. 355–371. IEEE (2021)
63. Liu, F., et al.: CATalyst: defeating last-level cache side channel attacks in cloud computing. In: 2016 IEEE International Symposium on High Performance Computer Architecture (HPCA), pp. 406–418. IEEE (2016)

64. Liu, F., Yarom, Y., Ge, Q., Heiser, G., Lee, R.B.: Last-level cache side-channel attacks are practical. In: 2015 IEEE Symposium on Security and Privacy, pp. 605–622. IEEE (2015)

65. Lou, X., Zhang, T., Jiang, J., Zhang, Y.: A survey of microarchitectural side-channel vulnerabilities, attacks, and defenses in cryptography. ACM Comput. Surv. (CSUR) **54**(6), 1–37 (2021)

66. Lyu, Y., Mishra, P.: A survey of side-channel attacks on caches and countermeasures. J. Hardware Syst. Secur. **2**(1), 33–50 (2018)

67. Malozemoff, A., Wang, X., Katz, J.: EMP-toolkit framework. https://github.com/emp-toolkit. Accessed 30 Jan 2023 (2022)

68. Martin, R., Demme, J., Sethumadhavan, S.: TimeWarp: rethinking timekeeping and performance monitoring mechanisms to mitigate side-channel attacks. In: 2012 39th Annual International Symposium on Computer Architecture (ISCA), pp. 118–129. IEEE (2012)

69. Moghimi, A., Irazoqui, G., Eisenbarth, T.: CacheZoom: how SGX amplifies the power of cache attacks. In: Fischer, W., Homma, N. (eds.) CHES 2017. LNCS, vol. 10529, pp. 69–90. Springer, Cham (2017). https://doi.org/10.1007/978-3-319-66787-4_4

70. Mohassel, P., Rosulek, M., Zhang, Y.: Fast and secure three-party computation: the garbled circuit approach. In: Proceedings of the 22nd ACM SIGSAC Conference on Computer and Communications Security, pp. 591–602 (2015)

71. Mohassel, P., Zhang, Y.: SecureML: a system for scalable privacy-preserving machine learning. In: 2017 IEEE Symposium on Security and Privacy (SP), pp. 19–38. IEEE (2017)

72. Mowery, K., Keelveedhi, S., Shacham, H.: Are AES x86 cache timing attacks still feasible? In: Proceedings of the 2012 ACM Workshop on Cloud Computing Security Workshop, pp. 19–24 (2012)

73. Mushtaq, M., Mukhtar, M.A., Lapotre, V., Bhatti, M.K., Gogniat, G.: Winter is here! a decade of cache-based side-channel attacks, detection & mitigation for RSA. Inf. Syst. **92**, 101524 (2020)

74. Nakamoto, A.: W-shield: protection against cryptocurrency wallet credential stealing. In: Workshop on Security and Privacy in E-Commerce 2018, pp. 71–107 (2018)

75. Nikolaenko, V., Weinsberg, U., Ioannidis, S., Joye, M., Boneh, D., Taft, N.: Privacy-preserving ridge regression on hundreds of millions of records. In: 2013 IEEE Symposium on Security and Privacy, pp. 334–348. IEEE (2013)

76. Ostrovsky, R., Paskin-Cherniavsky, A., Paskin-Cherniavsky, B.: Maliciously circuit-private FHE. In: Garay, J.A., Gennaro, R. (eds.) CRYPTO 2014. LNCS, vol. 8616, pp. 536–553. Springer, Heidelberg (2014). https://doi.org/10.1007/978-3-662-44371-2_30

77. Osvik, D.A., Shamir, A., Tromer, E.: Cache attacks and countermeasures: the case of AES. In: Pointcheval, D. (ed.) CT-RSA 2006. LNCS, vol. 3860, pp. 1–20. Springer, Heidelberg (2006). https://doi.org/10.1007/11605805_1

78. Page, D.: Theoretical use of cache memory as a cryptanalytic side-channel. Cryptology ePrint Archive (2002)

79. Percival, C.: Cache missing for fun and profit (2005)

80. Sahai, A., Seyalioglu, H.: Worry-free encryption: functional encryption with public keys. In: Proceedings of the 17th ACM Conference on Computer and Communications Security, pp. 463–472 (2010)

81. Saxena, A., Panda, B.: DABANGG: a case for noise resilient flush-based cache attacks. In: 2022 IEEE Security and Privacy Workshops (SPW), pp. 323–334. IEEE (2022)

82. Schneider, T.: Practical secure function evaluation. In: Informatiktage, pp. 37–40 (2008)

83. Schwarz, M., et al.: Automated detection, exploitation, and elimination of double-fetch bugs using modern CPU features. In: Proceedings of the 2018 on Asia Conference on Computer and Communications Security, pp. 587–600 (2018)

84. Schwarz, M., Weiser, S., Gruss, D., Maurice, C., Mangard, S.: Malware guard extension: using SGX to conceal cache attacks. In: Polychronakis, M., Meier, M. (eds.) DIMVA 2017. LNCS, vol. 10327, pp. 3–24. Springer, Cham (2017). https://doi.org/10.1007/978-3-319-60876-1_1

85. Sherali, H.D., Tuncbilek, C.H.: A squared-Euclidean distance location-allocation problem. Naval Res. Logist. (NRL) **39**(4), 447–469 (1992)

86. Songhori, E., Siam, H., Riazi, S.: Tinygarble framework. https://github.com/esonghori/TinyGarble. Accessed 30 Jan 2023 (2019)

87. Songhori, E.M., Hussain, S.U., Sadeghi, A.R., Schneider, T., Koushanfar, F.: TinyGarble: highly compressed and scalable sequential garbled circuits. In: 2015 IEEE Symposium on Security and Privacy, pp. 411–428. IEEE (2015)

88. Standaert, F.-X., Malkin, T.G., Yung, M.: A unified framework for the analysis of side-channel key recovery attacks. In: Joux, A. (ed.) EUROCRYPT 2009. LNCS, vol. 5479, pp. 443–461. Springer, Heidelberg (2009). https://doi.org/10.1007/978-3-642-01001-9_26

89. Tian, L., Jayaraman, B., Gu, Q., Evans, D.: Aggregating private sparse learning models using multi-party computation. In: NIPS Workshop on Private Multi-Party Machine Learning (2016)

90. Vattikonda, B.C., Das, S., Shacham, H.: Eliminating fine grained timers in XEN. In: Proceedings of the 3rd ACM workshop on Cloud Computing Security Workshop, pp. 41–46 (2011)

91. Whitnall, C., Oswald, E.: Robust profiling for DPA-style attacks. In: Güneysu, T., Handschuh, H. (eds.) CHES 2015. LNCS, vol. 9293, pp. 3–21. Springer, Heidelberg (2015). https://doi.org/10.1007/978-3-662-48324-4_1

92. Wu, M., Guo, S., Schaumont, P., Wang, C.: Eliminating timing side-channel leaks using program repair. In: Proceedings of the 27th ACM SIGSOFT International Symposium on Software Testing and Analysis, pp. 15–26 (2018)

93. Yao, A.C.C.: How to generate and exchange secrets. In: 27th Annual Symposium on Foundations of Computer Science (SFCS 1986), pp. 162–167. IEEE (1986)

94. Yarom, Y., Falkner, K.: Flush+ reload: a high resolution, low noise, l3 cache side-channel attack. In: 23rd {USENIX} Security Symposium ({USENIX} Security 14), pp. 719–732 (2014)

95. Zahur, S., Kerneis, G., Necula, G.: Obliv-C secure computation compiler. https://github.com/samee/obliv-c. Accessed 2 Feb 2023 (2018)

96. Zahur, S., Evans, D.: Obliv-C: A language for extensible data-oblivious computation. Cryptology ePrint Archive (2015)

97. Zahur, S., Rosulek, M., Evans, D.: Two halves make a whole. In: Oswald, E., Fischlin, M. (eds.) EUROCRYPT 2015. LNCS, vol. 9057, pp. 220–250. Springer, Heidelberg (2015). https://doi.org/10.1007/978-3-662-46803-6_8

98. Zhao, L., Iyer, R., Makineni, S., Newell, D., Cheng, L.: NCID: a non-inclusive cache, inclusive directory architecture for flexible and efficient cache hierarchies. In: Proceedings of the 7th ACM International Conference on Computing Frontiers, pp. 121–130 (2010)

Related-Tweak and Related-Key Differential Attacks on HALFLOOP-48

Yunxue Lin[1,2] and Ling Sun[1,2,3(✉)]

[1] Key Laboratory of Cryptologic Technology and Information Security,
Ministry of Education, Shandong University, Jinan, China
lingsun@sdu.edu.cn
[2] School of Cyber Science and Technology, Shandong University, Qingdao, China
[3] Quan Cheng Shandong Laboratory, Jinan, China

Abstract. HALFLOOP-48 is a 48-bit tweakable block cipher used in high frequency radio to protect automatic link establishment messages. We concentrate on its differential properties. Using the automatic method, we determine the lower bound for the number of active S-boxes and the upper bound for the differential probability for the conventional, related-tweak, and related-key differential attack settings. The newly identified 6-round related-tweak differential is utilised to initiate an 8-round related-tweak differential attack against the cipher. With $2^{33.27}$ chosen-plaintexts and $2^{92.71}$ 8-round encryptions, the 128-bit key can be recovered. In addition, we find an 8-round related-key differential with a probability of $2^{-46.88}$ and employ it to develop a full-round related-key differential attack. The full-round attack is marginal, and the 128-bit key can be retrieved using $2^{47.34}$ chosen-plaintexts and $2^{123.91}$ full-round encryptions. Despite the impractical complexity of the newly proposed attacks, the security of HALFLOOP-48 in the related-key attack setting is compromised. Therefore, we assert that caution is necessary to prevent misuse.

Keywords: Differential cryptanalysis · Related-tweak · Related-key · HALFLOOP-48

1 Introduction

HALFLOOP is a tweakable block cipher family. It was designed to encrypt protocol data units prior to transmission in automatic link establishment (ALE). The latest revision of MIL-STD-188-141D [1], the interoperability and performance standards for medium and high frequency radio systems issued by the United States Department of Defence, has standardised HALFLOOP.

All three variants of HALFLOOP, called HALFLOOP-24, HALFLOOP-48, and HALFLOOP-96, have the same 128-bit key size and different state sizes, 24-bit, 48-bit, and 96-bit, respectively. The three HALFLOOP variants are utilised in different generations of ALE systems: HALFLOOP-24 in the second generation (2G) system, HALFLOOP-48 in the third generation (3G) system, and HALFLOOP-96 in the fourth generation (4G) system.

C. Pöpper and L. Batina (Eds.): ACNS 2024, LNCS 14585, pp. 355–377, 2024.
https://doi.org/10.1007/978-3-031-54776-8_14

The HALFLOOP announcement is not accompanied by public cryptanalysis. Dansarie *et al.* [12] reported the first public cryptanalytic result on HALFLOOP-24 and proposed a variety of differential attacks [5] for ciphertext-only, known-plaintext, selected-plaintext, and selected-ciphertext scenarios. Despite its 128-bit key size, the attack results indicated that HALFLOOP-24 is incapable of providing 128-bit security.

Note that the security of HALFLOOP-24 has been extensively examined in [12], whereas the security of the remaining two HALFLOOP versions has been assessed using the time memory tradeoff attack. However, a non-generic attack for the remaining two versions is not provided. As stated in [12], designing the key schedule for block ciphers with small states requires significantly more care. If the key bits are not properly mixed with the state, the security of this type of cipher can be substantially lower than anticipated. In light of this observation, we are curious about the security of HALFLOOP-48, which also has a relatively small state.

The breaking of HALFLOOP-24 [12] depends on the slow spread of the tweakey schedule. It is possible to create a 6-round related-tweak differential characteristic with a probability of one, which enables full-round attacks on the cipher. However, in the case of HALFLOOP-48, it is not immediately apparent if a related-tweak differential characteristic with a high chance of occurrence exists. The potential for extending the attack on HALFLOOP-24 to HALFLOOP-48 remains uncertain.

Our contribution Motivated by understanding the security of HALFLOOP-48, we investigate its resistance to the differential attack, one of the most fundamental and powerful block cipher cryptanalyses. Given that HALFLOOP-48 exploits an 8-bit S-box, we employ the SAT method described in [22] for its rapid construction of SAT models for large S-boxes. We determine the lower bound on the number of active S-boxes and the upper bound on the differential probability using the automatic method for conventional, related-tweak, and related-key differential attack settings.

❶ The resistance of HALFLOOP-48 to the conventional differential attack is adequate. The longest differential characteristic with a probability greater than 2^{-47} spans three rounds, whereas the longest valid differential spans four rounds. Given that the complete version of HALFLOOP-48 consists of ten rounds, the security margin seems sufficient.

❷ In the related-tweak attack setting, the security of HALFLOOP-48 is acceptable. The longest differential characteristics and differentials with probabilities higher than 2^{-47} cover six rounds. The optimal differential is a 6-round differential with a probability of $2^{-29.48}$. Its validity is verified using randomly drawn plaintexts, keys, and tweaks.

❸ The vulnerability of HALFLOOP-48 to the related-key differential attack is low. The longest differential characteristic with a probability greater than 2^{-47} spans seven rounds, whereas the longest effective differential spans eight. An 8-round related-key differential with a probability of $2^{-46.88}$ is discovered.

Even though the probability of the 8-round differential is marginally higher than the critical value, it remains functional in a full-round attack.

We mount differential attacks against HALFLOOP-48 via the newly-identified differentials. A 6-round related-tweak differential is employed to initiate an 8-round related-tweak differential attack. The 128-bit key can be retrieved using $2^{33.27}$ chosen-plaintexts and $2^{92.71}$ 8-round encryptions. In addition, the unique 8-round related-key differential is used to launch a full-round related-key differential attack. $2^{47.34}$ chosen-plaintexts and $2^{123.91}$ full-round encryptions are required to recover the 128-bit key. Table 1 provides an overview of the complexity of the attacks. Due to their impractical complexity, the attacks described in this paper do not pose a real security risk to HALFLOOP-48. Nevertheless, caution must be taken to prevent misuse, as our study reveals no secure margin in the related-key attack setting.

Table 1. Overview of the attacks on HALFLOOP-48 reported in the paper.

Setting	Round	Data	Time	Memory (Byte)	Success Probability	Section
Related-tweak	8	$2^{33.27}$	$2^{92.71}$	$2^{36.85}$	90%	Sect. 5.1
Related-key	10	$2^{47.34}$	$2^{123.91}$	$2^{33.34}$	50%	Sect. 5.2

The paper is organised as follows. Section 2 introduces differential cryptanalysis and the specification of HALFLOOP-48. Section 3 represents the method for creating SAT models to search for differential characteristics of HALFLOOP-48. Section 4 exhibits the differential properties of the cipher in the conventional, related-tweak, and related-key attack configurations. The 8-round related-tweak differential attack and the full-round related-key differential attack are given in Sect. 5. Section 6 concludes the paper.

2   Preliminaries

This section begins with a review of differential cryptanalysis and its variants in the context of related-key and related-tweak attacks. The focus of the paper, HALFLOOP-48, is then introduced.

2.1   Differential Cryptanalysis

Biham and Shamir [5] were the first to define differential cryptanalysis. The basic procedure employs plaintext pairs (P, P') connected by a constant *difference* Δ_{in}. Several methods exist for defining differences, but the XOR operation is the most prevalent because, in the majority of instances, the XOR operation involves the keys in the encryption phase. The attacker then computes the differences between the corresponding ciphertexts (C, C') in an attempt to detect a difference Δ_{out} that occurs with a probability that is not random. The pair of differences $(\Delta_{in}, \Delta_{out})$ is called a *differential*. The *differential probability* of a differential $(\Delta_{in}, \Delta_{out})$ over an n-bit primitive E_K parameterised with a k-bit key K is computed as

$$\mathrm{Pr}_{E_K}(\Delta_{in}, \Delta_{out}) = \frac{\{x \in \mathbb{F}_2^n \mid E_K(x) \oplus E_K(x \oplus \Delta_{in}) = \Delta_{out}\}}{2^n}.$$

The *weight* of a differential is $-\log_2\left[\mathrm{Pr}_{E_K}(\Delta_{in}, \Delta_{out})\right]$. To guarantee a successful attack, the probability of a differential used in a differential attack must exceed 2^{1-n}.

Typically, evaluating the differential probability of a differential in order to discover a valid differential for a large-scale cipher involving numerous rounds is extremely challenging. The differential is usually localised by constructing *differential characteristics*, which track the difference after each round. Denote $(\Delta_{in} = \Delta_0, \Delta_1, \ldots, \Delta_r = \Delta_{out})$ an r-round differential characteristic of the differential $(\Delta_{in}, \Delta_{out})$. Suppose the r-round encryption E_K can be represented as the composition of r round functions as $f_{k_{r-1}} \circ f_{k_{r-2}} \circ \cdots \circ f_{k_0}$. Under the assumption that the round keys $k_0, k_1, \ldots, k_{r-1}$ are independent and uniformly random, the differential probability of the differential characteristic can be calculated as

$$\mathrm{Pr}_{E_K}(\Delta_0, \Delta_1, \ldots, \Delta_r) = \prod_{i=0}^{r-1} \mathrm{Pr}_{f_{k_i}}(\Delta_i, \Delta_{i+1}).$$

Since a fixed differential may contain a large number of differential characteristics, the probability of the differential can be computed as

$$\mathrm{Pr}_{E_K}(\Delta_{in}, \Delta_{out}) = \sum_{\Delta_1, \Delta_2, \ldots, \Delta_{r-1} \in \mathbb{F}_2^n} \mathrm{Pr}_{E_K}(\Delta_{in}, \Delta_1, \ldots, \Delta_{r-1}, \Delta_{out}).$$

In practice, exhaustively searching for all characteristics in a differential and accurately calculating its probability is impossible due to the limited computational resources available. A common way of handling this is to find the differential characteristics with a higher probability in the differential, and the summation of probabilities of these characteristics approximates the probability of the differential.

After obtaining an r-round differential $(\Delta_{in}, \Delta_{out})$ with probability p_0 ($p_0 > 2^{1-n}$), initiating an $(r+1)$-round differential attack against the $(r+1)$-round encryption $\tilde{E}_K = f_{k_r} \circ E_K$ is possible. The following is a summary of the fundamental attack procedure.

❶ Select N plaintext pairs (P, P') such that the difference between P and P' is Δ_{in}. Query the encryption oracle to obtain the pairs of ciphertexts (C, C') that correspond.

❷ Create a counter $Cnt[k_r^{(i)}]$ for each possible value $k_r^{(i)}$ of the subkey k_r, $0 \leqslant i \leqslant 2^n - 1$. For each pair (C, C'), determine the value of $f_{k_r^{(i)}}^{-1}(C) \oplus f_{k_r^{(i)}}^{-1}(C')$ for each $k_r^{(i)}$. If the equation $f_{k_r^{(i)}}^{-1}(C) \oplus f_{k_r^{(i)}}^{-1}(C') = \Delta_{out}$ is valid, increment the counter $Cnt[k_r^{(i)}]$ by one.

❸ If the threshold is set to τ, the key guess $k_r^{(i)}$ is sorted into a candidate list only if the counter value $Cnt[k_r^{(i)}]$ is at least τ.

From the attack procedure, the counter memorising the number of pairs validating the differential follows a binomial distribution $\mathcal{B}(N, p_0)$ under the correct key guess (cf. [7]). On the other hand, the probability of a pair satisfying the differential given an incorrect key guess is $p = 2^{-n}$. The counter follows a binomial distribution $\mathcal{B}(N, p)$.

Differential cryptanalysis, categorised as statistical cryptanalysis, always faces two errors. The probability that the correct key does not exist in the candidate list is denoted by α. Denote β the false alarm error probability, which is the probability that a wrong key guess survives in the candidate list. Consequently, the success probability P_S of the attack, which is the probability that the right key appears in the candidate list, is equal to $1 - \alpha$. According to the analysis in [7], when N is sufficiently large, α and β can be approximately calculated as

$$
\begin{aligned}
\alpha &\approx \frac{p_0 \cdot \sqrt{1 - (\tau - 1)/N}}{(p_0 - (\tau - 1)/N) \cdot \sqrt{2 \cdot \pi \cdot (\tau - 1)}} \cdot \exp\left[-N \cdot D\left(\frac{\tau - 1}{N} \middle\| p_0\right)\right], \\
\beta &\approx \frac{(1 - p) \cdot \sqrt{\tau/N}}{(\tau/N - p) \cdot \sqrt{2 \cdot \pi \cdot N \cdot (1 - \tau/N)}} \cdot \exp\left[-N \cdot D\left(\frac{\tau}{N} \middle\| p\right)\right],
\end{aligned}
\tag{1}
$$

where $D(p\|q) \triangleq p \cdot \ln\left(\frac{p}{q}\right) + (1 - p) \cdot \ln\left(\frac{1-p}{1-q}\right)$ is the Kullback-Leibler divergence between two Bernoulli distributions with parameters respectively being p and q.

2.2 Related-Key and Related-Tweak Differential Cryptanalyses

The difference between conventional differential cryptanalysis and related-key differential cryptanalysis is that the latter exploits the properties of differential propagation when plaintexts P and P', which can be identical, are encrypted using different keys. Formally, an r-round *related-key differential* is represented by the triple $(\Delta_{in}, \Delta_{out}, \Delta_{key})$, where Δ_{key} is the difference between the keys, and its probability is calculated as

$$
\Pr_{E_K}(\Delta_{in}, \Delta_{out}, \Delta_{key}) = \frac{\{x \in \mathbb{F}_2^n \mid E_K(x) \oplus E_{K \oplus \Delta_{key}}(x \oplus \Delta_{in}) = \Delta_{out}\}}{2^n}.
$$

Initialising related-tweak differential cryptanalysis is also possible for tweakable block ciphers (such as HALFLOOP-48, concerned in this paper). It employs differential propagation when P and P', which may be identical, are encrypted with the same key and distinct tweaks. We indicate a *related-tweak differential* with the triple $(\Delta_{in}, \Delta_{out}, \Delta_{tweak})$, where Δ_{tweak} represents the difference between the tweaks. Compared to related-key differential cryptanalysis, related-tweak differential cryptanalysis poses a more significant threat since the value of the tweak is publicly known to the adversary.

After obtaining an r-round related-key (resp., related-tweak) differential with a probability greater than 2^{1-n}, a related-key (resp., related-tweak) differential attack can be performed similarly to a conventional differential attack.

2.3 Specification of HALFLOOP-48

HALFLOOP [1] is a tweakable block cipher family with three distinct variants. HALFLOOP-48 employs 48-bit blocks and has 128-bit key K and 64-bit tweak T. Many operations in HALFLOOP-48 are derived from AES [2,11].

Initialisation. After receiving the plaintext $m = m[0]\|m[1]\|\cdots\|m[5]$, where $m[i] \in \mathbb{F}_2^8$, $0 \leqslant i \leqslant 5$, the internal state IS is set to

$$\texttt{IS} = \begin{bmatrix} m[0] & m[3] \\ m[1] & m[4] \\ m[2] & m[5] \end{bmatrix}.$$

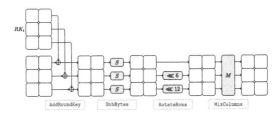

Fig. 1. Round function of HALFLOOP-48.

A single encryption round consists of the four operations depicted in Fig. 1: AddRoundKey (ARK), SubBytes (SB), RotateRows (RR), and MixColumns (MC). The number of encryption rounds is ten, and the final round replaces MixColumns with AddRoundKey. The definitions of the four operations are as follows.

AddRoundKey (ARK) The round key RK_i is bitwise XORed to the state in the i-th round.

SubBytes (SB) An 8-bit S-box S (cf. Table 2) is applied to each state byte, which is identical to the S-box used by AES.

RotateRows (RR) As shown in Fig. 1, this operation rotates the state rows to the left by a variable number of bit positions.

MixColumns (MC) Each 24-bit column is viewed as a polynomial over $\mathbb{F}_{2^8}$, and the irreducible binary polynomial is the same as that of AES: $m(x) = x^8 + x^4 + x^3 + x + 1$. Each column is multiplied modulo $x^3 + 1$ by a constant polynomial $c(x)$ expressed as $c(x) = x^2 + 2 \cdot x + 9$. This operation can also be expressed as a matrix multiplication with the matrix M over $\mathbb{F}_{2^8}$, where

$$M = \begin{bmatrix} 9 & 1 & 2 \\ 2 & 9 & 1 \\ 1 & 2 & 9 \end{bmatrix}. \tag{2}$$

Table 2. 8-bit S-box S of HALFLOOP. $x\|y$ is the 8-bit input, where $x, y \in \mathbb{F}_2^4$.

$S(x\|y)$	y															
		0	1	2	3	4	5	6	7	8	9	a	b	c	d	e	f
x	0	63	7c	77	7b	f2	6b	6f	c5	30	01	67	2b	fe	d7	ab	76
	1	ca	82	c9	7d	fa	59	47	f0	ad	d4	a2	af	9c	a4	72	c0
	2	b7	fd	93	26	36	3f	f7	cc	34	a5	e5	f1	71	d8	31	15
	3	04	c7	23	c3	18	96	05	9a	07	12	80	e2	eb	27	b2	75
	4	09	83	2c	1a	1b	6e	5a	a0	52	3b	d6	b3	29	e3	2f	84
	5	53	d1	00	ed	20	fc	b1	5b	6a	cb	be	39	4a	4c	58	cf
	6	d0	ef	aa	fb	43	4d	33	85	45	f9	02	7f	50	3c	9f	a8
	7	51	a3	40	8f	92	9d	38	f5	bc	b6	da	21	10	ff	f3	d2
	8	cd	0c	13	ec	5f	97	44	17	c4	a7	7e	3d	64	5d	19	73
	9	60	81	4f	dc	22	2a	90	88	46	ee	b8	14	de	5e	0b	db
	a	e0	32	3a	0a	49	06	24	5c	c2	d3	ac	62	91	95	e4	79
	b	e7	c8	37	6d	8d	d5	4e	a9	6c	56	f4	ea	65	7a	ae	08
	c	ba	78	25	2e	1c	a6	b4	c6	e8	dd	74	1f	4b	bd	8b	8a
	d	70	3e	b5	66	48	03	f6	0e	61	35	57	b9	86	c1	1d	9e
	e	e1	f8	98	11	69	d9	8e	94	9b	1e	87	e9	ce	55	28	df
	f	8c	a1	89	0d	bf	e6	42	68	41	99	2d	0f	b0	54	bb	16

Key Schedule The key schedule resembles that of AES-128 closely. Denote K and T as $K_0\|K_1\|K_2\|K_3$ and $T_0\|T_1$, respectively, where K_i $(0 \leqslant i \leqslant 3)$ and T_j $(j = 0, 1)$ are 32-bit words. K and T are utilised to generate a linear array of 4-byte words W_0, W_1, ..., W_{16}, which are then employed to create the round keys. The first four words are initialised with

$$W_0 = K_0 \oplus T_0, W_1 = K_1 \oplus T_1, W_2 = K_2, W_3 = K_3.$$

The remaining words are generated using the two functions listed below.

RotWord The function accepts the 4-byte input word $a[0]\|a[1]\|a[2]\|a[3]$, performs a cyclic permutation, and returns the output $a[1]\|a[2]\|a[3]\|a[0]$.

SubWord The function takes a 4-byte input word and applies the S-box S to each of the four bytes to generate a 4-byte output word.

Each subsequent word W_i $(4 \leqslant i \leqslant 16$ and $i \bmod 4 \neq 0)$ is the XOR of the two preceding words W_{i-1} and W_{i-4}. For words in positions i that are a multiple of four, $g = $ SubWord $\circ$ RotWord is applied to W_{i-1} before the XOR, and a round constant Rcon$_{i/4}$ is XORed with the result. The four round constants involved in the HALFLOOP-48 key schedule are

$$\mathrm{Rcon}_1 = 0\text{x}01000000, \mathrm{Rcon}_2 = 0\text{x}02000000,$$
$$\mathrm{Rcon}_3 = 0\text{x}04000000, \mathrm{Rcon}_4 = 0\text{x}08000000.$$

To obtain the round keys RK_0, RK_1, ..., and RK_{10} for HALFLOOP-48, it is necessary to repackage the 4-byte words into 6-byte words. The key schedule is illustrated in Fig. 2.

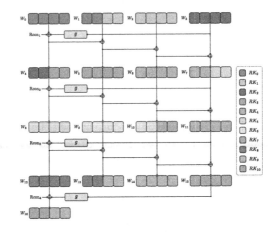

Fig. 2. Key schedule of HALFLOOP-48.

3 Automatic Search of Differentials

Identifying a differential with a non-negligible probability is the most crucial and challenging step in a differential attack. Matsui [17] presented the first systematic method, the branch and bound algorithm, to explore the optimal differential characteristic at EUROCRYPT 1994. When customised optimisations for particular ciphers are considered, branch and bound algorithms are unquestionably highly efficient [6,13]. Nevertheless, avoiding memory overload by carefully selecting search nodes is a test of both cryptanalysis and programming skills.

The introduction of automatic search techniques [18] has substantially facilitated the search for differential characteristics. The primary objective is to convert the problem of seeking differential characteristics into some well-studied mathematical problems. Using some publicly accessible solvers for these mathematical problems, the optimal differential characteristics can be identified. Since implementing automatic methods is relatively straightforward, it has been extensively utilised to search for distinguishers in various attacks.

Mixed integer linear programming (MILP), Boolean satisfiability problem (SAT), satisfiability modulus theories (SMT), and constraint satisfaction problem (CSP) are frequently encountered mathematical problems in the automatic search. The automatic search methods can be categorised based on the mathematical problems they resolve. MILP methods in [3,8,14], SAT method in [4,22], and SMT method in [15] can accomplish the search of differential characteristics for ciphers with 8-bit S-boxes. In this work, we select the SAT method in [22] for the rapid production of SAT models for S-boxes.

In this section, we describe the SAT models required to search for (related-key and related-tweak) differential characteristics of HALFLOOP-48, including models for linear operations, the S-box, and the objective function.

3.1 Boolean Satisfiability Problem

A *Boolean formula* consists of Boolean variables, the operators AND (conjunction, $\wedge$), OR (disjunction, $\vee$), and NOT (negation, $\neg$), as well as parentheses. The *Boolean satisfiability problem* is the problem of determining if an assignment exists for all Boolean variables such that the provided Boolean formula is valid. If so, the formula is referred to as *satisfiable*. Alternatively, if there is no such assignment, the formula is *unsatisfiable*. SAT is the first problem proven to be NP-complete [10], but very efficient solvers are now available to manage numerous actual SAT problems.

For distinguisher search, this paper utilises the solver CryptoMiniSat [20]. CryptoMiniSat requires Boolean formulas to be in *conjunctive normal form* (CNF), which is a conjunction of one or more *clauses*, each of which is a disjunction of (potentially negated) variables. CryptoMiniSat also supports *XOR clauses* composed of XOR of variables, which tremendously facilitates the model construction for HALFLOOP-48. Converting distinguisher searching problems into Boolean formulas in CNF is the most crucial phase in creating SAT models.

3.2 SAT Models for Linear Operations of HALFLOOP-48

In this section, for the m-bit vector Δ, the i-th bit ($0 \leqslant i \leqslant m - 1$) is denoted by $\Delta[i]$, while $\Delta[0]$ represents the most significant bit.

Model 1 (XOR, [16]) *For the m-bit XOR operation, the input differences are represented by Δ_0 and Δ_1, and the output difference is denoted by Δ_2. Differential propagation is valid if and only if the values of Δ_0, Δ_1 and Δ_2 validate all of the following XOR clauses.*

$$\Delta_0[i] \oplus \Delta_1[i] \oplus \Delta_2[i] = 0, 0 \leqslant i \leqslant m - 1.$$

We employ the procedure described in [23] to build the model for the MC operation. First, the *primitive representation* [21] $\mathbb{M}$ of the matrix M (cf. Eq. (2)) is created.

$$\mathbb{M} = \begin{bmatrix}
1 & 0 & 0 & 1 & 0 & 0 & 0 & 0 & 1 & 0 & 0 & 0 & 0 & 0 & 0 & 0 & 0 & 1 & 0 & 0 & 0 & 0 & 0 & 0 \\
1 & 1 & 0 & 0 & 1 & 0 & 0 & 0 & 0 & 1 & 0 & 0 & 0 & 0 & 0 & 0 & 0 & 0 & 1 & 0 & 0 & 0 & 0 & 0 \\
1 & 1 & 1 & 0 & 0 & 1 & 0 & 0 & 0 & 0 & 1 & 0 & 0 & 0 & 0 & 0 & 0 & 0 & 0 & 1 & 0 & 0 & 0 & 0 \\
0 & 1 & 1 & 1 & 0 & 0 & 1 & 0 & 0 & 0 & 0 & 1 & 0 & 0 & 0 & 0 & 1 & 0 & 0 & 0 & 1 & 0 & 0 & 0 \\
1 & 0 & 1 & 0 & 1 & 0 & 0 & 1 & 0 & 0 & 0 & 0 & 1 & 0 & 0 & 0 & 1 & 0 & 0 & 0 & 0 & 1 & 0 & 0 \\
1 & 1 & 0 & 0 & 0 & 1 & 0 & 0 & 0 & 0 & 0 & 0 & 0 & 1 & 0 & 0 & 0 & 0 & 0 & 0 & 0 & 0 & 1 & 0 \\
0 & 1 & 1 & 0 & 0 & 0 & 1 & 0 & 0 & 0 & 0 & 0 & 0 & 0 & 1 & 0 & 1 & 0 & 0 & 0 & 0 & 0 & 0 & 1 \\
0 & 0 & 1 & 0 & 0 & 0 & 0 & 1 & 0 & 0 & 0 & 0 & 0 & 0 & 0 & 1 & 1 & 0 & 0 & 0 & 0 & 0 & 0 & 0 \\
0 & 1 & 0 & 0 & 0 & 0 & 0 & 0 & 1 & 0 & 0 & 1 & 0 & 0 & 0 & 0 & 1 & 0 & 0 & 0 & 0 & 0 & 0 & 0 \\
0 & 0 & 1 & 0 & 0 & 0 & 0 & 0 & 1 & 1 & 0 & 0 & 1 & 0 & 0 & 0 & 0 & 1 & 0 & 0 & 0 & 0 & 0 & 0 \\
0 & 0 & 0 & 1 & 0 & 0 & 0 & 0 & 1 & 1 & 1 & 0 & 0 & 1 & 0 & 0 & 0 & 0 & 1 & 0 & 0 & 0 & 0 & 0 \\
1 & 0 & 0 & 0 & 1 & 0 & 0 & 0 & 0 & 1 & 1 & 1 & 0 & 0 & 1 & 0 & 0 & 0 & 0 & 1 & 0 & 0 & 0 & 0 \\
1 & 0 & 0 & 0 & 0 & 1 & 0 & 0 & 1 & 0 & 1 & 0 & 1 & 0 & 0 & 1 & 0 & 0 & 0 & 0 & 1 & 0 & 0 & 0 \\
0 & 0 & 0 & 0 & 0 & 0 & 1 & 0 & 1 & 1 & 0 & 0 & 0 & 1 & 0 & 0 & 0 & 0 & 0 & 0 & 0 & 1 & 0 & 0 \\
1 & 0 & 0 & 0 & 0 & 0 & 0 & 1 & 0 & 1 & 1 & 0 & 0 & 0 & 1 & 0 & 0 & 0 & 0 & 0 & 0 & 0 & 1 & 0 \\
1 & 0 & 0 & 0 & 0 & 0 & 0 & 0 & 0 & 0 & 1 & 0 & 0 & 0 & 0 & 1 & 0 & 0 & 0 & 0 & 0 & 0 & 0 & 1 \\
1 & 0 & 0 & 0 & 0 & 0 & 0 & 0 & 0 & 1 & 0 & 0 & 0 & 0 & 0 & 0 & 1 & 0 & 0 & 1 & 0 & 0 & 0 & 0 \\
0 & 1 & 0 & 0 & 0 & 0 & 0 & 0 & 0 & 0 & 1 & 0 & 0 & 0 & 0 & 0 & 1 & 1 & 0 & 0 & 1 & 0 & 0 & 0 \\
0 & 0 & 1 & 0 & 0 & 0 & 0 & 0 & 0 & 0 & 0 & 1 & 0 & 0 & 0 & 0 & 1 & 1 & 1 & 0 & 0 & 1 & 0 & 0 \\
0 & 0 & 0 & 1 & 0 & 0 & 0 & 0 & 1 & 0 & 0 & 0 & 1 & 0 & 0 & 0 & 0 & 1 & 1 & 1 & 0 & 0 & 1 & 0 \\
0 & 0 & 0 & 0 & 1 & 0 & 0 & 0 & 1 & 0 & 0 & 0 & 0 & 1 & 0 & 0 & 1 & 0 & 1 & 0 & 1 & 0 & 0 & 1 \\
0 & 0 & 0 & 0 & 0 & 1 & 0 & 0 & 0 & 0 & 0 & 0 & 0 & 0 & 1 & 0 & 1 & 1 & 0 & 0 & 0 & 1 & 0 & 0 \\
0 & 0 & 0 & 0 & 0 & 0 & 1 & 0 & 1 & 0 & 0 & 0 & 0 & 0 & 0 & 1 & 0 & 1 & 1 & 0 & 0 & 0 & 1 & 0 \\
0 & 0 & 0 & 0 & 0 & 0 & 0 & 1 & 1 & 0 & 0 & 0 & 0 & 0 & 0 & 0 & 0 & 0 & 1 & 0 & 0 & 0 & 0 & 1
\end{bmatrix}$$

is the matrix representation of M over $\mathbb{F}_2$. $\mathbb{M}_{i,j}$ is referred to the element of $\mathbb{M}$ in the i-th row and j-th column. The SAT model can then be constructed using XOR clauses.

Model 2 (Matrix Multiplication) *For matrix multiplication with the 24 × 24 matrix $\mathbb{M}$, the input and output differences are represented by Δ_0 and Δ_1, respectively. Differential propagation is valid if and only if the values of Δ_0 and Δ_1 satisfy all the XOR clauses in the subsequent.*

$$\bigoplus_{\{j \,\mid\, 0 \leqslant j \leqslant 23 \ s.t. \ \mathbb{M}_{i,j}=1\}} \Delta_0[j] \oplus \Delta_1[i] = 0, 0 \leqslant i \leqslant 23.$$

3.3   SAT Model for the S-Box of HALFLOOP-48

The probabilities of possible differential propagations $\Delta_0 \rightarrow \Delta_1$ for the 8-bit S-box S can take values from the set $\{2^{-7}, 2^{-6}, 1\}$. Motivated by the two-step encoding method described in [22], we introduce two Boolean variables u_0 and u_1 for each S-box to encode the differential probability of possible propagations.

$$V = \left\{ \Delta_0 \| \Delta_1 \| u_0 \| u_1 \;\middle|\; \begin{array}{l} \Delta_0, \Delta_1 \in \mathbb{F}_2^8, u_0, u_1 \in \mathbb{F}_2 \\ u_0 \| u_1 = \begin{cases} 1\|1, & \text{if } \Pr(\Delta_0 \rightarrow \Delta_1) = 2^{-7} \\ 0\|1, & \text{if } \Pr(\Delta_0 \rightarrow \Delta_1) = 2^{-6} \\ 0\|0, & \text{if } \Pr(\Delta_0 \rightarrow \Delta_1) = 1 \end{cases} \end{array} \right\}$$

is an optional set of values that may be assigned to the vector $\Delta_0 \| \Delta_1 \| u_0 \| u_1$. Accordingly, the weight of a possible propagation can be calculated as $u_0 + 6 \cdot u_1$. To ensure that $\Delta_0 \| \Delta_1 \| u_0 \| u_1$ never takes values outside of the set V, for each 18-bit vector $v \notin V$, we create the following clause[1] that may be a candidate for the SAT model of the S-box.

$$\bigvee_{i=0}^{7} (\Delta_0[i] \oplus v[i]) \vee \bigvee_{i=0}^{7} (\Delta_1[i] \oplus v[i+8]) \vee (u_0 \oplus v[16]) \vee (u_1 \oplus v[17]) = 1.$$

Note that this clause guarantees that $\Delta_0 \| \Delta_1 \| u_0 \| u_1$ will never equal v. These clauses comprise an initial version of the SAT model for the S-box. Because the size of the set $\mathbb{F}_2^{18} \setminus V$ is $2^{18} - 32386 = 229758$, using the initial version of the SAT model directly will inhibit the searching process of the automatic method. To reduce the size of the S-box model, we employ the Espresso[2] algorithm [9] to simplify the model. The final S-box SAT model is composed of 8728 clauses.

3.4 SAT Model for the Objective Function

We aim to discover differential characteristics with high probabilities. The objective function can be represented as $\sum_{i=0}^{\ell} u_i \leqslant w$, where u_i $(0 \leqslant i \leqslant \ell)$ are Boolean variables encoding the differential probability of possible propagations for S-boxes, and w is a predetermined upper limit for the weight of differential characteristics. The sequential encoding method [19] transforms this inequality into clauses.

Model 3 (Objective Function, [19]). *The following clauses provide validity assurance for the objective function* $\sum_{i=0}^{\ell} u_i \leqslant 0$.

$$\overline{u_i} = 1, 0 \leqslant i \leqslant \ell.$$

For the objective function $\sum_{i=0}^{\ell} u_i \leqslant w$ *with* $w > 0$*, it is necessary to incorporate auxiliary Boolean variables* $a_{i,j}$ $(0 \leqslant i \leqslant \ell - 1, 0 \leqslant j \leqslant w - 1)$*. The objective function is valid if the following clauses hold.*

---

[1] Given that $\Delta_0[i] \oplus v[i]$ equals $\Delta_0[i]$ or $\overline{\Delta_0[i]}$ contingent on the value of v_i, the expression is a clause.

[2] https://github.com/classabbyamp/espresso-logic contains a modern, compilable re-host of the Espresso heuristic logic minimizer.

$$\overline{u_0} \vee a_{0,0} = 1$$

$$\overline{a_{0,j}} = 1, \ 1 \leqslant j \leqslant w - 1$$

$$\left.\begin{array}{l} \overline{u_i} \vee a_{i,0} = 1 \\[4pt] \overline{a_{i-1,0}} \vee a_{i,0} = 1 \\[4pt] \left.\begin{array}{l} \overline{u_i} \vee \overline{a_{i-1,j-1}} \vee a_{i,j} = 1 \\[4pt] \overline{a_{i-1,j}} \vee a_{i,j} = 1 \end{array}\right\} 1 \leqslant j \leqslant w - 1 \\[4pt] \overline{u_i} \vee \overline{a_{i-1,w-1}} = 1 \end{array}\right\} 1 \leqslant i \leqslant \ell - 2$$

$$\overline{u_\ell} \vee \overline{a_{\ell-1,w-1}} = 1$$

3.5   Finding More Differential Characteristics in the Differential

We can identify differential characteristics with high probabilities using the models presented in Sects. 3.2 to 3.4. To improve the probability evaluation of the differential, we should fix the input and output differences in the automatic model and find as many other differential characteristics as feasible. An additional clause should be added to the SAT problem to prevent the solver from returning the same solution after obtaining a single differential characteristic. Assume that $v \in \mathbb{F}_2^\omega$ is a solution for the ω Boolean variables $x_0, x_1, \ldots, x_{\omega-1}$ returned by the SAT solver. Two index sets

$$v|_0 = \{i | 0 \leqslant i \leqslant \omega - 1 \text{ s.t. } v[i] = 0\} \text{ and } v|_1 = \{i | 0 \leqslant i \leqslant \omega - 1 \text{ s.t. } v[i] = 1\}.$$

are generated based on the value of v. Adding the clause

$$\bigvee_{i \in v|_0} x_i \vee \bigvee_{i \in v|_1} \overline{x_i} = 1$$

to the SAT problem guarantees that the solver will not find v again.

4   Differential Properties of HALFLOOP-48

This section demonstrates the differential properties of HALFLOOP-48 in the conventional, related-tweak, and related-key attack settings, which were derived using the method described in Sect. 3.

4.1   Conventional Differential Properties of HALFLOOP-48

In the standard differential attack, the lower bound on the number of active S-boxes, which are S-boxes with probabilistic differential propagations, and the upper bound on the differential probability are evaluated. Table 3 exhibits the outcomes from 1 to 10 rounds of HALFLOOP-48. The longest differential characteristic with a probability greater than 2^{-47} covers three rounds, and Fig. 3 depicts a 3-round differential characteristic with a probability of 2^{-33}.

Table 3. Differential properties of HALFLOOP-48.

Round	Standard setting		Related-tweak attack setting		Related-key attack setting	
	Active S-box	Probability	Active S-box	Probability	Active S-box	Probability
1	1	2^{-6}	0	1	0	1
2	4	2^{-24}	0	1	0	1
3	5	2^{-33}	0	1	0	1
4	8	2^{-50}	1	2^{-6}	1	2^{-6}
5	9	2^{-61}	3	2^{-20}	2	2^{-12}
6	12	2^{-78}	5	2^{-33}	5	2^{-30}
7	13	2^{-89}	8	2^{-53}	7	2^{-45}
8	16	2^{-105}	10	2^{-68}	7	2^{-47}
9	17	2^{-117}	13	2^{-88}	10	2^{-65}
10	20	2^{-133}	15	2^{-101}	12	2^{-80}

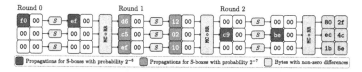

Fig. 3. A 3-round differential characteristic for HALFLOOP-48 with probability 2^{-33}.

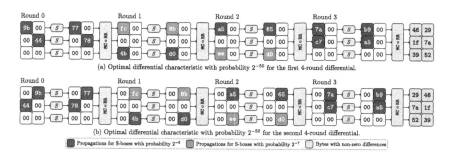

(a) Optimal differential characteristic with probability 2^{-50} for the first 4-round differential.

(b) Optimal differential characteristic with probability 2^{-50} for the second 4-round differential.

Fig. 4. Optimal characteristics for two 4-round differentials with probability $2^{-45.69}$.

We question the existence of a 4-round differential with a probability greater than 2^{-47}, although the probability of the optimal 4-round differential characteristic is less than 2^{-47}. To locate the solution, we narrow our search to four rounds and set the weight in the objective function of the SAT problem to 50. Four 4-round differential characteristics are obtained with a probability of 2^{-50}. After fixing the input and output differences in the SAT problem to those of the four newly discovered characteristics, we search for all differential characteristics with probabilities larger than 2^{-70} in the four differentials. Among the four differentials, we discover that two have accumulated probabilities of $2^{-45.69}$.

Figure 4 illustrates the best differential characteristics for these two differentials. Based on these results, we conclude that the resistance of HALFLOOP-48 to the single-tweak differential attack is high.

4.2 Related-Tweak Differential Properties of HALFLOOP-48

In the context of a related-tweak differential attack, the lower bound on the number of active S-boxes and the upper bound on the differential probability are determined. The test outcomes are shown in Table 3.

Table 4. Input differences for the 45 6-round related-tweak differential characteristics. The output difference is $\Delta_{out} = $ 0x160b53dbe0a1, and the tweak difference is $\Delta_{tweak} = $ 0xc9000000c9000000.

Trail	Δ_{in}	Trail	Δ_{in}	Trail	Δ_{in}
$\mathfrak{D}_0$	0xc9000000c950	$\mathfrak{D}_1$	0xc9000000c933	$\mathfrak{D}_2$	0xc90000005900
$\mathfrak{D}_3$	0xc9060000c900	$\mathfrak{D}_4$	0xc9920000c900	$\mathfrak{D}_5$	0xc9000016c900
$\mathfrak{D}_6$	0xc90000dac900	$\mathfrak{D}_7$	0xc90000f4c900	$\mathfrak{D}_8$	0xc9000010c900
$\mathfrak{D}_9$	0xc900005bc900	$\mathfrak{D}_{10}$	0xc900008ac900	$\mathfrak{D}_{11}$	0xc90000b2c900
$\mathfrak{D}_{12}$	0xc9000028c900	$\mathfrak{D}_{13}$	0xc900008cc900	$\mathfrak{D}_{14}$	0xc98f0000c900
$\mathfrak{D}_{15}$	0xc90000f6c900	$\mathfrak{D}_{16}$	0xc900007bc900	$\mathfrak{D}_{17}$	0xc90000c6c900
$\mathfrak{D}_{18}$	0xc90000ddc900	$\mathfrak{D}_{19}$	0xc90000bcc900	$\mathfrak{D}_{20}$	0xc90000a5c900
$\mathfrak{D}_{21}$	0xc90000dbc900	$\mathfrak{D}_{22}$	0xc90000aac900	$\mathfrak{D}_{23}$	0xc90000a7c900
$\mathfrak{D}_{24}$	0xc90000e1c900	$\mathfrak{D}_{25}$	0xc9000027c900	$\mathfrak{D}_{26}$	0xc900006bc900
$\mathfrak{D}_{27}$	0xc90000e8c900	$\mathfrak{D}_{28}$	0xc9000077c900	$\mathfrak{D}_{29}$	0xc9000081c900
$\mathfrak{D}_{30}$	0xc90000f0c900	$\mathfrak{D}_{31}$	0xc9000040c900	$\mathfrak{D}_{32}$	0xc9cc0000c900
$\mathfrak{D}_{33}$	0xc9250000c900	$\mathfrak{D}_{34}$	0xc99f0000c900	$\mathfrak{D}_{35}$	0xc9870000c900
$\mathfrak{D}_{36}$	0xc99e0000c900	$\mathfrak{D}_{37}$	0xc94e0000c900	$\mathfrak{D}_{38}$	0xc900002cc900
$\mathfrak{D}_{39}$	0xc9000084c900	$\mathfrak{D}_{40}$	0xc900008dc900	$\mathfrak{D}_{41}$	0xc90000d4c900
$\mathfrak{D}_{42}$	0xc900e400c900	$\mathfrak{D}_{43}$	0xc9000000c94b	$\mathfrak{D}_{44}$	0xc90000a9c900

The longest effective differential characteristic is six rounds long. The SAT solver reveals that 45 6-round related-tweak differential characteristics have a probability of 2^{-33}. These differential characteristics, denoted $\mathfrak{D}_0$, $\mathfrak{D}_1$, ..., $\mathfrak{D}_{44}$, have the same output difference $\Delta_{out} = $ 0x160b53dbe0a1 and tweak difference $\Delta_{tweak} = $ 0xc9000000c9000000. Table 4 displays the input differences of the 45 six-round characteristics. The 45 6-round related-tweak differentials generated by the 45 differential characteristics are then analysed. Fixing the input, output, and tweak differences in the SAT problem, we then search for all differential characteristics with probabilities greater than 2^{-60} for each of the 45 differentials. The probability of the optimal differential among them is $2^{-29.48}$, and the best differential characteristic within this differential is $\mathfrak{D}_{40}$. Figure 5 shows the 6-round related-tweak differential characteristic $\mathfrak{D}_{40}$. The validity of the differential is checked with 2^{32} randomly generated pairs of plaintexts, and the test is repeated using 32 random pairs of keys and tweaks. The probability of tests is $2^{-29.45}$ on average.

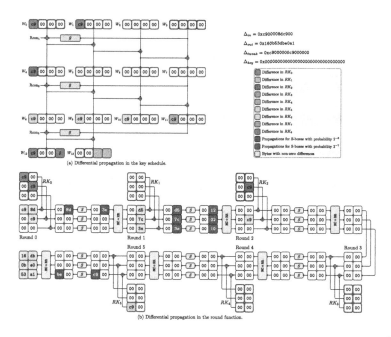

Fig. 5. 6-round related-tweak differential characteristic $\mathfrak{D}_{40}$ with probability 2^{-33}. δ is a non-zero difference, ensuring that $\texttt{0xc9} \rightarrow \delta$ is a valid propagation for the S-box.

Similar to the case in the conventional differential attack scenario, we question the existence of 7-round related-tweak differentials with probabilities greater than 2^{-47}, despite the probability of the optimal 7-round related-tweak differential characteristic being 2^{-53}. To determine the answer, we first discover eight 7-round related-tweak differential characteristics with probabilities of 2^{-53}. Then, we fix the input, output, and tweak differences of the SAT problem and look for all differential characteristics with probabilities greater than 2^{-70} for each of the eight 7-round differentials. All eight differentials have accumulated probabilities below 2^{-48}. Therefore, the optimal related-tweak differential that can be used in the differential attack consists of six rounds.

4.3   Related-Key Differential Properties of HALFLOOP-48

Note that if both the key and tweak differences are permitted to be non-zero, the conditions $\Delta T_0 = \Delta K_0$, $\Delta T_1 = \Delta K_1$, and $\Delta K_2 = \Delta K_3 = \text{0x00000000}$ will lead to trivial differential characteristics with all internal state differences being zero. Consequently, in the related-key attack setting, we focus on the differential properties of HALFLOOP-48 with non-zero key differences and zero tweak differences. The results of analysing the lower bound on the number of active S-boxes and the upper bound on the differential probability are presented in Table 3.

The longest related-key differential characteristic, with a probability greater than 2^{-47}, achieves eight rounds. We check with the SAT solver that there is only one 8-round related-key differential characteristic with probability being 2^{-47}, which is demonstrated in Fig. 6. The unique 8-round related-key differential generated by this characteristic is then analysed. We try to find all differential characteristics with probabilities greater than 2^{-70} within this differential and find that its accumulated differential probability is $2^{-46.88}$.

Since the probability of the 8-round differential is marginal, we also investigate the 7-round differential characteristics and differentials. There are five 7-round differential characteristics with probabilities of 2^{-45}, as determined by the SAT solver. The five differentials resulting from these differential characteristics are then evaluated. After fixing the input, output, and key differences in the SAT problem, we search exhaustively for all differential characteristics with probabilities greater than 2^{-70} for each of the five 7-round differentials. The experimental results indicate that the accumulative influence of these differentials is negligible, and their accumulated probabilities are nearly identical to 2^{-45}. Table 5 provides information on the five 7-round differentials.

Table 5. Information on the five 7-round related-key differentials.

Trail	Δ_{in}	Δ_{out}	Δ_{key}
$\mathcal{RD}_0$	0x0a002132f800	0x201090bdbf3c	0x0a0021324800213242000000000000000000
$\mathcal{RD}_1$	0x640008481000	0x232046d57c3e	0x6400084874000848100000000000000000
$\mathcal{RD}_2$	0x640008481000	0xe850c7d691c8	0x6400084874000848100000000000000000
$\mathcal{RD}_3$	0xc700260de800	0x61bd220c0636	0xc700260d8b00260d4c00000000000000000
$\mathcal{RD}_4$	0x640008481000	0x54bfc3c49889	0x6400084874000848100000000000000000

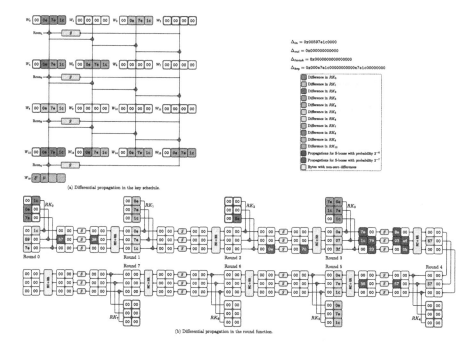

Fig. 6. 8-round related-key differential characteristic with probability 2^{-47}. δ' is a non-zero difference that ensures $\texttt{0x0e} \to \delta'$ is a possible propagation for the S-box. $\mu \oplus \texttt{0x0e}$ should be non-zero, and the propagation $\texttt{0x7e} \to \mu \oplus \texttt{0x0e}$ for the S-box should be valid.

5 Differential Attacks on HALFLOOP-48

This section describes the 8-round related-tweak differential attack (see Sect. 5.1) and the 10-round related-key differential attack (see Sect. 5.2) for HALFLOOP-48.

5.1 Related-Tweak Differential Attack on HALFLOOP-48

Using the 6-round related-tweak differential with probability $2^{-29.48}$ from Sect. 4.2, we launch an 8-round related-tweak differential attack in this subsection. In the attack, two rounds are added after the distinguisher, and the key-recovery process is depicted in Fig. 7. To reduce complexity, we swap the order of the $\texttt{MC} \circ \texttt{RR}$ operation in the 6-th round with the $\texttt{ARK}$ operation in the 7-th round. $\overline{RK}_7$ represents the equivalent round key $\texttt{RR}^{-1} \circ \texttt{MC}^{-1}(RK_7)$.

In the attack, $\mathcal{S}$ structures are prepared. There are 2^{24} plaintexts within each structure such that three bytes $P[0, 3, 4]$ of the state P traverse all possible values while the remaining bytes are fixed to random constants. Then, 2^{23} pairs with a difference of ΔP can be constructed with a single structure, bringing the total number of pairs to $N = \mathcal{S} \cdot 2^{23}$. Consequently, the attack has a data complexity of $\mathcal{S} \cdot 2^{24}$ chosen-plaintexts.

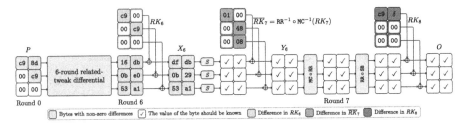

Fig. 7. 8-round related-tweak differential attack on HALFLOOP-48. As illustrated in Fig. 5(a), δ must satisfy certain conditions.

For each 56-bit possible value of $RK_5[5] \| RK_7[2] \| RK_8[0\text{-}2, 4, 5]$, we initialise an empty table $\mathbb{T}$. The value (Y_6, Y_6') is calculated and inserted into the table $\mathbb{T}$ for each pair (O, O') obtained from the encryption oracle. This step, which corresponds to line 8 of Algorithm 1, has a time complexity of $T_{\ell 8} = 2^{56} \cdot \mathcal{S} \cdot 2^{23} \cdot 2 = \mathcal{S} \cdot 2^{80}$ one-round encryptions. Then, we guess the value of $\overline{RK}_7[0]$ and compute $\Delta X_6[0]$ for every (Y_6, Y_6') in $\mathbb{T}$. The pairs that result in $\Delta X_6[0] \neq \mathtt{0xdf}$ are removed from table $\mathbb{T}$. This step, which corresponds to line 11 of Algorithm 1, has a maximum time complexity of $T_{\ell 11} = 2^{56+8} \cdot \mathcal{S} \cdot 2^{23} \cdot 2 \cdot 1/6 = \mathcal{S} \cdot 2^{85.42}$ one-round encryptions. Note that the number of pairs in $\mathbb{T}$ is reduced to $\mathcal{S} \cdot 2^{15}$ after this phase. Following this, the remaining five bytes of $\overline{RK}_7$ are guessed one at a time, with the specific procedure described in Algorithm 1. Time complexity during the enumeration of $\overline{RK}_7$ also includes $T_{\ell 15} = \mathcal{S} \cdot 2^{85.42}$, $T_{\ell 18} = \mathcal{S} \cdot 2^{77.42}$, $T_{\ell 21} = \mathcal{S} \cdot 2^{77.42}$, and $T_{\ell 24} = \mathcal{S} \cdot 2^{77.42}$.

Based on an analysis of Algorithm 1, the number of remaining pairs Cnt in $\mathbb{T}$ follows the binomial distribution $\mathcal{B}(N, p_0 = 2^{-29.48})$ for a correct key guess and $\mathcal{B}(N, p = 2^{-48})$ otherwise. We set the threshold τ for the number of right pairs at three and the success probability P_S at 90%. After plugging these values into Eq. (1), we find that $\mathcal{S} = 2^{9.27}$ and $\beta = 2^{-49.74}$. Consequently, the attack has a data complexity of $2^{33.27}$ chosen-plaintexts. The time complexity of enumerating $\overline{RK}_7 \| RK_8$ is $T_1 = (T_{\ell 8} + T_{\ell 11} + T_{\ell 15} + \cdots + T_{\ell 24})/8 = 2^{92.71}$ 8-round encryptions. $T_2 = 2^{128} \cdot \beta \cdot (1 + 2^{-48} + 2^{-96}) = 2^{78.26}$ 8-round encryptions are required to seek exhaustively for the remaining 32-bit key. The total time complexity of the attack is, therefore, $T_1 + T_2 = 2^{92.71}$ 8-round encryptions. The memory complexity of the attack is approximately $2^{33.27} \cdot 2 \cdot 6 = 2^{36.85}$ bytes, given that table $\mathbb{T}$ dominates memory consumption.

Algorithm 1: 8-round related-tweak differential attack

1   Create $\mathcal{S} \cdot 2^{23}$ pairs (P, P') from $\mathcal{S}$ structures
2   Obtain the value of (O, O') for each (P, P') by querying the encryption oracle
3   **foreach** *16-bit possible values of* $RK_5[5] \| RK_7[2]$ **do**
4   Compute the value of $(RK_8[3], RK'_8[3])$
5   **foreach** *40-bit possible values of* $RK_8[0\text{-}2, 4, 5]$ **do**
6   Initialise an empty table $\mathbb{T}$
7   **foreach** $\mathcal{S} \cdot 2^{23}$ *pairs* (O, O') **do**
8   Calculate (Y_6, Y'_6) and insert the result into $\mathbb{T}$
9   **end**
10   **foreach** *8-bit possible values of* $\overline{RK}_7[0]$ **do**
11   Compute $\Delta X_6[0]$ for each (Y_6, Y'_6) in $\mathbb{T}$
12   Remove from $\mathbb{T}$ the pair (Y_6, Y'_6) if $\Delta X_6[0] \neq \texttt{0xdf}$
13   **foreach** *8-bit possible values of* $\overline{RK}_7[1]$ **do**
14   Compute $\overline{RK}_7[2]$ with $\overline{RK}_7[0, 1] \| RK_7[2]$
15   Compute $\Delta X_6[1, 2]$ for each (Y_6, Y'_6) in $\mathbb{T}$
16   Remove from $\mathbb{T}$ the pair (Y_6, Y'_6) if $\Delta X_6[1, 2] \neq \texttt{0x0b53}$
17   **foreach** *8-bit possible values of* $\overline{RK}_7[3]$ **do**
18   Compute $\Delta X_6[3]$ for each (Y_6, Y'_6) in $\mathbb{T}$
19   Remove from $\mathbb{T}$ the pair (Y_6, Y'_6) if $\Delta X_6[3] \neq \texttt{0xdb}$
20   **foreach** *8-bit possible values of* $\overline{RK}_7[4]$ **do**
21   Compute $\Delta X_6[4]$ for each (Y_6, Y'_6) in $\mathbb{T}$
22   Remove from $\mathbb{T}$ the pair (Y_6, Y'_6) if $\Delta X_6[4] \neq \texttt{0x29}$
23   **foreach** *8-bit possible values of* $\overline{RK}_7[5]$ **do**
24   Compute $\Delta X_6[5]$ for each (Y_6, Y'_6) in $\mathbb{T}$
25   Remove (Y_6, Y'_6) from $\mathbb{T}$ if $\Delta X_6[5] \neq \texttt{0xa1}$
26   Count the number of pairs Cnt remaining in $\mathbb{T}$
27   **if** $Cnt \geqslant \tau$ **then**
28   Test exhaustively each of the 2^{32} master keys compatible with $\overline{RK}_7 \| RK_8$ using three plaintext-ciphertext pairs
29   **end**
30   **end**
31   **end**
32   **end**
33   **end**
34   **end**
35   **end**
36   **end**

5.2   Full-Round Related-Key Differential Attack on HALFLOOP-48

In the following, we employ the 8-round related-key differential with probability $2^{-46.88}$ from Sect. 4.3 to launch a full-round related-key differential attack. After the distinguisher, two rounds are added, and the key-recovery process is depicted in Fig. 8. Likewise, we use the equivalent round key $\overline{RK}_9 = \texttt{RR}^{-1} \circ \texttt{MC}^{-1}(RK_9)$ to reduce complexity.

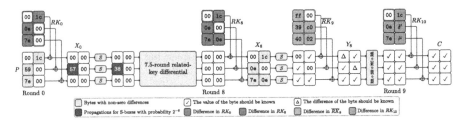

Fig. 8. Full-round related-key differential attack on HALFLOOP-48. As illustrated in Fig. 6(a), δ' and μ must satisfy certain conditions.

$\mathcal{S}$ structures are prepared for the attack. Each structure contains 2^{24} plaintexts such that three bytes $P[1\text{-}3]$ of the state P traverse all possible values while the remaining bytes are fixed to random constants. There are a total of $N = \mathcal{S} \cdot 2^{23}$ pairs involved in the attack.

For each possible 48-bit value of $RK_8[0,1] \| RK_{10}[0\text{-}3]$, we initialise an empty table $\mathbb{T}$. The value (Y_8, Y_8') is calculated for each pair (C, C') returned by the encryption oracle. If $\Delta Y_8[0,4] = \texttt{0xffc0}$, the pair $(Y_8[1\text{-}3,5], Y_8'[1\text{-}3,5])$ is inserted into $\mathbb{T}$. This step, which corresponds to line 8 of Algorithm 2, requires $T_{\ell 8} = 2^{48} \cdot \mathcal{S} \cdot 2^{23} \cdot 2 = \mathcal{S} \cdot 2^{72}$ one-round encryptions to complete. $\mathbb{T}$ contains approximately $\mathcal{S} \cdot 2^7$ pairs. Then we guess the value of $\overline{RK}_9[1]$ and calculate $\Delta X_8[1]$ for each pair in $\mathbb{T}$. The pairs in table $\mathbb{T}$ that result in $\Delta X_8[1] \neq \texttt{0x0e}$ are removed. This step, which corresponds to line 14 of Algorithm 2, has a maximum time complexity of $T_{\ell 14} = 2^{48+8} \cdot \mathcal{S} \cdot 2^7 \cdot 2 \cdot 1/6 = \mathcal{S} \cdot 2^{61.42}$ one-round encryptions. After this step, the number of pairs in $\mathbb{T}$ is reduced to $\mathcal{S} \cdot 2^{-1}$. Then, the three bytes $\overline{RK}_9[2,3,5]$ are estimated one at a time using the procedure described in Algorithm 2. During the enumeration of $\overline{RK}_9$, time complexity also incorporates $T_{\ell 17}$, $T_{\ell 20}$, and $T_{\ell 23}$. Each is capable of up to $\mathcal{S} \cdot 2^{61.42}$ one-round encryptions.

The number of remaining pairs Cnt in $\mathbb{T}$ follows the binomial distribution $\mathcal{B}(N, p_0 = 2^{-46.88})$ for a correct key guess and $\mathcal{B}(N, p = 2^{-48})$ otherwise, according to Algorithm 2. The threshold τ for the number of right pairs is set to one, and the success probability P_S is set to 50%. We determine $\mathcal{S} = 2^{23.34}$ and $\beta = 2^{-1.88}$ based on the property of the binomial distribution. Consequently, the data complexity of the attack is $2^{47.34}$ chosen-plaintexts. $T_1 = (T_{\ell 8} + T_{\ell 14} + T_{\ell 17} + T_{\ell 20} + T_{\ell 23})/10 = 2^{92.02}$ full-round encryptions are required to enumerate $RK_8[0,1] \| \overline{RK}_9[1\text{-}3,5] \| RK_{10}[0\text{-}3]$. Since the first round of the 8-round distinguisher always propagates the input difference $\texttt{0x57}$ to the output difference $\texttt{0x38}$, there are only four possible values for $X_0[1]$, namely $\texttt{0x00}$, $\texttt{0x57}$, $\texttt{0xaf}$, and $\texttt{0xf8}$. This restriction, which corresponds to line 28 of Algorithm 2, allows us to filter the $2^{128} \cdot \beta$ key candidates with a probability of 2^{-6}. The key schedule is viewed as a 2-round encryption. This step has a maximum time complexity of $T_2 = 2^{128} \cdot \beta \cdot 2/10 = 2^{123.80}$ full-round encryptions. The remaining master keys are then evaluated with three plaintext-ciphertext pairs, with a time complexity of $T_3 = 2^{128} \cdot \beta \cdot 2^{-6} \cdot (1 + 2^{-48} + 2^{-96}) = 2^{120.12}$ full-round encryptions. Therefore, the total time complexity of the attack is $T_1 + T_2 + T_3 = 2^{123.91}$ full-round encryptions. The memory complexity of the

---

Algorithm 2: full-round related-key differential attack

---

1 Create $\mathcal{S} \cdot 2^{23}$ pairs (P, P') from $\mathcal{S}$ structures
2 Obtain the value of (C, C') for each (P, P') by querying the encryption oracle
3 **foreach** *16-bit possible values of* $RK_8[0,1]$ **do**
4   **foreach** *32-bit possible values of* $RK_{10}[0\text{-}3]$ **do**
5   Compute $RK_{10}[4,5]$ with $RK_8[0,1]\|RK_{10}[0\text{-}3]$
6   Initialise an empty table $\mathbb{T}$
7   **foreach** $\mathcal{S} \cdot 2^{23}$ *pairs* (C, C') **do**
8   Calculate (Y_8, Y_8')
9   **if** $\Delta Y_8[0,4] = \texttt{0xffc0}$ **then**
10   Insert $(Y_8[1\text{-}3,5], Y_8'[1\text{-}3,5])$ into $\mathbb{T}$
11   **end**
12   **end**
13   **foreach** *8-bit possible values of* $\overline{RK}_9[1]$ **do**
14   Compute $\Delta X_8[1]$ for each pair in $\mathbb{T}$
15   Remove from $\mathbb{T}$ the pair if $\Delta X_8[1] \neq \texttt{0x0e}$
16   **foreach** *8-bit possible values of* $\overline{RK}_9[2]$ **do**
17   Compute $\Delta X_8[2]$ for each pair in $\mathbb{T}$
18   Remove from $\mathbb{T}$ the pair if $\Delta X_8[2] \neq \texttt{0x7e}$
19   **foreach** *8-bit possible values of* $\overline{RK}_9[3]$ **do**
20   Compute $\Delta X_8[3]$ for each pair in $\mathbb{T}$
21   Remove from $\mathbb{T}$ the pair if $\Delta X_8[3] \neq \texttt{0x1c}$
22   **foreach** *8-bit possible values of* $\overline{RK}_9[5]$ **do**
23   Compute $\Delta X_8[5]$ for each pair in $\mathbb{T}$
24   Remove from $\mathbb{T}$ the pair if $\Delta X_8[5] \neq \texttt{0x0e}$
25   Count the number of pairs Cnt remaining in $\mathbb{T}$
26   **if** $Cnt \geqslant \tau$ **then**
27   **for** 2^{48} *keys compatible with* $\overline{RK}_9[1\text{-}3,5]\|RK_{10}$ **do**
28   Compute $(X_0[1], X_0'[1])$ of the right pair(s)
29   **if** $X_0[1], X_0'[1] \in \{\texttt{0x00}, \texttt{0x57}, \texttt{0xaf}, \texttt{0xf8}\}$ **then**
30   Use three plaintext-ciphertext pairs to test the key
31   **end**
32   **end**
33   **end**
34   **end**
35   **end**
36   **end**
37   **end**
38   **end**
39 **end**

---

attack is approximately $2^{23.34} \cdot 2^7 \cdot 4 \cdot 2 = 2^{33.34}$ bytes, given that the table $\mathbb{T}$ dominates memory consumption.

6   Conclusion

This paper focuses on the differential property of the tweakable block cipher HALFLOOP-48 and presents its first public non-generic cryptanalysis. The search for differential characteristics and differentials is modelled as SAT problems. We use the SAT solver to determine the lower bound for the number of active S-boxes and the upper bound for the differential probability in the conventional, related-tweak, and related-key differential attack settings. Using the newly discovered 6-round related-tweak differential with probability $2^{-29.48}$, an 8-round related-tweak differential attack is launched against HALFLOOP-48. We also present a full-round related-key differential attack against HALFLOOP-48 using the newly obtained 8-round related-key differential with probability $2^{-46.88}$. Due to their impractical complexity, the attacks described in this paper do not pose an actual security risk to HALFLOOP-48. Nevertheless, caution must be taken to prevent misuse, as our analysis indicates no secure margin in the related-key attack setting.

Acknowledgements. The research leading to these results has received funding from the National Natural Science Foundation of China (Grant No. 62272273, Grant No. 62002201, Grant No. 62032014), the National Key Research and Development Program of China (Grant No. 2018YFA0704702), and the Major Basic Research Project of Natural Science Foundation of Shandong Province, China (Grant No. ZR202010220025). Ling Sun gratefully acknowledges the support by the Program of TaiShan Scholars Special Fund for young scholars.

References

1. Interoperability and performance standards for medium and high frequency radio systems. United States Department of Defense Interface Standard MIL-STD-188-141D
2. Specification for the advanced encryption standard (AES). Federal Information Processing Standards Publication 197 (2001)
3. Abdelkhalek, A., Sasaki, Y., Todo, Y., Tolba, M., Youssef, A.M.: MILP modeling for (large) S-boxes to optimize probability of differential characteristics. IACR Trans. Symmetric Cryptol. **2017**(4), 99–129 (2017)
4. Ankele, R., Kölbl, S.: Mind the gap - a closer look at the security of block ciphers against differential cryptanalysis. In: Cid, C., Jr., M.J.J. (eds.) Selected Areas in Cryptography - SAC 2018. LNCS, vol. 11349, pp. 163–190. Springer, Cham (2018). https://doi.org/10.1007/978-3-030-10970-7_8
5. Biham, E., Shamir, A.: Differential cryptanalysis of des-like cryptosystems. In: Menezes, A.J., Vanstone, S.A. (eds.) CRYPTO 1990. LNCS, vol. 537, pp. 2–21. Springer, Heidelberg (1991). https://doi.org/10.1007/3-540-38424-3_1
6. Biryukov, A., Roy, A., Velichkov, V.: Differential analysis of block ciphers SIMON and SPECK. In: Cid, C., Rechberger, C. (eds.) FSE 2014. LNCS, vol. 8540, pp. 546–570. Springer, Heidelberg (2015). https://doi.org/10.1007/978-3-662-46706-0_28

7. Blondeau, C., Gérard, B., Tillich, J.: Accurate estimates of the data complexity and success probability for various cryptanalyses. Des. Codes Cryptogr. **59**(1–3), 3–34 (2011)
8. Boura, C., Coggia, D.: Efficient MILP modelings for Sboxes and linear layers of SPN ciphers. IACR Trans. Symmetric Cryptol. **2020**(3), 327–361 (2020)
9. Brayton, R.K., Hachtel, G.D., McMullen, C.T., Sangiovanni-Vincentelli, A.L.: Logic Minimization Algorithms for VLSI Synthesis, The Kluwer International Series in Engineering and Computer Science, vol. 2. Springer, New York (1984). https://doi.org/10.1007/978-1-4613-2821-6
10. Cook, S.A.: The complexity of theorem-proving procedures. In: Harrison, M.A., Banerji, R.B., Ullman, J.D. (eds.) Proceedings of the 3rd Annual ACM Symposium on Theory of Computing, May 3–5, 1971, Shaker Heights, Ohio, USA, pp. 151–158. ACM (1971)
11. Daemen, J., Rijmen, V.: The Design of Rijndael: AES - The Advanced Encryption Standard. Information Security and Cryptography, Springer, Heidelberg (2002). https://doi.org/10.1007/978-3-662-04722-4
12. Dansarie, M., Derbez, P., Leander, G., Stennes, L.: Breaking HALFLOOP-24. IACR Trans. Symmetric Cryptol. **2022**(3), 217–238 (2022)
13. Kim, S., Hong, D., Sung, J., Hong, S.: Accelerating the best trail search on AES-like ciphers. IACR Trans. Symmetric Cryptol. **2022**(2), 201–252 (2022)
14. Li, T., Sun, Y.: Superball: a new approach for MILP modelings of Boolean functions. IACR Trans. Symmetric Cryptol. **2022**(3), 341–367 (2022)
15. Liu, Y., et al.: STP models of optimal differential and linear trail for S-box based ciphers. Sci. China Inf. Sci. **64**(5), 159103 (2021)
16. Liu, Y., Wang, Q., Rijmen, V.: Automatic search of linear trails in ARX with applications to SPECK and Chaskey. In: Manulis, M., Sadeghi, A.-R., Schneider, S. (eds.) ACNS 2016. LNCS, vol. 9696, pp. 485–499. Springer, Cham (2016). https://doi.org/10.1007/978-3-319-39555-5_26
17. Matsui, M.: On correlation between the order of S-boxes and the strength of DES. In: De Santis, A. (ed.) EUROCRYPT 1994. LNCS, vol. 950, pp. 366–375. Springer, Heidelberg (1995). https://doi.org/10.1007/BFb0053451
18. Mouha, N., Wang, Q., Gu, D., Preneel, B.: Differential and linear cryptanalysis using mixed-integer linear programming. In: Wu, C.-K., Yung, M., Lin, D. (eds.) Inscrypt 2011. LNCS, vol. 7537, pp. 57–76. Springer, Heidelberg (2012). https://doi.org/10.1007/978-3-642-34704-7_5
19. Sinz, C.: Towards an optimal CNF encoding of Boolean cardinality constraints. In: van Beek, P. (ed.) CP 2005. LNCS, vol. 3709, pp. 827–831. Springer, Heidelberg (2005). https://doi.org/10.1007/11564751_73
20. Soos, M., Nohl, K., Castelluccia, C.: Extending SAT solvers to cryptographic problems. In: Kullmann, O. (ed.) SAT 2009. LNCS, vol. 5584, pp. 244–257. Springer, Heidelberg (2009). https://doi.org/10.1007/978-3-642-02777-2_24
21. Sun, B., Liu, Z., Rijmen, V., Li, R., Cheng, L., Wang, Q., Alkhzaimi, H., Li, C.: Links among impossible differential, integral and zero correlation linear cryptanalysis. In: Gennaro, R., Robshaw, M. (eds.) CRYPTO 2015. LNCS, vol. 9215, pp. 95–115. Springer, Heidelberg (2015). https://doi.org/10.1007/978-3-662-47989-6_5
22. Sun, L., Wang, M.: SOK: modeling for large S-boxes oriented to differential probabilities and linear correlations. IACR Trans. Symmetric Cryptol. **2023**(1), 111–151 (2023)
23. Sun, L., Wang, W., Wang, M.: More accurate differential properties of LED64 and Midori64. IACR Trans. Symmetric Cryptol. **2018**(3), 93–123 (2018)

Users and Usability

How Users Investigate Phishing Emails that Lack Traditional Phishing Cues

Daniel Köhler$^{(\boxtimes)}$ [iD], Wenzel Pünter [iD], and Christoph Meinel

Hasso Plattner Institute, University of Potsdam, Potsdam, Germany
{daniel.koehler,wenzel.puenter}@hpi.de

Abstract. Phishing is still one of the prevalent threats targeting private persons and organizations. Current teaching best practices often advocate cue-based investigation methods. Previous research primarily confronted participants with phishing emails showing such indicators to assess the success of different education measures. Our large-scale mixed-methods study challenges the behavior of 4,729 participants with four phishing emails that lack technical cues. The phishing emails concerned entirely fictitious entities and were directed at participants in their private lives, recruited from the online education platform *openHPI*. For our analysis, we apply the human-in-the-loop model for interaction with phishing content to investigate participant behavior when their learned best practices for detection fail. The primary indicator of enhanced phishing resiliency observed in our study was awareness of missing context to the supposed entity. Such context is often successfully enhanced by web searches, significantly contributing to decreased phishing susceptibility.

Keywords: Phishing Investigation · Cybersecurity Awareness · User Study

1 Introduction

Phishing, social engineering delivered via emails and other communication channels [29], has been the primary initial access vector used by cyber threat actors in 2022 [6]. In phishing campaigns, the adversary often tries to trick users into entering sensitive information on a malicious website [29] or to lure the user into performing a self-harming action [7]. This goal is often achieved by impersonating a legitimate third-party entity known to the target and counterfeiting its website and branding.

Due to the high practical relevance of this threat vector, fellow researchers have published numerous works on technical and human aspects of phishing in the past. Examples include aspects of phishing emails that drive their persuasiveness [21,26], such as logos and images [37]. Other research on phishing has investigated how socio-demographic features of targets impact their susceptibility [11,13,28], or how technical measures such as highlighting external emails enhance protection [39]. Traditional phishing education often covers technical or

© The Author(s), under exclusive license to Springer Nature Switzerland AG 2024
C. Pöpper and L. Batina (Eds.): ACNS 2024, LNCS 14585, pp. 381–411, 2024.
https://doi.org/10.1007/978-3-031-54776-8_15

psychological cues and triggers used inside phishing emails, such as typosquatting, to sensitize users for these indicators. In professional contexts, such education is often performed using embedded phishing training programs [1,25]. For laypersons outside professional contexts, central (e.g., governmental) institutions attempt to provide cybersecurity awareness programs by similarly highlighting common cues to identify phishing [2,3,12]. With a population primed to expect and suspect learned cues and technical features of phishing emails, such as manipulated email senders and links, we investigate the following research question, to the best of our knowledge never explicitly studied before:

Research Question How do people investigate phishing emails that lack traditional (technical) cues for phishing?

We performed a mixed-methods study combining quantitative results from a phishing study with qualitative results obtained in a post-study survey. We designed the phishing study according to *Staged Innovation Design*, allowing us to introduce new participants and thereby study an unbiased group of participants in each of our four interventions. We studied a total of 4,729 participants in overly private contexts recruited from the online education platform *openHPI*, to which we sent more than 14,000 phishing emails, all concerning entirely fictitious entities, without technical indicators for phishing, such as manipulated email headers, links using typosquatting, or impersonation of other companies. We obtained quantitative insights into the target variables of *link click* and *data submitted*. In a separate publication, we investigated the quantitative results of participant's socio-demographic features towards the target variables, identifying that male participants, who are particularly young or old and of lower levels of education, are more susceptible to falling victim to phishing attacks [15].

To achieve additional qualitative insights into participants' investigation processes when challenged with the emails, we collected survey answers from 950 participants. We map participants' investigation approaches to the human-in-the-loop (HITL) model, which describes the process people follow for phishing investigation, as systematized in previous studies with smaller participant groups [20,33,35]. During our analysis in Sect. 6, we touch on human interaction with phishing content, from investigative approaches to time spent on web pages. We thereby foster three main contributions to the body of research:

Contribution 1 We map survey responses from a large-scale real-world phishing study to the HITL model contributing to the systematization of human phishing investigation behavior. We present three resulting taxonomies in Sect. 6.1.

Contribution 2 We observe that identification of (missing) context during the phases of *Expect* and *Suspect* in the HITL model significantly decreases *link click* and *data submission* rates of participants (cf. Section 7.1).

Contribution 3 In Sect. 7.2, we identify and discuss that web searches used to generate more context on the entity or topic posed in the email significantly helped participants identify our emails as phishing.

2 Background

Phishing is a form of social engineering that can be modeled as a cycle of interactions between attacker and victim, influencing a victim's trust and subsequent
actions [18]. Victims receive and assess phishing emails. Upon following phishing
links and visiting web pages, they face new, convincing information from attackers, which they must contextualize to decide how to act. These interactions can
be described using a human-in-the-loop model [5]. *Wash* and *Nthala* identified
a process that both experts [33] and non-experts [20, 35] follow when investigating a piece of (phishing) content, deriving the HITL model for phishing email
investigation. It consists of the following steps:

1. **Noticing** While viewing a piece of content (e.g., mail, website), humans
   extract features like the type of email, context, sender, layout, or URL format.
2. **Expecting** People subconsciously compare the noticed content features to
   their expectations.
3. **Suspecting** When features deviate from the expectation or trigger a learned
   cue, suspiciousness emerges.
4. **Investigating** When suspiciousness is raised, people begin with investigative behavior like hovering over or following links, reading the imprint, or
   contacting the sender.
5. **Deciding** Based on the investigation, humans decide how to interact with
   the content or collect more info.
6. **Acting** Depending on the result, people might respond differently to a message (e.g., continue, delete, or ignore).

3 Related Work

Fellow researchers have already studied various parts of the phishing landscape.
Previous studies on the effectiveness of cybersecurity awareness education, particularly phishing, usually focused on highlighting technical cues to identify
maliciousness [4, 26]. As such, fellow researchers have explored URLs [8, 27, 36],
spelling and grammar [10, 22], visual cues such as images and logos [10, 21, 22] as
only few of the core criteria used to assess phishing emails.

Other researchers have evaluated approaches such as story-based education
[34], which still used technical best practices such as *"Hover over a link to see
where it really goes to"* as taken from *Wash and Cooper's* 2018 study [34]. Contrasting, *Jensen et al.* have started to evaluate approaches to enhance mindfulness during email analysis [14]. Mindfulness in the respective study was triggered through considerations of the context of the email, such as *"Why would
the sender need me to do this?"*. The authors identify that while mindfulness
approaches help participants with high email skills, they cannot replace cue-
based approaches like those highlighted previously.

Mindfulness training, as used by *Nguyen et al.* [19] and *Jensen et al.* [14],
supports the assumption that more strongly assessing email context should be

the key to achieving more resilience against phishing attacks. Still, many educational programs we observed in the wild focus on rule-based phishing training. Such educational programs attempt to provide users with rules (e.g., *Check for the spelling of the domain*) to educate users on what they should be looking out for. However, to the best of our knowledge, analyzing emails without cues for phishing is missing from previous research.

Wash and *Nthala* have previously worked on the human-in-the-loop model, which we use as a foundation for our study. *Wash* initially interviewed 21 experts on instances where they successfully identified phishing attacks in an exploratory study [33]. Based on the HITL model, he derived a process that expert users follow to identify and assess phishing emails. Building on this process, *Wash, Nthala, and Rader* surveyed 297 non-experts from the US on their experiences with phishing emails [35], identifying that the investigation process of non-expert users is similar to the process of experts. *Nthala and Wash* verified the previous findings in a study with 31 non-expert users, sending them a phishing message and interviewing them on their experience with the email [20]. They highlight that non-expert users often depend on their social connections, unlike expert users who primarily rely on technical investigations.

The previous studies on HITL models relied on interviews. Hence, the number of participants was limited. In our study, we expand the number of studied users, further challenging them with a larger variety of emails, thereby contributing to contextualizing real-world phishing investigation processes. As we track participants' actual behavior, our study allows quantifying the success of individual investigation measures mentioned by the participants.

4   Method and Study Design

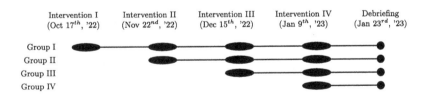

Fig. 1. Overview of our *Staged Innovation Design* study and timeline in which we ran it. *Debriefing* is explained in Sect. 4.2.

Our study's quantitative-qualitative mixed-methods approach combines a large-scale field study with a survey for qualitative reflection of participants' behavior during the study. The study has been designed according to *Staged Innovation Design* [32], whereby we introduce participant groups into the study across four different phishing interventions. During each intervention, participants receive a phishing email containing a link to a phishing website asking for personal data and credentials. For the analysis, we aggregated participant behavior across the emails. We use the terminology of *intervention* taken from educational research referring to the times in which researchers interact with study participants, such as sending a phishing email in our case. The interventions were distributed in approximately four-week intervals (cf. Figure 1) to exceed knowledge retention periods reported in previous studies [16]. One week after the last intervention, all participants received a debriefing email and were asked to participate in the optional post-study survey. The study targeted German-speaking participants.

4.1   Participant Recruitment

Participants were recruited from *openHPI*, an online education platform with over 100.000 registered users [17], where university lecturers provide free online courses on IT-related topics to the general public. Recruitment happened in the form of an additional consent available on the platform covering "Research at *HPI*", which learners of the platform could provide in their profile. The consent covered data processing and analysis outside the education platform and email communication in the context of research studies. Upon logging in to the platform during the study duration, learners received a one-time notification that the new consent was available. The default value for the consent was *off*, requiring users to actively opt-in to the study. Then, they could opt-in and -out of the study at any time during the study period. Studying real-world interactions with phishing content poses the challenge that many participants will never open phishing emails. Therefore, we did not set an upper limit on the number of participants for our study but included everyone providing consent during the study period.

4.2   Ethical Study Design

Studying human subjects requires researchers to closely consider ethical questions, such as the mental load on participants. Therefore, human subject studies should generally be assessed by an Institutional Review Board (IRB) and require consent from the subjects to be studied. Consenting to a study generally means that individuals who are fully informed about it actively agree to participate [24]. In cybersecurity, particularly phishing research, participants could provide informed consent, e.g., at the beginning of a lab study. However, providing all information on a study can lead to biases of the subject, altering the study results [9]. Instead, researchers can use deception by withholding essential information on the study design from participants [9]. Deception is only deemed an option if the study is of minimal risk to the participants and requires the researcher to *debrief* the participants upon completion, i.e., provide all previously withheld information.

Our study design uses deception upon participant recruitment. We did not inform consenting participants that we would perform a phishing study. The IRB of the University of Potsdam and the data protection officers of the conducting institute approved this study design. When visiting the online education platform *openHPI* starting in September 2022, learners could provide and revoke consent to receive email communication for research projects. Once they provided their consent, they would be included in every following iteration of our study. E.g., we included a learner who provided the consent on Dec 12th for the third and fourth iteration (cf. timeline in Fig. 1).

Phishing attacks are no unusual threat for any user of the Web and Internet. Hence, during the assessment of our study, the IRB agreed that the planned research, including deception to retrieve consent, poses minimal risks to participants. For our web pages, we ensured that no personal data, such as usernames, passwords, or address information, entered by the participants would be transmitted to our servers. All other data, e.g., reaction to an email and behavior on the web page, was collected in pseudonymized form, i.e., it was only labeled with a pseudonymized identifier, not a user's email address or username. All users were *debriefed* with the final email in January 2023, a week after intervention four of the study had been sent to all participants[1]. To ensure the debriefing email reached all participants, we sent it using the official email servers of *openHPI*. This provided a trust anchor for the users and ensured that the potential lack of reputation of our phishing domains did not limit email delivery. That debriefing email contained all information on the study, the researchers involved, consent and legal information, a link to the survey, and a link to revoke the provided consent. The user data was removed before further analysis if the consent was revoked. Twenty-one users revoked their consent throughout the study.

To keep the mental load on participants as low as possible, we included *debriefing information* in all our resources to be found whenever an in-depth investigation would be performed. Such were, e.g., hidden as white text inside the email, the web page's source code, and the web page imprint. Further, once participants, e.g., replied to the emails or contacted the supposed support email addresses, we also debriefed them. The debriefing contained the scientific and legal background of the study and information on how to resign from the study by withdrawing consent. The multi-staged nature of our study design poses the challenge to monitor when a participant has been debriefed and should be excluded from further analysis. We discuss the challenges arising from the debriefing of users in Sect. 7.3.

4.3   Email and Webpage Content Design

Figure 2 presents screenshots from all four emails and web pages sent to participants. Content and entities used across all emails were fictitious and created solely for this study. We prepared an email and webpage for each study intervention, which was designed based on real-world designs of similar companies. While similar in design to known companies, none of our emails featured traditionally taught technical cues of phishing emails, such as typosquatting in links. To maximize data on email and webpage interaction by users collected in

---

[1] Emails were sent and delivered to all participants throughout approximately one week for each iteration. This measure ensured that no sudden traffic spike from formerly little-known domains would put the respective domains on a spam list.

this study, we designed persuasive emails, basing various design decisions on the more convincing vectors identified in previous research. The emails relied on the more significant psychological vectors such as time pressure, trust, or financial loss [23,37]. To incorporate these vectors, we chose fitting topics for the emails: supposed package deliveries (emails I and IV), a mail from an energy company concerning rising energy prices (emails II), and a supposed payment confirmation (email III). Emails III and IV used a personal salutation to enhance the email delivery rates, while emails I and II relied on a generic salutation. This change was introduced to counteract emails being blocked as spam and is visible in a change of delivery rates as depicted in Table 1. Throughout all emails, we omitted any traditional cues of phishing emails, such as spelling mistakes. Further, we tried to include images or logos in each email to enhance persuasiveness [37].

Upon following a link from our phishing emails, users were presented with company web pages. These continued the email's theme and topic, persuading the users to enter personal information such as an address, username, or password. Besides, for example, a package tracking website as a landing page for emails I and IV, each domain hosted further web pages, such as the home page and an imprint of the fictional company.

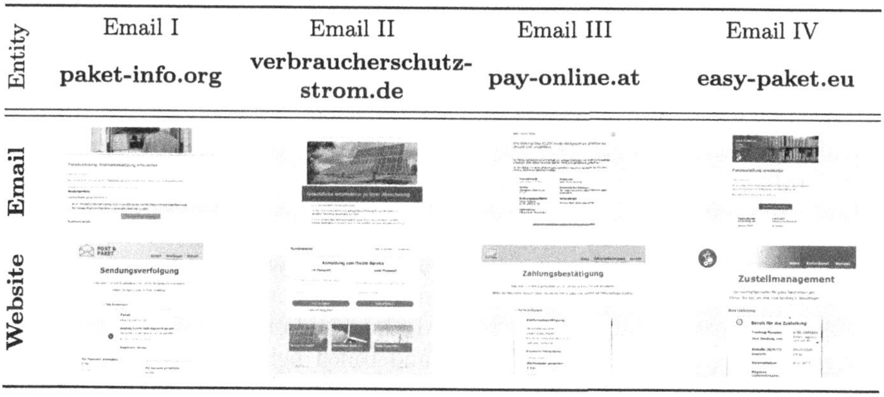

Entity	Email I **paket-info.org**	Email II **verbraucherschutz- strom.de**	Email III **pay-online.at**	Email IV **easy-paket.eu**
Email				
Website				

Fig. 2. Phishing content sent to the participants in the four iterations, ordered left to right. Large-scale images are available in the Appendix, Fig. 8, Sect. B.

The debriefing email informed participants of the nature of the study that had been conducted (cf. Sec. 4.2) and invited them to participate in our survey. To not impact the participants' alertness and, thereby, future reactions to our emails, the debriefing and survey could only be performed after the completion of the entire study. Due to the post-hoc nature of the survey, sent 3.5 months after the initial phishing emails, we expect some inaccuracies in participants' memories to occur. Such could be that participants only remember particularly important or surprising aspects of the emails [21]. We discuss this limitation in Sect. 8. In the survey (cf. Appendix, Sect. A), we retrieved (socio-) demographic information on the participants and their perception of the emails and web pages. Throughout the survey questions, participants could select pre-provided answers from multiple-choice lists and additionally provide free-text answers. For evaluation, *Wenzel Pünter*, second author of this manuscript, manually coded the free-text responses and mapped all responses to the HITL model.

To ensure an email contained no technical cues for phishing, we purchased all four domains, registered them with a new public IP address, and sent emails directly from these domains. As no impersonation was performed, links in the emails did not rely on special characters or typosquatting to counterfeit a third-party entity. In order to enhance our delivery rates, we sent a few hundred emails from the new domains to our inboxes at various webmail providers before sending the actual study emails. This preparation reduced the number of our emails being rejected by webmail providers. Across the interventions, we were able to improve our delivery rate to 99.70%[2] in the final iteration (cf. Table 1).

4.4 Data Collection and Cleaning

We obtained two datasets: the survey responses and the tracking data from the phishing campaign with four iterations. The tracking data covered all four stages of the funnel of phishing email interaction as described by the following actions:

1. **Delivery** Emails have been sent using a commercial gateway. The time of email delivery has been recorded for each email.
2. **Open** Dynamic elements tracked when the email was opened.
3. **Click**ing on a phishing link from the emails opened the website using HTTPS.
4. **Submit** The phishing website requested to enter personal data (username and password, or address), revealing a *debriefing* page upon submission.

The server recorded the timestamp, requested page, IP address, and user agent for the click and submit stages. The websites contained JavaScript-based tracking elements that allowed recording the load and unload timestamps, screen and window dimensions, scroll, mouse, and touch behavior, window visibility changes, input blurring, and focus events. The data recorded by the server, in particular, served as ground truth for the following analysis of user behavior on the web pages. To prepare the analysis, we performed data cleaning of the tracking data from our study. We reduced the web page requests to our servers which we included for further analysis from 6,881 to 5,275:

1. To analyze actual user behavior, automated mail sandbox and security system traffic were cleaned using ASN- and user-agent-based filtering. We excluded traffic from networks of carriers, hosting- and security service providers, as well as requests issued by non-browsers, such as bots, previews (iMessage or Discord), or headless browsers to remove automated reactions to our emails, ensuring our data contains only, e.g., link clicks by human users.

---

[2] This delivery rate is based on email server acceptance. Email classification, e.g., into the *junk/spam* folder as done by secondary filters, can not be tracked in our setup.

2. Automated traffic from commercial IP spaces was identified using a commercial dataset on IP addresses, allowing the filtering for traffic from data centers, VPNs, and anonymization services. Similar to (1.), we excluded highly-similar requests from commercial data centers assuming automated behavior.
3. *Debriefed* participants were accounted for by excluding any activity after a participant was exposed to a disclaimer on our web pages.

5   Overview of Study Data and Participant Population

The study included 4,729 participants, to which we sent 14,123 phishing emails. Of these emails, 6,027 (42.68%) have been opened, whereby 1,549 users (32.76%) clicked on the contained phishing links and 446 of these (28.79%) submitted personal data. 950 participants (20.09%) answered the post-study survey, whereby the number of responses varies across the questions. 26 participants (0.55%) replied to at least one of the phishing emails during the study, assuming the content was legitimate. In other email responses, participants, for example, highlighted that they liked the additional learning experience and that they were adequately prepared by any of the courses they previously took.

Table 1. Overview of the participation rates across the intervention funnel stages.

Iteration	I		II		III		IV	
	N	*Share*	N	*Share*	N	*Share*	N	*Share*
Sent	1,955		3,483		4,260		4,729	
Delivered	1,871	*95.70%*	3,360	*96.47%*	4,177	*98.05%*	4,715	*99.70%*
Opened	851	*43.53%*	1,218	*34.97%*	1,844	*43.29%*	2,114	*44.70%*
Clicked	311	*15.91%*	222	*6.37%*	359	*8.43%*	657	*13.89%*
Submitted	92	*4.71%*	35	*1.00%*	51	*1.20%*	268	*5.67%*
Replied	0	*0.00%*	0	*0.00%*	17	*0.40%*	9	*0.19%*

Table 2 provides an overview of participant demographic information as provided during our survey. A Kolmogorov-Smirnov test of the sample data shows a significant skew compared to the distribution of sexes and age groups ($K = 1.0000$, $p = 0.0286$) in Germany. The most deviation in age is explained by people aged 60+, who experience a lower Internet penetration rate.

Another demographic factor considered in the study is the level of education reached by participants. The responses have been categorized according to the UNESCO ISCED-2011 taxonomy [30]. 934 participants (98.32%) have reported their highest level of education, whereby 3 (0.32%) have reached Primary education, 36 (3.85%) Lower secondary education, 163 (17.45%) Upper secondary education, and 732 (78.37%) a Bachelor's degree or any equivalent higher level of education. Depending on their work situation, participants might have different exposure to phishing content and training. Therefore, working participants

Table 2. Overview of participant socio-demographic information as provided in the post-study survey. In total, 950 participants (20.09%) replied to the survey.

Feature	# Responses*	Statistics						
Gender	925 (97.37%)	**Gender**	Male	Female	Other			
		# Responses	722	195	8			
		Share	76.00%	20.53%	0.84%			
Age	934 (98.32%)	**Age Group**	< 20	20 − 29	30 − 39	40 − 49	50 − 59	60 − 69	> 70
		# Responses	13	59	103	164	253	209	133
		Share	1.37%	6.21%	10.84%	17.26%	26.63%	22.00%	14.00%
Level of Education	934 (98.32%)	**Degree of Education**	Primary	Lower Secondary	Upper Secondary	Bachelor's	Master's	Doctoral
		# Responses	3	36	163	157	483	92
		Share	0.32%	3.85%	17.45%	16.81%	51.71%	9.85%
IT Usage	Work: 773 (81.37%) Home: 869 (91.47%)	**Usage**	Always	Daily	Regularly	Rarely	Sporadically	Never
		# Responses	425	262	38	11	7	30
		Share	54.98%	33.89%	4.92%	1.42%	0.91%	3.88%
		# Responses	283	490	81	4	9	2
		Share	32.57%	56.39%	9.32%	0.46%	1.04%	0.23%
Work Industry †	811 (85.37%)	**Industry Code**	H	J	K	O	P	Q	other
		# Responses	39	478	45	124	193	53	94
		Share	4.81%	58.94%	5.55%	15.29%	23.80%	6.54%	11.59%

† Industry Codes according to UN ISIC Rev. 4 [31], e.g. **H**: Transportation and Storage, **J**: Information and Communication, **K**: Financial, **O**: Public Administration, **P**: Education, **Q**: Health and Social Work

were asked to state the industry they are currently working in. The responses were classified according to the UN ISIC Rev. 4 primary industry groups [31]. 811 (85.37%) working participants stated their industry in the survey, whereby 654 (68.84%) participants associated themselves with only one industry and 157 (16.53%) mentioned multiple. 58.94% of our participants associated themselves with the *Information and Communication* industry, followed by 23.80% in *Education* and 15.29% in *Public Administration and Defense*.

The earlier outlined distribution of participants shows a bias of the study sample compared to the general population of Germany concerning sex, age, level of education, and work industry. The studied population is overly male, has not reached the age group 60+, has an above-average education level, and primarily works in information technology, education, and the public sector. We surveyed that most participants use IT at least daily in both work (88.87%) and private (88.96%) contexts, thereby judging that we observe a group with a high affinity towards IT systems. We discuss the following two derived biases in our population in Sect. 7.3.

Bias 1 We observe the foremost discriminator from the average population and, thereby, potential bias to our study to be the overly technical population.

Bias 2 All participants were recruited from the online education platform *openHPI*, which offers particularly IT education. Therefore, our participants will likely be more interested in IT methods, tools, and technology.

6   Study Results

During our evaluation, we mapped participant responses from the survey to the different phases of the human-in-the-loop model introduced earlier. To ensure unbiased participant responses, we formulated our survey questions as broadly as possible (cf. Appendix, Sect. A). We applied the classification by manually labeling participants' (free-text) responses and mapping them to the different stages of the HITL model based on the reported actions. The following sections present the results of our classification.

6.1   Mapping of Responses to the Human-In-The-Loop-Model

Contribution 1 We contribute to the systematization of phishing investigation behavior by coding and mapping responses from participants of a large-scale study in overly private contexts to the HITL model.

As part of the survey, participants were asked to explain their actions for each phishing email received across the four iterations. Properties mentioned in the responses were classified according to the human-in-the-loop model introduced in Sect. 2 and manually clustered hierarchically. This section provides an overview of the explored answer space.

This section is structured alongside the human-in-the-loop model presented by *Wash et al.* [35], with the phases of *Notice, Expect, Suspect, Investigate, Decide* and *Act.* However, our study methodology partly limits the exact assignment of an answer to a precise stage in the model. For example, we asked participants which aspects of the mail caused their suspicion (*Suspect*). These differ from participants' expectations (*Expect*). Due to our study setup (*post-study questionnaire*), we could not interview participants on their *actual* expectations for, e.g., package delivery emails before sending our study emails and survey. Still, some answers did provide information on the participant's expectations, such as *P101: "Layout of the mail did not correspond to, e.g., UPS, DPD, etc.",* which provides us with the information that the participant would *Expect* a package delivery announcement via email to look like the ones they are used to. The answer, however, was provided because the layout of our email triggered the participant's suspicion. Therefore, we evaluate the two stages *Expect* and *Suspect* alongside each other.

HITL-Model: Notice. Fig. 3 summarizes the features that were *noticed* by participants. We manually mapped all free text answers to the respective questions (cf. Appendix, Sect. A.2: Q10, Q12) and structured them hierarchically. The observed features center around metadata, content, and context of the received emails, seen phishing websites, and conducted online searches to investigate the legitimacy of content. For example, 17 participants noticed that the *Email Salutation* (*Email ▶ Body ▶ Salutation*) was very *Generic*. In contrast, 17 [others] noted the *Personal* salutation we employed in emails III and IV. Similarly, a total of 40 participants noticed the *Email Sender's TLD*

($Email \blacktriangleright Sender \blacktriangleright Address \blacktriangleright Domain \blacktriangleright TLD$), for which some took particular notice of, e.g., .at, or .eu ($N_{.at} = 29, N_{.eu} = 5$). However, few observations do not match reality, only participants' perceptions, biased by imperfect memory. E.g., we sent all content in German but never in English, how some participants reported to have observed it (cf. Appendix, Fig. 9, $Email \blacktriangleright Locale$).

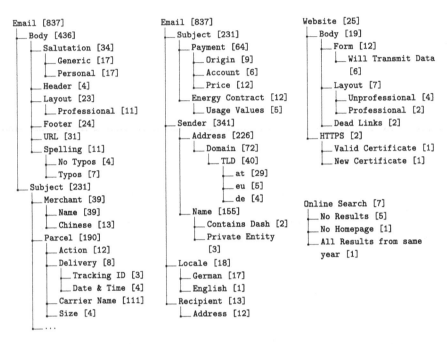

Fig. 3. Highlights of hierarchically structured *Noticed* properties named in survey responses. Participants *noticed* aspects within the **Email**, **Website** and during their **Online Searches**. [Numbers in brackets] refer to the count of mentions. Figure 9 in the Appendix, Sect. C shows the entire figure.

HITL-Model: Expect and Suspect. Properties that were *suspected* and thereby differ from what was *expected* by participants split into a context that is unique to the person itself (**Personal**) and expectations that emerge from a person's assumptions about the world and its relationships (**Global**). An overview of suspected and expected aspects mentioned in the survey is provided in Fig. 4. For example, 111 participants mentioned global expectations towards emails by *Logistics Carriers* (*Global* $\blacktriangleright$ *Entities* $\blacktriangleright$ *Companies*). Regarding *Personal* expectations, 12 participants reported to have had expected orders (*Personal* $\blacktriangleright$ *Activities* $\blacktriangleright$ *Orders*). In comparison, 184 participants claimed they were not expecting orders or, e.g., never ordered from foreign countries ($N = 4$).

Based on their observations and expectations, participants attempted to identify the context of the email. Often, they expressed either an event that required legitimate communication or different kinds of fraud, sometimes resulting from a

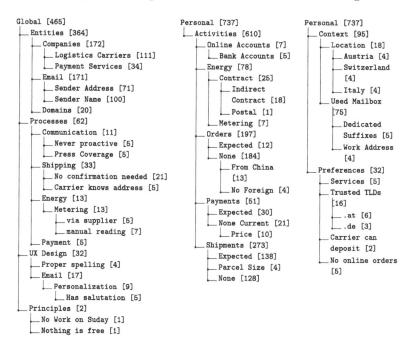

Fig. 4. Highlights of hierarchically structured *Expected* and *Suspected* properties named in survey responses. We differentiate between **Global** expectations that could be identical across participants and **Personal** expectations, e.g., of a concrete shipment. [Numbers in brackets] refer to the count of mentions. Figure 10 in the Appendix, Sect. C shows the entire figure.

data breach. Those participants who suspected fraud assumed their identity data was leaked from a service provider (N=20), phishing (N=2), spoofing (N=1), or domain-specific types of fraud associated with the message content like a fraudulent order (N=2), the abuse of a credit card number (N=6), or a compromised PayPal account (N=1). Typically, those who assumed legitimate communication suspected recent personal activities as the origin of the unwanted communication:

1. **Energy Price (Email II)** While the sent email was themed along governmental support programs in consequence of the Russian invasion of Ukraine in 2022, participants suspected legitimacy not because of this context but personal circumstances like a newly established supply contract (N=4) or the delegation of duties from the supplier (N=2) to an unknown third party.
2. **Payment (Email III)** Most of the participants who suspected the legitimacy of the payment email assumed that they missed the payment for an online order (N=13). Others believed the payment was misrouted (N=1) or the transaction was a pending refund (N=1).
3. **Logistics Services (Emails I and IV)** As with the payment message, most legitimacy assumptions centered around pending orders that participants were no longer aware of (N=22). Related events like a recent birthday (N=2), a Christmas parcel (N=1), or a current address change (N=1) can

also explain the unexpected delivery message. Several participants assumed a parcel to or from another person, like their spouse (N=1), a relative (N=1), or another third party (N=1).

HITL-Model: Investigate. Several participants mentioned how they investigated the legitimacy of the phishing content in each iteration. Investigation techniques performed by participants are - besides their representation in the HITL model - of significant interest to this study. The traditional analysis of, e.g., link targets or email headers does not provide insights in our study, as all phishing emails lacked technical cues for maliciousness. In the post-study survey, 884 participants (93.05%) reported their investigation methods. Figure 5 presents an overview of the distribution of participants' answers on their investigation techniques, contrasting with whether they fell for any of the received phishing emails.

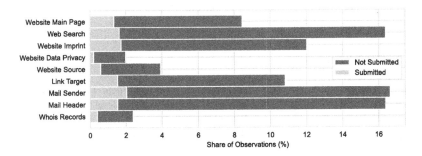

Fig. 5. Distribution of participants' qualitative survey answers on investigation techniques enriched with whether they had submitted any data during the study ($N = 844$).

In the free-text responses, participants mentioned that they aimed to fulfill two goals with their investigation: (a) collecting additional information and (b) verifying observations and assumptions with external information. One participant also mentioned an experiment-based approach, entering fake data and modifying URL parameters to test the web service.

Figure 6 presents the taxonomy of participant replies. Participant investigation techniques could be grouped around the email itself, the webpage, technical investigation procedures such as investigating name server records, or verification of the supposed content of the email through either context or social contacts. Sixty-four participants mentioned having investigated the imprint of our webpage. 56 participants mentioned using search engines to investigate the supposed companies, email sender, involved domains, or phishing URLs. Various other responses covered verification of the email content; examples include verifying the context by checking bank statements or attempting to match the phishing emails to originating orders. Other participants highlight getting help from social connections such as family members or colleagues to verify the email content, which confirms the earlier introduced findings by *Nthala and Wash* [20].

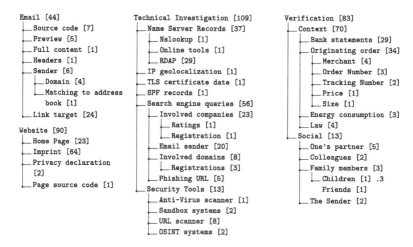

```
Email [44]                    Technical Investigation [109]    Verification [83]
└─Source code [7]             └─Name Server Records [37]        └─Context [70]
├─Preview [5]                  ├─Nslookup [1]                    ├─Bank statements [29]
├─Full content [1]             ├─Online tools [1]                ├─Originating order [34]
├─Headers [1]                  └─RDAP [29]                       │  ├─Merchant [4]
├─Sender [6]                  ├─IP geolocalization [1]           │  ├─Order Number [3]
│  ├─Domain [4]               ├─TLS certificate date [1]         │  ├─Tracking Number [2]
│  └─Matching to address      ├─SPF records [1]                  │  ├─Price [1]
│     book [1]                └─Search engine queries [56]       │  └─Size [1]
└─Link target [24]             ├─Involved companies [23]         ├─Energy consumption [3]
                               │  ├─Ratings [1]                  └─Law [4]
Website [90]                   │  └─Registration [1]            └─Social [13]
├─Home Page [23]               ├─Email sender [20]               ├─One's partner [5]
├─Imprint [64]                 ├─Involved domains [8]            ├─Colleagues [2]
├─Privacy declaration          │  └─Registrations [3]            ├─Family members [3]
│  [2]                         └─Phishing URL [5]                │  └─Children [1] .3
└─Page source code [1]        └─Security Tools [13]              │     Friends [1]
                               ├─Anti-Virus scanner [1]          └─The Sender [2]
                               ├─Sandbox systems [2]
                               ├─URL scanner [8]
                               └─OSINT systems [2]
```

Fig. 6. Hierarchical overview of *investigative* measures named in free text survey responses. Numbers in [brackets] refer to the count of mentions.

Those aspects of the participants' investigation, which targeted our phishing web pages, were measurable. As participants reported investigating the content, one could hypothesize that an increased amount of observed content reduces the chance of clicking on the phishing link or submitting data on subsequent web pages. However, content visibility and the device type (e.g., mobile or computer) did not show to be significantly correlated with data submission on the web pages. We further assessed user scroll distance and time spent with the web page as proxy factors for the investigation process.

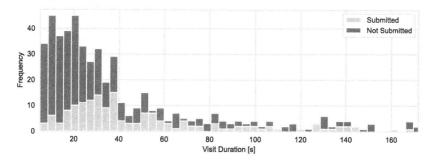

Fig. 7. Histogram of time spent on the phishing page before submitting data or leaving the page. The figure shows the 90% quantile of the long-tail distribution and how many users showed the respective behavior (*Frequency*).

When users visited our web pages, we could calculate the visit duration by investigating the time between JavaScript (JS) load and unload events on the webpage. We excluded requests without those events, as the disabled JS severely limits our tracking capabilities. On the first visit, the median time spent before leaving the webpage was 31,05 s. Figure 7 shows the histogram of visit durations. Tracking webpage blur events[3] showed that 645 participants (41.64%) left at least one of the phishing pages to other tabs or windows during their first visit to our page. We interpret this observation as a proxy factor to web research (e.g., Google search) on an entity or context provided on the webpage.

HITL-Model: Decide and Act. The *Decide* step in the cognitive human-in-the-loop model is hardly measurable in a field study. Based on the observed, expected, and suspected properties, participants *decided* that the seen piece of content is legitimate or illegitimate and acted upon it.

In the survey, 310 participants expressed different *Actions* in response to the content in free text answers: 149 participants (48.06%) reported that they deleted the respective email, 53 moved it to the junk folder, 35 (11.29%) contacted the authors, 25 ignored the content, 24 reported it to another entity, 16 admitted clicking on the link, four blocked the sender, three replied to the message assuming it was legitimate, and one person waited for subsequent messages. Two participants mentioned that they monitored their bank accounts in the subsequent days for malicious transactions. Those participants who reported the content to a third party forwarded it to their organizational IT department (N=10), to the RDAP abuse contact (N=3), to their bank (N=1), or filed a report to their local police (N=1).

6.2 Impact of Features on Participants' Reactions

In the previous sections, we outlined which behavior, investigation, or observation has been reported by participants. Building on our mixed-methods approach, we have aggregated both quantitative and qualitative data. The aggregated quantitative dataset on participant behavior in reaction to the phishing emails, such as *opened the phishing email, clicked on links*, or *submitted personal data* is presented in-depth in [15]. Earlier, we highlighted the overarching finding that young and old males of lower educational degrees are particularly susceptible to phishing attacks. Additionally, we presented an overview of the underlying data in Table 1 for statistical insights into the different interactions, and Table 2 for the socio-demographic background of our study population. Insights into the qualitative data as obtained through analysis of survey answers and mapping to the HITL model for phishing investigation are presented in this manuscript. Using both data sets, we can quantify the success of a specific method of investigation in decreasing a participant's susceptibility to phishing attacks. We assessed correlations between all observed features throughout the three phases of the HITL model, *Notice, Expect & Suspect*, and *Investigate* and participants' reactions to our phishing emails, such as *link click* or *data*

---

[3] Once every 800ms, the user's browser sent all events that occurred in the past time-frame to our server. This included blur events of the webpage in case users placed the open tab in the background.

submission. The correlations were computed using primarily *chi-squared* tests (χ^2) to identify significance in correlations and Spearman tests to identify the direction of impact for categorical variables. We use $\alpha = 0.05$ as a quasi-standard for significance. Table 3 highlights and groups our analysis's most essential and overarching observations.

Table 3. Highlights and overarching observations on elements noticed, or actions reported by participants throughout the HITL model, that correlate with interaction with our phishing emails. Full analysis available in Table 4 in the Appendix.

	Observation	Impact	Sig.	N_{true}	Type	Result	p
Notice	Noticing elements from email body (e.g., URLs, icons) correlates with increased interaction	⌃	✓	103	χ^2	15.909	0.000
	Noticing the senders' name or address significantly correlates with decreased interaction	▼	✓	70	χ^2	19.237	0.000
	Noticing the topic *parcel delivery*, significantly correlates with increased interaction	⌃	✓	53	χ^2	48.342	0.000
Expect. & Suspect	Lack of personal context significantly correlates with decreased interaction	▼	✓	652	χ^2	5.264	0.022
	Lack of knowledge of the entity significantly correlates with decreased interaction	▼	✓	35	χ^2	9.798	0.002
	Lack of knowledge about sender significantly correlates with decreased interaction	▼	✓	16	χ^2	5.941	0.015
	Not-expecting current shipments significantly correlates with decreased interaction	▼	✓	537	χ^2	37.150	0.000
	Expecting shipments and deliveries significantly correlates with increased interaction	⌃	✓	63	χ^2	112.082	0.000
Investigate	Investigating *email headers* significantly correlates with decreased interaction	▼	✓	362	χ^2	4.301	0.038
	User Y-axis scroll distance correlates with **not** submitting data on the webpage	▼	✓	1,549*	t	−9.3223	0.0000
	Webpage blur events (*as casual proxy for user web searches*) significantly correlates with **not** submitting any data	▼	✓	645	χ^2	8.5307	0.0035

Impact refers to increased or decreased susceptibility of participants.
Significance (**Sig.**) refers to whether the statistical evaluation reports significance given $\alpha = 0.05$.
* for the *t*-test, N refers to the entire amount of users that visited the webpage

7 Discussion and Contextualization of Results

The previous overview of the study results (Table 3) shows effects that require closer assessment and contextualization. In the following sections, we explore a few of the overarching measures applied and observations mentioned by participants during this study, which we observed to impact their susceptibility to phishing attacks.

7.1 Noticing, Expecting and Suspecting Context

Contribution 2 We observe that identification of missing context during the phases *Expect* and *Suspect* significantly decreases participants' susceptibility to phishing attacks.

The different steps and phases of the HITL model are closely connected. Whenever a participant *notices* a specific feature, they automatically compare it to their *expectation*. If that differs, the participant *suspects* illegitimacy. Due to the posthoc nature of our survey, we expect that most participants only reported features that have caused particular suspicion (*Limitation 1*). Across the stages *Notice*, *Expect*, and *Suspect* of the HITL model, we generally observe that email features denoting context, such as the sender, the topic, and particularly the entity covered in the email impact participant's susceptibility to react to it. Participants observing that they had no connection to the entity generally performed better, as most of them interpreted the email as SPAM or unrelated to them and chose to ignore or delete the email.

Contrasting, participants for which the email fit into a current context, such as, e.g., they were currently expecting a delivery or recently ordered something on the Internet, usually performed worse, expecting a shipment significantly correlated with increased susceptibility($N = 63, \chi^2 = 112.082, p < 0.001$). Vice-versa, participants' awareness that they are not expecting a shipment significantly correlated with decreased susceptibility ($N = 537, \chi^2 = 37.150, p < 0.001$).

7.2 Investigative Measures

Contribution 3 Web Searches are one of the most successful investigation techniques in cases in which an email lacks technical indicators and thereby significantly decrease users' susceptibility to falling for phishing attacks.

Generally, upon *Suspicion* during looking at, e.g., an email, participants should start to investigate the nature of the email. Investigation is typically a process in which users attempt to gain more information about, e.g., the context of an email. In many teaching programs, measures such as the investigation of email headers, URL targets, and email bodies are named. We observed some participants who knew (and applied) these methods among our participants. However, we further observed investigation techniques such as *looking at the main webpage* or *clicking on the link*. Such methods can expose the participant to dangers upon visiting a malicious website.

Participants who investigated, e.g., email headers, were less likely to further interact with our phishing content. This observation is surprising, as the emails were not forged, and no manipulation that would have been visible in email headers was applied. Further, *Zheng et al.* reported that displaying email headers does not reduce phishing susceptibility as users often fail to interpret them correctly [38]. Instead, we judge that email header investigation is a casual proxy for participants to be more aware of potential cybersecurity risks, which was the reason for decreased interaction.

Considering further investigation techniques, participants who scrolled a lot on the webpage were significantly less likely to submit data on the webpage ($N_{Visited} = 1,549, t = -9.3223, p < 0.001$). We interpret this measure as a proxy for users carefully interacting with and observing the webpage. In our questionnaire and free text answers specific to the emails, users reported investigation of the emails by web searches. Performing such web searches, users hoped to identify *"Who is actually behind the parcel service provider? Which corporation?" (P365)*. Throughout the study, a total of 741 participants reported having performed web searches to retrieve more context on the supposed entities. Performing a Web search has proven to be one of the techniques significantly correlated with decreased submissions of private data on our webpage ($N = 741, \chi^2 = 3.943, p = 0.047$). Overall, 13.73% of participants who did **not** perform web research submitted data in any of our phishing emails. In contrast, from those who performed web research, only 9.09% submitted personal data.

While we cannot track participant behavior after opening the email, we could track their behavior when visiting our webpage. One of the events we tracked is *webpage blur*, which occurs whenever a user selects any other tab in their browser but keeps our webpage open. We interpret webpage blur as a casual proxy for opening a new tab and performing a web search. This behavior significantly correlates with users not submitting data ($N = 645, \chi^2 = 8.5307, p = 0.0035$).

7.3 Biases and Limitations

(Non-) Technical Population Groups. One bias observed in our participant group (cf. Sec 5) is the difference between technical and non-technical people, e.g., expressed through jobs in IT and technology exposure. To test for the impact of IT affiliation, we compared different features throughout the HITL model between the two groups. We observe that the more technical features *noticed* by participants, such as the URL, are more often named among the IT population. In contrast, non-technical features, such as the personal salutation, were primarily noticed by people not affiliated with IT. Contextual aspects such as the email sender are noticed across both groups and contribute to not interacting with the email for both groups.

When assessing *Expected* and *Suspected* features inside the email, observations such as *Personal context significantly drives increased or decreased interaction* hold true independent of technicality. Similarly, throughout both groups, people who expected shipments, as reported in free text answers (cf. Figure 4), were more likely to click on the links and submit data on the web pages. One observed contrast between both groups is that IT-affiliated people expect and suspect more technical features, such as *parcel size*. However, that had no impact on increased or decreased susceptibility to phishing attacks in our study.

Regarding investigative measures, 352 IT-affiliated and 358 non-IT people have claimed to have performed (web-) searches. IT people were slightly better with their investigation, as only 8,89% of them submitted data, while 11,33% of non-IT people submitted data after having performed web searches. We observed advanced investigation techniques even among those participants who were not affiliated with IT. However, among this group of people, we observed a higher error rate in interpreting the results (two of four non-IT participants have still submitted data after checking with, e.g., VirusTotal). We claim that this misjudgment stems from suboptimal training in which the absence of indicators for maliciousness (e.g., alerts in VirusTotal) is automatically interpreted as a positive sign without questioning if the measure applied (checking a URL with VirusTotal) is actually reasonable for the current assessment.

When *acting* on an email, after having investigated it, we assessed whether a participant clicked on the link or submitted data to the webpage. Further reactions, as reported during mapping participants' answers to the HITL model (cf. Sec. 6.1), included moving an email to SPAM or reporting it inside the company. We observed that reporting the email to any third party (IT department, police, other institutions) was more often reported among non-IT participants.

Participant Group Recruitment. Our participants were recruited from the online education platform *openHPI*, on which free video-based online courses are offered. The platform mostly features educational courses on IT topics, such as programming, databases, AI, or cybersecurity. Earlier, we discussed observed differences between IT-affiliated participants and those participants who are employed, e.g., in jobs in public administration. Still, we assume that throughout all participants in all job roles, a particular interest in IT is apparent. Otherwise, they would not be enrolled in the platform. Therefore, we assume that the generalizability of our results towards the general public, particularly the non-IT population, is limited. Building on this thought, however, makes apparent that even those particularly interested in information technology (i.e., participants of our study) failed to correctly interpret indicators of mistrust such as missing context during our study. Replicating the study with a more representable population group would show less applied technical investigation techniques and an even higher failure rate to assess the study content as phishing correctly, matching results from related works.

Debriefing of Participants. Our study targeted real-world participants who had not received the entire disclosure of the study context upon providing consent to participate (cf. Section 4.2). Hence, participants are likely unaware of participating in a phishing study. Therefore, we were required to ensure that our study emails would not be propagated further beyond our study participants. While the emails should withhold brief investigation by participants, any more technical investigation of our emails or web pages by trained staff should easily refer to the research context of the study. Therefore, we included debriefing information at various points throughout the study design:

1. The emails contained debriefing as white text on a white background
2. The imprint of the webpages contained debriefing information
3. Upon submitting data to the webpage, participants were debriefed
4. Upon contacting the sender of the emails, we debriefed the participants

The hidden debriefing information in emails potentially impacts users with screen readers or those who viewed the emails in plain text. For the former, investigating the behavior of users with disabilities would be part of a larger research question covering the impact of assistance tools on (phishing) assessment practices. An appropriate analysis of this research question is out of scope for our study. For the latter, in the survey, only a few people (< 10) responded to have viewed the email in plain text. The practice is uncommon in our study population. As we can not track which participants have observed the debriefing information inside the email, we acknowledge the limitation. However, we must omit a detailed analysis of the practice in this manuscript.

With the different measures of debriefing in place, debriefed participants within each intervention needed to be excluded from the analysis. For example, for a user who submitted data and later further investigated the web page, that web page behavior should not be tracked and assessed. For debriefing measures two through four, we could technically track through requests to our web servers or emails to the contact addresses when the debriefing happened. In the data cleaning step three (Sect. 4.4), such participant behavior after debriefing was excluded from the dataset before further analysis.

8   Future Work

Our study targeted participants' investigative behavior of phishing content without traditional indicators for phishing. This increases the difficulty of email assessment, resulting in a relatively high time investment. To further study the human cost of phishing, a follow-up study using the same setup and observed data points could be developed studying phishing emails showing traditional cues for phishing, such as tampered email senders, illegitimate links, or spelling and grammar mistakes. Such analysis could provide interesting results, allowing further interpretation of the human cost of phishing attacks.

During our qualitative analysis of participants' answers, we observed the phenomenon of participants reporting, e.g., content in English, while all content was purely designed and distributed in German. This is likely because our survey was only sent posthoc, up to 3.5 months after the first phishing email (cf. study setup depicted in Fig. 1). On the other hand, participants could also be subject to the phenomenon of confirmation bias and thus misremember information. Further research studying this observation could be performed by interlacing the *Staged Innovation Design* with surveys to some participants, after which those would be removed from the future participant pool to ensure maintaining an unbiased study population while retrieving intermediate survey answers.

9   Conclusion

This manuscript presents the results of a large-scale mixed-methods study examining human-phishing interaction when confronted with emails that lack traditional cues for phishing. We provide three *human-in-the-loop* model taxonomies of 950 participants' phishing email investigation approaches. We observe the major contributor to phishing susceptibility in our study to be the identification of (missing) context. As expected, this is the only valid indicator for phishing in the study emails, as the fictitious entities had actual web pages, and no, e.g., links were manipulated. Participants unsure of the nature, entity, or subject of the emails reported to have performed web searches for further investigation. Verifying with our data on submissions of private data on the phishing web page, we could observe that the participants who mentioned having performed web research submitted sensitive data in 33.79% fewer cases than the cohort.

In our study, most users intuitively reacted well to the challenge of missing cues for phishing inside the emails. However, we also observed users who failed to make proper decisions. One reason might be users unaware of the implications of data disclosure to an attacker. We call on educators to highlight the risks of providing sensitive data to cybercriminals more prominently. Furthermore, concepts currently only employed in professional contexts, such as highlighting if an email is from an external organization, could also be beneficial in private contexts. E.g., a banner in email applications for emails where it is the first time the user has contact with the entity could help participants derive context.

Various qualitative answers by participants have shown that they assess their emails to know whether they are required to react. However, they need guidance and easily usable tools to support their investigation process. Hence, developing tools and measures to help laypersons investigate (phishing) emails securely should be prioritized in research and product development.

A   Appendix: Survey Instrument

The survey questions are translated from German for publication in this manuscript. The following sub-sections layout the survey instrument used to obtain the responses presented throughout the manuscript.

A.1   Demography

Q1: Please enter your email address.
Q2: How old are you?
Q3: Which gender would you associate yourself with?
Q4: Which is your highest level of education?
Q5: In which industry are you currently working? *(Multi-Select among primary industry groups according to UN ISIC Rev.4* [31]*)*

A.2   Phishing Emails and Reactions

Q6: In the past 4 months, we have sent 4 phishing emails as part of this study. In the following questions, we would like to know whether and how you reacted to the corresponding emails. You can view the four emails again here:
Q7: Have we successfully persuaded you to enter data during our campaign?

Q8: Which of the four phishing emails do you remember? (*Multi-Select*)
Q9: What was the major reason for a reaction to the email? (*Matrix-Select, one reason per email*)
- Curiosity
- Fear
- Pressure
- Financial Interest
- Trust
- Authority
- *I did not react to this mail.*
- *Prefer not to answer.*

Q10: Please provide more information on your reaction. (*Freetext*)
Q11: Which of the emails gave you the feeling that something was wrong? (*Multi-Select*)
Q12: Please explain your feelings on the emails. (*Freetext answer for each email*)
Q13: What did you do when you had off feelings with an email? (*Multi-Select*)
- Visit the main webpage
- Perform a web search
- View the website imprint
- View the website data privacy declaration
- Investigate the website source code
- Investigate the link target
- Investigate the sender
- Investigate the email header

Q14: Have you carried out any further checks? (*Freetext*)
Q15: Which precautions have you taken for your investigation? (*Multi-Select*)
- I did not take special precautions.
- VPN
- TOR
- Deactivate JavaScript
- Deactivate Cookies
- Use a special browser
- Use a sandbox / virtual machine
- Issue WHOIS / RDAP request for the IP / domain

Q16: Did you implement any other precautions or technical measures? (*Freetext*)

A.3   IT-Context and Sensitization

Q17: How often do you use IT-Devices for your work and in your leisure time?
Q18: Estimate, how many emails you receive per day in your private and work contexts.
Q19: Did you previously participate in courses or training for cybersecurity awareness?
Q20: Which types of trainings did.you previously participate in? (*Multi-Select*)
- Classroom training (including digital group training)
- Awareness information emails

- Test phishing emails (outside this study)
- Computer-based training
- Online courses
- Information videos
- Social media content
- Documentations (TV, Youtube)
- Podcasts and radio
- Print media (newspapers, flyer)
- Posters and billboard advertisement
- Other (*Freetext*)

Q21: How long ago did you participate in your last training?

Q22: Have you previously been affected by a security incident? (*Multi-Select*)

- Reacted to a phishing email
- Malware infection
- Lost a password
- Lost data
- Lost access to an account
- Stolen devices
- Lost money
- Other (*Freetext*)

B   Appendix: Large Scale Images of Phishing Content

The paper incorporates tiny graphics as an overview of the emails and webpages employed throughout the four iterations of our phishing study. Here, we provide the following images for readers who want to look at larger-scale variants.

C   Appendix: HITL-Model: Figures

Presented in the paper were shortened versions of the two taxonomies that highlight aspects which were more frequently named by study participants. However, in case fellow researchers would be designing similar studies, even answers from single participants could be helpful to understand what behavior to expect. Therefore, we present Figs. 9 and 10, showing the full range of participant responses to the survey on the respective stages in the HITL model.

Fig. 8. Large-scale screenshots of German phishing content sent throughout the four iterations.

D   Appendix: Resulting Correlations

In Table 3, we summarized the most important correlations we observed between our participant responses and their interaction with our phishing emails and web pages. The analysis has brought us to identify the highlighted observations as particularly important, e.g. because we further observed mentions of the aspects

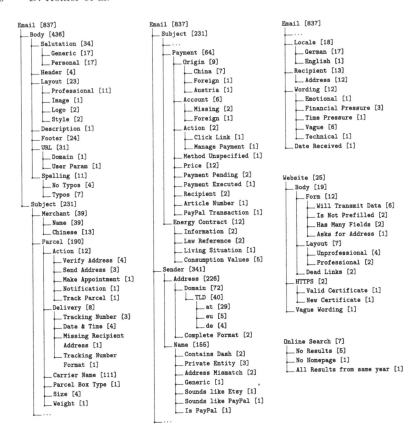

Fig. 9. Hierarchical overview of *noticed* properties named in survey responses. Participants *noticed* aspects within the *Email, Website* and during their *Online Searches.* * Numbers in [brackets] refer to the count of mentions.

in qualitative answers. Additionally, Table 4 provides an overview of all impactful aspects derived during our analysis. In the table, we group the findings by the iteration they were reported of, with *General* applying to answers given to general, overarching question not directly targeted towards single interventions. Inside each iteration, we differentiate between the different phases of the HITL interaction model: *Notice* (N), *Expect* (E), *Suspect* (S), *Investigate* (Inv.), and *Act* (A). We compare the performance of the group that reported the respective feature (*Share of Participants*) to the performance of the *General Population*. Depending on whether participants who reported the respective feature performed better or worse, we indicate whether the respective group of participants *reacted* (React.) more or less often than their peers. The reaction translates to the phishing susceptibility, as indicated in Table 3 in the manuscript. An increased amount of reaction and, thereby, increased susceptibility hereby indicates worse behavior. Below, we provide one example of how to read the table:

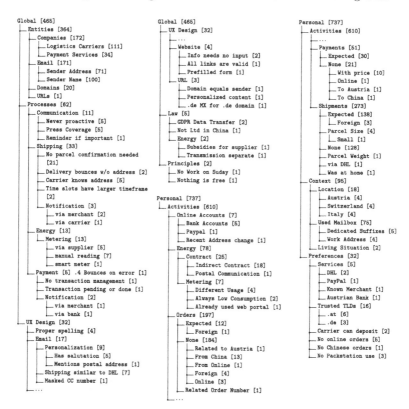

Fig. 10. Hierarchical overview of *expected* and *suspected* properties named in survey responses. We differentiate between *Global* expectations that could be identical across participants and *Personal* expectations, such as a concrete shipment. * Numbers in [brackets] refer to the count of mentions.

Reading Example: People that highlighted *General Expections* towards how (third party) entities perform email communication (`global/entities/email`) performed better than their peers. Out of the 32 people who highlighted the respective feature, only 3.1% *Clicked* on the links provided in the emails, while generally, 24% of participants clicked on the links provided. This observation is statistically significant, as confirmed with a χ^2 test for significance resulting in $p = 0.001$.

Table 4. Overview of all Correlations observed between Participant Responses clustered to the HITL model.

HITL	HITL Feature	Share of Participants	Interaction	General Population	React.	Sig.	N_{true}	χ² Test Result	p
Notice (N)	email/sender/name	12.5%	Clicked	24.0%	▼	✓	24	6.283	0.012
	email/sender	17.1%	Clicked	24.0%	▼	✓	70	19.237	0.000
	email/sender	8.6%	Submitted	7.0%	∧	✓	70	9.268	0.002
	email/body	50.5%	Clicked	24.0%	∧	✓	103	15.909	0.000
	email/body	32.0%	Submitted	7.0%	∧	✓	103	17.211	0.000
	email/body/parcel	77.4%	Clicked	24.0%	∧	✓	53	48.342	0.000
	email/body/parcel	52.8%	Submitted	7.0%	∧	✓	53	44.334	0.000
	email/body/footer	11.5%	Clicked	24.0%	▼	✓	26	7.583	0.006
	email/sender/address	17.3%	Clicked	24.0%	▼	✓	52	11.744	0.001
	email/sender/address	7.7%	Submitted	7.0%	∧	✓	52	6.567	0.010
General & Overall / Expect (E)	personal/activities	31.6%	Clicked	24.0%	∧	✓	636	4.925	0.026
	personal/activities	13.1%	Submitted	7.0%	∧	✓	636	6.390	0.011
	personal	31.4%	Clicked	24.0%	∧	✓	652	5.264	0.022
	personal	12.7%	Submitted	7.0%	∧	✓	652	3.891	0.049
	personal/activities/shipments/none	24.6%	Clicked	24.0%	∧	✓	537	37.150	0.000
	personal/activities/shipments/none	6.7%	Submitted	7.0%	▼	✓	537	63.413	0.000
	global/entities/email/sender	0.0%	Clicked	24.0%	▼	✓	16	5.941	0.015
	global/processes/energy/metering	100.0%	Clicked	24.0%	∧	✓	3	3.866	0.049
	global/processes/energy	100.0%	Clicked	24.0%	∧	✓	3	3.866	0.049
	global	0.0%	Submitted	7.0%	▼	✓	44	5.436	0.020
	global/entities/email	3.1%	Clicked	24.0%	▼	✓	32	10.850	0.001
	global/entities	5.7%	Clicked	24.0%	▼	✓	35	9.798	0.002
	global/entities	0.0%	Submitted	7.0%	▼	✓	35	4.043	0.044
	personal/activities/shipments/expected	90.5%	Clicked	24.0%	∧	✓	63	112.082	0.000
	personal/activities/shipments/expected	66.7%	Submitted	7.0%	∧	✓	63	184.949	0.000
Suspect (S)	legit/parcel/other-order	100.0%	Clicked	24.0%	∧	✓	6	4.762	0.029
	legit/parcel/other-order	100.0%	Submitted	7.0%	∧	✓	6	8.584	0.003
	legit/parcel	76.9%	Clicked	24.0%	∧	✓	26	14.182	0.000
	legit/parcel	65.4%	Submitted	7.0%	∧	✓	26	16.313	0.000
	legit	65.6%	Clicked	24.0%	∧	✓	32	7.594	0.006
	legit	53.1%	Submitted	7.0%	∧	✓	32	8.100	0.004
	fraud	23.5%	Clicked	24.0%	▼	✓	17	5.829	0.016
	fraud	11.8%	Submitted	7.0%	∧	✓	17	5.835	0.016
	legit/payment	0.0%	Submitted	7.0%	▼	✓	8	4.000	0.046
	fraud/identity	0.0%	Submitted	7.0%	▼	✓	8	4.000	0.046
Inv.	info/search	29.3%	Clicked	24.0%	∧	✓	741	4.191	0.041
	info/website/link	64.7%	Clicked	24.0%	∧	✓	17	7.550	0.006
Act	react	64.3%	Clicked	24.0%	∧	✓	14	9.820	0.002
	react	42.9%	Submitted	7.0%	∧	✓	14	20.560	0.000
Iteration 2 / Notice	email/sender/address/domain/tld	50.0%	Submitted	2.9%	∧	✓	2	5.508	0.019
	email/sender/name	3.4%	Clicked	18.2%	▼	✓	29	4.050	0.044
	email/sender/address/domain/tld/de	50.0%	Submitted	2.9%	∧	✓	2	5.508	0.019
Expect	personal/preferences/trusted-tld	50.0%	Submitted	2.9%	∧	✓	2	5.512	0.019
	personal/preferences/trusted-tld/at	50.0%	Submitted	2.9%	∧	✓	2	5.512	0.019
	personal/preferences	50.0%	Submitted	2.9%	∧	✓	2	5.512	0.019
Inv.	verify/energy-law	66.7%	Clicked	18.2%	∧	✓	3	10.616	0.001
	verify/energy-law	33.3%	Submitted	2.9%	∧	✓	3	5.876	0.015
	info/search/company	100.0%	Submitted	2.9%	∧	✓	1	19.502	0.000

(*continued*)

Table 4. (*continued*)

HITL		HITL Feature	Share of Participants	Interaction	General Population	React.	Sig.	N_{true}	χ^2 Test Result	p
Iteration 3	Notice	website	33.3%	Submitted	2.8%	∧	✓	3	4.742	0.029
		website/wording	100.0%	Submitted	2.8%	∧	✓	1	16.000	0.000
		website/wording/vague	100.0%	Submitted	2.8%	∧	✓	1	16.000	0.000
	Inv.	info/search	7.9%	Clicked	19.5%	▼	✓	547	5.923	0.015
	Notice	website	62.5%	Clicked	31.1%	∧	✓	8	6.593	0.010
		website/body	62.5%	Clicked	31.1%	∧	✓	8	6.593	0.010
		website/body/form	66.7%	Clicked	31.1%	∧	✓	6	5.483	0.019
Iteration 4	Expect	global/entities	6.6%	Submitted	12.7%	▼	✓	137	4.597	0.032
		global	6.2%	Submitted	12.7%	▼	✓	144	3.920	0.048
		global/entities/email/sender	13.6%	Submitted	12.7%	∧	✓	22	3.982	0.046
		personal	1.5%	Submitted	12.7%	▼	✓	199	6.091	0.014
		personal/activities/shipments/expected	45.8%	Clicked	31.1%	∧	✓	24	12.202	0.000
	Inv.	info/search	15.1%	Clicked	31.1%	▼	✓	535	18.303	0.000
		info/website/imprint	45.0%	Clicked	31.1%	∧	✓	20	9.208	0.002
		info/website	48.1%	Clicked	31.1%	∧	✓	27	16.680	0.000

References

1. Al-Daeef, M.M., Basir, N., Saudi, M.M.: Security awareness training: a review. Lecture Notes in Engineering and Computer Science (2017) iSBN: 2078-0958
2. Alharbi, A., Alotaibi, A., Alghofaili, L., Alsalamah, M., Alwasil, N., Elkhediri, S.: Security in social-media: awareness of phishing attacks techniques and countermeasures. In: 2022 2nd International Conference on Computing and Information Technology (ICCIT) (2022). https://doi.org/10.1109/ICCIT52419.2022.9711640
3. Alzubaidi, A.: Measuring the level of cyber-security awareness for cybercrime in Saudi Arabia. Heliyon **7**(1) (2021). https://doi.org/10.1016/j.heliyon.2021.e06016
4. Caputo, D.D., Pfleeger, S.L., Freeman, J.D., Johnson, M.E.: Going spear phishing: exploring embedded training and awareness. IEEE Security Privacy **12**(1), 28–38 (2014). https://doi.org/10.1109/MSP.2013.106
5. Cranor, L.F.: A framework for reasoning about the human in the loop (2008)
6. European Union Agency for Cybersecurity: ENISA Threat Landscape 2022 (2022). https://www.enisa.europa.eu/publications/enisa-threat-landscape-2022
7. Federal Bureau of Investigation: Business email compromise (2022). https://www.fbi.gov/how-we-can-help-you/safety-resources/scams-and-safety/common-scams-and-crimes/business-email-compromise
8. Fernando, M., Arachchilage, N.: Why Johnny can't rely on anti-phishing educational interventions to protect himself against contemporary phishing attacks? ACIS 2019 Proceedings (Jan 2019). https://aisel.aisnet.org/acis2019/42
9. Finn, P., Jakobsson, M.: Designing ethical phishing experiments. IEEE Technology and Society Magazine **26**(1), 46–58 (2007). https://doi.org/10.1109/MTAS.2007.335565conference Name: IEEE Technology and Society Magazine
10. Furnell, S.: Phishing: can we spot the signs? Comput. Fraud Secur. **2007**(3), 10–15 (2007). https://doi.org/10.1016/S1361-3723(07)70035-0
11. Greitzer, F.L., Li, W., Laskey, K.B., Lee, J., Purl, J.: Experimental investigation of technical and human factors related to phishing susceptibility. ACM Trans. Social Computi. **4**(2), 1–48 (2021). https://doi.org/10.1145/3461672

12. Innab, N., Al-Rashoud, H., Al-Mahawes, R., Al-Shehri, W.: Evaluation of the effective anti-phishing awareness and training in governmental and private organizations in Riyadh. In: 2018 21st Saudi Computer Society National Computer Conference (NCC), pp. 1–5 (Apr 2018). https://doi.org/10.1109/NCG.2018.8593144

13. Jampen, D., Gür, G., Sutter, T., Tellenbach, B.: Don't click: towards an effective anti-phishing training. A comparative literature review. Human-centric Comput. Inform. Sci. **10**(1), 33 (Aug 2020). https://doi.org/10.1186/s13673-020-00237-7

14. Jensen, M.L., Dinger, M., Wright, R.T., Thatcher, J.B.: Training to mitigate phishing attacks using mindfulness techniques. J. Manag. Inf. Syst. **34**(2), 597–626 (2017). https://doi.org/10.1080/07421222.2017.1334499, publisher: Routledge

15. Köhler, D., Pünter, W., Meinel, C.: Fishing for non-professional answers: Quantitative study on email phishing susceptibility in private contexts (2023). https://doi.org/10.13140/RG.2.2.21865.47201/1in Review

16. Kumaraguru, P., et al.: School of phish: a real-world evaluation of anti-phishing training. In: Proceedings of the 5th Symposium on Usable Privacy and Security, pp. 1–12 (2009)

17. Meinel, C., Willems, C., Staubitz, T., Sauer, D., Hagedorn, C.: openHPI: 10 Years of MOOCs at the Hasso Plattner Institute (2022)

18. Mitnick, K.D., Simon, W.L.: The art of deception: Controlling the human element of security. John Wiley & Sons (2003)

19. Nguyen, C., Jensen, M., Day, E.: Learning not to take the bait: a longitudinal examination of digital training methods and overlearning on phishing susceptibility. Eur. J. Inf. Syst. **32**(2), 238–262 (2023). https://doi.org/10.1080/0960085X.2021.1931494

20. Nthala, N., Wash, R.: how non-experts try to detect phishing scam emails. Workshop on Consumer Protection (May 2021). https://par.nsf.gov/biblio/10297019-how-non-experts-try-detect-phishing-scam-emails

21. Parsons, K., Butavicius, M., Pattinson, M., McCormac, A., Calic, D., Jerram, C.: Do Users Focus on the Correct Cues to Differentiate Between Phishing and Genuine Emails? In: ACIS 2015 Proceedings (Jan 2015). https://aisel.aisnet.org/acis2015/6

22. Parsons, K., McCormac, A., Pattinson, M., Butavicius, M., Jerram, C.: Phishing for the truth: a scenario-based experiment of users' behavioural response to emails. In: Security and Privacy Protection in Information Processing Systems, pp. 366–378. IFIP Advances in Information and Communication Technology, Springer, Berlin, Heidelberg (2013). https://doi.org/10.1007/978-3-642-39218-4_27

23. Rajivan, P., Gonzalez, C.: Creative persuasion: a study on adversarial behaviors and strategies in phishing attacks. Front. Psychol. **9** (2018)

24. Resnik, D.B., Finn, P.R.: Ethics and phishing experiments. Sci. Eng. Ethics **24**(4), 1241–1252 (2018). https://doi.org/10.1007/s11948-017-9952-9

25. Schroeder, J.: Advanced persistent training: take your security awareness program to the next level. Apress (Jun 2017). google-Books-ID: UjgoDwAAQBAJ

26. Siadati, H., Palka, S., Siegel, A., McCoy, D.: Measuring the effectiveness of embedded phishing exercises (2017). https://www.usenix.org/conference/cset17/workshop-program/presentation/siadatii

27. Stockhardt, S., et al.: Teaching phishing-security: which way is best? In: ICT Systems Security and Privacy Protection. pp. 135–149. IFIP Advances in Information and Communication Technology, Springer International Publishing, Cham (2016). https://doi.org/10.1007/978-3-319-33630-5_10

28. Sutter, T., Bozkir, A.S., Gehring, B., Berlich, P.: Avoiding the hook: influential factors of phishing awareness training on click-rates and a data-driven approach to predict email difficulty perception. IEEE Access **10**, 100540–100565 (2022). https://doi.org/10.1109/ACCESS.2022.3207272

29. The MITRE Corporation: CAPEC-98: Phishing (2021). https://capec.mitre.org/data/definitions/98.html

30. UNESCO Institute for Statistics: International standard classification of education: Isced 2011 (2012). https://uis.unesco.org/sites/default/files/documents/international-standard-classification-of-education-isced-2011-en.pdf

31. United Nations Department of Economic and Social Affairs: International standard industrial classification of all economic activities (2008). https://unstats.un.org/unsd/publication/SeriesM/seriesm_4rev4e.pdf

32. Wagner, N.: Instructional product evaluation using the staged innovation design. J. Instruct. Develop. **7** (1984)

33. Wash, R.: How experts detect phishing scam emails. Proc.ACM Human-Comput. Interact. **4** (2020). https://doi.org/10.1145/3415231

34. Wash, R., Cooper, M.M.: Who provides phishing training? facts, stories, and people like me. In: Proceedings of the 2018 CHI Conference on Human Factors in Computing Systems. ACM, New York (2018). https://doi.org/10.1145/3173574.3174066

35. Wash, R., Nthala, N., Rader, E.: Knowledge and capabilities that non-expert users bring to phishing detection, pp. 377–396 (2021). https://www.usenix.org/conference/soups2021/presentation/wash

36. Wen, Z.A., Lin, Z., Chen, R., Andersen, E.: What. hack: engaging anti-phishing training through a role-playing phishing simulation game. In: Proceedings of the 2019 CHI Conference on Human Factors in Computing Systems, pp. 1–12. CHI '19, ACM, New York, USA (May 2019). https://doi.org/10.1145/3290605.3300338

37. Williams, E.J., Polage, D.: How persuasive is phishing email? the role of authentic design, influence and current events in email judgements. Behav. Inform. Technol. **38** (Feb 2019). https://doi.org/10.1080/0144929X.2018.1519599

38. Zheng, S., Becker, I.: Presenting suspicious details in user-facing e-mail headers does not improve phishing detection. In: SOUPS @ USENIX Security Symposium (2022). https://api.semanticscholar.org/CorpusID:252996739

39. Zheng, S.Y., Becker, I.: Checking, nudging or scoring? evaluating e-mail user security tools, pp. 57–76 (2023). https://www.usenix.org/conference/soups2023/presentation/zheng

Usable Authentication in Virtual Reality: Exploring the Usability of PINs and Gestures

H. T. M. A. Riyadh[1,2(✉)], Divyanshu Bhardwaj[1,2], Adrian Dabrowski[1],
and Katharina Krombholz[1]

[1] CISPA Helmholtz Center for Information Security, Saarbrücken, Germany
{htma.riyadh,divyanshu.bhardwaj,adrian.dabrowski,krombholz}@cispa.de
[2] Saarland University, Saarbrücken, Germany

Abstract. Virtual Reality (VR) is becoming increasingly popular with its ability to offer new forms of interaction, user interface, and immersion not only for recreation but also for work, therapy, arts, or education. These new spaces need to be safeguarded by authentication similar to conventional IT systems. However, porting conventional interfaces to VR has often been found to be less than optimal as it fails to fully embrace the technology's potential and potentially disrupt the immersive experience. This paper evaluates and compares the usability of two major authentication methods for VR: 2D Personal Identification Number (PIN) and gesture-based authentication - with 40 participants. While prior research has shown promising results in authentication security, there is a lack of studies specifically on usability in VR. Our findings indicate that the type of authentication and the user's experience level affect usability, with gesture-based authentication having a higher usability score than a PIN and having faster authentication times. Hereby, users with less VR experience profited the most from a natural interaction mode for VR. The results suggest that developers should rather choose a native interaction mode in VR than try to port a familiar conventional interaction such as number pads for PINs.

Keywords: Virtual Reality · Usability · Authentication · PINs · Gestures

1 Introduction

Virtual Reality (VR) is an immersive technology that allows users to engage with computer-generated graphics in a virtual environment. In the wake of the COVID-19 pandemic, VR has become increasingly popular among researchers and consumers [2,5,37], resulting in a surge in revenue [42]. Although several authentication solutions have been offered for VR, usability studies related to VR authentication have not been given adequate consideration.

VR presents innovative methods of interacting with technology but questions the effectiveness and usability of traditional authentication techniques in

C. Pöpper and L. Batina (Eds.): ACNS 2024, LNCS 14585, pp. 412–431, 2024.
https://doi.org/10.1007/978-3-031-54776-8_16

this new realm. When using VR, users must authenticate themselves to access their confidential data. As such, it is crucial to safeguard users' data, ensuring their security and establishing trustworthiness through a seamless and user-friendly [35] authentication process in virtual reality. Presently, different authentication methods are being proposed, such as knowledge-based authentications like PIN [15], Pattern Lock [15], 3D Password [3], 3D Pattern [48], or biometric-based authentication [26,34,44]. Although these methods offer robust security, they often sacrifice usability.

To address the need for better authentication in VR, we conducted a between-subjects design user study with N=40 participants. Our research was guided by two key questions:

1. Does the authentication type impact the authentication usability in Virtual Reality?
2. Does the authentication usability vary based on the user's experience with Virtual Reality?

To address these inquiries, we explored two authentication methods: a 2D PIN and a gesture-based authentication. PIN is a well-established traditional authentication process that users frequently use daily. We used the classic 4-digit numerical PIN pad. In contrast, gesture-based authentication is a knowledge-based authentication process relatively new to most users. We utilized four single-hand alphabetic mid-air gestures in a 3D space. The gestures simulated drawing on a 2D touch surface.

Our study revealed that participants with prior experience generally performed better in PIN-based authentication, while no significant differences were observed in gesture-based authentication. These results suggest that experience may have less impact on performance when the design of the VR system follows natural interaction patterns. Interestingly, despite the widespread use of PINs in daily activities and authentication methods, our findings indicate that their performance decreases when used in VR. This could be attributed to the differences in input modalities, as gestures were found to be a more natural and intuitive means of interaction, leading to a better performance and usability.

Our research provides valuable insights into the naturalness of input modalities in VR, which can aid developers in implementing more effective authentication methods that are both user-friendly and secure. Additionally, our usability study enhances our comprehension of user interaction, which we hope can prove beneficial in the design of VR applications moving forward.

The rest of this paper is structured as follows: In Sect. 2, we provide some background knowledge to help our readers understand the work-related topics, terms, and technologies. After that, Sect. 3 dives deep into the previous work on VR authentication and usability. Section 4 outlines our study design, methodology, and a brief discussion about user study. Sections 5 and 6 characterize our results, followed by the discussion. Section 7 contains the conclusion and future work.

2   Background

This section provides the prerequisite context and information for readers to engage with the paper.

2.1   Virtual Reality

Virtual Reality (VR) is an advanced computer graphic-generated human-computer interface that simulates a realistic environment. In VR, users have the ability to immerse themselves in experiences that can either replicate real-world scenarios or transport them to entirely different environments. VR evolved from the early stages of computer graphics, which began in the mid-1960 s to the early 1970s. At that time, it was referred to as Artificial Reality. The term 'Virtual Reality' [30] was first coined by Jaron Lanier, the founder of VPL Research. Nowadays, VR uses a mixture of different senses like light, touch, sound, and tactile feedback to generate more natural experiences. Head-Mounted Display (HMD) is used in standard VR systems as a display device. Augmented Reality smart glasses augment the virtual world to the real world and allow users to interact in real-time [40]. Figure 1 demonstrates two popular forms of VR display devices.

VR is based on two core ideas: immersiveness and interactivity. VR is fully immersive because it is built in such a way that it keeps the user away from other environmental distractions by blocking surroundings selectively. One of the primary objectives of VR is to immerse users in a virtual environment in a way that makes them feel as if they are present in the real world. Achieving this requires taking into account factors such as human psychology, anatomy, user perspective, and environmental awareness [18]. The applications of VR are vast, from medical research and training simulations to online gaming, virtual shopping, and even conferences and meetings. Due to its widespread usage, the VR market has grown significantly [42], with its current size estimated at 28.42 billion USD in 2022, up from 21.83 billion USD in the previous year. As VR technology continues to evolve, it is becoming more accessible to people from all walks of life.

(a) Head Mounted Display (HMD)   (b) Augmented Reality Glass

Fig. 1. VR Display Device

2.2 Authentication

Authentication is the process of recognizing a user's identity. It ensures the prevention of unauthorized access to sensitive data. User identification usually can be done by sending a secret code/password to the system [10]. This secret passcode can consist of four factors: (1) Something you know e.g., password, pattern, etc. (2) Something you are e.g., biometric features, fingerprint, etc. (3) Something you own e.g., ID card (4) Something you do e.g., typing pattern, pupil movement. Accessing the storage, intercepting the communication channel, or disclosing information can compromise the security of a secret password [23]. Therefore, authentication is crucial for data protection from the end-user perspective. Various mechanisms, such as numeric PINs, fingerprints, biometric features, and pattern locks, can authenticate the true user. The usability of authentication hinges on finding the right balance between security and user experience. Complex authentication procedures may discourage users or result in insecure practices, such as overly simplistic passwords.

2.3 Usability

Usability is one of the fundamental properties of a system or a process that defines how easily, effectively, efficiently, and safely a task can be performed. It is a measure of user satisfaction in a specific context. Usability vastly depends on human behavior and psychology. The quality of a product, software, device, or service is sometimes measured by its usability study. The 1996 System Usability Scale (SUS) [9] by Brooke is frequently used to evaluate the usability of a system. Later, Peres et al. validated that SUS can be used to compare two more systems [36].

There exists a reciprocal relationship between usability and security [49]. When security is prioritized, usability may suffer. An illustration of this is the common requirement for 11-character passwords containing at least one uppercase, one lowercase, one number, or one special character. These complex passwords can be difficult for users to recall, reducing usability and prompting evasive behavior – which in turn lowers security. Therefore, usability is an integral consideration throughout the design process.

3 Related Work

3.1 Interaction in VR

Different input modalities are used to interact with the virtual environment in VR, such as controller tapping, gaze input, head pose, or body gestures. People are habituated to using a physical keyboard, mouse, device, or hard surface as an input medium. In a virtual environment, for example, typing on a virtual keyboard or deforming an object (e.g., Rubik's Cube) lacks haptic feedback. The missing feedback degrades the usability of the virtual input systems [14].

. UI designers try to work around this limitation. For example, tapping can mimic real-world interaction, and pointing-based interaction (e.g., a laser beam) in VR enjoys popularity. A study by Hale et al. [16] discourages using pointers as an input method because it does not follow the natural interaction of real life. They also emphasize the precision problem on small screens. However, Ballagas et al. [6] showed that on large public displays, pointer-based interaction is useful and, indeed increases usability. In our study, we adopted the previous studies and combined both pointers and tapping as interaction concepts in the development. See Table 5 in the Appendix for our adaptation decision.

3.2   Authentication in VR

At the time of writing, available devices such as HTC Vive[1], or Oculus Quest[2] provide high-end usability and portability [12,39]. These devices are wireless and self-contained with an in-built display screen. But in some cases, they lack seamless interaction. For example, the authentication process sometimes requires a second device or the removal of the headset. While VR does offer some options for seamless and continuous authentication [33,38,43], the usability of the authentication process has often been overlooked in favor of prioritizing security and overall VR experience.

From the users' perspective, seamless authentication is necessary. Taking off the VR set to provide a secret code breaks the immersion and the experience. Researchers have proposed various solutions for VR authentication. These solutions can be categorized into the following groups:

Traditional Authentication Methods: These are predominantly based on the "something you know" principle. Established authentication methods such as Personal Identification Numbers (PINs), patterns, or passwords are widely used and accepted. They are time efficient and well integrated in 2D devices like mobile phones [46]. Initial research claimed that 2D devices' authentication methods are not well suited in virtual reality [3], as they are vulnerable to observation attacks [19,31,46]. To bolster the security of PINs, Krombholz et al. [21] proposed incorporating a pressure-sensitive layer into screens that would provide an additional pressure dimension when entering PINs, mostly invisible to shoulder surfers. They evaluated these *force-PINs* in touch screen devices and showed that it could increase the entropy of PINs without sacrificing usability. Furthermore, Lu et al. [27] proposed 3D passwords as an alternative, assuming they would be more secure due to the added dimension, thereby preventing shoulder surfing attacks. However, recent works show that PINs can be used for authentication in VR [32,48]. A comparative study by George et al. [15] found that PINs are suitable in the VR space due to their fast input speed. This is because PINs can be easily input in VR by tapping or pointing; while drawing a pattern on a 2D or 3D surface can be challenging as it relies on motor skills [15].

---

[1] https://www.vive.com/.
[2] https://www.meta.com/quest/.

After considering all the options, we decided to use PINs as the baseline of a traditional method of authentication for our study.

Behavioural Biometric Authentication: Behavioral biometric authentication leverages the human behavior patterns such as body movements [25], head movements [43], or gestures [22,38]. Behavioral biometrics has recently become increasingly popular due to its ability to block guessing and shoulder-surfing attacks [27]. This authentication method can be categorized into gesture, gaze, and rhythm-based authentication. However, one major drawback of behavioral biometrics is its observability, making it unsuitable for most public settings. Furthermore, the HMD obstructs the participant's vision. In 2009, Hansen et al. [17] reviewed gaze-based studies from the past 30 years and proposed that gaze features have unique characteristics that could be utilized for authentication. Eye movements, blinking, velocity, and other behaviors are distinctive [11,28,41,49] and can be used successfully to authenticate users. However, these biometric features demand a high cognitive load and are less user-friendly. Consequently, Mustafa et al. [34] suggested using behavioral biometric features in conjunction with other security measures as an added layer of security in VR applications that require rigorous protection. They also highlighted the potential challenges of relying solely on behavioral biometrics in a large-scale setting.

Knowledge-Based Biometric Authentication: Knowledge-based biometric authentication is a hybrid authentication method that leverages the strengths of both knowledge-based and biometric authentication methods. It offers a higher level of security and accuracy by validating the user's identity through a combination of something they know (knowledge-based authentication) and something they are (biometric authentication). The knowledge-based component involves the user providing information only they should know, while the biometric component uses physiological or behavioral characteristics to identify the user. While knowledge-based authentication methods are robust against traditional attacks, researchers have found novel attacks that exploit human traces on smartphone touchscreens, such as smudge [4], thermal [1], and microbiological attacks [20]. In light of this, Mathis et al. [32] suggested including hand movement patterns during PIN entry as an additional layer of protection.

3.3   Usability Issues in VR Authentication

One of the critical components of immersive technologies is their ability to integrate into our lives seamlessly. To achieve this, continuous authentication can be a viable solution for VR usage [43]. As VR headsets cover the user's eyes, they become less aware of their surroundings, hindering their 'body and environment awareness' and skills [18]. Therefore, an implicit and smooth authentication process is essential for VR. Research conducted by Zhu et al. [49] found that if security measures are too stringent, usability tends to suffer. Overly complex passwords may increase security (in the short run) but lower usability and user-friendliness, prompting possible evasive user behavior (e.g., writing them down).

Table 1. Pros and Cons of authentication in VR by their category.

Traditional Authentication	
Pros:	**Cons:**
- Well established	-Not hands free
- Easy to transfer	-Interruption in interaction
Behavioural Biometric Authentication	
Pros:	**Cons:**
-Implicit interaction	-Low stability
-Continuous auth	-Depends on cognitive mode
-Not observable	-Expose user in public space
Knowledge-Based Biometric Authentication	
Pros:	**Cons:**
-Added extra layer of security	-Memorability
-Implicit interaction	
-Protection in public space	

There is always a trade-off between security and usability. Keeping a balance between them is a tedious task in the design process for an authentication mechanism. The main goal is to maintain an ecosystem where users are protected without feeling burdened.

4   Study Design and Implementation

Our study employed a between-subjects design, consisting of two groups that were further divided based on their VR experience. Using two distinct methods, we obtained user authentication data and followed up with questions regarding their usability, based on the System Usability Scale (SUS) [9]. One group was given a four-digit PIN, while the other used gesture-based authentication. A total of 40 (mean age=29.02, SD=6.78, 67.5% male) people participated in our study. The overview of our study design and population is shown in Fig. 2.

Participants were recruited through social media advertising and posters in public spaces, such as bus stops and cafeterias. The recruited individuals represented diverse study programs and had backgrounds in both technical and non-technical fields. Participants received no financial compensation, and the study was entirely voluntary.

Based on our experiment design, we determined that a between-subject study would be the most appropriate choice for our sample category. This was done to eliminate any potential learning and ordering effects for participants. Login time and SUS score usability metrics were measured throughout the user study. VR authentication application was developed using C# in Unity 3D, and Oculus Integration 46.0 SDK (OVR) was used for the interaction framework and

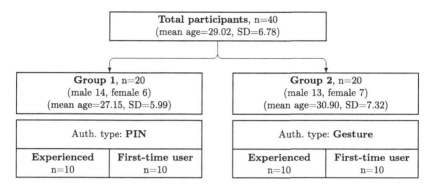

Fig. 2. Participant distribution for data collection.

displayed in Oculus Quest 2 HMD. Figure 3 shows the layout of the interface. Table 5, in the Appendix, summarizes our decision to select PIN authentication.

4.1 Methodology

The PINs had a four-digit length, and handwriting gestures comprised four symbols. Both were generated at random to ensure uniqueness among participants. We employed the login time calculation proposed by George et al. [15], which begins at the start of the virtual interface interaction and ends upon password entry via pointing and pressing the enter button. Wrist movements and relative wrist coordinates were used to identify gestures, with any four letters from the English alphabet (capitalized or lowercase) accepted for recognition. Stroke order and direction were disregarded to eliminate the need for users to remember during training/sample collection. This approach was inspired by the Point Cloud Recognizer [45] and adapted to accommodate 3D gesture recognition, utilizing the controller gyroscope and inbuilt HMD's camera to track hand and wrist positions and coordinates during movement.

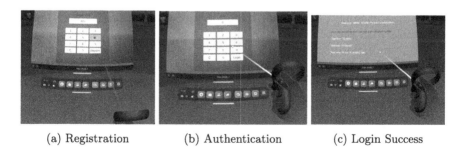

(a) Registration   (b) Authentication   (c) Login Success

Fig. 3. UI for 4-digit PIN

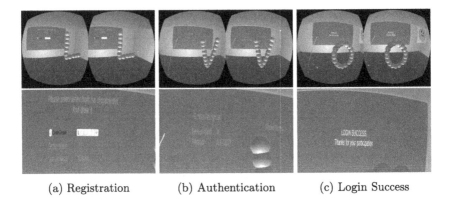

| (a) Registration | (b) Authentication | (c) Login Success |

Fig. 4. Different phases of gesture recognition authentication (full view and closeup)

4.2 Recruitment

We conducted the study with 40 university graduate students from various departments. Our recruitment strategy was informed by VR market analysis, which suggested that individuals between 16 and 34 are more likely to use VR [24]. Therefore, we focused on selecting participants falling within this demographic. Our selection process took into account prior experience with VR. Experienced users had used VR systems at least five times before, whereas first-time users had never interacted with VR before. There were no in-betweens. All participants possessed normal vision and were right-handed. They did not receive any financial compensation.

4.3 Data Collection

We divided our participants into two authentication groups. Figure 2 shows the participants' distribution for the data collection process.

Prior to commencing the study, we presented our research protocol and informed participants about our data collection methods. We proceeded to request their consent, giving them the opportunity to decline if they were not comfortable with the process. Following this, we provided a brief training session and introduced them to the VR setup and the input modality. We provided a tutorial to build familiarity with the authentication method (either PIN or gesture). Participants were then asked to enter their respective authentication type (PIN or gesture). During the trial run, most participants entered their authentication type once.

Participants were assigned a four-digit PIN or a four-letter gesture for the main experiment. Gestures incurred the additional step of registering them first (training the system). Subsequently, participants would authenticate themselves with those credentials once. The login time was measured from the beginning of the interaction until the authentication succeeds, i.e., if the user needed to re-enter because of a failed authentication, the total time across all the attempts was considered. Visual feedback in text form informs about the success or failure of the authentication.

In a post-study questionnaire, we collected users' usability evaluation of our authentication systems through a System Usability Scale (SUS) questionnaire [9]. SUS is a quantitative method to evaluate the usability of a system and provides a higher-level overview of the product from the user's perspective. SUS is also frequently used as a usability comparison tool between two systems [36].

4.4 Pilot Testing

Two participants who wore glasses encountered difficulties with our HMD. Specifically, one expressed that they could only see a blur while experimenting. As such, we limited recruiting to participants without corrective glasses. Additionally, our pilot study revealed that four participants favored a lighter-colored pointer. Thus, we changed the pointer color to a light blue when pointing to a button and a dim white when pointing somewhere else.

4.5 Data Analysis

Section 5.1 delves into the impact of authentication type on usability. We analyzed SUS scores for both PIN and gesture for all 40 participants without considering experience. To compare the difference between independent sample SUS scores for the two authentication types, we conducted the Wilcoxon Rank Sum Test [47].

Subsequently, in Sect. 5.2, we analyzed the impact of authentication type on login time. We conducted a statistical analysis to assess the performance of both methods. Since our data did not follow a normal distribution, we used the Independent-Samples Mann-Whitney U test [29], which is a non-parametric statistical analysis.

We furthered our analysis by factoring in experience to examine the impact of authentication types on both usability and login times. We repeated the tests mentioned above within each group for first-time and experienced participants for both PIN and gesture authentication types.

4.6 Ethical Considerations

No real credentials were used in the study. Our study was designed to minimize the need for personally identifiable information. We took steps to anonymize all data before processing it. Every participant was required to fill out a consent form and was free to ask questions and withdraw from the study at any time, both during and after participation. We made it clear that their decision to participate was entirely voluntary and that their privacy was paramount to us.

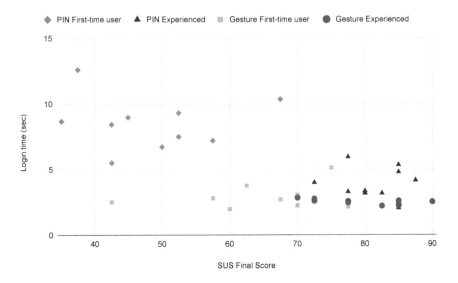

Fig. 5. Login times compared to SUS scores and participant groups

5   Results

Our findings show that experienced users rate the usability of PIN and gesture-based authentication equally and perform similarly on both, although PIN may take them more time to log in. However, first-time users, especially when using PINs, tend to perform significantly worse both in terms of usability and login time. Conversely, gesture-based authentication is generally faster and more readily embraced by those new to virtual reality. Figure 5 gives a broad overview of our results. The following sub-sections provide a detailed analysis of our findings.

5.1   Authentication Type and Usability

Wilcoxon Rank Sum Test shows that authentication type has a significant (Z=-2.320, p=0.02, rejection level=0.05) effect on system usability with a medium (r=0.37) effect size. On a five-point (1=strongly disagree, 5=strongly agree) System Usability Scale, participants show more preferences for gesture-based authentication. Table 2 presents the summary of the SUS score of each authentication method. Overall, our findings show that gestures have a higher acceptability than PINs. Thus, according to the classification from Bangor et al. [7], gesture authentication scores as 'Acceptable' while PIN scores only 'High Marginal' in acceptability.

5.2   Authentication Type and Login Time

Independent-Samples Mann-Whitney U Test shows that login time (mean=4.486, SD=2.706, median=3.195, n=40) statistically differs (p=.001 <

Table 2. SUS Score Summary

Authentication Type	Experience	Count	Mean	Min	Max	Grade Scale	Acceptability [7]
PIN	Experienced	10	81.25	72.5	87.5	B	Acceptable
	First-time user	10	48.25	35	67.5	F	Not Acceptable
	Overall	20	64.75	35	87.5	D	Marginal (High)
Gesture	Experienced	10	79.75	70	90	C	Acceptable
	First-time user	10	65.50	42.5	77.5	D	Marginal (High)
	Overall	20	72.63	42.5	90	C	Acceptable

.05) based on the authentication type. Login time depends on the authentication type. Our statistical test indicates a significant difference (U=30, Z=-4.599, p=.001) to gesture (mean rank=12.0, median=2.599, n=20) and PIN (mean rank=29.0, median=5.74, n=20). Gestures as an authentication method require less time to log in compared to PIN. This notable speed difference shows that users are able to log in at a faster pace when using gestures rather than a PIN. Table 3 summarizes the login time for each authentication method.

Table 3. Login time summary

Authentication Type	Experience	Count	Mean	SD	Min	Max
PIN	Experienced	10	3.94 s	1.17	2.06 s	5.96 s
	First-time user	10	8.54 s	2.0	5.51 s	12.61 s
	Overall	20	6.24 s	2.85	2.06 s	12.61 s
Gesture	Experienced	10	2.53 s	0.21	2.22 s	2.85 s
	First-time user	10	2.94 s	0.93	2.00 s	5.14 s
	Overall	20	2.73 s	0.69	2.00 s	5.14 s

5.3 PIN: Experienced vs. First-Time User

We also examined whether VR experience has an impact on usability. We found that participants with prior VR experience scored significantly (Z=-3.79, p=.001) higher on the SUS scale than first-time participants with a large effect size. Our results show that experienced participants are more confident using the PIN authentication and provide a high average score of 4.8/5 by answering question 9 (*[Q9] "I felt very confident using the system"*), whereas first-time users rate it as 2.5/5. From question 10 (*[Q10] "I needed to learn a lot of things before I could get going with this system"*), we can infer that first-time users may need some time to learn how to use the VR system. This may lead to a lack of confidence in using the PIN to log in to the system, affecting the time taken to log in. Based on the Independent-Samples Mann-Whitney U Test, we found that participants with VR experience take significantly less time (p=.001, Z=-3.704) to log in than those with no prior VR experience. Figure 6 compares the average SUS score for each question when using PIN for authentication while taking experience into account.

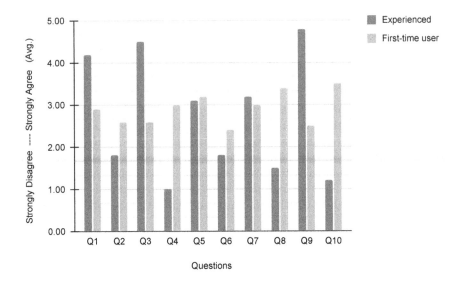

Fig. 6. Average SUS score of the individual questions for PIN

5.4   Gesture: Experienced vs. First-Time User

The Independent-Samples Mann-Whitney U Test demonstrates no significant difference (U=37, Z=.983, p=.353) in login time between experienced users (median=2.57, n=10) and first-time users (median=2.28, n=10). However, the same statistical test for usability shows that experienced users score significantly higher than first-time users (U=10, Z=-3.042, p=.002). It is worth noting that while the SUS score indicates experience has an impact on using gesture authentication, login time suggests otherwise. One possible explanation for this discrepancy is that PIN entry requires a specific motor task confined to a fixed surface area, whereas gesture authentication allows for more natural, free movement. Participants with no VR experience report feeling more confident using gesture authentication than PIN (Q9, score 3.7 vs. 2.5). Figure 7 compares the average SUS score for each question, when using gesture for authentication while taking experience into account.

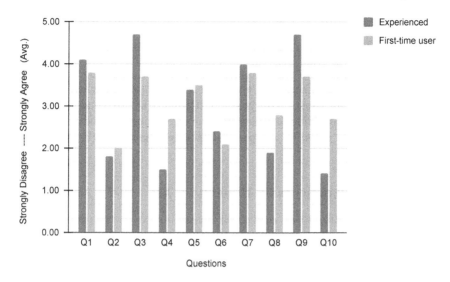

Fig. 7. Average SUS score of the individual questions for Gesture

6   Discussion

A developer can follow two major schools of thought when porting a process from conventional GUI to VR.

For one, focus on familiarity with the conventional 2D user interface and try to mimic that as closely as possible. The idea is to increase usability by tapping into what users already learned and know from the 2D world and thus reduce adaption costs.

The other school of thought is to increase usability by natively integrating it into the new medium at the expense of familiarity. The benefit here is the seamless and coherent integration into the advanced interaction capabilities and the internal working logic of the virtual world.

Our results clearly suggest that familiarity gains from the 2D world weigh much less than one might expect. Native VR methods that take advantage of the new UI style should be preferred. In our study, gesture-based handwriting authentication provided security levels similar to the 2D PIN while delivering the most benefits to first-time users and significantly improving the performance of experienced users.

6.1   Impact of Authentication Type on Usability in VR

Our findings indicate that authentication type influences usability. Participants found gesture authentication to be *acceptable*, while PIN was only rated as *marginally acceptable* [7]. Though PIN is established and one of the faster (1.5 s) [46] authentication methods in a mobile device, in our study, PIN authentication took 6.24 s on average, while gesture authentication took only 2.74 s. This login time difference affected the usability score, implying that if the established PIN is transferred to the VR space, there is a significant performance drop, reducing the usability.

The data demonstrates that conventional authentication methods, such as the PIN, may be less effective in the immersive VR world, where users prefer more natural interactions. Our study participants showed that they favored gesture-based authentication, emphasizing the importance of modifying authentication methods to cater to the particular requirements of VR and improve overall usability.

6.2   Impact of Experience on Usability in VR

Our findings also indicate that experience has an impact on the overall usability of the authentication system. For both the PIN and the gesture authentication method, experienced participants provided a higher usability score than first-time participants.

Familiarity and learning curves play a significant role in technology adoption, particularly in immersive environments like VR. The greater ease experienced by first-time participants with gestures suggests that incorporating natural and intuitive interactions has a shorter learning curve for newcomers, thereby facilitating a smoother transition into VR. This implies that VR applications aimed at a diverse user base, including beginners, may benefit from prioritizing user-friendly, gesture-based interactions. Additionally, adaptive VR interfaces that adjust authentication and interaction methods based on the user's experience level can enhance overall usability.

6.3   Limitations

By recruiting student participants from mostly technology-related fields, our sample only partially represents the general population. On the other hand, our recruitment selected participants that align with the market analysis of VR users [24], i.e., technology-affine aged between 16 and 35. Furthermore, we conduct our research in a lab setting that ensures a controlled environment, though expanding to diverse settings can enhance the generalizability of our results. We believe that our research provides a strong foundation for understanding the usability of PIN and gesture authentication in VR, and our findings hold valuable implications for improving the usability design of authentication methods.

7   Conclusion and Future Work

This paper assesses the usability of two distinct authentication methods in virtual reality - one utilizing a familiar number pad for PINs and the other a handwriting gesture. Based on factors such as login time and SUS score, it then pinpoints the factors that influence the usability of those VR authentication methods. The data shows that the type of authentication interaction and the user's proficiency in virtual reality significantly impact the authentication process's usability. In particular, the naturalness of interaction, such as with gesture-based authentication, is crucial for usability.

The research has shown promising directions regarding the usability of authentication in virtual reality. Moving forward, we aim to broaden our investigation to include more authentication methods and interaction styles. Furthermore, we intend to conduct our study in both laboratory and natural settings. Additionally, future work should examine how factors such as design, behavior, and context influence authentication usability.

A System Usability Scale

Table 4. Adapted System Usability Scale

	Strongly disagree	Strongly agree
1. I think that I would like to use this (PIN/Gesture-based) authentication system frequently in VR		1 2 3 4 5
2. I found the system unnecessarily complex		1 2 3 4 5
3. I thought (PIN/Gesture-based) authentication system was easy to use in VR		1 2 3 4 5
4. I think that I would need the support of a technical person to be able to use this system		1 2 3 4 5
5. I found the various functions in this system were well integrated		1 2 3 4 5
6. I thought there was too much inconsistency in this system		1 2 3 4 5
7. I would imagine that most people would learn to use this (PIN/Gesture-based) authentication system very quickly		1 2 3 4 5
8. I found the system very cumbersome to use		1 2 3 4 5
9. I felt very confident using (PIN/Gesture-based) authentication system in VR		1 2 3 4 5
10. I needed to learn a lot of things before I could get going with this system		1 2 3 4 5

Table 5. Decision table for PIN authentication type.

Input Modalities	
Pointer	Ray cast on the input surface, Controller tapping for selection, Both hand interaction [13,15]
Pointer on click	Two button presses are required for complete selection. Relatively slow, and not usable.
Tap (touch)	Adopt from the touch screen physical devices, Virtual typing is required. Left visual clues, vulnerable for observation attack [15]. Conflict with "Area Awareness and Skill", and "Body Awareness and Skill" as the user's eyes are covered with VR headset [18]. Not suitable for public place authentication. Screen/input surface size matters, suitable for (relatively) small surface [8].
Input Surface	
Large	Not suitable for our study, Touch is not suitable, Pointer requires a noticeable motor (wrist, hand, head) movements
Medium	For Pointing modalities, medium type surface is the best suitable [15]
Small	Adopt form the personal device such as smartphones. Suitable for touch interaction, Pointer interaction is harder because of the motor movements
Password Type	
PIN	Established and widely used, faster, usable and secure [15]
Pattern	Relatively slower, error-prone, sensitive motor task required
Other decisions	
Username	Not required,
Joystick selection	Required longer time, not suitable with Fitt's law [8]

References

1. Abdelrahman, Y., Khamis, M., Schneegass, S., Alt, F.: Stay cool! Understanding thermal attacks on mobile-based user authentication. In: Proceedings of the 2017 CHI Conference on Human Factors in Computing Systems, pp. 3751–3763 (2017)
2. Alsop, T.: VR device shipments by vendor worldwide 2017–2019 (2022). https://www.statista.com/statistics/671403/global-virtual-reality-device-shipments-by-vendor/
3. Alsulaiman, F.A., El Saddik, A.: A novel 3D graphical password schema. In: 2006 IEEE Symposium on Virtual Environments, Human-Computer Interfaces and Measurement Systems, pp. 125–128. IEEE (2006)

4. Aviv, A.J., Gibson, K., Mossop, E., Blaze, M., Smith, J.M.: Smudge attacks on smartphone touch screens. In: 4th USENIX Workshop on Offensive Technologies (WOOT 10) (2010)
5. Ball, C., Huang, K.T., Francis, J.: Virtual reality adoption during the COVID-19 pandemic: a uses and gratifications perspective. Telematics Inform. **65**, 101728 (2021)
6. Ballagas, R., Rohs, M., Sheridan, J.G.: Sweep and point and shoot: phonecam-based interactions for large public displays. In: CHI 2005 Extended Abstracts on Human Factors in Computing Systems, pp. 1200–1203 (2005)
7. Bangor, A., Kortum, P., Miller, J.: Determining what individual SUS scores mean: adding an adjective rating scale. J. Usability Stud. **4**(3), 114–123 (2009)
8. Bi, X., Li, Y., Zhai, S.: FFitts law: modeling finger touch with fitts' law, pp. 1363–1372 (2013)
9. Brooke, J., et al.: SUS-a quick and dirty usability scale. Usability Eval. Ind. **189**(194), 4–7 (1996)
10. Burrows, M., Abadi, M., Needham, R.: A logic of authentication. ACM Trans. Comput. Syst. (TOCS) **8**(1), 18–36 (1990)
11. Cantoni, V., Galdi, C., Nappi, M., Porta, M., Riccio, D.: Gant: Gaze analysis technique for human identification. Pattern Recogn. **48**(4), 1027–1038 (2015)
12. Craddock, I.M.: Immersive virtual reality, google expeditions, and English language learning. Libr. Technol. Rep. **54**(4), 7–9 (2018)
13. Doronichev, A.: Daydream labs: exploring and sharing VR's possibilities. Retrieved 10 April 2020 (2016)
14. Earnshaw, R.A.: Virtual Reality Systems. Academic Press (2014)
15. George, C., et al.: Seamless and secure VR: Adapting and evaluating established authentication systems for virtual reality (2017)
16. Hale, K.S., Stanney, K.M.: Handbook of Virtual Environments: Design, Implementation, and Applications. CRC Press (2014)
17. Hansen, D.W., Ji, Q.: In the eye of the beholder: a survey of models for eyes and gaze. IEEE Trans. Pattern Anal. Mach. Intell. **32**(3), 478–500 (2009)
18. Jacob, R.J., et al.: Reality-based interaction: a framework for post-wimp interfaces, pp. 201–210 (2008)
19. Khamis, M., Alt, F., Hassib, M., von Zezschwitz, E., Hasholzner, R., Bulling, A.: GazeTouchPass: multimodal authentication using gaze and touch on mobile devices. In: Proceedings of the 2016 CHI Conference Extended Abstracts on Human Factors in Computing Systems, pp. 2156–2164 (2016)
20. Krombholz, K., Dabrowski, A., Weippl, E.: Poster: The petri dish attack-guessing secrets based on bacterial growth (2018)
21. Krombholz, K., Hupperich, T., Holz, T.: Use the force: evaluating {Force-Sensitive} authentication for mobile devices. In: Twelfth Symposium on Usable Privacy and Security (SOUPS 2016), pp. 207–219 (2016)
22. Kupin, A., Moeller, B., Jiang, Y., Banerjee, N.K., Banerjee, S.: Task-driven biometric authentication of users in virtual reality (VR) environments. In: Kompatsiaris, I., Huet, B., Mezaris, V., Gurrin, C., Cheng, W.-H., Vrochidis, S. (eds.) MMM 2019. LNCS, vol. 11295, pp. 55–67. Springer, Cham (2019). https://doi.org/10.1007/978-3-030-05710-7_5
23. Lamport, L.: Password authentication with insecure communication. Commun. ACM **24**(11), 770–772 (1981)
24. Laricchia, F.: UK: VR headset owners by age 2023 (2023). https://www.statista.com/statistics/1362661/share-of-vr-headset-owners-by-age-uk/

25. Liebers, J., et al.: Understanding user identification in virtual reality through behavioral biometrics and the effect of body normalization. In: Proceedings of the 2021 CHI Conference on Human Factors in Computing Systems. pp. 1–11 (2021)

26. Lin, F., Cho, K.W., Song, C., Xu, W., Jin, Z.: Brain password: a secure and truly cancelable brain biometrics for smart headwear. In: Proceedings of the 16th Annual International Conference on Mobile Systems, Applications, and Services, pp. 296–309 (2018)

27. Lu, D., Lee, T., Das, S., Hong, J.I.: Examining visual-spatial paths for mobile authentication. In: WAY@ SOUPS (2016)

28. Luo, S., Nguyen, A., Song, C., Lin, F., Xu, W., Yan, Z.: OcuLock: exploring human visual system for authentication in virtual reality head-mounted display. In: 2020 Network and Distributed System Security Symposium (NDSS) (2020)

29. MacFarland, T.W.W., Yates, J.M.M.: Introduction to Nonparametric Statistics for the Biological Sciences Using R. Springer, Cham (2016). https://doi.org/10.1007/978-3-319-30634-6

30. Machover, C., Tice, S.E.: Virtual reality. IEEE Comput. Graphics Appl. **14**(1), 15–16 (1994)

31. Maguire, J., Renaud, K.: You only live twice or the years we wasted caring about shoulder-surfing (2015). arXiv preprint arXiv:1508.05626

32. Mathis, F., Fawaz, H.I., Khamis, M.: Knowledge-driven biometric authentication in virtual reality. In: Extended Abstracts of the 2020 CHI Conference on Human Factors in Computing Systems, pp. 1–10 (2020)

33. Miller, R., Ajit, A., Banerjee, N.K., Banerjee, S.: Realtime behavior-based continual authentication of users in virtual reality environments. In: 2019 IEEE International Conference on Artificial Intelligence and Virtual Reality (AIVR), pp. 253–2531. IEEE (2019)

34. Mustafa, T., Matovu, R., Serwadda, A., Muirhead, N.: Unsure how to authenticate on your VR headset? Come on, use your head! In: Proceedings of the Fourth ACM International Workshop on Security and Privacy Analytics, pp. 23–30 (2018)

35. Partala, T.: Psychological needs and virtual worlds: case second life. Int. J. Hum Comput Stud. **69**(12), 787–800 (2011)

36. Peres, S.C., Pham, T., Phillips, R.: Validation of the system usability scale (SUS) SUS in the wild. In: Proceedings of the Human Factors and Ergonomics Society Annual Meeting. vol. 57, pp. 192–196. SAGE Publications Sage CA: Los Angeles, CA (2013)

37. Petrock, V.: Us virtual and augmented reality users 2020 (2020). https://www.insiderintelligence.com/content/us-virtual-and-augmented-reality-users-2020

38. Pfeuffer, K., Geiger, M.J., Prange, S., Mecke, L., Buschek, D., Alt, F.: Behavioural biometrics in VR: Identifying people from body motion and relations in virtual reality. In: Proceedings of the 2019 CHI Conference on Human Factors in Computing Systems, pp. 1–12 (2019)

39. Phelan, D.: Google daydream VR review: comfy, capable and affordable but not enough content yet (2016). https://www.independent.co.uk/tech/google-daydream-view-vr-review-virtual-reality-pixel-xl-headset-is-it-worth-it-a7444226.html

40. Rauschnabel, P.A., Brem, A., Ro, Y.: Augmented reality smart glasses: definition, conceptual insights, and managerial importance. Unpublished Working Paper, The University of Michigan-Dearborn, College of Business (2015)

41. Rigas, I., Economou, G., Fotopoulos, S.: Biometric identification based on the eye movements and graph matching techniques. Pattern Recogn. Lett. **33**(6), 786–792 (2012)

42. Sergei Vardomatski: Council post: Augmented and virtual reality after COVID-19 (2021). Accessed 4 Nov 2022

43. Sivasamy, M., Sastry, V., Gopalan, N.: VRCAuth: continuous authentication of users in virtual reality environment using head-movement. In: 2020 5th International Conference on Communication and Electronics Systems (ICCES), pp. 518–523. IEEE (2020)

44. Sluganovic, I., Roeschlin, M., Rasmussen, K.B., Martinovic, I.: Using reflexive eye movements for fast challenge-response authentication. In: Proceedings of the 2016 ACM SIGSAC Conference on Computer and Communications Security, pp. 1056–1067 (2016)

45. Vatavu, R.D., Anthony, L., Wobbrock, J.O.: Gestures as point clouds: a $ p recognizer for user interface prototypes. In: Proceedings of the 14th ACM International Conference on Multimodal Interaction, pp. 273–280 (2012)

46. Von Zezschwitz, E., Dunphy, P., De Luca, A.: Patterns in the wild: a field study of the usability of pattern and pin-based authentication on mobile devices. In: Proceedings of the 15th International Conference on Human-Computer Interaction with Mobile Devices and Services, pp. 261–270 (2013)

47. Wilcoxon, F.: Individual Comparisons by Ranking Methods. In: Kotz, S., Johnson, N.L. (eds.) Breakthroughs in Statistics. Springer Series in Statistics. Springer, New York, NY (1992). https://doi.org/10.1007/978-1-4612-4380-9_16

48. Yu, Z., Liang, H.N., Fleming, C., Man, K.L.: An exploration of usable authentication mechanisms for virtual reality systems. In: 2016 IEEE Asia Pacific Conference on Circuits and Systems (APCCAS), pp. 458–460. IEEE (2016)

49. Zhu, H., Jin, W., Xiao, M., Murali, S., Li, M.: BlinKey: a two-factor user authentication method for virtual reality devices. Proc. ACM Interact. Mob. Wearable Ubiquitous Technol. 4(4), 1–29 (2020)

Living a Lie: Security Analysis of Facial Liveness Detection Systems in Mobile Apps

Xianbo Wang[iD], Kaixuan Luo[iD], and Wing Cheong Lau[(✉)][iD]

Department of Information Engineering, The Chinese University of Hong Kong,
Shatin, N.T., Hong Kong
{xianbo,kaixuan,wclau}@ie.cuhk.edu.hk

Abstract. Mobile apps are embracing facial recognition technology to streamline the identity verification procedure for security-critical activities such as opening online bank accounts. To ensure the security of the system, liveness detection plays a vital role as an anti-spoofing component, verifying that a selfie provided is from a live individual. Emerging facial recognition companies offer convenient integration services through mobile libraries that are widely utilized by numerous apps in the market. By analyzing 18 mobile facial recognition libraries, we reveal the protocol design and implementation intricacies of various systems. The investigation leads to the discovery of several system security issues in over half of the libraries, predominantly linked to the liveness detection module. These vulnerabilities can be exploited for low-cost identity forgery attacks without relying on media synthesizing technologies like deepfake. We scan 18,096 apps from an app market and identify 802 apps incorporating recognized facial recognition libraries, with over 100 million total downloads. More than half of the libraries examined exhibit weak security, with about 40% downstream mobile apps being affected. This study emphasizes the importance of system security in mobile facial recognition services, as the practical impact can be on par with or even surpass the extensively studied machine learning attacks.

Keywords: Mobile facial recognition · Liveness detection · Library vulnerability · Identity forgery · Protocol security

1 Introduction

The recent advancements in computer vision technology have led to the growth of automatic facial recognition services. Today, highly accurate facial recognition can be performed on consumer mobile devices. In addition to serving as an authentication method for tasks like unlocking screens, many security-sensitive mobile apps are utilizing facial recognition for identification purposes. Examples include using it for anti-money laundering (AML) in banking apps, age verification in gaming or gambling apps, and as a proof of identity on social media or crowdsourcing platforms. Among these applications, Electronic Know Your

C. Pöpper and L. Batina (Eds.): ACNS 2024, LNCS 14585, pp. 432–459, 2024.
https://doi.org/10.1007/978-3-031-54776-8_17

Customer (eKYC) process in the financial services industry is most common. Traditionally, opening a bank account requires physical presence of an individual in a bank with the identity document for prevention of fraudulent activities involving document forgery or identity theft. With recent advances in eKYC via mobile devices, the cumbersome in-person application process of various banking or financial services can be eliminated. For instance, many mobile banking apps now employ optical character recognition (OCR) to extract information on the identity document and utilize facial recognition technology to match the individual's live facial image with the reference photo obtained from the identity document or a trusted source. A challenge that is unique to the online eKYC scenario is the validation of the "liveness" status, which is not a problem in the offline scenario as it is straightforward for human bank tellers to verify such thing. Hence, *liveness detection*, which has the ability to distinguish between a real live person and fake entities like photos, masks, or pre-recorded videos, is critical for ensuring the security of a facial recognition system.

Given the privacy impact and economic interest, criminals are incentivized to conduct spoofing attacks against facial recognition systems for identity forgery. In many cases, instead of targeting a specific victim, professional identity forgers profit from mass identity fraud such as opening bank accounts under random victims' names for money laundering, creating multiple accounts to take advantage of new user rewards, or selling identity-verified accounts to scammers or users from restricted regions. As a matter of fact, massive number of stolen identity documents have been circulating in the underground markets. Sellers even bundle the identity documents with high-resolution photos of the victim and sell them at a low price [1]. The black market thrives the most in regions like China, where the facial recognition market has enjoyed rapid growth and wide adoption [2]. In our investigation, we find that stolen identity materials are sold at only around $3 per set. Worse still, with less than $100, one can buy a tutorial on bypassing certain mainstream mobile facial recognition systems adopted by commercial companies, with software included. News reports [3,4] have covered real legal cases where criminals forged videos of the victim to open bank accounts or forge tax invoices under the victim's identity.

Easy access to stolen identity documents and photos makes liveness detection a crucial component for facial recognition. By examining subtle traces like facial expressions, reflections, and video continuity, the liveness detection algorithm, usually in the form of a machine learning classifier, can determine if the input is from a real person in front of the camera. In recent years, deep learning-based image and video synthesis techniques, popularly known as deepfakes, have exposed vulnerabilities in facial recognition systems used in academia and industry, particularly in liveness detection [5]. Meanwhile, various mitigations have been proposed as summarized in a survey paper [6]. Activities within the aforementioned underground markets, alongside documented criminal cases, indicates a prevailing preference for conventional, manually-operated animation software and data injection attacks that exploit design or implementation vulnerabilities, rather than resorting to deepfake methodologies. This suggests that the technical and financial barriers to deploying deepfake attacks may be beyond the reach of typical criminals. Meanwhile, the fact that criminals can conduct non-deepfake attacks at scale raises an alarm in the security of current facial recognition systems.

Unfortunately, while synthetic media attacks on facial recognition systems have been widely discussed, there is a void in the security research focusing on the protocol design and system implementation aspects. In this work, we systematically analyze the security of mobile Software Development Kits (SDK) from mainstream facial recognition service providers.[1] By inspecting the internals of the system, we discover that numerous mobile facial recognition SDKs are susceptible to low-cost non-synthetic attacks. The underlying vulnerabilities stem from flawed protocol design or careless implementation, irrespective of the sophistication or reliability of the machine-learning algorithms employed for liveness detection. We conduct an extensive security analysis of 18 popular mobile facial recognition SDKs and reveal 10 of them have critical security issues. Based on these findings, we launch market-scale app scanning and identify over 300 apps that may be at risk of exploitation. To facilitate readers in acquiring a visual understanding of the attack, we provide a demonstration video [7] that showcases a proof-of-concept attack against a real mobile app with over 4 million total downloads. To summarize, this paper has made the following contributions:

- We delineate three typical system architectures of facial recognition systems in mobile apps, and reveal protocol design and implementation details.
- We uncover overlooked yet common weaknesses in the liveness detection systems of mobile facial recognition SDKs, which can lead to identity forgery attacks without the need for media synthesizing techniques like deepfake.
- We develop an SDK fingerprinting framework capable of scanning apps on the market and quantifying the impact of our findings. This framework is designed to be resistant to app hardening techniques.

2   Background

In this section, we introduce background information of facial recognition systems used in mobile eKYC, including their main components, high-level design patterns, and modes of liveness detection.

2.1   Facial Recognition Pipeline

Usually, the facial recognition pipeline consists of three major components, as illustrated in Fig. 1.

1. *Face detection*: The camera stream is first fed into the face detection module, which decides whether a given picture frame contains a human face and optionally returns the coordinates of the bounding box. Face detection is efficient and serves as an input filter to save subsequent processing work.

---

[1] For simplicity, we refer to cloud facial recognition service provider as *face cloud* and their mobile library as *face SDK* in this paper.

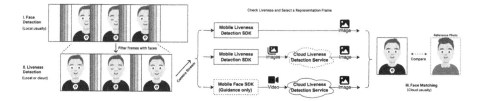

Fig. 1. Facial Recognition Pipeline.

2. *Liveness detection*: A single frame or a sequence of consecutive frames containing the face becomes the input of the liveness detection module. As a classifier, the liveness detection module can tell whether the input picture frames are captured from a live person.
3. *Face matching*: A single frame or several representative frames are chosen as the input for the face-matching module. This module determines whether the input face matches the reference face (from identity document or authority database) and returns the final result of the facial recognition process.

Given the computational capabilities and security measures of mobile devices, it is possible for the facial recognition service provider to distribute these components across various locations. Typically, the process of face detection takes place on the device itself, as most mobile devices possess sufficient computational resources for this task, and face matching is performed on the cloud, involving access to an authoritative database. In situations where a centralized face database is unavailable, the captured photo is compared to an image extracted from a scanned identity document. The implementation of liveness detection varies among vendors, with different modes being observed in practice. These modes will be discussed in detail in the following section.

2.2   Design Patterns of Mobile Facial Recognition Systems

While users interact with the facial recognition interface in the mobile app, there are several processes taking place in the backend of the system. Many apps depend on facial recognition service providers that offer SDKs tailored for popular mobile platforms like Android and iOS, simplifying the development process for app developers. These SDKs encapsulate complex implementations, including machine learning models, and offer developers a user-friendly Application Programming Interface (API). Some SDKs also handle network messaging with the providers' cloud server for the app. Although most of the functions remain hidden from app developers, they may still need to implement their own customized logic and send data to their own server in certain cases. By differentiating the placement of components in the facial recognition pipeline in Fig. 1, we can categorize the mobile facial recognition system into the following three patterns:

- *Pure Local*: The liveness detection and face matching both take place on the user's mobile device. This assures the best privacy but can only give an untrusted result.
- *Local-Cloud Mixed*: As the most security-sensitive step, face matching is commonly secured in the backend server. To save network bandwidth and optimize user experience, many systems perform initial liveness detection, especially video-processing ones, on the user's device. In some systems, a secondary image-based liveness detection is executed inside the cloud for an additional level of security.
- *Pure Cloud*: To ensure the reliability of data processing and verification, some providers incorporate liveness detection and face matching on the backend server, while the mobile SDK only help capture and upload face videos without much processing. However, this approach may have negative impact on user experience due to network delays and reduced app responsiveness.

The various settings outlined above necessitate the transfer of data across different locations, leading to varying protocol flows. We will delve into the internal system designs in Sect. 4.

2.3 Modes of Liveness Detection

There are many different liveness detection techniques. We can categorize them based on the mode of operation that can be observed by the users.

- *Static image*: Some can use a single image as the input. By inspecting static information like reflections, textures, Moire patterns, and image quality [8], it can differentiate live-captured image *vs.* image that was re-shot or transferred from the Internet.
- *Passive video*: The information that the model can learn from a static image is limited. Most liveness detection models require a video snippet or a sequence of consecutive frames as the input. Natural facial motions like eye blinking and mouth movement are useful for liveness detection. Another more recent method is to flash screens with different colors and infer liveness from the reflected lights [9].
- *Interactive video*: In addition to a natural video with a shown face, it is common for liveness detection systems to use an interactive approach where the user needs to perform specified actions such as blinking eyes, shaking the head, or reading a sequence of numbers.

The variety of the methods is not only displayed in academic works [10] but also in real products [11]. Many face recognition service providers even have multiple product lines, applying different techniques.

3 Threat Model

This paper focuses on the insecure protocol and implementation threats and considers attackers with practical capabilities and aim for low-cost attacks that are easy to scale. We are especially interested in the settings where the attacker performs traditional system attacks without involving computer vision technologies like deepfake. While recent studies [5,12] have shown that synthetic media technologies powered by deepfake or adversarial learning can deceive facial recognition or other machine learning models used in mobile apps, the practical threats for non-synthetic attacks have not been covered.

This work focuses on the *non-synthetic attacks with stolen identity materials* threat model. The goal of the attacker is to spoof the eKYC system and complete the identity-proofing process as a victim. We assume the attacker possesses clear face image(s) of the victim, like headshots or photo posted on social platforms, along with other essential personal information like name and identity card number. Be aware that these materials can be easily obtained in the underground market, as discussed in Sect. 1. The attacker has complete control over a test mobile device, on which he can modify the system, inject code, and perform various analyses against the vulnerable target app. There are two branches of techniques that attackers can apply. We call those attacks that exploit insecurity in the design or implementation to bypass the liveness detection as *injection attacks*, which are the focus of this study. We call those attacks that use computer-generated imagery (CGI) or more advanced deep learning approaches *synthetic attacks*.

In practice, apart from fundamental security threats such as the trustworthiness of client-side results, the cost of an attack plays a crucial role in assessing the actual threat. For example, when the verification process is conducted locally, attacking apps without any reverse engineering protection are considered *effortless*, whereas attacks that require non-trivial efforts like deobfuscation are deemed *laborious*. In cases where the liveness detection result cannot be forged through data replacement of code injection, non-synthetic attacks are deemed *impractical*.

4   Mobile Facial Liveness Detection Protocols

To systematically study face recognition SDKs, especially the liveness detection system in practice, we analyze the protocols of a number of mainstream SDKs in the market and propose a general framework to summarize their protocol flows. We then zoom into each part of the protocol and further analyze its design and implementation details.

4.1   General Protocol Flow

Mobile facial recognition systems, especially those provided as a cloud service, involve multiple entities, including a mobile app, a facial recognition SDK embedded in the mobile app, the app's backend server, the backend cloud of the facial recognition service provider, and authoritative data sources. Each entity invokes the others to exchange data. Figure 2 describes a high level protocol flow for common mobile facial recognition systems for identity verification purposes. Our study focuses on the liveness detection part of the protocol, which consists of three major phases:

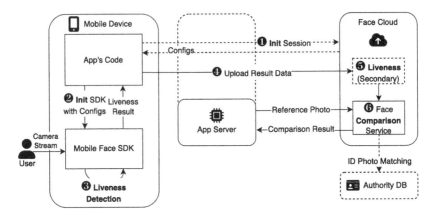

Fig. 2. Architecture of common facial recognition systems in mobile apps

1. *Initialization.* The mobile app initializes the embedded face SDK with optional configurations like liveness detection modes. In some system, the app needs to first contact the facial recognition service cloud to establish a session and fetch pre-defined configurations (❶, ❷). The session establishment step may be delegated through the app server. At the same time, the SDK may collect environment information like the operating system version, root status, and packages installed, so as to determine whether it is secure to proceed to the next phase, or to be passed to the service provider cloud for risk checking.

2. *Interaction and detection.* After initializing the SDK, the app can invoke the liveness detection process. Usually, the configurations during initialization stage determines the motion matching strategy. The order and types of motions in the sequence are usually randomized to prevent replay attack with pre-recorded video. Afterwards, the SDK or the app displays the liveness detection interface and guides the user to capture the face with required motions. The face video stream can be processed at different locations for liveness detection, as we discussed in Sect. 2.2. Some systems handle liveness detection locally (❸), some uploads the raw video clip to the cloud for liveness detection (❺), and others use a mixed strategy. Deep learning models are commonly employed under the hood for the purpose of classifying whether captured frames contain live face images.

3. *Result passing.* The liveness detection system produces a static image as its final output, which is then inputted into the face matching module (❻). Note that the data transmitted to the cloud (❹) can be intermediate result containing video, images, or metadata for further verification. To safeguard against on-path injection attacks, the data returned from the SDK can be encrypted or signed. Additionally, including a session identifier enables the cloud to authenticate the initialized settings.

4.2   Design and Implementation Details

Facial recognition service providers choose various architectures and designs of the system. As introduced in Sect. 2, depending on where each module is hosted, the system can have different architectures, which significantly affects the design of the protocol. In addition, each provider and app server can have heterogeneous implementations. These factors result in different protocol paths in Fig. 2. For a thorough description, we list 6 key differentiating characteristics of face SDKs, as depicted in Fig. 3, and discuss their implications.

(1) Protection of Business Logic. As some security-sensitive functions run on mobile devices, face SDK vendors tend to write more power-efficient code and employ various techniques to protect related code from reverse engineering. It is common to implement core modules like the liveness detection algorithm as a Native (compiled from C/C++) library. Native code has higher efficiency, especially for image processing and deep learning inferences. At the same time, Native binaries are generally harder to reverse than Java bytecode. Obfuscation techniques are also applied in some face SDKs with Native library obfuscation tools like OLLVM [13] or Java code obfuscator like ProGuard [14].

(2) Configurability. To enhance flexibility in usage, certain SDKs (*e.g.*, SDK A, D in Table 1) offer the option for apps to customize parameters that control the liveness detection process. These parameters commonly include the liveness detection mode, action settings such as the number of eye blinks required, and even the passing threshold for the liveness test. However, not all of these adjustable parameters are documented. We refer to them as *undocumented parameters* when they can be configured via API calls but are not described in the documentation. On the other hand, *implicit parameters* are not exposed through API calls but can be modified by altering the SDK. For instance, certain SDKs randomly generate the required action sequence within local code, which can be controlled by code modification. In systems that retrieve configurations from the cloud, these configurations may be linked to a session, and the cloud might verify the results using predefined configurations to prevent unauthorized modifications.

(3) Environment Checking. The purpose of environment checking is to ensure that the app runs in a secure environment, preventing code modification and hooking during facial recognition process. This checking can be done locally on the handset, allowing for the immediate termination of the facial recognition process if an unsafe environment is detected. Alternatively, it can be performed in the cloud using environment data collected from the SDK. Common environment values that are checked include the operating system version, root status, debugger processes, installed apps, motion sensor data, and hardware fingerprints such as MAC address and camera.

(4) Liveness Detection Location. The protocol flow for face SDKs that perform local liveness detection differs significantly from those that rely on the face cloud

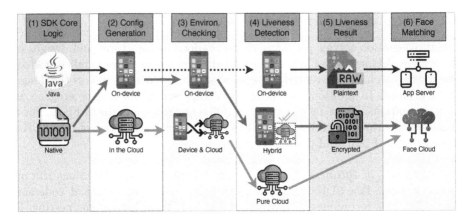

Fig. 3. Observed SDK design and implementation choices. Three arrow flows outline three typical patterns with different security levels.

for liveness checking. Typically, a liveness detection system requires a video clip as input to conduct checks such as frame continuity. However, for cloud liveness detection, the SDK needs to upload the video stream to a remote server, which can be bandwidth-intensive, especially for users with expensive cellular data plans. To address this, a commonly observed solution is to perform liveness detection on the device itself, implementing various techniques to prevent reverse engineering or injection attacks. Additionally, certain face SDKs (*e.g.*, SDK C, F, G in Table 1) combine both local and cloud liveness detection, utilizing different strategies for each. For example, they may conduct video-based detection on the device while performing static image liveness detection on the cloud for an additional layer of verification.

(5) Detection Result. After local liveness detection, results are returned and passed to the app. Each SDK defines different return values, which can consist of a boolean detection result r, a set of k images $M = \{M_i | 1 \leq i \leq k\}$, and environment information E. The returned data can contain combinations of these values. One common practice is to return $R = \{r, M\}$, consisting of a flag and a selected frame of the face image. Some return multiple frames corresponding to every matched actions (*e.g.*, SDK G in Table 1). To mitigate against data leakage or on-path attacks that replace the result, many SDKs encrypt values in the result, *e.g.*, $R_{enc} = \{r, M_{enc}\}$. Only the corresponding cloud service provider of the SDK is able to decrypt the data. Other SDKs return plaintext results but attach a signature $R_{signed} = \{r, M, signature\}$ to prevent result forgery.

(6) Photo Matching Location. Most facial recognition cloud service providers support face matching APIs. Either the API user needs to provide both the reference photo and the photo to match, or the cloud service provider has access to the authoritative face-image databases and can fetch the reference photo with an identity card number. The cloud API usually accepts images that are

encrypted by the SDK, therefore even the app server may not have access to the captured plaintext image. However, some app vendors are averse to sharing users' photos with another party, so some face SDKs (*e.g.*, SDK D, E in Table 1) return the plaintext image directly and let them handle the photo matching.

A Combination of Above Describes an SDK Design. The choice of different characteristics and their combinations can lead to varying levels of overall security. Figure 3 presents a comprehensive list of these characteristics. The three arrow flows depict three representative designs, with increasing levels of security robustness, arranged from top to bottom. The topmost flow represents SDKs that implement all functionalities within the client-side app code without much emphasis on hardening and protection. The middle flow illustrates a popular combination of choices found in many vendors, wherein core liveness detection is performed on the device, while additional checks are conducted in the cloud. This design usually includes a certain degree of environmental verification and data encryption. The bottom flow represents the most secure design among a few SDKs, where all essential detections are carried out in the cloud. Based on our observations, most SDKs are close to the second design mentioned. This suggests that majority design decisions are likely driven by usability considerations rather than security concerns. In Sect. 6, we present the results of our analysis of mainstream facial recognition SDKs we collected regarding to the above characteristics.

5 Weakness of Liveness Detection SDKs

We have identified multiple security weaknesses through our analysis of the protocol design and implementation details of liveness detection SDKs in the market. We believe some are conscious decision as a compromise for usability. We believe that some of these weaknesses may have been intentional compromises made in order to enhance usability. However, there are also evident design flaws that can be attributed to oversight or laziness, without any discernible advantage. These flaws have the potential to greatly lower the cost of attacks, thereby compromising the intended security standards. In this section, we introduce common security flaws we identified in real face SDKs or apps. Additionally, we discuss the potential security risks associated with these flaws.

5.1 Insufficient Client-Side Code Protection

Defense measures that enhance app resilience against reverse engineering and code injection attacks are a crucial aspect of mobile app security. These measures, including code obfuscation, packing, and anti-debugging, offer a cost-effective solution for increasing the difficulty of attacks. Many face SDKs and apps that utilize facial recognition services employ these techniques as their first line of defense against malicious actors. Figure 4 shows such examples. However, the level of defense varies among different products. For example, SDKs like H and K

(a) Control flow flattening in Native library   (b) Anti-debug in Native library

Fig. 4. Example of advanced client-side protections in face SDK

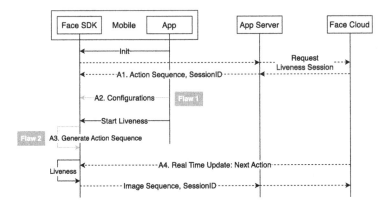

Fig. 5. Action sequence generation protocols in typical liveness detection systems.

in Table 1 only rename identifiers in Java, making it relatively easy to decompile Dalvik bytecode into readable Java code. Additionally, while placing core logic in Android Native libraries increases the difficulty of reverse engineering, skilled attackers can still manage it. Anti-debugging is another effective measure for enhancing client-side attack resilience. However, we have found that many SDKs do not perform environment checks, enabling dynamic code injection attacks. It is important to note that even with comprehensive obfuscation to prevent static reverse engineering, attackers can still analyze the app's runtime behavior and carry out code injection or data replacement attacks. Achieving high-quality code obfuscation and anti-debugging simultaneously is a challenging task, and the failure of either can lead to inadequate code protection, which is observed in many SDKs.

5.2   Insecure Protocol Design

Many security issues identified in face SDKs stem from insecure protocol designs. Rectifying these issues typically necessitates protocol modifications, which can be challenging to fix and push to products in a short term.

Predictable or Forgeable Action Sequence. For interactive liveness detection, the level of security largely depends on the comprehensiveness of the action sequence. Actions that are too simple may not provide significant security advantages compared to motionless liveness detection. Conversely, overly complex actions can be difficult to follow, especially for older individuals. In practical terms, we have observed that most motion-based liveness detection systems utilize a sequence of two to four standard actions, such as blinking and shaking the head. However, it is worth noting that attackers could potentially collect video clips of the victim engaging in these actions, enabling them to execute a replay attack. Therefore, it is crucial to randomize the action sequence in order to render such video preparation impractical. With four available action choices, there are 64 possible three-action sequences, resulting in sufficiently low odds for a prepared video clip to match. Figure 5 depicts the observed action generation protocol flows in different liveness detection systems, where $A1$ to $A4$ indicate alternative sources of action sequence.

We have identified certain SDKs (*e.g.*, SDK K in Table 1) that utilize a predetermined sequence of actions during the liveness detection process. This allows attackers to exploit the system by preparing a video in advance. They can accomplish this by purchasing a pre-recorded video from the underground market, extracting it from publicly available videos of the victim, or synthesizing it themselves. In addition, many SDKs provide an API for the app to configure the action sequence, as shown by $A2$ in the figure, where many apps simply feed a fixed action sequence. The situation is as bad for those liveness detection systems that put the sequence generation logic on-device ($A3$). Under the threat model where the attacker has full control of the device, the generated sequence can be tampered (Flaw 2). If the action generation logic and sequence data are fully contained in Native library with proper hardening, the attack may require more skills and time. But if any of these processes are exposed in the Java space, it is fairly trivial to control and modify the action sequence. The security implication is the same as using a predefined sequence. In extreme cases, the attacker can even specify a uniform sequence that only contains one type of action, *e.g.*, $A = (a_{eye}, a_{eye}, a_{eye})$.

For protocols that fetch an action sequence from the cloud ($A1$), the security depends on the design of the protocol. If the action sequence is associated with a liveness session, and the cloud checks the uploaded image frames or metadata for such binding, the system is considered secure since actions cannot be tampered. In an ideal protocol, the SDK should fetch the next action in real-time from the cloud during liveness as shown by $A4$. By also enforcing timeout policy, it make media synthesizing attack impractical.

Forgery of Liveness Detection Result. Many vendors of face SDKs opt to implement liveness detection on the client side in order to minimize data transmission overhead. However, the authenticity of the detection result is hard to guarantee due to the inherent limitations of local detection methods. Given that the attacker has control over the device, they can manipulate the code being executed and falsify the returned values. This can be achieved by injecting code into

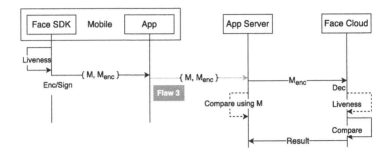

Fig. 6. Example of result passing flow after liveness detection in some protocols.

the SDK's code space or intercepting network traffic during the data upload to the app server, thereby enabling the substitution of the result, including the image, *i.e.*, from $R = \{r, M\}$ to $R' = \{r', M'\}$. To prevent code modification and injection attacks, SDKs employ environment checking like root detection and debugger detection. Nevertheless, it is inevitable that some attackers can bypass these checks, just with higher costs. Another mitigation being observed in practice is to encrypt or sign the result using either symmetric or asymmetric cryptographic tools, *e.g.*, $R = \{r_{enc}, M_{enc}\}$. Since it is harder for adversaries to analyze the logic in Native libraries, many SDKs perform the data encryption/signing in the Native code space before returning the result to the Java space. In this way, to modify the result or replace the raw image, the attacker must perform the injection attack on the Native code space, which builds some hurdles. When the SDK returns an encrypted detection result, but the selected picture frames are in plaintext, *i.e.*, $R = \{r_{enc}, M\}$, the security level is the same as the previous case. The attacker can just complete a liveness detection process by presenting himself to the camera to obtain $R' = \{r_{enc}, M'\}$, then replace the plaintext image M' with the victim's one M. No reverse engineering of the encryption algorithm is needed.

We observe that some SDKs (*e.g.*, SDK A, K in Table 1) return both raw and encrypted images in the result as shown by Flaw 3 in Fig. 6. Further analysis of the documentation and protocol reveals the possible reason for such a design: to give flexibility to app vendors who prefer to do image comparisons without sharing users' photos to the face cloud. We argue that this design goes too far in sacrificing security. The normal flow uploads the encrypted result to the face cloud for decryption, data integrity checks, and secondary cloud liveness verification. However, if an app vendor chooses the alternative flow, those additional protections are skipped, resulting in much lower attack cost. A better design is assigning an app-specific key pair to the SDK and app server for end-to-end encryption instead of exposing raw images on-path, which can retain the Native level obfuscation security.

Another type of flaw is the incorrect usage of cryptographic scheme. The SDK returns $R = \{r_{enc}, M_{enc}\}$ in both success and failure case. Note that the result and image data are encrypted separately, so the attacker can use the SDK and an encryption oracle to encrypt the victim's photo and replace it into a successful result. The detail of the attack is further explained in Appendix A.

5.3   Flaws in SDK Implementations

Apart from the protocol issues that happen during interactions between multiple entities, the implementation inside the SDK can also cause security problems.

Unrestricted Configurations. For tuning flexibility, some SDKs provide a set of APIs to configure parameters for liveness detection. Configurable parameters mainly fall into two groups: 1) parameters controlling the liveness detection mode and 2) parameters of the liveness detection model. Without proper restrictions, these parameters can significantly weaken the security of the liveness detection system. Even though all model parameters are essentially modifiable when the liveness detection runs locally, exposing a public Java API gives low-hanging fruits to the attacker, making the system more susceptible to code injection attacks. This weakness corresponds to Flaw 1 in Fig. 5.

Two common key security-sensitive parameters exposed in face SDKs are the action sequence and liveness score threshold. For example, one popular SDK we analyzed (SDK E in Table 1) provides an API setThreshold(float x), which allows setting a new action score threshold as $\theta' \in (0,1)$, while the default threshold is set to $\theta = 0.95$. This gives the attacker a convenient interface to alter the threshold to an abnormally small value, thus nullifying the action-matching mechanism. The initialization API of the same SDK consumes a list of actions expected from the user, *e.g.*, $A = \{a_{mouth}, a_{eye}, a_{head}\}$, which means the user needs first to open his mouth, then blink his eyes, finally node his head to complete the process. However, the SDK has no restriction on the number of actions, so the attacker can configure the action list as $\{a_{eye}\}$, or even an empty set $\varnothing$. With these abnormal settings, the action matching process drops its difficulty sharply or is even disabled totally. The simplified code snippet in Listing 1.1 illustrates the flawed action list processing logic in the SDK. This particular example exposes those APIs in the Java code, so it is under the *Java code injection* threat. Some other SDKs provide parameter-setting APIs in the Native library but hide them from Java interfaces. They have a higher obfuscation security level but are still vulnerable under the *Native code injection* threat model.

```
1  public void start(int[] motionList) {
2      if (motionList == null || motionList.length < 1) {
3          resultCode = ResultCode.OK;
4      } else {
5          beginLivenessDetection(motionList);
6      }
7  }
```

Listing 1.1. SDK code with flawed action list configuration logic.

Unprotected Model Files. Almost every face SDK supporting local liveness detection ships with machine-learning models in the app package. Some SDKs embed the models as standalone files and are not difficult to recognize. A recent tool ModelXRay [15] can identify the machine learning model files in Android apps, as well as analyze whether the model files are encrypted. Unencrypted model files are susceptible to modification and model replacement attacks. Attackers conducting *synthetic attacks* can alter parameters in the model to accept poorly synthesized videos.

Leakage of Captured Images or Video. During the real-time handling of camera streams, the system may need to cache certain image frames or a snippet of video for subsequent processing. Some face SDKs choose to save the cached data to the filesystem. In the Android system, files can either be stored in the internal storage that is only accessible by the app or in the external shared storage. In the latter case, captured face images or video can be stolen by a malicious app. We noticed that one SDK we analyzed (SDK D in Table 1) cache captured video during liveness detection and the selected image frames into the external storage, a path obtained with the `getExternalCacheDir()` method. Before Android 11, this location is accessible to any apps with the `READ_EXTERNAL_STORAGE` permission. Starting from Android 11, the external files are also isolated by apps [16]. However, another app with the special user-granted permission `MANAGE_EXTERNAL_STORAGE` can still access them.

UI Hijacking. In a normal use case, the user is expected to launch the liveness detection interface in the target app and proceed by following the instructions. The whole process assumes the user knows the context of the face authentication process. However, if a malicious app can invoke the interface of the target app and then display an overlay to hide the liveness detection context, the user may unknowingly finish the facial recognition. User interface (UI) readdressing attack has been witnessed in practice [17] for phishing with Android malware. Covering the liveness detection interface without interrupting the camera stream is possible when the SDK lacks proper implementation, as discussed in [18]. Combined with the previous image cache leak attack, a malicious app without camera permission can steal the user's photo from an app that embeds the vulnerable face SDK. Another possibility is to force the victim login into the attacker controlled account [19] or use the preemptive account hijacking attack [20], then perform the UI hijacking attack to steer the victim to complete the facial eKYC process. Thus, the attacker can gain access to the victim's account with greater permission, like withdrawing money from a mobile wallet.

5.4   Mistakes by App Developers

It is impractical for face SDKs to provide end-to-end facial recognition solutions to mobile apps. In practice, they implement the core functions and expect app developers to handle the rest. However, it is notoriously unrealistic to assume that app developers can implement everything securely.

Table 1. Protocol Design and Implementation Details of Mainstream Face SDKs

Face SDK	Interact Mode	SDK Code	Action Generation	Configurable	Env. Checking	Liveness Location	Liveness Results	Matching Location	UI Included	Cost of Attack
A	actions	N	—	$\theta, \mathbb{A}$	N	L	$\{r, M, M_{enc}\}$	C, S	✗	effortless
A′	actions	N	L	$\theta, \mathbb{A}$	N	L	M_{sign}	C	✗	effortless
B	flashing	N	C	∅	$N \wedge C$	L	M_{enc}	C	✓	laborious
B′	static	N	—	∅	$N \wedge C$	C	—	C	✓	impractical
C	actions	N	C	$\theta_s, \mathbb{A}_s$	$N \wedge C$	$L \wedge C$	$\{M_{enc}, E_{enc}\}$	C	✓	impractical
D	actions	N	L	$\theta, \mathbb{A}$	N	L	M	S	✗	effortless
E	actions	N	L	θ	N	L	M	S	✗	effortless
F	actions	N	C	$\theta_s, \mathbb{A}_s$	$N \wedge C$	$L \wedge C$	?	C	✓	laborious
G	actions	N	C	∅	$N \wedge C$	$L \wedge C$	M_{sign}	C	✓	laborious
H	actions	J	C	∅	J	L	M	C	✓	effortless
I	actions	N	—	$\theta_s, \mathbb{A}_s$	J	L	M	S	✓	effortless
J	static	J	—	∅	7	C	—	C	✓	impractical
K	actions	J	fixed	∅	7	L	$\{M_{enc}, M\}$	S	✓	effortless
L	static	N	—	∅	7	L	r	L, S	✗	effortless
M	actions	N	?	θ	7	L	$\{r, M_{enc}\}$	L, S	✗	laborious
N	static	N	—	θ	7	L	r	L, S	✗	effortless
O	actions	J	L	$\mathbb{A}$	7	C	—	C	✗	impractical
P	actions	N	L	$\mathbb{A}$	7	L	$\{r, M_{sign}\}$	S	✗	effortless

Some face SDKs return liveness results consisting of a boolean result, encrypted data, and a raw image. The app developer may select whatever value he needs as the liveness detection result without following the face SDK's designated usage. For example, some apps may only rely on the boolean result returned by the SDK and use an image frame extracted by the app for face comparison. These unexpected usages can render certain security mechanisms of the facial recognition system non-effective.

It is harder for app developers to handle things correctly, where even SDK providers make mistakes. Some SDKs (*e.g.*, SDK A, D, E in Table 1) delegate the implementation of the liveness detection UI to the app. Not surprisingly, most app developers would not consider the security threats when implementing the UI component. Worse still, the demo code with sample UI implementations provided by certain SDK provider (SDK E) also lacks proper hijacking protection, making app developers more likely to produce flawed implementations. The insecure image storage problem can also appear in apps when they obtain the returned images from the liveness detection module. A typical implementation uses the file system as an intermediate media that stores the resultant image before uploading the app server.

6 Empirical Study

Facial recognition services have been mushrooming in recent years. Many of them provide mobile SDKs, which can be found in many financial and government service apps. As an empirical security study of face SDKs, we first collect popular mobile face SDKs to analyze their security aspects. Then, we collect a set of high-profile mobile banking and cryptocurrency exchange apps to analyze the face SDKs they used and discuss their security impact. Finally, we build a static analyzer to scan apps at the market scale and present the distribution of face SDKs in practice.

6.1   Retrieval of Face SDKs

We collect a set of Android face SDKs from well-known providers. Most facial recognition service providers host a developer platform with configuration interfaces and documentation. In some cases, the face SDK can be downloaded from the platform. More often, we encounter providers that only allow verified enterprise developers to access their SDKs or platforms. For those cases, we try to search for public apps or GitHub repositories that contain the corresponding SDK using package names or other distinct strings. While most apps utilizing face SDKs are protected by commercial packers, we intentionally search for old version of apps with weak code hardening so that we can retrieve an analyzable copy of the target SDKs. In the end, we collected 18 face SDKs from 16 different providers. A few vendors provide SDK variants for different use cases or from different product lines. For example, the face SDK for financial apps can differ from the SDK for general apps in the provider.

6.2   Security Metrics of Face SDKs

Android SDKs are provided as Android library packages (.aar or .jar), which contain Java executables (.dex), native libraries (.so), and other resources such as machine learning models. After unpacking, we decompile the Java code to locate functions related to facial recognition. We usually cross-compare the code with the official SDK document to understand the purpose of located APIs. Then we check common security weaknesses we discussed in Sect. 5 for each SDK. We start from analyzing the relevant Java code, from which we can determine if any facial recognition functions are implemented in Native libraries. We further examine whether the app employs any obfuscation or anti-debugging techniques. We, as practiced Android security researchers, spend a maximum of five person-hours analyzing the Native library. Information we failed to obtain during such a time frame is treated as unknown and considered hard for attackers to obtain as well.

Table 1 presents the analysis results. When multiple modes of interaction are available in the same SDK, the analysis is based on the *actions* mode. In several columns of the table, N, J, C, L, S represent Native, Java, cloud, local, and app server, respectively. These indicate the location where the corresponding process is executed and have security implications. For example, actions generated on-device (L) cannot be remotely verified and are more susceptible to tampering. Environment checking implemented in Java is easier to bypass than those protected in Native libraries. SDKs that expose configuration functions allowing

Table 2. Financial Apps with Face SDKs

App	SDK	Packer	App	SDK	Packer
Wallet A	Q, A	—	Bank A	A	—
Wallet B	B	Tencent	Bank B	A, E	Bangcle
Wallet C	Q, K	DexGuard	Bank C	D	Bangcle
Wallet D	I	—	Bank D	D, E	Bangcle
Wallet E	E	—	Bank E	D, E	Bangcle
Wallet F	I, K	—	Bank F	B	Bangcle
Wallet G	A	Bangcle	CEX A	G, H	—
Wallet H	C	Ali	CEX B	R, G	Tencent

Table 3. SDK distribution in app market

SDK	# Apps	# App Downloads
B	297	113 million
F	192	7.7 million
A	153	6.6 million
E	123	15.3 million
D	85	3.1 million
G	80	4.7 million
Q	14	5.5 million
P	12	0.1 million
total (weak)	802 (294)	156 (25.2) million

unrestricted control of model thresholds (θ) or action sequence ($\mathbb{A}$) are considered insecure. Those whose configurations are bound to a remote session ($\theta_s, \mathbb{A}_s$) or those that provide no configuration API ($\varnothing$) do not have related issues. For *Liveness Results* column, r, M, E represent the detection result, images, and environment information, respectively. If a plaintext image or result returned by the SDK is used for comparison, it is easy for an attacker to perform data replacement attacks. Cells marked as *?* indicate that we cannot reach a conclusion within our analysis time-budget, mostly due to the difficulty of reverse engineering. Any weakness in the SDK has the potential to cause a security breakdown. We highlight design weaknesses in each characteristic columns and summarize the cost of attack in the last column. The underlined ticks in "UI Included" column indicate the official UI implementation has security issues mentioned in Sect. 5.3. Overall, a majority of the SDKs (10 out of 18) have design or implementation issues that can lead to low cost attacks (those labelled *effortless* in the last column). Only 4 SDKs enforce full cloud liveness detection and are impractical to attack without synthetic media.

6.3   Face SDKs in High-Profile Financial Apps

The dominant market for face SDKs is composed of financial mobile apps. Financial apps like mobile banking and online investment platform rely on eKYC for anti-money laundering (AML). Apart from identity documentation verification, substantial eKYC services utilize facial recognition, especially liveness detection, to prevent people from registering with forged or stolen identity documents. We collect a list of mainstream mobile wallet, mobile banking, and centralized crypto-currency exchange (CEX) apps that support account verification using facial eKYC. We manually analyze each of them to the extent that we know which face SDK is embedded in the app, whether the app is protected from reverse engineering using some packers as listed in [21]. Table 2 summarize our analysis results. We can see that most financial apps use the SDKs we have analyzed, including those with security issues. Some of them include multiple face SDKs for different functionalities. More than half of them are protected with commercial packers.

6.4   Market Scale Evaluation

When we analyze the protocol and implementation of face SDKs and investigate SDK usage in financial mobile apps, we have gathered a list of face SDKs. Some SDKs are made by renowned companies and have been seen in many apps. Some are created by startups and are only used by a few apps. We create a face SDK fingerprinting tool to scan Android apps at a market scale, which can help us understand 1) the mobile app market distribution of face SDKs and 2) whether popular face SDKs have better security.

Face SDK Fingerprints. We collected a database of face SDK fingerprints by examining a set of SDKs and those found in high-profile apps. Our fingerprints utilize unique package names, file names, and string content to identify a face SDK. The package name serves as a unique identifier for an SDK. However, if the code undergoes obfuscation with package renaming or the app is packed, the package name becomes inaccessible. On the other hand, file names, particularly those of the Native library and model files, typically remain unchanged even after obfuscation or packing, making them reliable SDK fingerprints. Additionally, certain strings found within files can also serve as effective fingerprints. An example of this is the license file included in the SDK, which may contain the name of the provider company or even a version number of the SDK.

Large-scale Scanning Results. Based on the collected fingerprints, we modify the open-source Android app identifier APKiD [22] to scan the facial recognition SDKs in Android. Our fingerprint dataset and the tool are available at [7]. We run the face SDK scanner on a set of 18,096 apps crawled from one popular Chinese Android app market in April 2022. Results are listed in Table 3. Among 802 apps that include at least one face SDK, about 40% of them contain a vulnerable SDK we analyzed. The total single-market downloads for these apps exceeds 20 millions. Considering the wide selection of Android app markets, the actual number of affected apps and users are much higher. We further count the category of apps that embed face SDKs and find that over a quarter of them are finance apps. We describe the detailed result in Appendix B.

6.5   Case Study

In this section, we elaborate on the details for realizing proof-of-concept attacks on two real-world mobile apps with millions of users. Besides the systematic analysis process as performed in Sect. 5, end-to-end attack hinges on the attacker's ability to circumvent common defense measures such as app packing and anti-debugging mechanisms, as well as exploiting app-specific mistakes.

The first app provides government service and has more than a million users. It requires identity document verification and facial liveness detection for registration to confirm the user is actually present. Bypassing this security feature could allow an attacker to hijack accounts with stolen IDs, creating a serious privacy threat. The app's code is protected by a strong packer, which prevents reverse-engineering with common tools. However, we show that vulnerabilities in the facial recognition SDK can be exploited without reverse-engineering the app. When reverse engineering of the target app is challenging and time-consuming, attackers may resort to directly analyzing the SDK code. Static files within this app reveals that the SDK being used is E in Table 1, which is vulnerable to the result tampering attack. The `onSuccess(int code, byte[] data)` function within SDK E is a key target for real-time image data manipulation via hooking. This task becomes complex when dealing with packed apps because function names are often obfuscated, making it unclear where to insert hooks. However, the consistent signatures of SDK interfaces allow us to align runtime function signatures with SDK functions and perform "blind" hooking. To initiate hooking in the app, we first bypass anti-debugging features, *e.g.*, by modifying the `TracerPid`. Subsequently, we probe the runtime memory to list methods accessed during facial recognition interactions. Through this process, we pinpointed the method `a(int i, byte[] b)`, which, given its signature and context within its class, corresponds to the target `onSuccess` method. This SDK-to-app attack scheme exhibits scalability, as an attacker can exploit all apps using a vulnerable SDK by employing the same approach, avoiding labor-intensive reverse-engineering process.

The second app serves as a platform enabling small businesses to sell certain services and functions as a transaction escrow, with reported monthly transactions exceeding $100 million. To combat money laundering, it mandates facial identity verification for users prior to withdrawal. However, our findings demonstrate that attackers can effortlessly bypass this security measure using another person's identity, thereby undermining the anti-money laundering system in place. After extracting files from the Android app package, we recognized a file associated with a widely-used SDK vendor A, as listed in Table 1. Our prior analysis revealed that A's SDK provides both encrypted data and plaintext results following facial liveness detection. The feasibility of a data replacement attack depends on the app's implementation. However, direct inspection of the app's code is impeded by a commercial packer. To circumvent this, we used the publicly available DexHunter tool [23] to extract the original byte-code from memory. Analysis of the decompiled application revealed that it utilizes a third-party library to interface with the facial recognition SDK A, streamlining SDK integration for developers. However, this library inappropriately uses unencrypted outputs from the SDK and applies its own basic encryption, which is easily compromised due to the simplicity of extracting the encryption key from the Java code. Consequently, an attacker could manipulate the app on a compromised device to carry out facial recognition with their own face, and then replace the encrypted result with one from a victim's image by exploiting the reverse-engineered encryption method.

7   Discussion on Mitigation

While more than half of the SDKs we analyzed exhibit flawed design or implementation, we also observed a few examples that demonstrate strong security measures. By studying both the positive and negative aspects of these examples, we can offer a reference design that encompasses robust security features and user-friendly functionality. Furthermore, we will briefly discuss potential future mitigations that address more fundamental issues.

Reference Protocol. While cloud-based video liveness. detection is the most secure and has a simple protocol, it has obvious drawbacks in user experience. Hybrid system that perform video-based local liveness detection coupled with few-image liveness in the cloud for double check can maintain reasonable security while keeping high usability. However, such system involves complex and error-prone multi-party protocol. One key security requirement is configuration integrity, which can be achieved by passing a configuration binding back along with the liveness result for cloud verification. The unpredictability of interaction sequence serves as an effective countermeasure against media synthesizing attacks; consequently, the best practice is to return the next action in real-time after the previous one is completed. Finally, the result integrity is of paramount importance. To prevent data replacement attack, the SDK should encrypt the data while hardening the encryption code, putting them in native library with code obfuscation and anti-debugging. A detailed description of the reference protocol is available in Appendix C.

Future Direction of Mitigation. Current mobile facial recognition systems, including the proposed reference protocol, rely on code obfuscation and risk checking as protection measures for client integrity. Google's SafetyNet Attestation API [24] enables third-party apps to conduct anti-abuse checks, including device integrity verification, but it is only available to Android devices with Google services. A trusted execution environment (TEE) like ARM's TrustZone enables client code execution integrity using hardware-level isolation and is utilized for fingerprint and face authentication on modern mobile devices [25]. However, none of the studied facial eKYC service providers utilize TEE. This could be due to several reasons like design complexity when remote image comparison is involved, insufficient computational power in TEE, and device compatibility. Although there are workarounds for some of these challenges, *e.g.*, as proposed in [26,27], no actual deployment has been observed in the market.

8   Related Work

The study of facial recognition security has gained attention with the growing popularity and importance of these technologies in real-world applications. Many studies concentrate on algorithm security, particularly the weaknesses in deep learning models that have been exposed in recent years. Adversaries can manipulate inputs to deceive the classifier using adversarial learning techniques [28,29], leading to numerous presentation attacks where the attacker can bypass the system using a carefully crafted mask or even an on-screen video [8,30]. Synthetic media attacks, especially those powered by deep learning (deepfake

[31]) to generate new image or video with specific facial expressions from static images, can be leveraged to fool liveness detection systems. Authors of [5] conduct empirical assessment on six cloud-based liveness detection APIs by submitting videos synthesized with various deepfake techniques and proved them vulnerable to deepfake attacks. Liveness detection systems in mobile apps we studied are more complex than cloud APIs because they do not directly utilize those APIs and instead involve multi-party communication. While not focusing on facial recognition, a recent work [12] shows that close to half of the real-world deep learning models used in Android apps are vulnerable to adversarial examples.

However, the security of mobile facial recognition systems in terms of system architecture or protocol design receives very limited attention from researchers. In reality, the security of these systems requires a comprehensive approach that considers various angles, such as input authenticity and result integrity. For instance, launching a synthetic media attack in mobile requires a valid data injection technique, as demonstrated in a Black Hat talk [32]. Model integrity is another factor that can pose a threat to the overall system security. Authors of [15] develop an automatic model extraction framework and show that some models embedded in mobile apps have weak protections.

In practice, the mobile facial recognition system involves multiple parties, including the user's device, the app's server, and the service provider's server, and any weak link can result in security and privacy issues. Despite numerous security vulnerabilities uncovered in other multi-party protocols on mobile platforms, such as payment and OAuth [33–35], the security analysis of liveness detection protocols remains a largely uncharted area. A recent study [36], independent to ours, explored the security aspects of the Cross-side Face Verification System, aligning with the Local-Cloud Mixed scenario presented in Sect. 2.2. Our research, however, covers broader types of mobile facial recognition system, namely, the Pure Local and Pure Cloud architectures where all verification steps are performed on-device or in the cloud respectively. In addition, security analysis of [36] are targeting apps, while we study each SDK, whose vulnerabilities affect all apps relying on it. While some findings are shared between [36] and this work, e.g., the data inconsistency problems and lack of environment checking, our study uncovers additional security concerns with detailed attack analysis, such as failure in data encryption scheme (see Sect. 5.2), unrestricted tampering with machine learning thresholds (Sect. 5.3), and vulnerability caused by insecure usage of SDK results (Sect. 5.4). Moreover, our analysis includes apps fortified with packing (Sects. 5.1 and refsec:casespsstudy), a common practice that substantially increases attack costs, which [36] does not take into account.

9   Conclusion

In this study, we examine the protocol design and SDK implementations of mobile facial recognition systems. Despite significant attention from industry and academia to the security of algorithms and models in facial recognition, the system security as a whole has been overlooked. We find that a number of these systems put the liveness detection process on the device, leading to vulnerabilities that allow for low-cost identity fraud attacks by data tampering or code injection, which are easy to carry out at scale. Our study of 18 SDKs highlights the common pitfalls and provides a reference protocol that can serve as a security guide for mobile facial recognition service providers.

Responsible Disclosure. We have sent vulnerability reports to all affected face SDKs and some highly impactful apps. However, many vendors are emerging AI companies founded in recent years, typically lacking a dedicated security team or established vulnerability reporting channels. We have endeavored to send our reports to the most appropriate contact available, such as the general support email or business contact. While many vendors have not responded at the time of writing, some have reacted to our reports. For instance, a prominent SDK provider met with us to explore potential fixes and discuss future cooperation. One popular app engaged with us proactively to address the issue, requesting anonymity due to the challenges associated with completely mitigating the vulnerability. Additionally, we observed a vendor discreetly removed their SDK from public access months after receiving our report. We acknowledge the complexities involved in thoroughly resolving these vulnerabilities; as discussed in Sect. 7, protocol redesign would necessitate significant engineering efforts, not to mention the complexities of compelling downstream mobile apps to update embedded SDKs. Consequently, we have chosen to maintain the anonymity of the SDK providers and applications in this paper.

Acknowledgement. This research was supported in part by the CUHK Direct Grant project#4055203 and the MobiTeC R&D Fund project#7105768.

A   Flawed Encryption Scheme and Oracle Attack

One type of insecure design is caused by incorrect use of the encryption scheme. Suppose an SDK returns $R = \{r_{enc}, M_{enc}\}$ regardless success or failure. The attacker can conduct liveness detection with the victim's static image. The process ends up with a failure that returns $R' = \{enc(\text{"failed"}), M'_{enc}\}$, which provides the attacker with an encryption oracle to encrypt arbitrary images. Therefore, the attacker can construct a valid R by first obtaining r_{enc} from a successful liveness detection of himself $enc(\text{"success"})$, then using the oracle to obtain a correctly encrypted image of the victim M'_{enc}, as illustrated in Fig. 7, successfully impersonating the victim.

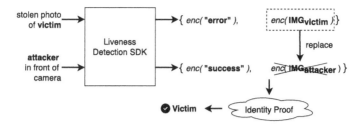

Fig. 7. Illustration of the image encryption oracle attack.

B   Face SDK Scanning Result of App Categories

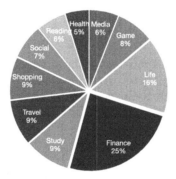

Fig. 8. Category distribution of apps with face SDKs.

We run the face SDK scanner on 18,096 Android apps, identifying 802 apps that include the SDKs we studied. We label the app category to which each app belongs, and Fig. 8 depicts the resulting distribution. As expected, the largest category is *Finance*, contributing a quarter of apps embedding face SDKs.

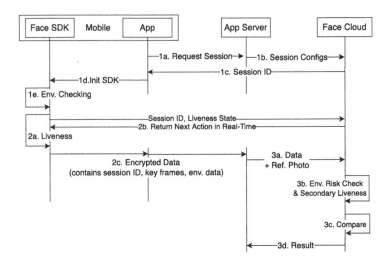

Fig. 9. A reference secure protocol for a facial recognition system with mobile-centric liveness detection.

The app market categorizes most government service apps in the *Life* group, making it the second largest category. Additionally, apps in the *Study* category usually utilize the face SDK for attendance taking. Some *Game* apps use facial recognition for age proof, in compliance with local regulations.

C   Reference Protocol with Security and Usability Consideration

By summarizing the knowledge of our analysis on many SDKs, we propose a reference protocol as depicted in Fig. 9 for a mobile-centric facial recognition system that provides reasonable security protections under a local-cloud mixed liveness detection setting. Several implementation details are worth highlighting in this protocol. The session configuration (1b) request sent from the app server to the face cloud requires an API secret so that the system is configurable, but only by an authorized entity. During liveness detection, after each liveness detection state, the next required action is determined by the cloud in real-time and returned through some persistent channel like WebSocket (2b). The purpose is to increase the difficulty of video synthesizing attacks. An alternative approach is to return the whole action sequences as encrypted data in (1c). After liveness detection, all result data are encrypted, and no raw data are exposed to the app server (2c). The app server must pass the encrypted data to the face cloud, where it can be decrypted and processed. The purpose of the secondary liveness checking (3b) is to validate whether the returned images match the action sequence of the session. Photo-based liveness detection can be performed as well to mitigate photo-synthetic attacks.

References

1. Baydakova, A.: For \$200, You Can Trade Crypto With a Fake ID. https://www.coindesk.com/policy/2021/10/19/for-200-you-can-trade-crypto-with-a-fake-id/
2. Liu, T., Yang, B., Geng, Y., Du, S.: Research on face recognition and privacy in china-based on social cognition and cultural psychology. Front. Psychol. **12**, 809736 (2021). https://www.frontiersin.org/articles/10.3389/fpsyg.2021.809736
3. Borak, M.: Chinese government-run facial recognition system hacked by tax fraudsters: report. https://www.scmp.com/tech/tech-trends/article/3127645/chinese-government-run-facial-recognition-system-hacked-tax
4. Tang, A.: How a young hacker breaks the facial recognition system of Xiamen Bank app. https://china-caixin-com.translate.goog/2020-03-12/101527373.html?_x_tr_sl=auto&_x_tr_tl=en&_x_tr_hl=en-US&_x_tr_pto=wapp
5. Li, C., et al.: "Seeing is living? rethinking the security of facial liveness verification in the deepfake era," in 31st USENIX Security Symposium (USENIX Security 22), pp. 2673–2690. USENIX Association, Boston, MA (2022)
6. Mirsky, Y., Lee, W.: The creation and detection of deepfakes: a survey. ACM Comput. Surv. (CSUR) **54**(1), 1–41 (2021)
7. MobiTeC, C.: Security analysis of facial liveness detection systems in mobile apps (2023). https://mobitec.ie.cuhk.edu.hk/facesdk
8. Ramachandra, R., Busch, C.: Presentation attack detection methods for face recognition systems: a comprehensive survey. ACM Comput. Surv.(CSUR) **50**(1), 1–37 (2017)
9. Tang, D., Zhou, Z., Zhang, Y., Zhang, K.: Face flashing: a secure liveness detection protocol based on light reflections. In: 25th Annual Network and Distributed System Security Symposium, NDSS 2018, San Diego, California, USA, February 18–21 (2018)
10. Chakraborty, S., Das, D.: An overview of face liveness detection. arXiv preprint arXiv:1405.2227 (2014)
11. Facia: The future of faical recognition (2023). https://facia.ai/wp-content/uploads/2023/05/The-Future-of-Facial-Recognition.pdf
12. Deng, Z., Chen, K., Meng, G., Zhang, X., Xu, K., Cheng, Y.: Understanding real-world threats to deep learning models in android apps. In: Proceedings of the 2022 ACM SIGSAC Conference on Computer and Communications Security, pp. 785–799 (2022)
13. Junod, P., Rinaldini, J., Wehrli, J., Michielin, J.: Obfuscator-llvm-software protection for the masses. In: IEEE/ACM 1st International Workshop on Software Protection. IEEE 2015, pp. 3–9 (2015)
14. 'Shrink, obfuscate, and optimize your app. https://developer.android.com/studio/build/shrink-code
15. Sun, Z., Sun, R., Lu, L., Mislove, A.: Mind your weight(s): a large-scale study on insufficient machine learning model protection in mobile apps. In: 30th USENIX Security Symposium (USENIX Security 21). USENIX Association, Aug. 2021, pp. 1955–1972 (2021)
16. Android Developers. Storage updates in Android 11. https://developer.android.com/about/versions/11/privacy/storage
17. Yan, Y., et al.: Understanding and detecting overlay-based android malware at market scales. In: Proceedings of the 17th Annual International Conference on Mobile Systems, Applications, and Services, 2019, pp. 168–179 (2019)

18. Wang, X., Shi, S., Chen, Y., Lau, W.C.: Phyjacking: physical input hijacking for zero-permission authorization attacks on android. In: Proceedings 2022 Network and Distributed System Security Symposium. NDSS (2022)

19. Fett, D., Küsters, R., Schmitz, G.: A comprehensive formal security analysis of OAuth 2.0. In: Proceedings of the ACM Conference on Computer and Communications Security, vol. 24–28-Octo, pp. 1204–1215 (2016)

20. Ghasemisharif, M., Ramesh, A., Checkoway, S., Kanich, C., Polakis, J.: O single Sign-Off, where art thou? an empirical analysis of single Sign-On account hijacking and session management on the web. In: 27th USENIX Security Symposium (USENIX Security 18), Aug 2018, pp. 1475–1492 (2018)

21. Duan, Y., et al.: Things you may not know about android (un) packers: a systematic study based on whole-system emulation. In: NDSS (2018)

22. rednaga. APKiD - Android Application Identifier. https://github.com/rednaga/APKiD

23. Zhang, Y., Luo, X., Yin, H.: DexHunter: toward extracting hidden code from packed android applications. In: Pernul, G., Ryan, P.Y.A., Weippl, E. (eds.) ESORICS 2015. LNCS, vol. 9327, pp. 293–311. Springer, Cham (2015). https://doi.org/10.1007/978-3-319-24177-7_15

24. Ibrahim, M., Imran, A., Bianchi, A.: Safetynot: on the usage of the safetynet attestation api in android. In: Proceedings of the 19th Annual International Conference on Mobile Systems, Applications, and Services, 2021, pp. 150–162 (2021)

25. Bianchi, A., et al.: Broken fingers: on the usage of the fingerprint api in android. In: oDSS (2018)

26. Zhang, D.: Trustfa: Trustzone-assisted facial authentication on smartphone. Tech, Rep (2014)

27. Bayerl, S.P., et al.: Offline model guard: Secure and private ml on mobile devices, In: Design, Automation and Test in Europe Conference & Exhibition (DATE). IEEE, pp. 460–465 (2020)

28. Kurakin, A., Goodfellow, I., Bengio, S.: Adversarial machine learning at scale. arXiv preprint arXiv:1611.01236 (2016)

29. Goswami, G., Ratha, N., Agarwal, A., Singh, R., Vatsa, M.: Unravelling robustness of deep learning based face recognition against adversarial attacks. In: Proceedings of the AAAI Conference on Artificial Intelligence, vol. 32, no. 1, (2018)

30. Sharif, M., Bhagavatula, S., Bauer, L., Reiter, M.K.: Accessorize to a crime: real and stealthy attacks on state-of-the-art face recognition. In: Proceedings of the 2016 ACM SIGSAC Conference on Computer and Communications Security, 2016, pp. 1528–1540 (2016)

31. Westerlund, M.: The emergence of deepfake technology: a review. Technol. Innov. Manage. Rev. 9(11) (2019)

32. Chen, Y., Ma, B., Ma, Z.: Biometric authentication under threat: liveness detection hacking, Black Hat USA (2019)

33. Al Rahat, T., Feng, Y., Tian, Y.: Oauthlint: an empirical study on oauth bugs in android applications. In: 2019 34th IEEE/ACM International Conference on Automated Software Engineering (ASE), 2019, pp. 293–304 (2019)

34. Shi, S., Wang, X., Lau, W.C.: Mossot: an automated blackbox tester for single sign-on vulnerabilities in mobile applications. In: Proceedings of the 2019 ACM Asia Conference on Computer and Communications Security, ser. Asia CCS '19. New York, NY, USA: Association for Computing Machinery, 2019, p. 269–282. https://doi.org/10.1145/3321705.3329801

35. Yang, W., Li, J., Zhang, Y., Gu, D.: Security analysis of third-party in-app payment in mobile applications. J. Inform. Secur. Appl. **48**, 102358 (2019). https://www.sciencedirect.com/science/article/pii/S2214212619301632
36. Zhang, X., et al.: Understanding the (in) security of cross-side face verification systems in mobile apps: a system perspective. In: IEEE Symposium on Security and Privacy (SP). IEEE Computer Society 2023, pp. 934–950 (2023)

Author Index

A

Alam, Manaar III-163
Alkadri, Nabil Alkeilani I-376
Andreeva, Elena II-433
Attrapadung, Nuttapong II-373
Avizheh, Sepideh III-74

B

Banegas, Gustavo II-101
Bao, Han I-213
Basso, Andrea I-432
Bemmann, Pascal I-351
Berger, Robin I-288
Berndt, Sebastian I-351
Bettale, Luk I-457
Bhardwaj, Divyanshu III-412
Bhattacharya, Sarani III-271
Bock, Estuardo Alpirez II-101
Boneh, Dan III-105
Bonneau, Joseph III-105
Boura, Christina II-485
Brisfors, Martin III-301
Brzuska, Chris I-3, II-101

C

Cachet, Chloe I-156
Carpent, Xavier I-26
Chen, Binbin II-283
Chen, Mingjie I-432
Chen, Rongmao I-351
Chmielewski, Łukasz II-101
Cimorelli Belfiore, Roberta II-163
Cogliati, Benoît II-433
Cong, Kelong II-133
Conti, Mauro I-183
Custódio, Ricardo II-3

D

Dabrowski, Adrian III-412
De Cosmo, Andrea II-163
Derbez, Patrick II-485

D (cont.)

Dey, Soumyajit III-163
Ding, Xia II-265
Doan, Thi Van Thao I-257
Dobraunig, Christoph II-460
Dörre, Felix I-288
Döttling, Nico I-376
Dowerah, Uddipana II-189
Dubrova, Elena III-301

E

Egger, Christoph I-3
Eldefrawy, Karim II-133
Emura, Keita I-237

F

Fan, Yongming II-340
Feneuil, Thibauld I-403
Feng, Zheyun III-217
Ferrara, Anna Lisa II-163
Forte, Domenic III-325
Fouotsa, Tako Boris I-432
Francati, Danilo I-135
Frederiksen, Tore Kasper I-58
Fuller, Benjamin I-156
Funk, Margot II-485

G

Ganji, Fatemeh III-325
Garman, Christina II-340
GhasemiGol, Mohammad II-313
Ghazvinian, Parsa II-313
Ghosh, Soumyadyuti III-163
Giron, Alexandre Augusto II-3
Gui, Jiaping III-241

H

Hamlin, Ariel I-156
Hanaoka, Goichiro II-373
Hashemi, Mohammad III-325
Heitmann, Nico III-190

Henze, Martin   II-241
Hiromasa, Ryo   II-373
Hwang, Seoyeon   I-26
Hwang, Vincent   II-24

J

Jee, Kangkook   III-241

K

Kahrobaei, Delaram   I-457
Kailus, Adrian   III-137
Kamimura, Junpei   III-241
Karmakar, Angshuman   III-271
Kern, Dustin   III-137
Koch, Alexander   I-288
Köhler, Daniel   III-381
Koseki, Yoshihiro   II-373
Krauß, Christoph   III-137
Krombholz, Katharina   III-412
Kumaresan, Ranjit   III-51
Kundu, Suparna   III-271
Kutas, Péter   I-432
Kwak, Hyesun   II-403

L

Lallemand, Virginie   II-433
Larangeira, Mario   I-88
Lau, Wing Cheong   III-432
Laval, Abel   I-432
Lazzeretti, Riccardo   I-183
Le, Duc V.   III-51
Lee, Dongwon   II-403
Li, Zhichun   III-241
Liberati, Edoardo   I-183
Lin, Yunxue   III-355
Lindstrøm, Jonas   I-58
Ling, Xi   II-283
Litos, Orfeas Stefanos Thyfronitis   III-28
Liu, Chi-Ting   II-24
Liu, Zhuotao   I-213
Lorek, Paweł   III-3
Lu, Tianbo   II-265
Luo, Kaixuan   III-432

M

Madsen, Mikkel Wienberg   I-58
Marco, Laurane   I-432
Mateu, Victor   II-3
Matsuda, Takahiro   II-373

Meinel, Christoph   III-381
Mennink, Bart   II-460
Minaei, Mohsen   III-51
Minier, Marine   II-433
Mitrokotsa, Aikaterini   II-189
Mondal, Puja   III-271
Moog, Sven   III-190
Mukherjee, Kunal   III-241
Mukhopadhyay, Debdeep   II-47, III-163

N

Naito, Yusuke   I-318
Nakamura, Toru   I-119
Nikolaenko, Valeria   III-105
Nishida, Yutaro   II-373

P

Patranabis, Sikhar   II-47
Pereira, Olivier   I-257
Perin, Lucas Pandolfo   II-3
Perret, Ludovic   I-457
Peters, Thomas   I-257
Phalakarn, Kittiphop   I-119
Podschwadt, Robert   II-313
Pu, Sihang   I-376
Puniamurthy, Kirthivaasan   I-3, II-101
Pünter, Wenzel   III-381
Purnal, Antoon   II-433

R

Raghuraman, Srinivasan   III-51
Ragsdale, Sam   III-105
Rezapour, Maryam   I-156
Rhee, John Junghwan   III-241
Riahi, Siavash   III-28
Riyadh, H. T. M. A.   III-412
Robben, Jeroen   II-217
Roy, Arnab   II-433

S

Saah, Gustave Tchoffo   I-432
Safavi-Naini, Reihaneh   III-74
Sakai, Yusuke   II-373
Sasaki, Yu   I-318
Schardong, Frederico   II-3
Schuldt, Jacob C. N.   II-373
Serror, Martin   II-241
Shang, Jiaze   II-265
Siewert, Hendrik   III-190

Sinha, Sayani   II-47
Smart, Nigel P.   II-133
Somorovsky, Juraj   III-190
Song, Yongsoo   II-403
Šorf, Milan   II-101
Spangsberg, Anne Dorte   I-58
Su, Xiangyu   I-88
Sugawara, Takeshi   I-318
Sun, Ling   III-355

T
Taguchi, Ren   II-79
Takabi, Daniel   II-313
Takayasu, Atsushi   II-79
Tanaka, Keisuke   I-88
Tang, Lu-An   III-241
Terner, Ben   II-133
Tsudik, Gene   I-26

U
Uluagac, Selcuk   I-183

V
Valle, Victor   II-3
Vanhoef, Mathy   II-217
Venturi, Daniele   I-135
Verbauwhede, Ingrid   III-271
Verbel, Javier   I-457
Visintin, Alessandro   I-183

W
Wagh, Sameer   II-403
Wagner, Eric   II-241
Wang, Long   I-213

Wang, Pengfei   I-88
Wang, Qi   III-241
Wang, Ruize   III-301
Wang, Xianbo   III-432
Wang, Yisong   I-213
Wehrle, Klaus   II-241
Wei, James   III-241
Wiedemeier, Joshua   III-241

X
Xu, Dongpeng   III-217
Xu, Haitao   II-283
Xu, Yuquan   II-340

Y
Yang, Bo-Yin   II-24
Yang, Yibin   III-51
Yasuda, Satoshi   II-373
Yu, Jiongchi   II-283
Yu, Xiao   III-241
Yung, Moti   III-3

Z
Zagórski, Filip   III-3
Zamani, Mahdi   III-51
Zhang, Fan   II-283
Zhang, Han   II-265
Zhang, Mengyu   I-213
Zhang, Naiqian   III-217
Zhang, Xiaoping   I-213
Zhao, Pengfei   II-265
Zhao, Ziming   II-283
Zhou, Zhihao   II-283

Printed in the United States
by Baker & Taylor Publisher Services